ARCHYTAS OF TAF

Archytas of Tarentum is one of the three most important philosophers in the Pythagorean tradition. He was a prominent mathematician who gave the first solution to the famous problem of doubling the cube, an important music theorist, and the leader of a powerful Greek city-state. He is famous for sending a trireme to rescue Plato from the clutches of the tyrant of Syracuse, Dionysius II, in 361 BC. This is the first extensive study of Archytas' work in any language. It contains original texts, English translations and a full commentary for all the fragments of his writings and for all testimonia concerning his life and work. In addition there are introductory essays on Archytas' life and writings, his philosophy, and the question of authenticity. Carl A. Huffman presents a new interpretation of Archytas' significance both for the Pythagorean tradition and also for fourth-century Greek thought, including the philosophies of Plato and Aristotle.

CARL A. HUFFMAN is Professor of Classics at DePauw University. He is the author of *Philolaus of Croton: Pythagorean and Presocratic* (1993) and contributor to *The Cambridge Companion to Early Greek Philosophy* (ed. A. A. Long) (1999).

ARCHYTAS OF TARENTUM

Pythagorean, Philosopher and Mathematician King

CARL A. HUFFMAN

Professor of Classics, DePauw University

CAMBRIDGE
UNIVERSITY PRESS

CAMBRIDGE UNIVERSITY PRESS
Cambridge, New York, Melbourne, Madrid, Cape Town, Singapore, São Paulo

Cambridge University Press
The Edinburgh Building, Cambridge CB2 2RU, UK
Published in the United States of America by Cambridge University Press, New York

www.cambridge.org
Information on this title: www.cambridge.org/9780521837464

First published 2005

Printed in the United Kingdom at the University Press, Cambridge

A catalogue record for this book is available from the British Library

Library of Congress Cataloguing in Publication data
Huffman, Carl A.
Archytas of Tarentum : Pythagorean, philosopher, and mathematician king / Carl A. Huffman.
p.   cm.
Includes bibliographical references and index.
ISBN 0 521 83746 4
1. Archytas, of Tarentum.   2. Mathematics, Ancient.   3. Pythagorean theorem.
4. Mathematicians – Greece – Biography.   5. Philosophy, Ancient.
6. Scientists – Greece – Biography.   1. Title.
QA31.H84   2004
510′.92 – dc22
[B]   2004049736

ISBN-13 978-0-521-83746-0 hardback
ISBN-10 0-521-83746-4 hardback

For Martha, David, Peter and John

Contents

vii

Figures

Preface

The last book devoted to Archytas was published over 160 years ago (Gruppe 1840). Even that work was not really a study of Archytas' thought but rather an unsuccessful attempt to argue that no authentic fragments of Archytas had survived from antiquity. It is not an exaggeration to say, then, that there has never been a book-length study of Archytas of Tarentum. There have not even been many shorter treatments. Erich Frank gave Archytas a fairly prominent role in his reconstruction of early Pythagoreanism (1923), but that reconstruction was eccentric and has been largely rejected by scholars. Essentially the only commentary has been that in Italian by Maria Timpanaro Cardini, as part of a three-volume commentary on all the Pythagoreans (1958–64). In recent years there have been a few important articles and sections of larger works dealing with isolated aspects of Archytas' work, notably his harmonic theory (e.g. Barker 1989, 1994; Bowen 1982; Cambiano 1998 and Lloyd 1990), but to say that Archytas has been neglected would be an understatement. Nonetheless, Archytas is one of the three most important figures in ancient Pythagoreanism (along with Pythagoras himself and Philolaus); we cannot hope to understand ancient Pythagoreanism without understanding Archytas. He was also an important philosopher, mathematician and political leader in his own right. Most scholarship on Greek philosophy during the first half of the fourth century has been devoted to Plato and the Academy. Archytas is a crucial figure for any attempt to understand Greek philosophy and mathematics outside of the Academy during this period and thus for understanding the broader environment in which both Plato and Aristotle developed as philosophers. It is astounding that Archytas, who represents the developed Pythagoreanism that "makes a direct and personal impact on Plato himself" (Guthrie 1962: 333) and whom Gregory Vlastos has called a "master metaphysician" and "a new model philosopher for Plato" (1991: 129), has never been the subject of a complete study.

My first goal is to provide as complete and as reliable a collection of the fragments and testimonia of Archytas as possible. Since this evidence is full of difficulties and much of it little studied, my second goal has been to provide a detailed commentary that addresses the major philosophical and philological issues. Finally, since the evidence is disparate and often technical, scholars have found it difficult to attain an overview of Archytas' achievement. I have tried to fill this lacuna with the introductory essays on Archytas' life and philosophy. The detailed arguments in support of the points made in the overview of Archytas' philosophy are found in the commentaries on the individual fragments and testimonia. One of the reasons that Archytas has been neglected is the technical nature of some of the evidence. I write primarily as a historian of ancient philosophy and a philologist. I have tried to make Archytas' technical work in mathematics and harmonic theory clear to other students of ancient philosophy and philology, but I am not a professional mathematician. Certainly I have no illusions of having produced that mythical beast, "the definitive edition"; my hope is that this edition will provide a reliable basis on which study of Archytas can build and that my interpretation of Archytas' philosophy will stimulate further work.

The standard collection of the fragments and testimonia of Archytas has been that in *Die Fragmente der Vorsokratiker* by H. Diels as revised by W. Kranz (6th edn. 1951–52, referred to as DK). DK collects the most important testimonia but does not pretend to be complete. In order to avoid confusion I have followed the numbering of fragments and testimonia in DK but have added approximately fifty testimonia to those found there. In some cases these are just additional sources, where DK has given the most important (e.g. A7 [the anecdote about not punishing in anger], A15 [doubling the cube], Fr. 1). There are a few brief reports having to do with Archytas' philosophy which DK overlooked (A7a [mentioned in the afterword but not included in DK]; A11a; A13, Text G; A19c; A21a). DK do not mention Iamblichus' reports about Archytas' role in the history of means (Fr. 2, Texts A–D) nor most of the references to Archytas in Iamblichus' *On the Pythagorean Life* (A6b). DK did not include a large number of testimonia having to do with Archytas' life and reception (e.g. Archytas as the teacher of Eudoxus: A6c; relations with Plato: A5a1, A5a2, A5b2, A5b3, A5b4, A5b5, A5b6, A5b7, A5b8, A5b9, A5b10, A5b11, A5b12, A5b13, A5c2, A5c3, A5c4, A5c5; reception A3a, A3b, A3c, A3d, A3e, A3f; miscellaneous reports about his life: A1a, A1b, A1c, A1d, A1e, A1f, A1g, A6a, A6d, A6e, A6f, A6g, B5a, B8b).

I print the same four fragments as DK, but the texts of those fragments differ from DK in a number of important ways. DK's version of Fragment 1 is particularly unreliable. With one major exception I have not done new collations of manuscripts for either the testimonia or the fragments and have instead relied on the best published editions. Fragments 3 and 4 come from Stobaeus, and my examination of the manuscripts of Stobaeus for my earlier work on Philolaus suggested that there would be little value in examining these manuscripts for Archytas (Huffman 1993: xvi). The exception is the manuscripts of Porphyry's commentary on Ptolemy's *Harmonics*. Porphyry is the major source for two of the fragments of Archytas (1 and 2) as well as two important testimonia (A17 and A18). Professor Thomas Mathiesen kindly made available to me his copies of the five major manuscripts of Porphyry's work so that I was able to carry out fresh collations of them (E = Vaticanus gr. 186, V^{187} = Vaticanus gr. 187, G = Vaticanus gr. 198, M = Venetus Marcianus gr. app. cl. VI/10, and T = Vindobonensis int. phil. gr. 176). My collations have revealed Düring's reports of these manuscripts to be quite unreliable. While the new readings do not radically change the meaning of the text, they have caused me to print a different text in a number of places, and I have given a full report of my findings in the apparatus. The translations of fragments and testimonia are my own unless otherwise indicated.

The dialect of the fragments presents a particularly thorny problem. The manuscripts preserve a hodgepodge of Attic, Doric and even Lesbian or Epic forms. There have been two basic approaches. We can try to restore the text uniformly to the Doric forms which we think that Archytas, as a native of Tarentum, was likely to have used. The difficulty is that there is no good model of fourth-century Doric prose to follow in restoring those forms. In the ancient world, Archytas was the model (see A6g). Blass (1884) corrected all forms to correspond to the Doric of the Heraclean Tables, but it is far from clear how close the Doric of the tables is to what Archytas might have used, and Blass' reconstruction undoubtedly differs from what Archytas wrote. The second approach is that followed by most editors, including DK, i.e. to print a text based on the best evidence of the manuscript tradition without, for the most part, trying to reconstruct unattested Doric forms. The result is a text which reflects the combination of Attic and Doric forms found in the manuscripts so that e.g. an Attic infinitive form will be found in one line and a Doric infinitive form in the next. Clearly such a text cannot reflect what Archytas wrote either, but, when one tries to correct even the most obvious conflicts between Doric and Attic forms, two problems arise, the above mentioned problem of what model of Doric prose to follow and the question of when to stop correcting. As a result of these difficulties, I have opted to follow the general approach of DK and thus only print the Doric forms when they are either found in the manuscripts or strongly suggested by the manuscript readings. My collations of the manuscripts of Porphyry have allowed me to restore some Doric forms. In a few instances, where the forms suggested by the manuscript tradition are extremely unlikely to have been used by Archytas, I have restored the typical Doric form (e.g. I have followed Cassio (1988) in printing διαγνώμεν in Fr. 1, line 1).

Greek authors are generally cited according to the abbreviations used in the *Greek–English Lexicon* of H. G. Liddell and R. Scott revised by H. S. Jones, with Supplement (1968 – referred to as LSJ). I have referred to Plato according to the Stephanus pages given in Burnet's Oxford Text; the treatises of Aristotle according to Bekker's Berlin edition; the fragments of Aristotle according to the numbering of the third edition of Rose (1886). Modern works are generally referred to by the author's last name and publication date. The abbreviations used for periodicals are generally those of *L'Année philologique*. Common abbreviations:

CAG   (1882–1909) *Commentaria in Aristotelem Graeca* (Berlin)

DK   Diels, H. (1952) *Die Fragmente der Vorsokratiker*, 6th edn., rev. W. Kranz, 3 vols. (Berlin), first edn. 1903

FGrH   Jacoby, F. (1923–) *Die Fragmente der Griechischen Historiker* (Berlin)

OCD   Hornblower, Simon and Spawforth, Antony (1996) *The Oxford Classical Dictionary*, 3rd edn. (Oxford)

RE   Pauly, A., Wissowa, G., and Kroll, W. (1893–) *Realencyclopädie der klassischen Altertumswissenschaft*

SVF   von Arnim, H. (1903–21) *Stoicorum veterum fragmenta* (Leipzig)

I have been working on this book for a long time, and there are a number of people and institutions who have kindly supported my work. A fellowship from the John Simon Guggenheim Foundation in 1995–96 allowed me to complete substantial parts of the book. DePauw University has aided my project in a number of ways, most importantly with a sabbatical leave in 1995–96 and a Fisher Fellowship, which allowed me to devote the Fall semester of 1999 to research and writing. Andrew Barker read the sections on Archytas' harmonic theory and was generous with his support and advice. Myles Burnyeat has read and commented on sections of my work and given me his own work in related areas, sometimes unpublished, to read. He has been unfailingly supportive of my project. Charles Kahn has provided invaluable help at a number of steps along the way, as well as sharing his own work with me. Geoffrey Lloyd has helped in many ways, including reading substantial parts of a draft of the book and sending me helpful comments. As always my mentor Alex Mourelatos has provided support at crucial moments. None of these people is responsible for the deficiencies that still remain, of course. The TLG disk has been an invaluable resource in my research, and the director of the Thesaurus Linguae Graecae, Maria Pantelia, generously carried out some searches for me on materials not yet available on the disk. Alan Cameron helped me with Testimonium A3f by identifying Joannes Geometres as the source. Friedrich Niessen translated the medieval Hebrew version of Ḥunayn's report on Archytas for me as well as providing expert commentary on it. Marwan Rashed kindly translated the testimonium from Ibn Abī Uṣaybiʿa for me. There are numerous other individuals who have aided me by reading parts of the manuscript, by responding to papers based on my work, or by helping with problems. I would particularly like to mention Bernard Batto, István Bodnár, Michael Chase, Patricia Curd, Martin Curd, Underwood Dudley, Daniel Graham, Paul Kissinger, Chris Kopff, Reviel Netz, Juli Rainbolt, Steven Strange, Andrea Sununu, Philip Thibodeau, Paul Woodruff, Nazik Yared, and Leonid Zhmud who provided expert comments on several parts of the manuscript. My wife Martha has taken time from her own work to read numerous drafts of my work as well as providing loving support. Finally, I would like to thank Michael Sharp, Jackie Warren, and Sinéad Moloney at Cambridge University Press for all their hard work in making the book possible. Linda Woodward deserves special thanks for her careful copy-editing, which saved me from many errors.

PART ONE

Introductory essays

CHAPTER I

Life, writings and reception

SOURCES

(The original texts and translations of the testimonia for Archytas' life are found in Part Three, Section One)

Archytas did not live the life of a philosophical recluse. He was the leader of one of the most powerful Greek city-states in the first half of the fourth century BC. Unfortunately he is similar to most important Greek intellectuals of the fifth and fourth centuries BC, in that we have extremely little reliable information about his activities. This dearth of information is all the more frustrating since we know that Aristoxenus wrote a biography of Archytas, not long after his death (A9). Two themes bulk large in the bits of evidence that do survive from that biography and from other evidence for Archytas' life. First, there is Archytas' connection to Plato, which, as we will see, was more controversial in antiquity than in most modern scholarship. The Platonic *Seventh Letter*, whose authenticity continues to be debated, portrays Archytas as saving Plato from likely death, when Plato was visiting the tyrant Dionysius II at Syracuse in 361 BC. Second, for Aristoxenus, Archytas is the paradigm of a successful leader. Elected general (*stratēgos*) repeatedly, he was never defeated in battle; as a virtuous, kindly and democratic ruler, he played a significant role in the great prosperity of his native Tarentum, located on the heel of southern Italy.

Archytas' connection to Plato is important in a number of ways, but it is helpful to begin by removing him from the shadow of Plato and the controversies surrounding the *Seventh Letter*, in order to see what we can determine about his life, independently of the Platonic tradition. To begin with, he was clearly a central figure in the Greek world, in the first half of the fourth century, both as an intellectual and as a man of action. He received a considerable amount of attention from important writers of the mid and late fourth century. These fourth-century authors are our most reliable sources and form the basis of what is trustworthy in

the two brief, extant lives of Archytas in Diogenes Laertius (A1) and the
Suda (A2). Aristotle wrote more books on Archytas than any other individual figure. He devoted three books to the philosophy of Archytas himself
and wrote another consisting of a summary of Plato's *Timaeus* and the writings of Archytas (see A13). Aristotle's pupil, Aristoxenus, appears to have
begun the tradition of peripatetic biography and wrote a life of Archytas,
thus putting him in the select company of Pythagoras, Socrates and Plato.
Aristoxenus was from Tarentum and began his philosophical career as a
Pythagorean, so that it is not a surprise that he should choose to write
a life of his countryman, but that choice also reflects the prominence of
Archytas. Aristoxenus' contemporary, Eudemus, another pupil of Aristotle,
referred to Archytas prominently in his history of geometry (A6, A14) and
his physics (A23–A24).

Whereas Aristotle's works on the philosophy of Archytas, now lost, do not
seem to have been much used in the doxographical tradition, Aristoxenus'
life undoubtedly lies behind much of the later biographical and anecdotal
tradition about Archytas. Diogenes Laertius mentions Aristoxenus twice in
his brief *Life of Archytas* (A1). Aristoxenus is explicitly named by Athenaeus
as the source for the debate on pleasure between Archytas and the Syracusan
hedonist, Polyarchus (A9). He is also likely to be the source for the story
of Archytas' unwillingness to punish in anger (A7) and may be the source
of a number of Cicero's reports about Archytas as well as, perhaps, those of
other Romans of the first century BC (see on A9a). Aristoxenus (born ca. 375)
was somewhere between fifteen and twenty-five years old when Archytas
died (360–350 BC), so he may have had some first-hand knowledge of his
subject. Moreover, as a native of Tarentum he will have had a number
of contacts there, most notably his father, Spintharus (A7), who was an
adult during Archytas' prime years at Tarentum. Aristoxenus was thus in
a position to possess very accurate information about Archytas' actions
and beliefs. The testimonia show that his *Life* was not a spare catalogue
of events but rather relied heavily on anecdote to make points about the
character of Archytas (A7). Aristoxenus also brought out Archytas' views
by dramatizing his meetings with other philosophers and putting speeches
into the mouths of both Archytas and his opponents (A9). The surviving
evidence suggests that Archytas was presented in a largely positive light, and
we might therefore suspect that the *Life* is primarily an exercise in uncritical
hagiography. Archytas' opponents, however, also appear to have been given
a fair hearing and are not simply straw men (Polyarchus in A9). Archytas
himself, moreover, seems to have been given a few foibles (A7 and A11).

It may thus be better to conclude that Aristoxenus' *Life*, while favorable, was not simply panegyric (Momigliano 1993: 76).

It is impossible to determine the chronology of Archytas' life with any certainty. Most reconstructions of it are based heavily on the problematic tradition about the dealings of Archytas with Plato, to which I will return below. The best estimate based on the remaining evidence is that Archytas was born sometime between 435 and 410 and died sometime between 360 and 350. Strabo clearly associates Archytas with the flourishing of Tarentum, after which the city entered a period of decline, which in turn led it to hire a series of mercenary generals to fight its wars (A4). Since the mercenaries start ca. 340, Strabo's account suggests that Archytas was gone by 350 at the latest. The *Erotic Oration* (A5c1) groups Archytas with Timotheus (died 355–4) and the fact that Archytas is listed after Timotheus might indicate that Archytas died after 355. The external history of the Greek city-states of southern Italy suggests that Tarentum was particularly likely to have flourished after 379, when Croton fell to Dionysius I (see below). This suggests a period of 379 to 360 for the height of Archytas' political activity in Tarentum.

The beginnings of Archytas' career are just as hard to pin down. The catalogue of geometers in Proclus' commentary on Book I of Euclid, which goes back to Aristotle's pupil Eudemus, connects Archytas with Leodamas of Thasos and Theaetetus as contemporaries of Plato (A6). These figures are not exact contemporaries, since Theaetetus is usually thought to have been born ca. 415, on the basis of Plato's dialogue which was named after him (see *RE* under Theaetetus), while Plato was born in 428–7, when Leodamas is also likely to have been born.[1] So far as Eudemus' evidence goes then, Archytas' birth should be dated somewhere between 435 and 410, since it is unlikely that he would have been more than twenty years different in age than those who are named as his contemporaries (Plato and Leodamas ca. 430 and Theaetetus ca. 415). This would make Archytas between 30 and 55 when Tarentum starts to emerge as a power in 380 and between 60 and 85 at death, if he died in 350. It is hard to see how he can be

---

[1] A certain Neoclides is said to be younger than Leodamas, but still the teacher of Leon, who was likely to have been born around 400, since he was a little older than Eudoxus, who was born ca. 390 (Procl., *In Euc.*, Prol. II, 66.18 ff.; See *RE* under Leodamas). We can make sense of all this if we assign the following birth dates: Leodamas ca. 430, Neoclides ca. 420, Leon ca. 400.

much older than Plato and still classed as a contemporary of Theaetetus, but he could be fifteen to twenty years younger than Plato. Whether born in 435 or 410 Archytas could quite plausibly be the teacher of Eudoxus (A6c) and could have written the *Harmonics* by the 370s, when Plato quotes from it in composing the *Republic* (530d; cf. Guthrie 1975: 437; Kahn 1996: 59).

FAMILY, TEACHERS AND PUPILS

Diogenes Laertius first identifies Archytas' father as Mnesagoras (A1), and the *Suda* adds the variants Mnesarchus and Mnasagetes (A2). Diogenes also tells us, however, that Aristoxenus gave his father's name as Hestiaeus. It is hard to see how Aristoxenus could have been wrong about something like this, given his sources, and we should therefore follow the *Suda* in preferring Hestiaeus as his father's name. Hestiaeus also appears under the heading of Tarentum in the catalogue of Pythagoreans preserved in Iamblichus (*VP* 267) and thus might be Archytas' father or son. None of the other names appear in the catalogue. The other names have a suspicious similarity to the name of Pythagoras' father, Mnesarchus (D.L. and Porphyry) or Mnemarchus (Iamblichus). We know nothing else about Archytas' father or family.

We also know surprisingly little about Archytas' teachers and pupils, given the doxographical tradition's interest in philosophical successions. There may already have been a Pythagorean community in Tarentum by 509, when according to Dicaearchus, Pythagoras took refuge there in his flight from Croton (Porph. *VP* 56). His visit was short-lived, since Dicaearchus goes on to say that Pythagoras and his followers soon suffered the same sort of persecution in Tarentum as they had at Croton, leading Pythagoras to flee to Metapontum. There continued to be Pythagoreans in Tarentum, however. In the middle of the fifth century, when the Pythagorean meeting place in the house of Milo at Croton was attacked (ca. 454), the only two Pythagoreans to escape, Lysis and Archippus, were Tarentines; Archippus is reported to have fled to Tarentum (Iamb. *VP* 250). Aristoxenus tells us that, after this attack on the Pythagoreans, all the Pythagoreans left Italy except for Archytas (Iamb. *VP* 250 = A6b). This report oddly associates Archytas with events twenty to thirty years before his birth but can be understood, if we step back and take a broader view. We know that both Philolaus and Lysis spent time in Thebes (Huffman 1993: 1–7). Aristoxenus also reports that the last Pythagoreans whom he knew, in the first half of the fourth century, came from the mainland: Phlius and the

Thracian Chalcidice (D.L. VIII. 46). It is in contrast to this general east-ward movement that Archytas can be described as alone remaining in Italy. Aristoxenus calls the last Pythagoreans students of Philolaus and Eurytus (who was an older pupil of Philolaus). He calls both Philolaus and Eurytus Tarentines, although Philolaus is elsewhere identified as coming from Croton. Philolaus was probably originally from Croton but, after his visit to Thebes, may have returned to Tarentum to teach in his old age (Huffman 1993: 6).

If Archytas was in his formative years (ages 15–30) in the late fifth or very early fourth century and became a Pythagorean in his maturity, it would be logical to assume that he had studied with the most important Pythagorean of the day, Philolaus (ca. 470–390 BC), who, as we have seen, might have spent his last years in Tarentum.[2] Certain aspects of Archytas' philosophy (see A20, A21 and the overview of Archytas' philosophy) make it plausible that Philolaus was indeed an important influence on him. Archytas may also have studied with Eurytus, since Theophrastus cites Archytas as the source for our most important testimony about Eurytus (*Metaph.* 6a = A13, Text H), but we know too little of Eurytus' views to trace any influence on Archytas. Archytas' use of his predecessors (see the philosophical overview) suggests that he might also have studied with non-Pythagoreans such as Hippocrates of Chios, but we have no direct evidence for this.

The *Suda* reports that Archytas had famous pupils, but the only exam-ple it provides is, rather problematically, Empedocles (ca. 492–432), who probably died before Archytas was born (A2). The only famous philoso-pher, who can be identified as a pupil of Archytas with some degree of confidence, is Eudoxus (ca. 390–340). Even here the evidence is meager; the sole source is Diogenes Laertius (A6c). Eudoxus will not have learned his famous hedonism (Arist. *EN* 1172b9–10) from Archytas, who attacked bodily pleasure (A9a), but Diogenes is, in fact, careful to say that it was specifically geometry that Eudoxus learned from Archytas. Archytas, whose solution to the duplication of the cube made him one of the leading geome-ters of the day and who did considerable work with proportions might well have been sought out by the young Eudoxus, who went on to develop the general theory of proportion found in Book 5 of Euclid and to con-struct a mathematical system to explain the motions of the heavenly bodies. One problematic tradition (A5b1–12), to which I will return below, makes Plato a pupil of Archytas. Aristoxenus presents Archytas as meeting with

---

[2] Cicero, however, is the only source to name Philolaus as Archytas' teacher (A5c2), and his report may not be based on an independent source but on the logic which I have just given.

associates in the sacred precincts of Tarentum, in order to walk about and discuss philosophical questions (A9). The only name which we can give to these associates is provided by the *Seventh Letter* and Plutarch, who identify Archedemus as one of Archytas' associates (A5, 339a–b; A5a1).[3]

The later tradition uniformly presents Archytas as a Pythagorean (D.L., *Suda*, Iamblichus, Strabo, Cicero etc.). The difficulty is in determining what exactly it means for him to be called a Pythagorean and to what extent it defines his thought. On the one hand, the Platonic evidence is mixed. Neither Archytas nor his associates are called Pythagoreans in the *Seventh Letter*, just as Philolaus is not called a Pythagorean in the *Phaedo*. When Plato quotes from Archytas' *Harmonics* at *Republic* 530d, however, he presents Archytas' words as what "the Pythagoreans say." Clearly in the realm of harmonics Archytas is labeled a Pythagorean, which indeed makes sense in light of Philolaus' earlier work in the area. On the other hand, Aristotle makes a distinction between "the so-called Pythagoreans," to whom he refers extensively in his extant writings and about whom he wrote two separate treatises, and Archytas, who is not called a Pythagorean in Aristotle's extant treatises and about whom Aristotle wrote three books distinct from those he wrote about the Pythagoreans (A13). All of this suggests that it may have been much more common in the later tradition than in the fourth century to simply label Archytas a Pythagorean. In the fourth century he may have been viewed as an important thinker in his own right, who was also a Pythagorean in his way of living and who developed themes treated earlier in the Pythagorean tradition by figures such as Philolaus. When Archytas' name was mentioned, the labels "philosopher" and "mathematician" may have popped into people's heads first and "Pythagorean" only second. In the later tradition, on the other hand, Archytas was first of all a "Pythagorean." Aristoxenus says that the last Pythagoreans, whom he knew of, were the pupils of Philolaus and Eurytus (D.L. VIII. 46). Was Archytas independent enough from the Pythagorean tradition that his pupils were not regarded as Pythagoreans?

ARCHYTAS AND TARENTUM

In contrast to some figures such as Philolaus, who were associated with several different cities in southern Italy, Archytas is universally associated

---

[3] It is true that Archedemus also appears in two surely spurious letters of Plato (II and III), but it is perfectly possible for such spurious letters to refer to historical figures. We know nothing further about Archedemus. It is tempting to suppose that it is Archytas' associate who figures in the title of one of Xenocrates' books: *Archedemus or Concerning Justice* (D.L. IV. 13.9)

with Tarentum. This suggests that he was both born there and also spent his entire life there. In order to make sense of Archytas' career in Tarentum, it is necessary to understand some features of the history of the city. According to the literary tradition, Tarentum was founded by colonists from Sparta in 706 BC (Strabo VI. 3.4; Brauer 1986: 3 ff.). It is situated where the heel meets the instep of the "boot" of Italy. Tarentum had by far the best harbor on the south coast of Italy, and it was a natural stopping point for ships sailing west from mainland Greece (Plb. x. 1). Initially, however, Tarentum was overshadowed by the Greek colonies founded by the Achaeans further west on the gulf of Tarentum: Croton and Sybaris.

On their arrival, the Greeks found the region around Tarentum occupied by native peoples known as Iapygians, who were divided into three main groups, the Messapii, who inhabited the heel of Italy, the Peucetii who were north of the Messapii and the Daunians who lived still further north (Plb. III. 88.4; there is much confusion in the use of these names). Tarentum's history was characterized by continuing conflict with these native peoples. Dedications at Delphi commemorated victories over the Messapians (Paus. x. 10.6) and Peucetians/Iapygians (Paus. x. 13.10) in the first half of the fifth century. Even more important was a defeat suffered by Tarentum and her ally Rhegium at the hands of the Iapygians in 473 (D.S. XI. 52). Herodotus says that this was the greatest slaughter of Greeks of which he knows; 3,000 soldiers from Rhegium alone died, with no number having been put to the Tarentine dead (VII. 170). Aristotle tells us that so many Tarentine nobles were killed in this battle that democratic elements in the state were able to change the constitution to a democracy from a constitutional government (*Pol.* 1303a). We know little of the constitution at Tarentum before this time, although Herodotus reports that a king, Aristophilides, was in power ca. 492 (III. 136). The new democracy still retained its traditional Dorian connections, taking the Peloponnesian side against Athens in the Peloponnesian War. Tarentum refused anchorage and water to Athens in 415 (Thuc. VI. 44), providing safety to the Spartan general Gylippus in 414 (Thuc. VI. 104) and finally sending ships to help the Peloponnesian cause, after the Athenian disaster in Sicily (Thuc. VIII. 91). The Athenians for their part were allied to Tarentum's traditional foes, the Messapians (Thuc. VII. 33).

Pressure from another native people, the Lucanians, and worries about the tyrant of Syracuse, Dionysius I, led the southern Greeks to form a league in 393, which included at least Rhegium, Croton, Thurii, Hipponium, Caulonia and Elea and in which Croton played the leading role (D.S. XIV. 91 and 100–06; Polyaenus VI. 11; Plb. II. 39; Purcell 1994: 387).

Dionysius I of Syracuse attacked Rhegium in 390, who appealed to the league for support, leading Dionysius to ally himself with the Lucanians (D.S. xiv. 100). Dionysius eventually came to control southern Italy as far as Thurii, with Croton falling in 379/8 (D.H. xx. 7; Justin xx. 5; Livy xxiv. 3; Caven 1990: 196). There is no indication either in the literary sources or from coinage that Tarentum played any role in the Italian league at this point. Evidence from coinage suggests but does not prove that her colony, Heraclea, was a member, and this might indicate that Tarentum was part of the alliance, at least insofar as it was directed against the Lucanians (Wuilleumier 1939: 65). It is more difficult to believe that Tarentum played any role against Dionysius I of Syracuse, since Syracuse was a Dorian colony like Tarentum and since Tarentum had been a virtual ally of Syracuse earlier during the Peloponnesian War and would later be the ally of Dionysius II of Syracuse. The evidence might be read as indicating that Tarentum was the ally of Dionysius I (Purcell 1994: 387). Whatever the exact situation, it is clear that Tarentum was not significantly involved in the conflicts with the Lucanians and Dionysius I in the years between 393 and 379. In general Tarentum must have benefitted from the decline of the other Greek cities in southern Italy, which resulted from those conflicts.

It is likely that Tarentum eventually became head of the Italiote league, whose meeting place was probably moved, some time after the fall of Croton ca. 378, to the Tarentine colony, Heraclea. The evidence is sketchy. What might be a federal coinage began to be issued around 380 in the form of diobols of identical type at Tarentum and Heraclea, which were imitated in other cities (Brauer 1986: 55–56; Purcell 1994: 388). The reverse of the coin had Heracles wrestling the Nemean lion, which suggests the centrality of Heraclea. The clearest assertion of Tarentum's leadership of the league by the literary tradition is found in the rather imprecise language of the entry for Archytas given in the *Suda* (A2). In that entry Archytas is said to have had the leadership of the Italian league and to have been chosen *stratēgos* both by his own citizens and by the Greeks of the area. The literary evidence for Heraclea as the meeting place for the league is also indirect. Strabo (vi. 3.4) reports that Alexander the Molossian, a mercenary general, who first served Tarentum and then became disaffected, tried to move the festal assembly of the Greek peoples of that region, which had been meeting in Tarentine territory at Heraclea, to Thurii, out of hostility to Tarentum. Alexander was involved in Tarentine affairs from 334–331 (Purcell 1994: 391). This suggests then that some time after the fall of Croton in 379/8 and before the time of Alexander in 334–331, the meeting place of the league was moved to Heraclea and also that, since Heraclea was a Tarentine colony, Tarentum was the leader of the league. It seems likely that this move occurred shortly after the fall of Croton, and it is indeed plausible that Tarentum's leadership of the league was encouraged by Dionysius I (Purcell 1994: 388).

If Archytas was born between 435 and 410, he will have spent his childhood or youth in a Tarentum that was aiding Syracuse and the Peloponnesian cause against Athens. He will have been between 20 and 45 when Dionysius I intervened in southern Italy, and between 30 and 55 when Croton fell, and Tarentum assumed leadership of the league. For about a thirty year period between 380 and 350 conditions were right for Tarentum to increase considerably in power amid the weakened Greek states in southern Italy and with Dionysius II, who was considerably weaker than his father, in control in Syracuse. Indeed, it is quite plausible to regard Tarentum as one of the most powerful of all Greek city-states in this period (Purcell 1994: 388). It is clear then that, although Archytas undoubtedly had great leadership ability and outstanding character, he was also fortunate to reach his maturity at a time when external conditions had favored Tarentum so significantly. Archytas was the right man, but it was also the right time for Tarentum.

Strabo reports that, at its height, Tarentum "possessed the greatest fleet of those in the region and sent to battle 30,000 footsoldiers, 3,000 cavalry, and 1,000 mounted javelin throwers" (Strabo VI 3.4 = A4).[4] These are impressive numbers. It is worth noting for comparison that, according to Thucydides, Athens had a total of 29,000 footsoldiers and 1,200 cavalry at the beginning of the Peloponnesian War (II. 13; see Gomme 1956 and Hornblower 1991 ad loc.), so that fourth-century Tarentum may have been comparable to fifth-century Athens in size. Strabo does not provide any precise dating for this description of Tarentum except that it occurred under the democracy (established in 473), and before the age of the mercenary generals (330s), but he associates Archytas with this flourishing, so it must belong to the first half of the fourth century. This may also be the period to which applies Florus' description of Tarentum as "capital of Calabria, Apulia and all of Lucania, . . . famous for its size, walls and port" and as "situated at the very entrance to the Adriatic sea, sending forth ships into all lands" (A4a).

---

[4] It is not clear whether the numbers Strabo gives apply just to Tarentum or whether they also include allied forces, but the most straightforward reading suggests that the numbers apply just to Tarentine forces. By ancient standards 4,000 is a very large cavalry, although Diodorus refers to cavalries of 1,000 to 3,000 in southern Italy and Sicily (Spence 1994: 30–31). Tarentum was, indeed, famous for her cavalry. Some of her coins display a cavalry rider (Spence 1994: 31). Military tactics of the third and second centuries may have been influenced by the Tarentine cavalry (Wuilleumier 1939: 666–68; Griffith 1935: 246 ff.).

It was of such a Tarentum that, according to Diogenes Laertius, Archytas was elected general (*stratēgos*) seven times (D.L. VIII. 79 = A1). Aelian (A1d) makes it six times, but Diogenes' report should be preferred, since he is likely to be following our best source, Aristoxenus, whom he cites twice elsewhere. We do not know how many generals were elected each year, but Archytas must have been a member of a board of generals, such as the ten *stratēgoi* at Athens. In addition to strictly military duties, the *stratēgoi* also had special political powers at Athens, either by custom or law, such as the ability to make proposals to the council and to have a role in convening and perhaps setting the agenda of the assembly (Hignett 1952: 245 ff.; Rhodes 1972: 43–46; Sinclair 1988: 81). It seems probable that Archytas had similar political powers at Tarentum, but there is no direct evidence.

It is usually assumed that Archytas served as *stratēgos* seven consecutive times (e.g. Wuilleumier 1939: 68 "sept fois de suite"), although Diogenes does not explicitly say this. He does, however, make the point, again presumably relying on Aristoxenus, that no one else served more than one year as *stratēgos*, since the law forbade it. It seems highly unlikely that the law would have allowed an individual to serve only one year in his entire life as general; the state would have needed the services of talented generals. The simplest solution is to suppose that Diogenes means that the law forbade individuals from serving as general more than one year *in succession* and Archytas was unusual in serving seven years in a row. At Athens there was no limitation on the number of times an individual could be elected *stratēgos*, either in succession or otherwise ([Arist.] Ath. LXII. 3; Hignett 1952: 244); it is generally accepted that Pericles served fifteen times in succession (Plut., *Per.* XVI. 3; Fornara 1971: 48). We are not told what mechanism allowed Archytas to serve seven times in a row, in the face of a law forbidding serving even two years in succession, but the most reasonable suggestion would seem to be that the law was suspended in Archytas' case by a vote, probably of the assembly. Indeed the report that Archytas served seven times is cited precisely as evidence for the general assertion that he was "admired among the multitude for every virtue." The implication is that the multitude was willing to override the law, which presumably existed in order to protect them from an individual gaining too much power through successive tenures as *stratēgos*, in Archytas' case, because of the trust they put in his character (A1c).

Archytas need not have served *only* seven times as *stratēgos*, as many scholars assume (e.g. Wuilleumier 1939: 68–69). Pericles served as *stratēgos* at Athens several times other than in his fifteen-year run from 443–429 (e.g. 454/3 and 448/7; Fornara 1971: 47 ff.). Nicias served 427–423, 421, and

418–413 (Fornara 1971: 56 ff.). Diogenes reports, on the authority of Aristoxenus, that Archytas was never defeated in battle and that, when he was driven to withdraw from the office by the envy of his opponents, the Tarentine forces were immediately defeated (D.L. VIII. 82 = A1). This story is usually taken to mean that at the end of his seven successive years Archytas withdrew from the office never to serve again. Such an assumption is not necessary nor even the most likely interpretation of Aristoxenus' story. It seems just as likely that the story went on to tell of Archytas' return to office, after his opponents' incompetence as generals had been revealed by his abdication. There is again a parallel with Pericles, who was removed from office by the Athenians only to be reinstated or reelected the next year (Fornara 1971: 55). There are no indications as to when Archytas served his seven successive years as *stratēgos* or when he might have served other terms. Strabo reports rather imprecisely that Archytas led the city "for a long time" (A4).

The *Suda* adds the further information that "he was the leader of the Italian league and was chosen general *autokratōr* by the citizens and the Greeks in that region" (A2). We know essentially nothing of the workings of the Italian league. Since Tarentum was evidently the leader of the league starting sometime in the 370s (see above) and Archytas was elected general at Tarentum, it follows that he must in some sense have been a leader of the league. It is less clear whether the members of the league also elected generals. The description of Archytas as general *autokratōr* is also hard to interpret. Exactly what the term means will depend on who was using it. In Plutarch's time the term *autokratōr* had become roughly equivalent to the Latin *imperator* (*Pomp.* VIII) and thus was a special title of honor given to a general after an important victory, while *stratēgos autokratōr* was the equivalent of the Latin *dictator* (Plb. III. 86.7). If the term goes back to Aristoxenus, however, the meaning may be quite different. Thucydides reports several instances in which a general at Athens was called *autokratōr*. The term indicates a grant of special powers, by which the general was freed in certain respects from his customary dependence on the assembly. Thus he could make a diplomatic agreement or certain military decisions without consulting the assembly. These special powers seem to be limited to very carefully defined circumstances and were nothing like a grant of absolute authority for the general to do as he wished. His actions were probably still subject to the later review of the people. The earliest example of such powers were those given to the leaders of the Sicilian expedition, who would have had difficulty in conferring with the Athenians on important decisions because of the distances involved (Thuc. VI. 8.2; see Gomme, Andrewes and Dover 1970: ad loc.; Pritchett 1974: 30 and 42; Hignett 1952: 248; Fornara 1971: 14 and 37 n. 34). Something like this use of the term is found in Syracuse. Hermocrates calls for the Syracusans to elect a small group of *stratēgoi autokratores* to deal with the Athenians (Thuc. VI. 72.5). If the term *autokratōr* is being applied to Archytas in something like this Athenian and Syracusan sense, the point would be that Archytas was given some latitude in carrying out diplomacy and special authority in making military decisions, while he was on campaign. The term does not suggest that he was free of oversight of the assembly or autocratic in the modern sense.

So far as we can tell, Archytas' campaigns will have been directed against the Tarentines' long time adversaries, the non-Greek peoples of Italy, such as the Lucanians and Messapians. We have no direct evidence for any of Archytas' campaigns, although one of Aristoxenus' anecdotes portrays him as having been away for a considerable time in a campaign against the Messapians (A7). We have no evidence for Tarentine campaigns against other Greeks during the period of Archytas' leadership.

Some scholars have thought it probable that Archytas used his mathematical expertise in order to help design mechanical devices to aid in the defense of Tarentum or in her campaigns against others (e.g. Diels 1965: 21–22; Wuilleumier 1939: 192; Gigante 1971: 69; Ciaceri 1927–32: II. 439). As I argue in the overview of Archytas' philosophy, however, the evidence for Archytas as an inventor of mechanical devices is quite limited. Moreover, whereas Plutarch describes the machines invented by Archimedes in order to help in the defense of Syracuse against the Roman siege (*Marc.* XIV ff.), there is no ancient evidence which connects Archytas directly to the design or construction of any military devices.[5] Diodorus asserts that

---

[5] Kingsley (1995a: 146, n. 54) argues that "in Plut. *Marc.* 14.3–6 the connection between Archytas' mechanics . . . and weaponry is made explicit." Plutarch does connect mechanics and weaponry in this passage, but it is not "Archytas' mechanics" that is connected to weapons. As Plutarch tells the story, mechanics becomes separated from philosophy because of Plato's complaints about the use of mechanics in geometrical proofs by Archytas and others. As a result of Plato's complaints mechanics was "ignored for a long time by philosophy" and "ended up as one of the arts of warfare." The clear implication is that it was some time after Plato's complaints that mechanics found a home as one of the arts of warfare, but this also means that it was some time after Archytas. Plutarch's remarks make good sense as referring to treatises on machines of warfare such as that of Biton in the third or second centuries BC. Kingsley also says that "Plutarch's mention of ὀργανικὰς καὶ μηχανικὰς κατασκευὰς in *Qu. conv.* 718e is again an allusion to weaponry," but in context this is improbable. Plutarch is again recounting Plato's complaint about Archytas' solution to the problem of doubling the cube. He describes that solution, in the words cited by Kingsley, as leading the problem "into constructions that use instruments and that are mechanical." Plutarch is thinking of mechanical instruments used to determine means such as Eratosthenes' mesolab. He is not saying that Archytas was trying to solve the problem of doubling the cube by using machines of war. Nor does Archytas' comparison of sound to a missile in Fragment 1 give us any grounds for concluding that he designed artillery.

the first Greek artillery was invented at Syracuse in 399 by craftsmen whom Dionysius had gathered from Italy, Greece and Carthaginian territory (XIV. 41.3). Dionysius used this artillery with success at Motya in 397 (D.S. XIV. 50.4). Given this new importance of artillery, it is not implausible that, as a successful *stratēgos*, Archytas will have had familiarity with its use in war (Cambiano 1998: 310). There is evidence that the use of artillery had spread to mainland Greece by 370, and it is likely to have reached southern Italy earlier (Marsden 1969: 65–67). This need not mean, however, that Archytas himself was engaged in designing artillery any more than Pericles' use of new devices in the siege of Samos made him an engineer (the designing may have been done by Artemon of Clazomenae. See Plut. *Per.* XXVII and D.S. XII. 28.3).

Archytas may have been exposed to new discoveries in artillery earlier than and independently of the work inspired by Dionysius. We have clear evidence that his fellow Tarentine, Zopyrus, was a prominent designer of an advanced form of Greek artillery known as the belly-bow (Biton 62 and 65). Until recently scholars have dated Zopyrus' activity to around the middle of the fourth century (Marsden 1971: 98, n. 52). Kingsley has now provided strong arguments, however, leading to the conclusion that Zopyrus was active in the last quarter of the fifth century (1995a: 149–55). Biton tells us that he created bows for Cumae and Miletus, and by far the most plausible time for such activity would be before Cumae was conquered by the Sabellians in 421 and before Miletus came under Persian control in 402. It is probable then that Zopyrus was one of the Italians invited to Syracuse by Dionysius I in 399, precisely because he had already developed prototypes of the new artillery. It may be that some improvements were made in Syracuse and that such artillery was thought to have been first developed only in 399, because the first clear evidence for its effective use was at Motya in 397. If this dating for Zopyrus is correct, then he belonged to the generation before Archytas, and it is probable that Archytas knew of his work, even if Zopyrus did much of his work outside Tarentum.

Diels (1965: 23) was quite right, moreover, to suggest that this Zopyrus may well be the same as the Zopyrus given in Iamblichus' catalogue of Pythagoreans from Tarentum (*VP* 267). It is important to recognize, however, that there is no necessary connection between Zopyrus' success in making artillery and his being a Pythagorean and no reason to assume that there was a school of specifically Pythagorean technicians at Tarentum with whom Archytas studied. We have no idea in what sense Zopyrus was a Pythagorean. He may simply have followed a Pythagorean way of life.

There is evidence that ancient technicians moved around considerably from city to city (Cambiano 1998: 307; Kingsley 1995a: 151–52; Burkert 1992), and the evidence we have for Zopyrus himself indicates that his belly-bows were developed not for Tarentum but for Miletus and Cumae at quite opposite ends of the Greek world (Biton 62 and 65). It is perfectly possible that he gained his technical knowledge from an equally itinerant craftsman rather than from a supposed school of Pythagorean technicians in Tarentum. Just as there has been a mistaken tendency by some scholars to think of the Pythagoreans any time that mathematics raises its head in an ancient text, so there is a danger of assuming that any technical work that involved mathematical expertise, especially if such work is completed in Italy, was carried out by the Pythagoreans. So Diels concludes that, when Dionysius is said to have gathered technicians from Italy, this is likely to be a reference to the Pythagoreans and especially to Archytas (1965: 21). As we have seen there is good reason to assume that Zopyrus was one of these technicians, but there is no reason to assume that technicians who came from Italy were always or even usually Pythagoreans. Nor are the technicians summoned by Dionysius from Greece proper and from Carthaginian territory likely to have been Pythagoreans. Applied mathematics is not the exclusive domain of the Pythagoreans (see e.g. Huffman 2002a).

There is, moreover, no obvious connection between the sort of mathematics which Archytas was pursuing and the type of artillery in use in his day and designed in part by Zopyrus. It is crucial to recognize that the types of artillery in use in the first half of the fourth century were non-torsion devices whose central component was the composite bow (Marsden 1969: 5–16). The "belly-bow" (*gastraphetēs*) had a curved end to the stock which could be rested against the archer's belly, thus allowing him to apply more force to pulling back the bow (Marsden 1969: 55). Zopyrus' versions of the belly-bow were advances in that they introduced a winch rather than relying upon the strength of a single man in order to bend the bow, and were mounted on a base so that, since they did not have to be manipulated by an individual, they could be larger and heavier. Zopyrus' biggest bow could shoot a six foot wooden missile which was 4.5 inches in diameter (Marsden 1969: 14). For the design of such bows sophisticated mathematics was not required. The solution to the problem of finding two mean proportionals in continued proportion, i.e. the solution to the problem of doubling the cube, which Archytas was the first to discover, is of no practical application in designing these bows. It was of importance in the development of later torsion artillery, which relied on "springs" of hair or rope, in order to determine spring-diameters. Such artillery was not likely to have been developed before 350 (Marsden 1969: 56–60), however, and the application of the mathematics of the two mean proportionals to it did not arise until even later, sometime in the third century (Marsden 1969: 39–41). We should conclude then that Zopyrus did invent important artillery devices but should not jump to the conclusion that this was a result of his being a Pythagorean or having studied specifically Pythagorean mathematics. Nor should we outrun the ancient evidence to conclude that Archytas was an engineering genius who outfitted Tarentum with mechanical devices to defend it against attack and designed artillery to take its enemies' towns. We have to rest content with the knowledge that he was a successful general and will have known something about the use of artillery because of that.

The best evidence suggests that Tarentum was a democracy for the entire time that Archytas was active in the city, although certainty is impossible. As we have seen, Aristotle says that there was a revolution leading to a democracy, when a great number of nobles were killed in a war with the Iapygians in 473 (*Pol.* 1303a; Diodorus supplies the date). Later, at *Politics* 1320b, Aristotle reports further features of the Tarentine constitution which suggest that it was a democracy. He comments on their division of magistracies so that some were elected and some were filled by the particularly democratic procedure of lot. Aristotle also praises the Tarentine policy of gaining the goodwill of the multitude by making some of the possessions of the wealthy available to the needy. Aristotle uses the present tense in describing these policies, and they are very much in accord with Archytas' statements about good government in Fragment 3 (see the commentary), so that it is reasonable to assume that Aristotle is describing the Tarentine government of the mid-fourth century, which still had the form familiar to and perhaps partially instituted by Archytas. Some of the features of the Tarentine constitution as described by Aristotle could be consistent with a government that was a compromise between oligarchy and democracy, but most of the emphasis is on the features that favor the multitude. A final passage in the *Politics* suggests again that Aristotle primarily thought of Tarentum as a democracy. In his discussion of kinds of democracies, Aristotle notes that Tarentum's democracy is based on an unusually large number of fishermen, as Athens' democracy was based on a large number of citizens who staffed the triremes (*Pol.* 1291b14 ff.).

Aristotle's evidence for democracy at Tarentum is supported by the few other surviving references to the government there in the later fifth and fourth centuries. Strabo reports that "the Tarentines were once exceedingly powerful, when they had a democratic government" (ἴσχυσαν δέ ποτε οἱ Ταραντῖνοι καθ' ὑπερβολὴν πολιτευόμενοι δημοκρατικῶς, A4) and ties this description to the time of Archytas. Diogenes Laertius similarly presents Archytas' success in Tarentum as a result of his popularity with the masses (A1 τοῖς πολλοῖς), just as the *Suda* presents him as chosen *stratēgos* by the citizens (A2 ὑπὸ τῶν πολιτῶν). It is, of course, quite likely that there was some civil strife between democrats and oligarchs in Tarentum, as there was elsewhere in the Greek world. It is thus possible that, at times between 473 and 350, there were periods of oligarchy, but there is not a scrap of direct evidence for oligarchy at Tarentum in this period and, as we have seen, considerable evidence for a democracy. Certainly we have to reject the suggestion of some scholars that, simply because Archytas was a Pythagorean or because Tarentum was a Spartan foundation, the government of Tarentum must have been an oligarchy, with only occasional bouts of democracy. Thus, Minar asserts, dogmatically and with no supporting evidence, first of the revolution in 473 that "this 'accidental' democratic triumph cannot have lasted for long" (1942: 88) and then that ". . . in the fourth century the aristocrats had matters fairly well under control" (1942: 90). Although Ciaceri rightly points out that the constitutional characteristics described in Aristotle do not necessitate a democracy, he is unjustified in sweeping away the clear testimony in Strabo and the clear implication in Aristotle that Tarentum was a democracy in the fourth century, merely on the supposition that Tarentum could not have lost the aristocratic leanings which it inherited from Sparta (1927–32: II. 446–47). It is true that Tarentum's colony Heraclea, founded in the 430s had officials named ephors as at Sparta, and it is thus plausible that Tarentum too had officials with this name. This tells us nothing, however, about how the ephors functioned at Heraclea or Tarentum, and there is no reason to assume that the government had to be an oligarchy because this name was used for officials. After all the title *stratēgos*, typical of Athenian democracy, was the title of the office Archytas himself held. Nor is there any reason to assume that Archytas disapproved of the democracy in Tarentum; Fragment 3 suggests that he supported the democratic reforms by which the rich gave to the poor.

ARCHYTAS' PRIVATE LIFE AND CHARACTER

We know virtually nothing about Archytas' private life. Anecdotes, even if they ultimately go back to Aristoxenus, provide a very unreliable source of information. These anecdotes suggest that Archytas owned an extensive estate, which was worked at least in part by slaves (A7), but this is what we would have expected of a prominent member of any Greek city-state at this time. Other anecdotes present Archytas as liking children and as allowing the children of his slaves into the dining room at dinner parties (A8). He was famous for designing a clapper with which to entertain children (A10). His philosophical discussions with his companions were evidently held in the sacred precincts in the city, which provided pleasant and uncrowded places to meet (A9).

The goal of most of the anecdotes in Aristoxenus' *Life of Archytas* must have been to illustrate Archytas' many virtues, and again it is doubtful how historically reliable these accounts are. Nonetheless, there are indications that Aristoxenus, while presenting Archytas in a positive light, was also able to see the weaknesses in his character, which he had to overcome. The central theme of the anecdotes is the importance of acting only under the direction of reason and never when controlled by our passions. Archytas distrusts bodily pleasure precisely because of its interference with intellect, which he regards as the best gift of gods to men (A9a). Under the sway of the most intense pleasures we are not able to reason at all. He refuses to punish slaves, who have neglected his estate in his absence, because he has been overcome by anger and believes that we should never let our emotions rather than our reason guide our actions (A7). Aristoxenus' presentation of this anecdote, while underlining Archytas' self-control, also suggests that Archytas was, in fact, prone to anger. His temper may have led him to want to swear, but in another story we are told of his temperance in restraining himself from actually uttering the offensive language, although he scrawled it on a wall instead (A11). Perhaps it was a bit of self-knowledge which led him to say that "just as it is difficult to find a fish without bones, so it is also difficult to find a man who does not possess some treacherous and prickly characteristic" (A11a). At any rate Archytas was not a dour recluse but enjoyed children (A8) and thought that even the highest intellectual achievement brought no satisfaction without a friend with whom to share it (A7a). Strabo connects the prosperity of Tarentum in the fourth century to Archytas' self-control and rejection of a life devoted to pleasure and regards the demise of Tarentum and its need to call in mercenary generals as a result of the wanton way of life (τρυφή) that arose after Archytas' death (A4). A number of scholars have noticed this moralizing shape to the history of Tarentum (e.g. Purcell 1994: 389), and it may in part go back to Aristoxenus' *Life of Archytas*.

THE DEATH OF ARCHYTAS AND HORACE'S "ARCHYTAS ODE"

Some scholars, following the ancient scholia (See A3a and A3b), have supposed that the speaker of Horace's famous "Archytas Ode" (1. 28 = A3) is Archytas himself and that we accordingly know that he died in a shipwreck, since the speaker says that he was "overwhelmed by the south wind in Illyrian waves." By identifying the Matine shore near which Archytas is said to be buried (line 3) with the shore near Mt. Garganus up the east coast of Italy above the heel of the boot, one completes the romantic picture of the *stratēgos* Archytas dying during one last expedition against the native peoples of the region (Ciaceri 1927–32: III, 4). This is almost certainly a misinterpretation of the ode, however. It would be awkward to have Archytas address himself in the first line of the poem and in line 14, but it is impossible for the Archytas who is addressed in the first line of the poem to be the same as the speaker of the poem who addresses himself as "me also" (i.e. in addition to you, Archytas, and the others whose deaths I have discussed) in line 21. There is, in fact, an overwhelming consensus that the poem is a monologue spoken by the corpse of a drowned sailor,[6] who first apostrophizes the great Archytas to make the point that death waits for us all, however remarkable our achievements, before turning to a passing sailor in order to beg burial in line 23 (West 1995: 132; Santirocco 1986: 62 ff.; Williams 1980: 5 ff.; Nisbet and Hubbard 1970: 317ff. [see their references for other interpretations of the poem]; Wilkinson 1945: 108 ff.; Wuilleumier 1939: 74–75 [see his references to earlier scholarship]).[7]

The dead sailor's assertion that "me too the south wind . . . has overwhelmed in the Illyrian waves" does not indicate that Archytas also died

---

[6] It is an intriguing suggestion that the speaker might be the Pythagorean Hippasus, who was supposedly drowned at sea for revealing Pythagorean secrets (Iamb. *VP* 88), and who has here come back from the dead to beg a passing sailor for the burial of an unburied Archytas (MacKay 1977). Yet, the first lines clearly do suggest that Archytas is buried, and none of the details of Horace's presentation of the speaker give any hint that he is Hippasus (e.g. no reference to his divulging of secrets). It is hard to see why Horace would introduce such a speaker and make no allusion to his peculiar history.

[7] Frischer has proposed a radically new reading of the poem in a learned and provocative article (1984). His interpretation is attractive in that it makes Horace's persona the speaker for the first twenty lines as he is in all the other odes. The problem is that, starting with *me* in line 21, the speaker has to change, since Horace cannot be describing himself as having died in a shipwreck. Frischer's solution to this problem is the suggestion that lines 21–36 of the poem are a quotation of the epitaph on Archytas' cenotaph before which Horace is imagined to be standing. This suggestion is highly problematic. He cites parallels for epitaphs incorporated into other Latin poetry of the golden age (1984: 94), but all these examples are much shorter than the supposed epitaph in the Archytas ode (2 lines as opposed to 15) and, most importantly, all are clearly introduced in the preceding text as epitaphs. Nothing in the immediately preceding lines of the Archytas ode suggests that a quotation of an epitaph begins in line 21. Frischer argues that *quoque* in line 21 is used inceptively and functions in effect as quotation marks to indicate the quotation of the epitaph. While he provides good examples of *quoque* used inceptively (1984: 92), these examples come from passages clearly marked in other ways as beginnings (e.g. the beginning of a book in Livy or Vergil). Moreover, it remains true that by far the most common use of *quoque* is as the copulative adverb "too," so that it is very unlikely that any reader would be tempted to interpret a *quoque* in the 21st line of a poem as an inceptive *quoque*, particularly when the *me* which begins the line is clearly in parallel to the *te* that begins the poem.

by shipwreck. The speaker has discussed a number of forms of death in the preceding twenty lines (including those of sailors in line 18) and is only asserting that he too, like all those discussed, has met the inevitable fate of death, although in his particular case the death came from shipwreck. There is simply no hint as to how Archytas died. Nor does the ode tell us anything about the nature of his tomb or burial beyond the conventional reference to a "small amount of dust" (line 3). We might hope that Horace is at least indicating that he knows of a tomb of Archytas "near the Matine shore" (line 3), but the exact reference of the adjective Matine has proved elusive (see Nisbet and Hubbard 1970: 322–23 for a full discussion). The connections of the adjective point to south-east Italy and some specifically to Tarentum but tell us little more than that Archytas was buried somewhere near Tarentum, which we would have guessed anyway. There is thus no indication that Horace wrote the ode with any specific knowledge about Archytas' death or tomb.[8]

RECEPTION

Although Horace's ode tells us nothing about Archytas' death (or life for that matter), it does provide important evidence for the Roman reception of Archytas in the first century BC. Apart from the fourth century BC, the first centuries BC and AD were clearly the period of Archytas' greatest fame in antiquity. In addition to Horace's ode, Propertius alludes once to Archytas (IV. 1b.77 = A3c), Varro once (B8), Vitruvius four times, and Cicero no less than eleven times. In the first century AD, Valerius Maximus refers to him three times, Quintilian once, Columella once, and the elder Pliny names him as a source six times. In part this is clearly due to a conscious attempt on the part of the Romans to claim Pythagoreanism as a native Italian philosophy and Archytas as a native Italian philosopher (see the commentary on A9a). Horace portrays Archytas as a loyal Pythagorean according to whose judgment, Pythagoras "was no mean authority on nature and truth" (lines 14–15). The description of Archytas as one "who measured the sea and the earth" is a reference to his fame as a geometer, since the Latin

---

[8] Frischer points out that tombs were not generally built near the shore and that the archaeological evidence suggests that such tombs were generally cenotaphs for people who died at sea and thus that Horace is imagining the speaker of the poem as standing before the cenotaph of Archytas, who died in a shipwreck (1984: 81 ff.). He is quick to point out that this need not mean that there really was such a cenotaph or that Archytas died in this way (1984: 80). In fact he argues that Horace has given Archytas a death at sea to make a symbolic point (1984: 83). It is also true that we need not take "near the Matine shore" literally as on or near the shore. Tarentum is in an obvious enough sense close to the shore.

terrae mensor is a literal translation of the Greek *geō-metrēs* (Nisbet and Hubbard 1970: 320) and fits Archytas' great geometrical skill as revealed in his solution to the problem of doubling the cube (A14–A15). On the other hand, the claim that he measured "the sands without number" may be a reference to Archimedes' work entitled *The Sand Reckoner*, since there is no evidence for a work of this sort by Archytas. Either Horace is confusing Archimedes and Archytas here, or as is more likely, he is not concerned with making careful attributions of mathematical achievements and treats the reckoning of the number of grains of sand as one of the marvelous achievements common to all mathematicians (Nisbet and Hubbard 1970: 321).[9]

What is, at first sight, most surprising is Horace's emphasis on Archytas' work as an astronomer who "investigated the heavenly realms and . . . traversed the rounded sky."[10] It is true that Archytas refers to astronomy as one of the four canonical sciences in Fragment 1, but there is no trace elsewhere of any particular achievement of Archytas in this field. Yet Propertius, writing shortly after Horace, also presents Archytas as a great astronomer (A3c). The astrologer of Propertius IV. 1 supports his

[9] Frischer argues (1984: 75–76 and n. 10) that the counting of grains of sand "was a proverbial expression for hybristically attempting the impossible" and uses this as an important point in his argument that lines 1–6 of the ode are sarcastic and not laudatory. This is one plausible interpretation of Horace's expression. Frischer's dismissal of a possible reference to the sand reckoner of Archimedes, however, does not really work. He makes the point that Archimedes' treatise does not claim to count the sand in the world but uses a grain of sand as a unit to determine the size of a finite universe. It is true, however, that many books are known mainly by their title and assumptions about their contents rather than a precise understanding of their actual argument. It seems to be quite possible that Horace never read the *Sand Reckoner* but, on the basis of the title and a common perception of it, sees it as an attempt to count the grains of sand. Such a perception does in fact get some support from the text of the *Sand Reckoner*. At the beginning, Archimedes refers to the belief that the number of grains of sand in the world is infinite and implies that he thinks that a number can be put to them, although he does not claim that he will actually count them. It seems to me quite possible that Horace is referring to the bold attempt of mathematicians to set a number to the grains of sand, which is to be contrasted to their burial by a few handfuls of dust, without assuming that the counting the sand is *per se* hybristic and silly.

[10] It is commonly said that Horace's description of Archytas as *aërias temptasse domos* suggests audacity or impiety on Archytas' part (Nisbet and Hubbard 1970: 324). Frischer uses this image of Archytas "storming heaven" as a key part of his interpretation of lines 1–6 as heavily sarcastic. It is true that *tempto* can convey this sense of hybristic audacity, but it is also used elsewhere in Horace with no such connotation. "Virtue, opening heaven wide for those not deserving to die, tries a path (*temptat iter*) denied to others" (*Odes* III. 2.21–22). Horace swears that in the Muses' company he "will gladly as a mariner essay (*temptabo*) the raging Bosphorus" (*Odes* III. 4.29–31). Indeed, as an Epicurean, Horace has no reason to think Archytas impious for investigating the heavens. It seems more likely that Horace is portraying Archytas as "essaying the heavens" in the sense of investigating, studying, or making trial of the heavens rather than as "storming the heavens." As the parallels above show, *tempto* often suggests the attempt to journey through or to some place and this fits perfectly Archytas' journey to the supposed edge of the heavens to prove that they are unlimited. *Tempto* suggests the audacity of great achievement without necessarily imputing hybris to the attempt.

ability to predict the future and "move the constellations on the bronze sphere" (either a bronze sphere with the constellations on it or an orrery, see Cic. *De Rep.* I. XV. 22; for orreries, see Keyser 1998), by claiming descent from the Babylonian Horops, who is in turn the offspring of Archytas. He also claims Conon of Samos, the third-century astronomer, mathematician and friend of Archimedes, as a forefather. Thus Archytas is joined with Conon as great Greek astronomers on whose work Babylonian astrology is based. It is always possible that these portrayals of Archytas are based on reports of his work in astronomy, which have not survived, but it is odd that they would have left no other ripple in the tradition.[11]

I would suggest that this image of Archytas as a master astronomer is based on Archytas' most famous argument as a cosmologist, the argument to show that the universe is unlimited. That argument corresponds to Horace's description in striking ways. The argument is a thought experiment. Archytas imagines himself at the supposed limit of the universe and then asks whether he would be able to extend a stick beyond the limit or not. Since our intuitions suggest that he would be able to extend the stick, Archytas asks us to advance to the new limit set by the end of the stick and asks the same question. In this way he will be able to go on extending his stick, advancing to the new limit and asking his question without limit so that the universe is shown to be unlimited (see A24 for a detailed discussion). Horace's description of Archytas as investigating or making trial of (*temptasse*) the heavens and traversing (*percurrisse*) the rounded sky matches well enough the repeated attempts to extend the stick and the repeated advances beyond the supposed limit. Horace's indication that Archytas did this "with his mind" (*animo* – line 5) corresponds exactly to the character of Archytas' argument as a thought experiment. Propertius makes Archytas more explicitly an astronomer dealing with the constellations, but Propertius is not an historian of science, and he may simply be embellishing Horace's picture of an Archytas who traverses the heavens and assigning to him the traditional accomplishments of an astronomer.

---

[11] It has been suggested that Archytas' investigation of the heavens and journey through the sky had nothing to do with astronomy but are instead references to an account by Archytas of a mystical journey of the soul through the heavens, which is the predecessor of Plato's story of Er in *Republic* x and of the ascent of human souls to the heavens in the *Phaedrus* (Morrison 1958: 215). There is, however, absolutely no trace of such a journey elsewhere in the evidence for Archytas, and Horace's description of Archytas is more plausibly explained by reference to the argument in A24, as I suggest in the next paragraph. Morrison is right that knowledge of astronomy conveys no hope of immortality to contrast with Horace's emphasis on Archytas' mortality, while a mystical journey of the soul might. Nonetheless, it is perfectly intelligible that Horace is contrasting Archytas' almost divine capability of surveying the whole cosmos with his mind with the inevitability of his death.

The first-century portrait of Archytas thus sees him as a master geometer (Horace and Vitruvius in A15c) and as a cosmologist/astronomer who has traversed the heavens with his mind (Horace, Propertius) but who found such investigations unsatisfying without a friend with whom to share them (Cicero – A7a). Horace ultimately emphasizes Archytas' achievements as a mathematician and cosmologist only to contrast them with the fact that, like all other men he will die and amount to only a few handfuls of dust. For the contrast to work, however, the image of Archytas' great accomplishments must first be established. Cicero adds to this the portrait, probably based on Aristoxenus, of an Archytas, who regards reason as our best guide and who, therefore, refuses to act in the heat of anger and is suspicious of bodily pleasure, which can obliterate our ability to reason (A9a; A7, Texts D and E).

Although the ancient reception of Archytas was almost uniformly positive, there are some traces of a tradition that was critical of him, particularly for the obscurity of his work in music theory. There are two verses satirizing Archytas by the sophist Bion of Borysthenes (335–245 BC). Bion (A3d) begins with a parody of Homer, *Iliad* III. 182, in order to portray Archytas as self-satisfied and pompous (ὀλβιότυφε, "happy in your conceit" as opposed to Homer's description of Agamemnon as ὀλβιόδαιμον, "of blessed lot"). Archytas is "born for the lyre" (ψαλληγενές) in contrast to Homer's Agamemnon, who is described as "born with the blessing of fortune" (μοιρηγενές). In the second line, Bion explains that Archytas' conceit is based on his devotion to the very technical and obscure controversies in musical theory about the structure of the tetrachord (cf. A16). His language with purposeful ambiguity describes Archytas as most experienced in the "quarrel over the *hypatē*" (*hypatē* refers literally "the highest string" on the lyre, but is the technical term for the lowest pitch in the tetrachord, cf. A16), while at the same time implying that the quarrel reaches the highest intensity.[12]

---

[12] It is not absolutely certain that Archytas of Tarentum is Bion's target here. It might be that it is rather Archytas from Mytilene, who is described as a musician by Diogenes Laertius (A1 – see further below), but whose date is uncertain. It is hard to say which Archytas would have been more famous in the third century, so that we cannot decide on those grounds. It could be said that a practicing musician was quarreling over the *hypatē*, but the use of the technical term works better as an attack on the obscurity of Archytas' musical theory. Diogenes Laertius seems to take it as an attack on Archytas of Tarentum, since he comments immediately after the verses that Bion "made fun of both music and geometry." The pairing of music with geometry suggests that Diogenes thought that the target was not practical music but the technical music theory which was a branch of mathematics alongside geometry (Archytas B1 and Plato, *R.* VII). For further discussion of this issue and Bion's verses on Archytas see Kindstrand 1976: 194–97.

In the early tradition and up to the fourth century AD, Archytas is, strikingly, never connected to the religious and mystical side of Pythagoreanism. In the fourth century AD, however, Eunapius describes Archytas as emulating the wisdom of Pythagoras, which is associated with the inquiry about the gods (A6d). Much later, in the eleventh century AD, Psellus describes Archytas as pursuing the secret wisdom which Pythagoras began. Archytas and Pythagoras are said to use occult powers and contemptible spells in order to disturb what should not be disturbed (the dead?) and to foretell the future (A6f). It is hard to tell whether Eunapius or Psellus (or their sources) are referring to actual texts ascribed to Archytas, in which there is appeal to occult powers or inquiry about the gods, or whether they (1) know of this side of Pythagoreanism, (2) know that Archytas was one of the most prominent members of the Pythagorean tradition, and then (3) simply assume that he was involved in the same sort of inquiries as were ascribed to Pythagoras. The second possibility is supported by the fact that Eusebius, writing not long before Eunapius, expressly asserts that Archytas nowhere claimed to have wisdom about the gods and how to enter into discourse with them (A6e). Thus, there is little evidence in the tradition for Archytas as the sort of Pythagorean sage who professes to have special wisdom about the gods. Certainly his use of the "bull-roarers," which were employed in some initiation rituals, as one example among many in his discussion of acoustics (Fr. 1) is no grounds for assuming that Archytas had any closer tie to mystery religion than the average Greek, although it is possible that as leader of his city he may have officiated at some mystery ceremonies (Kingsley 1995a: 164). In the medieval period, however, under the name Architas, he became one of the great wise men of the ancient world and works such as *Lumen animae* and *De mirabilibus mundi* assign to him magical remedies for bodily ills and special knowledge about miraculous features of the natural world (see the appendix on spurious writings).

OTHER MEN NAMED ARCHYTAS

Any attempt to reconstruct the life and writings of Archytas is complicated by the existence of other figures named Archytas in the ancient tradition. There are three texts which refer to "Archytas the elder." Photius says that Plato became the "pupil of Archytas the elder (πρεσβυτέρου)" (A5b10) and Apuleius reports that Plato "studied with the Pythagoreans Eurytus of Tarentum and the older (*senior*) Archytas" (A5b7). There was controversy in the ancient tradition as to whether Plato or Archytas was the teacher whom the other followed (see further below), and the texts in

Photius and Apuleius probably arise from a polemic against the view that Plato was the teacher of Archytas (Burkert 1972a: 92, n. 42). Such a polemic would naturally have asserted that Archytas was the elder. The third text is not quite so easy to explain in this way. A passage in Iamblichus' *On the Pythagorean Life* gives a list of Pythagoreans who as young men studied with Pythagoras in his old age (*VP* 104 = A6b). Most of the figures on the list cannot possibly have studied with Pythagoras and the list looks like an attempt to show that all the great names in early Pythagoreanism had studied with the master (e.g. Philolaus, Eurytus, Lysis, Empedocles). It is in Archytas' case that the anachronism is most pronounced, and it is possible that a later commentator recognized that it was impossible for the famous Archytas to have studied with Pythagoras and thus introduced an "Archytas the elder" in order to remove the chronological impossibility. This creation of an "Archytas the elder" might also explain the assertion in the *Suda* that Archytas was the teacher of Empedocles (A2), although in Iamblichus Empedocles is listed alongside Archytas as a fellow student of Pythagoras. However these three texts are to be explained, it seems unlikely that there was more than one Archytas in the Pythagorean tradition. There is only one Archytas listed in the catalogue of Pythagoreans at the end of Iamblichus' *On the Pythagorean Life*, a catalogue that probably goes back to Aristoxenus.

Xenophon refers to an Archytas as eponymous ephor at Sparta in 405 BC (*Hell.* II. 1.10 and 3.10). Athenaeus knows of an Archytas who wrote an *Art of Cookery* and who gargled hot water so that he could eat hot food and thus get more than others who could not (XII. 516c; I. 5f; cf. *Suda* s.v. ὀψοφαγία and Φιλόξενος). Plutarch quotes a line from the poet Archytas of Amphissa (*Quaest. Graec.* 295a), who is probably a contemporary of Euphorion and Eratosthenes in the third century BC (Athen. III. 82a; Stob. IV. 32.1.15). Diogenes initially lists four men with the name Archytas including the philosopher (A1). The fourth on the list is described as a writer of epigrams and might be the same as Archytas of Amphissa. The other two on the list produce problems.

The second, a *mousikos* (the term is applied to both music theorists and practicing musicians, cf. its application to Aristoxenus at Athen. XII. 545a) from Mytilene, is potentially hard to distinguish from our Archytas, who was famous for his work in music theory. There are, however, only a few passages that could be references to the musician from Mytilene. There seems no reason to reject Diogenes' anecdote as applying to the musician who, when chided for his weak voice, said that his instrument would speak for him (D.L. VIII. 82). It seems most probable that the Archytas *harmonikos*, who is said by the Peripatetic Chamaeleon (350 – after 281 BC) to have discussed the erotic poetry of Alcman (Athen. XIII. 600f), is Archytas of Mytilene, since songs by Alcman might have been part of his repertoire, while we have no other evidence that Archytas of Tarentum engaged in analysis of poetry. Finally, although Athenaeus reports that many Pythagoreans, including Archytas, played the flute and that Archytas wrote a treatise on flutes (IV. 184e = B6) and although Archytas does use flutes as examples in his acoustic theory (B1), it is also quite possible that there was confusion in the tradition and that the treatise on flutes was by Archytas of Mytilene.

The third Archytas on Diogenes' list is the author of a treatise *On Agriculture*. The problem is that Varro identifies Archytas the Pythagorean (B8) and Columella (B8a) Archytas of Tarentum as having written about matters having to do with agriculture (*agri cultura* – Varro) and husbandry (*rusticis rebus* – Columella). Is Diogenes then wrong to think that it was a separate Archytas who wrote the treatise *On Agriculture*? It is important to note that neither Varro nor Columella ascribes a book specifically entitled *On Agriculture* to Archytas. Varro makes clear that the fifty odd authors whom he names as relevant to agriculture have written on a variety of topics (*alius de alia re*). Aristotle and Theophrastus are present on both Varro's and Columella's lists, and neither of these authors wrote a treatise *On Agriculture*. It is presumably the various Theophrastan and Aristotelian treatises on plants and animals that are at issue. Pliny also lists an Archytas as one of the foreign authorities for his *Natural History* some six times (B8b; at I. 10c.6 he is specifically identified as Archytas of Tarentum). The books of Pliny's *Natural History* for which Archytas is cited as an authority deal with animals (Book 8), birds (Book 10), fruit trees, including vines and olives (Books 14, 15, and 17), and farm crops, including plowing and weather (Book 18). Aristotle and Theophrastus, along with Democritus, are also cited as authorities for each of these books. There is no indication of the title of the book(s) of Archytas on which Pliny drew.

It could be then that there was just one treatise *On Agriculture* circulating under the name of Archytas on which Varro, Columella and Pliny all drew and to which Diogenes refers, but that, whereas Diogenes regards the book as by a separate Archytas, the other authors regard it as by Archytas of Tarentum. Given the proliferation of pseudo-Archytan treatises by the first century BC and the fame of Archytas of Tarentum in that period, it is more likely that a treatise by another Archytas is being ascribed to the famous Archytas than the reverse. On the other hand, in addition to the treatise *On Agriculture* to which Diogenes refers, there may have been treatises by Archytas of Tarentum on plants and animals or a general cosmological treatise in which plants and animals were discussed on which Varro, Columella and Pliny drew. What particularly suggests this is testimonium A23a, which deals with the shape of the parts of plants and animals. While it is not impossible that such a discussion could have occurred in a work entitled *On Agriculture*, it seems more likely that it came from a treatise on plants or animals in general, such as those of Theophrastus and Aristotle. If this is so, then Diogenes may be right that the treatise *On Agriculture* is by a different Archytas, but Varro, Columella and Pliny may not be drawing on, or not drawing solely on that work but rather from writings on plants and animals by Archytas of Tarentum, of which A23a is our clearest indication.

After describing his four men with the name Archytas, Diogenes continues "Some say that there was also a fifth, an architect, whose book *On Mechanism* has been preserved. It has the following beginning, 'I heard the following from Teucer of Carthage'." The initial list of four men with the name Archytas is likely to be derived from Demetrius of Magnesia's *On Poets and Writers of the Same Name* (ca. 50 BC), which is Diogenes' usual source for homonymous writers (D.L. I. 38; Mejer 1978: 38–39). The introduction of the information about this fifth Archytas with the expression "some say" simply indicates that Diogenes is changing sources and is no indication that the material is less reliable. It is typical of Diogenes to add material from other sources to what he found in Demetrius (e.g. VIII. 46–47; Mejer 1978: 38–39). Diogenes makes no attempt to reconcile this report about a book *On Mechanism* by another Archytas with his comments a few lines later about Archytas of Tarentum's contribution to mechanics. It is important to note that Diogenes identifies the fifth Archytas as an architect and quotes the first line of the book in what is a clear attempt to prove that such a book existed.[13]

The only other evidence for a book on mechanism ascribed to an Archytas is Vitruvius' mention (B7 = VII , praef. 14) of Archytas in a long list of names of authors who had written about machines (*de machinationibus*). Vitruvius refers to Archytas on three other occasions. In each of these cases the emphasis is on his mathematical ability. Two of them occur in a passage in Book IX (praef. 13–14 = A15c), where Archytas is praised along-

---

[13] If we knew anything about the Teucer of Carthage mentioned in the first line of the book, we might be in a better position to decide whether Archytas of Tarentum was the author, but I have not found any other reference to Teucer of Carthage in ancient literature. Certainly it is a tantalizing idea that Archytas had contacts with Carthaginian writers. Archytas made it a practice to discuss his predecessors' work (see the philosophical overview), so that it would be in character for him to begin a work by expressing his debt to a predecessor.

side Eratosthenes for providing a solution to the problem of doubling the cube. This passage follows Eratosthenes (A15) in emphasizing the abstract geometrical character of Archytas' solution in terms of a semicylinder and is innocent of the false story later found in Plutarch, according to which Archytas used an instrument to solve the problem (see on A15). Archytas is also listed as a master of astronomy, geometry and music and called a mathematician at 1.1.17 (A1b).[14] It is striking that in the three cases where Archytas is praised for his mathematical abilities, he is identified as Archytas of Tarentum, whereas the author of the work on machines is simply Archytas. On the whole the evidence of Vitruvius suggests that he knew of a book by an Archytas on machines and he probably assumed that Archytas of Tarentum was meant, although there is a slight chance that he knew it was by another Archytas and hence did not identify him as from Tarentum. Diogenes' description of the fifth Archytas as an architect is intriguing in light of this testimony of Vitruvius. Vitruvius does not call his Archytas an architect, but Vitruvius' work was entitled *On Architecture*, so that it is possible that someone trying to correct or explain Vitruvius' reference to an Archytas who wrote on machines differentiated him from Archytas of Tarentum by calling him an architect. The paroemiographical tradition ascribes the invention of Archytas' clapper to Archytas the builder (τέκτων – A10, Text A), and this might also be a reference to the tradition that there was an Archytas who was an (ἀρχι)τέκτων.

Diogenes' citation of the first line makes it very likely that there was indeed in circulation a treatise *On Mechanism* ascribed to an Archytas. Is this book likely to be a genuine work of Archytas of Tarentum, which some wanted to deny to be his work, or is it likely to be in fact by a different Archytas? The story could be told either way, and certainty is not possible on this question. It is true, nonetheless, that Eratosthenes (A15 – third century BC), who clearly knew Archytas' work, characterized him as too theoretical and Athenaeus Mechanicus (A1a – first century BC), who also implies familiarity with Archytas' work describes it as "utterly removed and separated from practical considerations." As time goes on, the general trend in the ancient tradition is to move from this early presentation

---

[14] At the end of the list of names, Vitruvius appends the following relative clause: "who left to posterity many mechanical devices and sundials, which were discovered and explained by means of mathematics and natural science." This is confusing, since the passage that led up to the list of names emphasized their work as theoretical mathematicians rather than as technicians. It seems clear that Vitruvius is not claiming that all the authors in the list created mechanical devices and sundials. At any rate, when he comes to discuss sundials at IX. 8.1, he does not mention Archytas and mentions only Aristarchus, Apollonius and Scopinas from the seven names listed in Book 1. Nor do we have any other indication that Philolaus, who is also mentioned in the list, created any mechanical devices.

of Archytas as too theoretical to Plutarch's later version of an Archytas
who was the founder of mechanics and attacked by Plato for introducing
instruments into geometry. Given this general tendency in the tradition, it
seems more likely that a work on machines by an obscure Archytas would
come to be falsely associated with the famous Archytas of Tarentum, who
was also incorrectly being presented as having incurred Plato's wrath for
using instruments in mathematics, than that a genuine work of Archytas
on machines would be denied him. This conclusion would agree with my
argument in the philosophical overview that the evidence for Archytas' work
in mechanics has been radically overstated. The reports about Archytas'
clapper (A10) and his wooden dove (A10a), which should probably be
accepted as genuine, do not presuppose a technical presentation in a work
like *On Mechanism* and could well have derived even from Aristoxenus'
Life of Archytas.

WRITINGS

It is disappointing that neither Diogenes Laertius nor anyone else in the
ancient tradition provides us with a list of the writings of Archytas. Our
evidence for his writings depends largely on the book titles given by ancient
sources, when quoting his fragments; such sources are notoriously unreliable. The issues related to the various titles given to the works from which
the fragments of Archytas derive are discussed in detail in the commentary
on each fragment. Archytas' most important work appears to have been the
Harmonics. Fragment 1 is the beginning of this book, and Fragment 2 is also
likely to derive from it. The detailed accounts of Archytas' harmonic theory found in Ptolemy and Porphyry (A16–A18), as well as Boethius' report
of Archytas' proof to show that a superparticular ratio cannot be divided
into equal parts (A19), are all likely to be based on the *Harmonics*. This
then was a treatise that began with a discussion of the basic principles of
acoustics, defined the three types of mean which are of importance in music
theory, and went on to present Archytas' mathematical descriptions of the
tetrachord in the three main genera (chromatic, diatonic and enharmonic).
A second work, *On Sciences*, may have been a more general discussion of
the value of the mathematical sciences for human life and, in particular,
for the construction of a just state (Fr. 3). A third work entitled *Discourses*
(Διατριβαί) is more difficult to define because of the difficulty in determining the exact meaning of the title; it may have focused on ethical issues
and the application of mathematics to such issues (Fr. 4). It is, of course,
far from clear that any of these three titles go back to Archytas himself, and
they may be creations of the later tradition.

Beyond these specific titles, the nature of the testimonia for Archytas suggest that he produced works in other areas as well. It seems possible that he produced an account of the cosmos resembling the typical Presocratic treatise or Plato's *Timaeus*. Commentary on Archytas' views on optics, the unlimited extent of the cosmos, matter, and motion, which are found particularly in the Peripatetic tradition, may all be inspired by such a book (A13, A23, A23a, A24, A25). A work on definitions seems likely to lie behind Aristotle's comments in A22 (see also A12). Perhaps a biological treatise set forth the views alluded to in A23a, although this material may also derive from the more general cosmological treatise. It might be that a work on arithmetic set out Archytas' views on the nature of the one and other numbers (B5a, A20 and A21), but it is also possible that these reports are based on passing comments in other works such as the *Harmonics*. Did Archytas produce some sort of a treatise on geometry or solid geometry, in which his solution to the problem of doubling the cube (A14–A15) was presented? Finally, it is important to note that a number of testimonia, especially for Archytas' ethical views, derive from Aristoxenus' *Life of Archytas* rather than from any treatise of Archytas (A7, A9, A9a, A7a?, A8?, A11?, A11a?). It is possible that even Archytas' argument for the unlimited universe (A24), his account of vision (A25), or some of his definitions (A12, A22) in fact derive from anecdotes in Aristoxenus rather than from treatises of Archytas. All in all, it looks as if we have evidence for something like five or six treatises by Archytas.

The many writings to which the later tradition refers (*Suda* = A2) are likely not to be a reference to these five or six alone but also to include the considerable number of spurious treatises collected in Thesleff. Gregory of Corinth, in the twelfth century AD, refers to Archytas' writings as a model of Doric prose (A6g). Since Gregory never in fact uses Archytas for examples in his discussion of the details of the Doric dialect, it is likely that he did not know Archytas directly and that he is relying on the earlier tradition for his assertion of Archytas' importance as a model. He gives as his sources John Philoponus (sixth century AD) and Tryphon, a grammarian of the time of Augustus. So one or both of these authors knew of an extensive body of Archytas' writings, which again may have contained both genuine and spurious writings. It is important to note that the passage in Gregory does not show definitively that Tryphon knew of Archytas' writings as Thesleff suggests (1972: 74). To make Archytas the model for Doric prose is not necessarily to be seen as great praise for Archytas' style, since there were few other Doric prose writers.

As we have seen, it is uncertain whether the treatises *On Flutes* (B6), *On Machines* (B1 and B7), and *On Agriculture* (B1 and B8), which were in

circulation under the name of Archytas, were in fact by him or by other
men of the same name. The treatise *On the Decad* mentioned by Theon
(B5) might be by Archytas, but the treatise by Philolaus with which it is
paired is spurious (Huffman 1993: 347–50), thus suggesting that the same
may be true of the treatise under Archytas' name as well. Jerome's reference
to Archytas' discussion of odd numbers (B5a), if it is a reference to a specific
text, might be a reference to *On the Decad* or to some other lost work of
Archytas on arithmetic.

ARCHYTAS AND PLATO

Archytas was arguably most famous in the ancient tradition and is most
famous today for having rescued Plato from the tyrant of Syracuse,
Dionysius II, in 361. Both in Diogenes Laertius' life of Archytas (A1) and in
the *Suda* (A2) the first thing asserted about Archytas, after identifying his
city-state and father, is that he saved Plato from Dionysius. The quickest
way to identify Archytas then becomes as the friend of Plato (e.g. Mathieu
1987). This has left Archytas in the shadow of Plato, and for this reason I
have first tried to paint a portrait of Archytas that is largely independent of
the Platonic connection. That connection is more problematic than appears
at first sight. Modern scholarship has, indeed, already begun to call into
question the exact nature of the relationship between Archytas and Plato
(Lloyd 1990). Close examination of the ancient tradition shows that there
was, in fact, already considerable debate in antiquity as to how we should
understand the ties between the two men.

The most famous source of the story for Archytas' rescue of Plato and
for his relationship to Plato in general is the *Seventh Letter*, which purports
to be by Plato and in which Plato describes his involvement with the affairs
of his Syracusan friend Dion and Dionysius II, tyrant of Syracuse. The
authenticity of that letter and the extent to which we can use it as a reliable
source for the history of Plato or Archytas are matters of considerable
controversy to which I will return shortly. Before examining the letter,
however, it is worthwhile surveying the ancient tradition about Archytas'
connection to Plato, which appears to be independent of the letter. There are
two main strands to that tradition and they are, at first sight, contradictory.
The first strand portrays Archytas as the Pythagorean master at whose feet
Plato sat, while the second argues that Archytas was a nobody until he
studied with Plato. Each of these strands deserves close study.

The first strand is represented by texts A5b1–b13. The earliest source may
be Plato's pupil Hermodorus (D.L. III. 6) in the fourth century BC, but

Cicero in the first century BC is the first to mention Archytas explicitly, and the tradition continues until Tzetzes in the twelfth century AD. There is considerable variation from passage to passage but two elements are crucial: (1) Upon the death of Socrates in 399, Plato, at age 27, cast about looking for new teachers and new sources of wisdom. (2) One of the places where Plato sought instruction was the Pythagorean school in southern Italy and Sicily, and Archytas is regularly listed as one of the Pythagoreans whom Plato sought out. In addition to Archytas, Cicero (A5b2) lists Timaeus, Arion and Echecrates of Locri (so also Valerius Maximus in A5b6) along with Philolaus (A5b1). Philodemus simply reports that Plato went to visit the Pythagoreans without naming names (A5b4). Diogenes Laertius is the only source to give names of the Pythagoreans whom Plato visited and not name Archytas; Diogenes, perhaps on the authority of Plato's pupil Hermodorus, says that Plato visited Philolaus and Eurytus (D.L. III. 6; see Huffman 1993: 5). Apuleius, in the second century AD has Plato visit Archytas and Eurytus at Tarentum (A5b7). In the later tradition Archytas alone is mentioned as the teacher of Plato (Olympiodorus A5b9 [sixth century AD] and Photius A5b10 [ninth century AD]), and Plato is firmly assigned the position as ninth in the succession from Pythagoras (A5b10). The most colorful version of this tradition is the latest, that of Tzetzes in the twelfth century, who combines the story of Plato studying with Archytas with another famous story according to which Dionysius I became angry with Plato on his first visit to Sicily and gave Plato to a merchant or a Spartan admiral to be sold into slavery (Riginos 1976: 86–92). In Tzetzes' unique version the Spartan admiral, Polis, sells Plato to Archytas, who thus becomes Plato's master in both the economic and philosophical sense (A5b12–13). Tzetzes may have been partially inspired by Diodorus' version of the story, according to which Dionysius sold Plato directly and Plato was bought, evidently in Sicily, and sent back to Greece by unnamed philosophers (D.S. XV. 7.1; See Riginos 1976: 91).

The second strand is represented by texts A5c1 to A5c3. This tradition also goes back to the fourth century and appears in Demosthenes' (?) *Erotic Oration* (A5c1), which can be dated between 350 and 325 BC, even if it is not by Demosthenes.[15] The central features of this strand are: (1) Archytas is

---

[15] For a good survey of the debate about the authorship and date of the *Erotic Oration* see Clavaud 1974: 83–89. The majority of scholars have found its contents and style to differ too greatly from the rest of the Demosthenic corpus for it to be by Demosthenes. Clavaud, however, argues that it is easier to explain it as an atypical work by Demosthenes, perhaps used for teaching, than to explain how such an unusual work would come to be included in the corpus of Demosthenes' work, if it were not by Demosthenes. Clavaud dates it to 340–323 on a number of grounds. The strongest evidence

presented as primarily a political figure who only achieves power and fame
after and because of studying with the philosopher Plato; (2) Archytas and
Plato are just one of a series of statesman/ philosopher pairs, being joined
by Pericles/Anaxagoras, Alcibiades/Socrates and Timotheus/Isocrates.
Cicero adds some more statesman/philosopher pairs (Critias/Socrates!,
Epaminondas/Lysis and Agesilaus/Xenophon) and introduces an interesting change regarding Archytas and Plato. He makes Philolaus rather than
Plato the philosopher who influenced the statesman Archytas and correspondingly introduces Dion as the statesman whom Plato improved (A5c2).
The obvious explanation for this is that Cicero regarded Pythagoreanism
as a native Italian philosophy and did not want to make one of its most
famous exponents, Archytas, dependent on the Athenian, Plato. Philodemus, although earlier in A5b4 presenting Plato as going to Italy to study
with the Pythagoreans, in A5c3 lists Archytas as one of the pupils of Plato.
Plutarch and Aelian (A5c4–5) do not explicitly make Plato the teacher
of Archytas, but Plutarch lists Archytas along with the statesmen Pericles,
Dion and Epaminondas and portrays Archytas as primarily a politician who
participated in philosophy only to the degree that he could. Aelian pairs
Archytas with Solon as figures who did not simply live a quiet philosophical
life but who were both men of action and philosophers.

To which of these traditions about the connection of Archytas to Plato
does the *Seventh Letter* subscribe? There has been a tendency to say that the
letter shows Archytas as the friend of Plato and to thus assimilate the letter
to the first tradition, which makes Archytas Plato's Pythagorean master.
Closer examination of the letter indicates, however, that it is much closer
to the second tradition, which makes Plato Archytas' teacher. There is not
the slightest hint in the *Seventh Letter* that Plato ever regarded himself
as the pupil of Archytas. In fact, as Lloyd has shown, the implications
of the letter are that from Plato's point of view, Archytas' judgment in
philosophical matters is not very reliable (Lloyd 1990). Plato reports that
letters kept coming from Archytas (and others) which praised Dionysius'
progress in philosophy to the skies (A5, 339d–e), when as the sequel showed,
Dionysius understood little or nothing about Plato's philosophy. This can

is the reference to Timotheus and Archytas (A5c1), who seem to be presented as dead but who are
explicitly called "more recent examples" than Pericles and Alcibiades. Of course someone writing
200 years after the death of Timotheus and Archytas could technically refer to them as more recent
than Pericles, but, when we survey the past in this way for models, a reference to "more recent"
examples inevitably suggests that we will not be dealing with examples that are still in the distant
past but rather to examples that are drawn from recent history. Timotheus died shortly before 354,
so that the author of the *Erotic Oration* must be writing somewhere between 350 and 325, in order
to describe Timotheus' career as "recent."

only suggest either that Archytas did not have a firm grasp on Platonic philosophy or that for political reasons he was willing to deceive Plato about Dionysius' progress in philosophy, in order to persuade Plato to return. The letter may go even further and suggest that the half-baked philosophy that Dionysius thought he had learned was taught him by Archytas or even that Archytas was so out of touch with Platonic philosophy that he conversed with Dionysius, because he hoped to learn Platonic philosophy from him (Lloyd 1990: 165 and 168). So Archytas is hardly presented as the Pythagorean master with whom Plato studied; he is rather presented as someone who had an imperfect grasp of Plato's philosophy.

Archytas is first mentioned in the letter, when Plato is describing Dionysius II's attempt, after Plato's departure in 367/6, to get Plato to return to Syracuse (A5, 338 c–d). Plato initially resists this attempt. He reports that Archytas then visited Dionysius and along with others engaged in philosophical discussion with Dionysius, on the mistaken assumption that Plato had taught Dionysius II the principles of Platonic philosophy during his first visit with him in 367/6. We might argue that it is just the "others" who made this mistake but the implication is rather that Archytas did not understand that Dionysius had been a failure as Plato's pupil. Plato explains Archytas' visit to Dionysius by pointing out that before departing in 367/6 he had established hospitality and friendship between Archytas and those in Tarentum and Dionysius. These are the earliest dealings between Archytas and Plato that are explicitly established in the letter. The normal assumption, however, is that in order to establish these relations Plato himself must have previously established friendly relations with Archytas and his associates at Tarentum. Indeed, later, at 339e, Plato refers to his guest-friends and companions in Tarentum (ξένους τε καὶ ἑταίρους) and at 350a to Archytas and his other friends (φίλους) in Tarentum. It seems unlikely that he would have established those ties for the first time at the same time as he was arranging ties between Archytas and Dionysius II in 367/6, so it is not unreasonable to assume that he established connections with Archytas earlier. The *Seventh Letter* presents Plato as journeying to both Italy and Sicily, when he was about forty (388/7), when Dionysius I was still in power, although no specifics are given as to whom he visited (324a, 326b–d). It is natural to see this visit as the one described in tradition one above (Texts A5b1–13) and attested already by Hermodorus. So the *Seventh Letter* does seem to agree with the first tradition in having Plato journey to southern Italy and Sicily not long after the death of Socrates and in having Plato make connections with Archytas at this time, but, as we have seen, the nature of those connections is clearly quite different than is suggested by the first tradition. Far from alluding to any new intellectual enlightenment that he achieved as a result of the trip, the Plato of the *Seventh Letter* mainly complains of the devotion to hedonism that he found in Italy and Sicily (326b–d).

On the other hand, the letter presents Plato as taking the lead in establishing relations between Archytas and Dionysius II, relations that are said to be of considerable political importance (339d–e), so that the letter seems to be portraying Plato as partially responsible for Archytas' political success, which matches the relationship to be found between Plato and Archytas in the second tradition.[16] What exactly does the letter envisage as Plato's role? One interpretation would be that Plato establishes a relationship of hospitality and friendship between the city-state of Tarentum and Dionysus II as leader of Syracuse. On this reading "Archytas and those in Tarentum" at 338c–d is a reference to Archytas as the political leader of Tarentum.[17] Plutarch, in his life of Dion, is clearly following the letter closely, in that he uses the same language as the letter to describe the relationship (A5a1, XVIII. 5.4 – "friendship and hospitality," φιλία καὶ ξενία). Plutarch also says, however, that the relationship was established by Plato between Dionysius, on the one hand, and Archytas and the Pythagoreans, on the other. It might be that Plutarch is simply assuming that the Pythagoreans controlled the government, but the more obvious reading is that Plato established the relationship not between the states of Tarentum and Syracuse but between individuals. Plutarch uses the expression φιλία καὶ ξενία in several other passages and it always involves a relation between individuals (e.g. Solon v and Lysander XIX). The letter presents Archytas and those in Tarentum as urging Plato to come back to Syracuse, because otherwise the friendship would be destroyed and as pointing out that the friendship was of no small importance with regard to affairs of state (339d–e). Some might regard this as evidence that the friendship was between city-states all along, but it seems to be evidence that it was instead between individuals. There is no need to point out the political importance of the connection, if it has been a straightforward political connection all along.

What sort of relationship, then, does the *Seventh Letter* suggest was first established between Plato and Archytas in 388/7 and to which Archytas

---

[16] The probably spurious *Ninth Letter* also gives Plato the role of Archytas' master in politics.

[17] That there was, at some point during the reign of Dionysius II, a relationship of friendship between the two states is indicated by the story in Athenaeus (xv. 700d), reported on the authority of the poet Euphorion (b. 275 BC), that Dionysius dedicated a lampstand in the town hall at Tarentum, which could hold as many lamps as there were days of the year. Herman 1987: 132–35 gives examples of powerful rulers who became *xenoi* of whole states. Aristoxenus also mentions ambassadors sent by Dionysius II to Tarentum, one of whom was Polyarchus (A9).

appealed in trying to persuade Plato to return to Sicily in 361? Plato refers to his guest-friends and companions (ξένους τε καὶ ἑταίρους) in Tarentum at 339d–e and to Archytas and his other friends (φίλους) in Tarentum at 350a. There can be no doubt then that, according to the *Seventh Letter*, in an important sense Archytas was Plato's friend. At the same time, it must be recognized that the concept of φιλία in antiquity even more than that of friendship in the modern world embraced a wide range of relationships. At the forefront of the relationship which Plato says he has with Archytas and which he establishes between Archytas and Dionysius II is the concept of the guest-friend. Such friends serve as hosts to one another when one party visits the other's city and such friends have obligations to be of service to one another even when not visiting. It is important to note, however, that Aristotle explicitly labels the friendship of hosts and guests as an example of friendship for utility (*EN* 1156a30). Aristotle points out that such friends do not necessarily spend much time together or even find each other's company pleasant.[18] Each finds the other pleasant only to the extent that he expects some good from him (*EN* 1156a26 ff.). The *Seventh Letter* presents Plato and Archytas as having just such a relationship. Dionysius expects that Archytas will have some influence over Plato because of their guest-friendship, and this is the basis on which Archytas appeals to Plato to return. Archytas and Plato's other guest-friends in Tarentum also are quick to point out the political disadvantage that will result for them, if Plato does not return. It is precisely to this relation that Plato appeals at the end, when he feels that his life is in danger in Syracuse and on the basis of which Archytas arranges for an embassy be sent from Tarentum asking for Plato's release.[19] On the other hand, if we are looking for a close personal friendship, the *Seventh Letter* suggests that it is not Archytas but rather Archedemus, one of Archytas' associates, who was Plato's friend in this sense. It is Archedemus whom Dionysius sends to Plato on a trireme, because he judged that Plato thought the most of Archedemus of all those in Sicily (339a–b). It can of course be pointed out that "all those in Sicily" would not include Archytas, who is from Tarentum, but matters are not so clear, since Archytas is in Sicily at this point and since Archedemus is identified as an associate of

---

[18] See Herman 1987: 17: "The partners involved in ritualised friendship . . . were presumed to be bound by mutual affection. This affection, however, imitated the outward manifestations but not the inward spirit of kinship: ritualised friends were not supposed to love each other, but to behave as if they did."

[19] See Herman 1987: 129 for a list of services typically performed by guest-friends. The services that Archytas and Plato carried out for one another as guest-friends are enough to explain their appearance on the list of great Pythagorean friends in Iamblichus' *On the Pythagorean Life* (127 = A6b), a list that may go back to Aristoxenus. See also on A7a.

Archytas. It could also be that Archytas is too important to send, but the most direct reading of the letter suggests that it is Archedemus and not Archytas who is Plato's most intimate if not most powerful friend.

It has become common to follow Wuilleumier in arguing that the *Seventh Letter* shows that Archytas served his seven consecutive terms as *stratēgos* from 367–361 (1939: 68–69). The argument is that Archytas must have been in a position of authority in 367 for Plato to have established a relation of hospitality and friendship between Archytas and those in Tarentum, on the one hand, and Dionysius, on the other, and that he must similarly have been in authority to arrange for the ship and embassy to be sent from Tarentum to plead for Plato's release in 361. Since Archytas will have served exactly seven years, if he also served for the five years between these two dates, the coincidence was too great to overlook. We have seen, however, that the friendship and hospitality established in 367 may well have been a personal rather than an explicitly political connection; Archytas need not have been in power for such a relationship to be established. It is true that it might have been easier for Archytas to promote the sending of the ship and the embassy in 361, if he were *stratēgos*, but he could have succeeded in bringing this about, even if he did not hold the office at the time. The fact that the period from 367 to 361 is seven years may well simply be a coincidence, and the argument that it was just these years that Archytas served rests on the unspoken assumption that he only served as *stratēgos* for the seven year period. As was argued above this is a very questionable assumption. The most that the *Seventh Letter* shows us is that Archytas was politically active in the period between 367 and 361, and it is surely best to admit that we do not know the exact years when Archytas served as *stratēgos*.

Up to this point I have ignored the thorny question of the authorship of the *Seventh Letter* and have been content simply to describe the manner in which it portrays the connection between Archytas and Plato. The issue of the nature of the *Seventh Letter* is far too complex to address fully here, and I remain undecided on its authenticity.[20] There are, however, three basic possibilities, which are relevant to our understanding of Archytas. First, if the letter is by Plato, then we can be reasonably confident about the basic train of events that it recounts, although we cannot, of course, assume that Plato is an invariably reliable witness. We could also regard the letter as presenting us with Plato's own view of his connection to Archytas. Second, if the letter is by one of Plato's close associates, then it is again presumably

---

[20] See Appendix to this chapter entitled "The authenticity of the *Seventh Letter*."

fairly reliable in its account of events, but this time the author may have his own point to make about those events, including the connection between Plato and Archytas. Finally, the letter might be a work of literature, which is neither by Plato nor his close associates but is something more like a novel. In this case it is possible that the author not only presented the chain of events under an interpretation which served his purposes but also changed or invented events. It would then be extremely difficult to say what reliable information we could derive from the letter about Archytas' connection to Plato.

There are good reasons to think, however, that, even if the letter is primarily a literary rather than a historical document, its originality is in its interpretation of events rather than in the invention of them. Independently of the *Seventh Letter*, we have evidence which suggests that the sequence of events which it describes is basically historical. According to D.L. III. 6, Hermodorus, one of Plato's associates, attested to Plato's trip to Italy not long after Socrates' death so that the tradition of a trip in 388/7 is quite plausible (Huffman 1993: 5). The *Erotic Oration* (ca. 350–325 BC) also clearly envisages direct contact between Archytas and Plato. Again, while authors such as Plutarch and Nepos base their accounts of Plato's activities in Italy and Sicily heavily on the *Seventh Letter*, it is certain that they had other sources and did not always follow the letter. This means both that they regarded the *Seventh Letter* as providing a basically sound, although not unassailable, account of events and also that other ancient authors had talked about Plato's visits to Sicily.[21]

There is some evidence that, even in the specific case of Plato's dealings with Archytas, Plutarch had access to at least one account which was independent of the *Seventh Letter*. Plutarch says emphatically that Archytas and his Pythagorean followers provided themselves as "sureties" (ἀναδόχους) for the agreement between Dionysius II and Plato, which led to Plato's return in 361 (*Dion* XVIII. 5.4). Accordingly, when Archytas rescues Plato from Dionysius, he makes explicit reference to their role as guarantors of Plato's safety (XX. 2 ἀναδόχους). There is no trace of Archytas and his friends serving as formal sureties for Plato's safety in the *Seventh Letter*. In

---

[21] Edelstein (1966: 41–46) provides important evidence that the ancient historians (notably Plutarch), on occasion showed distrust of the account of events in the *Seventh Letter* and preferred to follow other accounts. Plutarch particularly notes the divergence between the *Seventh Letter* and other accounts concerning the way in which Plato parted from Dionysius (Dion xx). Since we do not have the texts of historians who dealt with Sicily in this period, such as Timaeus and Ephorus, it is impossible to be certain whether they really presented accounts, which were independent of the *Seventh Letter*, of Plato's activities in Sicily, but the evidence suggests that they did.

the letter, Archytas urges Plato to return to Sicily by emphasizing the danger for the political relationship between Tarentum and Syracuse, if Plato refuses to come, and by eulogizing the progress that Dionysius has made in philosophy. Plutarch makes no mention of either of these points. Again, in the letter, when Plato is in danger from the peltasts, the appeal to Archytas is presented as something Plato devised then and there (μηχανῶμαι 350a) to obtain his safety rather than as an appeal to something that had been agreed to in advance. Plutarch's account looks like an independent version of events rather than an elaboration of what is presented in the letter. While it is not impossible that Plutarch or his source invented the whole theme of sureties, the definiteness with which he asserts it, repeating the word "sureties" twice, suggests that he is following another source, which shows that Plato's third trip to Sicily and Archytas' involvement in that trip was attested independently of the *Seventh Letter*. It seems best then to regard the *Seventh Letter* as presenting a basically accurate sequence of events but to recognize that those events are presented under an interpretation which may be motivated by literary purposes, and is hence just one interpretation among many.

In Plutarch's presentation, as in that of the *Seventh Letter*, it is clearly Plato who is the star attraction and Archytas is playing the role of someone trying to persuade the great man. Nepos' *Life of Dion* (A5b5) goes even further in this direction. Nepos explicitly says that Plato came to Tarentum during the reign of Dionysius I (presumably the visit of 388/7) and that his fame was so great that it was carried into Sicily. Dion became inflamed with the desire to meet Plato and Dionysius acceded to his wish and had Plato brought to Syracuse. Other ancient accounts suggest that Plato went to Sicily in order to see Mt. Aetna (Riginos 1976: 73), but Nepos' account again fits the strand of the tradition which makes Plato and not Archytas the great philosopher.

It seems to me that there is a way to make sense of the two main strands of the tradition regarding Archytas and Plato, which also accords with what we find in the fragments of Archytas and the dialogues of Plato, especially *Republic* VII. The evidence seems fairly solid that Plato did indeed make a trip to southern Italy not too long after the death of Socrates. If we ask why Plato might have made such a trip, it seems quite plausible that he wanted to meet some of the leading thinkers in the area, and Archytas would certainly seem to fall into this class, so that the first strand of tradition is correct in asserting that Plato went to Italy at least in part to see Archytas. If this visit took place close to the traditional date of 388/7, it is likely that Tarentum was just at the beginning of its rise to dominance in southern Italy and that Archytas was not yet the leading figure in Tarentine politics. Thus, the second strand of tradition would be correct in asserting that Archytas only became dominant in Tarentum after he had associated with Plato, although it need not be correct that this success was a result of his contact with Plato.

The crucial point is to ask what it was that Plato hoped for from a visit with Archytas. The first tradition supposes that he was hoping for Archytas to replace Socrates as his philosophical master. Yet, what the surviving fragments and testimonia about Archytas show us is that he was above all a master mathematician. If we then turn to the one place in his writings where Plato appears to allude to Archytas, his reference at *Republic* 530d to Archytas' assertion in Fragment 1 that the sciences are akin to one another, we find again that it is as a master of *mathēmata* that Plato appeals to Archytas. Shortly after this, he describes and criticizes Pythagorean work in harmonics (531c), which sounds very much like that of Archytas (A16). Just a little earlier Plato has described the field of solid geometry as not yet really in existence, although he concedes that it has made some progress because of its considerable charm (528c). Certainly one of the most charming early achievements of solid geometry is Archytas' solution to the problem of doubling the cube. I submit then that if we want to know why Plato went to visit Archytas in Tarentum and what his attitude to Archytas was, the answers are found in Book VII of the *Republic*, which was written sometime in the 370s, and that these answers suggest a way in which the two strands of the later tradition about Archytas and Plato can be connected. Plato had become fascinated with mathematics and the aid it might give in solving philosophical problems. He did seek out Archytas as the first tradition suggests but not as a Pythagorean master to replace Socrates as his teacher, as is also suggested by that tradition, but rather as one of the leading authorities on *mathēmata*, on mathematics. Plato did indeed find that Archytas was a master in these areas, but he is critical of Archytas, as he is of other mathematicians, for not realizing the ultimate philosophical value of mathematics. Far from regarding Archytas as his master in philosophy, Plato regards him as, in a number of ways, misguided.

So Plato is indeed the friend of Archytas in that they established a relationship of guest-friendship in 388/7 which obligated them to do their best to further each other's interests. Plato tries to help Archytas politically by connecting him to Dionysius II and Archytas will come to Plato's aid when he is in danger at Syracuse. During Plato's visit they undoubtedly spent considerable time in discussions, and Plato must have sought and received instruction in mathematics from Archytas. Plato will also, however, have had serious debates with Archytas on what the true value of the *mathēmata* was. Archytas, in turn, may have asked Plato for instruction in dialectic. Archytas, however, did not become a Platonist and Plato did not become a Pythagorean, or Archytan. Archytas and Plato were guest-friends and civil but competitive colleagues in the world of ancient science and philosophy; neither was the master of the other. To judge by the three works he devoted to Archytas, Aristotle may have been more sympathetic to Archytas the philosopher than Plato was. (For more on the relation of Archytas' philosophy to those of Plato and Aristotle, see the last section of the philosophical overview.)

APPENDIX TO CHAPTER 1: THE AUTHENTICITY OF THE *SEVENTH LETTER*

Letters as a genre are particularly open to suspicions about authenticity, since they were relatively easy to forge in order to sell to libraries of the Hellenistic period, which were collecting as much Greek literature as possible, and because the rhetorical schools employed, as an exercise, the composition of letters by famous people (Morrow 1962: 3–4). These *a priori* concerns apply particularly to the shorter Platonic letters. The *Seventh Letter* is obviously a special case, since it is so long and complicated that it is hard to imagine either that someone composed it in order to make a little profit or that it can have been a school exercise. If it is a forgery, we need to suppose different motivations for it. Most would agree that it is a defense of Plato against various attacks that had been made concerning his involvement in Sicilian affairs (Finley 1977: 80; Schofield 2000: 298–99). Lloyd has pointed out that the letter also serves in part as a defense against charges that Plato owed important aspects of his philosophy to the Pythagoreans (1990). Both of these defenses would make most sense in the second half of the fourth century, when the events in Sicily were still in people's minds and when there was already a tendency to associate Plato (Aristotle, *Metaph.* 987a29 ff.) and the early Academy (Burkert 1972a: 82) with the Pythagoreans. With the passage of time it becomes more and more common to assimilate Plato to the Pythagoreans and less and less likely that someone would want to assert Plato's independence from them.

The collection of thirteen Platonic letters which has come down to us was already present in Thrasyllus' collection of Plato's writings in the first century AD (D.L. III. 61). Cicero clearly refers to the *Seventh Letter* in the first century BC (*Tusc.* V. 35.100). Letters were part of the collection of Plato's writings made by Aristophanes of Byzantium around 200 BC (D.L. III. 62), but we cannot be sure which letters were included in this collection. Thus we have evidence that the *Seventh Letter* was surely in existence before 50 BC and perhaps in existence before 200 BC. It is puzzling, if the letter is by Plato, that Aristotle makes no reference to it, especially when he is discussing matters dealt with in the letter, such as Dion's activities in Sicily.

At the present time no one argues that all the letters are authentic. Opinions on the *Seventh Letter* are divided, although a greater number of scholars have favored its authenticity. The table in Brisson (1987: 72) shows 23 scholars in favor of authenticity and only 3 against in the years between 1906 and 1983, although the table is incomplete and does not include significant opponents of authenticity such as Shorey (1933: 40–41), Cherniss (1945: 13) and Vlastos (1981: 202). In the recent *Cambridge Companion to Plato* (Kraut 1992), Irwin is against authenticity (78–79, n. 4) and Penner is in favor (130). In the *Cambridge History of Greek and Roman Political Thought*, Schofield is "hesitantly" against authenticity (2000: 299–300). A number of recent studies of other aspects of Plato's thought have assumed or supported the authenticity of the *Seventh Letter* (Lewis 2000; Kahn 1996: 48; Sayre 1995: xviii–xxiii; White 1976), although Keyser 1998 attacks the authenticity of the philosophical digression in the *Seventh Letter*, because of its connections to *Letter 2*, which he argues to be spurious. Both Morrow (1962) and Brisson (1987), in their editions of the letters, accept its authenticity, although Edelstein (1966), in the last full study of the *Seventh Letter*, argued against it (see the critique in Solmsen 1969). Guthrie (1978) and von Fritz (1971) accepted the authenticity, while Gulley (1972) argued against it. Studies of the style of the letter have in general shown it to be compatible with the style of the *Laws*, which Plato would have been writing about the same time (Ledger 1989; Brandwood 1969; Wilamowitz-Moellendorf 1919–20; Raeder 1906; Ritter 1888). Levison, Morton and Winspear (1968) judge the letter spurious on stylistic grounds, but their examination was very limited in scope and Brandwood 1969 raised well-founded doubts about their approach, as does Deane 1973. Caskey 1974 also raises some doubts about authenticity, but on the basis of very limited stylistic criteria. It is commonly said that, even if the letter is not by Plato, it shows such familiarity with the events in Sicily and Plato's philosophy that it must have been written in the first or second generation after Plato's death by a Platonist steeped in Plato's style, and is accordingly a relatively reliable source for the history of Plato's activities in Sicily (Westlake 1994: 693; Brunt 1993: 319–25; Finley 1977: 80; Shorey 1933: 40–41). Schofield says that the letter is "the work of an ingenious and powerful writer, steeped in Plato's writings and his habits of thinking and expression" but hesitantly concludes that the writer is not Plato, because of the letter's lack of wit and because it is in conflict with Plato's aversion to self-disclosure (2000: 300). Some scholars do not find it possible to come to a firm conclusion about authenticity (Brunt 1993: 324; Lloyd 1990; Finley 1977: 80).

CHAPTER II

The philosophy of Archytas

Archytas of Tarentum fits the popular conception of a Pythagorean better than anyone in the Pythagorean tradition, including Pythagoras himself. He was a distinguished mathematician; indeed we know of no other Pythagorean who even approached the mathematical prowess, which Archytas displays in his stunning solution to the problem of doubling the cube, the so-called Delian problem (A14). He also showed the typical Pythagorean interest in the mathematics of music, but again his analysis of the music of his day is by far the most sophisticated piece of harmonic theory in the early Pythagorean tradition (A16). Finally, he was elected leader of his city-state, Tarentum, seven consecutive times and his accomplishments in the political sphere are more impressive and better documented than those in the legends about Pythagoras (see "Life, writings and reception" above). Thus, we have the Pythagorean whom some have seen as the model for Plato's philosopher king (Guthrie 1962: 333). It is true, nonetheless, that Archytas has received relatively little attention from scholars of the history of ancient philosophy, let alone the educated community as a whole. He might justly be labeled "the lost Pythagorean." Pythagoras has, of course, garnered the most attention, in large part because of his enormous importance in later antiquity (see, e.g., O' Meara 1989). The legend of Pythagoras has recently been debunked to some extent, and a more accurate appreciation of his accomplishment has been achieved (Burkert 1972a, Huffman 1999a: 66–75). As a result Philolaus of Croton, who wrote the first book in the Pythagorean tradition, has emerged from the shadow of Pythagoras and come to be recognized as an important Presocratic thinker (Huffman 1993; Kirk, Raven and Schofield 1983; Barnes 1982; Burkert 1972a). How are we to explain the continuing neglect of Archytas?

To some extent Archytas has suffered, like all later Pythagoreans, from the tendency to regard Pythagoreanism as a monolithic philosophical system, which all ultimately derives from Pythagoras himself. This view is enshrined in numerous histories of Greek philosophy, in which Archytas is included not in the fourth century as a contemporary of Plato but rather as a footnote to the treatment of Pythagoras in the late sixth century. Thus, Archytas is discussed on pages 333–36 of Volume 1 of Guthrie's *History of Greek Philosophy*, at the end of the section on Pythagoras and right before Xenophanes, who was born over 100 years before Archytas. For the same reason, the fragments of Archytas are found in the standard collection of the fragments of the Presocratic philosophers edited by Diels and Kranz, although Archytas, as a contemporary of Socrates' pupil Plato, can hardly be considered a Presocratic.

It is important to emphasize that this tendency to treat Archytas as a footnote to Pythagoras and Presocratic Pythagoreanism is an artefact of the Neopythagorean tradition in later antiquity and is directly contradicted by Aristotle's approach in the years shortly after Archytas' death. In his extant works, Aristotle has almost nothing to say about Pythagoras himself. In his comments on Pythagorean philosophy, he always refers to a fifth-century Pythagoreanism, which is closely connected to Philolaus (e.g. *Metaph.* 985b23 ff.) and to which he devoted two treatises, which are now lost. Archytas, on the other hand, is never called a Pythagorean by Aristotle and is not grouped with the other Pythagoreans whom Aristotle discusses. Instead, Aristotle wrote three separate books on Archytas himself and a fourth which consisted of summaries of passages from the writings of Archytas and Plato's *Timaeus* (A13). Thus Aristotle devotes almost twice as much attention to Archytas as he devotes to fifth-century Pythagoreanism. For Aristotle, then, Archytas would appear to have been a far more important philosopher than either Pythagoras or Philolaus. For Aristotle, Archytas stands outside the shadow of Pythagoras, in which the later tradition placed him, and is an important philosopher in his own right.

A second and probably equally important reason for the neglect of Archytas is precisely his eminence as a mathematician. Over 100 years ago, the great German scholar, Zeller, set the tone by arguing that we could learn little about Pythagorean philosophy from Archytas, because most of the genuine fragments and testimonia focus on extremely technical mathematics and harmonic theory (1923: 1. 1.375). Scholars have found it difficult to discover Archytas' basic philosophical principles or even if he had any.[1] Nonetheless, the testimonia and fragments cover a wide range of topics:

---

[1] Frank (1923) made one of the few attempts to reconstruct Archytas' philosophy, but his reconstruction is completely unreliable, because it makes virtually no use of the primary evidence which we do have for Archytas (e.g. Frs. 1–4, A14, A16, A22, A23, A23a etc.) and relies instead on reading between the lines in Plato and arbitrarily transferring doctrines ascribed to Pythagoras and Eurytus to Archytas (e.g. A13, Texts F and H).

political theory, the emotions, pleasure, definition, motion, and cosmology, along with technical disciplines such as harmonics, geometry, arithmetic and optics. Such a breadth of interest at least encourages us to think that Archytas did not just work in the technical disciplines and either that he did have a consciously unified philosophical outlook or that there may be a unity implicit in his work. I will argue that Archytas' technical work in the various mathematical sciences was both based on and radically transformed an all-encompassing view of the cosmos and the place of humanity in it, which he inherited from his predecessor Philolaus. The Archytan philosophical system that emerges from this transformation has at its core the mathematical sciences in which Archytas excelled, and in particular the science of ratio and proportion, which he called logistic.

ARCHYTAS AS A MATHEMATICIAN

In coming to an appreciation of Archytas' intellectual accomplishment, it is essential to confirm at the beginning that he was an important and rigorous mathematician; indeed he was one of the most prominent mathematicians of his generation. That this was the ancient view of his significance is confirmed by the history of geometry written by Aristotle's pupil, Eudemus of Rhodes, and preserved in part by Proclus. Archytas is listed along with Theaetetus of Athens and Leodamas of Thasos as the three dominant geometers of Plato's generation, by whom "the theorems were increased in number and brought into a more scientific order" (A6). One of the theorems to which Eudemus is referring is undoubtedly Archytas' solution to the problem of doubling the cube, which Eudemus described in detail (A14). Archytas was the first to provide a solution to this famous problem, and scholars have generally recognized its brilliance and rigor. Heath describes it as "the most remarkable of all [the solutions]" and as a "bold construction in three dimensions" (1921: 246); Mueller hails it as "a *tour de force* of the spatial imagination" (1997: 312, n. 23). We have two other substantial testimonia for Archytas' work in mathematics, both dealing with mathematics relevant to harmonic theory: (1) Archytas' proof to show that there is no mean proportional between numbers in superparticular ratio (A19), which leads to the important recognition that the octave, fifth, fourth, and whole tone, all of which correspond to superparticular ratios (e.g. 2/1, 3/2, 4/3 and 9/8), cannot be bisected; (2) Archytas' mathematical analysis of the three primary musical scales of his day (A16). The ancient tradition indeed recognizes Archytas' preeminence in the mathematics of harmonic theory. In his *Harmonics*, Ptolemy identifies Archytas as having "engaged in the study of music most of all the Pythagoreans" (A16: 6–7). Although Ptolemy is critical of Archytas' work in some respects, he spends a considerable amount of time on Archytas' harmonics and clearly regards him as one of the two most significant harmonic theorists of the fourth century, along with Aristoxenus, of whom Ptolemy is even more critical. The description of Archytas' analysis of the structure of the three main types of tetrachord, which Ptolemy preserves (A16), shows that Archytas is much more sophisticated than his predecessor Philolaus and leaves little doubt that Archytas was the leading harmonic theorist of his day.

It is important to get a just appreciation of Archytas' accomplishments as a mathematician, because there has been a tendency to both inflate and deflate his abilities. Van der Waerden's assessment of Archytas is responsible for a great deal of confusion, because he somewhat paradoxically inflates the extent of Archytas' achievements in mathematics, while at the same time calling into question the quality of Archytas' work (1963: 152–55). Van der Waerden's suggestions that Archytas was responsible for Book VIII of Euclid's *Elements* and for the treatise on the mathematics of music known as the *Sectio Canonis*, which is ascribed to Euclid in the ancient tradition, although often repeated by later scholars (e.g. Knorr 1975: 244), are almost certainly erroneous. His argument for assigning Book VIII to Archytas is based on an analysis of Archytas' style as unclear, prolix and illogical, an analysis which is subjective in the extreme and based on faulty evidence (see the commentary on A19). Using an equally subjective analysis of Book VIII as also "confused" and "illogical," van der Waerden then produces the *non sequitur* that it must be by Archytas as well, as if confusion and illogical thinking had to be limited to Archytas. Unlike Book VIII the *Sectio Canonis* clearly does draw on Archytas' work, but equally clearly cannot be by Archytas. Both the theory of pitch and the analysis of the diatonic and enharmonic tetrachords found in the *Sectio* contradict what we find in the testimony for Archytas' harmonics (see further the commentary on Fr. 1 and A19).

Burkert also presents a puzzling picture of Archytas' abilities, which seems to be a result of the context in which he discusses Archytas and a consequent failure to integrate the diverse evidence for his mathematical work into a whole. The primary focus of Burkert's epoch making book is on Pythagoras and Philolaus. He only mentions Archytas insofar as Archytas sheds light on this earlier Pythagoreanism. One of Burkert's central theses is that Pythagoras was not engaged in rigorous mathematics, and he argues that the same is true of Philolaus. This means that there is little or no rigorous mathematics in the Pythagorean tradition before Archytas, and, for Burkert's story to hold together, Archytas must appear to be making the first tentative steps in the direction of mathematical rigor and not to be a polished mathematician. Thus Burkert describes the proof in A19 as "a mathematics still feeling its way along an uncertain path" (1972a: 446). Similarly, Archytas' music theory is characterized as in part "mere arithmology" (1972a: 386), as resulting from trial and error manipulation of ratios (1972a: 389, n. 17) and as failing both to describe actual music and to apply mathematical principles consistently (1972a: 386). Unfortunately this picture of an Archytas who mixes arithmology and trial and error calculation with the first stumbling steps towards mathematical proof is very hard to reconcile with the Archytas who provided the stunning solution to the duplication of the cube, which Burkert himself calls a "decisive geometrical achievement" (1972a: 449). It is perfectly possible for someone to be better in one branch of mathematics than another, but it is implausible to suppose that someone could deploy the mathematical rigor and sophisticated argumentation found in Archytas' solution to the duplication of the cube and be completely confused about how to construct a logical argument in arithmetic. Burkert's presentation of such a schizophrenic Archytas requires us to look very closely at his analysis of Archytas' proof in A19 and his account of Archytas' harmonic theory.

Such examination shows that A19 is not evidence for Archytas' confusion about mathematical reasoning but important evidence both for the value which Archytas put on rigorous proof and for his ability to carry out such reasoning. Archytas' achievement in A19 is not the *tour de force* which his duplication of the cube is; but it is the foundation on which the later argument in the *Sectio Canonis* is built, and the level of rigor in argumentation is comparable to what is found in the duplication (see the commentary on A19). The supposed confusions in Archytas' harmonic theory largely evaporate on close examination. There is arithmology in A17, but A17 is not a report of Archytas' own views but rather Archytas' report of some of his predecessors' views. Archytas appears to have made it a practice to begin from the work of his predecessors (see below), and there is no reason to believe that he approved of the arithmological practices of the harmonic theorists whom he describes in A17 any more than that he approved of Eurytus' method of identifying things with numbers, which he also reports (A13, Text H). Burkert's complaint that Archytas' ratios for the tetrachords do not correspond fully to Greek musical practice reflects Ptolemy's similar complaint, but Winnington-Ingram's careful analysis has shown that Ptolemy is misled by the musical practice of his own day (1932: 207). Aristoxenus, writing not long after Archytas' death, allows us to confirm that Archytas' ratios do correspond to the musical practice of his contemporaries (Winnington-Ingram 1932: 208). Burkert's supposition that Archytas manipulated seven of the nine ratios by trial and error techniques so that they were superparticular in form (roughly n + 1/n, e.g. 5/4), in order to correspond to his *a priori* postulate that the ratios of all melodic intervals should have this form, refutes itself, since by such techniques Archytas could have easily made all nine ratios superparticular. Archytas' harmonic theory does accurately describe important aspects of the musical practice of his day and does so on the basis of a clear understanding not just of the types of tetrachord in use in his day but also of a common method of tuning, as Barker has shown (1989: 50). Archytas' account of the tetrachords is based on a consistent application of this "method of concordance" and the harmonic and arithmetic means (on all these issues regarding Archytas' harmonics, see the commentary on A16). Archytas succeeds remarkably well in finding the numbers that govern the harmonies heard in the music of his day, and his procedure corresponds to Plato's description of the Pythagoreans as searching for numbers in "heard harmonies" (*R.* 531c). Plato regards this as a misdirected enterprise, since it focuses on the phenomenal world, but he never suggests that Archytas carried out the enterprise in anything other than a rigorous way.[2]

A detailed account of the sophistication of Archytas' mathematical abilities is hard to achieve, since in no case do we have Archytas' mathematical reasoning preserved in his own words. Both A14 and A19, however, show at a minimum that Archytas recognized the requirements for a formal deductive proof; there is a clear statement of what is to be proven and what is given, the proofs proceed by logical steps, in one case the proof has the form of a *reductio ad absurdum*, and a considerable body of mathematical knowledge is appealed to in each proof. If we were to ascribe these features to Archytas' editors (Eudemus/Eutocius and Nicomachus/Boethius) rather than Archytas himself, it would be very hard to say why those same editors thought that Archytas had proved anything worth preserving.

---

[2] Mueller, in his excellent survey of Greek mathematics in the sixth through fourth centuries (1997), presents a puzzling portrait of Archytas, which has some of the same defects as Burkert's account and perhaps for the same reason, i.e. Archytas is not central to his purposes. First, like Burkert, he takes virtually no account of Archytas' most important achievement in mathematics, the duplication of the cube, mentioning it only in a two-line footnote, although he calls it "a *tour de force* of the spatial imagination" (312, n. 23). Second, like Burkert, he treats A17 as if it were a report of Archytas' own views rather than what it purports to be, an account of the views of his predecessors, and uses A17 as the basis for his conclusion that Archytas went in for "mathematical mystification" as well as "mathematical reasoning" (289). Finally, he accepts Burkert's view that mathematical *a priorism* played a central role in Archytas' description of the tetrachords in A16. I argue in detail against such a view in the commentary on A16.

Evaluation of Archytas' mathematics is also complicated by the lack of information about what Greek mathematics as a whole looked like in Archytas' day. About the only pre-Archytan mathematical argumentation which we have is Hippocrates of Chios' work on lunes. Archytas' duplication of the cube shows the same high level of rigor and logical argumentation as Hippocrates' work. Archytas and Hippocrates also appeal to a very similar body of geometrical knowledge (see on A14). Archytas builds on another of Hippocrates' achievements, the reduction of the problem of doubling the cube to the problem of finding two mean proportionals, but he surpasses Hippocrates by finding a solution to the latter and hence the former problem. Archytas' construction, which involves the intersection of two curves on the surface of a semicylinder, is more complex and imaginative than anything we find in Hippocrates' work on lunes and draws on material in solid geometry such as will later appear in Book XI of Euclid. The geometry which Archytas uses to demonstrate that the two lines which result from this construction are the desired two mean proportionals, however, is comparable to what we find in Hippocrates (material later found in Euclid 1–4 and 6). All of this suggests that Archytas had mastered the techniques of his predecessor and then raised them to a higher level in order to solve problems that his predecessor could not.

One of the large gaps in our knowledge concerns the form of the body of geometrical knowledge that Hippocrates and Archytas employed. Did Archytas appeal to an *Elements of Arithmetic* or an *Elements of Geometry*, written either by himself or by someone else? If so, what exact form did these works have? In particular how did their conception of the starting points or elements of geometry compare with those later found in Euclid? There is no way to answer these questions definitively (see the commentary on A14). We know that Eudemus attributed the first work on the elements of geometry to Hippocrates (Procl., *In Euc.* 66) so that he must have made some distinction between more and less fundamental principles in geometry. As Lloyd has pointed out, however, some evidence suggests that he may have considered a proposition, which itself required proof, as a geometrical starting point, thus raising doubts as to whether his elements started from first principles which were indemonstrables such as Euclid's definitions, postulates and common notions (1979: 109). On the other hand, Archytas' rigor in the presentation of the proofs in A14 and A19 would be pointless, if the geometrical and arithmetical knowledge to which he appeals were not itself established in a rigorous way. Archytas' practice thus suggests that he could refer to an *Elements of Geometry*, perhaps that of Hippocrates, but the precise nature of these works and how they compare to what we find later in Euclid cannot be decided given the present state of the evidence.

Eudemus does not ascribe an *Elements* to Archytas, but he does explicitly say that Archytas contributed to the scientific ordering of geometrical theorems (A6), which thus indicates that he too was to some extent concerned with the structure of geometry as a science. It is hard to see how Archytas can have contributed to the "scientific ordering" of the theorems, as well as discovering new theorems, unless he produced at least some sort of revised version of an earlier *Elements*. Archytas' interest in definitions, to which Aristotle attests (see A22), and his comments on the structure of the sciences in Fragment 1 (see below) go further to support the supposition that he was centrally concerned with the question of what counted as first principles in mathematics and that he had made distinctions between more and less fundamental principles in each of the four disciplines, which he mentions in Fragment 1. While the evidence is too meager to tell us what sort of elements of geometry, arithmetic or astronomy Archytas was working with, Fragment 1 does give us some evidence about the structure of his science of harmonics. One of the central characteristics of the way in which Archytas develops that structure is his explicit reliance on the work of his predecessors, and before we look at the structure of Archytas' harmonics as a whole, it is important to clarify the way in which Archytas uses his predecessors.

ARCHYTAS AND HIS PREDECESSORS

Fragment 1 preserves what is probably the beginning of Archytas' *Harmonics*, his most famous book in antiquity. The first words of the fragment consist precisely of praise for some of his predecessors, who are identified as "those concerned with the sciences" (τοὶ περὶ τὰ μαθήματα). The immediately following lines make clear that Archytas is thinking of predecessors in the four sciences of astronomy, geometry, logistic (his name for the science concerned with numbers – see Fr. 4) and music. In Fragment 2, Archytas does not explicitly refer to any predecessors, but he is implicitly taking over the three means which are relevant to music (the arithmetic, geometric and harmonic means) from harmonic theorists before his time. A17 is a report of Archytas' detailed account (thirty-seven lines) of the procedure used by some Pythagoreans to rank the various musical concords in terms of degrees of concordance. Finally, in A13, Text H, Archytas is the source for the curious attempt by Eurytus, a Pythagorean of the generation immediately preceding him, to demonstrate the number associated with individual things in the world, by setting out the number of pebbles required in order to create a picture of the thing in question. Archytas' references to his predecessors' views are thus striking both for their number, given the relatively few surviving fragments and testimonia, and also for the detail in which the views are presented. Can we say anything more precise about whom he regarded as his predecessors and how he made use of them?

In some cases his predecessors were clearly Pythagoreans. Eurytus is explicitly mentioned in A13, Text H, and unnamed Pythagorean harmonic theorists are discussed in A17. The origin of the three means described in Fragment 2 is not identified, and we do not know who first originated them, but it is plausible that the Pythagorean Hippasus knew of them in the first half of the fifth century and that Archytas is drawing on him. Some scholars have assumed that, when Archytas referred to "those concerned with the sciences" at the beginning of Fragment 1, he must have again been referring to Pythagoreans. In this case, however, it seems much more likely that the reference is broader and includes all those who have contributed to the four sciences mentioned, whether they are Pythagorean or not. Certainly Archytas gives no indication that he is limiting the reference to Pythagoreans; the expression "those concerned with the sciences" is quite general. Moreover, surely when Archytas thought of his predecessors in geometry, he must have thought of non-Pythagoreans such as Hippocrates of Chios, on whose work his solution to the problem of doubling the cube depended (see A14). Who then were these predecessors in the sciences, upon whom Archytas heaps such praise in Fragment 1?

Since no names are given, we must rely on arguments from probability. As has just been suggested, Hippocrates of Chios will be at the top of the list, if we are looking for geometers, whom Archytas could have regarded as his predecessors, and Theodorus of Cyrene is another plausible candidate. Eudemus identifies Hippocrates along with Theodorus as the two leading geometers in the period immediately preceding Archytas and specifically says that Hippocrates was the first to write about the elements of geometry (Procl. *In Euc.* 66.4–8). The evidence for specifically Pythagorean geometry before Archytas is much more sketchy. The geometrical accomplishments assigned to Pythagoras by Proclus (*In Euc.* 65.16–21) are commonly recognized as the creation of the later tradition. There is evidence that Pythagoreans worked on the application of areas, but it is hard to assign a date to this work (Procl. *In Euc.* 419.15–18). Hippasus, in the early fifth century, is connected to work with the dodecahedron (Iamb. *Comm. Math.* 78.27–36 and *VP* 132.11–23 = DK 18A4), and von Fritz reconstructed a method by which Hippasus might have discovered incommensurability using the dodecahedron (1945a), but there is no direct testimony that Hippasus discovered incommensurability, let alone that he used the method von Fritz proposes. Certainly none of this Pythagorean work has the close connection to Archytas' work in geometry, which Hippocrates' work does.

If we turn from geometry to astronomy, Archytas particularly singles out predecessors who have handed down clear distinctions about the speed of the stars and their risings and settings. This is presumably a reference to the determination of the periods of the five planets, sun and moon and to calendars of the parapegmata type, which listed such astronomical phenomena as the risings and settings of constellations for each day of the year (Dicks 1970: 84 ff.). The years between 430 and 400, when Archytas was growing up, were a particularly active period for this type of astronomy, and it is not surprising that Archytas should be impressed with the accomplishments of his predecessors in this area. Archytas' predecessor in the Pythagorean tradition, Philolaus, was the first to incorporate the moon, sun and five planets into an astronomical system in the correct order according to their periods (Huffman 1993: 260–61), although we do not know for sure how he obtained this information. Hippocrates' fellow Chian, Oenopides devised a fifty-nine year cycle (DK 41A9), in which to reconcile the periods of the sun and moon, and Meton and Euctemon of Athens used a nineteen year cycle (Heath 1913: 293). Euctemon and Meton also provided equinox and solstice information that was incorporated into parapegmata calendars. There is evidence that the atomist Democritus devised a parapegma (D.L. IX. 48), and the existence of this calendar is confirmed by use of information derived from Democritus in the calendar attached to Geminus' *Isagoge*, including information about the risings and settings of constellations (DK 68 B14). Works on the planets and celestial phenomena are also reported for Democritus (D.L. IX. 46–47). Philolaus, Oenopides, Euctemon, Meton and Democritus are thus all likely to be in Archytas' mind when he refers to his predecessors in astronomy.

Democritus is particularly intriguing for his connections to Archytas. In addition to his work in astronomy, Democritus also wrote books on geometry, arithmetic and acoustics (D.L. IX. 47). Archytas' other predecessors in arithmetic/logistic are the most difficult to pin down. It is traditional to refer to a Pythagorean arithmetic of the fifth century that was based on figurate numbers, i.e. numbers represented by pebbles set out in certain shapes. Becker has also reconstructed some of the theorems of early Pythagorean arithmetic on the basis of Euclid's *Elements* (for a good recent treatment of this early Pythagorean arithmetic, see Mueller 1997: 294–98).

This early Pythagorean arithmetic is almost completely a modern reconstruction, however, and it makes little sense to speculate whether Archytas drew on it or not. In harmonics, his predecessors appear to have been a mixture of Pythagoreans and non-Pythagoreans. The acoustic theory presented in Fr. 1 may owe something to Archelaus' definition of sound as well as to Democritus; Archytas' interest in sounds too small to be heard could be a response to Zeno's millet seed argument and his discussion of sounds too large to be heard may be connected to Lasus of Hermione (see pp. 136–37). On the other hand, A16 indicates that Archytas employed Philolaus' diatonic tetrachord in devising his own chromatic tetrachord. Hippasus, in the generation even before Philolaus, is associated with work on the means used by Archytas in Fr. 2 (see the commentary) and with an experiment to demonstrate the connection between whole number ratios and the basic concords (octave, fourth and fifth), an experiment which, unlike those ascribed to Pythagoras, would actually have worked (DK 18A12; Huffman 1993: 148).

This survey of Archytas' likely predecessors suggests, then, that when he referred to "those concerned with the sciences," he had a very wide range of thinkers in mind, including both Pythagoreans and non-Pythagoreans. What stance, then, does Archytas maintain toward his predecessors' achievements, both in Fragment 1 and elsewhere? In some cases, he accepts the work of his predecessors and builds on it. This is very clear in Fragment 1. Archytas begins with praise of those concerned with the sciences and spends the first seven lines providing a general characterization of their contribution to knowledge. When he turns to the specific topic of music in line 7, he starts with what his predecessors contributed ("first they reflected that . . .") and continues to present their views in indirect statement in lines 7–18 until, in line 18, he switches to direct statement and begins to state his own thesis about pitch. Lines 7–18 are more than just a report of his predecessors' views; they also serve as Archytas' own account of the basic principles of harmonics. Similarly, in Fragment 2, Archytas is clearly taking over the three means from his predecessors, although he renames one of them and adds his own additional characterization of each mean.

Archytas' stance towards his predecessors is much less clear in A17. In this case he describes in some detail certain unnamed Pythagoreans' attempt to rank the musical concords according to degree of concordance. The testimonium makes perfectly clear that this is not a direct report of Archytas' views but his report of the views of others. We are not told what Archytas thought of this attempt. There are, however, two small indications that he rejected it. First, A17 is quite explicit that Archytas is reporting the views of others; if these were views that he also adopted, we might have expected some statement to that effect. Second, the mathematical procedure used to rank the concords in A17 confuses the ratios that govern the concords with the arithmetical difference between the two terms in the ratio, which is a confusion that someone who had as much expertise with ratio as Archytas did (Fr. 2, A14, A16 and A19) would be unlikely to endorse.

The last explicit example of borrowing from a predecessor, unlike the first three, is unlikely to come from the *Harmonics*, although we cannot be sure of its origin. Theophrastus tells us that it was Archytas who reported the unusual procedure by which Eurytus, a Pythagorean who seems to fall between Archytas and Philolaus in age, demonstrated the connection between numbers and individual things in the world, e.g. a man or a horse, by setting out pebbles in such shapes (A13, texts H and I). In this case we again have no explicit indication of what Archytas thought of Eurytus' procedure. It is tempting, however, to regard it as a sort of intermediate case. On the one hand, Archytas might well have been sympathetic with Eurytus' project, which was probably inherited from Philolaus, i.e. to describe the phenomenal world in terms of number, to find numbers in things (see below). On the other hand, other indications suggest that Archytas thought that ratios and proportions were a more promising way of expressing the numerical structure of the world than the simple identification of individual numbers with things (e.g. man = 273). Archytas, then, appears to have had a complex relationship to the work of his predecessors. In some cases he accepts it wholesale as the foundation on which he builds his own contributions (Frs. 1 and 2), while in others he may praise the goals of his predecessors while rejecting their conclusions (A13), and finally in some cases he may have treated his predecessors as simply misguided (A17).

Archytas' attitude towards his predecessors can be further clarified in light of the epistemology that he presents in Fragment 3. Archytas develops his epistemology from what is almost a commonplace in the Greek intellectual tradition (see the commentary on Fragment 3): "it is necessary to come to know those things which you did not know, either by learning from another or by discovering yourself." He develops this commonplace in a startling way, given the typical stereotype of Pythagoreanism. Pythagoreans are often portrayed in the later tradition and in modern scholarship not as innovators but rather as preserving the revelation of the master, Pythagoras. The only argument required in support of their philosophical positions is the classic appeal to authority: "he himself (i.e. Pythagoras) said it" (αὐτὸς ἔφα, *ipse dixit*). This model of learning may not be just an artefact of the later tradition but also may go back to Pythagoras himself. Barnes (1982: 146) has suggested that Heraclitus' famous criticism of Pythagoras for "polymathia" (B40, B129) may get most of its force not from the emphasis on the many subjects that Pythagoras pursued but from his having pursued them largely by learning from others (μανθάνειν) rather than from personal discovery. If so, Archytas is on Heraclitus' side of this debate rather than on that of Pythagoras. In Fragment 3, while Archytas seems willing to accept that we do learn from our predecessors, it is clear that he regards discovering things for ourselves as preferable: "Learning is from another and belongs to another, while discovery is through oneself and belongs to oneself." This seems to mean that what we hear and accept from another may be accepted uncritically without real understanding, while our own discovery is based on a process of reasoning that is our own.

Given this emphasis on discovery through reasoning, it is not surprising that the testimonia and fragments of Archytas emphasize proof and argumentation and that these features are much more prominent in Archytas than in his Pythagorean predecessor Philolaus. As we have seen Archytas does employ rigorous mathematical proof in A14 and A19, but the *reductio* form of A19 and the imagination of the construction in A14 are also paralleled by Archytas' penchant for the use of the thought experiment in his argumentation outside of mathematics. Thus, in A24 we are to imagine ourselves at the edge of the universe and asked whether we could extend our hand or not, and in A9a we are to imagine ourselves in the throes of the most intense pleasure imaginable and asked whether we would be able to calculate in such a state. These thought experiments are in effect *reductio* arguments, in that in each case we accept our opponents' position, i.e. that there is an edge to the universe or that the most intense pleasure is the goal of our life, and then show the absurd results that follow. Archytas presented his philosophy as a combination of what he had "learned from another" and his own discoveries, which were bolstered by argumentation of the most imaginative sort.

Archytas' use of his predecessors is significant in several ways. First, it is clear that Archytas is not a Pythagorean who is content to repeat the words of the master and attribute any discoveries he makes on his own to that master. Archytas is a Pythagorean who emphasizes that discovery for oneself is best and that what one discovers belongs to oneself. At the same time, Archytas explicitly builds on the achievements of his predecessors in a way which contrasts with the Presocratic emphasis on innovation concerning first principles and rejection of one's predecessors, but which looks forward to Aristotle's systematic use of his predecessors in developing his own views. Archytas can be seen as a bridge between Presocratic egotism

(Lloyd 1987a: 56 ff.) and Aristotle's famous assertion that each thinker "says something about the nature of things" (*Metaph.* 993b1–2). Archytas' attitude is also paralleled in the Hippocratic treatise *On Regimen*, insofar as that author advises us to take over from our predecessors what they understood correctly, while correcting them where they went astray and adding our own new insights (*Vict.* 1). It may be that Archytas was influenced by Greek medical thought in developing his epistemology, but it also seems very plausible to suppose that the strongest influence came from the four sciences which Archytas mentions in Fragment 1, since the development of each of these sciences in the late fifth century clearly would have suggested that progress in understanding the world was cumulative in nature. Archytas only succeeded in doubling the cube because of what Hippocrates had accomplished before him. We need to turn now to the question of why it was that he thought the sciences were so central not just to epistemology but to all of human intellectual endeavor and indeed, as we will see, to all of human life.

ARCHYTAS ON THE VALUE OF THE SCIENCES

Archytas' praise for "those concerned with the sciences" cannot help but remind us of Plato's discussion of a similar set of sciences in *Republic* VII. Indeed, Plato seems to be assuming Archytas' set of four sciences in his discussion and very pointedly adds a fifth, stereometry or solid geometry (528a), the sad state of which he ascribes in part to its arrogant practitioners (528c), among whom Plato probably includes Archytas (see the commentary on A15). The differences between Plato and Archytas are not limited to the number of the sciences, however. There are even greater differences concerning the precise nature of these sciences and hence concerning what it is that makes the study of them valuable. Plato values the sciences for their ability to turn the eye of the soul from the sensible to the intelligible world, from the world of becoming to the world of being (521d). Plato's persistent emphasis on the intelligible at the expense of the sensible causes him to redefine astronomy and harmonics so that they no longer deal with the visible heavens and audible concords, and instead become the science of true speed and true slowness (529d) and the science of concordant numbers (531c) respectively. Exactly how we are to understand these new sciences is a matter of controversy (see e.g. Mourelatos 1980 and Mueller 1980). Plato does not regard even these purified sciences as the highest study, however, but as preparation for the highest study, dialectic. *Republic* VII is thus a radical document which praises the value of the sciences but which accompanies that praise with a critique of their current practice and a transformation of what it means to be a science that significantly alters the nature of sciences such as astronomy and harmonics.

If we turn to Archytas' praise of the sciences in Fragment 1, there is little in common with Plato. There is no reference to Plato's distinction between the sensible and intelligible realm and hence no description of the ability of the sciences to turn the soul from the sensible to the intelligible or to purify the soul. It is quite clear that Archytas' astronomy does deal with the visible heavens, with the risings and settings of the stars and planets (Fr. 1, lines 4–5). Indeed, both in their number and in their nature, it would appear that Archytas' sciences are precisely those that Plato is proposing to transform in *Republic* VII. On what grounds, then, does Archytas praise the sciences, if not on these Platonic grounds? The first seven lines of Fragment 1 are the best evidence we have for Archytas' view of the sciences as a whole, and close scrutiny of them allows us to see the outlines of his conception.

What is initially striking about Archytas' presentation of the sciences in Fragment 1 is the epistemological vocabulary which he uses to describe and to praise them. Archytas uses the verb διαγιγνώσκειν and its cognate noun διάγνωσις three times in the first five lines in order to characterize the activity of those concerned with the sciences. Archytas' emphatic usage of διαγιγνώσκειν is unparalleled in a philosophical text and says something important about how he understands the sciences. The verb basically means "to distinguish one thing from another." The verb and its cognate noun are typically used to indicate that one thing is being distinguished from its opposite, e.g. a true from a false friend (E. *Hipp.* 926). It does not always refer to the distinction of opposites, however, and can refer to our attempt by a variety of means to distinguish the distinct entities in the world around us; Heraclitus (Fr. 7) is reported to have said that, if all things turned to smoke, the nostrils would "distinguish" things (from one another). In the first words of Fragment 1, then, Archytas is saying that "those concerned with the sciences make distinctions well" (καλῶς . . . διαγνῶμεν).[3]

Why should Archytas suppose that the ability to make such distinctions is particularly characteristic of those concerned with the sciences? His thesis gains some plausibility, if we think of a science which he does not mention,

---

[3] The best parallels for Archytas' emphasis on making distinctions are found in the Hippocratic corpus. Indeed, the whole model of science envisaged by Archytas finds intriguing parallels in the Hippocratic corpus, where there is a similar focus both on making distinctions and also on paying attention to the whole and the part. See the note on διαγνῶμεν in line 1 of Fragment 1. That there should be parallels between Archytas' thought and the Greek medical tradition is not a complete surprise, since Archytas' predecessor Philolaus had a developed medical theory (Huffman 1993: 289 ff.).

biology, in which the ability to distinguish and classify plays a large role. In his biological treatises, Aristotle uses the verb διαγιγνώσκειν to describe the distinctions made between male and female and young and old animals (*HA* 613a16 and 501b11). Plato's comments about the sciences in *Republic* VII may also shed some light. One of the things that Socrates particularly values about the sciences is that they take as objects things which are not adequately grasped by sense perception but which are always presented to the senses with their opposites, so that reason has to be summoned in order to distinguish the two opposites which are presented together in sensation (521c ff.). For example, the ring finger appears to the senses as both large (in comparison to the little finger) and small (in comparison to the middle finger), so that our reason is called in to consider what the true nature of the large and small really is. Archytas need not accept Plato's metaphysical thesis that these objects only exist in the intelligible realm to agree that geometers must distinguish the straight from the curved and arithmeticians the odd from the even. Accordingly, I propose the following hypothesis: Archytas is arguing that those concerned with the sciences are good at making distinctions, because making distinctions is a central activity of the sciences.

Archytas makes a second claim about those concerned with the sciences in the next sentence. He argues that it is precisely because those concerned with the sciences make good distinctions "concerning the nature of wholes" that "they were likely to see well how things are in their parts." It is not initially clear exactly what Archytas means by wholes and parts here. Since he refers to "wholes" in the plural rather than to "the whole," Archytas is probably not referring to the (whole) universe and its parts. The plural instead suggests that, in each science, there is a whole or a set of wholes, which those concerned with the sciences distinguish, and that, because of their good discernment of these wholes, they are able to see well how things are in their parts. I, therefore, propose a second hypothesis: Archytas is arguing that scientists begin by carefully distinguishing and defining the universal concepts of the given science (the wholes) and that, because they have done so, they are also able to understand the particular objects or particular types of objects considered by the science (the parts).[4] Archytas gives an

---

[4] Archytas' distinction between the whole and the parts in Fr. 1 is reminiscent of Aristotle's distinction (e.g. *APr* 24a16 ff.; *Int.* 17a39; *Metaph.* 1060b32) between the universal (καθόλου) and particular (κατὰ μέρος, ἐν μέρει). I do not agree with Cambiano (1998: 312, n. 52), however, that this gives us any reason to doubt the authenticity of Fr. 1. It seems to me not at all implausible that Aristotle may have been in part influenced by passages like Fr. 1 in developing his distinction and the terminology with which he expresses it. We know that he studied Archytas carefully. It is much less plausible

instructive example of what he means by the scientists' clear vision of things in their parts: the clear set of distinctions that astronomers have handed down "concerning the speed of the stars" (i.e. the periods of the planets, sun and moon) "and their risings and settings" (i.e. of constellations). Venus can be distinguished from Jupiter by its different period of revolution and constellations can be distinguished from each other by their different pattern of risings and settings in the night sky. Thus, an astronomer may start with a set of distinctions about general concepts such as motion, but he will end up being able to give accurate accounts of the motion of specific astronomical bodies such as the constellations, planets, sun and moon.[5]

The hypotheses about Archytas' view of the sciences, which I have presented above, can be tested by looking at the specific science which is the subject of the book of which Fragment 1 is the beginning, harmonics. We are limited again by fragmentary evidence, but we do have about the first thirty lines of Archytas' discussion of harmonics (Fr. 1, lines 7–43), a second fragment from the treatise (Fr. 2) and a number of testimonia about its contents (A16, A17, A18 and A19). If Archytas' treatment of harmonics corresponds to my proposed model of Archytan science, that correspondence will be strong support for the model.

Archytas' presentation of harmonics begins precisely as the proposed model would suggest, with a series of distinctions concerning the wholes or universal concepts of the discipline. The fundamental concept ("the whole") in harmonics is sound, and according to Archytas it is precisely with sound that his predecessors began (lines 7–8 πρᾶτον . . . . ψόφον). No definition of sound is offered, but the conditions under which sound arises are clearly set out. These conditions involve a second major concept, that of an impact (πλαγά). No sound can arise without an impact (line 8). Next, Archytas reports, his predecessors concluded that impacts, in turn, cannot arise without the collision of bodies in motion. They then distinguished two different circumstances in which collisions occur, either when bodies meet from opposite directions or when one body is overtaken and struck by another body moving in the same direction but at a greater

---

to suppose that Fr. 1 was forged on the basis of Aristotle, because the language of Fr. 1 does not in fact correspond to Aristotle very closely. The only close similarity is the use of the expression κατὰ μέρος in line 3 of Fragment 1. Aristotle's term for "universal" (καθόλου) does not appear in Fr. 1. The pseudo-Pythagorean treatises, however, tend to be characterized by rather precise repetition of the terminology of the Platonic or Aristotelian original. Thus, the term καθόλου appears some 14 times in the pseudo-Archytas treatises (e.g. Thesleff 3.19; 14.15; 17.9; 19.10; 22.12) and is what we would expect in Fr. 1, if it were a forgery. Fr. 1 may well provide us, then, with a glimpse into the origins of Aristotle's distinction.

[5] See the Appendix to this chapter entitled "Archytas and the Platonic method of division."

velocity (lines 9–13). Having now defined the circumstances under which sound arises in terms of the impacts resulting from the collisions of moving bodies and having distinguished two ways in which such collisions arise, Archytas' predecessors made another distinction, between sounds that we perceive (line 18) and sounds that we do not perceive (lines 13–14). As long as an impact has occurred there is a sound, whether the sound is perceived or not. Three different circumstances in which we do not hear sounds are then distinguished (lines 14–16). In some cases the impact is too weak to affect our ears, in others the impact in itself might have been large enough but, because of the distance from us, does not reach our ears with enough force and, finally, in some cases, the impact is excessively large so that it will literally not fit into our ears. This latter case may be an attempt to explain why we do not hear the famous music of the spheres. At this point (line 18), Archytas turns to the sounds that can be heard and switches from an indirect report of the distinctions made by his predecessors, which he evidently accepts, and starts making distinctions of his own. Sounds that we do hear are then distinguished in terms of high and low pitch. High-pitched sounds are ones that travel rapidly from the impact to our senses and low-pitched sounds are those that travel slowly (lines 18–20). The rest of Fragment 1 consists of a series of examples given to illustrate this thesis, which is summarized in the last two lines (42–43).

Thus, the first lines of Archytas' direct treatment of harmonics (Fr. 1, lines 7–20) consist precisely of the distinction of the central concept or "whole" relevant to harmonics, sound, followed by further distinctions within that whole (inaudible sounds, audible sounds, high pitched sounds and low-pitched sounds). These distinctions are made in terms of the conditions under which first sound itself and then the various subdivisions of sound arise. The discussion of these conditions involves appeal to other concepts such as impact, collision, bodies and motion. These first lines on harmonics give ample illustration of what Archytas meant in saying that those concerned with the sciences are good at making distinctions and that they begin by making distinctions about the nature of wholes.[6] The final goal of the science according to the model I have proposed, however, is not knowledge of these initial divisions or parts of sound but rather knowledge

---

[6] As the Appendix to this chapter suggests, there may be connections between Archytas' distinctions of wholes and Plato's method of division. It should be clear, however, from the distinctions which Archytas outlines at the beginning of his *Harmonics*, that he was not always thinking either of genus/species distinctions or that the distinctions were dichotomous at each step. For a defense of Platonic division and a discussion of the variety of principles that may have governed how it was carried out see Ackrill 1970.

of the true nature of each individual sound. Can any sense be made of this in terms of what we know of the rest of the contents of Archytas' *Harmonics*?

It is likely that, after having distinguished between high and low pitch, Archytas turned to the discussion of different intervals of pitch and made a further distinction between intervals that are concordant and intervals that are discordant. It is at this point that the discussion would have shifted from the consideration of sound in general to musical sound. Testimonium A18 seems to reflect Archytas' discussion of the factor which distinguishes concordant intervals from discordant intervals: in the case of concords the ear has the impression of a single note. It is also clear that Archytas went on to argue that intervals can be represented by ratios of numbers and that the numbers in the ratio are the numbers of the quick and slow motions which produce high- and low-pitched notes respectively (A19a). He then undoubtedly introduced the ratios of numbers that correspond to the three main concords: the octave (2:1), the fourth (4:3) and the fifth (3:2). Evidently he then discussed attempts of his predecessors to make further distinctions among these concords and to arrive at a means of ranking concords, although it is doubtful that he approved of their practice (A17).

At this point Archytas probably turned to discussion of the inner structure of an octave. Fragment 2 probably belongs to this context, because it distinguishes the three means relevant to music: the geometric, arithmetic and harmonic means. Insertion of the arithmetic mean in the octave will divide it into a fourth and a fifth in descending order (e.g. if the octave is 12:6, the arithmetic mean is 9 and $12/9 = 4/3$ which is the fourth and $9/6 = 3/2$ which is the fifth). Insertion of the harmonic mean will divide the octave once again into a fourth and a fifth, but this time the order of the fifth and fourth is reversed (e.g. 8 is the harmonic mean between 12 and 6 and $12/8 = 3/2$, which is the fifth and $8/6 = 4/3$, which is the fourth). It is natural to want to divide the octave in half, but this turns out to be impossible. It is not possible to find a geometric mean in the octave (e.g. there is no x such that 12:x :: x:6). This was undoubtedly known to Archytas' predecessors but Archytas, in accordance with his rigorous mathematical outlook, made an important new contribution here by proving that it is impossible to put a geometric mean into any ratio of the form $n + 1/n$ (A19). In doing so Archytas showed not just that the octave could not be divided in half but also that the same was true of the fourth, the fifth and the whole tone (9/8) as well.

It seems very likely that Archytas ended his *Harmonics* with his account of the inner structure of the fourth in the three main genera: the diatonic, the chromatic and the enharmonic. As we have seen, the octave is divided into a fourth and a fifth. The fifth, however, consists of a fourth + a whole tone ($3/2 = 4/3 + 9/8$), so that the whole octave can be viewed as two fourths joined by a whole tone. Thus, in constructing a scale an octave in length, the key issue was how to divide the fourth. In Archytas' day there were basically three different ways (genera) in which musicians divided the fourth, which then produced three main types of scale: diatonic, chromatic and enharmonic. Philolaus had discussed only one genus, the diatonic, and he presented a version of that genus which resulted from repeated applications of the arithmetic and harmonic mean but which did not correspond to any musical scale actually in use. Archytas, on the other hand, abandons Philolaus' diatonic and presents us with a diatonic which does correspond to a tuning that was actually used by the musicians of his day. Even more significantly the same is true for each of the other genera; Archytas adopts a chromatic and an enharmonic tetrachord that corresponds to scales used by practicing musicians. He defined the intervals in the diatonic tetrachord by the ratios $9/8$, $8/7$ and $28/27$, those in the chromatic by the ratios $32/27$, $243/224$, and $28/27$, and those in the enharmonic by the ratios $5/4$, $36/35$, and $28/27$.

The science of harmonics is thus an excellent example of what Archytas meant when he said that those concerned with the sciences understood the true nature of each individual thing; harmonic science allows us to determine mathematically the particular intervals that we hear musicians playing. Archytas was not able to determine most of these ratios by direct measurement. The Greeks simply did not have the capability of making measurements accurate enough to identify a ratio such as $243/224$. Archytas arrived at these ratios by starting from the ratios that governed the basic concords (the octave [$1/2$], fourth [$3/4$] and fifth [$2/3$]), which could be determined by measurement, and then mathematically manipulating these ratios. He did not, however, simply manipulate these ratios to arrive at ratios which he judged to be proper on some *a priori* grounds, as is sometimes maintained. Instead, he manipulated them in light of the tuning practice which he observed musicians using (see the commentary on A16), so that the ultimate basis for Archytas' mathematical description of the three types of tetrachord is actual musical practice, i.e. what he saw musicians doing. We can now see clearly why Plato is upset with Pythagorean harmonics (by which he undoubtedly means Archytan harmonics) in *Republic* VII. His complaint is precisely that Archytas directs harmonics towards the sensible world, that Archytas sees the goal of harmonics as to determine the numbers of "heard harmonies" (531c, ταῖς συμφωνίαις ταῖς ἀκουομέναις).

This dispute between Archytas and Plato is further exemplified in Plato's *Timaeus*, where the mathematical structure of the world soul (35a ff.) corresponds to Philolaus' diatonic scale, which is constructed solely by the application of mathematical means with no appeal to music we actually hear. There is no trace of Archytas' divisions of the tetrachord in the *Timaeus*. The ultimate object of Archytan science is the sensible particular, not the structure of the intelligible world.

Fragment 1 makes one further statement about the sciences and, in contrast to much of the rest of Archytas' account of the sciences, this statement struck a responsive chord in Plato. Archytas ends his introductory remarks on the sciences with the assertion that the four sciences he has identified are all akin (ἀδελφεά). Plato picks up and slightly modifies this idea in *Republic* VII. Socrates asserts that astronomy and harmonics are kindred sciences, "as the Pythagoreans say" (530d). His repetition of Archytas' word (ἀδελφαί) makes it very likely that he has the beginning of Archytas' *Harmonics* specifically in mind. Moreover, although Socrates initially just mentions harmonics and astronomy as akin, while Archytas referred to the kinship of all four sciences, at 531d Socrates is emphatic that study of the sciences is valuable only insofar as it brings out the community, kinship and affinities of all the sciences (κοινωνίαν . . . ξυγγένειαν . . . οἰκεῖα). Plato explains the kinship of astronomy and harmonics with the remark that they are akin in that astronomy deals with visible motion while harmonics deals with audible motion (530d). In Fragment 1 Archytas does not give an explicit explanation of the kinship. The assertion of kinship is given in support of the suggestion that just as clear distinctions have been made concerning astronomy, geometry and numbers, so also harmonic theorists have given us clear distinctions about the particular phenomena of music. Archytas makes the point clearly only in the case of astronomy, where he specifies the phenomena which are explained (the speeds, risings and settings of the heavenly bodies), and skips over geometry and logistic quickly in order to get to his main interest, music. Plato's initial limitation of the kinship to astronomy and harmonics may be a reflection of this feature of Archytas' text. The kinship that Archytas sees must, therefore, reside in the similar structure of all the sciences. Just as the clear discrimination of wholes in astronomy leads to accurate knowledge of particular astronomical phenomena so, because of the similar structure of all the sciences, we can expect the same results in harmonics.

Since detailed examination of one of Archytas' sciences, harmonics, thus supports my initial hypothesis about his understanding of the nature and value of the sciences as a whole, it is appropriate to see how that understanding might apply to the other three sciences. In each science the first step is to distinguish the relevant "wholes," or basic principles and continue by making further distinctions within these wholes. The ultimate goal of each science, however, is not simply to establish an appropriate set of distinctions but to gain knowledge of particulars. In music the fundamental concept or whole is sound and the ultimate goal is to gain knowledge of the musical intervals we hear in actual music, by identifying the mathematical ratios which describe those intervals. In astronomy the fundamental concept is presumably motion, and the ultimate goal is to specify the periods of the planets and their risings and settings, presumably again in mathematical terms.[7] In geometry it seems likely that there were several fundamental concepts (e.g. point, line, surface, solid) and that the ultimate goal would be to describe mathematically the physical objects that fill the world: plants, animals, inanimate objects, and artefacts (e.g. statues and temples). Finally, in the science of number, logistic, the fundamental concepts are the unit and number. There will have been further distinctions of different types of number starting with odd and even and also examination of ratios of numbers and different types of ratios as well as proportions and different types of proportions. In this case the ultimate goal will be to quantify in various ways the objects in the physical world. It is clear, however, that logistic will have a special position within the sciences, because, while it does have as its own proper object the counting and multiplying and dividing of objects in the world, it is also involved in each of the other sciences, insofar as their accounts of the sensible particulars are all given in terms of numbers, ratios and proportions. Harmonics ends up by defining heard harmonies in terms of ratios just as astronomy ends up defining the periods of planets in terms of numbers.

One way of understanding Archytas' approach to the sciences is to suppose that he is developing and carrying on the project already set out by his predecessor Philolaus. Philolaus argued that we only gain true knowledge of things insofar as we can give an account of them in terms of numbers (Fr. 4). We have no explicit statement of this thesis in Archytas

---

[7] I do not mean to suggest that Archytas was practicing mathematical astronomy based on the systematic recording of astronomical data in terms of the angular position of an object in the sky or that he was trying to provide a detailed account of planetary motion, taking into account such phenomena as retrograde motion. His astronomy was mathematical only insofar as it tried to determine and reconcile the periods of the sun and the moon and other planets and to tie the rising and setting of constellations to numbered days of the month. Archytas' conception of the mathematical nature of astronomy may, however, have been influential in the earliest attempt to explain planetary motion, that of Eudoxus, who may have been his pupil. See Goldstein and Bowen 1983, although I think that they preserve too rigid a separation between astronomy and cosmological speculation.

(unless A21a can be read this way), but his sciences seem to be directed at providing just the sort of account of the phenomenal world that is called for by Philolaus. Philolaus only took the first steps in this project, by associating certain numbers with certain concepts (e.g. justice = 4), by describing the overall structure of the cosmos in terms of the diatonic scale (Fr. 6a), by taking into account the periods of the planets in his astronomy, and by noting numerical structures in biology (B13). Archytas appears to have been much more successful in carrying out the project, e.g. he is able to give a more sophisticated account of musical phenomena. In particular he focuses more on the role of proportion in explaining phenomena than on individual numbers. Proportion is used in an attempt to describe different sorts of motions and the biological structure of plants and animals, which results from those motions (A23a). Proportion is also applied to human behavior and in particular to the workings of the just state (Fr. 3). It is significant that numbers are employed in both Philolaus and Archytas in the attempt to explain particulars or at least kinds of particulars.

Philolaus' more fundamental principles were limiters and unlimiteds. It appears that once again Archytas may have taken over this basic thesis but developed it in a much more sophisticated way. Archytas' theory of definition, which Aristotle praises, can be best understood as based on the distinction between limiters and unlimiteds. One of the examples of Archytan definitions given by Aristotle is the definition of calm-at-sea, which is one word in Greek (γαλήνη) and which is defined by Archytas as "levelness" of "sea." Aristotle interprets this in terms of his own distinctions as a definition involving both the form (levelness) and the matter (sea). It is more likely, however, that Archytas was thinking in terms of Philolaus' metaphysical system, according to which sea is an excellent example of an unlimited and levelness is what limits the sea (see A22). Given this interest in definition, what we would have expected, then, is that Archytas would have attempted to arrive at definitions of the wholes which serve as the foundation of each of his sciences and that these definitions would be formulated in terms of his general theory of definition, according to which each definition has both a limiting and unlimited component. It is puzzling, then, that, in his *Harmonics*, while he specifies the conditions in which sounds arise, he does not provide a definition of sound or the other concepts which he discusses. There is the possibility, however, that in geometry and logistic Archytas did start from definitions of the point and the unit respectively (A22). Whatever role definition may have played, Archytan science begins with universal concepts or wholes, which are not specified in terms of numbers and ends up with concrete particulars which are. This mirrors Philolaus' initial account of the world in terms of limiters and unlimiteds and his thesis that the individual things in the world will be known through number.[8]

We do not have any explicit statement that Archytas saw himself as following Philolaus in the ways I have just suggested.[9] It is striking, however, that one of the few things we know about Eurytus, who appears to fall between Philolaus and Archytas chronologically, is that he tried to find numbers in things and went so far as to give the specific number of such things as a man or a horse. As we have seen, our ultimate source for this report about Eurytus is Archytas. Given Archytas' method of beginning with the work of his predecessors, it seems quite plausible to suppose that Archytas first identified the project of finding numbers in things as originating with Philolaus and then described the attempt to carry out the project by Philolaus' successor, Eurytus. It is common for modern scholars to ridicule Eurytus and to suppose that Theophrastus must be speaking ironically, when he appears to praise Eurytus for not resting content with general principles but instead going on to explain how those principles can explain particular cases (A13 – Text H). I suspect, rather, that Theophrastus is here reflecting his source Archytas, who may well have praised Eurytus for at least attempting to carry out Philolaus' project, although Archytas thinks that he himself can do better. The conspicuous absence of any reference to Archytas' metaphysical principles in the doxographical tradition (with the possible exception of A21a) may then not be the result of a defective tradition but rather accurately reflect the historical situation; Archytas did not present a new metaphysical system but instead gave some real content to Philolaus' system which is dramatic but short on specifics.

One odd feature of Archytas' account of the physical world is paralleled in an aspect of Philolaus' system, which drew comment from Aristotle. The

---

[8] There is one further possible connection between Archytas' conception of science and Philolaus, to which I allude in the Appendix. Philolaus developed a method of "*archai*," which involved finding the minimum number of starting points ("*archai*"), which had to be posited in order to explain a given phenomenon (Huffman 1993: 78 ff.). Thus, in order to explain the cosmos as a whole, three principles must be posited (limiters, unlimiteds and *harmonia*), while in order to explain disease a different set of three principles must be posited (bile, blood and phlegm). It may be that the wholes that Archytas sees as the foundation of each of the sciences are a development of these starting points of Philolaus. This suggestion would be strengthened, if we were sure that Archytas was responsible for the definitions of the point as the starting point of the line and the unit as the starting point of number, which appear in Aristotle's *Topics* (see A22).

[9] Although there is no direct testimony that Archytas followed Philolaus in adopting limiters and unlimiteds as basic principles, a close connection between Archytas and Philolaus regarding first principles is supported by the doxographical tradition's explicit assertion that Archytas followed Philolaus in his treatment of the one (A20 and A21).

Pythagoreans' focus is resolutely on the physical world, but they employ explanatory principles (mathematics) that are more appropriate for a different sort of reality. Aristotle thought that, in explaining physical reality, the Pythagoreans needed to say much more about physical principles (*Metaph.* 989b30). The evidence suggests that Archytas showed a wide interest in physical phenomena, discussing motion (A23 and A23a), the parts of animals and plants (A23a), the extent of the universe (A24), optics (A25), and, of course, acoustics (Fr. 1). There is even the possibility that he had something to say about matter and the fifth element, aether (A13). His treatments of acoustics and optics, however, show a characteristic tendency to present what could be described as a bare bones physical theory. In neither case does he seem to have anything to say about the medium of sound or sight, air and light respectively. There is evidence that he tried to describe motion mathematically but no indication that he discussed the natural motion of the different elements as did Aristotle. There is remarkably little evidence for discussion of the physical elements. It looks as if, after distinguishing the basic concepts in a given field, Archytas focused on the mathematical description of physical entities rather than bothering to account for their specifically physical properties.

LOGISTIC AS THE FUNDAMENTAL SCIENCE

If the goal of the sciences, according to Archytas, is to give an account of the sensible world in terms of numbers, it should follow, as I have already suggested, that the science of number would have a particularly prominent place among Archytan sciences. The preeminence of the science of number, which Archytas calls logistic, is strikingly confirmed by Fragment 4. In Fragment 4, Archytas asserts that "logistic seems to be far superior indeed to the other arts in regard to wisdom" and then describes its superiority over geometry in particular, saying that it puts demonstrations into effect where geometry is deficient and even surpasses geometry in dealing with shapes. Before looking in more detail at Archytas' reasons for regarding the science of number as superior to the other sciences, it is important to examine the significance of the name which he gave that science, logistic.

In Fragment 1, Archytas simply describes the science as "concerned with numbers" (περὶ . . . ἀριθμῶν, lines 5–6) without assigning it a name. When he praises logistic at the expense of the other sciences, and in particular at the expense of geometry in Fragment 4, there is little doubt, however, that he is referring to the science of number (see the commentary on Fr. 4). In using "logistic" rather than "arithmetic" as the name for the science of numbers, Archytas is in agreement with Plato. In *Republic* VII, Socrates begins by using both the names arithmetic and logistic for the first of his five sciences (525a), but, as the discussion develops, arithmetic drops out and it is clear that logistic is the preferred term (λογιστικῷ 525b, λογιστικήν 525c, λογισμῶν 536d – see also *Tht.* 145a and the commentary on Fr. 4). The definitions of arithmetic and logistic given in the *Gorgias* suggest that logistic comes to be used as the term for the science of numbers as a whole, because it builds on arithmetic. According to these definitions, arithmetic is concerned to classify different sorts of numbers, without paying attention to their specific quantity, starting with the distinction between even and odd (451b). Logistic, on the other hand, deals with the quantity of number and in particular with what quantity numbers have in relation to one another (Pl., *Gorgias* 451c). Logistic thus has as a central concern relative quantity, i.e. ratio and proportion (Klein 1968: 24). The three means applied to music in Fragment 2 of Archytas are thus, *qua* means, the subject of logistic (e.g. in the case of the geometric mean, the extreme term a has the same quantity relative to the mean term b as the mean term b has to the other extreme c, so that a:b :: b:c). Archytas' choice of logistic as the name for the science of numbers thus suggests that the real value of that science is what it tells us about ratio and proportion (see further the commentary on Fr. 4, line 1).[10]

As we have seen above, in Fr. 1, Archytas treats the sciences as one big happy family; they are akin to one another, because they all have a similar structure. In Fragment 4, however, Archytas appears to be making logistic the head of the family. At first sight, he appears thereby to be introducing discord into the Pythagorean family, since Philolaus had earlier called geometry the source and mother-city (ἀρχὴ καὶ μητρόπολις) of all the sciences (A7a). This image of geometry as the mother-city which sends out the other sciences as colonies is genealogical and diachronic. It matches well with what we know of the historical development of Greek mathematics. Geometry does indeed seem to be the first of the sciences to develop a structure in which certain first principles or elements are postulated on which, in turn, a structure of proofs is built (Proclus, *In Euc.* 66.7). So more than anything else the image of geometry as the mother-city suggests that Philolaus is making an historical point about the

---

[10] Cambiano, in his excellent article, also argues that logistic should not be understood as simple calculation with the natural numbers but rather as dealing with proportion (1998: 313–15). His interpretation and my interpretation of the role of logistic in Archytas, although developed independently of each other, come to quite similar conclusions. See also his development of the connection between Eurytus and Archytas (316–24).

sciences. Geometry was the first science to gain a scientific structure, and it then inspired "colonies" in other sciences. Is Archytas disputing this point, when he asserts the priority of logistic in Fragment 4?

It is important to note that Philolaus' assertion of the priority of geometry is problematic even for Philolaus. Elsewhere in the fragments of his book it would appear that number and hence logistic/arithmetic is primary. In Fragment 4 he asserts that ". . . indeed all the things that are known have number. For it is not possible that anything whatsoever be known or understood without this." If, however, we make the Aristotelian move of recognizing two senses of priority, the problem can be resolved. Number is prior in the sense that, without it, we cannot have secure knowledge of anything. However, secure knowledge of the world is not what we begin with. In terms of what is known to us, the world is first of all to be understood, according to Philolaus, as a combination of limiters and unlimiteds. The first line of his book makes no overt mention of number but rather asserts that "Nature in the world-order was fitted together both out of things which are unlimited and out of things which are limiting, both the world-order as a whole and all the things in it" (Fr. 1). Limiters and unlimiteds are very broad categories, but one of the primary things that Philolaus is referring to is the imposition of shape and structure on indeterminate continua including stuffs. In this sense, Philolaus is doing geometry from the first, as is clear in his cosmogony, which famously begins with a central fire that is conceived as coming to be in the center of a cosmic sphere (Fr. 7). So, for Philolaus, we see the world first in terms of geometry. However, even in Fragment 1 we were warned that number was coming. For the limiting shapes and the unlimited stuffs are "fitted-together" by the principle of *harmonia* which is numerical for Philolaus. Limiters and unlimiteds are held together by numerical ratios, and in Fragment 6 Philolaus' example of this "fitting-together" is the diatonic scale. For Philolaus geometry is the mother-city of the sciences insofar as our first experience of the world is in terms of geometry; hence, geometry is the first of the sciences to develop a scientific structure which is then exported to the other sciences. However, none of this contradicts his assertion that we will not have a firm grasp of the world until we understand the numbers in accord with which it is put together. It is only these numbers that give us secure knowledge.

Archytas' assertion of the priority of logistic can be understood in the same way. He may well agree with Philolaus that, historically speaking, geometry was the first science to receive a truly scientific structure, but in Fragment 4 he stresses that in other respects, i.e. with regard to wisdom and in putting demonstrations into effect, logistic is superior to the other sciences. Scholars have had difficulties even with this assertion in terms of what we know of the relative sophistication of geometry and arithmetic in Archytas' day. Burkert was led to assume that Fragment 4 must be spurious, since a distinguished mathematician like Archytas could not have asserted that the science of number was superior to geometry, when geometry was able to deal with irrational magnitudes and arithmetic was not. Other scholars have responded that arithmetic is employed to complete proofs, even proofs concerning incommensurability, that geometry alone cannot (see the commentary on Fr. 4), so that Burkert's doubts are misplaced. Closer reading of Fragment 4, however, suggests that Archytas' praise of logistic is not focused on the issue of irrational magnitudes or indeed on the relative capacity of geometry and logistic to complete proofs, but is rather based on somewhat different grounds.

It is crucial to pay attention to the language in terms of which logistic is praised at the expense of the other sciences: it is far superior in regard to wisdom (σοφίαν), it deals with what it wishes more concretely (ἐναργεστέρω) than geometry, and it completes demonstrations (ἀποδείξιας) where geometry is deficient, even if those demonstrations involve shapes. The two crucial words are "wisdom" and "concretely." σοφία can refer to a specific craft or skill, but the context suggests that here in Fragment 4 it is more likely to have its broader sense which picks out an intellectual virtue of the highest level and broadest importance, i.e. wisdom (see the commentary on Fr. 4). Archytas is not saying that logistic is superior to the other sciences *qua* sciences but rather that logistic has more to contribute to our understanding of the most important things and hence of how to live our lives than any of the other sciences. It contributes more to the all-encompassing sort of wisdom which the guardians of Plato's *Republic* have and which makes the whole state well governed and wise (428d). Archytas, however, differs radically from Plato, when specifying the nature of this wisdom. Logistic is not superior to the other sciences by providing the clear vision of the intelligible realm for which Plato calls. Archytas says that logistic is superior because it deals with whatever it wishes more concretely (ἐναργεστέρω) than the other sciences. The fundamental meaning of the adjective ἐναργής, from which the adverb ἐναργεστέρω derives, is "visible, palpable, in bodily form." If we take the adverb in this fundamental sense, Archytas is saying that calculation makes palpable what geometry leaves undetermined. Geometry works at too high a level of abstraction. Archytas appears to be locating wisdom in the exact opposite realm from Plato; wisdom has to do not with the intelligible and invisible but with the visible and palpable.

Precisely what Archytas means by arguing that logistic deals with things more palpably or more concretely becomes clearer, when we consider his final assertion that logistic completes or puts into effect demonstrations where geometry fails, even when those demonstrations have to do with shapes. How can logistic possibly be superior to geometry in dealing with shapes, when shapes such as triangles, circles, spheres etc. would appear to be the proper subject matter of geometry? Logistic is superior, indeed indispensable, whenever we want to create or describe a specific concrete object of whatever shape. In order to create a sculpture we cannot rest content with a purely geometrical description, we will have to assign specific proportions and measurements, i.e. numbers, to the various parts of the statue. Thus, the Argive sculptor Polyclitus asserts that a beautiful statue comes to be "through many numbers" not "through many shapes" (Fr. 2 – see Huffman 2002a). Logistic is the master science because it is through number and proportion that individual objects in the sensible world are both created and understood (Cambiano 1998: 322 also makes the connection to Polyclitus). This leads us finally to Archytas' assertion that logistic "completes demonstrations" where geometry fails. This has usually been taken to mean that logistic can complete proofs where geometry fails, but close examination of Archytas' language again suggests something different. The verb translated above as "complete" (ἐπιτελεῖ) in fact usually means "to put into effect" something that exists only in thought or word. This fits well with the line of interpretation I have been developing. The point is that it is logistic that allows one to put into effect what geometry can only demonstrate abstractly.[11]

There is a second dimension to this superiority of logistic. Precisely because we need numbers in order to create and understand concrete objects, numbers and numerical relations have a clarity and persuasiveness that go beyond the other sciences. This persuasiveness is not limited to the description of the physical world, however, but also has a prominent role in human behavior and in particular in the functioning of the just state. The second half of Fragment 3 of Archytas is a hymn to the value of "calculation" (λογισμός) in establishing the state. Archytas is not talking about the technical science of calculation (λογιστικά) here, as he was in Fragment 4, but rather about the practical ability to understand numerical calculations, including not just addition and subtraction but also basic

---

[11] Cambiano, for slightly different reasons, agrees that Fr. 4 of Archytas is not in conflict with A7a of Philolaus, because Philolaus is praising geometry as the beginning of the sciences, while Archytas praises logistic as what completes them (1998: 313, n. 54; 315).

proportions. This is an ability that is shared by most human beings, and it is on that shared ability that the possibility of a just state rests. Basing the state on the common human ability to calculate thus has a leveling effect and leads Archytas to support a more democratic constitution than Plato. This practical use of calculation (λογισμός) is ultimately grounded in the science of logistic, but one does not have to be a master of the science in order to do calculations and understand basic proportions. Unlike Plato, Archytas does not make the expert mathematical knowledge of a few a requirement for a good state to arise. Archytas argues that it is the clarity of proportion that convinces the rich to give to the poor and that persuades both parties that "they will have what is fair" (Fr. 3, line 10), but in order to agree that they have what is fair both rich and poor must be able to calculate. It is the clarity of proportion which has the power to do away with the constant striving for more (πλεονεξία) which produces strife in the state (Fr. 3, lines 6–7). It may be this fragment of Archytas to which Plato alludes in the *Gorgias*, when he has Socrates chide Callicles for ignoring geometric equality (508a), i.e. the sorts of equality he would appreciate, if he paid attention to mathematics. Archytas also argues that it is proportion which undergirds the legal system, preventing crime by demonstrating the unfairness of the unjust act and suggesting the fair punishment once a crime has been committed (Fr. 3, lines 10–14). Archytas is in effect arguing that most people recognize that "numbers don't lie" and emphasizing the importance of number and proportion in obtaining the agreement (ὁμόνοια – Fr. 3, line 6) necessary for a stable state.

Calculation is the foundation not just of the healthy state but also of the good life for an individual. The persistent theme in the testimonia which we have for Archytas' moral philosophy, testimonia which consist mainly of anecdotes, is that our actions should only be governed by reason and never by our emotions or the pursuit of pleasure. Archytas refused to punish the serious misdeeds of his slaves, because he had become angered (A7); similarly he restrained himself from swearing in anger, writing out his curses on a wall instead (A11). He argued that there was no greater evil for human beings than bodily pleasure, because there was nothing more opposed to reason than pleasure (A9a). Aristoxenus presented Archytas as developing this point in response to his own version of Plato's Callicles, Polyarchus of Syracuse, who argued that nature calls on us to pursue pleasure and that lawgivers, by bringing us all to one level, unnaturally curtail our individual attempt to get more of it for ourselves (A9). Archytas asks us (and Polyarchus) to imagine someone in the throes of the greatest bodily pleasure (sexual orgasm?) and argues that we must agree that a person in such a state is not able to reason. Thus, the more we succeed in obtaining bodily pleasure the less we are able to reason. It is far from clear to what extent the intellectual vocabulary used in these testimonia goes back to Archytas himself. This is particularly true in the last case discussed above, where all we have is Cicero's Latin version of Archytas' words. It is striking nonetheless that calculation once again has a prominent role. Cicero says that, in the state of most intense pleasure, we are able to engage in no mental activity (*nihil agitare mente*), and in particular are not able to achieve anything by calculation (*ratione*) or by deliberation (*cogitatione*). On the other hand, Archytas clearly did not think that all pleasures were disruptive; he enjoyed playing with children (A8) and regarded the pleasures of friendship as central to a good life (A7a). It may be that for Archytas the central point was that, since calculation is the intellectual virtue which governs our proper relations with others in the state and since, when it is developed further into the science of logistic, calculation is also crucial to our knowledge of the world, the key to living a good life is keeping our ability to calculate free from the hindrances imposed by certain emotions and the pursuit of bodily pleasure; it is quite literally our sense of proportion that we must struggle to preserve.

In light of the emphasis on logistic in Fragment 4 and calculation in Fragment 3, it is not surprising that, when we look at Archytas' distinctive contributions to the understanding of the world, it is his use of ratio and proportion that particularly stands out. In music theory he discovered the ratios that govern the three main types of scale in the music of his day (A16). He gave a rigorous account of the three types of proportion used in music and renamed one of them (Fr 2). He was evidently the first to prove the important point that superparticular ratios, such as those that govern the musical concords, cannot be divided in half. He may have attempted to define different types of motion in terms of different types of proportion (A23a). He was clearly interested in the ratios between the periods of the planets, sun and moon, although we do not know of any unique contribution of his in this area (Fr. 1). Of course, Archytas was most famous for having discovered the two mean proportionals that solve the problem of doubling the cube.

There is one final use to which Archytas put proportion. He thought that it was useful as a tool for discovering new knowledge, i.e. as a heuristic device. Aristotle's testimony clearly shows that Archytas was interested in definitions (A22), and, as we have seen, it may be that his interest in definitions was spurred in part by the role which making distinctions played in his conception of science. The nature of the definitions which Aristotle reports for Archytas suggests that he may have used proportion as a way to arrive at new definitions. In the *Topics* (108b24), Aristotle emphasizes the role which the consideration of similarity plays in developing definitions and gives as an example that *galēnē* in the sea is the same as *nēnemia* in air. These are the terms whose definitions Aristotle elsewhere associates with Archytas (A22), and Aristotle's statement of the role of similarity here is in essence an appeal to the proportion, *galēnē*:sea :: *nēnemia*:air. If we define calm-on-the-ocean (*galēnē*) as levelness of sea, we may use this definition in order to try to arrive at a definition of windlessness (*nēnemia*) as a certain state of air. We do so by setting up a proportion, as levelness is to sea so x is to air, and then solving for x. What is it that bears the same relation to the air as levelness to sea? This formulation of the proportion leads us to recognize that we need to look for what is similar in the two ratios, and Aristotle suggests that the common idea is calm. In the *Rhetoric*, Aristotle praises Archytas for his ability to see what is similar in things that differ greatly, giving as an example Archytas' assertion that an altar and an arbitrator are the same (A12). Here we know that the value of "the ratio" is something like "protecting a suppliant," and we know that both an altar and a person who is an arbitrator can do this. The question is how to define the differing but analogous (proportional) ways in which the altar and the arbitrator carry out this function. Exactly how Archytas conceived of the role of proportion in formulating definitions must remain conjectural, but the nature of his definitions and Aristotle's testimony make it very probable that proportion did serve a heuristic role.

Fragment 3 of Archytas may provide confirmation of the central role of proportion not only in discovering new definitions but in discovery in general. The first part of that fragment distinguishes two ways of gaining knowledge, learning from another and discovery on one's own (lines 1–2). As we have seen above, both learning and discovery have a role to play, but the highest value is clearly placed on discovery. The question then becomes how we are to make discoveries. The first answer that Archytas gives is the obvious but not very helpful answer, that we need to inquire (lines 3–4); we need to seek an answer to our puzzlement. How are we to do that? The text appears to be defective at this point. We are told that in order to seek we must have knowledge, but not told what sort of knowledge. The context suggests that Archytas' point is that in order to seek we must know how to calculate (λογίζεσθαι), since the remainder of the fragment focuses precisely on calculation (λογισμός). If this is so, Archytas is arguing that it is impossible to seek new knowledge, unless we know how to calculate (see the commentary on Fr. 3). For Archytas calculation and the science on which it is based (logistic) are most of all focused on proportion, so we might conjecture that Archytas is arguing that proportion is not just helpful in seeking and discovering definitions; it is the key to seeking and discovering all new knowledge.

OPTICS AND MECHANICS

In the *Posterior Analytics* Aristotle presents four pairs of sciences, in which one science is mathematical in nature and studies "the reason," while the science paired with it is subordinate to the mathematical science and focuses on the phenomena or the facts (78b34 ff.). Thus, arithmetic (mathematical harmonics) is paired with an harmonics which focuses on what we hear and mathematical astronomy is paired with the study of astronomical phenomena. Those who pursue the superordinate science study the universal while those who pursue the subordinate study the particular. This description of the sciences has some tantalizing connections with Archytas' presentation of the sciences in Fragment 1, where science starts with wholes and ends with individual things, except that Archytas seems to regard each of the sciences as a unity and does not break them into pairs as Aristotle does. The remaining two pairs of sciences introduce two sciences which did not appear either in Plato's list of sciences in Book VII of the *Republic* or in Fragment 1 of Archytas: optics and mechanics. Optics is said to be subordinate to geometry and mechanics to solid geometry. If these sciences did not exist or were not sufficiently prominent in the early fourth century for Plato and Archytas to mention them, we might suppose that they first came into their own in the middle of the fourth century and that this explains Aristotle's mention of them. There are other ways to explain Plato's and Archytas' silence; Plato might have known of them but chose not to mention them on philosophical grounds (they focus on the phenomenal world). Archytas might have included them as the parts of geometry that dealt with individual things but not treated them as separate sciences. Again Aristotle's mention of them may not so much indicate that the sciences were already in good form in his day as that they were emerging and his remarks may rather look forward to works such as Euclid's *Optics* and the *Mechanical Problems* preserved in the Aristotelian corpus, works which probably appeared in the generation or two after Aristotle's death.

If optics and mechanics had emerged as independent disciplines prior to the writing of the *Posterior Analytics*, however, Archytas would *prima facie* be a strong candidate as the person responsible for their development. In the case of optics we do have evidence that Archytas developed a theory of vision and of the phenomena involved in mirrors (A25). His Pythagorean predecessor Philolaus seems to have dealt with optical issues in developing his theory of the sun and his non-Pythagorean predecessor, Hippocrates of Chios, explained the tail of a comet in terms of reflection of the visual ray (see on A25). Even more striking is Aristotle's testimony that the Pythagoreans thought that the study of optics was in a state of agreement "because it was based on diagrams [i.e. geometry]" (A25, Text C). This seems to be suggesting that the Pythagoreans made a point which was similar to the point that Aristotle makes in the *Posterior Analytics*, i.e. that optics is a subordinate science to geometry. It indicates that the Pythagoreans had recognized that optics is based on geometrical principles. The question is whether this development was due to Archytas or whether it goes back even before Archytas to Pythagoreans of Philolaus' generation. The best solution may be to suppose that work in optics goes back to the generation of Philolaus but that it was only with Archytas that it became organized enough to be recognized as such by Aristotle. Whether Archytas saw it as such or as a part of geometry remains unclear (see on A25).

Archytas' work in optics has gone largely unnoticed by scholars (with the notable exception of Burnyeat). He has, however, often been hailed as the founder of mechanics. The name mechanics in Greek (μηχανική) is derived from the word for machine (μηχανή), and ancient mechanics can be defined as "the description and explanation of the operation of machines" (Knorr – *OCD*). The earliest surviving treatise in mechanics, the *Mechanical Problems* ascribed to Aristotle but probably dating to the third century BC, begins with problems having to do with a simple machine, the lever. The most detailed discussions of mechanics are the much later treatises by Heron (*Mechanics*, first century AD) and Pappus (*Mathematical Collection* VIII, fourth century AD), both of Alexandria. Pappus in particular gives a more complex account of what is meant by mechanics: "According to Pappus' first, and probably foremost, definition, mechanics is in particular an inquiry into the movement, rest and local motion of bodies in the universe. It studies the causes of phenomena that happen according to nature . . . and also determines the occurrence of phenomena that go against nature . . . It thus has both a productive part – it acts on nature [e.g. through machines] – and a cognitive one – it aims to understand nature" (Cuomo 2000: 104). Pappus maintains that there is both a theoretical part of mechanics, which is heavily mathematical, and a practical part (1022.13–15). The most important mechanical arts from the point of view of practical utility are identified as (1) the art of devising machines to lift great weights; (2) the art of devising machines of war such as the catapult;

(3) the art of devising water lifting machines; (4) the art of inventing amazing devices (automata); and (5) the art of constructing spheres as models of the heavens (VIII.2, 1024.12–1025.4). Given the interest in describing physical phenomena in mathematical terms, which I have ascribed to Archytas above, it might seem inevitable that Archytas should have shone in the field of mechanics as just described. What seems like an inevitable development does not always actually occur, however. While Archytas may have been an important precursor to later developments, there is little reliable evidence that he founded the discipline of mechanics.

It is important to note that no writer in the tradition of ancient Greek mechanics ever ascribes any work in the field of mechanics to Archytas; he is scarcely mentioned at all.[12] There is no mention of Archytas in the pseudo-Aristotelian *Mechanical Problems*, nor in Heron's or Pappus' mechanics, nor in Archimedes, nor in the treatises on machines of war by Heron, Biton and Philon, nor in the treatises on automata by Heron and Philon.[13] Either these authors did not know that Archytas was the founder of their discipline or they chose not to mention it. This silence is puzzling but not conclusive, particularly given the large amount of ancient work on mechanics which has not survived. It is also worth noting that Archytas does not mention mechanics, either when he lists the sciences in Fragment 1 or elsewhere in the surviving fragments. We have seen, however, that Archytas might

---

[12] Athenaeus Mechanicus (first century BC) is the only author in the Greek mechanical tradition to mention Archytas (A1a). His point is that Archytas' work is no help at all in writing a practical treatise on mechanics or for devising a mechanical device, because it is "utterly removed and separated from practical considerations." His concession that Archytas' work is "not without use for gaining instruction in basic principles" suggests to me that he is thinking of Archytas' contribution to the mathematics that came to serve as part of the foundation of mechanics (i.e. the duplication of the cube), rather than to any treatise on mechanics by Archytas. For Vitruvius' ascription of a book on machines to Archytas (B7, cf. A1b) see the section on "Other men named Archytas" above.

[13] Krafft (1970: 143 ff.) argues that, at *Laws* 893b ff., Plato refers to a central thesis of the *Mechanical Problems* (what Krafft calls the principle of the unequal concentric circles [XI]) and that the *Mechanical Problems* thus may be a genuine work of Aristotle written early in his career. He offers as an alternative that Plato is referring to an earlier treatise upon which the *Mechanical Problems* drew and that this earlier treatise was the work of Archytas. His arguments for this latter conclusion are mostly quite weak (e.g. Archytas had shown some interest in circular motion [A23a. Note, however, that for Archytas circular motion is natural, while in the *Mechanical Problems* it is not.] and was a friend of Plato [on this issue see my overview of Archytas' life]). His argument is seriously undercut by his treatment of a text from the surely spurious Archytan treatise on categories, which is quoted by Simplicius (*CAG* VIII. 128. 18–20), as genuine (147 ff., see Szlezak 1972: 41, 120–21 for commentary). There are some possible connections between the discussions of motion in Archytas and in the *Mechanical Problems* (see the commentary on A23a), and it is not impossible that the peripatetic text drew on Archytas' views on motion, but this in no way requires that Archytas wrote a treatise on mechanics and Krafft's speculations about an Archytan treatise on mechanics (which are followed by Schürmann 1991: 48 ff.) far outrun the evidence.

have seen mechanics as a part of geometry (or solid geometry) and seen no reason to name it separately.

What then is the evidence that has led some scholars to suppose that Archytas was the founder of the science of mechanics? Plutarch's dramatic story of Plato's anger at Archytas and others for employing instruments and mechanical constructions in order to solve the problem of the duplication of the cube (A15a and A15b) has played a central role; Plutarch asserts that Eudoxus and Archytas "set in motion this prized and famous science of mechanics" (A15b). Plutarch is not merely ascribing to Archytas some mathematics relevant to mechanical problems; he is ascribing to him the actual construction of a mechanical device (A15b, lines 8–9) to determine the two means necessary to the duplication of the cube, what Eratosthenes calls a mesolab or "mean getter" (so also Cambiano 1998: 296). Close examination of this story, however, shows that it is almost certainly false and was probably created as a sort of foundation myth for the science of mechanics (see my detailed arguments in the commentary on A15 and Cambiano 1998, esp. 299–300). Archytas' solution to the duplication of the cube, in fact, employs no instruments and no mechanical motion; our earliest commentary on Archytas' solution, that of Eratosthenes, emphasizes that Archytas' solution was highly abstract and could not be put into practice. He describes it precisely as "hardly mechanical" (δυσμήχανα). We must wipe Plutarch's story from our minds, if we are to have an accurate view of Archytas.

It is not clear whether Plutarch himself (ca. AD 100) invented the story of Archytas' mechanical solution to the doubling of the cube or whether it was a creation of the earlier tradition. Plutarch's version of the story was very influential, however, and it appears to lie at least partially behind the other primary text on which scholars have relied in making Archytas the founder of mechanics, Diogenes Laertius (ca. AD 200). Here is Diogenes' report of three accomplishments of Archytas that are potentially relevant to mechanics:

(1) He was the first to systematize mechanics by using mathematical first principles, and (2) he was the first to apply the motion appropriate to instruments to a geometrical proof, seeking to find two mean proportionals by cutting the semicylinder, in order to duplicate the cube. And (3) in geometry he was the first to discover the dimension of the cube [i.e. solid geometry], to use Plato's language in the *Republic*. (D.L. VIII. 83 = A1)

The second point above is very likely to have been derived from Plutarch and hence provides no independent evidence for Archytas' work in mechanics. The key expression "motion appropriate to instruments" (κίνησιν ὀργανικήν) in Diogenes certainly looks like a reflection of Plutarch's repeated reference to "constructions that use instruments" (ὀργανικὰς . . . κατασκευάς A15a, lines 6–7; ὀργανικῶν . . . ὀργανικὰς . . . κατασκευάς A15b, lines 4 and 6–7). The manuscript version of the third point makes the nonsensical assertion that Archytas was the first to discover the cube. The allusion to the *Republic* suggests that what lies behind the corrupt manuscript tradition is a scholion on the assertion in the *Republic* that the dimension of the cube (= the discipline of solid geometry) had not been invented yet (528b); such a scholion might have ascribed the invention to Archytas.[14] Archytas' solution to the problem of doubling the cube could with some justification lead someone to argue that Archytas had founded the discipline of solid geometry. If this is the correct way to clarify Diogenes' third point, however, it says nothing about Archytas' work in mechanics.

We are left then with the first point above, that Archytas was the first to systematize mechanics by using mathematical first principles. It could be that this assertion too is derived from Plutarch's presentation of Archytas as someone who began to set in motion the science of mechanics, but the language does not match anything that we have in Plutarch very closely. The reference to the systematization of mechanics is somewhat reminiscent of Proclus' report that Archytas helped to put geometry in a more scientific order (A6). As we have seen above, moreover, it was commonly recognized that, while mechanics properly speaking dealt with physical bodies and machines, there was also a theoretical part of mechanics which was largely mathematical and essentially identical with geometry or stereometry. The discovery of how to find the two mean proportionals which solve the problem of the duplication of the cube is of enormous importance for mechanics, since the solution to this problem allows one not just to double a cube but to construct solid bodies that are larger or smaller than a given solid body in any given ratio. Thus, if a working model of a machine (e.g.

---

[14] There are two problems with the manuscript text: (1) it is absurd to say that Archytas invented the cube, (2) Plato does not refer directly to Archytas in the passage of the *Republic* to which most scholars think Diogenes is referring (528b). On the basis of the passage in the *Republic*, I adopt the text κἀν γεωμετρίᾳ πρῶτος <τὴν τῶν> κύβων <αὖξην> εὗρεν, ὥς φησι Πλάτων ἐν Πολιτείᾳ, which asserts that Archytas was the first to discover solid geometry. Plato is just cited for the rather odd expression "the dimension of the cube" as a way of describing solid geometry and not as having referred to Archytas. A later commentator on the *Republic* then adds the information that this discipline, which Plato says at 528b had not been discovered, was in fact discovered by Archytas. The manuscript variant κύβην with its nonsensical ending may reflect Plato's αὖξην. The text may first have been corrupted to τὴν τῶν κύβην by an error in copying and the resultant nonsense later corrected to κύβον.

a catapult) can be devised, a larger version can be created maintaining all the proper proportions of the parts, provided that we know how to find the two mean proportionals. In his work on mechanics Pappus cites the three theorems proved geometrically by the ancients, which are most important for constructing machines; the determination of the two mean proportionals is second on the list (1028.18–21). Thus, Archytas was the first to solve geometrically one of the three theorems most relevant to the construction of machines.

I suggest that this is what is behind the assertion reported by Diogenes that Archytas was the first to systematize mechanics by using mathematical first principles. Archytas proved a theorem in geometry which is central to mechanics and that proof crucially depends on some sort of systematic presentation of mathematical first principles. Diogenes' report fits the rest of the evidence for Archytas very well, then, if we take him to mean that Archytas was the first to start to organize the mathematical first principles on which the science of mechanics would be constructed. The wording in Diogenes more naturally suggests that the discipline of mechanics was already in existence and that Archytas put it in order by providing mathematical first principles, but this would be a natural way for someone, who was writing after mechanics was an established science, to describe Archytas' achievement. Nothing in Diogenes' report requires us to assume that Archytas contributed to anything other than the geometrical aspect of mechanics. I should stress that I am not here reverting to the view of Tannery (1887: 128) who took it as a given that Archytas was on principle concerned only with pure mathematics and on these grounds dismissed all testimony suggesting that Archytas contributed to practical mechanics. My interpretation of Archytas' view of the sciences suggests that he was indeed interested in applying mathematics to physical objects, so that he would have no objection to practical mechanics on scientific grounds. My point is that the evidence in Diogenes Laertius gives no indication that Archytas did anything other than work in a quite abstract way on the mathematics that was relevant to mechanics.[15]

---

[15] Heiberg 1925: 67 takes a similar view. Krischer (1995) is right to point out that Aristotle's mention of a science of mechanics (*APo.* 76a24, 78b37), which is subordinate to geometry (stereometry), shows that some sort of science of mechanics existed at that time. There is nothing to indicate that this is a reference to any work of Archytas, however. Aristotle's remarks are more plausibly read as a reference to a science of mechanics, which was developing in the Lyceum (Hussey 1983: 185 ff.) and which would lead to the *Mechanical Problems*. The rest of Krischer's argument for Archytas as the founder of mechanics fails because of his reliance on a passage of Simplicius (*CAG* VIII. 128.18–20) as a fragment from Archytas' treatise on mechanics (pp. 63 and 67), when that passage is in reality from the pseudo-Archytan treatise on categories (Szlezak 1972: 41, 120–21). Krischer suggests that the reference to a "maker of machines" (μηχανοποιός) as someone who can save whole cities at

If we turn to actual mechanical devices that have been attributed to Archytas, a whole new series of problems arise. First, there is some simple misinformation in circulation. It is sometimes asserted, without any substantiating evidence (because there is none, so far as I can see), that Archytas invented the screw and pulley (Bluck 1947: 114; Brauer 1986: 48; Mustilli 1964: 18; Singer 1956: 631, 632, 677). Second, some scholars (e.g. Diels 1965 and Cambiano 1998) have suggested that Archytas was responsible for devising machines of war for his native Tarentum. No ancient text assigns such machines to Archytas, however, and the suggestion that he built or designed them is based on a series of questionable assumptions (see further my account of Archytas' life). A report in Aristotle assigns to an Archytas the invention of a clapper which was used in order to keep toddlers amused (A10). The later tradition assigns this to a separate Archytas who was a builder. The clapper is probably the work of Archytas of Tarentum (see the commentary on A10), but it is a very simple toy and should be seen as further testimony for Archytas' love of children rather than as evidence of his ability as an inventor of mechanical devices.

The single substantial mechanical device that can with some plausibility be assigned to Archytas is the famous flying wooden dove (A10a). Our evidence about the dove is sketchy, but the most reasonable reconstruction shows that this was not a dove that flew on its own, but a dove that was part of a mechanism and that was connected by a string to a counterweight through a pulley, so that, when motion was initiated by a puff of air, it "flew" from a lower to an upper perch which was part of the mechanism. Such a device shows some similarity to devices in the later tradition of Greek automata, and it does not seem impossible that Archytas could have devised it (see the commentary on A10a). We know from Diogenes Laertius, however, that there was a book on mechanics in circulation, which some people thought was the work of a different Archytas (A1 – see my comments on "Other men named Archytas"). Is the wooden dove the work of this putative Archytas *mēchanicos* instead (so Tannery 1887: 128)? Our sources for the dove are both late (Favorinus and Aulus Gellius in the second century AD), but they both clearly mean to ascribe the dove to Archytas of Tarentum. Since there is no great improbability involved in assigning the dove to

Gorgias 512b is likely to be a reference to Archytas, since there can have been few people who were both engineers and saved their city. Socrates is speaking quite generally here, however, and the maker of machines who sometimes saves whole cities is no more a reference to a specific person than the reference to the ship pilot who saves lives. There are likely to have been quite a number of engineers who helped their cities in important ways. The engineer Artemon is reported to have aided Pericles in the siege of Samos in 441 (Plut., *Per.* xxvii and D.S. xii. 28.3).

Archytas, we should follow these authorities and accept the dove as the work of Archytas, while recognizing that there are some grounds for doubt.

What can we finally conclude about Archytas' role in the development of the science of mechanics? When the dust has cleared there remain only two reliable ancient testimonia connecting Archytas to mechanics: Diogenes Laertius' assertion that Archytas worked on the mathematics relevant to mechanics and Archytas' dove. The "flying" dove is clever, but it does not constitute evidence that Archytas was the founder of the discipline of mechanics or even that he thought there was such a discipline. It is difficult, moreover, to see any connections between the dove and Archytas' work in mathematics that is relevant to mechanics. The most prudent conclusion would seem to be that Archytas did important work in aspects of solid geometry that would later serve as part of the mathematical foundation of the discipline of mechanics. Some later historians of mechanics could thus view him as having laid the mathematical foundations of mechanics, and their views are reflected in Diogenes Laertius' report, although we have no evidence to suggest that Archytas saw himself as founding a new science; he may well have simply seen himself as making an important contribution to geometry. He also, probably quite independently of his work in mathematics, showed an interest in devising toys and wonder-inducing mechanical devices. This activity certainly supports the conclusion that he had none of Plato's disdain for the physical world and that he did not see the work of a craftsman as beneath him. Archytas was thus one of the crucial forerunners who established the preconditions for the emergence of a discipline of mechanics. He did this in three ways. First, he was willing to apply mathematics to the physical world, which led to his praise of logistic for putting the demonstrations of geometry into effect (Fr. 4). Second, he developed a demonstration in solid geometry (the duplication of the cube), which is crucial to mechanics. Third, he was himself willing to devise a mechanical device, the wooden dove. None of these three accomplishments, however, would seem to justify us in concluding that Archytas had defined a distinct discipline of mechanics or that he was the author of a treatise specifically on mechanics. Such an account of his connection to mechanics would explain the universal silence concerning Archytas in the later tradition of Greek mechanical writers.

CONCLUSION: ARCHYTAS, PLATO AND ARISTOTLE

At this point it should be clear that the sciences are at the center of Archytas' philosophical achievement. He made significant contributions to the development of three of them: harmonics, geometry and logistic. In addition, he put forth an important thesis about the nature and value of the sciences, which led him to conclude that logistic was the most important of the sciences. He also argued that the common human ability to calculate and understand ratio and proportion, of which logistic is the rigorous scientific counterpart, is the basis for a stable and just society as well as for the good life of the individual. Archytas' conception of the sciences was thus the foundation of his moral and political philosophy. It is not surprising, then, that the Platonic text which makes the clearest allusion to Archytas is Plato's own account of the sciences in Book VII of the *Republic*. What is not commonly noticed, but what emerges from the account of Archytas presented above, is that Plato and Archytas were in serious disagreement. Scholars have typically emphasized the continuities between Plato and the Pythagoreans (e.g. Kahn 2001: 49 ff.) and overlooked the fact that the only mention of the Pythagoreans in the Platonic corpus turns out to be a criticism of them for seeking numbers in heard harmonies rather than ascending above the phenomena in order to consider which numbers are inherently concordant and which not and why (*R.* 530d ff.). Plato's criticisms of the nascent science of stereometry similarly take Archytas to task for focusing on individual problems posed by the phenomenal world rather than studying the geometrical solids for their own sake (see A15). Although the central books of the *Republic* are clearly in part directed at a very broad audience of philosophers and would-be philosophers, it is seldom recognized that one of their primary functions is to persuade a specific group of philosophers, the Pythagoreans and especially Archytas, of the errors of their ways and to convince them (1) that they must recognize the crucial distinction between the intelligible and sensible world, and (2) that because of a failure to make this distinction they have been mistaken about the true value of mathematics.

There is no indication that Archytas was persuaded by Book VII of the *Republic* to abandon his own conception of the value of the sciences. He seems rather to have tenaciously refused to make the split between the intelligible and sensible, for which Plato called. This may be one of the reasons that Aristotle found Archytas so attractive and spent so much time studying him (A13). Aristotle's admiration for Archytas is most obvious in his account of Archytan definitions in the *Metaphysics* (A22). Those definitions make clear that, for Archytas, as for Aristotle later, form does not exist in separation from matter and the basic entities of the world are complexes of matter and form, not separable Platonic forms. Archytas thought in terms of limiters and unlimiteds rather than Aristotelian form and matter but, as Aristotle saw, his definitions are always of the composite of limiter and unlimited, form and matter, and not of form separate from matter. Aristotle was also undoubtedly attracted by Archytas' insistence that the goal of the sciences was to give knowledge of the physical world and that mathematics was about ordinary perceptible objects (see Barnes 1995: 83–88 for a brief account of Aristotle's view of mathematics). We have seen that Aristotle's conception of subordinate sciences in the *Posterior Analytics* may have connections to Archytas' account of the sciences.

It is unclear whether Archytas provided any systematic account of the world in the form of a cosmology as Plato went on to do in the *Timaeus*. There is a small group of testimonia dealing with topics in physics, which could have figured in such an account: the argument that the universe is unlimited (A24), the discussion of the cause of motion (A23), the attempt to describe different sorts of motions in terms of mathematical proportions (A23a), the attempt to explain the shape of parts of animals and plants (A23a), and the account of vision (A25). With the exception of the first case, however, we have only the most exiguous evidence for Archytas' views in these areas. If these testimonia do derive from a systematic cosmology, it is strange that no trace of the basic principles of Archytas' cosmology (with the doubtful exception of A21a) or of the overall structure of his cosmos has survived in the doxographical tradition. As I have suggested above, another alternative would be to suppose that Archytas did not present a new account of the basic principles and structure of the cosmos but adopted those of Philolaus and instead directed his attention to using the sciences in order to work out that cosmos in detail. The surviving testimonia on physical topics would then have their origin in Archytas' development of each of the sciences; his optics could be seen as a development of geometry and his theory of motion may have developed within the science of astronomy. In some cases the arguments may have been responses to specific challenges to the Philolaic cosmology. This may be the case with Archytas' most famous argument (A24), which might be directed against Plato and defends not just the Philolaic view of the cosmos but also the atomist view and indeed the dominant view among the Presocratics, i.e. that the universe is unlimited. This view survived in Epicureanism, which borrowed and developed Archytas' argument. Plato and Aristotle, however, agreed in rejecting Archytas' position, although Aristotle calls Archytas' argument the most important argument for the existence of the unlimited (*Ph.* 203b23).

Archytas has often been supposed to lie behind the eponymous Italian statesman cum astronomer of Plato's *Timaeus* (20a, 27a). The figure of Archytas which has emerged from this overview suggests a somewhat different connection to the *Timaeus*. Aristotle, to be sure, wrote a book which appears to have been a summary of the *Timaeus* and the writings of Archytas (A13). The traditional view of Archytas' relation to the *Timaeus* would suppose that Aristotle's purpose was to summarize passages which showed the connection between Plato and Archytas, but my presentation of Archytas and some of the ancient evidence suggests that Aristotle's emphasis may have been more on the differences than the similarities and that Archytas came off rather better than Plato. One piece of evidence which points in this direction is Aristotle's pupil Eudemus' brief allusion to Archytas theory of motion (A23). After criticizing Plato for identifying the uneven or the unequal with motion, Eudemus concludes "it is better to say that these are causes [of motion] just as Archytas does." Again, when Apuleius reports early Greek accounts of vision he puts Archytas in contrast with Plato in describing the visual ray as "either filtered forth from the middle of our eyes, mixed with external light and thus made one, as Plato thinks, or derived from our eyes alone without any external support, as Archytas thinks." The contrast between Plato and Archytas in this passage may be due to Apuleius, but it is also possible that it reflects an earlier source such as Aristotle or Eudemus. Indeed, it is possible that Archytas himself presented the argument for his view of the visual ray with Plato in mind. Plato was wrong to suppose that the visual ray needs external support; the ray extends from the eye just as our arm can extend from our body without any external support (see the commentary on A25). The tension evident in the ancient tradition between Platonic and Archytan views on topics in physics suggests that Plato may have characterized the figure of Timaeus in ways that might remind us of Archytas, not out of emulation of Archytas but rather to suggest that Timaeus is in competition with Archytas; Plato gives us not the great statesman from Tarentum but rather a statesman from another south Italian state, Locri. Two of the interlocutors, Hermocrates and Critias seem to be historical figures, Timaeus appears to be the invention of Plato. Plato's dialogue begins by noticing the absence of a fourth interlocutor, someone who is prevented from attending by some infirmity (17a); is it Archytas who is absent because of a philosophical infirmity that prevents him from being Plato's spokesman in the *Timaeus*?

Archytas' refusal to distinguish between the sensible and the intelligible means that he would be unwilling to make Plato's central distinction between the works of reason (29e–47e) and the works of necessity (48b–68d) in the *Timaeus*. In Plato the works of reason are teleological, they are directed at what is best. Plato argues that it would be better for the cosmos to be one, whole, perfect and self-sufficient and that it cannot have these qualities if there is anything outside of it (32c ff.). Since there is nothing outside the cosmos, the cosmos itself, although it is alive, has no need for sensory organs (33c – there is nothing outside to perceive) or legs or hands (33d–34a). Thus it is on strictly *a priori* grounds that the cosmos is limited rather than unlimited; it is better that it be so. Plato concedes, however, that, if the cosmos is limited, there must be an edge to the cosmos and describes the world soul as stretched from the center to the edge (36e πρὸς τὸν ἔσχατον οὐρανόν). Archytas rejects this teleological argument and counters it with an argument that is based on our ordinary assumptions about the nature of the phenomenal world. The cosmos itself might not have arms, but imagine yourself at the edge, which Plato concedes that the universe has, would you be able to extend your arm or a stick beyond that edge or not? For Archytas the arbiter of truth is not *a priori* arguments of what is best but rather our own experience of the phenomenal world.

Another of the important works of reason is the construction of the world soul. The mathematical ratios to which this construction appeals undoubtedly have their origin in Greek harmonic theory, since they correspond to a standard method of tuning, "the method of concordance by which musicians established the outlines of their patterns of attunement" (Barker 1989: 51). Nonetheless these ratios do not correspond to any of the scales actually used by the musicians of Plato's day. In this passage of the *Timaeus*, Plato is doing the sort of harmonics which he prescribed in the *Republic*; he does not examine the numbers in the music he hears performed around him but rather puts aside the phenomena to focus on ratios that he finds concordant on *a priori* grounds. Consequently, when Plato presents these ratios in the *Timaeus* he makes no allusion to their origin in music. Again, Archytas could not have been a spokesman for this view, since it is precisely the numbers of the harmonies heard in the phenomenal world that are of interest to him (A16). Archytas' ratios for the diatonic, enharmonic and chromatic scale appear nowhere in the *Timaeus*.

If Plato's works of reason are missing from Archytas' view of the cosmos so correspondingly are the works of necessity. The works of necessity are purely mechanistic and thus provide explanations solely in terms of matter in motion. Some phenomena are to be explained by reason alone, others as a combination of reason and necessity, with reason successfully persuading necessity to cooperate, but others are solely the work of necessity (Strange 1985). At the foundation of these works of necessity is Plato's receptacle of being which is characterized by random and disordered motion. For Plato the motion which has its origin in the phenomenal world is identified with the uneven, with the unbalanced and chaotic state of the receptacle, and is to that extent ultimately undescribable by mathematics. Archytas seems to think that while motion and change may result from inequality or unevenness (A23), all motion can be described mathematically (A23a). For Archytas there is no irregular motion in Plato's radical sense; there are no aspects of the world which are the result of necessity alone. Plato thinks that acts of perception, such as sight, must depend not just on reason but on auxiliary causes which are the work of necessity and hence are, in a fundamental way, fallible. Hence, Plato does not give a mathematical account of optics in the *Timaeus*. The visual ray that proceeds from our eye cannot confront the phenomenal world on its own but in part depends on the support of something outside of us (45b ff.). Not so for Archytas. For Archytas the visual ray is controlled by intelligence and does not require external support (A25); it does not depend on the erratic workings of Plato's wandering cause.

Thus, Archytas is not just in disagreement with Plato's *Timaeus* on a few peripheral issues. The cosmos of the *Timaeus* is fundamentally un-Archytan. Plato does not usually make people who are still living characters in his dialogues, so Archytas may have been excluded from the *Timaeus* on those grounds alone. Even if Archytas were dead at the time of publication of the *Timaeus*, however, Plato would have had no choice but to absent him from the discussion and introduce a new south Italian of his own invention, who could present a mathematical view of the cosmos, which was in accord with Plato's conception of the value of mathematics. We thus reach the paradoxical conclusion that the "Pythagoreanism" of the *Timaeus* is only apparent; the *Timaeus* represents a radical reworking of the Pythagorean tradition by Plato, while Archytas' use of mathematics may have produced more influence on Aristotle's philosophy of mathematics than on Plato (see above).

Aristotle notoriously calls for principles to explain the physical world which are themselves physical and rejects Plato's attempt to derive the world from mathematical principles (e.g. the geometrical solids). He is, indeed, often blamed for cutting science off from mathematics (Solmsen 1960: 259–62). It may therefore seem perverse to suggest that Aristotle had significant connections to a Pythagorean like Archytas. There can be no doubt that Aristotle was critical of the bare bones quality of Archytas' physics, which focused mostly on mathematical description rather than physical properties. It remains true that, in addition to the similarities in metaphysics and theory of science mentioned above, there are some significant similarities between Archytas' and Aristotle's employment of mathematics. The use of calculation that lies behind Aristotle's distributive and retributive justice is closer to Archytas' vision of the role of mathematics in the state than Plato's (see Fr. 3). Plato's state depends on the expert mathematical knowledge of the guardians. The famous passage on the nuptial number stresses the difficulty and complexity of determining the truly concordant number which should govern human procreation, and hence the inevitable failure of human understanding to instantiate it, with the consequent failure of even the ideal state (545d ff.). Archytas and Aristotle stress the accessibility of the concept of proportion and its ability to produce agreement and justice in the state; in Archytas' case the basic human ability to understand proportion evidently led him to replace Plato's philosopher kings with a democracy. Aristotle uses mathematics in an Archytan way even in some aspects of his physics. If Aristotle's dynamics, for example, are "a bold attempt to bring physical phenomena within the grip of generally mathematical ratios" (Hankinson 1995: 147; see *Cael.* 273b30 and *Ph.* 249b29, 215a24), that attempt may owe a great deal to Archytas. Archytas was the prophet who preached that the ultimate goal of the scientists' good discernment of universal concepts was an accurate account of physical phenomena in terms of ratio and proportion.

APPENDIX TO CHAPTER II: ARCHYTAS AND THE PLATONIC METHOD OF DIVISION

Archytas' conception of the sciences finds an interesting parallel in Plato's account of the ideal science of rhetoric at *Phaedrus* 270b ff. In this passage, Socrates argues that, both in the case of rhetoric and in the case of medicine, there is a nature that we must determine, the nature of the soul in the one case and the nature of the body in the other, if we mean to be scientific and not content with mere empirical routine. Plato's further suggestion (270c) that one cannot know the nature of the soul without knowledge concerning τῆς τοῦ ὅλου φύσεως ("the nature of the whole") is closely paralleled by the language of Archytas' claim that scientists start from good discernment concerning τᾶς τῶν ὅλων φύσιος ("the nature of wholes"). It is striking that Phaedrus draws a parallel with Hippocrates of Cos' treatment of the body in terms of the nature of the whole, since Archytas' account of the sciences shows connections to the Hippocratic corpus (see note 3 above). What exactly Plato (or Hippocrates) means by "the whole" has been a matter of intense controversy (e.g. Mansfeld 1980, Lloyd 1975: 172 ff., Joly 1961, Kucharski 1939). Is it (1) the whole universe, (2) the whole body or soul, (3) the whole body-soul complex, or (4) the whole of whatever subject is being discussed? Fragment 1 of Archytas, as obscure as it is, may on this point be clearer than Plato. My interpretation of Archytas suggests that if Plato were following Archytas on this point, interpretation 4 would be the best reading of the *Phaedrus*.

The *Phaedrus* passage is just one of several statements of what is known as Plato's method of collection and division. The method is practiced in the *Sophist* and *Statesman*, and another theoretical statement of it is given in the *Philebus* (16c–17a), where it is presented as a development of a method of "the men before our time." I have shown elsewhere that this method of the men before our time has close connections to Philolaus' method of *archai* (Huffman 2001). The *Philebus* passage also has connections to Archytas. Instead of starting from a "whole" as he does in the *Phaedrus* and as Archytas does in Fragment 1, in the *Philebus*, Plato starts from a "one." This may well be just a different terminology for the same thing, however. The first example that Plato gives is precisely the science of harmonics which, as in Fr. 1 of Archytas, is said to start from sound as the one (17b), and, although the divisions of sound by no means exactly match those in Archytas, in two important ways they do mirror his procedure: one of the central divisions is into high and low pitch and the divisions of sound end with a specification of scales (17d). The similarities between Fragment 1 of Archytas and Plato's *Phaedrus* and *Philebus* are not such as to allow us to be certain whether or not either author directly influenced the other. Plato and Archytas may have independently developed similar approaches to science, which originated partly in Greek medicine and partly in the philosophy of Philolaus.

CHAPTER III

The authenticity question

[Note: This discussion should be supplemented with the sections on authenticity in the commentary on each of the genuine fragments and testimonia and by the more detailed discussion of specific pseudo-Archytan treatises in the appendix on spurious writings.]

In the case of most ancient authors, if a medieval manuscript or an ancient source ascribes a given text to that author, we assume that the text is genuine until proven otherwise. There are of course works ascribed in the ancient tradition to prominent authors, such as Plato and Aristotle, which modern scholars with good reason regard as spurious. The number of genuine works of Plato and Aristotle, however, far outnumber works judged to be spurious. This situation is almost completely reversed in the Pythagorean tradition. Thesleff's collection of spurious Pythagorean texts (1965) runs to some 245 pages. Out of the forty-four authors listed in Thesleff, in the case of only two, Archytas and Philolaus, are most modern scholars willing to agree that even some authentic fragments also survive, although there are some reliable testimonia about a few others (e.g. Hippasus and Eurytus). In the case of Archytas there are approximately 45 pages and 1,200 lines of almost certainly spurious texts collected in Thesleff, in contrast to the 7 pages and 100 lines of text in DK, which most scholars have accepted as authentic. Thus, in terms of number of lines, the amount of authentic material is less than 10 percent of the amount of spurious material. Archytas is far and away the most prominent figure in the pseudo-Pythagorean tradition, accounting for about 20 percent of the total spurious material in Thesleff's collection (45 of 245 pages), more than Pythagoras himself (30 pages). Given the nature of the Pythagorean tradition in general, then, and the Archytan tradition in particular, the assumption is usually that a text is spurious, until good reasons are given for regarding it as genuine.

There are, however, a great deal of early and reliable testimonia about Archytas' work, which shows that he was an important figure in the philosophy of the fourth century and that his genuine work was available to his contemporaries and immediate successors. Aristotle discusses Archytas' theory of definition in the *Metaphysics* (A22) and the *Rhetoric* (A12) and is reported to have written a total of four books dealing with Archytas (A13); Aristotle's pupil, Eudemus, preserved Archytas' method of doubling the cube in his history of geometry (A14), reports Archytas' argument to show that the universe is unlimited in extent (A24) and discusses his theory of motion (A23); another of Aristotle's pupils, Aristoxenus, wrote a *Life of Archytas*, which was rich in anecdotes (e.g. A7, A9); Plato appears to quote from Archytas' *Harmonics* in *Republic* VII (530d). There can be little doubt, then, that there were works of Archytas available in the fourth century BC. His prominence in the pseudo-Pythagorean tradition has in fact suggested to scholars that the dialect and style of Archytas' genuine works were the primary model for the pseudo-Pythagorean writings, at least for those written in Doric (Thesleff 1972: 61; Burkert 1972b: 100). It is then very likely that fragments from both genuine and spurious works of Archytas survive. There is, however, no quick way of distinguishing spurious from genuine. At first sight the fragments will appear to share a common dialect and style. Authenticity can only be determined by examining each fragment in detail.

The first step is to clarify the nature of the treatises which are commonly accepted as spurious. There are three central characteristics that apply both to the pseudo-Pythagorean writings in general and to the pseudo-Archytan writings in particular, although not all characteristics apply to all treatises and, when they do apply, they apply in varying degrees to different treatises. First, a number of treatises are directly based on passages of Plato and Aristotle and are close paraphrases of the Platonic and Aristotelian texts, sometimes following them word for word. Examples of this include the most famous of pseudo-Pythagorean texts, the treatise of Timaeus Locrus, which takes Plato's *Timaeus* as a model, and the treatise of Ocellus, which has passages that are very close to Aristotle's *On Generation and Corruption*. Among the pseudo-Archytan writings, *Concerning the Whole System of Categories* and *On Opposites* follow Aristotle's *Categories* closely, while a passage in *On Intelligence* (39.4–25) provides a paraphrase of Plato's account of the divided line in *Republic* VI.

Second, even when the pseudo-Pythagorean texts do not paraphrase a specific text from Plato and Aristotle, they make prominent use of Platonic and Aristotelian distinctions, employing Platonic and Aristotelian technical terminology. A number of pseudo-Pythagorean treatises employ Plato's tripartite soul, described in Plato's exact terminology (λογιστικόν = rational, ἐπιθυμητικόν = appetitive, and θυμοειδές = high-spirited, e.g. "Kallikratidas" 103.5 and "Metopos" 118.1–4). Among the pseudo-Archytan treatises, *On Principles* is replete with Aristotelian vocabulary and distinctions, such as ὑποκείμενον ("substrate"), τόδε τι εἶναι ("essence"), and μορφή ("form," 19.19–20 Thesleff). Some caution is needed in this case, however, since the isolated use of a term, which has a technical significance in Plato or Aristotle, e.g. εἶδος ("form"), need not be a sign of spuriousness, since such terms often have uses other than the technical Platonic or Aristotelian ones (cf. Archytas Fr. 4). It is particularly the use of complexes of such terms that are telltale signs, such as the use of εἶδος ("form") with one of the expressions used by Plato to indicate participation of particulars in forms (e.g. μετέχειν, cf. pseudo-Archytas, *On Intelligence*, 38.14–15 Thesleff).

Third, a number of pseudo-Pythagorean treatises work in what is obviously a Platonic or Aristotelian framework but improve on Aristotle or Plato by taking into account further developments in the philosophical tradition. The treatise of Timaeus Locrus takes into account criticisms of Plato's *Timaeus* (Ryle 1965: 176–78). Many pseudo-Pythagorean treatises particularly draw on the work of authors of the first century BC such as Antiochus, Arius Didymus, Eudorus and Philo of Alexandria. The fact that there are two separate pseudo-Archytan treatises, *Concerning the Whole System of Categories* and *On Opposites*, which draw on Aristotle's *Categories* reflects Andronicus of Rhodes' decision, in the first century BC, to separate the last six books of Aristotle's *Categories*, known as the *postpraedicamenta*, which deal with opposites, from the first nine books on categories proper. The pseudo-Archytan treatise *On the Good and Happy Man*, while dealing with issues first raised in Aristotle's *Nicomachean Ethics*, has clear connections to later work by Antiochus and Arius Didymus, while the pseudo-Archytan *On Moral Education* has close ties to Carneades' account of the goal of human action (Burkert 1972b: 30–38). In the area of metaphysics, *On Principles* follows Eudorus in positing a principle above the monad and dyad (Dillon 1977: 120–21).

The motivations for the pseudo-Pythagorean treatises as well as their time and place of origin remain matters of controversy. Burkert has shown that Zeller's thesis, which assigned all of the pseudo-Pythagorean treatises to the first century BC or later is untenable and that some pseudo-Pythagorica were produced already in the third century BC (1961). The treatise of Timaeus Locrus (first mentioned in Nicomachus) is dated to the first century AD and that of Ocellus (first mentioned in Varro) to the first half of the first century BC. With regard to the treatises forged in Doric, which are collected by

Thesleff and among which the pseudo-Archytan treatises figure so prominently, however, Burkert and more recent scholars have tended to suggest
that a date between 150 BC and AD 100 is most reasonable (Burkert 1972b:
40–41, Centrone 1990: 41–45 and 1994b, Moraux 1984: 606–07), in contrast to Thesleff who argued that they were composed in the third century
BC and originated in southern Italy (1961 and 1972: 59). Burkert has very
plausibly argued that they were most likely to have been composed in Rome
as part of the invasion of Roman intellectual life by Greek philosophy, an
invasion in which Archytas played a prominent role (1972b: 41–44; see also
my section on Archytas' life), while Centrone has gone back to Zeller's
position that they originated in Alexandria, because of similarities to the
works of Philo of Alexandria (1990: 30–34, 41–44).

    Why did people choose to write such treatises under the names of early
Pythagoreans? There is no single answer to this question. Some of the
standard motivations for forgeries may have been involved. In some cases
the forger may have been interested in making money by selling a rare
Pythagorean treatise to a book collector such as King Juba II of Lybia
(first century AD), who, Olympiodorus tells us (*CAG* XII. 1: 13), had a
passion for Pythagorean treatises (Thesleff 1961: 54). We don't have many
complete pseudo-Pythagorean treatises, but the ones that we do have are
not particularly long, and the shorter the treatise the more likely it is that a
forger would undertake it. It is possible that some treatises were rhetorical
exercises (Morrow 1962: 3–4). This would particularly apply to some of
the letters preserved, although letters, because of the ease of forging them are
also likely candidates to be forgeries for profit. Some letters, however, were
forged in order to authenticate other forgeries. Thus the correspondence
between Archytas and Plato which deals with the writings of Ocellus may
have been produced to authenticate the Ocellus forgery (Harder 1966: 39 ff.;
for another view see Thesleff 1962: 16 ff.), and a letter from Plato to Dion
may have had a similar function in relation to books forged in Pythagoras'
name (Burkert 1961: 19). Burkert has suggested that the letter of Lysis
plays the same role for the *Pythagorean Memoirs* which were excerpted by
Alexander Polyhistor (1961: 17–28).

    One problem that might be raised about the forgery for profit explana-
tion is why, on this explanation, so many of the treatises are forged in the
names of otherwise unknown or very obscure Pythagoreans. Some have
thought that the obscurity of most of the authors suggests a sort of genuine local Pythagorean tradition, probably in southern Italy, which produced the treatises. It is true that a forgery in the name of Pythagoras
himself or Archytas would probably attract more notice, but it does

not seem impossible to me that a book buyer might be interested in buying the work of a hitherto unknown member of the early Pythagorean school. Discovering an unknown has its own romance. About half of the pseudo-Pythagorean authors in fact appear in Iamblichus' catalog of Pythagoreans (*VP* 267), which probably goes back to Aristoxenus. This catalog may well have served as one source from which forgers might adopt their pseudonyms in order to give the treatises the stamp of authenticity (Burkert 1972b: 92).

Although money and the rhetorical schools may have in part motivated the pseudo-Pythagorean writings, their distinctive characteristics show that the primary motivation was to glorify the Pythagoreans at the expense of Plato and Aristotle. The treatises can be seen as providing the Pythagorean originals on which Plato and Aristotle drew (e.g. Moraux 1984: 642–43). That this was a central motive of the authors of the pseudo-Pythagorean texts and that they were successful is shown by Iamblichus' and Simplicius' acceptance of pseudo-Archytas' *Concerning the Whole System of Categories* as a genuine treatise, which antedated Aristotle (Simpl. *In Cat.*, *CAG* VIII. 2.9–25) and Syrianus' acceptance of Ocellus as the source of *On Generation and Corruption* (*CAG* VI. 1.175). Since most of the pseudo-Pythagoreans write in a Doric that seems to be modeled on that of Tarentum in southern Italy and since the most prominent author is "Archytas," who is from Tarentum, the treatises may also be motivated by the desire to glorify Italy and Pythagoreanism as an Italian philosophy (Burkert 1972b: 44). Archytas was a prominent figure in Roman literature of the first century BC, and it is tempting to suppose that this prominence led to the desire for a few more texts than had actually survived.

The improvements on Plato and Aristotle which are drawn from later philosophy and particularly from the philosophy of the first century BC, may just be a further attempt to glorify the early Pythagoreans, by showing that they not only anticipated Plato and Aristotle but in fact had anticipated criticisms of Plato and Aristotle; they thus present the true doctrine, from which Plato and Aristotle had deviated. On the other hand, it is also possible to view some of the pseudo-Pythagorean treatises as attempts to do philosophy in a style that is not sanctioned by the contemporary philosophical schools. If the Academy of the third and second centuries did not go in for metaphysical speculation, such speculation might have been done in the guise of Pythagoreanism, where it was more acceptable (Burkert 1961: 236). The pseudo-Pythagorean treatises also differ from Plato and Aristotle in their manner of presentation. For the most part, they present bald statements of philosophical positions and elaborate divisions and subdivisions of certain concepts without giving any argumentation to support these positions or divisions. This style suggests that they were something like catechisms of philosophical views common in the period of middle Platonism and militates strongly against the idea that they could really represent the texts in which these ideas were developed for the first time, the seed from which Platonism and Aristotelianism grew (Moraux 1984: 666).

What we do not find in the pseudo-Pythagorean treatises collected in Thesleff's edition is evidence for the clever forger, who produces Pythagorean texts which use only archaic terminology and concepts which predate Plato and Aristotle. The only nods in the direction of such authenticity is the use of the Doric dialect, the continuation of early Pythagorean interests such as the connection of music to philosophy and the prominence of the conception of harmony, and the occasional coinage of Pythagorean terms for Aristotelian concepts (e.g. ὠσία/ἐστώ = ὕλη. See also Moraux 1984: 633 and 644). One might argue that the reason we do not have evidence for clever forgeries is precisely because such forgeries are accepted as authentic and hence not included in Thesleff's collection. This argument has some force, but it would still be surprising that we have no example of a botched attempt in this direction, a treatise which is trying to be archaic but clearly fails. Further reflection suggests that it is not surprising that there are not "clever" forgeries. The motivation for such forgeries would have to be largely monetary and such forgeries would require a very high level of scholarship, in order to determine what Pythagoreanism in the fifth and early fourth centuries should look like. Obviously a treatise written to look like the work of someone taking the first tentative steps towards later Platonic and Aristotelian ideas would do little to glorify the early Pythagoreans. Such a composition would require an enormous amount of work and would be pointless, when people were clearly willing to accept forgeries that were much simpler to produce, such as the pseudo-Pythagorica which have survived.

Some have complained of the style of the fragments commonly accepted as genuine, such as Fragments 1 and 3, and taken the repetition and the generality of the presentation as signs of spuriousness. Yet, that style can be paralleled to some extent in the ethical fragments of Democritus, who lived in the generation before Archytas. Archytas' genuine writings were the latest, most mature and probably most extensive in the early Pythagorean tradition. It would then be natural for forgers to seize on his genuine writings as the model for the style and dialect of a spurious treatise, so that similarities to the dialect and the style of some of the pseudo-Pythagorean writings does not indicate that a given fragment of Archytas is spurious. The focus of our scrutiny must be on the concepts, distinctions and terminology used. Even here there is a final problem. Archytas is the contemporary of Plato and had contact with him. Thus, whereas clear Platonic distinctions ascribed to a figure like Philolaus, who lived two generations before Plato, are sure signs of spuriousness, we might suppose that Archytas' writings could show substantial similarity to Plato and other authors of the first half of the fourth century who were his contemporaries. This consideration should lead us to expect that Archytas confronted some of the same problems which faced Plato and indeed there are clear examples of this. Polyarchus presents the same challenge to Archytas in A9 as Callicles does to Plato in the *Gorgias*. Similarly, Fragments 1 and 4 show that Archytas is intensely interested in the relationship between the branches of mathematics, as is Plato in *Republic* VII. On the other hand, we would not expect Archytas' responses to these problems to be identical to Plato's or to employ just the same distinctions and just the same vocabulary as Plato, which is what we find happening in the pseudo-Pythagorean treatises.

Although Gruppe, in the last book devoted solely to Archytas, contended that not one of the fragments handed down under Archytas' name could be genuine (1840: 121), the general consensus of scholarship over the last hundred years is represented by the collection of four genuine fragments and some twenty-five testimonia in DK. Zeller's conclusions agree with the position of DK, and he provides a good summary of earlier German scholarship (1923: 1.1: 375–77 and, on the pseudo-Archytan writings, III.2: 119–23). Timpanaro Cardini (1962: 262–385) adds a few testimonia but is in basic agreement with DK. There have been some divergences from this consensus. Delatte (1922) argued that the fragments of *On Law and Justice* should be added to the canon of authentic works, and the issue is still unsettled (see the appendix on spurious fragments). Burkert, on the other hand, expressed grave doubts about the authenticity of the four fragments accepted by DK and gave some arguments against Fragments 1 and 4 (1972a: 220, n. 14; 379, n. 46). I believe that Burkert's doubts about these fragments are ultimately unfounded (see the commentary for detailed discussion) and accept basically the same canon as DK, although for somewhat different reasons, and supplemented by a number of testimonia overlooked by DK.

Let us now examine the principles on which this canon of fragments and testimonia is based. The broad criterion of authenticity implied by DK's collection was that fragments which used technical mathematics or that were derived from treatises on mathematics were less likely to be forged than treatises which dealt with more general metaphysical or ethical issues. Thus Fragments 1–3 are presented as all coming from one heavily mathematical work, *Harmonics*, and Fragment 4, while coming from a treatise entitled *Discources*, has a mathematical focus. This criterion is in need of modification in some respects. Some pseudo-Pythagorean writings, including the most famous of all, that of Timaeus Locrus, involve relatively complicated mathematics (Thesleff 1965: 210–13. See also the text discussed by Burkert 1961: 28–43). It is true that, in the case of Timaeus Locrus, the mathematics involved is to some extent based on the mathematics of Plato's *Timaeus*, but it does go beyond what is found in Plato. Thus, the presence of complicated mathematics is not in itself a sign of authenticity; pseudo-Pythagorean texts may employ and develop mathematical ideas already present in the tradition. On the other hand, it is implausible to suppose that a forger would be a creative mathematician, who would develop important new mathematical insights and then assign them to an ancient Pythagorean. Thus, the solution to the problem of doubling the cube assigned to Archytas is such a *tour de force* of creative mathematics that it could not be assigned to a forger, even if we did not have the excellent authority of Aristotle's pupil Eudemus, that the solution was that of Archytas (A14). The same argument shows that Archytas' mathematical description of the tetrachord (A16) is genuine as is the proof that there is no mean proportional between numbers in superparticular ratio (A19).

Difficulties remain for the four fragments accepted as authentic in DK. None of these fragments involve creative mathematics. Fragments 1 and 3 involve virtually no mathematics at all. Fragment 4 briefly discusses the relative merits of geometry and logistic but employs no actual mathematics. Fragment 2 does define the arithmetic, geometric and harmonic means, but these are relatively simple mathematical concepts, which could easily have been borrowed from earlier texts. DK evidently accepted Fragments 1–3 as authentic on the suppositions that (1) they all came from the same book, *Harmonics*, and (2) that this was the same book in which Archytas gave the mathematical descriptions of the tetrachords, which are reported in Ptolemy (A16). Since the material in A16 must be genuine, and Fragments 1–3 came from the same book, Fragments 1–3 also must be genuine. This argument works reasonably well for Fragments 1 and 2. Fragment 3, however, is nowhere said to come from the *Harmonics* and it is hard to see how it would fit in such a work, given the content of Fragments 1 and 2 (see the commentary on Fragment 3). It is described as coming from a work *On Sciences* (or *On Mathematics*) but, as we have seen, this is no guarantee of its authenticity.

Thus, the principle that forgers do not do creative mathematics provides a little support for Fragments 1 and 2, insofar as they can be assumed to come from the same book as A16 and A19, and no support for Fragments 3 and 4. The criterion that provides the greatest support for all four of these fragments is that they do not fit the central characteristic of the pseudo-Pythagorean writings; they make no attempt to assign prominent Platonic or Aristotelian conceptions to Archytas. Fragments 1–4 clearly reflect a state of development of their subject matter that is appropriate to the first half of the fourth century (acoustical theory [Fr. 1], theory of means [Fr. 2], the response to *pleonexia* [Fr. 3] and the distinction between logistic and geometry [Fr. 4]. See the commentaries on the individual fragments for detailed support of this point). Fragment 4 is the most problematic, because it is so short that it is impossible to be sure of the type of work from which it came. Nonetheless, none of these four fragments in themselves perform the function of the pseudepigrapha; none of them glorify Archytas by appropriating Platonic, Aristotelian and later conceptions. In order for them to be forgeries we would have to suppose that we have too little of the text to see that they in fact plunder Plato and Aristotle or we would have to suppose that they are the work of that mythical creature the clever forger, who with consummate scholarship only assigns to Archytas ideas that are independent of Plato and Aristotle and that are plausible in the first half of the fourth century. What these fragments show us is an Archytas who is grappling with some of the same sorts of problems which confronted Plato, but who gives different answers to them.

The authenticity of other testimonia for Archytas is secured by the early date and/or reliability of the source in which they are preserved. Aristotle guarantees Archytas' account of definitions (A22, A12), Eudemus Archytas' famous argument that the universe is unlimited (A24) and his obscure theory of motion (A23). Aristotle or one of his early successors supports the authenticity of A23a as does the original and idiosyncratic content, which is unlikely to be the work of a forger. Porphyry, although a late source, had access to material from Archytas' genuine work on harmonics (as did Ptolemy) and thus his testimonia on Archytas' harmonic theory are likely to be reliable (A17 and A18). In some cases the source of the information is late (e.g. A25, Apuleius) but the content of the testimonium makes sense for the first half of the fourth century and distinguishes Archytas' view from that of Plato and Aristotle rather than identifying them. Other testimonia agree with Aristotle's testimony about early Pythagoreanism rather than Platonic and Aristotelian views and thus make little sense as forgeries (A20–A21), while some testimonia are in agreement with the reliable testimonia for Archytas' views on harmonics, although too general in content to tell us much new about Archytas' views (A19a–c).

A large number of testimonia fall into the problematic category of anecdotes. The pseudo-Pythagorean writings collected by Thesleff do not employ such anecdotes so that these testimonia for Archytas are not likely to be derived from forged texts. As a genre, though, such anecdotes about the lives and beliefs of philosophers are not reliable and the same anecdote is often reported for several philosophers (see e.g. Riginos 1976). Anecdotes are subject to repeated retelling and are not a genre in which historical accuracy is particularly valued. Some of the testimonia for Archytas are special cases, however, in that they derive from Aristoxenus' *Life of Archytas* and, as I have argued in the account of Archytas' life, Aristoxenus was in a position to have relatively accurate information about Archytas' life and beliefs and did not engage in simple hagiography. Thus, testimonia such as A7, A9 and A9a, which are cited as from Aristoxenus' work or are very likely to be from that work, come at the very beginning of the anecdotal tradition about Archytas and are as "authentic" as any anecdotes about Archytas are likely to be. A number of other anecdotes may well be ultimately based on Aristoxenus' work, but certainty is impossible (A7a, A8, A11, A11a). There is another tradition of anecdotes which focuses on Archytas' solution to the problem of doubling the cube (A15). This tradition does not seem to be connected to Aristoxenus and undoubtedly involves some fabrication, particularly in the attempt to assign a mechanical solution of the problem to Archytas, which may serve as a sort of foundation myth for the discipline of mechanics (see on A15). Finally, there are the testimonia about Archytas' inventions, which have no connections to the pseudo-Pythagorean writings and are only problematic because they might in fact be the work of someone else with the name Archytas (see the essays on Archytas' life and philosophy).

PART TWO

Genuine fragments

CHAPTER I

Fragment 1

A. Porphyry, *On Ptolemy's Harmonics* 1. 3 (Düring 55.27–58.4)

τὰ μὲν δὴ τοῦ Πτολεμαίου περὶ τῆς κατὰ τοὺς ψόφους ὀξύτητος καὶ βαρύτητος τοιαῦτα· τὰ μὲν παρ᾽ αὐτοῦ ἐπινοηθέντα, τὰ δὲ καὶ παρὰ τῶν πρὸ αὐτοῦ εἰλημμένα.

δεῖ δὲ καὶ ἡμᾶς, καθάπερ ἐπηγγέλμεθα, ἐπιστῆσαι τῷ ζητήματι, εἰ καὶ ἐν πολλοῖς μέρεσι τῆς ἐξηγήσεως τὴν ἑαυτῶν φθάσαντες ἤδη γνώμην ἀπεδείξαμεν. ὅτι μὲν τοίνυν ἡ τῆς τοιαύτης αἰτίας ἀπόδοσις παλαιά τις ἦν καὶ παρὰ τοῖς Πυθαγορείοις κυκλουμένη, καὶ διὰ τῶν ἔμπροσθεν μὲν ἀπεδείξαμεν. παρακείσθω δὲ καὶ νῦν τὰ Ἀρχύτα τοῦ Πυθαγορείου, οὗ μάλιστα καὶ γνήσια λέγεται εἶναι τὰ συγγράμματα. λέγει δ᾽ ἐν τῷ Περὶ μαθηματικῆς εὐθὺς ἐναρχόμενος τοῦ λόγου τάδε·

καλῶς μοι δοκοῦντι τοὶ περὶ τὰ μαθήματα διαγνώμεν καὶ οὐδὲν ἄτο- 1
πον ὀρθῶς αὐτούς, οἷά ἐντι, περὶ ἑκάστου φρονέν. περὶ γὰρ τᾶς τῶν 2
ὅλων φύσιος καλῶς διαγνόντες ἔμελλον καὶ περὶ τῶν κατὰ μέρος, 3
οἷά ἐντι, καλῶς ὀψεῖσθαι. περί τε δὴ τᾶς τῶν ἄστρων ταχυτᾶτος 4
καὶ ἐπιτολᾶν καὶ δυσίων παρέδωκαν ἁμῖν σαφῆ διάγνωσιν καὶ περὶ 5
γαμετρίας καὶ ἀριθμῶν καὶ οὐχ ἥκιστα περὶ μωσικᾶς. ταῦτα γὰρ 6
τὰ μαθήματα δοκοῦντι εἶμεν ἀδελφεά. πρᾶτον μὲν οὖν ἐσκέψαντο, 7

1 τοὶ] Por. METV¹⁸⁷G, Nic. (om. GPSH, Philop. *in Nic.* ad loc. τὸ add. PS), Asclep. *in Nic.* ad loc. τοι Blass   διαγνώμεν] Blass   διαγνώμεναι Nic.   διαγνῶναι Por.   οὐδὲν] Nic.   οὔθεν Por.   **2** ὀρθῶς αὐτούς] αὐτοὺς ὀρθῶς Nic. (Cμ om. ὀρθῶς)   οἷά ἐντι] om. Por. ἕκαστον Por. ρ ἑκάστῳ Nic. H   ἑκάστων Blass   φρονέν] Blass   φρονέειν Nic.   θεωρεῖν Por.   τᾶς] Por. τῆς Nic. (τᾶς Gm, τὰς P)   περὶ γὰρ τᾶς τῶν ὅλων φύσιος καλῶς] τοιγὰρ περὶ τῶν καθόλου καλῶς Iambl. *VP* 160, *In Nic.* 6.20–22   **4** καλῶς] om. Por. ὀψεῖσθαι] ὀφεσθαι Por.   **4–6** περί τε … μωσικᾶς] Por. (om. σαφῆ; μουσικᾶς) περί τε (τι G₁P) δὴ τᾶς γεωμετρικᾶς (γεωμετρίας G₂CμΗΝΓ) καὶ ἀριθμητικᾶς καὶ σφαιρικᾶς παρέδωκαν ἁμμιν (ἄμμι H) σαφῆ διάγνωσιν, οὐχ ἥκιστα δὲ καὶ περὶ μουσικᾶς (μουσικῶν P, μωσικᾶς CμΗΓ) Nic. (τᾶς γεωμετρίας καὶ μουσικᾶς καὶ ἀριθμητικᾶς S; καὶ σφαιρικᾶς om. G₁P)   **6** ταῦτα γὰρ] Por., Nic. (ταῦτα δὲ P)   **7** εἶμεν] Por. METV¹⁸⁷G, Iamb. *in Nic.* 9.4, *Comm. Math.* 31.7 ἔμμεναι Nic.   ἤμεν Düring ἀδελφεά] Por., Nic.   ἀδελφά Iamb. *in Nic.* 9.5, *Comm. Math.* 31.7 post ἀδελφεά Nic. add.   περὶ γὰρ ἀδελφεὰ τὰ τοῦ ὄντος πρώτιστα δύο εἴδεα τὰν ἀναστροφὰν ἔχει (περὶ γὰρ ἀδελφεὰ om. G₁)   **7–43** πρᾶτον … πολλῶν γέγονεν] om. Nic.

ὅτι οὐ δυνατόν ἐστιν εἶμεν ψόφον μὴ γενηθείσας πληγᾶς τινων ποτ᾽ 8
ἄλλαλα. πλαγὰν δ᾽ ἔφαν γίνεσθαι, ὅκκα τὰ φερόμενα ἀπαντιάξαντα 9
ἀλλάλοις συμπέτῃ. τὰ μὲν οὖν ἀντίαν φορὰν φερόμενα ἀπαντιάζοντα 10
αὐτὰ αὑτοῖς συγχαλᾶντα, τὰ δ᾽ ὁμοίως φερόμενα, μὴ ἴσῳ δὲ τάχει, 11
περικαταλαμβανόμενα παρὰ τῶν ἐπιφερομένων τυπτόμενα ποιεῖν 12
ψόφον. πολλοὺς μὲν δὴ αὐτῶν οὐκ εἶναι ἁμῶν τᾷ φύσει οἵους τε 13
γινώσκεσθαι, τοὺς μὲν διὰ τὰν ἀσθένειαν τᾶς πλαγᾶς, τοὺς δὲ διὰ τὸ 14
μᾶκος τᾶς ἀφ᾽ ἁμῶν ἀποστάσιος, τινὰς δὲ καὶ διὰ τὰν ὑπερβολὰν τοῦ 15
μεγέθεος· οὐ γὰρ παραδύεσθαι ἐς τὰν ἀκοὰν ἁμῖν τὼς μεγάλως τῶν 16
ψόφων, ὥσπερ οὐδ᾽ ἐς τὰ σύστομα τῶν τευχέων, ὅκκα πολύ τις ἐκχέῃ, 17
οὐδὲν ἐγχεῖται. τὰ μὲν οὖν ποτιπίπτοντα ποτὶ τὰν αἴσθασιν ἃ μὲν ἀπὸ 18
τᾶν πλαγᾶν ταχὺ παραγίνεται καὶ <ἰσχυρῶς>, ὀξέαφαίνεται, τὰ δὲ 19
βραδέως καὶ ἀσθενέως, βαρέα δοκοῦντι εἶμεν. αἰ γάρ τις ῥάβδον λαβὼν 20
κινοῖ νωθρῶς καὶ ἀσθενέως, τᾷ πλαγᾷ βαρὺν ποιήσει τὸν ψόφον· αἰ 21
δέ κα ταχύ τε καὶ ἰσχυρῶς, ὀξύν. οὐ μόνον δέ κα τούτῳ γνοίημεν, 22
ἀλλὰ καὶ ὅκκα ἁμὲς ἢ λέγοντες ἢ ἀείδοντες χρήζομές τι μέγα φθέγξ- 23
ασθαι καὶ ὀξύ, σφοδρῷ τῷ πνεύματι φθεγγόμενοι. ἔτι δὲ καὶ τοῦτο 24
συμβαίνει ὥσπερ ἐπὶ βελῶν· τὰ μὲν ἰσχυρῶς ἀφιέμενα πρόσω φέρεται, 25
τὰ δ᾽ ἀσθενέως, ἐγγύς. τοῖς γὰρ ἰσχυρῶς φερομένοις μᾶλλον ὑπακούει 26
ὁ ἀήρ· τοῖς δ᾽ ἀσθενέως, ἧσσον. τωὐτὸ δὲ καὶ ταῖς φωναῖς συμβήσε- 27
ται· τᾷ μὲν ὑπὸ τῶ ἰσχυρῶ τῶ πνεύματος φερομένᾳ μεγάλᾳ τε εἶμεν 28
καὶ ὀξέᾳ, τᾷ δ᾽ ὑπ᾽ ἀσθενέος μικκᾷ τε καὶ βαρέᾳ. ἀλλὰ μὰν καὶ τούτῳ 29
γά κα ἴδοιμες ἰσχυροτάτῳ σαμείῳ, ὅτι τῶ αὐτῶ φθεγξαμένω μέγα μὲν 30
πόρσωθέν κ᾽ ἀκούσαιμες· μικκὸν δέ, οὐδ᾽ ἐγγύθεν. ἀλλὰ μὰν καὶ ἕν γα 31
τοῖς αὐλοῖς τὸ ἐκ τῶ στόματος φερόμενον πνεῦμα ἐς μὲν τὰ ἐγγὺς τῶ 32
στόματος τρυπήματα ἐμπῖπτον διὰ τὰν ἰσχὺν τὰν σφοδρὰν ὀξύτερον 33
ἆχον ἀφίησιν, ἐς δὲ τὰ πόρσω, βαρύτερον· ὥστε δῆλον ὅτι ἀ ταχεῖα 34

---

9 ἀπαντιάξαντα] in marg m. a. T   ἀπαντ᾽ ἄξαντα codd.   11 συγχαλᾶντα, τὰ] Diels
συγχαλᾶν, τὰ METV¹⁸⁷G   12 παρὰ] Stephanus περὶ codd.   13–18 πολλοὺς . . .
ἐγχεῖται] cf. Por. 81.7–11   13 εἶναι] Por. 81.7 ἔστιν Por. 56.16   15 μῆκος V¹⁸⁷g (56.18),
V¹⁸⁷M (81.8) τοῦ] Por. 81.9, 56.19 τῶ Düring 81.9   16 μεγέθεος] μεγάθεος 81.9 EMV¹⁸⁷
ἐς ¹] 56.19 εἰς 81.10   17 οὐδ᾽ἐς] Blass οὐδέ codd. τὰ] τὸ 81.11 σύστομα] σύστημα p
(56.20) σύσταμα MV¹⁸⁷G (81.11)   17–18 ἐκχέῃ – ἐγχεῖται] 81.11 METV¹⁸⁷ ἐγχέῃ –
ἐγχεῖται 56.21 METV¹⁸⁷G ἐκχέῃ – ἐκχεῖται 81.11 G αἴσθασιν] T αἴσθησιν MEV¹⁸⁷G
19 <ἰσχυρῶς>] Blass   20 ἀσθενέως] scripsi ἀσθενῶς codd. βαρέα] βραδέα Mg
21 καὶ] METV¹⁸⁷G τε καὶ Düring   22 κα τούτῳ] Blass κατὰ τοῦτο codd. κα τούτῳ
<τοῦτο> Düring   23 ἁμὲς] Blass ἅμες MTE ἅμε V¹⁸⁷ ἅμμες G τι] Blass εἰ
codd.   24 post φθεγγόμενοι lacunam indicavit Diels φθεγγόμεθα· αἴ τι δέ <κα μικκὸν καὶ
βαρύ, ἀσθενεῖ>. καὶ τοῦτο Blass   26–27 ἀσθενέως . . . ἀσθενέως] MTV¹⁸⁷ ἀσθενῶς . . .
ἀσθενέως E ἀσθενῶς . . . ἀσθενῶς G   27 τωὐτὸ] Blass τοῦτο codd.   29 ὀξέᾳ . . .
βαρέᾳ] T ὀξεῖα . . . βαρεῖα MEV¹⁸⁷G μικκᾷ] METV¹⁸⁷ μικρᾶG   30 κα ἴδοιμες] (κα
ἴδοιμες) Blass κατείδοιμες codd. ἰσχυροτάτῳ] Blass ἰσχυρῷ τόπῳ codd. σαμείῳ] Blass
σαμίω codd.   31 μικρόν G   34 ἐς] Wallis ὡς codd.

κίνασις ὀξὺν ποιεῖ, ἁ δὲ βραδεῖα βαρὺν τὸν ἄχον. ἀλλὰ μὰν καὶ τοῖς 35
ῥόμβοις τοῖς ἐν ταῖς τελεταῖς κινουμένοις τὸ αὐτὸ συμβαίνει· ἡσυχᾷ μὲν 36
κινούμενοι βαρὺν ἀφίεντι ἄχον, ἰσχυρῶς δέ, ὀξύν. ἀλλὰ μὰν καὶ ὅ γα 37
κάλαμος, αἴ κά τις αὐτῶ τὸ κάτω μέρος ἀποφράξας ἐμφυσῇ, ἀφήσει 38
<βαρέαν> τινὰ ἁμῖν φωνάν· αἱ δέ κα ἐς τὸ ἥμισυ ἢ ὁπόστον <ὦν> μέρος 39
αὐτῶ, ὀξὺ φθεγξεῖται· τὸ γὰρ αὐτὸ πνεῦμα διὰ μὲν τῶ μακρῶ τόπω 40
ἀσθενὲς φέρεται, διὰ δὲ τῶ μείονος σφοδρόν. 41

εἰπὼν δὲ καὶ ἄλλα περὶ τοῦ διαστηματικὴν εἶναι τὴν τῆς φωνῆς κίνησιν
συγκεφαλαιοῦται τὸν λόγον ὡς·

ὅτι μὲν δὴ τοὶ ὀξεῖς φθόγγοι τάχιον κινέονται, οἱ δὲ βαρεῖς βράδιον, 42
φανερὸν ἁμῖν ἐκ πολλῶν γέγονεν. 43

διὰ μὲν δὴ τούτων καὶ τῶν ἔτι πρόσθεν παρακειμένων, ὅτι Πυθαγόρειος
καὶ παλαιά τις δόξα ἦν αὕτη, ἧς προύστη ὁ Πτολεμαῖος, τὰ μὲν
αὐτὸς ἐργασάμενος, τὰ δ' ἐπιδραμὼν ὡς κυκλιζόμενα, αὐτάρκως ἡμῖν
ἐπιδέδεικται.

35 κίνησις MTE   ποιοῖ ME   **37** ὅ γα] V¹⁸⁷   ὅσα TE   ὅτου ἁ GM   **38** αἴ κά τις]
GT   ἔκατις MEV¹⁸⁷   αὐτῶ] codd.   αὐτῷ Düring   **39** <βαρέαν>] Mullach   κα] Düring
καὶ METV¹⁸⁷G   ὁπόστον] ἀπόστον p   <ὦν>] Blass   **40** αὐτῶ] codd.   αὐτῷ Düring
41 φέρεται] codd.   ἐκφέρεται Düring   μείονος] μείζονος G

Such, then, are the views of Ptolemy concerning height and depth in sounds.
Some of them are his own invention, but others have been taken from those
before him.

But it is also necessary that I, just as I promised, dwell on the question,
although I have already before this demonstrated my opinion in many
parts of the commentary. That such an explanation was given among the
ancients and was in circulation among the Pythagoreans, I have shown
through what I have said before. But now in addition let the words of
Archytas the Pythagorean, whose writings most of all are said to be indeed
genuine, be cited. In *On Mathematics*, just as he begins the discourse, he
says the following:

Those concerned with the sciences seem to me to make distinctions well,
and it is not at all surprising that they have correct understanding about
individual things as they are. For, having made good distinctions concerning
the nature of wholes they were likely also to see well how things are in their
parts. Indeed concerning the speed of the stars and their risings and settings
as well as concerning geometry and numbers and not least concerning
music, they handed down to us a clear set of distinctions. For these sciences

seem to be akin. Well then, first they reflected that it is not possible that there be sound, if an impact of some things against one another does not occur; they said that an impact occurred whenever things in motion came upon and collided with one another. Some moving in opposing directions, when they meet, make a sound as each slows the other down, but others moving in the same direction but not with equal speed, being overtaken by the ones rushing upon them and being struck, make a sound. Indeed many of these sounds cannot be recognized because of our nature, some because of the weakness of the blow, others because of the distance of separation from us and some because of the excess of the magnitude. For the great sounds do not steal into our hearing, just as nothing is poured into narrow-mouthed vessels, whenever someone pours out a lot. Well then, of the sounds reaching our perception those which arrive quickly and strongly from impacts appear high in pitch, but those which arise slowly and weakly seem to be low in pitch. For if someone should pick up a stick and move it sluggishly and weakly, he will make a low sound with his blow, but if quickly and strongly, high. Not only by this would we recognize the fact, but also whenever either speaking or singing we wish to voice something loud and high, since we speak with a violent breath. But further this also happens, just as with missiles. Those which are hurled strongly are carried far, those weakly, near. For to those moving vigorously the air yields more and to those moving weakly less. The same thing will also happen with vocal sounds. The one carried by a strong breath will turn out to be loud and high, the one by a weak one, soft and low. But indeed we can also see this fact from this strongest sign, that we can hear the same man speaking loudly from far off but speaking softly not even from near at hand. But indeed also in flutes, the breath moving from the mouth and falling into the openings near the mouth produces a higher sound because of the great force, but that falling into the holes further away, produces a lower sound. So that it is clear that quick motion makes a high sound and slow motion a low sound. But indeed the same thing also happens to the rhomboi which are whirled in the mysteries. If they are moved calmly, they produce a low sound but, if forcefully, a high sound. But also indeed, a reed, if someone, having blocked the lower part of it, blows in it, he will, you know, produce a low sound. But if he blows into the half or whatever part of it, it will sound high. For the same breath is carried weakly through a long distance and strongly through a shorter distance.

Having said other things about the motion of voice being according to intervals he summarizes the argument thus:

It has become clear to us from many things that high notes move more quickly and low ones more slowly.

Through this text and those cited still earlier, I have shown sufficiently that this was an ancient Pythagorean doctrine, which Ptolemy championed, having worked out some aspects himself, while running over other aspects lightly, since they were in general circulation.

B. Porphyry, *On Ptolemy's Harmonics* (Düring 80.28–81.16; for the apparatus and the text of the quotation from Archytas see Text A above)

τοιαῦτα μὲν καὶ τὰ τοῦ Ἀριστοξένου. εἰ μέντοι, ὡς φασιν οἱ Πυθαγόρειοι, ἡ τοῦ παντὸς ἁρμονία διὰ μέγεθος ψόφων ὑπερβάλλει ἡμῶν τὴν ἀκοήν, μείζων ἂν εἴη ὁ ὅρος τῶν ψόφων τῶν τῆς ἀκοῆς. ἔχοι γὰρ ἂν καὶ ὀξυτάτους καὶ βαρυτάτους φθόγγους ἡ τοῦ παντὸς ἁρμονία, ὧν ἡμῶν ἡ ἀκοὴ ἀπολείπεται.

γράφει οὖν ὁ Ἀρχύτας, οὗ καὶ πρόσθεν τὴν λέξιν παρεθήκαμεν περὶ τῶν ψόφων τάδε.

πολλοὺς μὲν . . . οὐδὲν ἐκχεῖται

ἀλλὰ περὶ μὲν τούτων ἀρκείτω ταῦτα. φανερὸν δ᾽ ἐκ τούτων, ὅτι αὕτη μὲν καθ᾽ ἑαυτὴν ἡ τοῦ μέλους τάξις νοουμένη τὴν αὔξησιν ἐπ᾽ ἄπειρον ἂν δόξειε λαμβάνειν, εἰς μέντοι τὴν φωνὴν ἢ καὶ τὴν ἀκοὴν τιθεμένη, οὐκ ἐπ᾽ ἄπειρον ἴσχει τὴν διάστασιν, ἀλλ᾽ ὁρίζεται ὑπὸ τῆς ἡμετέρας δυνάμεως.

Such are the words of Aristoxenus. If, however, as the Pythagoreans say, the harmony of the whole universe exceeds our hearing on account of the magnitude of the sounds, the limit of sounds would be greater than the limits of hearing. For the harmony of the whole would comprise both the highest and lowest sounds, with regard to which our hearing fails.

Archytas, whose text we also cited before, writes the following things about sounds:

Indeed many of these sounds cannot be recognized because of our nature, some because of the weakness of the blow, others because of the distance of separation from us and some because of the excess of the magnitude. For the great sounds do not steal into our hearing, just as nothing is poured into narrow-mouthed vessels, whenever someone pours a lot.

But let these things be enough on this topic. It is clear from these things that this intelligible ordering of melody, in itself, would seem to increase without limit, but, if it is transferred to the voice and the hearing, it does not have an unlimited extension but is limited by our ability.

C. Nicomachus, *Introduction to Arithmetic* 1. 3.3 (p. 6.8–7.6 Hoche; for the apparatus see Text A above)

οὐκ ἄρα τούτων [sc. ἀριθμητική, μουσική, γεωμετρία, σφαιρική] ἄνευ δυνατὸν τὰ τοῦ ὄντος εἴδη ἀκριβῶσαι οὐδ᾽ ἄρα τὴν ἐν τοῖς οὖσιν ἀλήθειαν εὑρεῖν, ἧς ἐπιστήμη σοφία, φαίνεται δέ, ὅτι οὐδ᾽ ὀρθῶς φιλοσοφεῖν· ὅπερ γὰρ ζωγραφίη συμβάλλεται τέχναις βαναύσοις πρὸς θεωρίης ὀρθότητα, τοῦτό τοι γραμμαὶ καὶ ἀριθμοὶ καὶ ἁρμονικὰ διαστήματα καὶ κύκλων περιπολήσιες πρὸς λόγων σοφῶν μαθήσιας συνεργίην ἔχουσιν, Ἀνδροκύδης φησὶν ὁ Πυθαγορικός. ἀλλὰ καὶ Ἀρχύτας ὁ Ταραντῖνος ἀρχόμενος τοῦ ἁρμονικοῦ τὸ αὐτὸ οὕτω πως λέγει·

καλῶς μοι δοκοῦντι τοὶ περὶ τὰ μαθήματα διαγνώμεναι καὶ οὐδὲν ἄτοπον αὐτοὺς ὀρθῶς, οἷά ἐντι, περὶ ἑκάστου φρονέειν. περὶ γὰρ τᾶς τῶν ὅλων φύσιος καλῶς διαγνόντες ἔμελλον καὶ περὶ τῶν κατὰ μέρος, οἷά ἐντι, καλῶς ὀψεῖσθαι. περί τε δὴ τᾶς γεωμετρικᾶς καὶ ἀριθμητικᾶς καὶ σφαιρικᾶς παρέδωκαν ἄμμιν σαφῆ διάγνωσιν οὐχ ἥκιστα δὲ καὶ περὶ μωσικᾶς. ταῦτα γὰρ τὰ μαθήματα δοκοῦντι ἔμμεναι ἀδελφεά.

περὶ γὰρ ἀδελφεὰ τὰ τοῦ ὄντος πρώτιστα δύο εἴδεα τὰν ἀναστροφὰν ἔχει. καὶ Πλάτων δὲ ἐπὶ τέλει τοῦ τρισκαιδεκάτου τῶν νόμων . . .

Without these [arithmetic, music, geometry, sphaeric], then, it is not possible to be exact about the forms of being nor to discover the truth in the things that are, the knowledge of which is wisdom, and, it appears, not even to philosophize correctly. For just as painting contributes to handicrafts with regard to correctness of theory, so lines and numbers and harmonic intervals and revolutions of circles provide a contribution towards learning wise discourses, says Androcydes the Pythagorean. But Archytas of Tarentum as he begins his *Harmonics* also says the same thing, in about these words:

Those concerned with the sciences seem to me to make distinctions well, and it is not at all surprising that they have correct understanding about individual things as they are. For, having made good distinctions concerning the nature of wholes they were likely also to see well how things are in their parts. Indeed concerning geometry and arithmetic and sphaeric they handed down to us a clear set of distinctions and not least also concerning music. For these sciences seem to be akin.

This is so, because they are concerned with the two primary forms of being which are akin. And Plato at the end of the thirteenth book of the *Laws*. . .

D. Iamblichus, *On the Pythagorean Life* 160 (90. 11–20 Deubner; cf. *In Nic.* 6.16–7.2, Pistelli)

καὶ γὰρ τῇ τούτων [sc. τῶν κυρίως ὄντων] καταλήψει συμβέβηκε καὶ τὴν τῶν ὁμωνύμως ὄντων παρομαρτεῖν, οὐδὲ ἐπιτηδευθεῖσάν ποτε, οἷα δὴ τῇ καθόλου ἐπιστήμῃ ἡ τοῦ κατὰ μέρος. "τοιγὰρ περὶ τῶν καθόλου," φησὶν Ἀρχύτας, "καλῶς διαγνόντες ἔμελλον καὶ περὶ τῶν κατὰ μέρος, οἷά ἐντι, καλῶς ὀψεῖσθαι." διόπερ οὐ μόνα οὐδὲ μονογενῆ οὐδὲ ἁπλᾶ ὑπάρχει τὰ ὄντα, ποικίλα δὲ ἤδη καὶ [τὰ] πολυειδῆ θεωρεῖται, τά τε νοητὰ καὶ ἀσώματα, ὧν τὰ ὄντα ἡ κλῆσις, καὶ τὰ σωματικὰ καὶ ὑπ' αἴσθησιν πεπτωκότα, ἃ δὴ κατὰ μετοχὴν κοινωνεῖ τοῦ ὄντως γενέσθαι.

For it turns out that the apprehension of things that exist homonymously also accompanies the apprehension of these things [sc. things truly existent], even when such apprehension is never pursued, just as the knowledge of the particular accompanies the knowledge of the universal. "Therefore, having made good distinctions about about universals," Archytas says, "they were likely also to see well about particulars, what sort of things they are." Wherefore, the existing things are not single, of one kind, or simple, but they are already observed to be varied and of many kinds, both the intelligible and the incorporeal things, for which the name is "the existing things," and the corporeal things and the things that fall under the purview of sensation, which by participation share in true being.

E. Plato, *Republic* 530d

κινδυνεύει, ἔφην, ὡς πρὸς ἀστρονομίαν ὄμματα πέπηγεν, ὡς πρὸς ἐναρμόνιον φορὰν ὦτα παγῆναι, καὶ αὗται ἀλλήλων ἀδελφαί τινες αἱ ἐπιστῆμαι εἶναι, ὡς οἵ τε Πυθαγόρειοί φασι καὶ ἡμεῖς, ὦ Γλαύκων, ξυγχωροῦμεν. ἢ πῶς ποιοῦμεν; οὕτως, ἔφη.

It is likely, I said, that as the eyes have been made for astronomy, so the ears have been made for musical motion, and these sciences are some kin of one another, as the Pythagoreans say and we, O Glaucon, agree. Or do we? Yes we do, he said.

F. Iamblichus, *On Nicomachus' Introduction to Arithmetic* (p. 9.1–7 Pistelli; cf. *De Communi Mathematica Scientia* pp. 31.4 ff., Festa)

διότι περὶ ἀδελφὰ τὰ ὑποκείμενα καταγενομένας, εὔλογον ἀδελφὰς καὶ τὰς ἐπιστήμας ταύτας νομίζειν, ἵνα μὴ ἀπαιδευτῇ τὸ Ἀρχύτειον "ταῦτα γὰρ τὰ μαθήματα δοκοῦντι εἶμεν ἀδελφά," ἀλλήλων τε ἐχόμενα τρόπον ἀλύσεως κρίκων ἡγεῖσθαι, καὶ εἰς ἕνα σύνδεσμον καταλήγοντα [Festa, καταλέγουσαν or -λήγουσα codd.], ὥς φησιν ὁ θειότατος Πλάτων ...

Wherefore, since they are concerned with underlying realities that are akin, it is reasonable to think that these sciences are akin, so that we do not fail to learn the lesson of the words of Archytas, "For these sciences seem to be akin," and it is reasonable to think that they hold on to one another like rings in a chain, ending in one common bond, as the most divine Plato says ...

G. Joannes Philoponus, *On Nicomachus' Introduction to Arithmetic* (p. 7 Hoche)

κα. ἐπιστήμην (Nic. *Ar.* 4.20 Hoche)] ... καὶ Ἀρχύταν δὲ τὸν Ταραντῖνον τὰ αὐτὰ παρίστησι λέγοντα· δωρίζουσι δὲ πάντες οὗτοι· "καλῶς γάρ μοι δοκοῦντι, φησὶν ἐκεῖνος, περὶ τὰ μαθήματα διαγνώμεναι." δοκοῦντι ἀντὶ τοῦ δοκοῦσι περὶ τὰ μαθήματα· τὰ γὰρ πληθυντικὰ τῶν ῥημάτων δι' ἑνικοῦ μετοχικοῦ ἐκφέρουσι, δοκοῦντι ἀντὶ τοῦ δοκοῦσι καὶ ποιοῦντι ἀντὶ τοῦ ποιοῦσι λέγοντες· τὸ δὲ διαγνώμεναι ἀντὶ τοῦ διαγνῶναι.

κβ. οἷά ἐντι (Nic. *Ar.* 6.19 Hoche)] τουτέστιν οἷά εἰσιν· ὑπὸ γὰρ τὰ καθόλου τελοῦσι τὰ καθέκαστον· ὅτι δὲ περὶ τὸ ποσὸν μετὰ τὰς οὐσίας ἡ πᾶσα σχεδὸν τῶν ὄντων θεωρία συνέστηκεν, ἐν ᾧ καὶ αἱ δ' εἰσι μαθηματικαὶ ἐπιστῆμαι, ὡς δείξαντες ἔφθημεν.

κγ. ἀδελφεὰ (Nic. *Ar.* 7.4 Hoche)] Δύο εἴδη τά, εἰς ἃ τὸ ποσὸν διαιρεῖται· τὸ γὰρ ποσὸν διαιρεῖται εἰς τὸ συνεχὲς καὶ τὸ διωρισμένον. ἐπειδὴ οὖν ἀδελφά ἐστι τὰ β εἴδη ἐξ ἑνὸς γένους τοῦ ποσοῦ προελθόντα, εὐλόγως ἄρα καὶ αἱ περὶ αὐτὰ ἐπιστῆμαι ἀδελφαί εἰσιν· ἀριθμητικὴ μὲν καὶ μουσικὴ περὶ τὸ διωρισμένον ποσόν, γεωμετρία δὲ καὶ ἀστρονομία περὶ τὸ συνεχές.

21. knowledge (Nic. *Ar.* 4.20 Hoche)] ... And he cites Archytas of Tarentum as one who says the same thing. All of this is in Doric. "For they seem [*dokounti*] to me," he says, "to have good discernment [*diagnōmenai*] about the sciences." *Dokounti* instead of *dokousi* about the sciences. For they express the plural of verbs through the singular of the participle,

saying *dokounti* instead of *dokousi, poiounti* instead of *poiousi*. *Diagnōmenai* is instead of *diagnōnai*.

22.　*hoia enti* (Nic. *Ar.* 6.19 Hoche)] i.e. *hoia eisin*; For the particulars belong under the universals. It has been established that pretty nearly the whole investigation of existing things is concerned with quantity after being, and the mathematical sciences have to do with quantity, as I showed before.

23.　akin (Nic. *Ar.* 7.4 Hoche)] Two forms, the ones into which quantity is divided; for quantity is divided into what is continuous and what is discontinuous. Since then the two forms are akin, having come forth from one genus, quantity, reasonably therefore the sciences concerning them are akin; arithmetic and music are concerned with discontinuous quantity, geometry and astronomy are concerned with continuous quantity.

H. Asclepius of Tralles, *On Nicomachus' Introduction to Arithmetic* (p. 28 Tarán)

κ.　καλῶς μοι δοκοῦντι (Nic. *Ar.* 6.17–18 Hoche)] ταῦτα ὁ Ἀρχύτας λέγει, δωρίζει δὲ οὗτος, τῷ δοκοῦντι οὖν δωρικῶς ἀντὶ τοῦ δοκοῦσι. τοὶ περὶ τὰ μαθήματα διαγνώμεναι ἀντὶ τοῦ οἱ περὶ τὰ μαθήματα διαγνῶναι· διαγνώμεναι γὰρ ἀντὶ τοῦ διαγνῶναι, τοὶ δὲ ἀντὶ τοῦ οἱ. τὰ γὰρ ἄρθρα τῶν πληθυντικῶν εὐθειῶν μετὰ τοῦ τ στοιχείου προφέρονται.

κα.　ἐντί, περὶ ἑκάστου (Nic. *Ar.* 6.19 Hoche)] ἀντὶ τοῦ ἐστί· τὸ γὰρ ἐστὶν ἐντί φασιν. "οἷά ἐντι" ἀντὶ τοῦ ὁποῖά εἰσιν. "εἶμεν ἀδελφεά" ἀντὶ τοῦ εἶναι συγγενῆ, ἐπειδὴ αἱ δ περὶ τὸ ποσὸν καὶ πηλίκον καταγίνονται· ἀριθμητικὴ μὲν καὶ μουσικὴ περὶ ποσόν, γεωμετρία δὲ καὶ ἀστρονομία περὶ πηλίκον.

κβ.　περὶ γὰρ ἀδελφεά (Nic. *Ar.* 7.2–3 Hoche)] συγγενεῖς εἰσιν αἱ ἐπιστῆμαι αἱ τέσσαρες, ἐπειδὴ περὶ συγγενῆ β, τό τε ποσὸν καὶ τὸ πηλίκον, καταγίνονται. καὶ ἁπλῶς ὃ λέγει τοιοῦτόν ἐστιν· ὅτι καλῶς μοι δοκοῦσι ποιεῖν οἱ διαγινώσκοντες τὰ μαθήματα, οἱ γὰρ τὴν τοῦ ὅλου φύσιν εὑρηκότες ἔμελλον ἂν καὶ κατὰ μέρος εἰδέναι. διέγνωσαν οὖν ἀστρονομίαν καὶ γεωμετρίαν καὶ ἀριθμητικὴν καὶ μουσικήν, ἐπειδὴ ἐκ τούτων ἡμῖν προσγίνεται τὸ τέλος.

κγ.　οὐχ ἥκιστα δέ (Nic. *Ar.* 7.1 Hoche)] ἀντὶ τοῦ μάλιστα δέ.

20.　They seem to me [to discern] well . . . (Nic. *Ar.* 6.17–18 Hoche)] Archytas says these words. He writes in Doric, with *dokounti* as the Doric form instead of *dokousi*. *Toi peri ta mathēmata diagnōmenai* instead of *hoi peri ta mathēmata diagnōnai*. For *diagnōmenai* is instead of *diagnōnai*, *toi* instead of *hoi*. For the articles of the nominative plural are prefixed with the letter tau.

21.   *enti*, concerning each (Nic. *Ar.* 6.19 Hoche)] Instead of *esti*; for they express *esti* as *enti*. *Hoia enti* instead of *hopoia eisin*. *Eimen adelphea* instead of *einai suggenē*, since the four are concerned with multitude and magnitude; arithmetic and music concerning multitude and geometry and astronomy concerning magnitude.

22.   For concerning [the primary forms of being which are] akin . . . (Nic. *Ar.* 7.2–3 Hoche)] The four sciences are relatives, since they are concerned with the two relatives, multitude and magnitude. Put simply what he means is something like this: That the ones who distinguish the sciences seem to me to do well, for they, having discovered the nature of the whole, would be likely also to know the parts. So then they distinguished astronomy and geometry and arithmetic and music, since it is from these that our goal is achieved.

23.   But not least (Nic. *Ar.* 7.1 Hoche)] Instead of "but especially."

Authenticity

Porphyry introduces his quotation of Fragment 1 with the assertion that the writings of Archytas "most of all are said to be indeed genuine" (Thomas [1939: 1. 5] translates μάλιστα . . . γνήσια as "mainly genuine" but, while μάλιστα has the sense of "about" with numbers, I can find no parallel for the translation "mainly" used with a simple adjective as here). It thus appears that Porphyry is well aware of controversy concerning the authenticity of Pythagorean texts but accepts the common view at his time that Archytas' writings, including *Harmonics*, from which Fragment 1 comes, are most (of all such writings) genuine. Fragment 1 was regarded as authentic by DK and most modern scholars have followed their lead. The only detailed attack on its authenticity is that of Burkert (1972a: 379 n. 46). I have responded to Burkert's doubts in an earlier article (Huffman 1985; see also Bowen 1982) and will not repeat all of those arguments here. Barker came down in favor of authenticity (1989: 39 n. 42). Burkert's most serious doubts about the fragment are based on the defective text of lines 4–7, which is printed in DK, and are removed once the text is clarified. In the comments on the context of the fragment below and in the commentary on the Greek text, I give further support for the text of lines 4–7, which I first presented in my article.

There are a few additional points that should be raised about the issue of authenticity. First, the vocabulary of the fragment suggests that it is authentic. It is not filled with the technical Platonic and Aristotelian terminology that is characteristic of the pseudo-Pythagorean writings. There is some unusual technical vocabulary in the fragment, but this vocabulary points more towards authenticity than the reverse. Some seven words are relatively rare: συγχαλάω appears nowhere else, ἀπαντιάζω is found only in two other places, the earliest of which is Procopius, περικαταλαμβάνω, σύστομος, ἐμφυσάω are all rare but find parallels in Aristotle, the Aristotelian *Problems*, Theophrastus, and Aristophanes. τεῦχος is rare in prose with the sense "vessels," but there are parallels in Xenophon and the Hippocratic corpus. ἦχος is a later form that appears first elsewhere in the Aristotelian *Problems*. If the parallels for the rare vocabulary only occurred in late authors, as is the case with ἀπαντιάζω, we might suspect that we were dealing with a late forger. But most of the rare vocabulary finds its parallels in technical treatises of the fourth century such as the Aristotelian *Problems*, Aristotle's biological works, and Theophrastus. Since Archytas is above all known for his technical work not only in acoustics but also in geometry, it is surely more plausible to explain the fourth-century technical vocabulary in Fragment 1 as the work of Archytas himself rather than as the work of a later forger. Such a forger would be more likely to draw either on the vocabulary of his own day or on the vocabulary that he found in mainstream Platonic and Aristotelian texts. In particular we would expect to see parallels with distinctive vocabulary used by Plato and Aristotle in their accounts of acoustics, which we do not.

Second, as the commentary below makes clear, the conceptual content of the fragment also finds most parallels in fifth- and early fourth-century authors; there is no trace of acoustical doctrines later than Plato. Indeed, the presentation of the central acoustical thesis of the fragment suggests that it is the work of Archytas rather than a later forger. At first sight the reverse might appear to be true. Since the most important acoustical thesis of the fragment, that pitch is determined by the speed with which the sound travels, was adopted by Plato and, in a modified form, by Aristotle, we might suppose that Fragment 1 was forged, in order to provide the Pythagorean text from which Plato and Aristotle "stole" this doctrine. It is a problem for this supposition that Aristotle's more refined version of the thesis is not found in Fragment 1, since Pythagorean forgeries tend to incorporate improvements developed in the later tradition into the texts that they assign back to early Pythagoreans. What is most striking about the presentation of the theory of pitch in Fragment 1, however, is that it confuses pitch with volume, in a way that is not found in Plato, Aristotle, or the later tradition. In Fragment 1 all and only high-pitched sounds are loud, while low-pitched sounds are always soft. It is very hard to explain why a forger, who had the texts of Plato, Aristotle and later thinkers in front of him, in which volume and pitch are not confused, would want to assign such a confusion back to Archytas. The whole purpose of such forgeries is to show the genius of the Pythagoreans. It is much more reasonable to conclude that Archytas wrote Fragment 1, and that the confusion between pitch and volume reflects the actual state of development of acoustic theory at his time. In the *Timaeus*, Plato accepts Archytas' proposed connection between the speed of transmission of a sound and its pitch, but he takes a step beyond Archytas in clearly distinguishing volume from pitch. If we could be sure that lines 15–18 are a reference to the doctrine of the harmony of the spheres, this would be yet another sign that the fragment was written by Archytas. The explanation given for our inability to hear the harmony in these lines is unique in the ancient tradition, and we would expect a forger to provide the more usual explanation found in Aristotle (see the commentary below).

Of course the earliest testimony to the authenticity of Fragment 1 of Archytas is Plato, in his reference to the Pythagorean doctrine of "kindred sciences" at *Republic* 530d (Text E). Burkert thought that the mention of "kindred sciences" in Fragment 1 was simply evidence of the forger taking a line from Plato to add authenticity to his work. Once we have recognized that the rest of the fragment shows none of the characteristics of the forgeries in the Pythagorean tradition, however, the reference to "kindred sciences" in Fragment 1 can be taken at face value as a statement of the doctrine to which Plato refers. Nothing in Plato's reference requires that he knew of the doctrine from a written source, so it need not be a specific reference to Fragment 1. Nonetheless, the doctrine of the kinship of the sciences is stated prominently at the beginning of Archytas' book, *Harmonics*, and it would be natural for Plato to think of this, as he himself begins consideration of the science of harmonics in the *Republic*. It is thus not implausible that Plato is virtually quoting Archytas here.

Context
There are significant differences between the texts of Fragment 1, which are preserved by our two primary witnesses, Porphyry and Nicomachus. It will therefore be necessary to carry out a thorough examination of the methods of both Porphyry and Nicomachus and the context in which they preserve Fragment 1. The whole of the fragment (forty-three lines) is

preserved only in Porphyry's commentary on Ptolemy's *Harmonics* (56.5–
57.27 Text A). Porphyry also quotes lines 13–18 of Fragment 1 again, later
in his commentary (81.7–11 Text B), and in doing so refers back to his first
quotation of the fragment. Nicomachus, in his *Introduction to Arithmetic*,
preserves just the first five lines of Fragment 1 (Text C). Later commentators
on Nicomachus quote parts of the five lines preserved by Nicomachus in
their commentaries but seem to be strictly limited to Nicomachus for their
knowledge of the fragment (Texts D, F and G).

Although Porphyry (AD 234 – ca. 305) is writing later than Nicomachus
(ca. AD 100), his testimony seems to be completely independent of Nicomachus, both because he quotes so much more of the fragment and also
because his version differs significantly from Nicomachus', in the first seven
lines, where the two quotations of the fragment overlap. The most significant bond between these two sources is their shared assertion that what
they are quoting comes from the beginning of Archytas' book. Nicomachus'
phrase "beginning the *Harmonics*" might possibly be interpreted to mean
just "in the beginning section of the *Harmonics*" rather than as a guarantee that he is quoting the actual first words. However, Porphyry's phrasing
almost certainly indicates that he is quoting the first words of the book ("just
[εὐθύς] as he begins the discourse" or "immediately upon beginning"). Simplicius (*In Phys. CAG* IX. 161.14–15) uses a similar phrase, "immediately at
the beginning" (εὐθὺς ἐν ἀρχῆ), of the first lines of Fragment 17 of Empedocles. Simplicius does leave off the first two words in his quotation at
161.9, but it is still clear that "immediately at the beginning" indicates that
he is giving the first lines of the text which he has quoted earlier.

That Porphyry intends the phrase "immediately upon beginning" to
refer to the literal beginning of Archytas' book is also supported by the
fact that Porphyry quotes the first seven lines at all. They have nothing to
do with the purpose for which he quotes from Archytas, i.e. to illustrate
Archytas' theory of pitch. Their inclusion in the quotation makes sense
only on the assumption that they are the literal beginning of the book and
that Porphyry, wanting to quote lines 7–43, thought that he might as well
start with the beginning. If the first seven lines are not the beginning of
the book and the whole fragment comes from just the beginning part of
the book, it is hard to see why Porphyry would not have started with the
material in line 7.

Porphyry and Nicomachus cite Fragment 1 for radically different purposes, which influence their quotation of the fragment. They also display
strikingly different degrees of fidelity in presenting Archytas' words. Nicomachus' *Introduction to Arithmetic* is primarily intended as a systematic

treatise on arithmetic and does not focus on the history of the subject. There are very few quotations from earlier authors, and the quotations which are given do not serve primarily to make historical points, where accurate quotation is important. The quotations instead appear in the early chapters of the work, in order to elucidate the metaphysical system which Nicomachus deploys and also to illustrate the importance of the study of the sciences. In Chapters 2 and 3 Nicomachus argues that there are two basic forms of being, magnitude and multitude (2. 4–5). Magnitude at rest is studied by geometry and in movement by sphaeric (Nicomachus' term for astronomy), while multitude as absolute quantity is studied by arithmetic and as relative quantity by music (3. 1–2). Nicomachus there- fore concludes that these four sciences (arithmetic, music, geometry and sphaeric) are necessary for understanding the truth about reality. Lines 1–7 of Archytas are quoted in support of this last conclusion.

It is crucial to note that, in introducing the passage from Archytas, Nicomachus indicates that he will not be presenting a completely accurate quotation but rather somewhat of a paraphrase: "Archytas of Tarentum, as he begins his *Harmonics*, also says the same thing, *in about these words*" (οὕτω πως – "something like this"). It is also important to realize that Nicomachus has a general tendency to paraphrase the texts that he cites, even where he does not emphasize that he is paraphrasing. In the first three chapters of Book 1 of the *Introduction to Arithmetic*, he quotes from the Platonic corpus three times, all with no indication that he is doing anything other than quoting literally. In the first case his quotation of five lines from *Timaeus* 27d is indeed accurate. However, both of the other quotations (3. 5, *Epin.* 991d ff.; 3. 7, *R.* 527d) show very significant divergences from the accepted text. In both passages Nicomachus has a tendency to simplify, to make the references more explicit and to use different verbs. Where Plato talks of "a certain organ of the soul" (*R.* 527d), Nicomachus gives "eye of the soul," and thus, when Plato goes on to say that this organ is more valuable than "thousands of eyes," Nicomachus has to say "than thousands of *bodily* eyes." In the *Epinomis* passage, the text says "if anyone will pursue these matters in any other way, it is necessary that he call in fortune, as we say." Nicomachus' "quotation" is "if anyone pursue *philosophy* in another way, it is necessary that he call in fortune as a *helper*." These are clear examples of paraphrasing, but relatively harmless paraphrasing. In other places the meaning is more radically altered. In the *Republic* where Plato says that "it is no trifling task but very difficult to realize that there is in every soul an organ . . . ," Nicomachus has "it is very difficult nay impossible" and attaches the phrase not to the description of the eye or organ of the soul that follows but rather to the previous assertion "that these are useless studies that I recommend." In the *Epinomis* where Plato (or whoever is the author of the *Epinomis*) has "without these never will any happy nature arise in cities," Nicomachus gives "without these there is never a path"; Plato's "happy nature" and "cities" are gone and instead we have "a path". Thus, Nicomachus' normal procedure in citing texts involves significant paraphrasing. What are we to make of his admission, in quoting Archytas, that Archytas only said "something like the following?" Before examining this question further, it will be helpful to turn to Porphyry for a moment, for purposes of comparison.

Porphyry quotes Fragment 1 of Archytas as part of his commentary on Book 1, Chapter 3 of Ptolemy's *Harmonics*. In this chapter Ptolemy is presenting his account of high and low pitch. Porphyry's professed goal in quoting Fragment 1 is to show that Ptolemy is adopting an ancient view on pitch, although Porphyry admits that Ptolemy has developed it quite a bit. This is consistent with one of the general goals of Porphyry's commentary, which is to identify the sources upon which Ptolemy is drawing, since Ptolemy himself frequently relies heavily on his predecessors without acknowledging the debt (Por. 5. 7 ff.). So Porphyry should be contrasted with Nicomachus both in regard to his purpose for quoting Fragment 1 (to illustrate Archytas' theory of pitch rather than his view on the sciences as a whole) and also in regard to his general purpose in writing his treatise; Porphyry's purpose is strongly historical, while Nicomachus, whose treatise is systematic, has little interest in history.

We have seen that Nicomachus indicates that his quotation of the fragment is only approximate. What can we determine about the quality of Porphyry's quotation? The evidence suggests, as I will show below, that he is presenting what he takes to be the literal text of the fragment without paraphrase or abridgement, except in one place where he explicitly marks an abridgement. Other scholars have thought otherwise. Since Nicomachus does include a line in the fragment, after ἀδελφεά in line 7, which does not appear in Porphyry, Blass concluded that Porphyry must have cut out a considerable amount of material at this point in the text (1884: 577). In support of this conclusion he refers to another passage where Porphyry explicitly says that he is "altering a few parts of the text (λέξεως) for the sake of brevity" (25.7). It is simply erroneous, however, to conclude from this latter passage that Porphyry habitually abridges his material. In a number of other passages he emphasizes that his quotation is literal. The key word here is λέξις, which seems to be equivalent to our "text" and picks out the literal text of the author in contrast to the commentary on it. At 96.7 he asserts that "Aelian says the following, in exactly these words" (κατὰ λέξιν tr. Barker 1989: 231), and at 33.17, again in reference to Aelian, that he will "provide the literal text" (τὴν λέξιν παραγράψομεν, "transcribe exactly" Barker 1989: 231). That λέξις has the sense "literal text" is also clear from the passage Blass quoted at 25.7. Porphyry there talks of altering a few parts τῆς λέξεως, and, in order for this comment to have any force, the meaning has to be "of the (literal) text." All of this suggests that Porphyry is in fact careful in presenting quotations. In the majority of cases, when presenting a quotation, however, Porphyry simply uses the form "x writes (or says) the following." This is the case with Archytas Fragment 1, where Porphyry says of Archytas "In *On Mathematics*, just as he begins the discourse, he says the following." What is Porphyry's practice of quotation likely to be in such places in general and in the case of Fragment 1 in particular?

Since Porphyry in his commentary is seeking precisely to provide the texts that Ptolemy has used without acknowledgment, we would in general expect him to be careful in quotation, unless he tells us otherwise. In order to consider the matter in more detail, however, we can take Chapter 3 of Porphyry's commentary as a test case. In this long chapter (29.27–78.3), he provides eighteen different quotations from other authors. Of these fifteen are of the "neutral" form and are introduced with a simple "he says" or "he writes" (λέγει, φησί, γράφει), while the other three are marked as literal quotations by the use of λέξις (31.27–28, 33.18, 61.19). In the case of a number of the quotations, it is not possible to check Porphyry's accuracy, because he is the only source we have for the text. This is the case, for example, with his quotation of the long excerpt from Theophrastus' lost *On Music* (61.16–65.15). Nine of the passages, however, come from texts that have been preserved elsewhere, two in Plato and seven in Aristotle. All nine are introduced in the "neutral" format. Of these nine two are very short, a line or less, and in these two cases Porphyry does present a paraphrase. These passages are not in fact quotations but rather quick summaries of the Platonic or Aristotelian view (48.32 and 39.10). The other seven passages, which are all longer, are very close to the currently accepted text (Plato, *Timaeus* 46.4; Aristotle, *Categories* 41.13, 42.30; Aristotle, *De Anima* 47.14, 49.15, 49.22, 52.15). There are of course textual variants and small differences in word order, but there is no evidence for unacknowledged abridgement or paraphrasing. Most revealing is the quotation from the *Categories* at 41.3. In this case Porphyry first quotes three lines of text, then marks a break (four lines are left out) and finally continues with eleven more lines. In another case he similarly distinguishes two texts of Aristotle as coming from different contexts rather than running them together (49.15 ff.). Thus, the evidence of Chapter 3 suggests that, while Porphyry will present one-line paraphrases of a given author's view, when he presents quotations that are longer than a line, those quotations are intended to be literal rather than paraphrases, and he is in the habit of marking any abridgements or breaks between quotations. His use of the word λέξις in some cases emphasizes the literal nature of the quotation but appears to be primarily a stylistic variant in introducing quotations rather than an indication that other quotations, which are introduced without a reference to λέξις, are presented as less than literal.

If we return then to Porphyry's quotation of Fragment 1 of Archytas, since this is a long quotation in the neutral format, we should assume that Porphyry is presenting it as a literal quotation and that he would not abridge it without indication. He does in fact indicate one abridgement at the end of the quotation, between lines 41 and 42, and gives a brief summary of the material abridged. The indication of abridgement at this point surely suggests that the rest of the fragment is not abridged. Moreover, there is a further striking confirmation that Porphyry is not paraphrasing or abridging without indication in his quotation of Fragment 1 and of my general conclusion about Porphyry's practice regarding quotations which are introduced in the neutral way. At 81.7–11 Porphyry quotes lines 13–18 of Fragment 1 again. Two important things should be noticed here. First, Porphyry is again revealed as careful in his quotations: with the exception of a few minor variations, which could easily have arisen in the transmission of the manuscripts, the two quotations of these lines are identical. Second, and this is the more important point, in introducing the quotation at 81.5–6, Porphyry says "Archytas, whose (literal) text (λέξιν) we have also provided before, writes the following about sounds." The mention of λέξις here shows that Porphyry regarded the original quotation of Fragment 1 at 56.5, where λέξις was not used, as a literal quotation and also indicates that, when Porphyry presents quotations in the neutral format, he is intending them to be understood as literal quotations.

We can now see that Blass' suggestion that, in the case of Fragment 1, Porphyry quotes the first seven lines and then without comment drops a number of lines before picking up with Archytas' account of pitch (1884: 577), is not at all in accord with Porphyry's practice of quotation elsewhere, nor indeed in accord with his practice in quoting Fragment 1 itself, since he clearly indicates an abridgement at the end of the quotation. Moreover, Blass' suggestion really makes Porphyry's procedure in quoting Fragment 1 unintelligible. Blass rightly sees that Porphyry is mainly interested in the material on pitch in lines 7–43. He then bizarrely supposes that Porphyry quotes the first seven lines, although they are irrelevant to his purposes, and then leaves out a number of other lines as irrelevant before quoting the text he is really interested in. Why quote the irrelevant lines 1–7 in the first place?

The obvious answer is that they were the first seven lines of Archytas' book and that the material in which Porphyry was interested began in line 7, so that it seemed logical to just start at the beginning of the book. If as Blass supposes, the lines in which Porphyry was interested were not lines 7–43 but rather, e.g. lines 25–60, it immediately becomes unintelligible as to why Porphyry would jump to lines 1–7, then decide to leave out lines 8–24, and then finally quote the material he was interested in all along. Surely, in this case he would have simply quoted lines 25–60 without lines 1–7. Thus both Porphyry's general practice of quotation and the peculiar features of his quotation of Fragment 1 show that he is not likely to have used abridgement.

With this understanding of Porphyry, we can now return to Nicomachus' presentation of the first seven lines of Fragment 1 and in particular to what he meant in saying that Archytas said "something like the following." Comparison with Porphyry's version of the first seven lines of Archytas makes it reasonably clear that Nicomachus paraphrases parts of the passage to make its relevance to the context in the *Introduction to Arithmetic* clearer. In the first three lines Porphyry's and Nicomachus' versions are very similar and differ primarily in dialect forms. When it comes to the list of sciences in lines 4–6, however, there are very significant differences between Porphyry's version ("Indeed concerning the speed of the stars and their risings and settings as well as concerning geometry and numbers and not least concerning music . . .") and Nicomachus' version ("Indeed concerning geometry and arithmetic and sphaeric . . . and not least also concerning music"). Even apart from what we have discovered about Porphyry and Nicomachus as sources and by looking just at these two texts in themselves, Nicomachus' version is much more suspect. Everything in Porphyry's language can be paralleled from authors of the fifth and fourth centuries BC. Nicomachus' use of the word "sphaeric," on the other hand, is very problematic. Sphaeric properly speaking deals with the geometry of the sphere as it applies to astronomy (Heath 1921: 11; Neugebauer 1975: 11. 755). It appears as the title of a work by Theodosius of Bithynia (fl. 100 BC). As a subject matter it goes back at least to the beginning of the third century BC and is found in Autolycus' *On the Moving Sphere* and Euclid's *Phaenomena*, which may in turn draw on earlier work. It is unclear, however, how early the term sphaeric itself was in use. Older histories of astronomy (Heath 1921) of course assign it to Archytas on the basis of this passage of Nicomachus, but there is no trace of the term in Plato or Aristotle.

Our worries about the usage of the term sphaeric are confirmed when we note that it is Nicomachus' own standard term for astronomy, the term that he has used shortly before (3.2) this "quotation" from Archytas and shortly afterward (3.7, 5.2). This fact along with Nicomachus' general tendency to paraphrase suggests that he has rewritten the list of sciences in what is, for him, more modern terminology, which allows the relevance of the Archytas passage for Nicomachus' own discussion to stand out. Porphyry, on the other hand, has no reason whatsoever to change the language of these lines. His main interest, as we have seen, is in the acoustic theory that follows in lines 7–43.

In line 7, the famous description of the sciences as akin, Nicomachus and Porphyry are back in agreement. However, apparently as the last line of his quotation, Nicomachus presents a sentence that is not found in Porphyry at all. The sentence gives an explanation of the assertion that the sciences are akin: "For they are concerned with the two primary forms of being which are akin." Some of the features of the language of this line show that it must be, at least in part, considerably later than Archytas (Huffman 1985: 346). The analysis of Porphyry and Nicomachus as sources, which I have given above, also sheds important light on this sentence. First, as argued above, it is very unlikely that Porphyry is purposely abridging his quotation to cut out this line or a longer passage. It of course remains possible that the line fell out of the text through transmission, either before Porphyry's time or after. If we look at the content of the line in its context in Nicomachus, however, it appears much more likely that the additional line is due to Nicomachus. In its context in Archytas, there is no explanation of the enigmatic phrase "the two primary forms of being." We can, of course, come up with a number of plausible conjectures that might fit Archytas (Barker 1989: 40 n. 44 suggests the visible and the audible; see the detailed commentary), but there would still be a puzzle as to why he used such enigmatic terminology with no explanation. In its context in Nicomachus, however, there is nothing puzzling about "the two primary forms of being" at all. They have been the central focus of Nicomachus' discussion in the previous pages. At 3.4 he says that all things are either magnitudes or multitudes and that wisdom is the knowledge "of these two forms." Shortly afterwards in Chapter 3, just a few lines before quoting Archytas, Nicomachus distinguishes the four sciences and says that without these it is not possible to deal accurately with "the forms of being." Thus, it appears that, just as Nicomachus introduced his term sphaeric into the list of sciences in his paraphrase of Archytas, so here he adds a line at the end which connects Archytas to the central thesis which he, Nicomachus, has been developing about the connection between the four sciences and the two primary forms of being.

Further, the expression "the two primary forms" is easily paralleled in Nicomachus' style. Later in his work Nicomachus will describe the even and the odd as the "two primary forms" (1. 6.4 πρώτιστα εἴδη δύο) of scientific number, prime numbers as "the primary form" (1. 11.2 πρώτιστον εἶδος) of the three kinds of odd numbers, and the multiple ratio as "the primary form" (1. 18.1 εἶδος . . . τὸ πρώτιστον) of "the greater." It is thus clear that "primary forms" (πρώτιστα εἴδη) or "primary form" (πρώτιστον εἶδος) is typical Nicomachean jargon used to pick out the first species in a genus or the most important species in a genus.

In light of the freedom with which Nicomachus paraphrases Plato, it is possible that this last line is to be understood as part of his paraphrase of Archytas. Think back to the "path" that replaced Plato's "happy nature" in the "cities." Nicomachus might think that this sentence, although not literally found in the text of Archytas, is part of the gist of what Archytas is saying. Nicomachus expresses the sentence in his own terminology, in order to show its relevance to his immediate point. The γάρ in the additional sentence would then indicate Nicomachus' unpacking of what Archytas meant by saying that the sciences were akin: they are akin because they deal with the two primary forms of being which are akin. In this case the Doric forms in the additional sentence would be Nicomachus' own doing and show that the whole was thought to be a paraphrase of Archytas. Cassio (1988) has shown that Nicomachus "improves" on Archytas' Doric by adopting poetic forms in other cases and suggests that it is thus not implausible that he would Doricize this sentence, even if it is his own composition.

It appears more likely, however, that Nicomachus intended the additional sentence as a comment on Archytas and did not mean it to be understood as part of his paraphrase. To begin with, the additional sentence has the regular singular verb form with the neuter plural subject, while the immediately preceding sentence has the plural verb form with the neuter plural subject. Such variation between two adjoining sentences is not easy to attribute to one author, and it would make more sense if Archytas was responsible for the first usage and Nicomachus for the second. If the sentence is Nicomachus', γάρ introduces his own comment on the fragment of Archytas, which he has just cited: (what Archytas says is right) "For the sciences have to do with the first two forms of being which are akin." Nicomachus' treatment of the quotation of the *Epinomis*, which immediately follows his quotation of Archytas, strongly supports this understanding of the additional sentence introduced by γάρ. Immediately after the quote from the *Epinomis*, Nicomachus continues with a further elaboration on the text introduced by γάρ. In this case we have the text of the *Epinomis* to tell us where the *Epinomis* stops and Nicomachus begins. If we did not have that text, however, it would be very difficult to be sure when Nicomachus' comments start. Here is the passage in D'Ooge's translation:

The one who has attained all these things in the way I describe, him I for my part call wisest, and this I maintain through thick and thin. For it is clear that these studies are like ladders and bridges that carry our minds from the things apprehended by sense and opinion to those comprehended by the mind and understanding, and from those material, physical things, our foster-brethren known to us from childhood, to the things with which we are unacquainted, foreign to our senses, but in their immateriality and eternity more akin to our souls, and above all to the reason which is in our souls.

Only the first line comes from Nicomachus' quotation of the *Epinomis*, the long second sentence is pure Nicomachus, but there is no obvious break in the flow of the text, and I suspect that, if the *Epinomis* had not survived, all of this would be regarded as deriving from it. Fortunately, Porphyry's more careful and longer quotation of Fragment 1 of Archytas helps us to see, in this case too, where Archytas ends and Nicomachus begins.

While Nicomachus' further elaboration on the *Epinomis* goes on for several lines, his comment on Archytas is a single sentence, which is in turn immediately followed by the quotation from the *Epinomis*, which is introduced by the words "And Plato . . . (καὶ Πλάτων . . .). The fact that Nicomachus' comment on Archytas is sandwiched between two quotations explains how it has come to be tinged with Doric dialect. A scribe, seeing the beginning of the quotation from Archytas clearly marked and then a few lines later a separate quotation from Plato clearly marked by the words "And Plato . . .", assumed that everything in between was Archytas. The one-sentence comment of Nicomachus, which fits seamlessly with the quotation of Archytas in terms of sense, is not recognized for what it is. The third word in this sentence would have been written ἀδελφῇ by Nicomachus, but, in the context of the Doric form ἀδελφεά at the end of the quotation from Nicomachus just three words earlier, it is naturally "corrected" to the Doric form. This might in turn have led to the correction of εἴδη, which Nicomachus would have written, to εἴδεα, although the two corrections are not really parallel and it is not clear that this is what Archytas would have written (Buck 1955: 39). Once these changes are made, it is the easiest of all corrections to change the Attic eta to the Doric long alpha to give τὰν ἀναστροφάν for τὴν ἀναστροφήν, and that is the extent of the Doric dialect in the sentence. If the sentence had in fact been written by Archytas, we would have expected πράτιστα rather than the πρώτιστα that is preserved in the manuscripts of Nicomachus (Buck 1955: 94). In the next sentence, which is the first sentence of the section preserved only by Porphyry, we find Archytas using the form πρᾶτον and not πρῶτον. Thus our scribe copying Nicomachus was sophisticated enough to make obvious corrections to Doric forms but not more subtle changes. Too much weight cannot be attached to the appearance of πρώτιστα rather than πράτιστα, however, because the manuscript tradition has so much trouble with dialect forms.

The evidence of Nicomachus' practice in quotation and the similarities between the additional sentence and his own style and thought provide overwhelming evidence that the additional sentence was not part of the text of Archytas but an addition by Nicomachus. There is no reason to excessively censure Nicomachus for his treatment of Fragment 1 of Archytas or even his paraphrases of Plato. Unlike Porphyry, he is not trying to make a historical point about the origin of certain ideas, he is expounding a thesis about the nature of reality and our ability to know it. He rewrites Archytas' list of sciences in modern terminology but, after all, he warns us that it was only "something like this" that Archytas wrote. The mistaken addition of his comment on Archytas to the text of Archytas is his fault only in that he did not clearly mark the end of his quotations.

I will now briefly examine the other, less-important, witnesses to the text of Fragment 1, which are presented in Texts D, F, G and H. Iamblichus' commentary on Nicomachus' *Introduction to Arithmetic* gives some further support for the thesis that the sentence about "the two primary forms of being" is Nicomachus' comment on Archytas. At 9.1–7 (Text F above) Iamblichus identifies the sentence "for these sciences seem to be akin" as "the saying of Archytas." He quotes just this sentence and does not add the further comment that these sciences are "concerned with the two primary forms of being." Instead, this latter idea is part of the introduction to the quotation of the line from Archytas and is implicitly presented as part of Nicomachus' reasoning rather than as an idea going back to Archytas. Iamblichus, after summarizing Nicomachus' account of the relation between the four sciences and the two primary forms, says that "since these sciences arise concerning underlying realities that are akin, it is reasonable to consider these sciences to be akin as well." All of this is presented as paraphrase of Nicomachus' reasoning, and it is only after this that Archytas' statement about the kinship of the sciences is quoted. Iamblichus' treatment of the passage is too loose to allow for any certain conclusions, but, on the whole, Iamblichus' procedure rather supports the conclusion that he regarded the comment about "the two primary forms of being which are akin" (in Iamblichus' language "the underlying realities that are akin") as belonging to Nicomachus. It is possible, then, that, when Iamblichus was writing (200 years after Nicomachus), Nicomachus' comment had not yet been Doricized in the transmission of the text and thus appeared to Iamblichus to clearly belong to Nicomachus.

Iamblichus' commentary on Nicomachus does not proceed line by line and is a parallel treatise on arithmetic inspired by Nicomachus rather than a strict commentary. We have two later commentaries on Nicomachus, dating from the sixth century AD, those of John Philoponus and Asclepius of Tralles, which do take the form of scholia on Nicomachus' text (Texts G and H). These commentaries are similar to one another and are perhaps based on the lectures of their teacher, Ammonius son of Hermeias (Tarán 1969: 5 ff.). It is important to note that both Asclepius and Philoponus comment on the line added by Nicomachus with the first three words as a lemma. In this lemma the Doric form ἀδελφεά appears so that the sentence had already been Doricized in at least some manuscripts by the sixth century. On the other hand, both commentaries also interpret the "two primary forms of being" in terms of the metaphysical theory set out by Nicomachus in the preceding pages. If they regard the added sentence as by Archytas, they seem either to assume that Archytas and Nicomachus have the same metaphysical theory or to interpret the sentence in Nicomachean terms, because it makes sense in those terms and they have no further information as to what Archytas might have meant by it. Asclepius, in fact, provides a paraphrase of the Archytas fragment, but that paraphrase deals just with the praise of those who distinguished the sciences and does not include the comment about the kinship of the sciences or the two forms of being.

There is one final context in which a sentence from Fragment 1 appears. Iamblichus (Text D above) quotes lines 2–4 of Archytas: "For, having discerned well concerning the nature of wholes they were likely also to see well how things are in their parts." What is striking about Iamblichus' quotation is that, like Nicomachus, he has slightly rewritten the text of Archytas in light of his own terminology. The last part of the sentence matches the text as constituted from the versions quoted in Porphyry and Nicomachus. In the first part of the sentence, however, Iamblichus has replaced Archytas' somewhat obscure expression "concerning the nature of wholes" (περὶ γὰρ τᾶς τῶν ὅλων φύσιος) with "concerning universals" (τοιγὰρ περὶ τῶν καθόλου). Iamblichus introduces the quotation to support the idea that "knowledge of the particular accompanies the knowledge of the universal" and has simply paraphrased Archytas' text to make clear that, when Archytas talks of "the nature of wholes," Iamblichus understands him to mean "universals." Thus Iamblichus shows the same willingness as Nicomachus to "update" the text of Archytas for the sake of clarity.

The title of Archytas' book

As we have seen, Nicomachus and Porphyry agree that Fragment 1 is the beginning of a book of Archytas, but they disagree about the title of that book. Paradoxically, Porphyry, who is mainly interested in the book for its harmonic theory, gives it the more general title *On Mathematics*, while Nicomachus who is interested precisely in what Archytas has to say about mathematics in general, gives it the more specific title *Harmonics*. It is, of course, quite possible that the book came to be known under different names. The title *Harmonics*, however, is more likely to be the original. The bulk of the fragment is focused on harmonics rather than mathematics in general. One might argue that this is true just of what is preserved and that Archytas went on to talk of the other sciences later in the book. But the rhetoric of the first six lines is all designed to highlight music: after praise of the sciences in general, Archytas gives a list of the sciences in which music is mentioned last but said to be "not least." When the rest of the fragment then goes on to focus precisely on music, it would be very odd, if later on in his book Archytas returned to the other sciences. They have been mentioned only to introduce music and then be dismissed. It is also easy to explain how the treatise would come to have the alternative title *On Mathematics*. The first seven lines focus precisely on the mathematical sciences (τὰ μαθήματα) as an introduction to the main topic of harmonics, and someone judging just by those introductory lines could well have thought the title *On Mathematics* more appropriate than its true title, *Harmonics*.

Archytas and the sciences: Fragment 1, lines 1–7

(For commentary on Fragment 1 see also Barker 1989 and Bowen 1982.) Archytas begins his *Harmonics* with a seven-line proem in which he praises "those concerned with the sciences" for their ability to make distinctions, identifies a group of four related sciences (astronomy, geometry, logistic, and harmonics), in which good distinctions about wholes have led to proper understanding of individual things, and effects a transition to his main topic, harmonics. These lines are crucial to understanding Archytas' philosophy as a whole and raise a number of important questions: (1) Whom, both in terms of broad groups and in terms of specific individuals, is Archytas designating with the expression "those concerned with the sciences"? (2) What relationship does Archytas envisage between the discoveries of his predecessors and his own work? (3) Why does Archytas emphasize the ability of those concerned with the sciences to make distinctions well? (4) What does he intend by the contrast between "the nature of wholes" and "things in their parts"? (5) What does he mean by saying that the sciences are related? (6) In light of the answers to these first five questions, what point, finally, is Archytas making about the value of the sciences? I have addressed all of these questions in my overview of Archytas' philosophy. There are, however, two questions about these first seven lines on which I would like to expand briefly here. (Technical points about the language of these lines are dealt with in the line-by-line commentary at the end.)

First, does the expression "those concerned with the sciences" refer only to Pythagoreans? I have argued in the overview that Archytas is referring to a wide range of thinkers, including both Pythagoreans and non-Pythagoreans. Many scholars have assumed that, since Archytas was a Pythagorean, he must be writing in a narrowly Pythagorean tradition and for a Pythagorean audience. Accordingly, when he refers to "those concerned with the sciences," we should understand him to mean "the Pythagoreans concerned with the sciences," and, when he goes on to describe the acoustic theory of his predecessors in lines 7–18, we should again understand that he is referring just to his predecessors who were Pythagorean (e.g. Zhmud 1997: 198; Lasserre 1954: 36). Bowen, who recognizes that much of the progress in the sciences was not Pythagorean, tries to finesse the issue by referring to "a Pythagorean reformulation of Greek scientific culture" (1982: 86). It is better simply to recognize that Archytas is not referring exclusively to Pythagoreans. After all, he refers quite generally to "those concerned with the sciences" and makes no mention of Pythagoreans. If Plato, Aristotle, any Presocratic, indeed, just about any philosopher we can think of referred to "those concerned with the sciences," this would be read as a remark about the general scientific tradition and not as "Platonists concerned with the sciences" or "Heracliteans concerned with the sciences."

In the case of the Pythagoreans, however, an extra assumption is in play, the assumption that Pythagoreans ran a closed shop and worked only in their own tradition and in particular were wont to assign their own views back to Pythagoras or other early Pythagoreans, in part to glorify Pythagoras and in part to gain authority for the views they were presenting (e.g. Barker 1989: 31 n. 9; Bowen 1982: 83–86). There is evidence to make such an assumption reasonable in many cases in the later Pythagorean tradition. Such an assumption accounts for the vigorous tradition of Pythagorean pseudepigrapha, where the forged work can gain authority from its ascription to an early Pythagorean. It is illegitimate, however, to assign such an attitude uncritically to early Pythagorean figures such as Philolaus and Archytas. As I have shown in the overview, Archytas' reference to the sciences in Fragment 1 presupposes the work of many non-Pythagoreans, and the epistemology which he develops in Fragment 3, while valuing the work of his predecessors, does not call for uncritical acceptance of his predecessors' work and in fact puts the highest value on innovation. It is also significant that Aristotle, who wrote two treatises on Pythagoreanism, wrote separate treatises on the work of Archytas, which suggests that Aristotle saw him as a figure whose importance was not limited to the Pythagorean tradition (A13). Finally, Fragment 1 works very poorly as an appeal to authority, since neither Pythagoras nor any other authority figure is explicitly named. There is not even an implicit allusion to Pythagoras as an unnamed "wise man," or to the Pythagoreans as "wise men." All we have is the perfectly neutral expression "those concerned with the sciences."

Second, what significance is there to the names and order of the four sciences presented in lines 4–6? A peculiarity in the presentation suggests that both the ways of naming the sciences and the order of the sciences are dictated by Archytas' particular rhetorical purposes in this passage and do not reflect his typical names for the sciences or a hierarchy of sciences. The peculiarity is the way in which astronomy is presented. In contrast to the other three sciences, which are identified by their subject matter expressed in a single word (geometry, numbers and music), astronomy is identified more elaborately as concerned with "the speed of the stars and their risings and settings." The emphasis here is on concrete observational data. The reason for this emphasis becomes clearer in light of Archytas' overall point about the sciences in the preceding lines. He has emphasized that the scientists' discernment about wholes allows them to "think correctly about individual things as they are." "The speed of the stars and their risings and settings" are examples of just this sort of knowledge of particulars. So astronomy is listed first and under this heavily empirical description as providing a clear example of Archytas' point that discernment about "the nature of wholes" leads one to see the parts clearly. He does not feel the need to go on to illustrate this point for geometry and the science of numbers and simply lists them briefly by subject matter. It may well be that Archytas felt that astronomy provided better examples of concrete particulars known through number than geometry or arithmetic. Music is listed last in the order, once again because of Archytas' immediate purposes. Fragment 1 is the beginning of a work precisely on harmonics and music is put last for rhetorical effect (it is emphatically "not least") and to mark the transition to the main focus of the book.

The list of four sciences in Fragment 1 is in reality a list of four subject matters in which those concerned with the sciences have provided clear distinctions about particular things. Geometry is the only case where the description of the subject matter corresponds to the name of the science.

Fragment 4 suggests that Archytas' name for the science concerned with numbers was logistic. The title of the book from which Fragment 1 comes suggests that the name for the science concerned with music was harmonics. Finally, it seems likely that Archytas like Plato used the name astronomy rather than an awkward periphrasis in terms of subject matter such as "the science concerned with the speed of the stars and their risings and settings." Archytas' names for the four sciences are thus likely to have been logistic, geometry, astronomy and harmonics. Fragment 4 clearly suggests that logistic had a special position among the sciences for Archytas (see the overview of Archytas' philosophy), but beyond that there is no evidence of a hierarchy among them.

The acoustic theory of Archytas: Fragment 1, lines 7–43

The account of acoustic theory, which Archytas presents in Fragment 1, falls into three parts. In lines 7–13 Archytas discusses the conditions necessary for any sound to arise at all, i.e. that there be an impact of bodies against one another. In lines 13–18 he discusses sounds that are not heard because of deficiencies in our nature, e.g. sounds that are not heard because of the distance between us and the colliding bodies. Finally, in lines 18–43, Archytas considers sounds that are heard and states his central thesis about the cause of high and low pitch in such sounds: sounds "which arrive quickly and strongly from impacts appear high in pitch, but those which arrive slowly and weakly seem to be low in pitch." The bulk of the passage (lines 20–41) is taken up with the extensive evidence he provides for this thesis drawn primarily from acoustic "experiments," from experience with the human voice, and from the functioning of musical instruments. I will consider each of these three major sections in turn. See Barker (1989: 39–42) and Bowen (1982) for other discussions of the passage.

Lines 7–13, which discuss the conditions necessary for sound to arise at all, are presented not as the product of Archytas' own research but as an account of what his predecessors and contemporaries ("those concerned with the sciences" in line 1) have accomplished. Since Archytas is so general in his reference to these people, it seems unlikely that he is thinking of any specific text or author. It is more likely that he is presenting what he takes to be the *communis opinio* concerning the origin of sound, a *communis opinio* with which he seems to agree and which serves as his own statement about the origin of sound. Since Fragment 1 constitutes the first lines of Archytas' book, *Harmonics*, and since there do not seem to be any breaks in the presentation of the first forty-one lines, we can take it that we are here provided with the first principles of Archytas' theory of sound. That this

is his chosen starting point is made clear by the emphatic "first" (πρᾶτον)
with which the lines begin.

The central thesis about the origin of sound is stated quite generally
and without any initial reference to musical sound: sound (ψόφος) cannot
arise unless there is an impact (πληγή) of some things against one another.
As Barker points out, this is the earliest explicit statement of a "familiar
theme in fourth-century and later acoustics" (1989: 40 n. 45). It can be
found in Plato, Aristotle, and the Euclidean *Sectio Canonis* among others
(see Barker for references). This broad similarity can lead us to overlook
some significant differences, however.

For a variety of reasons scholars have wanted to connect Archytas closely
with the *Sectio Canonis* ascribed to Euclid (see the commentary on A19).
Some have even made Archytas the virtual author of the work and based
much of their reconstruction of Archytas' work on the mistaken assumption
that he is the author of the *Sectio Canonis* (Frank 1923: 174; Lasserre 1966a:
177; van der Waerden 1943: 169–70). At first sight the acoustic theory at
the beginning of the *Sectio* might seem to support this close connection,
since it explicitly says that an impact (πληγή) is necessary for anything to
be heard. But the *Sectio* develops this theme in ways of which there is no
trace in Archytas. First, while Archytas leaves it as an implicit assumption
that motion must exist (φερόμενα) before impacts of bodies can arise, the
first line of the *Sectio* makes this point a central theme: "if there should
be calm with no movement, there would be silence." Second, the *Sectio* is
clearly thinking of musical sound from the beginning rather than of sound
in general, since φθόγγοι, which can refer to sounds in general but which
comes to mean "notes" and must have this meaning in the preface to the
Sectio (149.17 etc., see Bowen 1991b: 169), is used rather than Archytas' more
neutral ψόφος ("noise," "sound"). Moreover, the motions that are discussed
in the *Sectio* are immediately characterized in terms of being "closer packed"
or "more widely spaced," which clearly suggests a vibrating string of which
there is no trace in Archytas. Most importantly, the *Sectio* will also go on
to present a theory of pitch that differs from Archytas (see below), and the
analysis of the enharmonic and diatonic genera in the *Sectio* differ from
what we find in Archytas (A16). Thus, while the *Harmonics* of Archytas may,
in a general sense, be seen as the ancestor of the preface to the *Sectio*, the
differences between the two treatises are more striking than the similarities
(see also the commentary on A19).

Plato (*Tim.* 67b) shares with Archytas the emphasis on the necessity of
an impact for sound to arise, and the theory of pitch that he presents is
the same as that of Archytas. Plato does not mention Archytas' colliding

bodies, however, and instead says that sound (Plato's word is φωνή, which usually means "voice") is "an impact of air, coming through the ears, and impinging on the brain and blood" (tr. Barker). Archytas says surprisingly little about air (it is mentioned later in line 27), or about the ear and human perception (but see line 16). Archytas' account is in fact closest to what we find in Aristotle's *De Anima* (419b4 ff.). Aristotle mentions not only impact but specifically the impact of one thing against another as in Archytas, and he uses Archytas' general word for sound (ψόφος). Once again, however, Aristotle develops a number of themes not found in Archytas. In particular he emphasizes and discusses in detail the medium in which sound moves, air, which Archytas does not initially discuss at all and which he never discusses directly. Aristotle's discussion of the influence on sound of the differing nature of the bodies that collide (e.g. bronze vs. wool) has no counterpart in Archytas. It thus appears that Archytas' quite simple point about the origin of sound has, not unnaturally, been developed extensively by later thinkers.

If we look carefully at the language that Archytas uses in lines 7–13, some striking results follow. His language is indeed resolutely general in content and not tied specifically to music. In this sense Archytas' presentation of his predecessors' views coincides with the praise he has just bestowed on them: they begin with the nature of the whole, with motion and sound in the cosmos as a whole, before turning to the specific science of harmonics. We have already seen that ψόφος is clearly a neutral word for sound with no musical connotations. φερόμενα, which appears three times, picks out "bodies in motion," whose motion is controlled by natural law rather than any human purpose. It is, in fact, a common term in fourth-century science and cosmology (Plato, *Lg.* 889b, *Phdr.* 261d). Aristotle uses the word twice specifically in reference to the Pythagorean view that "the bodies which are moved (φερόμενα) in the heaven are ten" (*Metaph.* 986a10, cf. *Prob.* 910b36) and it is common in the *Problems* and *Mechanical Problems* (e.g. 852b and 915b18). It is possible to make some even more specific suggestions about the origins of Archytas' account of sound. First, Aristotle's discussion of the famous Pythagorean doctrine of the harmony of the spheres at *De Caelo* 290b ff. shows clear connections with the language and concepts used in Archytas' discussion of sound. In reporting the reasons for which the Pythagoreans supposed that the heavenly bodies made a harmonious music by their motion he says "as many things as are . . . moved (φέρεται) create noise (ψόφον) and impact (πληγήν)." Here are all the central terms of Archytas' discussion. Since Archytas is explicitly referring to his predecessors and since Aristotle usually means the Pythagoreans of the middle or later part of the fifth century when he talks of Pythagoreans, Fragment 1 of Archytas and Aristotle seem to confirm one another regarding Pythagorean acoustics in the late fifth century.

This is not the end of the matter. Archytas' discussion of the origin of sound also shows connections specifically to the atomic theory of Democritus. To begin with, we should note that the term "impact" (πληγή), which, as we have seen, becomes a standard feature of post-Archytan acoustic theory, was a central concept in atomic theory in the generation before Archytas. Simplicius reports that "Democritus says that by nature the atoms are motionless, and that they move by impact" (πληγῇ), and similar accounts are found in other sources (DK 68 A47). It is in fact clear that the atomists explained atomic motion in terms of a chain of impacts of atoms that stretched back *ad infinitum* (Furley 1987: 149). The common use of this term is, of course, not enough to show the influence of Democritus on Archytas. Archytas' discussion of the two cases in which impacts arise, however, further supports the idea that Democritus may have been one of "those concerned with the sciences," whose views Archytas is presenting. Archytas envisages impacts arising either when bodies moving in opposite directions meet and "slow each other down," or when bodies move in the same direction but at different speeds, so that the faster moving bodies catch up with and strike the slower moving. These two cases have little applicability to musical sound but make perfect sense in terms of the discussion of the impacts of atoms. The case in which bodies moving in different directions strike each other is standard in descriptions of atomic motion and its role in the generation of the cosmos (e.g. D.L. IX. 31), but even more striking is Archytas' second case, in which swifter moving bodies are supposed to catch up with and strike bodies moving more slowly in the same direction. A famous passage in Book II of Lucretius' *De Rerum Natura* (216 ff.) argues that atoms must swerve occasionally, if there are ever to be any impacts between atoms, precisely because all atoms naturally fall downward at the same speed. Thus according to Lucretius and his master Epicurus, at the atomic level, Archytas' second case cannot occur: since all atoms move at the same speed in the void, faster moving atoms cannot catch up with and strike slower moving atoms. Lucretius goes out of his way, however, to argue against an unidentified "someone" (*aliquis* II. 225), who supposes that heavier atoms might catch up with lighter ones as they fall. Some have argued that this is not a reference to Democritus but rather to "anyone who holds this theory" (Bailey 1947: II. 844), but Democritus may not have anticipated Epicurus in positing a "theoretical downward 'rain' of atoms" (Furley 1987: 151). The evidence for Democritus' views on atomic motion is meager and contradictory, but there is some evidence that, unlike

Epicurus, he did think that the atoms moved at different speeds (Furley 1987: 149; O' Brien 1981: 315 ff. esp. 329). Whether Democritus believed that Archytas' second case applied to atoms or not, the Lucretius passage shows that the discussion of that case has a natural place in atomism.

None of these parallels can prove that Archytas had atomists in mind, when he presented his discussion of the impacts of bodies, which are required for sounds to arise; we have seen that late fifth-century Pythagorean acoustics as reported by Aristotle discussed similar issues. Moreover, as Frank noted (1923: 384), Plato too (*Lg.* 893e) discusses moving bodies (φερόμενα) that meet one another from opposite directions (ἐξ ἐναντίας ἀπαντῶσι). These similarities, however, show only that Plato and Archytas are both using the vocabulary of late fifth- and early fourth-century physics. Plato says nothing about sound here and his descriptions of the meetings of bodies and the results of those meetings differ significantly from what we find in Archytas. Nor is there any trace in Archytas of the ten types of motion that Plato identifies. Certainly, in terms of the evidence we have, the atomists provide the most likely origin for Archytas' remarks on impacts. The persistent tradition that connects Democritus to the Pythagoreans and which even makes him the pupil of Philolaus (D.L. ix. 38) suggests that there may have been mutual influence between Pythagoreans and atomists in the late fifth century.

We do have evidence for a number of Presocratic accounts of sound, including the account of Democritus, preserved in Theophrastus' *De Sensu* and the doxographic tradition (see Beare 1906: 93 ff.). There can be little doubt that Archytas was familiar with some of these explanations, but it is hard to be sure how his discussion of sound is related to them, because of the difference in purpose between his account of sound and the purpose of the doxography on the Presocratics. Theophrastus and the doxography are primarily interested in Presocratic theories of sensation and thus focus on the mechanism of hearing. The theories discussed in the doxography (those of Alcmaeon, Empedocles, Anaxagoras, Democritus and Diogenes of Apollonia) all emphasize the role of air in hearing as well as the structure of the ear and head. Archytas does not directly address these topics and instead focuses on the generation of sound prior to our perception of it. This is not surprising, when we remember that Archytas is not writing a treatise on sensation here but rather on harmonic theory. He will discuss the limitations of our hearing in lines 13–18, and, in his theory of concordance in A18, it appears that Archytas emphasized the difference between what we hear and what is really the case. It may thus be that Archytas subscribed to some variation of one of the Presocratic accounts of hearing, which served as a basis for these remarks. On the other hand, it may be that, like his

predecessor Philolaus, Archytas was more interested in the basic principles
and mathematical laws that governed sound than in explaining the physical
mechanism of hearing.

Apart from discussions of the mechanism of hearing, there is little evidence for Presocratic accounts of sound. Theophrastus (*Sens.* 59) says that
the general Presocratic view was that sound (φωνή) is a movement of air
(κίνησις τοῦ ἀέρος). This is certainly consistent with what Archytas will say
about sound, but Archytas' emphasis on the necessity of impacts of bodies
for sound to arise is generally lacking in Presocratic accounts. Empedocles
(A86) has the organ of hearing striking (παίειν) the air in the ear (see also
Diogenes of Apollonia A21), and the doxography on Anaxagoras talks of
the blow of the breath on the external air in vocal sound (A106). The most
promising parallel for Archytas is Archelaus, the student of Anaxagoras and
teacher of Socrates. In Diogenes Laertius (II. 17 = DK60 A1) we are told
that he was the first to say that the origin of sound (φωνή) is "the blow on
the air" (τὴν τοῦ ἀέρος πλῆξιν). This might just refer to vocal sound, in
which case Archelaus would be close to Anaxagoras (A106), but it may be a
more general statement on the origin of sound. If we take the doxography
literally, the emphasis on the necessity of "blows" or "impacts" for the generation of sound in general would begin with Archelaus in the middle of
the fifth century. Democritus, who is perhaps twenty years younger than
Archelaus, might have found this account of sound congenial to his atom-
istic view of the world. It should be emphasized, however, that, although
there are good reasons for speculating that Democritus had such a view of
sound, all that is preserved in the doxography is his account of hearing.
The evidence of Archelaus, Democritus, and the Pythagoreans who argued
for the doctrine of the harmony of the spheres suggests that in the late fifth
century a consensus had emerged that impacts of objects were required
for sound to arise and it is this consensus that Archytas is presenting in
Fragment 1.

There is also a tradition that assigns important acoustical research to
other early Pythagoreans and in particular to Pythagoras himself, so that
some may be inclined to suppose that it is this narrowly Pythagorean tradition rather than a more general Presocratic tradition upon which Archytas
is drawing. Most of these experiments are designed to show the correspondence between the whole number ratios and the octave, fourth, and
fifth. Scholars have shown, however, that the majority of these acoustic
"experiments" simply would not have worked (see Burkert 1972a: 375 ff.; see
Zhmud 1997: 187 ff. for a more sympathetic account of these experiments).
He believes that Pythagoras worked out a scientific theory of harmonics on

the monochord, but evidence for Pythagoras' work with a monochord is all late). The exception is the story associated with Hippasus, according to which bronze disks of equal diameter but with thicknesses in the appropriate ratios were used (schol. to Plato, *Phaedo* 108d4 = DK18 A12; see Barker 1989: 30–31). So it is quite possible that Hippasus is one of "those concerned with the sciences," to whom Archytas is referring. The point to emphasize is that, while Hippasus and the Pythagoreans who argued for the harmony of the spheres (Aristot. *De Caelo* 290b, see below) show that Pythagoreans did work on acoustic theory, the evidence cited above for other Presocratic theories shows that such work was not limited to or predominantly carried out in Pythagorean circles. Nothing in his basic remarks on acoustics in lines 7–13 nor in his later description of acoustic "experiments" in lines 20–41 shows any specific connection with Hippasus' experiment or the other experiments in the Pythagorean tradition. As we will see below, there does seem to be some connection between what Archytas says in lines 13–18 about sounds that we do not hear and specifically Pythagorean acoustics, but there are also connections to Zeno's paradoxes. On the whole, Fragment 1 suggests that Archytas is drawing on a general Greek tradition of exploration into acoustic issues rather than just a Pythagorean one.

In lines 13–18, Archytas, still reporting and evidently accepting the views of his predecessors, goes on to emphasize that sounds do not have to be heard in order to exist. This emphasis is in strong contrast to Plato's account of sound in the *Timaeus*, where sound is defined as "a blow by the air passed through the ears to the brain and blood and reaching to the soul" (67b). Plato goes on to define hearing as the motion caused by this blow, which starts in the head and reaches the liver, so that if the motion does not reach the liver presumably there is no hearing. His definition also suggests that, if a blow by the air does not impinge on the brain and blood, there is no sound at all. For Archytas, on the other hand, as long as there is an impact between two bodies there is sound and in line 13 he stresses that "*many* of them . . . are not able to be discerned." The sounds are there, the problem is with our nature. He goes on to identify three general cases in which we are unable to hear sounds: (1) when the impact of the colliding bodies is weak, (2) when the distance between us and the colliding bodies is large, (3) when the magnitude of the sound is excessive. The first case could well deal with impacts between tiny bodies such as atoms, which we do not hear because of their small size, regardless of the force of impact, or with impacts between larger bodies that lightly bump each other. In the second case, stronger impacts become equivalent to the weaker impacts of the first case, because of their distance from us. There seems to be an implicit assumption here that sounds are impeded by the air that intervenes between us and the colliding bodies, so that, if the distance is large enough, the sound does not reach us at all.

Some scholars have suggested that Archytas' account of sounds that are too weak for us to hear might have been a response to Zeno's paradox of the millet seed (Barnes 1982: 258; Cherniss 1964: 159 n. 71). There is no clear evidence that Archytas or his predecessors had Zeno in mind, when discussing sounds that are too weak to be heard. Consideration of Zeno's paradox can, however, help to clarify the nature of the theory described by Archytas. There is some debate as to exactly how the paradox worked, but its most theatrical version is a dialogue between Zeno and Protagoras (Simplicius *in Ph.* 1108.18–25 = DK29 A29). It is natural to assume that Protagoras is chosen as the interlocutor, because he is committed to the view that, if we cannot hear a sound, then there is no sound. He is then compelled to answer Zeno that a single millet seed falling makes no sound, since we cannot hear it. Yet he also concedes that a bushel of millet seeds falling does make a sound. Since there is a ratio, in terms of physical size, between the bushel and the single seed, there ought to be a ratio between the sound of the bushel and the sound of a single seed, so that the single seed will make a sound after all. Zeno's point may well be that it is absurd for the sound of the whole bushel falling to be made up of the "no-sounds" of the individual seeds falling. How can a sound arise from components that make no sounds? It seems to me that Protagoras has a genuine problem here, since for him sound bursts inexplicably into existence when it reaches the threshold of hearing.

Archytas, on the other hand, argues that sound does not need to be heard in order to exist, and arises whenever there is an impact of two bodies against one another. If this is so, adding small sounds, which we cannot hear, can quite reasonably create a larger sound, which is above our threshold of hearing and hence audible. Thus Zeno's argument has no force against the view described by Archytas, since Archytas does not limit sound to audible sound. On the other hand, there is not sufficient evidence to conclude with Cherniss that Archytas "admitted the existence of an infinite range of sound below the level of audibility" (1964: 159 n. 71). In order to know whether Archytas had such a doctrine, we would have to know more about how he conceived the material composition of things.

The most intriguing case is the third one, where sounds are not heard "because of the excess of their magnitude." Archytas says that such sounds cannot "slip into" our ears, and he explains what he means with an analogy. Just as someone, who tries to pour a great amount (either of a liquid or a solid such as sand – see the commentary on lines 17–18) into a vessel with a narrow mouth, ends up getting nothing in the vessel, so great sounds poured on our ears do not get in. So, if we try to pour a great quantity of sand into a coke bottle all at once, little or no sand will get in at all. This analogy does suggest that the people who advocated the view Archytas is describing and Archytas himself, since he evidently accepts that view, think of sound as a material, such as sand or water, moving from place to place by locomotion (Bowen 1982: 89) and having spatial characteristics. Lasus of Hermione, who was active at the end of the sixth century BC, would appear to have had such a view of sound and hence may have been one of the predecessors to whom Archytas is referring. Aristoxenus (*Harm.* I. 3.21) tells us that Lasus regarded notes as having "breadth" (πλάτος). We do not know exactly what Lasus meant by "breadth" (see Barker 1989: 128 n. 12 for some speculations), but it might be compatible with a view that regarded certain sounds as too broad to be able to enter our ears.

Archytas gives no indication that he has any specific cases in mind as examples of these great sounds that cannot get into our ears. Porphyry, however, interprets the passage as a reference to the harmony of the spheres or the "harmony of the whole" as he calls it (Text B). The idea that the heavenly bodies make sound when they move and that this sound is harmonious may well go back to the early days of Pythagoreanism long before Archytas, although it was not tied to any astronomical system that was worked out in detail (Huffman 1993: 279 ff.). Aristotle's account of the doctrine in the *De Caelo* (290b12 ff.) does emphasize that, because of the size and speed of movement of the heavenly bodies, the Pythagoreans thought they should produce a sound that is "incredible in magnitude" (ἀμήχανόν τινα τὸ μέγεθος). Thus it is not implausible that Archytas' reference to "the excessive magnitude" (τὰν ὑπερβολὰν τοῦ μεγέθεος) of some sounds is a reference to the sound of the planets and stars in their orbits.

If Archytas is referring to the harmony of the spheres, he is giving a different explanation for our inability to hear this harmony than is found elsewhere in the tradition. The earliest explanation is given by Aristotle in the *De Caelo* passage, which is discussed above (290b12 ff.). According to Aristotle's Pythagoreans, there is no problem about the harmony of the spheres entering our ears. The sound of the harmony reaches our ears, but, since it has been there from the moment of our birth, we have no conception of silence, with which to compare it, and hence do not perceive the harmony. The harmony of the spheres, as loud as it is, becomes the neutral background against which we perceive other sounds. We are like blacksmiths, who through habit do not notice the din around them. Cicero gives an account that may ultimately be based on Aristotle's, but which has some significant differences (*Rep.* VI. 18–19). In Cicero's account, as in Aristotle's, the sound of the harmony does reach our ears, they are filled with it (*oppletae*), but Cicero suggests, as Aristotle does not, that our hearing is harmed by the loud noise. He says that as a result we have no duller sense than hearing. The later tradition shows still further variation. In his *Handbook* (Chapter 3), Nicomachus promises that, in his fuller treatise on music, he will explain why we do not hear the harmony. It is not clear that he ever got around to such an explanation, since Boethius, who seems to be following Nicomachus' fuller treatise, only comments that there are "many reasons" why we do not hear the harmony (*Inst. Mus.* I. 2). Plutarch gives a clearly Platonic interpretation, in which he suggests that most souls cannot hear the harmony because they are hindered by bodily obstructions and affections (*Quaest. Conv.* 745e). Aristides Quintilianus (III. 20) similarly says that the harmony is imperceptible because our hearing has been corrupted by the body. The silence of the later tradition about Archytas' explanation of our inability to hear sounds of excessive magnitude is a strong argument for the authenticity of Fragment 1. Forgeries in the Pythagorean tradition do not develop new ideas but rather try to show that Pythagoreans such as Archytas had the same view as Aristotle or Plato and hence had anticipated them.

In lines 18–20, Archytas turns from sounds that we cannot discern to those that do enter our perception. He divides these latter into sounds of high and low pitch and provides his explanation of differences in pitch: sounds that arrive quickly and forcefully appear high pitched and those that arrive slowly and weakly appear low pitched. This explanation may well be Archytas' own. Such an understanding of pitch is very common from Archytas' contemporary Plato onwards, but there is no trace of it among the Presocratic theories of sound before Archytas (Anaxagoras, Democritus etc.), so that Archytas appears to be the pivotal figure.

A single passage in Theon (59.4 ff.) has sometimes been used to argue that Lasus and Hippasus had anticipated Archytas on this point (Zhmud 1997: 197 ff.; Bowen 1982: 84; but see Burkert 1972a: 382 n. 60, 377 n. 36 and Barker 1989: 31 n. 9). Theon says that Lasus and Hippasus "accompanied (?) the speeds and slownesses of the movements through which the concords . . ." At this point the grammar of the sentence becomes corrupt and a lacuna is usually posited. The subject becomes a singular and the sentence continues ". . . thinking in numbers he constructed such ratios in vessels." Theon goes on to describe an experiment that is supposed to demonstrate the ratios governing the basic concords by filling vessels to various levels with liquid. Interpretation of the passage is complicated by the obviously corrupt text. There are particular problems with the verb συνέπεσθαι. It means "to follow along with" or "accompany" and usually takes a dative case. Here it makes no sense to talk of Lasus and Hippasus as "accompanying the speeds," and τάχη is in the wrong case. Scholars have usually tried to translate the verb as "to pursue" but this is hard to parallel. Even if this translation is accepted, it is hard to be sure whether "pursuing the speeds and slownesses" is based on anything that can be traced to Lasus or Hippasus or whether this language belongs to Theon or his source. It is precisely here that there is a lacuna in the text. Given the uncertainty of the text, it is far from impossible that the reference to "speeds" has its origin in a marginal gloss which has entered the text. Certainly the experiment using vessels which follows is usually cited to illustrate the simple whole number ratios that correspond to the octave, fourth and fifth, and such an experiment does not seem very useful for making the point that pitch is dependent on the speed with which sound travels. Since there is no trace of this doctrine of pitch elsewhere before Archytas, it seems ill advised to base much on this confused passage of Theon (see also A19a).

It is precisely with the introduction of the thesis about pitch, moreover, that Archytas abandons the indirect statement construction, which he has been using since line 9 (ἔφαν) in reporting his predecessors' views. The remainder of the fragment is in direct statement. It is possible that this shift of construction is just a matter of style to give more vividness to the account, but Archytas, who clearly has no hesitations about mentioning his predecessors, makes no mention of them in the rest of the fragment (lines 18–43). When he summarizes the central thesis about pitch in lines 42–43, moreover, he gives no credit to anyone else (e.g. he does not say "*they* have made clear to us from many things . . ."), but he presents the thesis as having become clear from the many examples that he, Archytas, has just provided. Thus both the direct construction and also Archytas' failure to mention his predecessors in the rest of the fragment make it more probable that he is now stating his own views. Fragment 1 thus confirms the conclusion reached above from the secondary sources: Archytas originates the thesis that pitch depends on the speed with which sound travels. (Barker 1989: 31 n. 9, who does not note the shift from indirect to direct discourse, suggests that the thesis does originate with Archytas, but that he is following Pythagorean convention in presenting his own views as those of his predecessors. As I have argued in the overview of Archytas' philosophy, however, there is strong evidence that Archytas is not following such a convention.)

Archytas' idea that pitch depends on the speed with which a sound reaches us "remained the dominant theory throughout antiquity" (Barker

1989: 41 n. 47). It was accepted by Plato in the *Timaeus* (67a ff., and 80a ff.) and by the writers of the Aristotelian *Problems* (e.g. XI. 3) and the Peripatetic *De Audibilibus* (803a). Aristotle modified the view (*De Anima* 420a–b) and Theophrastus rejected it outright (Por. *In Ptol.* 62.31 etc.). Archytas seems to have had a correct intuition in associating high pitch with speed, but he misunderstood the role of speed: pitch does not depend on the speed with which a sound reaches us but rather on the frequency of impacts in a given period of time. Thus a string that vibrates rapidly produces more impacts in a given period of time and is perceived as producing a higher-pitched sound than a string that vibrates less rapidly. All sounds, regardless of their pitch, travel at an equal velocity, if the medium is the same. The author of the *Sectio Canonis* is closer to the correct view (148.9 ff.; Barker 1989: 192 n. 2).

In lines 20–41, which take us up almost to the end of the fragment, Archytas provides evidence for his explanation of pitch. The fact that Archytas devotes so much space to providing evidence for this theory provides further evidence that it is his own invention. His proliferation of examples suggests that he expects his audience to need convincing and hence that the theory is something new and not something from the earlier tradition to which Archytas can expect his audience to assent with little or no argument. Before looking at the evidence he presents, it is important to emphasize two features of Archytas' account of sound up to this point. First, he has taken no explicit account of the medium through which sound travels. The closest he will come to doing so is in line 27, where, in discussing the analogy between sound and a missile, he talks of the air yielding to the missile to a greater or lesser degree, depending of the force with which it is hurled. He also discusses the breath that produces an impact, either in speaking or singing (lines 24 and 28) or in wind instruments (*auloi* or a reed – lines 32 and 40), but this breath is one of the bodies that collides with another body to produce an impact and not the medium through which sound is transmitted.

Second, Archytas has not so far and never does define what a sound is in Fragment 1. It is possible that he did so in material that has been lost, but the beginning of his account of acoustics, which is what we have in Fragment 1, is precisely where we would have expected such a definition. He has discussed the conditions under which a sound arises, i.e. when there is an impact of two bodies, but he has not described the nature of this sound which arises. His practice is simply to talk of a "sound" (φθόγγος, ἦχος) or "voice" (φωνή) without further definition. It is usual and reasonable, in light of the analogies that Archytas uses, to assume that he thinks of a sound as a missile of air (e.g. Barker 1989: 9) and that Plato is following

Archytas, when he says that sound is "a blow *of air*" on the brain and blood. Bowen (1982: 92) says that "sound is supervenient to the air that carries it" rather than being identified with the airy projectile, but I see no basis for this in the text of Archytas. It is precisely the relationship between sound and the medium, air, that Archytas does not analyze. According to Frank, Archytas thought that sound was incorporeal movement, not air that has been struck but the act of impact itself. Archytas was supposedly led by this basic insight about sound to a dynamic view of the world, in which body is a mere sense impression, which arises from the true realities which are ever changing motions (1923: 176). Archytas does not say, however, that sound is an incorporeal motion in Fragment 1 or even that it is an impact (πληγή). Archytas says that impact is necessary for a sound to arise, but this is not the same as saying that sound is an impact. The word motion (κίνασις) appears only once, in line 35, and it is there applied to the motion of the breath in wind instruments and does not figure in a definition of sound. Frank also tries to support his thesis on the basis of Plato's *Timaeus*, which he supposed to be influenced by Archytas, but again Plato does not simply define sound as an incorporeal blow but as a blow of air (ὑπ' ἀέρος 67b). Archytas' presentation of sound is in sharp contrast to Aristotle's subtle and nuanced discussion of both the medium of sound and the nature of sound itself (*De Anima* 419b ff.).

The evidence that Archytas goes on to provide for his theory of pitch is important for the study of the use of experiments by the early Greeks. Indeed acoustics and Pythagorean acoustics in particular is often singled out as the first area in which the Greeks carried out significant empirical research (Lloyd 1979: 144–45; Zhmud 1997: 187 ff.; Senn 1929). Most of what Archytas presents is drawn from everyday experience, including experience of missiles hurled in war and of bull-roarers whirled in religious ritual but also experience with singing and playing musical instruments. Scholars have rightly understood this evidence as more in the nature of illustrations than of experiments designed to test an hypothesis. Nonetheless, in several of the examples, it is quite possible to see Archytas as repeating what might first have been noticed in experience, in order to confirm an hypothesis (e.g. waving a stick at various speeds, shouting, whirling the bull-roarers). In his final example we might see him as actively changing lengths of reed in order to test his theory of pitch. There does not, however, seem to be a clear distinction made between experiment and simple observation or demonstration (Zhmud 1997: 200). Indeed, the simplicity and everyday nature of Archytas' examples are enough to make one doubt whether a systematic program of acoustic research going back to Pythagoras, such as is constructed by Zhmud, can really have existed.

If we compare Archytas' list of illustrations for his acoustic theory with other similar lists of experiments in the later tradition (e.g. Theon 59.3 ff. and 66.22; Ptol. *Harm.* 1. 8; Nicom. *Ench.* 6), some further interesting points emerge. First, two of Archytas' examples are unparalleled in the later tradition. No one else mentions the example of the waving stick or the *rhomboi* ("bull-roarers"). Second, a number of traditional experiments, including some assigned back to Pythagoras himself, do not appear in Archytas. Archytas says nothing about bronze discs, hammers, or vessels filled to various levels with liquid. Most strikingly of all he says nothing of experiments with strings. There are no weights hung from strings, no stringed instruments, and not a single string stretched over a ruler (*kanōn*). He does share with the later tradition an emphasis on experiments with wind instruments such as *auloi* and the reed or *kalamos*, which may be connected to the *syrinx* (see the commentary on line 38). Bowen (1982: 98) reasonably suggests that the emphasis on wind instruments might have its origin in Archytas' desire to explain vocal sound through its resemblance to such instruments. This does not explain, however, the puzzling absence of all mention of strings in Archytas' introductory account of sound and pitch. He may well have referred to examples derived from strings elsewhere in his *Harmonics*, but it is surprising that in this rather long list of examples to illustrate his theory of pitch strings are not mentioned.

Archytas' first illustration of and argument for his theory of pitch is that of a stick, which produces a high-pitched sound when moved swiftly and forcefully and a low-pitched sound when moved slowly and weakly. It isn't clear whether Archytas thinks of the stick as waved back and forth repeatedly or of a single stroke of the stick through the air (which is supported by the singular πλαγᾷ in line 21). It appears that Archytas is right to say that a stick moved quickly does produce a sound of a higher pitch than one moved slowly. It is his explanation of this phenomenon that is at fault. He evidently thinks of the stick as sending out missiles of air whose speeds depend on how swiftly the stick is moved, with the faster missiles perceived as higher-pitched sounds. The closest parallel elsewhere in the tradition of acoustic theory to Archytas' use of the stick as an example is perhaps Boethius' mention of someone waving his hand (*Inst. Mus.* 1. 3). It is important to note that, while in stating his theory of pitch in lines 18–20 Archytas referred to the speed with which sounds travel from the impact to our ears, his first example is stated in terms of the speed and force of the motion which generates the sound (i.e. the stick). He does not at this point try to show that the speed and force of the motion which generates the sound determines the speed and force with which the sound then travels (Bowen 1982: 89), but he will return to this connection below.

The next piece of evidence comes from speaking and singing. Whenever we want to say something loud and high pitched we speak with a violent (forceful) breath. It might be that Archytas has in mind the picture of a singer straining and applying force to hit a high note, but extra force is in fact also required to hit an especially low note. Note that Archytas does not distinguish between volume and pitch here. The violent breath leads both to a loud cry and a high-pitched one. In the case of the stick only pitch was mentioned and this new example supports it by showing that violent breath, just like the violent waving of the stick, produces a high-pitched sound, but now the sound is loud as well. This means that all and only high-pitched sounds will be loud. Plato (*Tim.* 67c), Aristotle (*Gen. An.* 786b ff.) and later authors in the Peripatetic tradition corrected Archytas on this point (Barker 1989: 41 n. 48; 61 n. 28) by separating volume from pitch.

Rather than introducing another example of sound, Archytas now tries to explain further the effect of speaking with a violent breath. He does this by introducing the analogy of shafts (βέλη) hurled or shot in war (e.g. arrows, javelins). Those that are hurled forcefully go far and those that are hurled weakly land near, since the air yields more to those moving forcefully and less to those travelling with little force. It would appear that the shaft corresponds to the sound, and the forceful throw that propels the shaft corresponds to the forceful breath that propels the sound. This analogy seems to apply primarily to the magnitude of the sound and only to pitch insofar as Archytas has equated high pitch with loud sound. The shaft that travels far is analogous to a sound that is loud and high pitched. We know that for a shaft to go far it must be hurled with force, so we understand that, in order to produce a loud sound, we must use a forceful breath. Although it is clear that the sound is compared to a missile, it is not made clear what sort of a missile sound is. Comparison with later accounts suggests (e.g. [Arist.] *Prob.* XI. 6) that it is probably to be understood as a missile of air, but it may be, as argued above, that Archytas simply leaves the physical nature of sound unanalyzed.

Archytas now returns from the missile analogy to the human voice. There is some repetition here. The voice was first considered in lines 23–24; the missile analogy is then introduced in lines 24–27 in order to help us understand the voice; Archytas rounds out the section by returning to the voice again in lines 27–31, so that the missile analogy is framed by discussions of the voice. In lines 23–24 Archytas only considered loud and high-pitched voices, while in lines 27–31 he also considers soft and low-pitched voices, so that he seems to be simply underlining the parallel between the missile analogy and the voice. Pitch is reintroduced as parallel to volume. The voice that is propelled by the strong breath is loud and high pitched and analogous to a missile hurled forcefully; that propelled by a weak breath is soft (small – μικκᾷ) and low pitched and analogous to a missile hurled less forcefully.

Archytas then presents what he says is the strongest evidence (ἰσχυροτάτῳ σαμείῳ – a play on words?) for "this." This evidence once again, as in the case of the missile, applies primarily to the volume of the sound rather than the pitch. When the same person speaks loudly we hear her from far off, but if she speaks softly not even when we are close by. The emphasis on "the same person" speaking seems to be an attempt to eliminate all other variables except the volume of the sound. Why is this "the strongest evidence"? What is special about this example? The example emphasizes the connection between shouting and our ability to hear the sound at a long distance. The preceding discussions of the voice (lines 23–24 and 27–29) talk solely in terms of pitch and volume and say nothing about the distance the voice travels. Lines 29–31, however, connect the force of the vocalization and the distance a sound travels. The missile analogy suggests that the distance a sound travels depends on the force of its movement, since the air yields more to something that is moving more forcefully (lines 24–27). So the example in lines 29–31 provides the "strongest evidence" for the thesis that the force used in producing a sound determines the force with which it travels. It is this thesis that cements the analogy between the missile and the voice. Archytas has now shown that the force of the impact which creates a sound determines the force with which it travels and hence the distance it travels. In modern terms, he has shown that the amplitude of a sound wave depends on the force of the blow creating the sound and that the larger the amplitude the further a sound will carry before being dampened by the medium. As noted above in the discussion of the example of the stick, it is precisely this connection between the force of the blow and the speed/force with which the sound travels that Archytas needed to demonstrate.

There is nothing here that supports the idea that a forceful breath always leads to a high-pitched sound, however. The mistaken connection of high pitch with great volume seems to have been most of all suggested by the stick example where forceful movement of the stick back and forth seems on the surface to produce both a loud and a high-pitched sound. Moreover, since the stick is moving rapidly, it is easy to make the mistaken assumption that the sound produced not only will be loud and carry far but also will move more rapidly than a sound created by a less forceful movement of the stick. This mistaken connection is then perhaps supported by the example of a singer straining for a high note where force again seems tied to high pitch and loud volume. Here common experiences should have shown Archytas that a low-pitched sound can also be loud and requires considerable force to sing.

Now for the first time (lines 31–34), Archytas draws an example from musical instruments. He appeals to experience with the *aulos*, a reed instrument comparable to a modern oboe with finger holes drilled into the pipe (Barker 1984: 14–15). *Auloi* are very commonly used as examples in Greek writings on acoustics (e.g. [Arist.] *Prob.* XIX. 23; See Barker 1989: 41 n. 50). The *aulos* is used to support only the point that pitch depends on the force of the breath, and, in this case, there is no mention of the magnitude of the sound (34–35 "quick motion makes a high sound and slow motion a low sound"). The point is that the breath which strikes the holes closer to the mouth will strike them with greater force and it is from these holes that the higher-pitched notes are produced. The breath will strike the holes further away from the mouth with less force, because of their distance from the mouth, and from these holes lower-pitched notes are produced. As in the case of the stick example, force and speed are equated. The breath gets to the holes closer to the mouth more quickly and more forcefully and thus produces higher-pitched sounds. Archytas then makes the same point with an example drawn from religious ritual. The *rhomboi* or "bull-roarers" were pieces of wood or metal whirled around at the end of strings to produce a whistling noise as part of certain rites (see the commentary ad loc.). Once again the point is made in terms of pitch alone; if they are whirled gently, they produce a low-pitched sound, but if forcefully, a high-pitched sound.

The final example once again comes from the realm of musical instruments. Archytas says that, if someone stops a reed at the lower end, he will produce a low-pitched note by blowing in it, whereas, if he stops it halfway up or at any other point, he will produce a high note. This procedure may be connected to the musical instrument known as the *syrinx*, one form of which is well known as the "Pan-pipe" (see the commentary on line 27). In this example Archytas emphasizes that the breath is the same, i.e. that we blow equally hard, and says that the movement of the breath will be weaker over a longer distance and stronger over a shorter distance, so that once again the breath traveling the shorter distance will produce the higher-pitched note. This is the first example in which Archytas refers to anything like precise measurements. He talks of "half or whatever other part," whereas previously the discussion had all been in general terms of what is stronger and weaker, nearer and farther.

At this point Porphyry breaks in and tells us that he is abridging his quotation from Archytas, before ending his quotation with two final lines in which he says Archytas "sums up his point as follows": "It has become clear to us from many things that high notes move more quickly and low ones more slowly." Two points should be emphasized here. First, in this summary sentence, Archytas states his thesis solely in terms of pitch, just as he first introduced the point solely in terms of pitch (lines 19–20), although in the intervening lines he has tied high pitch to loud volume. Second, Porphyry says that, in the material that he has not quoted (the material skipped between lines 41 and 42), Archytas "said other things about the movement of voice being according to intervals." Porphyry refers to "intervallic voice" in several other passages (6.23; 9.34–10.1 etc.) and this term is usually introduced as part of a distinction developed by Aristoxenus between "continuous" and "intervallic" movement of the voice (*El. Harm.* 1. 8.13 ff.). In the case of continuous movement, the voice is in constant motion and does not stop at any particular pitch. This movement is said to be characteristic of speech. In the case of intervallic movement, the voice comes to rest at one pitch and then another. This movement is characteristic of singing. Porphyry is then saying that, in the lines he has left out, Archytas described the voice as moving in intervals. But what is Archytas likely to have said on this topic?

In context Archytas' remarks would seem to need to be yet another in his list of examples which illustrate the thesis that high-pitched sounds are the result of vigorous motion and low-pitched the result of weak motion. This does not seem to be a very likely place to make a formal distinction between continuous and intervallic motion such as is found in Aristoxenus. The immediate context has, in fact, shown that the *aulos* and the reed do produce sound in an intervallic manner: If the *kalamos* is stopped half way up, it produces a sound higher than if stopped at the bottom. It is not explicitly stated but clear to any student of Greek harmonics that the first note will be the interval of an octave higher than the latter. Thus, the natural thing for Archytas to go on to say about the voice is that it behaves in the same way as the *aulos* and the *kalamos*. That Archytas might have done just this is strikingly confirmed by the chapter of Ptolemy's *Harmonics* on which Porphyry is commenting, when he quotes Fragment 1. In that chapter (1. 3; p. 9.2 Düring), Ptolemy makes the exact same point about the *aulos* that Archytas has made in lines 31–35. He then immediately turns to vocal sound and says that, in this case, the windpipe serves as a sort of natural *aulos* (αὐλῷ γάρ τινι φυσικῷ 9.6 Düring). The pitch of vocal sounds is then described as differing depending on the distance between the position on the windpipe where the sound originates and the outside air which is struck (see Barker 1989: 282 n. 35). I suggest, then, that Archytas also drew a parallel between the *aulos* (or the reed) and the voice and described the movement of the voice as intervallic, insofar as it behaves in the same way as the movement of the sound of the *aulos*, where the pitch depends on distances between the striking force (breath) and the thing struck, the hole. There is no way of knowing exactly how Archytas formulated the point, and it is not likely that it was expressed in just the same way as in Ptolemy. We can imagine, however, that he would have emphasized that high notes occur because the breath originates in the upper part of the windpipe and thus strikes the outside air with great force, while a lower note originates lower in the windpipe and thus strikes the external air with less force.

If we look back over Archytas' presentation of basic acoustic theory in Fragment 1, it is clear that he had an enduring influence on Greek writings on acoustics but also that there is much in his account that is peculiar to him or that was modified or added in the later tradition. Peculiar to Archytas are his treatment of colliding bodies, his discussion of sounds that we do not hear, the stick and bull-roarer examples, and his mistaken connection between volume and pitch. The later tradition universally corrected Archytas on this latter point, introduced an emphasis on the need for motion at the beginning of the account of sound (see especially *Sect. Can.* 148–49), and most importantly placed examples of vibrating strings, which are absent from Fragment 1 of Archytas, in the forefront. Despite all of these differences, there is a basic pattern in Archytas' presentation that is preserved in the later tradition (Ptol. *Harm.* 1. 3; Aelian [Por. *In Ptol.* 33.16 ff.]; Adrastus or Theon [Theon 50.4 ff. and 60.13 ff.]; Nicom. *Ench.* 4 and 10; Boethius *Inst. Mus.* 1. 3). This pattern had three elements: (1) the thesis that a blow is necessary for sound, (2) some sort of connection between the speed or force of the blow and pitch, (3) the use of the examples of *auloi* and reeds (or *syringes*) to emphasize the importance of the distance between the striker and the thing struck in determining pitch. Ptolemy evidently followed Archytas in comparing the voice to an *aulos*.

There have been a great variety of assessments of the organization and style of Archytas' presentation in Fragment 1. Van der Waerden complained of the "unbearable prolixity" and "lack of clearness, not to say confusion" (1963: 152) and Burkert too found aspects of the fragment "allusive" and unclear (1972a: 380 n. 46). Bowen argues that Archytas "articulates a definite and coherent view of how sound propagates" but admits that "the style is more 'literary' than one would expect" (1982: 98). It is crucial to recognize that both Burkert and van der Waerden were working with the text in DK, which includes unwarranted repetition and obscurity in the first six lines. Once the textual problems are resolved, a number of the reasons for their complaints are removed. The confusions in the theory of pitch and volume, despite Bowen's protestations, do produce some lack of clarity in presentation of the second part of the fragment and the series of illustrative examples is infected with this lack of clarity as well as having some repetition. Similarly the concept of sound is not defined and the medium of sound is left largely unexamined. On the other hand, there is no real confusion about what the central theses of the fragment are.

Even more importantly there is a clear and logical structure to the presentation at the macro level. This structure becomes clear once we recognize Archytas' model of science as starting from distinctions about wholes and moving to distinctions about individual phenomena (see the overview of Archytas' philosophy). Archytas is in fact presenting an elements of music, although his elementalizing differs considerably from that suggested by Bowen (1982: 87–88). After a proem praising the method of the sciences in general and introducing music in particular, Archytas applies that method to harmonics. He focuses on sound as the whole on which harmonics focuses, identifies an impact as necessary for any sound to arise, discusses the conditions under which impacts arise, distinguishes two classes of sounds (audible and inaudible), considers the cases in which sounds are inaudible, turns to sounds that we do hear, presents a thesis about the factors that govern their two main characteristics, pitch and volume, and then provides a series of illustrative examples.

It is important to note that, while Archytas certainly implies that sound is quantitative in the examples of the *aulos* and reed, he gives no explicit argument for the quantitative nature of sound in Fragment 1 such as we find e.g. in *Sect. Can.* 149, Nicom. *Harm.* 4, Ptol. *Harm.* 1. 3 (both Barker 1989: 281 n. 30 and Bowen 1982: 94 and 97 suggest that he does). It is quite possible, however, that he went on to argue explicitly for the quantitative nature of sound in a later section of the *Harmonics*. Ptolemy built the quantity/quality controversy into his discussion from the beginning (1. 3). Nicomachus' *Handbook* (4), however, makes the point that pitch "comes about in relation to quantity" and is "ordered according to number" at exactly the point where Fragment 1 of Archytas breaks off, after the initial statement of the thesis about pitch and the illustrative examples. So it is not at all unlikely that Archytas went on explicitly to connect quantity and number with pitch. The acoustical physics that he has developed is certainly suited to such a development (Bowen 1982: 96). We do not know with certainty what the rest of Archytas' *Harmonics* contained, but I have provided an account of its likely contents in the overview of Archytas' philosophy.

Detailed commentary

Line 1 δοκοῦντι – This is the normal Attic contraction. In Doric we might expect δοκέοντι which is read by Blass. For the text and dialect of the fragment see the preface.

τοί – This is the standard Doric form of the article in the nominative plural masculine (Buck 1955: 100). It appears in most manuscripts of Porphyry and half the manuscripts of Nicomachus, although Hoche did not read it in his text of Nicomachus. It is much more likely that this unusual form fell out of the text in transmission (the apparatus shows the confusion that arose in transmission) than that it was added, and τοί should be read in the text of both Porphyry and in Nicomachus. For the idiom τοί περὶ τὰ μαθήματα ("those concerned with the sciences" or "the experts in the sciences") see Plato, *Phd.* 69c8 οἱ περὶ τὰς τελετάς ("those concerned with the initiations") and Aristotle, *Pol.* 1342b23 τῶν περὶ τὴν μουσικήν ("those concerned with music").

διαγνῶμεν – The manuscripts of Porphyry read the typical Attic infinitive form διαγνῶναι. διαγνώμεναι, which is found in the manuscripts of Nicomachus, is adopted by DK and is the *lectio difficilior*, but it is problematic. It is in fact an epic and Lesbian form, while the normal Doric form is διαγνῶμεν, which is what Blass prints. Cassio (1988) argues persuasively that Nicomachus has a tendency to attribute poetic forms to Pythagorean writers on the mistaken assumption that they are the proper Doric forms and that the normal Doric form is what Archytas wrote in this case. Wackernagel (1914: 102 n. 1) had earlier explained the ending -μεναι, by suggesting that the normal Attic ending, -ναι, might have been written over the Doric form (διαγνῶμεν), in order to explain it and then worked its way into the text. Similarly, the Doric ending, -μεν, might have been written over the Attic infinitive form (διαγνῶναι) as a correction and then entered the text.

One of the unusual things about Fragment 1 is its epistemological vocabulary. διαγιγνώσκω and its cognate noun διάγνωσις occur three times in the first five lines. Moreover, it seems to be used to designate the type of epistemological activity that Archytas most wants to commend and that he regards as characteristic of the sciences (see the overview of Archytas' philosophy). Of course διαγιγνώσκω is a relatively common verb in Greek with the meaning "to distinguish one thing from another" or "to discern." In political and judicial contexts, it comes to mean "to decide," since decisions are usually based on distinctions (e.g. between the innocent and the guilty). The emphatic position of διαγιγνώσκω in Fragment 1, however, is unparalleled in a philosophical text and only finds a real parallel in the Hippocratic corpus (see below).

The noun and verb only appear once each in the Presocratics. According to Aristotle, Heraclitus said that, if all things turned to smoke, the nostrils would "distinguish" (διαγνοῖεν) things (from one another). It is not completely clear, however, if the use of διαγιγνώσκω here belongs to Heraclitus or to Aristotle (*De Sensu* v. 443a23 = Fr. 7). In Fragment 226, Democritus asserts that free speech is characteristic of freedom but that the discernment (διάγνωσις) of the right time (to speak) is a risky business. In Thucydides the verb is applied both to political officials and to the people as a whole as deciding legal cases and as making political decisions, but it also has the meaning of "discern" or "distinguish." Thus, on the occasion of an important vote, a Spartan ephor is unable to discern on which side the shout was louder (1. 87.2.2). When some people chided the Spartans captured at Plataea by suggesting that the real Spartans died in the battle, one of them responded that arrows would be worth a lot if they could "distinguish" the brave (IV. 40.2.6). In the next century Isocrates refers to Paris' difficulty in making a distinction as to which of the three goddesses was most beautiful (*Helen* 42.3).

While διαγιγνώσκω is not a technical term for Plato, he uses it fairly frequently and especially in contexts where an expert is called upon to use his expert knowledge to determine/distinguish/discriminate whether something is done well or badly in his field of expertise. Thus Socrates asks Ion whether it belongs to the art of the doctor to distinguish well whether Homer speaks correctly in a passage dealing with medicine (*Ion* 538c5). In the *Theaetetus* (150b2), the verb is used in the comparison between Socrates and the midwife as those who can distinguish between true and false offspring. Aristotle uses both the verb and noun very infrequently, but, interestingly enough, one of its few uses is in the passage in the *De Caelo* (290b28), where he is discussing the Pythagorean theory of the harmony of the spheres. The Pythagoreans explain our inability to hear the music of the spheres as resulting from our having heard the sound from birth, for they say that the discrimination (διάγνωσιν) of voice and silence is by contrast with one another.

The most important set of texts in which the verb is used comes from the Hippocratic corpus. There are around fifty uses of the verb and its cognate noun in the corpus. The primary meaning once again is "to distinguish" two things, usually in the context of a certain expertise. In *Airs, Waters and Places* (10.1) it is a matter of distinguishing whether the year will be healthy or unhealthy, and in *Regimen in Acute Diseases* (11.66, 11.84) it is crucial "to distinguish" the types of weakness in disease, whether the weakness arises from starving or pain etc. Again in *Wounds of the Head* instructions are given as to how to distinguish the one who is going to die and foretell what is going to happen (19.13). In *The Nature of Man* one must make the distinction between diseases that arise from regimen and those that arise from air. Of course diagnosis is a common medical term in the modern world as well, but the term has a much broader sense in the ancient texts and is not limited to distinguishing which disease the patient is suffering from.

Two passages from the Hippocratic corpus are particularly interesting, in that they treat making distinctions as a central intellectual activity and connect it to knowledge of parts and wholes, just as Archytas does in Fragment 1. In *Regimen* 1. 2 the author sets out the proper method for the treatment of human regimen and διαγιγνώσκειν appears as a central concept right from the beginning:

I say that he who is going to write correctly about human regimen must first know and distinguish (διαγνῶναι) the nature of man as a whole. He must know from what things it was constituted to begin with and distinguish (διαγνῶναι) by which parts it is controlled.

The author then lists a great number of things that the doctor must know and distinguish. It is interesting, in light of Archytas Fragment 1, that the risings and settings of stars are included. Again at *Epidemics* 1. 23 when the author stops to state his methodology the verb διαγιγνώσκειν appears prominently:

The following were the circumstances attending the diseases, from which I made my determinations (διεγινώσκομεν), having learned both from the common nature of all and from the particular nature of the individual: from the disease, the patient, the regimen prescribed . . .

He goes on to list a great number of factors that he uses in his determinations. There are two crucial things about these passages in *Regimen* and *Epidemics*: first, they provide a clear parallel for Archytas' use of διαγιγνώσκειν as a central epistemological term and thus suggest a possible connection between Archytas' view of the sciences and Hippocratic medicine; second, they are both also tied to Archytas Fragment 1 by a methodology that emphasizes the need to study both the whole and the part in order to make proper distinctions. *Epidemics* refers to "the common nature of all" and "the particular nature of each" whereas *Regimen* talks of "the nature of man as a whole" and "the parts by which it is controlled." Since we have no reliable evidence which attests to any work in medicine by Archytas, it may be surprising that his conception of science shows the influence of the Hippocratic tradition. We should remember, however, that Archytas' predecessor and possible teacher, Philolaus, had a developed medical theory (Huffman 1993: 289 ff.). Since the dates of *On Regimen* and *Epidemics* I are so uncertain, it is also not beyond the realm of possibility that it was Archytas who influenced these texts.

2 αὐτούς – Blass prints the regular Doric accusative plural masculine ending -ως here and consistently throughout the fragment. The manuscripts usually have the Attic -ους but see τὼς μεγάλως in line 16.

οἶά ἐντι – Plato frequently uses this expression to identify the real nature of something as opposed to the way it appears. Thus at *Republic* 598a Socrates first asks if the painter imitates the works of the craftsman. Having secured agreement here, he then asks whether the painter imitates these works "as they really are or as they appear "(οἶα ἔστιν ἢ οἶα φαίνεται). In some cases this expression may indicate a reference to the form (e.g. *R.* 472c). In other cases, however, forms are clearly not involved. Thus at *Apology* 19a Socrates says that he knows that it will be difficult to overcome the slander, which has long been circulated against him, and that he is not unaware of the "true nature" (οἶόν ἐστιν) of his task. The phrase is also found a number of times in Aristotle (e.g. *EN* 1116b8 and *Metaph.* 1024b22). In Fragment 10 Democritus says that it has been made clear that "in reality (ἐτεῆ) we do not grasp each thing such as it is or is not" (οἶον ἕκαστον ἔστιν ἢ οὐκ ἔστιν, see also Fr. 8). Archytas' usage is thus in accord with the philosophical vocabulary of the late fifth and early fourth centuries. His use of οἶά ἐντι does not commit him to any particular philosophical position other than a general recognition that there can, in at least some cases, be a tension between the way things appear and the way they really are. Such a recognition can already be found in Archytas' predecessor Philolaus, Fragment 5 (Huffman 1993), and is evident in Archytas' own account of concordance (A18) and indeed in his recognition here in Fragment 1 that some sounds cannot be heard because of the nature of our senses (line 13). Certainly there need be no reference to Platonic forms here, since οἶά ἐστι does not always imply reference to a form even in Plato. Archytas is thus saying that those concerned with the sciences have a correct understanding of individual things "as they are" or of "the true nature" of each thing, rather than just a familiarity with the way things appear.

ἑκάστου – This is the reading of virtually all the manuscripts of both Nicomachus and Porphyry. DK follow Blass in printing ἑκάστων which is found in no manuscript. The motivation for this latter reading appears to be to secure agreement with the plural οἶά ἐντι. LSJ s.v. gives a number of examples, however, where ἕκαστος in the singular is used in apposition to plural nouns, so that it seems well within typical Greek usage to follow the manuscripts and print ἑκάστου.

φρονέν – I have followed Blass (1884) in restoring the normal Doric infinitive form for the Attic φρονεῖν (see Buck 1955: 122). Nicomachus followed by DK reads φρονέειν, which is epic and quite unlikely to be what Archytas wrote but may represent what Nicomachus thought Archytas should have written (Cassio 1988). Porphyry has θεωρεῖν which Bowen (1982) prints. Both verbs will work in context and both are possible at Archytas' date. θεωρέω is a much more common verb than φρονέω, however, in both Porphyry's *Commentary on the Harmonics of Ptolemy* and Nicomachus' *Introduction to Arithmetic*; φρονέω is, in fact, very rare in both texts, appearing just once in Porphyry and only once in Hoche's word index to Nicomachus. It is thus much more likely that θεωρεῖν replaced φρονέειν in the text of Porphyry than that the reverse happened in Nicomachus.

φρονεῖν usually indicates intelligent awareness in general, although in Aristotle it came to have the narrower sense of "practical intelligence" (Irwin 1985: 411). Von Fritz (in Mourelatos 1993: 84) argues that in the late fifth century νοεῖν and φρονεῖν were synonyms and "covered any intellectual function that was not sense perception in the narrowest sense of the word." It is thus translated in a wide variety of ways: to think, to understand, to be intelligent, to be wise. Since there is an emphasis on the "real nature" (οἷά ἐντι) of something in the context in Archytas, it is best to understand the phrase to mean "to grasp correctly with the intelligence" or "have correct understanding."

4 ὀψεῖσθαι – The Doric future (Buck 1955: 115). Here and elsewhere Blass gives η for the ει that is the result of contraction.

περί τε δὴ τᾶς τῶν ἄστρων ταχυτᾶτος . . . – Porphyry and Nicomachus diverge radically in the text of this list of sciences. DK prints a strange amalgam of the two texts. In the discussion of the context of Fragment 1 given above, I argue that Nicomachus has rewritten the passage in his own terminology and that we should accept Porphyry's text. I follow Bowen, however, in adding the adjective σαφῆ from Nicomachus' text in order to further characterize διάγνωσιν, since to say simply that "they handed down discernment to us" rather than "clear discernment" seems hopelessly flat. In lines 1–3, moreover, Archytas repeatedly uses an adverb with the verbs διαγιγνώσκω and φρονέω in order to further define them (καλῶς is used three times and ὀρθῶς once), so that it would be odd to leave διάγνωσιν unqualified here.

5 ἁμῖν – This is what Porphyry gives us, but the more normal Doric is ἁμίν (Buck 1955: 98), which Blass prints.

6 μωσικᾶς – This is the reading of a few of the manuscripts of Nicomachus and is printed by DK and Blass. Since it is the *lectio difficilior* and more likely to be the Doric form (LSJ s.v.), it is to be preferred to μουσικᾶς which is found in Porphyry.

7 εἶμεν – The Doric form is εἶμεν or ἦμεν (Buck 1955: 128). Düring reads ἦμεν throughout the fragment, but this appears to be based on his mistaken report of the readings of the manuscripts. He reports εἶμεν only for g, but, in reality, all five major manuscripts (METV¹⁸⁷G) read εἶμεν throughout the fragment except at 57.11 where E and V¹⁸⁷ seem to have ἦμεν, although the reading is not perfectly clear.

ἀδελφεά – Attic has ἀδελφός, -ή, -όν but other dialects, including Doric have ἀδελφεός, -ά, -όν (Buck 1955: 132; LSJ ἀδελφός and ἀδελφή). The adjective seems to mean primarily "kindred" in Plato. At *Phaedo* 108b it appears twice, once of people who engage in killings or "other such things which are kindred of these" and once of the "deeds of kindred souls." See also *Phaedrus* 276 d and Sophocles, *Antigone* 192.

6–7 ταῦτα γὰρ τὰ μαθήματα δοκοῦντι εἶμεν ἀδελφεά – Immediately following this statement of the kindred nature of the sciences, the text of Nicomachus has another short sentence that explains why the sciences are kindred: περὶ γὰρ ἀδελφεὰ τὰ τοῦ ὄντος πρώτιστα δύο εἴδεα τὰν ἀναστροφὰν ἔχει ("For they are concerned with the first two forms of being which are akin"). This sentence is not found in Porphyry but has been included in the text of DK and appears in all translations. I first argued that the sentence is, in fact, a remark of Nicomachus' and should be excluded from the text, in Huffman 1985. I have argued even more extensively for this position in the section on the context of Fragment 1 above. Since the line appears in one of our sources and not in the other, the onus of proof seems to be equally divided between those who would include it and those who would exclude it. Close examination of the sentence shows that the arguments are overwhelmingly in favor of excluding it and following Porphyry's text. Briefly put, the reasons for excluding the sentence are (1) it does not appear in Porphyry who provides the whole text of Fragment 1 (43 lines to Nicomachus' 7) and who is generally accurate in his quotations; (2) it would be the last line in Nicomachus' quotation of the fragment and Nicomachus has a practice of offering explanatory comments on quotations and of failing to make clear where quotations end; (3) the content of the sentence, especially the reference to "the first two forms of being," has no clear meaning in Archytas but matches almost exactly the terminology and concepts that Nicomachus himself uses in the immediately preceding and following passages; (4) the grammar of the sentence diverges from the immediately preceding one, which suggests a different author (the use of the singular rather than the plural with a neuter plural subject), and some features of the language suggest Nicomachus' date rather than Archytas' (ἀναστροφάν). The only reason for hesitation in excluding the sentence is that it does have some Doric forms. I think that this can be explained in terms of the transmission of the manuscripts (see on the context of the fragment above).

Barker (1989: 40 n. 44), in partial response to point 3 above and in light of *Republic* 530, suggests that for Archytas the two primary forms of being might be the visible and the audible. This is a plausible conjecture, although Barker himself notes that it leads to an awkward scheme in which geometry and astronomy are tied to the visible (we might, however, argue that astronomy is also connected to the audible), music to the audible, and arithmetic to both. But it is precisely a conjecture; there is no evidence elsewhere in the testimonia or fragments of Archytas to support it. It would be very awkward, moreover, for Archytas to use a phrase like "the two primary forms of being" without further explanation and, since Fragment 1 was the beginning of his book, there is no place for him to have provided such explanation (Bowen 1982: 85–86 suggests that the phrase "the two primary forms of being" is to be understood as the thesis that "all things are number," but then there would only be one primary form of being). On the other hand, the distinction between two primary forms of being, magnitude and multitude, is the central theme in Nicomachus' *Introduction to Arithmetic*, in the pages leading up to the quotation of Fragment 1. When we find that this sentence, which makes perfect sense in its context in Nicomachus as a piece of Nicomachean metaphysics and which is at the least very obscure, if assigned to Archytas, does not appear in our other witness to the text, surely it is straining our credulity to suppose that Archytas just happened to have a metaphysics involving two primary forms of being as did Nicomachus and that the sentence in which he alluded to this metaphysics just happened to be preserved only by Nicomachus and not Porphyry.

7 πρᾶτον – This is the normal Doric form.

8 ψόφον – ψόφος means "a noise" or "sound." Plato talks of the "sound of the winds" at *R.* 397a, and it is also used of footsteps and knocking at the door (see LSJ s.v.). Aristotle makes a clear distinction between ψόφος as a sound and φωνή ("voice") as a ψόφος that means something (*De An.* 420b33). The context certainly suggests that for Archytas too ψόφος is a general word for "sound" or "noise."

ποτί – This is the usual west Greek for πρός (Buck 1955: 108).

9 ὅκκα – This is west Greek (ὅκα κα) for ὅτε ἄν (Buck 1955: 104).

ἀπαντιάξαντα – ἀπαντιάζω appears only here and in the next line, before the sixth century AD. After that it appears once in Procopius (*De Bellis* VII. 13.16.3) and once in Michael Psellus (*Chronographia* V. 31.10). But there is no problem about the meaning. The meaning of "to meet," which we would expect from the similarity to ἀπαντάω, works well in the context.

10 συμπέτη – ἔπετον is the Doric second aorist of πίπτω. συμπίπτω seems to have its basic meaning of "meet violently," "fall together" or "collide" here and refers to the actual contact of the two moving objects, whereas ἀπαντιάζω seems to refer to their entering into the same vicinity with each other. We can "meet" someone without literally bumping into them. A good parallel is a description of the formation of hail found in Antiphon (DK87 B29) where actual collision is emphasized: "whichever of the colliding factors (τῶν ξυμπιπτόντων) is overpowered, is condensed and compressed" (tr. Freeman 1948; see also Empedocles DK31 B59, Plato, *Lg.* 889b and Democritus DK68 A43 and 57). Archytas uses the verb in another sense ("happen," "turn out to be") in Fragment 2. Both ἀπαντιάζω (ἀπαντιάω) and συμπίπτω take a dative, and ἀλλάλοις, which is positioned between them, is probably to be understood as going with both of them. The exact same sort of construction is found in the next line where αὐτὰ αὐτοῖς is framed by ἀπαντιάζοντα and συγχαλᾶντα and goes with both of them.

11 συγχαλᾶντα – συγχαλάω is a *hapax legomenon*. χαλάω has both a transitive sense ("slacken," "loosen") and an intransitive sense ("become slack" or "become loose"). With the dative it can mean to yield or give way to someone, and this sense would work well here: "Objects that move in opposite directions meet and give way to one another" (or "are slowed by one another"). The συν- prefix emphasizes that the slowing down is mutual, that the objects slow down "with" one another ("themselves with themselves"). Düring's report of the manuscripts as reading συγχαλᾶντα is wrong. The five major manuscripts all clearly read the infinitive συγχαλᾶν followed by a stop and then τά going with the following δ'. Nonetheless, Diels' συγχαλᾶντα, τά is preferable, because, on the manuscript reading, there is no mention of a sound resulting from the impact of the bodies moving in opposite directions; they are simply said to slow each other down. Diels' reading takes ποιεῖν ψόφον in lines 12–13 as going with both the μέν and the δέ clause.

12 περικαταλαμβανόμενα – περικαταλαμβάνω appears first elsewhere in Theophrastus (*HP* IV. 2.5) and in the Aristotelian *Problems*. At *Problems* 946b39 it refers to clouds "hemmed in" by the mountains and hence condensed. In *De Mundo* (400b1) it refers to people "overtaken" by a stream of lava. This latter meaning, "overtaken," fits best in the context in Archytas. The manuscripts have περὶ τῶν ἐπιφερομένων which yields no sense and Stephanus' correction to παρὰ τῶν ἐπιφερομένων (overtaken "by the ones rushing upon them") should be accepted, but παρά is still somewhat awkward.

16 παραδύεσθαι – This verb is used at *Iliad* XXIII. 416 during the chariot race at the funeral games for Patroklos. Antilochus says that he will "get by" Menelaus in a narrow part of the course. Again in the *Republic* during the discussion of dangerous modes of music, which should not be allowed into their state, Socrates says that the guardians must build their guard-house here, since this sort of lawlessness "creeps in" or "insinuates itself" unnoticed (424d cf. Arist. *Pol.* 1307b32). It thus appears that the prefix παρα- implies "getting by" something where the path is guarded or narrow. Archytas' use of the verb is appropriate in suggesting that large sounds are not able to "get by" the narrow opening of the ear.

17 σύστομα – This is a rare word that led to confusion in the manuscript tradition, as is clear from the apparatus. It does appear in Aristotle's *Parts of Animals* (662a24) where it refers to some animals having a mouth that is "more contracted" (συστομώτερα), while others have a wider mouth (μεγαλόστομα), which can be used in self-defence.

τευχέων – This word clearly has the meaning "vessels" here, which is rare in prose. It is never used this way in Plato or Aristotle, but it does appear in Xenophon of a jar (*An.* v. 4.28) and in the Hippocratic corpus (*Loc. Hom.* 24) of the "vessels" of the body.

17–18 ἐκχέῃ . . . ἐγχεῖται – Düring's misreporting of the manuscripts has led to lots of confusion here. The reading that I print is the reading of most of the manuscripts at 81.11 (METV[187]). ἐκχέῃ . . . ἐκχεῖται, which is what Düring prints, only appears in manuscript G at 81.11. DK print ἐγχέῃ ... ἐγχεῖται which is the reading of all manuscripts at 56.21. It seems more probable that the differing prefixes ἐκ-/ἐγ would be made the same in the course of transmission than that identical prefixes would be differentiated. Moreover, on the reading of DK, there is a certain lack of logic in talking about someone "pouring in a lot" (πολύ τις ἐγχέῃ), when the point is that nothing is poured in. The force of the reading which I have adopted is in the contrast between "a lot out" and "nothing in." On Düring's reading, the last statement, that "nothing is poured out" makes no sense, since clearly we are assuming that a great amount is poured out.

Some scholars have assumed that Archytas is comparing sound to a liquid here (Bowen 1982: 89; Lloyd 1979: 145 n. 99). However, ἐγχέω can also be used of solids. At Homer, *Od.* 11. 354 it is used of barley meal poured into bags. The analogy, whether it is thought of in terms of liquids or solids, does suggest that Archytas thought of sound as a physical substance that traveled from place to place by locomotion.

20 ἀσθενέως – Düring's apparatus led to confusion here and in lines 21, 26 and 27. As Düring reports, ἀσθενῶς is the reading of all five primary manuscripts in line 20, while in line 21 all the manuscripts give ἀσθενέως. Düring, however, does not report the variants in lines 26 and 27. Three manuscripts give ἀσθενέως in both lines 26 and 27. Since ἀσθενέως is more typical of Doric and since it is read by the majority of manuscripts in three of its four occurrences, it seems best to read ἀσθενέως in all four instances. It is hard to see why Archytas would have used one form in three places and the other in the fourth.

ῥάβδον – In the *Odyssey* (x. 238) Circe's ῥάβδος is her magic wand with which she turns men into pigs, but the word clearly has the general meaning of stick or rod, which can be used for a number of different purposes. It appears three times in Plato, once in reference to a fishing rod (*Soph.* 221a) and twice as a rod used for punishing people, particularly the young (*Lg.* 700c; *Ax.* 367a). Eudemus does use it to refer to a stick held by a teacher as he talked and perhaps used to swat inattentive students (Fr. 88 = Simpl. *In Phys.* 732. 31–32). Archytas seems to be fond of ῥάβδοι as one appears again in A24, in his famous demonstration that the universe is unlimited in extent.

23 ἁμές – This is the correct accentuation of the Doric form (Buck 1955: 98). Düring reported all manuscripts as having ἄμμες, which is a Lesbian form, whereas only G in fact reads it. The other manuscripts have ἄμες and ἄμε which clearly reflect the correct Doric form.

24 φθεγγόμενοι – The syntax of the sentence that ends here is not as smooth as one would like, but the sentence is coherent nonetheless, and there is no reason to resort to Blass' extensive supplement nor to posit a lacuna as in DK. The meaning is "not only would we recognize ['it'] (an object must be supplied = 'the truth that swift and forceful motion produces a high-pitched sound') by this [previous example] but also, whenever in speaking or in singing we wish to voice something loud and high-pitched." At this point we have a complete sentence, but Archytas introduces a subordinate clause with a circumstantial participle, in order to make clear how this example is parallel to the previous example of the stick: "since we speak with a forceful breath."

ἔτι δὲ καὶ – For this combination see Thucydides 1. 80. Archidamos, the Spartan king, is explaining why the Athenians are a different sort of opponent than the Spartans are used to. He points out that the Athenians live far away, are experienced on the sea, have great wealth, and have a population greater than any other Greek state at the time. As a climax he adds "but further they also (ἔτι δὲ καὶ) have many allies who are subject to tribute." Archytas has illustrated his point about pitch first with the example of the stick, then with the example of the voice, and now further supports the point by drawing an analogy with missiles.

29 and 31 μικκᾷ . . . μικκὸν – This typical Doric form should be read in both lines. Düring's text is misleading on line 21 (57.9), since he prints μικρᾷ as if it were the reading of all manuscripts, yet only G has this reading. All the rest have μικκᾷ.

34 ἆχον – ἦχος is a later form of ἠχή. It appears in the *Problems*, which are the work of Aristotle's school, and in the *De Audibilibus*, which may or may not be by Aristotle (Barker 1989: 98). Archytas' use of the masculine is thus the earliest on record. Archytas seems to be using it as a simple synonym for ψόφος, which has been his general word for sound up to this point.

36 ῥόμβοις – A ῥόμβος ("bull-roarer") is defined as "a piece of wood attached to a cord which was spun around in the mysteries in order to make a whistling sound" (sch. Clem. Al. *Protr.* 2.17.2). See also the scholion to Athenaeus 525e (Loeb Vol. v p. 370, n. 2); Barker 1989: 41 n. 51; West 1992: 122; and Mathiesen 1999: 172–73. It is mentioned in Euripides' *Helen* (1362) in association with the rites of the Great Mother. In Theocritus (2.30) it is made of bronze and associated with Aphrodite, and at *A.P.* vi. 165 it is used in Dionysiac mysteries. For its use in Orphic initiations see West 1983:

157. Gow has a good note and pictures of ῥόμβοι in an appendix (1952:
II. 44 and Plate 5). Bowen suggests that the ῥόμβος may have been used
in religious rituals important to the Pythagoreans (1982: 91), but it could
just as well be that Archytas had seen or heard of it used in rituals that had
no special tie to Pythagoreanism. We know that there was an important
cult of Aphrodite, who is associated with the ῥόμβος, in Tarentum, but
there is little evidence that Aphrodite was a particularly important deity
for the Pythagoreans. Nothing in Fragment 1 justifies Smith's conclusion
that Archytas was a devotee of Orphic initiations (1976: 134 etc.). The bull-
roarer was also used as a toy and would have thus been easily available for
detailed study (*AP* vi. 309). Other evidence suggests that Archytas had an
interest in toys (A10).

38 κάλαμος – This word has the general meaning of "reed" but acquires
a series of special meanings depending on what the reed is used for. Here it
refers to a reed used to produce music as in a reed pipe (Pi. *O.* 10.84). The
syrinx was a kind of pipe made up of one (called *monokalamos*) or many
(called *polykalamos* and familiar as the "Pan pipe") such reeds (Barker 1984:
16; 1989: 462 n. 24). The *monokalamos syrinx* had finger holes in the side
and the *polykalamos* had the different reeds tuned by being filled with wax
to various levels. The *syrinx*, however, had no mouthpiece and was usually
played by blowing across the opening of the reed, whereas Archytas talks of
blowing into the reed and of the breath as traversing the various distances
(τόπω line 40) in the reed. But Archytas may have thought that, when
one blew across the opening of a pipe, the breath still entered the reed,
reflected off the wax used to block the reed, and came back out (see the
commentary on A19a, line 3). Barker suggests that Archytas is referring to
experiments with just one pipe here (1989: 42 n. 52), but the language is
loose enough that he might have been thinking of a Pan pipe with multiple
reeds, stopped at different lengths with wax.

αἴ κά τις – Note that Buck (1955: 140) says that the typical west Greek
order would be αἴ τίς κα.

ἀποφράξας – This verb appears mainly in technical contexts in works
such as the Hippocratic corpus, Plato's *Timaeus* (91c), and in the Aristotelian *Problems* (870a10) and often refers to passages in the body being
"blocked."

ἐμφυσῇ – ἐμφυσάω is a comparatively rare verb that is mainly attested in
technical scientific contexts. It does not appear in Plato. It appears several
times in Aristotle's biological works and in the Aristotelian *Problems* with
the meaning "inflate" or "distend." In Archytas the meaning is clearly "blow

into" and the best parallel for this is Aristophanes' *Wasps* 1219, where it refers to the flute girl having blown into the flute.

42 φθόγγοι – Archytas began his discussion of sound by using exclusively the word ψόφος (lines 8, 13, 17, 21). He then introduces the word φωνή with reference to the human voice (27) and comes back to it, when discussing the reed (39). In between these two uses of φωνή he uses ἦχος to describe the sound of the *aulos* and of the bull-roarer (34, 35, 37). Thus it is a bit surprising to have φθόγγος appear here for the first time in the sentence that summarizes the whole passage. φθόγγος does acquire the specialized meaning "note" but is also commonly used to mean simply "sound." Since Archytas' discussion has moved from general acoustic principles to a series of examples drawn from music, he may have unconsciously moved to a term which has more musical connotations but he may also use φθόγγος simply for variety of expression.

CHAPTER II

Fragment 2

Porphyry, *On Ptolemy's Harmonics* 1. 5 (Düring 92.9–94.28)

ὅτι μὲν οὖν διαφέρει λόγος ὑπεροχῆς δῆλον. ὅτι δ᾽ ὁ λόγος καὶ ἡ σχέσις τῶν πρὸς ἄλληλα συμβλητῶν ὅρων καλεῖται καὶ διάστημα, παραστήσομεν. . . . (92.25) ἀλλὰ καὶ Δημήτριος . . . κατὰ τοῦ αὐτοῦ τὸ διάστημα τῷ λόγῳ τίθεται, καὶ ἄλλοι δὲ πολλοὶ τῶν παλαιῶν οὕτω φέρονται. καθάπερ καὶ Διονύσιος ὁ Ἁλικαρνασσεὺς καὶ Ἀρχύτας ἐν τῷ Περὶ μουσικῆς καὶ αὐτὸς ὁ στοιχειωτὴς Εὐκλείδης ἐν τῇ Τοῦ κανόνος κατατομῇ ἀντὶ τῶν λόγων τὰ διαστήματα λέγουσιν. ὁ μὲν γὰρ Εὐκλείδης λέγει . . . (93.5) Ἀρχύτας δὲ περὶ τῶν μεσοτήτων λέγων γράφει ταῦτα.

μέσαι δέ ἐντι τρῖς τᾷ μουσικᾷ. μία μὲν ἀριθμητικά, δευτέρα δὲ ἁ 1
γεωμετρικά, τρίτα δ᾽ ὑπεναντία [, ἂν καλέοντι ἁρμονικάν]. ἀριθμητικὰ 2
μέν, ὅκκα ἔωντι τρεῖς ὅροι κατὰ τὰν τοίαν ὑπεροχὰν ἀνάλογον, ᾧ πρῶ- 3
τος δευτέρου ὑπερέχει, τούτῳ δεύτερος τρίτου ὑπερέχει. καὶ ἐν ταύτᾳ 4
<τᾷ> ἀναλογίᾳ συμπίπτει εἶμεν τὸ τῶν μειζόνων ὅρων διάστημα 5
μεῖον, τὸ δὲ τῶν μειόνων μεῖζον. ἀγεωμετρικὰ δέ, ὅκκα ἔωντι οἷος ὁ 6
πρῶτος ποτὶ τὸν δεύτερον, καὶ ὁ δεύτερος ποτὶ τὸν τρίτον. τούτων δ᾽ 7
οἱ μείζονες ἴσον ποιοῦνται τὸ διάστημα καὶ οἱ μείους. ἁ δ᾽ ὑπεναντία, ἂν 8
καλοῦμεν ἁρμονικάν, ὅκκα ἔωντι <τοῖοι, ᾧ> ὁ πρῶτος ὅρος ὑπερέχει 9
τοῦ δευτέρου αὐταύτου μέρει, τούτῳ ὁ μέσος τοῦ τρίτου ὑπερέχει τοῦ 10

---

1 ἐντι τρῖς] Wallis   ἐντι τρισί V¹⁸⁷G   τᾷ μουσικᾷ] τᾷ μωσικᾷ (an ταὶ μωσικαί?) Blass   μία] G
μίαν V¹⁸⁷   2   [ἂν καλέοντι ἁρμονικάν] seclusi   3   ἔωντι] Mullach, Blass, Düring   ἐόντι
V¹⁸⁷G   τὰν τοίαν] Blass   τὰν τωίαν V¹⁸⁷G ᾧ] Blass   ὢν codd.   πρῶτος] V¹⁸⁷G   πρᾶτος
Mullach, Blass, Düring, DK   4   τούτῳ] Düring   τωυτῷ Blass τούτου V¹⁸⁷G   4–5   ἐν
ταύτᾳ <τᾷ>] Mullach   ἐνταῦθα codd.   5   εἶμεν] V¹⁸⁷G   ἦμεν Düring   ἤμεν Blass
6   ἁ] Wallis   τὰ V¹⁸⁷G om. Blass   ἔωντι] Mullach, Blass, Düring   ἐόντι V¹⁸⁷G   οἷος] Blass
οἷς V¹⁸⁷G   εἷς ρ   ὡς Wallis   7   πρῶτος] V¹⁸⁷G   πρᾶτος Mullach, Blass, Düring, DK
9   ἔωντι] Mullach, Blass, Düring   ἐόντι V¹⁸⁷G   <τοῖοι· ᾧ>] Diels <ᾧ> Blass   πρῶτος]
V¹⁸⁷G   πρᾶτος Mullach, Blass, Düring, DK   10   αὐταύτου] DK, Düring   αὐταύτω Blass
ἀνταύτου V¹⁸⁷G

τρίτου μέρει. γίνεται δ' ἐν ταύτᾳ τᾷ ἀναλογίᾳ τὸ τῶν μειζόνων ὅρων   11
διάστημα μεῖζον, τὸ δὲ τῶν μειόνων μεῖον.   12

ἐν γὰρ τούτοις τὸν λόγον τῶν ὅρων διάστημα κέκληκεν, οὐ τὴν ὑπε-
ροχήν. οἱ δ' Ἀριστοξένειοί φασι . . . (94.22) τὸ δὲ ὑπολαμβάνειν, ὅτι
ἰδίως ἐπὶ μὲν τῆς ὑπεροχῆς διάστημα λέγεται, οὐκέτι δὲ καὶ ἐπὶ τοῦ
λόγου καλεῖται τὸ διάστημα, πῶς οὐκ ἄτοπον εἶναι δόξειε διὰ τὰ
προειρημένα Δημητρίῳ τε καὶ Παναιτίῳ, Ἀρχύτᾳ τε καὶ Διονυσίῳ καὶ
αὐτῷ τῷ Στοιχειωτῇ καὶ ἄλλοις πολλοῖς κανονικοῖς, καταχρησαμένοις
τῷ διαστήματι ἀντὶ τοῦ λόγου;

Πέφηνε μὲν οὖν, ὅπως καὶ ἀντὶ τοῦ λόγου τὸ διάστημα λαμβάνηται,
καὶ οὐ πάντως λόγος διαστήματος ἕτερον, ὡς δοκεῖ τισι.

(92.9) That ratio (*logos*), then, differs from excess (*hyperochē*) is clear. But
that the ratio (*logos*) and the relation of the terms which are compared
with one another is also called an interval (*diastēma*), I will [now] show . . .
(92.25) But Demetrius too . . . regards interval (*diastēma*) as the same as ratio
(*logos*), and many others of the ancients follow this usage. Just as Dionysius
of Halicarnassus, and Archytas in *On Music*, and the element man himself,
Euclid, in *The Division of the Canon*, speak of intervals (*diastēmata*) rather
than ratios (*logoi*). For Euclid says . . . (93.5) And Archytas speaking about
the means writes these things:

"There are three means in music: one is the arithmetic, the second geometric and the third sub-contrary [, which they call "harmonic"]. The mean
is arithmetic, whenever three terms are in proportion by exceeding one
another in the following way: by that which the first exceeds the second, by
this the second exceeds the third. And in this proportion it turns out that
the interval of the greater terms is smaller and that of the smaller greater.
The mean is geometric, whenever they [the terms] are such that as the first
is to the second so the second is to the third. Of these [terms] the greater
and the lesser make an equal interval. The mean is subcontrary, which we
call harmonic, whenever they [the terms] are such that, by which part of
itself the first term exceeds the second, by this part of the third the middle
exceeds the third. It turns out that, in this proportion, the interval of the
greater terms is greater and that of the lesser is less."

For in this passage he has called the ratio (*logon*) of the terms and not the
excess (*hyperochēn*) an "interval" (*diastēma*). But the followers of Aristoxenus
say . . . (94.22) But how would it not seem strange to assume that "interval"
(*diastēma*) is properly used of the "excess" (*hyperochē*), but that "interval" is
not also used of "ratio," in light of the things said above by both Demetrius

and Panaetius, by both Archytas and Dionysius and by the element man himself and many other canonists, who used "interval" (*diastēma*) instead of "ratio" (*logos*)?

It has become clear, then, that "interval" (*diastēma*) is also used for "ratio" (*logos*) and that a ratio (*logos*) is not absolutely different from an interval (*diastēma*), as some people think.

Text A. Iamblichus, *On Nicomachus' Introduction to Arithmetic* 100.19–101.11 (Pistelli)

μόναι δὲ τὸ παλαιὸν τρεῖς ἦσαν μεσότητες ἐπὶ Πυθαγόρου καὶ τῶν κατ᾽ αὐτὸν μαθηματικῶν, ἀριθμητική τε καὶ ἡ γεωμετρικὴ καὶ ἡ ποτὲ μὲν ὑπεναντία λεγομένη τῇ τάξει τρίτη, ὑπὸ δὲ τῶν περὶ Ἀρχύταν αὖθις καὶ Ἵππασον ἁρμονικὴ μετακληθεῖσα, ὅτι τοὺς κατὰ τὸ ἡρμοσμένον καὶ ἐμμελὲς ἐφαίνετο λόγους περιέχουσα. ὑπεναντία δὲ πρότερον ἐκαλεῖτο, διότι ὑπεναντίον τι ἔπασχε τῇ ἀριθμητικῇ, ὡς δειχθήσεται. ἀλλαγέντος δὲ τοῦ ὀνόματος οἱ μετὰ ταῦτα περὶ Εὔδοξον μαθηματικοὶ ἄλλας τρεῖς προσανευρόντες μεσότητας τὴν τετάρτην ἰδίως ὑπεναντίαν ἐκάλεσαν, διὰ τὸ καὶ αὐτὴν ὑπεναντίον τι πάσχειν τῇ ἁρμονικῇ, ὡς δειχθήσεται· . . . οἱ δὲ νεώτεροι τέσσαρας ἄλλας τινὰς προσανεῦρον . . .

In antiquity there were only three means, in the time of Pythagoras and the mathematicians around him: the arithmetic, the geometric, and third in order, the mean which was once called subcontrary, but the name of which was changed to harmonic by Archytas and Hippasus and their followers, because it manifestly embraced the ratios of what is harmonic and melodic. It was called subcontrary before, because it had characteristics that were contrary to the arithmetic mean, as will be shown. But, after the name was changed, those who came later, Eudoxus and the mathematicians around him, having discovered three other means in addition, called the fourth mean properly subcontrary, because it also had characteristics contrary to the harmonic mean, as will be shown . . . The moderns discovered some four additional means . . .

Text B. Iamblichus, *On Nicomachus' Introduction to Arithmetic* 113.12–113.21 (Pistelli)

καὶ αἵδε μὲν αἱ τρεῖς μεσότητες πρὸς τῶν παλαιῶν μόναι λόγου ἠξιοῦντο . . . αἱ δὲ ἐπὶ ταύταις τρεῖς ἀπ᾽ Ἀρχύτου καὶ Ἱππάσου παραδοχῆς καὶ αὐταὶ ἠξιώθησαν, ὧν ἡ πρώτη, τετάρτη δὲ

συναριθμουμένη τῶν ἐξ ἀρχῆς τριῶν, ἰδίως ὑπεναντία ὡς ἔφαμεν κέκλ-
ηται, διὰ τὸ ὑπεναντίον τι πάσχειν τῇ ἁρμονικῇ . . .

And these three means were alone taken into account by the ancients . . .
But the three means next to these were also themselves thought worthy
of acceptance by Archytas and Hippasus, of which the first, the fourth
counting the three means from the beginning, is properly called subcontrary as we said, because it has characteristics contrary to the harmonic
mean . . .

Text C. Iamblichus, *On Nicomachus' Introduction to Arithmetic* 116.1–7 (Pistelli)

εἴρηται καὶ περὶ τῶν ἑξῆς ταῖς πρώταις τριῶν μεσοτήτων, αἷς καὶ οἱ
ἀπὸ Πλάτωνος μέχρις Ἐρατοσθένους ἐχρήσαντο, ἄρξαντος ὡς ἔφαμεν τῆς εὑρέσεως αὐτῶν Ἀρχύτα καὶ Ἱππάσου τῶν μαθηματικῶν. τὰς
δ' ὑπὸ τῶν μετὰ ταῦτα νεωτέρων περί τε Μυωνίδην καὶ Εὐφράνορα
τοὺς Πυθαγορικοὺς προσφιλοτεχνηθείσας τέσσαρας οὔτε παραλείπειν
ἄξιον.

We have spoken also about the second set of three means, which people from
Plato to Eratosthenes used, the mathematicians Archytas and Hippasus
having begun the discovery of them, as we said. But it is not right to leave
out the four means added by the art of the moderns who came afterwards,
the Pythagoreans Myonides and Euphranor and their followers.

Text D. Iamblichus, *On Nicomachus' Introduction to Arithmetic* 118.19–119.3 (Pistelli)

τὰ νῦν δὲ περὶ τῆς τελειοτάτης ἀναλογίας ῥητέον ἐν τέσσαρσιν ὅροις
ὑπαρχούσης καὶ ἰδίως μουσικῆς ἐπικληθείσης διὰ τὸ τοὺς μουσικοὺς
λόγους τῶν καθ' ἁρμονίαν συμφωνιῶν τρανότατα ἐν αὐτῇ περιέχεσθαι.
εὕρημα δ' αὐτήν φασιν εἶναι Βαβυλωνίων καὶ διὰ Πυθαγόρου πρώτου
εἰς Ἕλληνας ἐλθεῖν. εὑρίσκονται γοῦν πολλοὶ τῶν Πυθαγορείων αὐτῇ
κεχρημένοι, ὥσπερ Ἀρισταῖος ὁ Κροτωνιάτης καὶ Τίμαιος ὁ Λοκρὸς
καὶ Φιλόλαος καὶ Ἀρχύτας οἱ Ταραντῖνοι καὶ ἄλλοι πλείους, καὶ μετὰ
ταῦτα Πλάτων ἐν τῷ Τιμαίῳ λέγων οὕτως . . .

We must now speak about the most perfect proportion, which consists of
four terms and is properly called musical, because the musical ratios of
the concords in harmony are most clearly embraced in it. They say that
it is a discovery of the Babylonians and that it came into Greece through

Pythagoras first. At any rate, many of the Pythagoreans are found using it, such as Aristaeus of Croton and Timaeus of Locri, and the Tarentines Philolaus and Archytas, and many others, and afterwards Plato in the *Timaeus*, speaking as follows . . .

Authenticity

The authenticity of this fragment has not often been questioned, in large part because of its mathematical subject matter. The terminology of the fragment, particularly the initial use of ὑπεναντία (subcontrary) for the third mean and the introduction of the new name "harmonic," suggests a pre-Platonic date (see further the detailed commentary on line 2 below). *On Law and Justice*, whose authenticity is doubtful, does refer to the subcontrary mean and applies the same comparison of the means as is presented in Fragment 2 to political constitutions. This may be a rare case in which a genuine fragment of Archytas is used as the basis for a text forged in Archytas' name (see the discussion of *On Law* in the appendix on spurious fragments). Apart from this connection to *On Law and Justice*, nothing in the language or ideas of the fragment gives rise to suspicion, unless one were to feel that it reads rather more like a textbook than the work of an original thinker such as Archytas. The fragment does not just summarize previous knowledge, however, as I will show below, and the same pattern of summary of previous knowledge followed by an account of Archytas' innovations can be seen in Fragment 1 as well.

The context in Porphyry (see also Düring [1934] 177–78)

Porphyry quotes this fragment of Archytas in the section of his commentary that serves as an introduction to his remarks on Chapter 5 of Book 1 of Ptolemy's *Harmonics* (10.23 ff.). Chapter 5 of Ptolemy is entitled "Concerning the principles adopted by the Pythagoreans in their postulates concerning the concords." After his remarks on the last few lines of Chapter 4 of Ptolemy, which introduced the distinction between concords and discords, Porphyry outlines Ptolemy's next few chapters saying "So, having entered into the discussion of concords, he [Ptolemy] first examines the Pythagorean arrangement of them and only then gives his own views. I will make a different beginning in my commentary on these matters" (90.3–5). Porphyry's "different beginning" consists of a six-page discussion of the way certain technical terms have been used by a variety of writers on music theory. His remarks mainly focus on three terms: ratio (*logos*), interval (*diastēma*), and excess (*hyperochē*). After a preliminary discussion of these terms, he takes it as settled that *logos* (ratio) differs from *hyperochē* (excess 92.9). Porphyry then says that he will show that *logos* is also called *diastēma*. He says that the ancients usually use *diastēma* instead of *logos* and as a first illustration quotes "the divine Plato" in the *Timaeus* (36a–b), where he notes that Plato talks of the hemiolic interval (*diastasis* = *diastēma*), when he clearly means the hemiolic ratio (*logos*).

Porphyry goes on to say (92.22) that most of the canonists and Pythagoreans talk of intervals (*diastēmata*) instead of ratios (*logoi*), and, in a list of such people, we get the first mention of Archytas (92.28 ff.). Porphyry says that "Dionysius of Halicarnassus and Archytas in *On Music* and the element man Euclid himself in *The Division of the Canon* speak of *diastēmata* in place of *logoi*." After quoting Euclid first, he turns to Archytas, at 93.5, and quotes Fragment 2. After the quotation, he says that "in these lines he (Archytas) has called the ratio (*logos*) of the terms and not the excess (*hyperochē*) an interval (*diastēma*)." After yet further discussion of the meaning of *diastēma* in non-musical contexts, Porphyry agrees that if someone wants to use the term *diastēma* in a non-technical sense to mean excess (*hyperochē*) that is acceptable. Porphyry asserts, however, that to assume that *diastēma* is properly applied to *hyperochē* and not used for *logos* is strange in light of the fact that "Demetrius and Panaetius, Archytas and Dionysius, and the element man himself [i.e. Euclid] and many other *kanonikoi* used *diastēma* in place of *logos*" (94.24–26). Finally Porphyry summarizes his comments on *diastēma* (94.29) by recapitulating that some identify it with the ratio (*logos*) of two terms, while others identify it with the difference between two terms or, put another way, the excess (*hyperochē*) of one term over the other. Thus it is clear that Porphyry quotes Fragment 2 of Archytas for one purpose only, to show that he uses the term *diastēma* (interval) for the ratio (*logos*) of terms.

From what work of Archytas does Fragment 2 come?

Porphyry says that this fragment comes from Archytas' book *On Music* (Περὶ μουσικῆς). Indeed, although the subject of the fragment, means, belongs properly to arithmetic, the first sentence of the fragment shows that the focus here is on the relevance of means to music. In terms of subject matter, music theory, it would then make sense to assign this fragment to the same book as Fragment 1, which appears to be the beginning of a treatise on music, and many scholars have done this (D' Ooge et al. 1926: 22; Zeller 1923: III. 2.120; DK includes Frs. 1–3 in the *Harmonics*). Porphyry is also one of our sources for Fragment 1, however, and says that it came from a book entitled *On Mathematics*, although Nicomachus assigned it to *Harmonics*. As I have argued in the commentary on Fragment 1, Nicomachus' title for the book from which Fragment 1 came, *Harmonics* (ἁρμονικὸς [λόγος]), seems the most plausible.

We are still left with a problem in the case of Porphyry. If we assume that Porphyry had complete books of Archytas in front of him, it seems a little strange that he would take Fragments 1 and 2 from the same book and yet cite that book by a different title in the two cases. Carelessness in citation of titles is common in the ancient world, however, and I do not think that it is impossible that Porphyry could have given two different titles for the same book. Any modern scholar can think of times when he has given a mistaken title to a work, which was readily available to him, either out of laziness or on the assumption that he did remember the title correctly. It could, however, be the case that Porphyry did not have the complete text of a book of Archytas, but was working from fragments quoted in other sources. Indeed, if Archytas' book were available we might have expected that Porphyry and others in this period, when the interest in Pythagoreanism was great, would have quoted more extensively from it. If Archytas' books were not available, the two different titles would be due to his sources. The title *On Music* could have been derived from the appearance of the word music in the first line of Fragment 2, just as the title *On Mathematics* may have come from the mention of the *mathēmata* in the first line of Fragment 1. Since we have no clear reason to posit two separate treatises on music, it seems simpler to suppose that all of the fragments and testimonia about Archytas' music theory came from one book, which was most probably titled *Harmonics*.

Andrew Barker has suggested to me that Porphyry's remarks could be explained on the assumption that there was a book of Archytas entitled *On Mathematics* in which there was a section devoted to music, which was known as *On Music* or *Harmonics*. Even if both Fragments 1 and 2 came from the section on music, as their content suggests, Porphyry or his source might well in one case cite Fragment 1 as from *On Mathematics*, using the title of the treatise as a whole, and then Fragment 2 as from the specific section *On Music*. My only difficulty with this is that the rhetoric of Fragment 1 sets up a comparison between music and the other sciences, which works well as an introduction to a treatise on music, but which would be very awkward if the treatise had already discussed or were going on to discuss the other sciences.

Archytas' account of the three means (see also D' Ooge et al. 1926: 21–22 and Barker 1989: 42–43)
Archytas was not the first to discover the arithmetic, geometric and harmonic (subcontrary) means, although he probably coined the term "harmonic" for the third mean (see the section on the history of the means

below). Nonetheless, Fragment 2 may well be the first text in which these means were set out as a group and defined carefully. As at the beginning of Fragment 1, Archytas is setting out what he thinks his predecessors have accomplished. This clear statement of the means discovered by them probably served as preparation for two of Archytas' own original contributions to harmonics: his proof that, in the case of superparticular ratios, no geometric mean can be found (A19) and his account of the way in which the tetrachords in each of the three musical genera are divided, an account which relies heavily on the harmonic and arithmetic mean (A16).

There are two things worthy of note in the presentation of means in Fragment 2: (1) the definitions of the three means and the progressions in which they occur, (2) the further characterization of each of the three means in terms of a comparison of the ratios of the greater terms in each progression with the ratio of the lesser terms in each progression. In defining the three means, Archytas necessarily also defines the progressions in which the means occur, since the mean is the middle of three terms in a progression. The arithmetic mean is defined in terms of the amount by which the terms in the progression exceed the following term: the first term exceeds the second by the same amount as the second exceeds the third term ($a-b = b-c$; e.g. 12, 9, 6. Here 12 exceeds the 9 by 3 and 9 in turn exceeds the third term, 6, by the same amount, 3. The mean is 9). The geometric mean is defined next. As the first term is to the second term so the second term is to the third ($a/b = b/c$; e.g. $12/6 = 6/3$; 6 is the geometric mean). In modern terms this is a proportion; the first term has the same ratio to the second term as the second term has to the third. The last mean to be defined is the harmonic. It is defined in terms of the amount by which the successive terms in the progression exceed each other, as was the arithmetic mean. The first term exceeds the second term by the same part of itself as the part of the third term by which the second term exceeds the third term, $(a-b)/a = (b-c)/c$ (e.g. 12, 8, 6; 12 exceeds 8 by 4, which is 1/3 of 12, while 8 exceeds 6 by 2, which is 1/3 of 6; 8 is the harmonic mean).

After defining each mean, Archytas characterizes them in terms of the comparison of the interval of the greater terms in the progression with the interval of the lesser terms. He is probably using the term "interval" (διάστημα) to refer to the musical interval that we hear (*pace* Porphyry who takes it that *diastēma* just means ratio here), and this shows that the musical application of the means is indeed in the forefront of his mind (see the commentary on line 5). In the case of the arithmetic mean, the interval of the greater terms is less and the interval of the lesser terms is greater ($12/9 < 9/6$). Since the geometric mean is defined in terms of equality

of ratios, the greater and lesser terms of course make an equal interval (12/6
= 6/3). Finally, in the case of the harmonic mean, the interval of the greater
terms is greater and of the lesser terms, lesser (12/8 > 8/6). Archytas does
not explicitly tell us what we are to make of these comparisons, although he
may have done so in the section of his *Harmonics* that followed Fragment 2
(note that the pseudo-Archytan *On Law and Justice* [34.4–34.10 Thesleff]
applies the same comparisons to a political context; see my appendix on
spurious fragments).

    Three points should be made about these comparisons. First, both the
arithmetic and harmonic means are defined in terms of the excess of the
terms of the progression over each other, whereas the geometric mean is
defined in terms of equality of ratio of the terms. Second, the geometric
mean and progression is in the middle of the other two means and hence
is, in a sense, a mean between them. Third, these comparisons explain the
earlier term "subcontrary" or "reversal" (ὑπεναντία) for the third mean (see
the end of the next section). In the arithmetic mean the ratio of the second
and third terms is excessively big, in the harmonic mean it is the ratio
between the first and second terms that is excessively big. The arithmetic
and harmonic means are thus the "reversal" of each other and the geometric
mean is in the middle. Archytas' presentation underlines this point, insofar
as he discusses the geometric mean second, between the arithmetic and
harmonic mean.

*Archytas and the history of means (see also Heath 1921: 84–86; Thomas 1939:
1. 110 ff.; Burkert 1972a: 440 ff.; Mueller 1997: 278 ff.)*
Most of the information on the history of means in Greek thought comes
from Iamblichus' commentary on Nicomachus' *Introduction to Arithmetic*.
Nicomachus himself says that the first three proportions, the same three
discussed in Archytas Fragment 2, were "acknowledged by all the ancients,
Pythagoras, Plato and Aristotle." He then mentions that there are three
more subcontrary to these, without saying anything about their origin,
before finally mentioning four more discovered by "the moderns" to bring
the total to ten (II. 22). Iamblichus goes into some more detail in several passages in his commentary on Nicomachus but the different passages unfortunately present contradictory information. In Text A, Iamblichus does
present a coherent story and Zhmud has argued plausibly that Iamblichus'
ultimate source here is Eudemus, although corruptions have also occurred in
transmission (Zhmud 2002: 270–72). For Pythagoras and the mathematicians of his time there were only three means: arithmetic, geometric, and
subcontrary. The name of this third mean was changed to harmonic by

the schools of Archytas and Hippasus (ὑπὸ δὲ τῶν περὶ Ἀρχύταν . . . καὶ Ἵππασον). After the name was changed, mathematicians in the school of Eudoxus discovered the fourth, fifth and sixth means and called the fourth subcontrary. Iamblichus concludes by saying that the ancients and their successors thus thought that there were six means but that the moderns added four more. It is problematic that the use of the name "harmonic" for the third mean is associated both with Archytas and Hippasus, since their work was separated by about 100 years. Apart from that, however, we have an intelligible account, which agrees with what Nicomachus says.

In Text B, Iamblichus starts by asserting again that "the first three means alone were taken into account by the ancients" but then diverges from his earlier account, by saying that the next three were thought worthy of acceptance "from/by Archytas and Hippasus." The phrasing of the last passage is awkward but suggests that Archytas and Hippasus were associated with the discovery of means 4–6. Eudoxus, who was associated with the discovery of means 4–6 in Iamblichus' earlier account, has disappeared and is also missing from Iamblichus' final account of the history of the means a few pages later (Text C). In his last account of the history of the means, in Text C, Iamblichus seems to try to combine the two accounts he has given so far, when he first says that the second three means were used by those from Plato to Eratosthenes (thus agreeing more or less with the version which ascribed their discovery to the school of Eudoxus), but then adds that Archytas and Hippasus "began" the discovery of them. What it means "to begin" the discovery of the means as opposed to actually discovering them is obscure. It would appear that Iamblichus is trying to reconcile two different versions of the history of the means, in one of which Eudoxus discovered means 4–6 and in the other of which Archytas discovered them. Thus he presents an account in which Archytas begins the discovery of means 4–6 and Eudoxus finishes the discovery.

Fragment 2 seems to support the view that Archytas knew only of the first three means, since it asserts dogmatically that "there are three means." The qualification, however, that it is *in music* that there are three means leaves open the possibility that he did know of other means which were not relevant to music. Certainty is not possible, but it seems most reasonable to accept Iamblichus' earlier account (100.19 ff.), which assigned to Archytas and his followers the change of name of the third mean from subcontrary to harmonic and to Eudoxus and his followers the discovery of means 4–6. In this version both Archytas and Eudoxus have an intelligible role to play. It is interesting that the change of name of the third mean is not mentioned explicitly in Iamblichus' later two accounts (113.12 ff.; 116.1 ff.), and this suggests an explanation for the confusion over the discovery of means 4–6. The change of name might have been elided out of some versions of the tradition leaving both Archytas' and Eudoxus' name but only one discovery for them to share. Accordingly a version springs up, in which Archytas was responsible for the discovery of the means. Iamblichus knows of both versions and gives the fullest version first, in which Eudoxus discovers means 4–6, but later tries to reconcile the two versions by supposing that Archytas "began" the discovery of means 4–6.

Let us now look more closely at the change of the name of the subcontrary mean to the harmonic mean. Is Iamblichus likely to be right that this was the innovation of Archytas, and how are we to explain Iamblichus' mention of Hippasus, who lived a hundred years before Archytas, as also having introduced the new name? One simple explanation is to assume that Archytas quoted Hippasus as having introduced the name and that in the later tradition "Archytas says that Hippasus . . ." became "Archytas and Hippasus say . . ." (Tannery 1912: II. 190), but this does not take into account the actual text of Fragment 2. It seems to have gone unnoticed that there is an important ambiguity in Fragment 2 itself about the change of the name. In the second line of the fragment, when the third mean is first introduced, it is first called "subcontrary," but this is quickly qualified with the words "which they call harmonic." We might well wonder who "they" are. DK translate the phrase as "the so-called harmonic" (*sogenannte harmonische*). This translation implies that Archytas was just giving another common name for the third mean, without having any particular people in mind as the "they," who gave the name. But, while the translation "so-called" is common for the passive of καλέω, this is not the usual meaning for the active (LSJ s.v. II). Moreover, scholars have not properly appreciated the fact that, in lines 8–9, when Archytas turns to his detailed treatment of the third mean, once again he introduces it under the name "subcontrary" but this time qualifies it with the expression "which *we* call harmonic." No mysterious "they" this time. Oddly enough, this difference between lines 2 and 8–9 does not seem to be noted in DK and the translation in lines 8–9 is identical to the translation in line 2, "the so-called harmonic."

What is striking is of course that, in the passages discussed above, Iamblichus in fact credited the school of Archytas (along with the school of Hippasus) as the originators of the name "harmonic" for the third mean and, here in lines 8–9 of Fragment 2, Archytas can be seen as claiming exactly that "harmonic" is the name that "we" give to the subcontrary. It might be argued that the "we" here refers to Pythagoreans in general, but, despite frequent claims to the contrary, there is not good evidence that

Archytas primarily saw himself as handing down an earlier Pythagorean tradition (see the commentary on Fr. 1), and it is more likely that "we" refers to himself. Thus Fragment 2 can be plausibly read as evidence both that knowledge of the first three means existed before Archytas and that he was responsible for introducing the name "harmonic" for the third mean. Fragment 2 also emerges as a very plausible source for a large portion of Iamblichus' account of the history of the means. But what are we to make of the "they" back in line 2? To begin with, it does not seem intelligible to keep "they" in line 2 and "we" in lines 8–9; Archytas is either identifying "harmonic" as his name for the third mean or as the name used by a "they," who might have been specified in the lines preceding Fragment 2 in his book. To be sure it is always possible that the name was invented by the unknown "they" and then used by Archytas himself as well, but to use the two different expressions six lines apart without making clear what is going on would surely have to be classified as carelessness on Archytas' part.

There is another explanation. I suggest that, in the original text of Archytas, there was no phrase "which they call harmonic" in line 2. Archytas initially introduces the mean under its traditional name "subcontrary." When he turns to more detailed consideration of this mean in lines 8–9, however, he points out that he uses the name "harmonic" for this mean. A later commentator on the text, noticing the new name in lines 8–9, goes back to line 2 and writes, in the margin or above the line next to the mention of the third mean, the phrase "which they [i.e. Archytas and his followers] call harmonic." This gloss later becomes incorporated into the text.

It is tempting to suppose that the contradiction between line 2 and lines 8–9 of Fragment 2 is what in fact gave birth to the confusion in Iamblichus as to whether Hippasus or Archytas coined the name "harmonic." One tradition may have started from the "we" in lines 8–9, naturally assuming that Archytas is claiming the name for himself, and another tradition could have begun from the "they" in line 2. Since all three means were assumed to go back to Pythagoras himself, it would be necessary to find some later "they," who changed the name from "subcontrary" to "harmonic." Hippasus and his followers are the logical candidates, since Hippasus is the Pythagorean who is most famous for his contributions to music theory between Pythagoras himself and Archytas.

There is one other report in the tradition which assigns the origin of the name "harmonic" for the third mean to yet another source. Nicomachus (II. 26.2) reports that "some who follow Philolaus" explain the name "harmonic" mean "from its attendance on all geometric harmony, and . . . say 'geometric harmony' is the cube from its having been harmonized in all three dimensions." If this report is to be accepted, Iamblichus would be wrong to assign the term "harmonic mean" to Archytas, and it would go back at least to Philolaus. Indeed, if Nicomachus' report is read as saying that Philolaus explained an already existing term, Hippasus would become the likely originator of the term. The report concerning Philolaus is problematic in a number of ways (Huffman 1993: 168–71), however. The most important point is that the explanation of the origin of the term "harmonic mean" assigned to Philolaus makes much less sense than the explanation assigned to Archytas and Hippasus by Iamblichus.

According to Iamblichus, the third mean was called harmonic because "it seemed to embrace the ratios of what is harmonic and melodic." Now, the harmonic mean does allow us to divide the octave into a fourth and a fifth (12:8 :: 8:6, where 12:8 is a fifth and 8:6 is a fourth), with the fourth as the lower interval. Moreover, in traditional Greek scales the note which was given the name "middle" (*mesē*) was a fourth above the lower note of the octave (*hypatē*) and a fifth below the upper note (*nētē*), so it has exactly the position of the third mean (if we assume that larger numbers go with higher notes, which is admittedly not a universal practice). Thus, since the third mean determines the middle note in the standard Greek scale or *harmonia*, it would be natural to call that mean the harmonic mean (Burkert 1972a: 441). It may be that Archytas was motivated to change the name from subcontrary to harmonic simply because it played this central role in music. It is not clear, however, that this third mean encompasses *all* the ratios of what is harmonic and melodic, which is what Iamblichus' report implies. The arithmetic mean also divides the octave into a fourth and a fifth (12:9 :: 9:6, where 12:9 is a fourth and 9:6 is a fifth). Indeed, both of these means were used in describing the division of the octave according to the method of attunement known as the "method of concordance." This method is illustrated in Philolaus Fragment 6a, where the *harmonia* is constructed first by inserting the harmonic mean but then the arithmetic mean is added as well. Moreover, neither of these two means allow us to construct a series of octaves, for which we need the geometric mean (12:6 :: 6:3). Thus, it is better perhaps to understand Archytas as having followed the simpler reasoning given above or to have thought not that the harmonic mean by itself is adequate to describe musical harmony, but rather that, as the third mean taken with the previous two means, it "embraced the ratios of what is harmonic and melodic." Either of these two explanations of the reason for Archytas' use of the term "harmonic" is readily intelligible.

The explanation assigned to Philolaus is much less so. Here the key is the connection of the third mean to the cube. The third mean is said to be connected to the cube, because the cube has 12 sides, 8 angles and 6 faces. If we were impressed with this parallel, it might seem reasonable to call the third mean the "cubic mean." In order to arrive at the name "harmonic" things get very convoluted. The explanation appears to be that the cube was given the special name "geometric harmony" by Philolaus. Even given this, it would appear more natural to try to call the mean "geometric" on the basis of this name for the cube. For Philolaus the world is full of harmonies; it is one of the central principles of his cosmos; to assign the third mean the title "harmonic," because it has a relation to just one of these many harmonies, seems arbitrary in the extreme. Although some have tried to assign the cube a special role in Philolaus' cosmology, the evidence for this is late and in tension with the earlier and more reliable evidence (Huffman 1993: 168–71). Since Nicomachus does not refer to Philolaus directly but rather to "some" who agree with Philolaus, it appears that Nicomachus' report is ultimately based on a later source which appeals to Philolaus as an authority, rather than on any text of Philolaus. That source appears to be giving a far-fetched reinterpretation of the term "harmonic mean," in light of later concerns.

Certainty about the origin of the name "harmonic" for the third mean is impossible to reach given the state of our sources. However, Fragment 2 of Archytas is the only relevant primary text, and the most natural reading of Fragment 2 is that Archytas' predecessors, including Philolaus called the third mean "subcontrary," while Archytas tells us that he himself calls it "harmonic." This primary testimony is in turn supported by Iamblichus' report. To be sure his report may be largely based on Fragment 2, but his further explanation of why Archytas used the name "harmonic" does fit with Archytas' musical practice elsewhere (A16). This is better than to follow Nicomachus' report about Philolaus, which is based on no primary evidence and which in fact conflicts with the early evidence for Philolaus.

Because Fragment 2 of Archytas is the first text to give clear definitions of the arithmetic, geometric and harmonic means, Archytas is sometimes virtually treated as their discoverer (Lasserre 1966a: 181–82). We have seen, however, that the doxography assigns them back to Archytas' predecessors, often to Pythagoras himself. Indeed, Fragment 2 clearly implies that the three means had been discovered before Archytas. The first line of the fragment might at first sight be read as Archytas' triumphant announcement of his discovery of the three means in music, but, when we find later in the fragment that he is changing the name of the third mean from "subcontrary" to "harmonic," this clearly implies that this mean, at least, existed earlier under a different name. Thus, in Fragment 2, as in Fragment 1 and elsewhere, Archytas is consciously building on the work of his predecessors. A fragment of Eudemus confirms that the three means were known in the early fourth century, before Plato's use of them in the *Timaeus*, and suggests that the third mean was indeed called "harmonic" at this point (Pappus *Comm. on Euclid* X 1.1; 2.17 [63,138 Junge and Thomson] – not in Wehrli). Eudemus says that Theaetetus (414–369 BC) used the three means to classify different types of irrational lines, and uses the name "harmonic" for the third mean. It is of course, not certain that "harmonic" is Theaetetus' usage rather than Eudemus', but if it does belong to Theaetetus, who was slightly younger than Archytas, it would be the first testimony, outside Fragment 2, to Archytas' new name for the third mean.

It remains unclear exactly how far back before Archytas knowledge of the three means can be traced. In the passages cited above, we have seen that Nicomachus and Iamblichus assign knowledge of the means to Pythagoras and there is yet a further testimony which suggests this. In Text D, Iamblichus, commenting on "the most perfect proportion" introduced by Nicomachus (II. 29), reports that "they say that it is the discovery of the Babylonians and through Pythagoras first came into Greece. At least many of the Pythagoreans are found to have used it, e.g. Aristaeus of Croton, Timaeus of Locri, and Philolaus and Archytas of Tarentum and many others, and after these Plato in the *Timaeus* . . .". The "most perfect proportion" is also called "musical" by Iamblichus and consists of four terms (a, a+b/2, 2ab/a+b, b). The primary example of such a proportion is 12:9 :: 8:6 which is important in music theory, since it employs both the harmonic and arithmetic mean. Iamblichus is right to say that Philolaus used it, since Fragment 6a (Huffman) clearly suggests awareness of this proportion.

There is one final comment to be made on the theory of means, which served as the background to Archytas' work. What is the origin of the term "subcontrary" for the third mean? As we have seen Archytas' description of the arithmetic and harmonic means suggests a sense in which the latter is the subcontrary or "reversal" of the former and the later tradition used precisely the points that Archytas raises in Fragment 2 in order to explain the term (see the note on ὑπεναντία below). There is some evidence to suggest, however, that this use of the term might have originated with Archytas' predecessor and possible teacher, Philolaus. In Fragment 6a, Philolaus seems to identify the harmonia which holds the world together with the octave. He then first divides the octave by going up a fourth from the lowest note of the octave and then up a fifth to the highest note of the octave (i.e. constructing the harmonic mean) and then reverses this by going down a fourth and then a fifth (i.e. constructing an arithmetic mean). Philolaus does not talk explicitly in terms of means here so that we do not know what terminology he would have used. It is significant though that, in his description of the cosmos in Fragment 17, Philolaus makes the point that the cosmos began to come to be at the middle and came to be in the same way upwards as downwards. Thus, according to Philolaus the things above the middle are the reversal (ὑπεναντίως) of those below. The connection with the "subcontrary" (ὑπεναντία) mean (the reversal of the arithmetic) suggested by the language may not be accidental. Looking at the cosmos from the outside, Philolaus' point is that the parts which occur at the bottom of the top half of the universe will occur at the top of the bottom half of the universe, just as, in the octave as described by Philolaus, the fourth occurs at the top, when the arithmetic mean is used, and at the bottom, when the harmonic mean is used. This is a striking parallel between music theory and the structure of Philolaus' cosmos, which goes along with similar parallels developed in Fragment 6a. It also suggests that Philolaus might well have used the term "subcontrary" or "reversal" to refer to the harmonic mean. In that case, Philolaus will have been one of the earlier thinkers whose terminology Archytas is improving, when he replaces the term subcontrary with harmonic.

Detailed commentary

Line 1 μέσαι – This term for a mathematical mean is derived from the adjective μέσος ("middle"). Its feminine gender may reflect its origin in geometry where it was understood originally to agree with εὐθεῖα ("straight line" see e.g. Euclid VI. 13; so also Aristotle *de An.* 413a19) and thus perhaps suggests that the Greek theory of means was first developed geometrically. The feminine noun μέση is also used in music theory, however, first to refer to the "middle" string (χορδή) in the seven-string lyre and then as the name for one of the standard notes in Greek scales, the note a fourth up from the lowest note (*hypatē*). This use is attested already in Philolaus Fr. 6a, in the second half of the fifth century. Arithmetically this note is a harmonic mean within the octave, and it does not seem impossible that the feminine μέση, signifying "mean," has its origin in these musical connections rather than in the geometrical connection suggested above. Note that, in line 10 below, Archytas uses the masculine μέσος agreeing with ὅρος (term) when discussing the harmonic proportion. Thus it is hard to explain the feminine term as having arisen in arithmetical treatments of proportion. μεσότης also comes to be used for mean (Pl. *Ti.* 36a; Arist. Fr. 47, *EN* 1107a2; Iamb. *passim*, Nicom. *passim*) and is used interchangeably with μέση (e.g. Arist. *Metaph.* 996b21, 1093a29). Pappus uses the two terms interchangeably in close proximity (III. 11.28 – 68.17 Hultsch).

τρῖς – This is the nominative plural form in Heraclean and some other dialects (Buck 1955: 95) and is suggested by the corrupt manuscript reading here. However, in line 3, all manuscripts have τρεῖς.

τᾶ μουσικᾶ – Here and throughout the fragment we find the long alpha, which Attic and Ionic changed to eta (Buck 1955: 21).

ἁ – The article is odd here, given that it is omitted in the parallel cases in this sentence, but there is manuscript evidence for it, and we may want to see it as unconscious variation on Archytas' part.

2 ὑπεναντία – As I have shown above, this fragment may well be the source for Iamblichus' report that the third mean was originally called "sub-contrary" (ὑπεναντία) rather than "harmonic" (ἁρμονική). The absence of ὑπεναντία from Plato and Aristotle and its rarity in the later tradition, suggest that it is genuine early terminology. Its early use in the Pythagorean tradition is supported by Philolaus' use of ὑπεναντίως in Fragment 17 (see the discussion of the history of means above). On the other hand, a parallel for the name "subcontrary" is found in the treatise *On Law and Justice*, which is ascribed to Archytas but of doubtful authenticity (see the appendix on spurious fragments). Nicomachus' explanation of the term subcontrary (*Ar.* II. 23.6; II. 25.2; see also Iamb. *In Nic.* 110.17 ff.) ultimately relies on Archytas' description of the means here in Fragment 2 (see "Archytas' account of the three means" above).

[ἂν καλέοντι ἁρμονικάν] For the meaning of this expression and its apparent contradiction with καλοῦμεν in line 9 below, see the comments on the history of means given above. For the reasons given there, I think that the phrase is likely to be an intrusive gloss. One argument against this suggestion could be based on the uncontracted form of the verb, which is more likely to go back to Archytas, than to be due to a marginal gloss. This is a difficulty, but once the gloss enters the text it become fair game for attempts to "correct" to Doric forms. The manuscripts were subject both to attempts to correct to Doric forms and to the natural tendency to use the more normal Attic forms. These contradictory tendencies explain the odd mixture of Attic and Doric forms in the manuscripts.

3 ὄκκα – For the form see Fragment 1, line 9.

ὑπεροχάν – Note that the arithmetic mean is defined in terms of the numerical "excess" of one term over the other. The terms in the arithmetic proportion are separated by an equal number (e.g. the equal number is 3 in 12:9 :: 9:6). However the interval (διάστημα line 5) between the terms, their ratio, is not the same.

ἀνάλογον – This word has its origin in the phrase ἀνὰ λόγον ("according to a due λόγος") but comes to be written as one word and to be used "practically as an undeclinable adjective" (Heath 1925: II. 129; see Euclid v. Def. 6; VII. Def. 20). So here it functions as an undeclinable adjective modifying ὅροι ("three terms *proportional* by exceeding one another in the following way . . ."). To say that the three terms are ἀνάλογον is to say that the relationship between the first and the second is in some way similar to the relationship between the second and the third. The nature of the similarity of these relationships is then defined in terms of the numerical excess of the first term over the second, and the second over the third. See the commentary on ἀναλογία in line 5.

3–4 πρῶτος – V[187] and G have πρῶτος throughout Fragment 2. The normal Doric form, πρᾶτος, was mistakenly reported by Düring and later editors followed him.

5 ἀναλογία – An *analogia* always involves two pairs of things (e.g. A&B and C&D). In an *analogia* we focus on the relationship between the objects in each of the pairs and assert that there is a similarity between the relationship of the objects in one pair and the relationship of the objects in the other pair. This similarity is the *analogia*. Thus an *analogia* exists when A has a relation to B that is similar to the relation that C has to D. When the four terms are all different, the *analogia* is called discontinuous, but the second and third terms in the *analogia* can be the same, so that e.g. A has a relation to B which is similar to the relation that B has to C. This is called a continuous *analogia*. In this case B is called a mean between A and C. Strictly speaking "mean" just applies to this middle term of the *analogia,* but the whole *analogia,* in which a mean occurs, is sometimes called a mean.

If we look at the usage of Plato and Aristotle, it is clear that properly speaking the similarity referred to in an *analogia* was "sameness of ratio," so that A:B :: C:D (e.g. 2:4 :: 8:16). In terms of a continuous *analogia* this picks out the *analogia* in which the geometric mean occurs (e.g. 2:4 :: 4:8, where 4 is the geometric mean between 2 and 8). Plato only uses the term *analogia* six times, and, in several cases the context is too loose to

be sure of his precise meaning. At *Timaeus* 31c–32c, however, it is clear
that the term *analogia* means the continuous geometric *analogia*, what
we would call a continuous geometric proportion, or just a continuous
proportion (Cornford 1937: 45ff.). When Plato discusses the arithmetic
and harmonic means at *Timaeus* 36a ff., he does not use the term *analogia*.
Similarly, at *EN* 1131a31, Aristotle defines *analogia* as "equality of ratio"
(ἡ γὰρ ἀναλογία ἰσότης ἐστὶ λόγων), and, a few lines later he tells us
that "the mathematicians call this sort of *analogia* geometrical *analogia*"
(1131b13).

With the mention of "this sort of analogia," Aristotle has prepared us for
the idea that, although properly speaking *analogia* refers just to the geometric proportion and particularly to the continued geometric proportion,
there are also, speaking more loosely, other sorts of *analogia*. In several places
Aristotle refers to the "arithmetical analogia" (e.g. *EN* 1106a36), although it
is perfectly clear that it will not fit Aristotle's earlier definition of *analogia* as
"equality of ratios," (in the arithmetic progression 12, 9, 6, the ratio 12:9 is
not equal to the ratio 9:6). It appears that from the more precise definition
of "equality of ratio" there developed a looser sense in which any similarity,
which could be defined in accordance with a mathematical account (ἀνὰ
λόγον), could constitute an *analogia*. In its broadest sense Aristotle uses
analogia to refer to any similarity in the relationships between two pairs of
things. Thus, in the biological works, a scale has the same relation to a fish
as a feather does to a bird (*HA* 486b17).

The later Greek mathematical tradition accurately mirrors what is found
in Plato and Aristotle. Theon's definition of ἀναλογία as "similarity or
sameness of more ratios than one" (82.6) is very reminiscent of Aristotle's.
Theon also knows of a tradition through Adrastus, who wrote a commentary on the *Timaeus*, according to which only the geometric mean was
proportion or ἀναλογία in the proper sense (106.15). Heath gives a good
discussion of the rest of the later tradition and concludes that originally
only the geometric proportion was called ἀναλογία but that in later usage
the word was applied to all the means (1925: II. 292–93). If this is so, we
are already dealing with the expanded use of the term in Archytas. He is
working with a meaning of ἀναλογία that corresponds to Aristotle's second sense above. Lines 2–3 suggest that an ἀναλογία arises whenever at
least three terms are such that the relation between the first and the second
and the relation between the third and the fourth are similar in accord with
a mathematically defined account or formula (ἀνὰ λόγον). The nature of
this account is what distinguishes between the three different ἀναλογίαι
in Fragment 2. There is no indication that, for Archytas, the geometric,

or for that matter, any one of the three, is more of an ἀναλογία than the others. In fact, the term is used explicitly only of the arithmetic (here in line 5) and harmonic (line 11) means and not of the geometric, although there is no reason to doubt that Archytas would have called the geometric mean an ἀναλογία. ἀναλογία also appears in Testimonium A23a of Archytas where the "ἀναλογία of equality" appears to be a reference to the arithmetic ἀναλογία.

εἶμεν – See the commentary on Fr. 1, line 7. Düring prints ἦμεν here which may be a misprint (as the apparatus in DK suggests), since all the major manuscripts in fact have εἶμεν.

διάστημα – Porphyry quotes Fragment 2 precisely to show that Archytas used διάστημα in a sense equivalent to λόγος (see the discussion of the context above). The usage here and in lines 8 and 12 clearly supports Porphyry up to a point. In line 3, Archytas has defined the arithmetic mean in terms of "excess," the first term exceeding the second by the same amount as the second exceeds the third (e.g. 12:9 :: 9:6). Here in line 5, however, he says that the διάστημα of the greater terms is less and of the lesser terms greater so that διάστημα cannot be the same as the excess. Andrew Barker has pointed out to me, however, that this does not necessarily mean that Porphyry is right to think that Archytas understood διάστημα to be simply equivalent to the ratio (λόγος) of the terms, where the greater terms produce a smaller ratio (e.g. 12:9) than the lesser (e.g. 9:6). διάστημα might have the simple meaning of "interval" in the musical sense of the interval which we hear (see e.g. Pl. *Phlb.* 17c11). This interval would of course be analyzed as a ratio by Archytas, but διάστημα still need not mean the same thing as *logos*.

7 ποτί – For the form see Fragment 1, line 8.

10 αὐταύτου – For this west Greek form of the reflexive see Buck (1955: 99).

CHAPTER III

Fragment 3

Stobaeus IV. 1.139 (88.5–89.8 Wachsmuth–Hense) ἐκ τοῦ Ἀρχύτου
Περὶ μαθημάτων

Iamblichus, *On General Mathematical Science* 11 (44.10–17 Festa)
διόπερ ὁ Ἀρχύτας ἐν τῷ Περὶ μαθηματικῶν λέγει·

δεῖ γὰρ ἢ μαθόντα παρ' ἄλλω ἢ αὐτὸν ἐξευρόντα, ὧν ἀνεπιστάμων   1
ἦσθα, ἐπιστάμονα γενέσθαι. τὸ μὲν ὦν μαθὲν παρ' ἄλλω καὶ ἀλλότριον,   2
τὸ δ' ἐξευρὲν δι' αὔταυτον καὶ ἴδιον· ἐξευρὲν δὲ μὴ ζατοῦντα ἄπορον   3
καὶ σπάνιον, ζατοῦντα δὲ εὔπορον καὶ ῥάδιον, μὴ ἐπιστάμενον δὲ   4
<λογίζεσθαι> ζητεῖν ἀδύνατον.   5
στάσιν μὲν ἔπαυσεν, ὁμόνοιαν δὲ αὔξησεν λογισμὸς εὑρεθείς.   6
πλεονεξία τε γὰρ οὐκ ἔστι τούτου γενομένου καὶ ἰσότας ἔστιν· τούτω   7
γὰρ περὶ τῶν συναλλαγμάτων διαλλασσόμεθα. διὰ τοῦτον οὖν οἱ πέν-   8
ητες λαμβάνοντι παρὰ τῶν δυναμένων, οἵ τε πλούσιοι διδόντι τοῖς   9
δεομένοις, πιστεύοντες ἀμφότεροι διὰ τούτω τὸ ἶσον ἕξειν. κανὼν δὲ   10
καὶ κωλυτὴρ τῶν ἀδικούντων <ἐὼν> τοὺς μὲν ἐπισταμένους λογίζεσθαι   11
πρὶν ἀδικεῖν ἔπαυσε, πείσας ὅτι οὐ δυνασοῦνται λαθεῖν, ὅταν ἐπ' αὐτὸν   12
ἔλθωντι· τοὺς δὲ μὴ ἐπισταμένους, ἐν αὐτῷ δηλώσας ἀδικοῦντας,   13
ἐκώλυσεν ἀδικῆσαι.   14

1 ἢ μαθόντα] Stob.   μαθόντα Iamb.   ἄλλω] Orelli ἄλλων Iambl. ἄλλου Stob. ὧν
ἀνεπιστάμων] Blass ὧν ἐπιστάμων Stob. ὧν ἂν ἐπιστάμων Iambl. (Festa) ὧν ἂν αὐτῶν
ἐπιστάμων Iambl. (Blass)   2 ὦν] Stobaeus M οὖν Stobaeus A ὧν Iamb. μαθὲν] Iamb.
μαθεῖν Stob. ἄλλω] Iamb. ἄλλου Stobaeus ἀλλότριον] Stobaeus ἀλλοτρία Iamblichus
3 δι' αὔταυτον] Blass διὰ τ' αὐτὸν Iamb. (Blass) αὐτὸν δι' αὐτοῦ Stob. ἴδιον] Iamb. Stob.
ἰδίᾳ Diels ἐξευρὲν] Iamb. ἐξευρεῖν Stob. μὴ ζατοῦντα] Iamb. μὴν ζητοῦντα Stob.
3–4 ἄπορον . . . ζατοῦντα δὲ] om. Stob.   4 ἐπιστάμενον] Iamb., Stob. ἐπιστάμονα
Canter, Blass   5 <λογίζεσθαι>] scripsi   6–14 στάσιν . . . ἀδικῆσαι] om. Iambl.   7
τε] om. A ἔστιν] Meineke ἐστίν MA   9 διδόντι] Canter διδόντες MA   10 τούτω]
Gesner τούτων MA ἕξειν] A ἕξειν M   11 <ἐὼν>] Blass λογίζεσθαι] Pflugk
ὀργίζεσθαι MA (ὀργ- M) τῷ ὀργίζεσθαι Gesner   12 ἔπαυσε] Gesner παύσας MA
12 αὐτὸν] MA αὐτὸ Gesner

(Stobaeus) From the *On Sciences* of Archytas:

(Iamblichus) Wherefore Archytas says in the *On Things Scientific*:

For it is necessary to come to know those things which you did not know, either by learning from another or by discovering yourself. Learning is from another and belongs to another, while discovery is through oneself and belongs to oneself. Discovery, while not seeking, is difficult and infrequent but, while seeking, easy and frequent, but, if one does not know <how to calculate>, it is impossible to seek.

Once calculation was discovered, it stopped discord and increased concord. For people do not want more than their share, and equality exists, once this has come into being. For by means of calculation we will seek reconciliation in our dealings with others. Through this, then, the poor receive from the powerful, and the wealthy give to the needy, both in the confidence that they will have what is fair on account of this. It serves as a standard and a hindrance to the unjust. It stops those who know how to calculate, before they commit injustice, persuading them that they will not be able to go undetected, whenever they appeal to it [sc. as a standard]. It hinders those who do not know how to calculate from committing injustice, having revealed them as unjust by means of it [i.e. calculation].

Authenticity
Fragment 3 was accepted as authentic by DK and most scholars have followed them. It is true, however, that Fragment 3 is quoted by Stobaeus immediately after four selections from the pseudo-Archytan treatise, *On Law and Justice* (see the context below). DK seem to have regarded Fragment 3 as authentic and the other selections as spurious, primarily because Fragment 3 is said to come from a work on mathematics, which they regarded as the same work from which Fragments 1 and 2 derived. There are problems with this approach. The use of technical mathematics as a criterion for authenticity is not foolproof (see the section on authenticity in the introduction). Moreover, it is unlikely that Fragment 3 came from the same book as Fragments 1 and 2 (see below), and what we have of Fragment 3 suggests rather a treatise on epistemology and the role of mathematics in the state than technical mathematics. It is necessary, therefore, to consider the content of the fragment very carefully.

As the detailed commentary below indicates, there is nothing in the language or concepts of the fragment that connect it to the typical pseudo-Pythagorean treatises. To put the argument more positively, the language and concepts used in Fragment 3 make excellent sense for someone writing in the late fifth and first half of the fourth centuries. The discussions of *homonoia* and *pleonexia* fit particularly well with the discourse on these topics during this period. There are many parallels in language with Democritus and early Plato. The concept of equality presented also matches the early fourth-century discourse without making the distinctions in types of equality typical of the middle of the fourth century.

In addition to these linguistic considerations, there are two strong arguments for authenticity, based on the agreement of Fragment 3 with external sources for the history of Tarentum and the life of Archytas. First, the somewhat unique *modus vivendi* worked out between rich and poor, which Aristotle ascribes to the Tarentum of his day (*Pol.* 1320b10 – probably at the time of or shortly after the death of Archytas), is very reminiscent of the emphasis put on the rich giving to the poor in Fragment 3. Second, Aristotle's pupil Aristoxenus, presumably writing in the second half of the fourth century, not long after Archytas' death, presents Archytas as arguing against the case for *pleonexia* put by a certain Polyarchus (A9), which is again very much in accord with Archytas' concern about *pleonexia* in Fragment 3. These two specific confirmations of the authenticity of the content of Fragment 3 combined with the general agreement in the level of discourse between Fragment 3 and other texts of the late fifth and early fourth centuries and with the absence of any specifically Platonic or Aristotelian distinctions, should make us reasonably confident that Fragment 3 is authentic.

Context

Stobaeus and Iamblichus quote Fragment 3 in two quite different contexts. Book IV. I of Stobaeus has 161 excerpts from ancient authors, which are devoted to the subject Περὶ πολιτείας (*On the Republic*). Fragment 3 of Archytas is entry 139. The chapter starts with a number of selections from Greek drama, but goes on to passages from the orators, Democritus and Thucydides among others. Selections 97–131 are from Plato and more Platonic passages occur after Fragment 3 of Archytas as well. The four selections immediately before Fragment 3 (135–38) are from the spurious *On Law and Justice* by "the Pythagorean Archytas" (see my appendix on spurious works and Thesleff 1965: 33.1–35.30) and 132 is also from a spurious treatise ascribed to Archytas, but no title for the work from which it comes is given (Thesleff 1965: 47.23). A number of the other entries have Pythagorean connections. Number 49 is from Aristoxenus'

Pythagorean Precepts. Others are from pseudo-Pythagorean writings: 80 and 81 are ascribed to "Pythagoras," 93–95 to "Hippodamos the Pythagorean," 96 and 133 to "Diotogenes the Pythagorean." Immediately following Fragment 3 are excerpts from Plutarch, Aesop and Demosthenes. Thus, there does not seem to be any real principle of order in this chapter of Stobaeus except somewhat of a tendency to present the excerpts from one author in a cluster or clusters, as is the case with Archytas.

Stobaeus says that Fragment 3 is "from the *On Sciences* of Archytas" (ἐκ τοῦ Ἀρχύτου Περὶ μαθημάτων). Hense points out that from the standard form in Stobaeus (e.g. 133 and 135) we would have expected the work to have been introduced as Ἀρχύτα Πυθαγορείου ἐκ τοῦ Περὶ μαθημάτων ("Of Archytas the Pythagorean, from *On Sciences*"). He suggests that the difference may be intended to indicate that these words are from the Tarentine Archytas and not the forger, but it is unclear why he thinks this. The article probably does not go with the name (i.e. not "the Archytas") but still goes with the title of the book, as is shown by other entries in Stobaeus (e.g. IV. 1.142 ἐκ τῶν Δημοσθένους Φιλιππικῶν, 144 ἐκ τῶν Ἀριστοτέλους Χρειῶν), so that the only real difference from the form used at 135 is the lack of the adjective Pythagorean and the use of the Attic form of the genitive. Not calling Archytas a Pythagorean might suggest his independence of the (pseudo)-Pythagorean tradition, but this seems a lot to read into the expression. In the end this way of introducing the selection seems to be an insignificant variation.

Iamblichus, on the other hand, quotes Fragment 3 for its epistemological content and makes no reference to political theory. He quotes just the first four lines in Chapter 11 of his *De Communi Mathematica Scientia*. The focus of this chapter is the function of mathematical science, which is explained in terms of the Platonic theory of recollection. Iamblichus begins by distinguishing mathematical science from understanding (*nous*) in a number of ways. Unlike understanding, mathematical science cannot gain knowledge entirely by itself but must be roused to knowledge from outside. Unlike understanding it involves seeking and discovering and is always advancing from some lack of knowledge to its fulfillment. Mathematical knowledge arises after learning provided by a teacher leads the way and is followed by discovery. The principles provided by the teacher cause the soul to be reminded of the true forms in mathematics. It is at this point that Iamblichus quotes lines 1–5 of Archytas Fragment 3, in order to show that mathematical knowledge is the joint product of learning from a teacher and discovery.

After quoting the fragment, Iamblichus further explains the nature of mathematical science by means of a detailed explication of the fragment. First, he points out that Archytas establishes learning (from another) as the starting point of mathematics. This learning is then followed by discovery. Although the second is primary in power, given human nature and our fall into the world of becoming, we must first go through a process of recollection initiated by learning from another and then make what we recollect our own through discovery. Iamblichus then further explicates the fragment by paraphrasing and explaining a number of passages. In one sense, learning from another and discovery are two means of gaining knowledge, but in another sense they are one. He supports this last point by paraphrasing line 2 of the fragment: for whenever we take over the sciences "from another and as belonging to another" at that time we make them our own by our own efforts. Iamblichus clearly interprets the last words of lines 4–5 in terms of the theory of recollection: "it is impossible to seek, if we do not know" (45.7–8). It is because of our prior knowledge that discoveries in the sciences are "easy and frequent for the one who seeks" and "difficult and infrequent for the one who does not seek" (cf. Archytas Fr. 3. 3–4). He concludes by saying that the practice of the sciences is a path from learning to seeking and discovery. Since mathematical science gets its start by learning from another (*mathēsis*) and cannot arise without this, it also takes its name (*mathēmatikē*) from this learning. Iamblichus' interpretation of the fragment helps to understand the problematic lines 4–5, although his assumption that the fragment is espousing the theory of recollection is suspect (see the commentary on lines 4–5).

Is Fragment 3 one fragment or two?

It has long been noticed that the first five lines of Fragment 3 do not, at least according to the text given in the manuscripts, cohere very well with lines 6–14. Blass rightly noticed that the style of the two sections is very similar and accordingly felt that they did belong together (1884: 581–82, so also DK). He assumes a lacuna after the first four lines to explain the apparent break in thought. DK print no break between the parts but, in the apparatus, notice the problematic connection between the two parts. Iamblichus quotes only the first five lines, but his failure to quote lines 6–14 says nothing about the continuity of the two parts. He is interested in the epistemology of lines 1–5 and has no reason to quote lines 6–14, which focus on the state. Stobaeus, on the other hand, quotes the passage precisely for what it has to say about the state, since it is presented under the heading "On the Republic." The first five lines have nothing to do with the republic, and it is hard to see why he quotes them. The answer of DK and Blass is that Stobaeus originally quoted some intervening material which connected lines 1–5 with lines 6–14 and that this material was lost in transmission. It is possible to suppose that this lacuna contained some remarks about human discoveries that would lead more naturally into the discussion of the discoveries that led to the state. There is no necessity to suppose that there is an extensive lacuna between the two parts of Fragment 3, however. The original unity of the fragment as well as the intelligibility of line 5 of the fragment can be seen once we recognize that one word, <λογίζεσθαι>, has fallen out of the text (see the commentary on lines 4–5). Stobaeus or whoever originally excerpted the fragment had a text of Archytas with λογίζεσθαι and hence excerpted lines 1–14 as a coherent unit. In the course of transmission λογίζεσθαι dropped out, and both Stobaeus and Iamblichus found the text in this later version. The unity of the fragment is thus the focus on the value of calculation, first as the basis for all inquiry and then for the contributions it makes to the state.

From what book does Fragment 3 come?
Stobaeus and Iamblichus are in very close agreement on the title of the book from which Fragment 3 comes. Stobaeus cites it as from *On Sciences* (Περὶ μαθημάτων). Iamblichus, using the adjective "scientific" rather than the noun "sciences," cites it as from *On Things Scientific* (Περὶ μαθηματικῶν). This variation is easily explained by the fact that Iamblichus uses the adjectival form several times in the surrounding context, and his focus is in fact on "mathematical/scientific knowledge" (43.13). Thus it seems likely that he cited the title of Archytas' work using the adjectival form, because that form was at the front of his mind.

Fragment 3 appears, then, to come from a work which was known as *On Sciences*. The question immediately arises as to whether this is the same book from which Fragments 1 and 2 come. Indeed it is a common assumption that Fragments 1–3 all come from the same book (e.g. DK and Zeller 1923: III. 2.120). Porphyry in fact cites Fragment 1 as coming from Περὶ μαθηματικῆς, *On Mathematics*. It seems most likely, however, that the book from which Fragments 1 and 2 came was properly called *Harmonics* (see the commentary on Fr. 1). Nonetheless this book was also known as *On Mathematics* as Porphyry's citation shows, so that its title is no bar to assuming that Fragment 3 belonged to it as well. It is, nonetheless, difficult to see how Fragment 3 could fit into the book from which Fragments 1 and 2 come. Fragment 1 is identified as the beginning of a book (see the commentary on Fr. 1). It gives us a brief general account of all the sciences as an exordium to the study of harmonics as well as providing the beginning of the detailed discussion of harmonics. Fragment 2 (cited as from *On Music*) would fit well in a later part of the detailed discussion of the mathematics of harmonics. Fragment 3, on the other hand, is very much an exordium as well, and it is thus hard to see how to fit a second exordium into the *Harmonics*. Moreover, Fragment 3 makes no mention of music and instead focuses on scientific thinking at a very general level and on the role of such thinking in the state. All of this seems much more appropriate as an exordium to a more general book *On Sciences*. Blass (1884: 584) suggests that Fragments 1–3 could come from only one book, if that book, after starting with music, turned to the other three sciences in turn. Fragment 3 could then be understood as coming from the exordium to the section on logistic. His suggestion seems to be that the book was known both as *Harmonics* and *On the Sciences* in antiquity. Blass' suggestion is ingenious, but the structure of Fragment 1 strongly suggests that it is the beginning of a book specifically on music (see the commentary on Fr. 1) rather than part of a larger book on all the sciences, and there would be no place in such a book for Fragment 3. It seems best to conclude that Fragments 1 and 2 came from a book entitled *Harmonics* and that Fragment 3 came from a separate work *On Sciences*. This latter work can be understood either as a work devoted to the value of the sciences for human life in general, which accordingly touched on their role in the state, or as a work devoted to discussing the sciences in a more technical fashion, in which Fragment 3 was part of an introduction serving as a protreptic to the study of the sciences by pointing out their value even in ordering the state.

Importance of the fragment

Fragment 3 focuses on two topics. First, it addresses a problem in epistemology: How do we gain new knowledge? Second, it examines the conditions that lead to a unified city-state, which is free from discord. These seem rather disparate themes, and scholars have been led to wonder if the first five lines, which treat the epistemological theme, really belong with lines 6–14, which deal with the political problem. The unity is provided by the concepts of discovery and calculation and becomes clearer once the text is clarified. In the first five lines, Archytas argues that there are two ways to gain new knowledge, learning from another and discovery on our own. He clearly suggests that discovery is best, because what we discover is in some sense our own; we do not depend on someone else for our understanding of it. Discovery, however, rarely occurs by chance; we must follow some process of inquiry in order to facilitate the discovery of new knowledge. Archytas then suggests that inquiry too has prerequisites. It is at this point that the text of the fragment becomes problematic. He clearly says that some sort of knowledge is required in order to inquire. Iamblichus understood this as a reference to the Platonic theory of recollection, i.e. that we must have prior knowledge of what we are looking for, in order to find it; finding it is, in fact, just recollecting what we already knew. There is no support for this reading in the text itself other than the bare suggestion that we must have some knowledge in order to inquire. It would be more plausible, in context of the rest of Fragment 3, to suppose that Archytas simply means that we must start from knowledge initially provided by a teacher, in order to be able to use inquiry to discover something new. Thus a teacher might provide the basics of the discipline and a methodology, which the student uses in order to make new discoveries. The difficulty with this interpretation is again that too much needs to be read into the text. The text as transmitted is inadequate to produce sense. It is likely that a phrase further defining the knowledge required for inquiry has fallen out of the text, and the remainder of Fragment 3 clearly suggests that what we need to know in order to inquire is how to calculate (see the detailed commentary).

If this is the correct way to clarify an obscure text, Archytas is arguing that the crucial prerequisite for the inquiry that leads to new knowledge is the ability to calculate. In Greek as in English, the word for calculation can refer to rational thought in general, but the rest of Fragment 3 heavily emphasizes the quantitative features of calculation (λογισμός), so that it is more likely that Archytas is thinking of calculation primarily in a mathematical sense. The science of calculation, called λογιστική in Fragment 4, studies the properties of numbers that form the basis for practical calculation and in particular studies proportions. It is the application of this science that Archytas sees as indispensable for inquiry. Although no clear explanation is given of how calculation serves as the basis for inquiry in Fragment 3, we might speculate that the use of proportion in forming definitions, which seems to lie behind the definitions in Testimonium A22, is an example of what Archytas has in mind.

The description of the process of learning in lines 1–5 has important implications for our understanding of Pythagorean education. The traditional picture of Pythagorean teaching, based in part on texts such as Iamblichus' *On the Pythagorean Life*, assumes the *ipse dixit* model, which calls on the student to memorize the precepts of the master and allows little scope for debate and questioning (see Lynch 1972: 56–57 for an example of this understanding of Pythagorean teaching). Archytas, in lines 1–5 of Fragment 3, on the other hand, puts the primary value not on learning from another but on discovery for oneself through inquiry. Testimonium A9 also shows that Archytas did not follow the *ipse dixit* model and suggests that open discussion of issues, in which the most extreme positions were entertained, was part of the process leading to discovery. In Fragment 3, Archytas is arguing that discovery is something that occurs in the individual and that such discovery is the result of two factors: (1) a process of seeking which, according to A9, included canvassing a wide variety of opinions, (2) the ability to calculate, which allows us to sort through the opinions and generate new knowledge from what we already know. The model of teaching and learning that Archytas has in mind, then, is clearly focused on discovery for ourselves and discovery of new knowledge through the use of calculation rather than on preserving the teaching of the master.

In the next section of Fragment 3, Archytas begins by describing the results of the discovery of calculation for human beings and in particular for the city-state. Lines 1–5 showed the need for calculation in order to reach new knowledge, and lines 6–14 give an example of the generation of new knowledge, the knowledge that ensures a concordant city-state. The problem of civil strife and the search for a way to ensure concord or *homonoia* were prominent themes in late fifth- and early fourth-century thought. Archytas' contribution to this discourse is his insistence that it is calculation and the application of proportion which will stop strife and increase concord, by establishing equality among the citizens in place of the continual drive to have more than others (*pleonexia*). He can hardly expect his citizens to all be masters of the science of calculation and proportion (*logistikē* – see Fr. 4) or to devote themselves to proofs such as he developed himself (A19). Nor does Fragment 3 suggest imposing a master mathematician as a philosopher king to rule the state in accordance with abstruse mathematical principles. Instead, Fragment 3 assumes that all citizens can grasp and apply the most important principles discovered by *logistikē*. In Fragment 3, Archytas appears as a moderate democrat, who thinks that calculation shows that the rich should give to the poor, but also that the clarity of the calculation will convince both parties that they have what is fair. The crucial feature of calculation to which Archytas is appealing is its ability to produce agreement. It produces agreement among rich and poor but also between all individuals in the state in their dealings with one another. Those tempted to injustice, who are able to use calculation, are shown by the clear light of calculation that their injustice cannot be hidden. Figures do not lie. Those not able to calculate may commit injustice, but, when brought to trial, they are revealed as unjust precisely by calculation. The calculation of judge and/or jury leads to their conviction and probably sets the penalty, both of which hinder them from further injustice. It may also be that through the legal proceedings the criminal comes to understand how to calculate and hence can use calculation as a standard in order to avoid future injustice. The master of *logistikē* has something to teach his fellow citizens, but it is the accessibility and clarity of mathematics to all citizens which allows it to be the foundation of a just state.

Fragment 3 makes sense as the background to a number of passages in Plato. Thus, Archytas is likely to be one of the wise men whom Socrates praises in the *Gorgias* (507e ff.) for the rejection of *pleonexia* and the recognition of the power of "geometric equality" (i.e. the study of proportion – see below). In the *Euthyphro*, Plato is clearly struck by the point that Archytas is making. At 7b ff. Socrates uses some of the same language as Fragment 3 to stress that appeal to calculation (ἐπὶ λογισμὸν ἐλθόντες, cf. Fr. 3, lines 12–13, ἐπ᾽ αὐτὸν ἔλθωντι) allows us to quickly settle disagreements (περί γε τῶν τοιούτων ταχὺ ἂν ἀπαλλαγεῖμεν, cf. Fr. 3, line 8, περὶ τῶν συναλλαγμάτων διαλλασσόμεθα) and reach concord (cf. *Alc. 1* 126c). There is some implication that a similar science concerning moral issues would be beneficial. Indeed, in the *Protagoras* Socrates envisages expanding the science of measurement to pleasure and pain (356d). It seems clear, nonetheless, that Plato saw difficulties in supposing that mathematical calculation could solve moral problems. Can calculation itself, for all its clarity, help us to determine what the values are to which it should be applied (cf. e.g. Irwin 1977: 298, n. 41). Pleasure at first sight appears to be a possible candidate as the common coinage to which calculation can be applied, but the *Philebus* shows that Plato came to see that pleasure was not uniform in nature. Already in the *Republic* Plato seems to have come to believe that the mathematics which governs the just state and human morality is extremely complicated; the famous passage on the nuptial number suggests that the mathematics of morality is perhaps too complicated even for the philosopher kings to master (546d). Archytas has a more democratic vision in which all citizens are able to grasp enough mathematics to ensure a just society.

Although Aristotle makes no direct mention of Archytas in developing his political theory and his theory of justice, there is much in what Aristotle says that is illuminated, if we assume that the ideas in Archytas Fragment 3 were one of Aristotle's starting points. To begin with areas of disagreement, Aristotle clearly had his doubts about Archytas' attempt to equate political science with the science of calculation. This can be seen in Aristotle's famous assertion that political science does not admit of the same degree of exactness as some sciences (*EN* 1094b12 ff.). Moreover, Aristotle argues that concord (*homonoia*), which is the focus in Archytas Fr. 3, cannot be equated with agreement in just any area and specifically says that agreement in an area of mathematics (the example given is astronomy) is not equivalent to political concord (*EN* 1167a24). This can be read as a direct criticism of Archytas' position that agreement between rich and poor about mathematical calculation and proportion leads to political concord. Indeed, distributive justice, which deals with the fair distribution of goods and power in the state, is ultimately based on some sort of criterion of desert, and it is concerning this criterion that disagreement arises between rival factions in the state such as democrats and oligarchs. We have no indication in Fragment 3 of how Archytas thought calculation could produce concord about such a criterion.

On the other hand, Aristotle's theory of justice can be seen as building directly on Archytas' insight regarding the connection between justice and calculation in Fragment 3. Indeed, Aristotle's account of the "special virtue" of justice (*EN* 1130b30) provides excellent examples of what Archytas may have meant by the application of calculation to problems of justice. The two types of special justice, distributive justice and corrective justice, are each identified with a mathematical proportion. Distributive justice is the equal according to the geometric proportion and corrective justice is the equal according to the arithmetic proportion (*EN* 1131a29 ff. and 1131b32 ff.). Distributive justice takes into account the relative worth of two citizens and assigns them goods that are in proportion to that relative worth; it is thus favored by aristocrats. Corrective justice ignores any differences in relative worth and treats each citizen as of equal worth, giving each an equal share; it is thus favored by democrats. Aristotle's account clarifies a puzzling aspect of Fragment 3 of Archytas, i.e. how different sorts of mathematical proportion might have been used in the just ordering of the state. Archytas may have thought that even more proportions than the arithmetic and geometric were relevant. We might suppose that Archytas had anticipated some of the important distinctions in Aristotle's theory of justice (e.g. distributive and corrective justice), but there is nothing in Fragment 3 to suggest this. Fragment 3 makes most sense as a programmatic statement highlighting the central role of mathematical proportion in political science to which both Plato and Aristotle responded and on which they both built.

Detailed commentary

Lines 1–2 δεῖ . . . γενέσθαι – In this line Archytas argues that there are two ways to gain knowledge which we do not have: by learning it from another or by discovering it ourselves. This thought finds parallels in a number of passages of Plato. In the famous "autobiographical" section of the *Phaedo*, Socrates envisages just the two possibilities found in Archytas Fragment 3 (οὔτ' αὐτὸς εὑρεῖν οὔτε παρ' ἄλλου μαθεῖν οἷός τε ἐγενόμην, 99c; cf. also 85c7, ἢ μαθεῖν ὅπῃ ἔχει ἢ εὑρεῖν). The *Cratylus* also uses the "learn or discover" formula but is even closer to Archytas Fragment 3 in that ἐξευρίσκω is used instead of simply εὑρίσκω. "Do we say that it is impossible to learn or discover things any other way than either having learned the names or having ourselves discovered what they are?" (ἢ τὰ ὀνόματα μαθόντας ἢ αὐτοὺς ἐξευρόντας οἷά ἐστι, 438b1–3). The similarities between these passages in Plato and Fragment 3 of Archytas need not be taken as evidence of Pythagorean influence on Plato or Platonic influence on Archytas. The thesis that in order to gain knowledge one must either learn it from another or discover it oneself is not a technical doctrine that belongs to a specific school of philosophy, but is a common-sense observation that is also found in the general Greek intellectual tradition. This is made clear by Fragment 843 of Sophocles: "Things that can be taught I learn, things that can be discovered I seek, things that can be prayed for I seek from the gods" (τὰ μὲν διδακτὰ μανθάνω, τὰ δ' εὑρετὰ ζητῶ, τὰ δ' εὐκτὰ παρὰ θεῶν ᾐτησάμην).

ἀνεπιστάμων . . . ἐπιστάμονα – Both of these adjectives are attested before Archytas. The latter appears already at *Odyssey* XVI. 374 and the former is found both in Herodotus (IX. 62) and Thucydides (VII. 67). ἀνεπιστάμων is Blass' emendation, which has been accepted by all later editors. Stobaeus has ἐπιστάμων, which Timpanaro Cardini (1962: 374) tries to defend, although printing Blass' emendation. Timpanaro Cardini understands the passage to mean that we gain *conscious* knowledge of things (ἐπιστάμονα γενέσθαι) which we before knew *unconsciously* (ὧν ἐπιστάμων ἦσθα). This reads far too much into the text. For such an interpretation to be tenable the crucial words "conscious" and "unconscious" would surely need to be expressed. Stobaeus' text, which asserts that "you come to know those things which you knew," is nonsense. Moreover, Iamblichus' text of the passage, ὧν ἂν ἐπιστάμων ἦσθα, gives strong support to Blass' emendation. In any attempt to make sense of this reading, the ἂν would have to be taken with ἦσθα and thus form part of a contrary to fact condition, but such a condition is totally out of place here. Blass' correction of ἂν ἐπιστάμων to ἀνεπιστάμων quickly restores sense to the sentence as a whole ("you come to know those things which you did not know") and at the same time explains the nonsensical reading found in Iamblichus as resulting from a mistaken division between words. Stobaeus' reading ἐπιστάμων is then either the result of a copyist omitting the non-sensical ἂν, once it had become separated from ἐπιστάμων, or an example of a polar error, where the copyist writes the exact opposite of the actual text (see Kopff 1975).

2–3 ἀλλότριον . . . ἴδιον – This is the reading of the manuscripts of Stobaeus and the text that Blass prints. The manuscripts of Iamblichus have ἀλλοτρία... ἴδιον, which is what Festa prints in his edition. Diels suggested ἰδίᾳ so that DK and Hense's edition of Stobaeus print ἀλλοτρίᾳ . . . ἰδίᾳ. At first sight ἀλλοτρίᾳ would appear to be the *lectio difficilior* and this probably led Diels to accept it and to propose the parallel change to ἰδίᾳ. Whereas ἰδίᾳ is common as an adverb meaning "privately," ἀλλοτρίᾳ is, however, unparalleled in this adverbial use ("with another's help" – DK). Moreover, ἰδίᾳ would have to bear the meaning "with one's own help," which is not its normal sense and, such a translation of the passage makes it redundant: "from another and with another's help . . . through oneself and with one's own help." What is the difference between "through oneself" and "with one's own help"? Stobaeus' text gives a better sense: "to learn is from another and belongs to another, but to discover is through oneself and belongs to oneself." Here ἴδιον and ἀλλότριον agree with the articular infinitives. As Blass notes, the expression is a bit bold, since to say that "to learn belongs to another" seems to mean that *what* we learn belongs to another and correspondingly *what* we discover is our own. The passage is clearly highly rhetorical, however, and such a transfer of the epithet to the verb from the noun does not seem too difficult. ἴδιος is usually contrasted with κοινός ("private vs. public") and ἀλλότριος with οἰκεῖος ("another's vs. one's own," e.g. Pl. *R.* 343c), but there are a few examples of ἴδιος and ἀλλότριος ("one's own vs. another's") being set in contrast as they are in Archytas (e.g. Arist. *de An.* 420a18; Pl. *R.* 610a).

   How then can we explain the reading ἀλλοτρίᾳ in Iamblichus? If we look at Iamblichus' explication of the passage we find that he interprets it in terms of mathematical knowledge (43.13) and τὰ μαθήματα. Thus, when he paraphrases Archytas, he does so in terms of learning τὰ μαθήματα:

"for whenever we take over the sciences as from another and belonging to another . . ." (45.2–3). Thus Iamblichus uses the neuter plural ἀλλότρια to agree with μαθήματα. This use of the neuter plural by Iamblichus could have then been read back into the text of Archytas either by Iamblichus himself, given his conceptualization of the situation, or in the manuscript tradition. This was in turn corrupted to the adverbial use of the dative, because the neuter plural had nothing to agree with in the context in Archytas.

3 ἐξευρὲν . . . ζατοῦντα – These two verbs, "to discover" and "to seek," are naturally and commonly paired. Seeking leads to discovery (e.g. Soph. Fr. 843 and Xenophanes Fr. 18). At *Cratylus* 436a, Socrates asks whether, when we discover the names of things, we also discover the things themselves, "or is this just the means of being instructed and there is some other way of seeking and discovering" (ἢ ζητεῖν μὲν καὶ εὑρίσκειν ἕτερον δεῖν τρόπον, μανθάνειν δὲ τοῦτον). This passage is also important as once again contrasting seeking/ discovering with learning. ἐξευρίσκω can mean simply "discover" but can also imply more effort as in "find out" or "invent." It is so used in Heraclitus Fr. 45 "You could not find out (ἐξεύροιο) the limits of the soul by going, even traveling every road, it has such a deep logos."

3–4 ἄπορον . . . εὔπορον – The use of the noun, adjective and verb formed on the roots απορ/ευπορ to express the contrast between what is difficult and what is easy is very common in the Greek of Archytas' time. Democritus Fr. 106 provides a close parallel to Archytas' use of the adjectives agreeing with infinitives used as substantives: "In good fortune it is easy (εὔπορον) to find a friend, but in bad fortune the most difficult (ἀπορώτατον) of all things." In Plato's *Symposium* (204b7), the father of love is εὔπορος while his mother is ἄπορος.

4 σπάνιον . . . ῥᾴδιον – This contrast is not very common and in fact seems to involve an ellipsis in thought. Properly, what is easy (ῥᾴδιον) should be contrasted with what is difficult (χαλεπόν) and not with what occurs infrequently (σπάνιον). What is difficult does occur infrequently, however, and what is easy occurs frequently so that σπάνιον and ῥᾴδιον could come to be used in opposition. Since we already have the contrast between difficult (ἄπορον) and easy (εὔπορον) in Archytas Fr. 3 and since σπάνιον (infrequent) comes first in the contrast, "infrequent" and "frequent" seem to be the best translations. Democritus Fr. 232 provides a good parallel for the use of σπάνιον: "The pleasures that occur most infrequently (σπανιώτατα) delight the most." The contrast between σπάνιον and ῥᾴδιον is rare. I find no examples in the Presocratics, the Hippocratic or Plato. Aristotle has a few passages that while not precise parallels show how the contrast could arise. Thus at *EN* 1109a29 Aristotle says that to find the mean in anger does not belong to everyone and is not easy (ῥᾴδιον), wherefore what is good is rare (σπάνιον) and praised (cf. *MM* i. 9 and *EE* 1235b).

4–5   μὴ ἐπιστάμενον δὲ <λογίζεσθαι> ζητεῖν ἀδύνατον – This is the most problematic passage in the fragment. The central difficulty is in explaining the force of the participle "not knowing" (μὴ ἐπιστάμενον). I favor the solution of supposing that an infinitive, λογίζεσθαι, governed by μὴ ἐπιστάμενον has fallen out of the text. Before discussing this emendation, however, it is important to review the three major ways of understanding the unemended text. First, some scholars understand μὴ ἐπιστάμενον as parallel to μὴ ζατοῦντα in line 3 and as governing the infinitive ζητεῖν, while ἀδύνατον is an adjective parallel to the other adjectives in lines 3–4 (easy/difficult; frequent/infrequent) and, like them, in agreement with ἐξευρὲν in line 3. Thus the phrase is understood to mean "if, however, one does not know how to seek, discovery is impossible" (Freeman 1948: 80; Merlan 1953: 9; Timpanaro Cardini 1962: 374–75). Grammatically and stylistically there is nothing wrong with this interpretation. There seems to be an insuperable problem for this interpretation in terms of sense, however. In lines 3–4, discovery is said to be "difficult and infrequent," if one does not seek (presumably we might chance upon the right answer) but "easy and frequent," if we do seek. Archytas is not going quite so far as to make seeking a sufficient or even necessary condition for discovery but rather asserting that seeking makes discovery much more likely than if we do not seek. He does recognize that discovery sometimes occurs, even if we do not seek. The first reading of lines 4–5, on the other hand, says that, if we do not know how to seek (and thus do not seek), discovery is not just "difficult and infrequent" but simply "impossible." This reading of the passage thus has Archytas contradict himself in the space of two lines, saying first that, if we do not seek, discovery is difficult and infrequent but possible and then, in the next line, saying that, if we do not seek (because we do not know how), discovery is completely impossible.

The sequence of thought in lines 1–5 also argues against this first interpretation of lines 4–5. In lines 1–3, the distinction between learning and discovery as ways of gaining knowledge is made, and discovery is identified as the best way to gain knowledge. Lines 3–4 then discuss the conditions under which discovery arises: it is said to be much easier and more frequent, if one inquires. At this point we would expect not another statement about the conditions for discovery (which is what the first interpretation gives us) but rather a statement about inquiry, which has just been identified as crucial to discovery. For these two reasons, then, the first reading of the passage must be rejected.

DK take a second possible line of interpretation, by understanding ζητεῖν in line 5 to go both with the participle and also with the adjective "impossible." They give the translation "für den freilich, der es nicht versteht, ist das Suchen unmöglich" ("for the one who does not understand it the search is impossible"). This interpretation avoids the problems outlined above, by not asserting that discovery is impossible and by understanding the focus to be on inquiry rather than discovery, but it introduces other problems. First, such a double use of the infinitive is a very awkward and unnatural construction. If μὴ ἐπιστάμενον is taken with ζητεῖν, the reader will most naturally understand ἀδύνατον to go with ἐξευρὲν and thus fall into the first interpretation. Second, the sense of the last part of the sentence becomes very weak. It is almost a tautology to say "if one does not know how to seek, it is impossible to seek." The first three lines of the fragment establish the crucial importance of seeking. What the logic of the passage calls for, then, is some sort of statement of the conditions which make seeking possible. The bare assertion that in order to seek one has to know how to seek without further comment, is vacuous. DK are in fact forced to posit a lacuna, in which the transition to the second part of the fragment was effected, and they may have supposed that further explanation of the conditions for seeking was also provided in the lacuna.

A third interpretation does away with the difficulties involved in the first two interpretations but introduces some difficulties of its own. On this interpretation ζητεῖν is the subject of the clause and parallel to ἐξευρὲν in line 3. It is thus asserted that "it is impossible to seek, if one does not know." This is the interpretation of Iamblichus. What does the sentence mean, read in this way? We are told that "it is impossible to seek, if we do not know," but it is unclear what we do not know. Iamblichus supposes that Archytas is arguing that we must have some sort of prior knowledge of that which we are seeking in order to seek and that this prior knowledge is to be understood in terms of Plato's theory of recollection: Archytas is solving Meno's paradox (how can we seek something we do not know?), in the same way that Plato did, by supposing that we do in some sense know what we are seeking. It is possible to seek the answer, because we already have the answer in us and simply need to recollect it.

It may be that modern scholars have avoided this interpretation because it seems to assign the doctrine of recollection to Archytas. The fragment would be of dubious authenticity, since it would be following the pattern of the pseudepigrapha, in assigning a prominent Platonic idea back to a Pythagorean. This general line of interpretation of the last clause in lines 4–5 need not, however, entail the doctrine of recollection. None of the Platonic vocabulary for recollection, most notably *anamnēsis* itself, is used. It is true that, since this is such a short fragment, it is not impossible that the text did go on to use such language. The fact, however, that Iamblichus, who is interpreting the fragment as referring to the doctrine of recollection, does not quote further or refer to any such language strongly suggests that Archytas did not say anything more which was indicative of the doctrine of recollection than we see here in Fragment 3. If Archytas gave no further explication of μὴ ἐπιστάμενον, it is a tremendous overinterpretation to read the doctrine of recollection into these two words.

What sense can we make of this third reading of the clause without Iamblichus' assumption that it refers to the doctrine of recollection? Iamblichus' discussion provides a clue (see my discussion of the context of the fragment above). Archytas is asserting that it is not possible to seek, if one does not know. If "not knowing" is not qualified in any way, the most reasonable interpretation is that one cannot seek, if one does not know anything about the matter in question. Now this would indeed introduce Meno's paradox, if Archytas thought that discovery was the only way to get knowledge and that one must seek in order to discover. Archytas explicitly says, however, that there are two ways to get knowledge, either by discovery or by learning from another. The first part of the fragment could be seen as having a sort of ring composition. Two ways of gaining knowledge are identified: learning from another or discovering by oneself. Discovering by oneself is shown to be preferable, as the only way to get knowledge that is really your own. Discovery is then said to be most easily attained by inquiry. Finally, inquiry is said to require knowledge. There is no assertion, however, that this knowledge must be the sort of knowledge that is acquired by discovery. Archytas might think that we begin by learning from others; such knowledge is not the best sort, since it does not really belong to us, nonetheless we need it in order to be able to inquire. Learning from a teacher gives us an initial familiarity with a field and a method of inquiry, which then allows us to go on to gain knowledge that is truly our own through discovery. This reading makes better sense than the first two and is reasonable for someone of Archytas' date, but there are serious problems with it. First, it is stylistically and syntactically odd to leave μὴ ἐπιστάμενον with no object or complement. Second, this interpretation calls upon us to read a considerable amount into μὴ ἐπιστάμενον. Indeed, if this were Archytas' point, he would surely have written not μὴ ἐπιστάμενον but rather μὴ μαθόντα ("not having learned") in order to clearly illustrate the ring composition and emphasize the relationship between learning from another and discovery. Finally, as with the first two interpretations, the third interpretation provides no obvious connection between line 5 and what follows. All modern interpreters have been forced to posit a lacuna between the two parts of the fragment in order to explain the apparent lack of connection between the two parts, although some (e.g. DK and Timpanaro Cardini) only mention the lacuna in their notes without actually indicating it in the text.

Since there are serious difficulties with the three proposed readings of the manuscript text, an emendation is called for. As in the third interpretation, I suggest that ζητεῖν be understood as parallel to ἐξευρὲν and as modified by ἀδύνατον. Having identified seeking as crucial to discovery, Archytas is now stating the conditions necessary for seeking to be successful. He makes the point negatively by asserting that "it is impossible to seek" under certain conditions. These conditions are expressed by the circumstantial participle μὴ ἐπιστάμενον, also as in interpretation three. Interpretation three, however, left the circumstantial participle undefined. The text provides no explicit answer to the obvious question, "If we do not know what?," and an answer has to be supplied from the context. One major problem with the manuscript text is thus the lack of a complement for μὴ ἐπιστάμενον. The other problem with the text is the lack of connection between line 5 and the rest of the fragment. We need an emendation that addresses both of these problems. I suggest that an infinitive, λογίζεσθαι, depending on the participle and specifying "what we do not know" has fallen out of the text. The correct text is thus μὴ ἐπιστάμενον δὲ <λογίζεσθαι> ζητεῖν ἀδύνατον: ". . . but, if one does not know how to calculate, it is impossible to seek" (cf. τοὺς μὲν ἐπισταμένους λογίζεσθαι just six lines later). A copyist, confronted by the two consecutive infinitives and understanding the construction of the passage along the lines of the first interpretation outlined above, according to which ἀδύνατον goes with ἐξευρὲν, removed the first infinitive, perhaps regarding "to calculate" as a gloss on "knowing how to seek."

This emendation solves both of the problems for the manuscript text. First, it restores sense to line 5, by specifying what it is that we do not know. Archytas' point is that discovery does not occur reliably unless we make the effort to seek an answer, but it is impossible to seek an answer, i.e. to investigate a problem, unless we know how to calculate. Calculation is used here in the sense that it has in the rest of Fragment 3, where calculation is the model for rational thought (see below). Second, the emendation neatly addresses the apparent lack of connection between the two parts of the fragment by recognizing the role of λογισμός, the central concept in the second part of the fragment, in the epistemology set forth in the first part of the fragment. The other major connection between the first and second part of the fragment is the use of the participle "discovered" (εὑρεθείς) in line 6, which can be understood as picking up on the prominent theme of discovery in the first four lines. Significantly this participle modifies precisely "calculation" (λογισμός). Thus, the first section of the fragment ends with the recognition of the need to know how to calculate, in order to carry out the investigation which leads to discovery. The second part of the fragment then starts from the discovery of calculation itself and describes the discoveries which follow from it and which lead to a stable state.

6 στάσιν... ὁμόνοιαν – Archytas is here using two of the central concepts in late fifth- and fourth-century political thought: discord (civil strife) and concord. The evidence suggests that the concept of *homonoia* or concord first emerged in the late fifth century as a response to the *staseis* or civil wars between democrats and oligarchs that shook city-state after city-state. As de Romilly remarks, one could even say that we observe the birth of the need for this concept in the course of reading Thucydides' history (1972: 199). The word does not occur in Homer, Herodotus, or the tragedians but appears twice each in Democritus and Thucydides before becoming very common after 404, particularly in the orators and sophists. In Thucydides it occurs in contexts of conflict between democrats and oligarchs at Athens (VIII. 75.2 and 93.3). Democritus Fr. 250 says that "It is from concord (ὁμονοίης) that it is possible for city-states to accomplish great things and fight wars, otherwise it is not possible," and Fr. 255 connects concord with the powerful helping the poor just as in Archytas Fr. 3. Similarly Democritus attacks *stasis* in Fragment 249 as good neither for those who conquer nor for those conquered. The concept of *homonoia* or concord among citizens is thus born from the need to defend the city against imminent disintegration, because of the strife between democrats and oligarchs. The sophists also seem to appeal to such a concept in their accounts of the basis of the state. Antiphon wrote a treatise of which very little survives, which was entitled *On Concord* (44a; 63; 67). Plato makes concord a crucial element of his ideal state and relates it to friendship and to the virtue of temperance (σωφροσύνη). He also in some contexts defines it in terms of shared beliefs (ὁμοδοξία), for which he is criticized by Aristotle (*EN* 1167a22–8), who also treats concord as an important political and moral concept (*EN* IX. 6;

cf. *EE* VII. 7 and *MM* II. 12). For Aristotle "concord" is a term used when discussing questions of action and questions of great importance for the city. He defines concord as political friendship (for the development of the concept of *homonoia* from Plato to the Stoics see Schofield 1991: 128–29).

It is thus clear from the history of the concept of *homonoia* that there is nothing surprising in Archytas using it, since it emerged as a central concept at about the time that he might have begun to write and continued to be a central theme in political thought throughout his lifetime. Archytas' distinctive contribution to this theme is his emphasis on the crucial role of calculation in establishing concord. None of the other texts from the period highlight the role of calculation in this way. The texts in the pseudo-Pythagorean tradition, on the other hand, tend to mirror the characteristics of the Platonic and Aristotelian treatments of *homonoia*. "Aresas" works precisely with the Platonic tripartite soul (νόος, θύμωσις, ἐπιθυμία Thesleff 50.11–12) and says that when each part has been ordered according to the harmonizing proportion *homonoia* and *homophrosuna* arise. The Platonic analogy between the soul and the city is also the context for the use of *homonoia* by "Damippos" (68.29). The pseudo-Pythagorean "Ecphantus" (81.22) shows Aristotelian influence in the claim that "Friendship in the city by aiming at some common goal shows the concord (*homonoia*) of the whole."

Archytas' account of concord in Fragment 3 as dependent on calculation, far from showing the influence of Platonic and Aristotelian discussions, in fact, seems to be one of the targets of both Plato and Aristotle. Aristotle emphasizes that concord is not agreement in just any area but rather agreement about practical ends of importance. His example of an area in which agreement would not constitute concord is precisely a mathematical science, astronomy. Agreement about things in the heavens lacks the bond of friendship which is necessary for true concord (*EN* 1167a25). Aristotle could similarly be supposed to respond to Fragment 3 by pointing out that agreement in mathematical calculation does not constitute concord and that Archytas is making an illegitimate leap in supposing that the science of calculation is the science of the state. Similarly the Platonic *Alcibiades I* recognizes that it is the friendship of the citizens, understood as concord, which makes the state good (126c), but in what follows arithmetic is said to produce "concord" about numbers only, and it is argued that some other art must produce concord in the state. The *Alcibiades I* may not be by Plato, but the same train of thought that rejects the literal application of numerical calculation to moral problems can be found in undoubtedly genuine dialogues (e.g. *Euthphr.* 7b ff., *Prt.* 356e). Plato is clearly more tempted by the analogy between the mathematical sciences and moral science than Aristotle, but he does not seem to accept Archytas' assertion that it is calculation which is the science that produces concord in the state.

λογισμὸς εὑρεθείς – λογισμός is the central concept of the second portion of Fragment 3, and, if we read <λογίζεσθαι> in line 5, its appearance here in line 6 is well motivated. The first five lines of the fragment point to the need for the ability to calculate in order for human beings to engage in the inquiry that leads to the discovery of new knowledge. The second part of the fragment then begins with an account of the marvelous things that follow from the discovery of calculation. There is a bit of a paradox here: if the knowledge of how to calculate is required for the inquiry that leads to discovery, how are we to explain the discovery of calculation? Does the discovery of calculation require calculation? Given the emphasis on discovery in the first part of the fragment (ἐξευρίσκω appears three times in five lines), it is indeed impossible not to think of what is said about discovery there, when the discovery of calculation is introduced in line 6. Archytas might have addressed this paradox in what followed Fragment 3. It is striking that he uses the simple form of the verb εὑρίσκω, when talking about the discovery of calculation, in contrast to the compound verb ἐξευρίσκω, which seems to imply the arduous process involved in humans finding things "out." Calculation may be something that is initially just found by chance rather than something that is figured out by a process of inquiry. Indeed, it is not uncommon for the Greeks to present such innate human abilities as calculation as the gift of the gods. It is in just such a context that we find a parallel for Archytas' reference to the discovery of calculation. In the *Phaedrus* (274c8), Plato reports that it was the Egyptian god Theuth who "discovered calculation" (λογισμὸν εὑρεῖν). It may well be that we should understand lines 6–14 as picturing the effect on society produced by the first discovery of calculation. This reading is supported by the use of the aorists in lines 6, 12 and 14, although they could also be gnomic aorists.

What exactly is this λογισμός, which is discovered? λογισμός has two basic meanings. It has a narrow meaning of "counting" or "numerical calculation" and in this sense is often paired with number (ἀριθμός). It is thus used to describe an Athenian general "counting up the days" (Th. IV. 122). In the *Euthyphro* Socrates argues that if they had a disagreement about which number was greater they could easily settle it by appealing to "numerical calculation" (ἐπὶ λογισμὸν ἐλθόντες 7b10) and in the *Phaedrus* (274c), as we have seen, it is listed along with number, geometry and astronomy as discoveries of the Egyptian god Theuth. It is most commonly used, however, in a more general sense of "the exercise of reason in rational inference and thought" (Irwin 1985: 422) with no reference to numbers. Thus in the funeral oration it refers to the rational calculation which the Athenians use in evaluating the risks of an action and which produces hesitation in other states (λογισμὸς ὄκνον φέρει) but not in Pericles' Athens (Th. II. 40). It is used in a wide range of Greek authors to refer to the rational part of a human being as opposed to the passions (Plato *R.* 439d1; cf. Chrysippus *SVF* III. 95.3). It is what distinguishes human beings from animals, which live just by impressions (Arist. *Metaph.* 980b28), and adults from children, who from the beginning have spirit (θυμός) but may never partake of *logismos* (Plato *R.* 441a9; cf. Arist. *Pol.* 1322b). Democritus uses it to contrast the soul with the body, arguing that perfection of the soul corrects the inferiority of the body but that physical strength without reason (λογισμοῦ) does not improve the mind (Fr. 187).

Probably because of this widespread use to refer in general to "the exercise of reason" or the "rational part" of a human being, λογισμός is not defined more precisely in most systems of Greek philosophy. Plato uses it as a general term but not as a technical term for a specific mental faculty. One source (Aët. IV. 21 = *SVF* II. 227.25) reports that the Stoics used it as an alternate name for "the commanding faculty" (τὸ ἡγεμονικόν), but it does not in fact appear very often in this use, and the normal Stoic word for reason is simply λόγος (for the Epicurean use of ἐπιλογισμός, see Sedley 1973: 27). Aristotle is the exception in that he does give it a technical sense. In classifying the states of the soul that grasp truth, he joins λογισμός with opinion as states that admit of falsehood in contrast to understanding (ἐπιστήμη) and comprehension (νοῦς), which are always true (*APo.* 100b7). λογισμός itself, however, does not occur as frequently in this sense as the verb λογίζεσθαι or the adjective form with the article, τὸ λογιστικόν. Thus, at *EN* 1139a11 ff., Aristotle divides the rational part of the soul into τὸ λογιστικόν "the rationally calculating part" and τὸ ἐπιστημονικόν "the scientific part." The scientific part deals with necessary truths whereas the rationally calculating part deals with what can be otherwise.

The Pythagorean pseudepigrapha characteristically use *logismos* in the context of Platonic and Aristotelian distinctions. In *On Virtue* by "Theages" *logismos* is used as the name for the rational part of the Platonic tripartite soul, in contrast to the two irrational parts, *thumos* and *epithumia* (Thesleff 1965: 190.8 ff.; see also 192.22 ff.). Again in a spurious treatise assigned to Archytas himself, *On the Good and Happy Man* (Thesleff 1965: 14.1 ff.), we are told that in order for a man to be *phronimos* he must from youth have exercised his mind (*dianoia*) in reasoning (λογισμοῖς), sciences (μαθημάτεσσι), and areas of inquiry that involve precision (ταῖς ποτ᾽ ἀκρίβειαν θεωρίαις). These distinctions seem to assume the Aristotelian identification of *logismos* as a mental faculty which deals with what can be otherwise in contrast to the faculties involved in the mathematical sciences and more precise inquiries. In Fragment 3 there is no suggestion that λογισμός is one part of a Platonic tripartite soul or that it is used in the Aristotelian sense as an intellectual state that admits of falsehood.

When we are told that *logismos* is required for all inquiry in lines 4–5 and in lines 12–13 that it keeps us from acting unjustly when we consult it, the general translation "rational calculation" might appear most plausible (so Despotopoulos 1987). Nonetheless, the language and rhetoric of Fragment 3 as a whole make most sense if Archytas is using it in the narrower sense of "numerical calculation." When first introduced *logismos* is associated with a series of words that refer to quantitative concepts. It is said to "increase" (αὔξησεν) "sameness of thought" (ὁμόνοιαν) and to produce "equality" (ἰσότας). It encourages proper relations of giving and taking between rich and poor because each party trusts that through this (λογισμός) they will have "what is equal" (τὸ ἴσον). λογισμός is also described as a κανών, which in its most basic sense refers to a carpenter's rule and is often paired with the word μέτρον ("measure"). Similarly it is said to stop πλεονεξία, which literally refers to the "desire for more." All of these connections make clear that Archytas is emphasizing quantitative relations and hence the meaning "numerical calculation." If we take *logismos* to mean simply "rational calculation" the passage loses its rhetorical force. Why in particular would we expect "rational calculation" to help us to establish equality and banish excess? It is precisely "numerical calculation" that helps here. The problems of the state are presented in purposefully quantitative terms in order to suggest that numerical calculation is the answer even in the political domain. It is numerical calculation that can help us to understand "equality" (I am here adopting a slightly different position than in Huffman 2002b: 262).

It is natural to connect the praise of λογισμός here in Fragment 3 with the characterization of λογιστικά as the preeminent mathematical science in Fragment 4. λογιστικά is there the science of number that underlies practical calculation and puts special emphasis on the relative quantity of numbers (see the commentary on Fragment 4). Since λογισμός is presented in Fragment 3 as accessible to all members of society, rich and poor alike, it is not likely to be the scientific study of calculation and proportion, i.e. *logistikē*. The average citizen would hardly be expected to develop proofs in this area. It is more likely that Archytas envisages *logismos* as a basic understanding first of calculation (i.e. modern arithmetic) but more importantly also of proportions, such as the three means found in Fragment 2. Such an understanding of λογισμός is clearly reflected in the opening words of Plato's *Statesman* (257a ff.). When Theodorus treats the sophist, statesman and philosopher as if they are of equal value and hence in an arithmetic proportion, Socrates points out that in fact they differ so much in worth that they cannot be expressed in a proportion (ἀναλογίαν), although proportion is the specialty of Theodorus' art. What is this art in which Theodorus is a specialist? He is described as "a master in calculations and things having to do with geometry" (τοῦ περὶ λογισμοὺς καὶ τὰ γεωμετρικὰ κρατίστου). A little later, he identifies his error as one having to do with calculations (λογισούς 257b). Fragment 4 and this passage of Plato's *Statesman* remind us, then, that the "numerical calculation," which the context of Fragment 3 suggests as a meaning for λογισμός, includes, as a prominent part, the understanding of basic proportions.

It has even been suggested that in Fragment 3 λογισμός means not just numerical calculation in general but has the more specific meaning of "geometric proportion" (Harvey 1965–66). Such a usage would be unparalleled, however. So far as I can see λογισμός never means simply proportion, let alone a specific sort of proportion such as geometric proportion. Harvey provides no parallel for this usage and himself admits that "calculation" is what we would expect the term to mean (1965–66: 140–41). An understanding of λογισμός as a general art of numerical calculation, which includes an understanding of basic proportions, can account for the features of Fragment 3 that led Harvey to suppose that Archytas intended the term to mean "geometric proportion." Since numerical calculation includes the study of all sorts of proportion, it is no surprise that some of what it accomplishes is ascribed to geometric proportion elsewhere (e.g. the abolition of *stasis* [Arist. *Pol.* 1301b26–27] and *pleonexia* [Pl. *Gorg.* 508a]). Certainly the general study of proportion will help us to understand cases where geometric proportion is applicable, but it also equips us to make use of other sorts of proportion. The major passages in both Plato and Aristotle, which Harvey quotes as illustrations of the efficacy of geometric proportion in politics, both in fact make the point that for the state to be effective both arithmetical and geometric proportion need to be applied (Pl. *Lg.*, 757e and Arist. *Pol.* 1301b27–1302a8). Fragment 3 of Archytas also explicitly claims that both the rich and the poor will be satisfied through the use of *logismos*. We have every reason to suppose, then, that Archytas saw *logismos* as including both of the proportions commonly applied to politics in the later tradition, the arithmetic and the geometric, and it is also conceivable that he thought other sorts of proportions were applicable as well. The same point can be made about the evidence we have for the government in Archytas' own Tarentum. Aristotle presents the Tarentine government as democratic but says that it should be emulated for having features that both appeal to the multitude and allow for good government by having some magistracies chosen by election rather than lot, a procedure that favors the upper class (*Pol.* 1320b10). Tarentum thus has once again the sort of government that makes use of both the arithmetic proportion to favor democrats and the geometric proportion to favor oligarchs.

There is therefore no reason to assume that Archytas limited the scope of numerical calculation simply to the application of the geometric proportion. Fragment 3 is praising the general efficacy of numerical calculation and its use of proportion in addressing political problems. An appreciation of proportion encourages people to make connections between different things of value in society. A person is not granted x amount of goods or y amount of rights in a vacuum, but these quantities exist in proportion to other values in society, e.g. basic human needs or the relative contributions of an individual to society as a whole. The key issue is to bring people's attention to the various values in society and the different ways in which they can be connected. If members of the state can see the coherence of the ways in which the values are connected, then concord can be achieved and discord banished.

7 πλεονεξία – Archytas here asserts that once calculation has arisen "wanting more than one's share" (πλεονεξία) does not exist while "equality" (ἰσότας) does. The basic meaning of the verb πλεονεκτέω is "to have more" or "to claim more" usually in the bad sense of "be greedy" but also in a more neutral sense of "to have an advantage." The noun πλεονεξία also can simply mean "advantage" or "gain" with no negative connotation, but more often it means "having or desiring more than one ought" and thus means "greed," "unjust advantage," "selfishness," or "arrogance" in different contexts. Plato gives the noun its widest meaning as the cosmic vice of "encroachment" at *Laws* x. 906c, where he says that it manifests itself as disease in bodies, pestilence in seasons and years, and injustice in cities and constitutions (cf. *Symp.* 188b).

Both the verb and the noun seem to be first used in the mid-fifth century by Herodotus, who uses them each once (VIII. 112.1 and VII. 149.3). There is only one occurrence of the noun or verb in the Presocratics (Dem. B86). *Pleonexia* becomes a central concept in the thought of the late fifth century and in the analysis of civic strife in that period by Thucydides. It figures prominently in Plato's presentation of both Thrasymachus in the *Republic* and Callicles in the *Gorgias* and also appears in the treatise known as the *Anonymus Iamblichi*. Both the verb and noun then become reasonably common in authors of the fourth century (e.g. Plato, Isocrates, Xenophon and Aristotle) and are found in prose authors from that point onward. Some of the pseudo-Pythagorean writers use *pleonexia* in connection with the Platonic tripartite soul. Cleinias (Thesleff 1965: 108.12) argues that there are three causes of injustice: "love of pleasure" (φιλαδονία), "greed" (πλεονεξία), and "love of reputation" (φιλοδοξία). Metopos (118.23) connects this threefold origin of evil with the three parts of the soul: *pleonexia* is associated with the rational part of the soul, while love of honor is associated with the spirited part and pleasure with the appetitive part (see also Diotogenes 73.10).

The usage of *pleonexia* in Fragment 3 shows none of the characteristics of these pseudo-Pythagorean texts, but it does have several points of contact with the debate about *pleonexia* in the late fifth and first half of the fourth centuries. First, Archytas implies that *pleonexia* was a characteristic of the original state of human beings, which is banished by the discovery of calculation (see the commentary on εὑρεθείς above). A prominent theme in late fifth-century thought similarly connects *pleonexia* to what is by nature in contrast to what is by convention. Both Thrasymachus in the *Republic* and Callicles in the *Gorgias* argue that one should "strive to have more" than others and "to overreach" them (*Grg.* 483c; *R.* 344a) and that it is natural for every creature to pursue "self-advantage" (*R.* 359c; cf. *Lg.* 875b6). It is only custom that forces us to honor equality instead (*R.* 359c). Second, Archytas clearly sees *pleonexia* as the major cause of discord in the state. This connection is particularly prominent in Thucydides. *Pleonexia* is used three times in the account of the revolution on Corcyra and is assigned a central causal role for the party strife: "The cause of all these things was desire for power on account of greed (*pleonexia*) and personal ambition" (III. 82.8). In this passage, *pleonexia* seems to be ascribed to both the oligarchic and democratic parties on Corcyra, but will come to be identified as the particular vice of the oligarchs.

In Diodotus' speech in the Mytilenian debate, wealth is particularly identified as producing arrogant "overreaching" (*pleonexia* – III. 45.4). Thus *pleonexia* seems to be associated with the abuse of power by either a tyrant or a wealthy oligarchy. This becomes most explicit later in Isocrates when he claims to condemn oligarchies and "special privileges" (*pleonexias*) and praise "equalities" and democracies (VII. 60.3). Aristotle also makes the connection between *pleonexia* and oligarchy. In *Politics* V. 2 Aristotle discusses the origins of party strife and at 1302b7 asserts that "when those in power act insolently and are greedy (πλεονεκτούντων) people form factions against one another and against the government . . ." The greater tendency towards *pleonexia* of those in power or with wealth is again asserted at *Politics* 1297a10 ff. "the encroachments of the wealthy corrupt the government more than those of the people." There is no evidence for this development in Fragment 3 of Archytas, where it appears that both the rich and the poor are persuaded to avoid *pleonexia* by calculation.

Archytas' response to *pleonexia* in Fragment 3 also has connections to other late fifth- and early fourth-century responses. The treatise known as the *Anonymus Iamblichi* rejects the position of a Callicles or a Thrasymachus, by arguing that human beings cannot survive on their own and require a political community in order to live a good life, while political communities in turn cannot exist unless laws replace unrestrained *pleonexia*: "It is not necessary to strive to have more (ἐπὶ πλεονεξίαν ὁρμᾶν) nor to think that the power to get more (τὸ κράτος τὸ ἐπὶ τῇ πλεονεξίᾳ) is virtue and that to listen to laws is cowardice . . ." (DK II. 402. 21). Archytas does not explicitly develop this argument, although the clear implication of Fragment 3 is that a stable political community is a good thing and that such a community is impossible, if *pleonexia* holds sway. What is distinctive about Archytas is his reliance not just on law but on numerical calculation in order, to combat *pleonexia* This brings us closest to Socrates' response to Callicles in the *Gorgias*. Socrates argues that it is in fact equality that underlies the natural order, and that Callicles praises *pleonexia* because he has neglected geometry and "geometric equality" (508a). No appeal is made to the cosmic order in Fragment 3, but its emphasis on calculation and the equality that results from calculation as the cure for *pleonexia* is strikingly parallel to Socrates' position in the *Gorgias*.

The stumbling block for supposing that Plato is making a direct reference to Archytas is Socrates' use of the term "geometric equality." Dodds (1959: 339; see also Vlastos 1981: 195, n. 119) represents the traditional interpretation, which takes "geometrical equality" in a technical sense to refer to the "aristocratic" equality that took into account merit in contrast to "arithmetic" and democratic equality that just distributes an equal amount regardless of merit (see the commentary on ἰσότας below). Archytas, on the other hand, while he does describe the geometric mean in Fragment 2, makes no mention of geometry here in Fragment 3, and, as we have seen, it is not likely that he is limiting the use of *logismos* to the geometric mean. Thus, the specific emphasis on the geometric mean in the passage in the *Gorgias* does not make much sense as a reference to Archytas Fragment 3, where the geometric mean is not singled out. It is doubtful, however, that Plato is using the expression "geometric equality" as a technical term equivalent to "geometric mean." To begin with a linguistic point, the expression "geometric equality," far from being a technical term in the discussion of sorts of equality or sorts of means, does not appear elsewhere in Plato, nor does it appear in other authors of the fourth century who distinguish different sorts of equality, such as Aristotle or Isocrates. As Burkert has pointed out (1972a: 78, n. 156), moreover, it would be at least awkward for Socrates to claim that Callicles neglects specifically this sort of equality, since Callicles would be to a degree happy with the idea that the "better" man should receive more in proportion to his worth, as the geometric mean directs (see also Irwin 1979). Indeed, in the context, the point is that Callicles' *pleonexia* is so extreme as not to recognize any sort of limitation or order, and an appeal to one specialized sort of equality is out of place.

It looks then as if "geometric equality" is not a technical term, with which Plato expects his reader to be familiar but rather a term that Plato is coining for the specific context. We need to look more carefully then at that context. I would suggest that, in the context in the *Gorgias*, the expression means "the sort of equality that is studied by geometers" and that Plato regards geometers as studying all sorts of equality, i.e. all sorts of means and proportions (for the relation between the two terms see the commentary on ἀναλογία in Fragment 2) and not just what came to be known as the "geometric mean." Socrates is thus chiding Callicles for neglecting the study of means and proportion in general rather than inexplicably and inappropriately singling out the geometric mean. Indeed, when Plato refers to geometry, he often means more than simply geometry in the narrow sense of plane and solid geometry. In this very passage of the *Gorgias* Socrates goes on to rebuke Callicles for neglecting "geometry" (γεωμετρίας γὰρ ἀμελεῖς). If "geometry" is taken to mean specifically plane or solid geometry, this is surprising, since nothing Socrates has said suggests that it is in these specific fields that Callicles is lacking. A passage somewhat earlier in the *Gorgias* makes even clearer how Plato is using the term geometer. At 465b7 Socrates says that he is going to act like the geometers, and what he goes on to do is to provide a proportion (as cosmetics is to gymnastics so sophistry is to legislation). This view of geometry as not simply including plane and solid geometry but also the theory of proportion can be seen in Euclid's *Elements* where Books v and vii–x are devoted to the theory of proportion and Books vii–x focus particularly on numbers. From some points of view geometry thus comes close to being equivalent to mathematics as a whole.

There are other passages in Plato where he is more concerned to make distinctions among the mathematical disciplines. Thus in *Republic* VII geometry seems to be limited to plane geometry, with even solid geometry separated off as the discipline of stereometry. The study of proportions would appear to be included under logistic (also called arithmetic) or under harmonics. The beginning of the *Statesman* is interesting in this regard. Theodorus is there said to have in effect made the mistake of regarding the relation between the statesman and philosopher in terms of the arithmetic rather than the geometric mean. Theodorus has made a mistake in his art, and this art is at first identified as the art "of one who is authoritative concerning calculations and things geometrical" (τοῦ περὶ λογισμοὺς καὶ τὰ γεωμετρικὰ κρατίστου). This suggests that one way to describe a great mathematician is to identify him as a master of logistic and geometry. It is interesting to note, however, that unlike the *Gorgias*, where geometers are identified as those concerned with proportions, here in the *Statesman*, Theodorus goes on to describe his mistake in the use of proportion as a mistake in calculation (τὸ περὶ τοὺς λογισμοὺς ἁμάρτημα, 257b).

It thus appears that, in some contexts, geometry is used very broadly to include not only plane and solid geometry but also the theory of proportions and number theory. So when Socrates contrasts the erotic necessity that will lead the guardians in his Republic to mate with one another, with "geometric necessity" (458d), it seems more likely that he is thinking of the rigor of mathematical proof in general than specifically plane geometry (Adam glosses "geometrical necessity" as the "so-called 'necessity' of mathematical reasoning"). This tendency to encompass all of mathematics under geometry is probably in part the result of the fact that rigorous proof appeared first in geometry in the narrow sense. The context at *Gorgias* 508a and Socrates' earlier reference to geometers at 465b make clear that in the expression "geometric equality" Plato is using "geometrical" in its broader sense. The same sort of thing seems to be going on in the famous story that there was a sign over the entrance to the Academy forbidding anyone who had not studied geometry to enter (Riginos 1976: 138). We don't know whether the story is true or when it originated, but presumably it was not just geometry but mathematics in general that was meant. Once we recognize that by "geometrical equality" Socrates means something closer to the study of proportion, it is clear that he is calling on Callicles to study the *logismos* which Archytas describes in Fragment 3 and that in this section of the *Gorgias* Plato is, at least in part, thinking of Archytas (Huffman 2002b: 268–69).

That Fragment 3 was in fact part of a larger attempt by Archytas to argue against the sort of glorification of *pleonexia* championed by Plato's Callicles and Thrasymachus receives startling confirmation from a section of the *Life of Archytas* written by Aristotle's pupil Aristoxenus. One fragment of this work preserved in Athenaeus (XII. 545a ff. = Archytas A9) presents the story of a meeting between Archytas and the hedonist Polyarchus. Polyarchus argues that nature bids us to follow pleasure; lawgivers unnaturally try to reduce the human race to one level and bar all citizens from luxury by creating the virtues. Polyarchus explicitly mentions *pleonexia* at 546b, where he seems to identify it as the main enemy of the lawgivers and hence as the central concept of his way of life: "when the lawgivers were fighting against the whole class of having more (τῷ τῆς πλεονεξίας γένει) the praise of justice was first extended." A version of Archytas' response to this speech as presented by Aristoxenus is found in Cicero (*De Sen.* XI. 39 ff. = Archytas A9a). It is most striking that in Fragment 3 *logismos* (calculation) brings all goods to the state, while in Cicero the primary attack on pleasure is precisely that it overthrows *mens* (reason), the best gift of the gods to men. Moreover, the first evils arising from pleasure, according to Cicero's Archytas, all have to do with the state. As I have argued in the commentary on Testimonia A9 and A9a, these reports from Aristoxenus, while inevitably involving some embellishment, are not likely to be total fabrication. Fragment 3, with its attack on *pleonexia*, may well have been one source used by Aristoxenus in developing the story of the meeting between Polyarchus and Archytas, as well as a source for Plato's *Gorgias*.

ἰσότας – Equality is clearly a central concept in Fragment 3 appearing both here and again in line 10. As the remarks on *pleonexia* given above make clear, some thinkers in the late fifth century portrayed "equality" as a convention contrary to nature pursued by the weak who, not being in reality equal, were content to be declared "equal" to their betters. In general, however, the concept of equality had overwhelmingly positive, if also imprecise, connotations, and ἰσότας here in Fragment 3 is clearly a positive term. In order to evaluate the use of ἰσότας further, it will be necessary to give a brief overview of the development of the concept of equality in the fifth and first half of the fourth centuries.

The concept of equality was particularly associated with the rise of democracy. The term ἰσονομία is important in this connection. First attested in a drinking song of the late sixth century celebrating the overthrow of the tyrants at Athens (Ostwald 1969: 121–30), it appears in a number of fifth-century authors such as Herodotus (cf. the famous debate on constitutions in Persia at III. 80.2–82) and Thucydides. Ἰσονομία is the abstract principle of political equality that becomes embodied in provisions such as those that allow citizens an equal chance to be elected to office and an equal chance to formulate policy (Ostwald 1969: 113). It is thus much more than simple equality before the law or constitutional government (Vlastos 1981: 163–66). It is closely connected to democracy, but, unlike democracy, it does not designate a type of constitution but is rather a "banner" that can be used to evaluate constitutions (Vlastos 1981: 173–74). As the principle of political equality, it naturally fits democracy best and its use normally suggests that a democracy is at issue, but it can be used of other sorts of government insofar as they embody principles of political equality (of the oligarchy at Thebes at Thucydides III. 62.3–4). In the fourth century ἰσονομία is largely replaced by either τὸ ἴσον or ἰσότης, which are somewhat more general concepts (Ostwald 1969: 182). Nonetheless, even these terms keep a close connection to democracy as can be seen in passages such as *Areopagiticus* 60.3, where Isocrates says that, in his writings, he will be found "condemning oligarchies and special privileges (πλεονεξίαις) and praising equal rights (ἰσότητας) and democracies."

Isonomia's ("equality of political rights") application on occasion to constitutions other than democracies may be based on the use of equality (τὸ ἴσον, ἰσότης) in the late fifth century as a broad concept, which is closely associated with and sometimes identified with concord, justice and friendship (Guthrie 1969: 149). Both Plato and Aristotle refer to the proverb that "equality (*isotēs*) is friendship" (*Lg.* 757a6; *EN* 1168b8), and in Stobaeus this bit of traditional wisdom is assigned to Pythagoras himself (II. 23.4 = 257.3 W). The most important passage illustrating this broad concept of equality comes from Jocasta's speech in Euripides' *Phoenissae* (531 ff.). She urges her son Eteocles to honor equality (ἰσότητα), which binds friends, cities and allies together. She appeals to the equality obvious in the natural order of the world, the equality of night and day, in order to urge Eteocles to treat his brother equally. Some scholars have wanted to see a specifically Pythagorean background to Jocasta's speech (Mueller-Goldingen 1985: 104, n. 68), but the ideas usually identified as Pythagorean, that the cosmos has a general order and that this order can provide a moral model for mortals, are not exclusively Pythagorean. It is an idea common to a number of Presocratics that equality is what preserves the order of nature, that cosmic equality is what guarantees cosmic justice (Vlastos 1970: 57).

In the late fifth and the first half of the fourth centuries, the ideal of equality as a unifying force as well as democracy's predominant claim to the concept became controversial. It is clear that oligarchs made use of the connotation of τὸ ἴσον as not simply what is numerically equal but as what is "fair" (Vlastos 1981: 184–85, n. 78), in order to turn the democratic call for equality/fairness back on itself. In a speech in Book VI of Thucydides (38.5), the Syracusan democrat Athenagoras reports the view of "some people" that democracy is neither intelligent nor fair (ἴσον). That equality had become a deeply problematic concept in the first part of the fourth century is clear from Plato's famous criticism of democracy in the *Republic* (VIII 558c5–6) as "distributing a sort of equality (ἰσότης) to both equal and unequal."

In response to these difficulties about the simple conception of equality there arose a distinction between two different sorts of equality, which is clearly attested not only in Plato but also in Isocrates and Aristotle. At *Laws* 757b Plato distinguishes between the two sorts of equality which, he says, have one name but which, for the most part, have contrary effects. The first is "the equality in measure, weight, and number" which every state and lawgiver can institute by simply using the lot. The second, the truest and best equality, is not easy for everyone to see. This equality "distributes more to the greater and less to the lesser"; "it distributes what is appropriate to each according to proportion" (κατὰ λόγον). Plato regards this latter equality as true justice, but, practically speaking, it must be tempered to some extent by the equality of the lot to appease the masses. Isocrates refers to this same distinction at *Areopagiticus* 21 (cf. *Nicocles* 14 ff.), when he talks of "the two accepted kinds of equality, one which distributes the same to all and the other which distributes what is fitting to each." The first type of equality is called unjust, since it holds that the good and bad should receive the same honors, while the second is just in rewarding and punishing according to the worth (κατὰ τὴν ἀξίαν) of the individual.

Aristotle makes use of this distinction between the two kinds of equality in a number of passages, most clearly at *Politics* 1301b30 ff. where he says "equality (τὸ ἴσον) is of two kinds, equality in number and equality according to worth (κατ' ἀξίαν)." Aristotle goes on to say that by equality in number he means "what is the same and equal in multitude or magnitude" and by equality according to worth he means what is equal "by proportion" (λόγῳ). The examples he gives of each form of equality are the arithmetic (3:2 :: 2:1) and geometric (4:2 :: 2:1) means. Aristotle argues that to form a constitution exclusively in accord with either one of the types of equality is bad and that each type of equality should be used for some things. Other notable discussions of the two sorts of equality by Aristotle are found at *Politics* 1301a9 ff., 1280a7–25, and *EN* 1131a9 (for a complete list and discussion of the appearance of the two equalities in later Greek thought see Harvey 1965–66. In these passages Aristotle particularly notes equality's traditional connection with justice. It is important to note, however, that Aristotle seems to be arguing against the sort of naive praise of equality that is found in the *Phoenissae*. Far from arguing that equality is always a cohesive force, at *Politics* 1301b29 he argues that striving for equality is the primary cause of party strife.

With this overview of the development of the concept of equality in the late fifth and early fourth centuries as background, we are now in a position to see where Fragment 3 of Archytas fits into the debate. One central point stands out. There is no hint of the distinction between two sorts of equality that is made in Plato's *Laws*, Isocrates and Aristotle (Harvey 1965–66: 106–07 tries to import the distinction into the fragment by mistakenly interpreting λογισμός as "geometric proportion"; see the commentary on λογισμός above). The usage of ἰσότας and τὸ ἴσον in Fragment 3 seems to have the same set of conceptual connections as we see in the idealization of *isotēs* in Euripides' *Phoenissae* minus the cosmic overtones. There is no sense that Archytas is using equality with scare quotes around it or that his praise for equality depends on what sort of equality is meant. Fragment 2 shows that Archytas was one of the leading figures in dealing with different sorts of proportions, and he was hence in a position to apply these means to politics and proclaim the difference between the arithmetic equality of the democrats and the geometric equality of the oligarchs. Fragment 3, however, shows that he did not do so. The firm distinction between the two sorts of equality seems to be established only in the latter part of the first half of the fourth century, although questions about the democratic ideal of equality are already present in Thucydides and Plato's *Republic*. It is hard to see how Fragment 3, with its unified conception of equality, could have been written after the clear contrast between the two sorts of equality has arisen and this suggests that it belongs to the very beginning of the fourth century.

The conception of equality in Fragment 3 also appears to bear some of the traditional democratic overtones. It is true that it is presented as something that satisfies both the rich and the poor and thus can hardly be so radical a concept as to call for equal redistribution of land. Nonetheless, the assumption seems to be that the poor should receive from the rich and that the rich should give to those in need. Equality is thus not being invoked to make sure that the best men get what they deserve but rather that the poor get what they need; the poor, however, get only what they need. Equality is a check against the greed (πλεονεξία) of the poor as much as that of the rich, and it is because of this that concord arises. Such an understanding of Fragment 3 is confirmed by Aristotle's description of Tarentum as a moderate democracy (*Pol.* 1320b9–14).

While equality is an important concept in Fragment 3, it is not the focus of the fragment. Archytas is not trying to solve the problem of political discord by distinguishing different sorts of equality; he seems to be writing in an environment where distinct aristocratic and democratic conceptions of equality have not yet become hardened positions. Archytas instead is focusing on the ability to calculate and to determine mathematical proportions (λογισμός) as the salvation for the state. One sort of proportion need not be intrinsically better than another and which should apply will depend on the circumstances. There may still be disputes on which sort of proportion to apply in a given instance, but the crucial first step in gaining any sort of concord among citizens is to get them to recognize that it is the clarity of mathematical relations which serves as the basis for agreement.

8 περὶ τῶν συναλλαγμάτων διαλλασσόμεθα – διαλλάττω can mean "to exchange," but, in the context in Fragment 3, it has the common more specific meaning of "to exchange enmity for friendship" or "to reconcile." It occurs already in Empedocles in the sense of "change" or "exchange" (35.15 and 17.12) and appears in Thucydides with the meaning "reconcile" (II. 95 etc.). The verb is used frequently in fourth-century authors such as Plato, Aristotle and Isocrates. I have found no parallel for its use with συνάλλαγμα nor very many parallels for its use with περί. The best such parallel comes from Archytas' contemporary Isocrates (III. 33.6), who talks about "making reconciliation with others about their complaints" (πρὸς δὲ τοὺς . . . περὶ τῶν ἐγκλημάτων διαλλαττόμενος).

The verb clearly has a place in the popular moral tradition and refers to the reconciliation that the good man seeks or accepts, when an injustice has been committed against him. Among the supposed sayings of Chilon of Sparta, one of the Seven Sages, as reported by Stobaeus (III. 1.172) we find "If you are treated unjustly, seek reconciliation (διαλλάσσου), if you are treated insolently, get revenge." διαλλάσσου seems to be a middle here. Plato may allude to this traditional wisdom at *Symposium* 213d, where Socrates, upon the entrance of Alcibiades, asks Agathon to "either reconcile (διάλλαξον) us or, if he uses violence, defend me." The middle is used at *Protagoras* 346b, where good men, if they feel anger at some wrong, are said to calm themselves and seek reconciliation (διαλλάττεσθαι, cf. Arist. *EN* 1126a28). Here in Archytas, the reconciliation seems to apply to the citizens as a whole and may have some reference to civil strife, which is mentioned in line 6. Its use for the reconciliation of warring factions in a polis is paralleled in Plato *Menexenus* 244a and Isocrates Letter VIII. 3.1. In Fragment 3, the middle form indicates that by calculation "we will reconcile ourselves" or "we will seek reconciliation."

συνάλλαγμα is a less common word, which does not seem to come into use until the fourth century. It is not found in Plato but occurs some eleven times in Aristotle and is also found three times in Demosthenes and once in the Hippocratic corpus (*Medic.* 1). The corresponding verb, however, does occur in the fifth century (e.g. Thuc. 1. 24). Archytas Fragment 3 thus contains one of the earliest uses of the noun. The noun has both the narrow sense of "monetary transaction" (e.g. D. *In Tim.* 213.3 – this is better than "contract") and a broader meaning of "dealing," "transaction," or even "interaction." This broader meaning can be seen when Aristotle says that one species of justice has to do with rectification in "dealings with others" and then divides these *sunallagmata* into those that are voluntary and those that are involuntary, the voluntary being things such as sales and loans, whereas some of the involuntary are "secret" such as theft or adultery, while others are "forcible" such as assault and murder. At *EN* 1103b14 Aristotle says that "it is by our actions in our dealings (ἐν τοῖς συναλλάγμασι) with people that we become just or unjust." Thus, in the summary of Plato's philosophy in Diogenes Laertius (III. 91.3), justice is defined as "to act justly in our associations (κοινωνίαις) and dealings" (συναλλάγμασι). The translation "partnerships and commercial transactions" given in the Loeb is unnecessarily narrow.

The most intriguing parallel for Archytas Fragment 3 is a fragment from Aristoxenus' *Life of Archytas* preserved in Athenaeus (A9). Lawgivers are said to "write statutes concerning dealings with others (συναλλαγμάτων) and all other matters thought essential for political community (κοινωνίαν)." συναλλάγματα is translated as "contracts" in the Loeb, but again this seems overly narrow given the quite general context. The word seems to identify all the "dealings" we have with others where there is scope for justice and injustice, whereas the "other matters" turn out to be issues of dress and general way of life, which are more private. Since Aristoxenus is from Tarentum, his usage at the least provides a nice parallel for συναλλάγματα in Fragment 3 and at the most could show the influence of Archytas' own writings on Aristoxenus' *Life of Archytas*.

The next sentence in Fragment 3 goes on to discuss the relations between rich and poor, which are likely to be "monetary transactions." While such transactions clearly do count as συναλλάγματα, however, they are introduced here as specific examples of a more general concept. Our "seeking reconciliation concerning dealings with others" is introduced as evidence for the previous assertion that, once calculation has arisen, *pleonexia* does not exist, while equality does. But, while *pleonexia* does often refer to greed for money, it usually has a much wider range of application and in fact applies to all dealings with others, in which we can be at an advantage or at a disadvantage. Thus, it surely seems best to take συναλλάγματα to refer to just such "dealings." The monetary dealings between rich and poor are then introduced as a specific example, because they are the most crucial for the health of the state.

8–10 οἱ πένητες λαμβάνοντι παρὰ τῶν δυναμένων, οἵ τε πλούσιοι διδόντι τοῖς δεομένοις – The discord produced in the state by the conflict between the rich and the poor is a common theme in Greek history and political thought during the late fifth and fourth centuries (Lintott 1982). Plato famously argues that all cities, except for the ideal city are in fact not one city but at least two, which are at enmity with one another. He uses some of the same language as Archytas in describing them as "the city of the poor (πενήτων) and the city of the rich" (πλουσίων *R.* 422e9). According to Aristotle, some thought that all civil discord arose because of disputes about property (*Pol.* 1266a38). Archytas clearly envisages reducing or eliminating this tension by having the rich give to the poor. There is no suggestion of redistribution of wealth so that all citizens have an equal allotment; Archytas instead calls for the rich who have the ability (τῶν δυναμένων) to help those with real need (τοῖς δεομένοις). This is also the recommendation of Aristotle, who says that the truly democratic statesman will make sure that the multitude is not excessively destitute (*Pol.* 1320a24). It is highly significant that, when Aristotle goes on to give examples of this practice, one of his examples is precisely Tarentum. He does not mention Archytas, but, since he uses the present tense, he seems to be referring to the Tarentum of the middle of the fourth century and hence to Tarentum shortly after the ascendancy of Archytas. Aristotle says that Tarentines gain the goodwill of the multitude by making property common for the use of the needy (τοῖς ἀπόροις, *Pol.* 1320b12). It is hard not to think that this is an allusion to the same policy recommended in Fragment 3 and that, since Aristotle clearly studied the writings of Archytas in order to write his three-book study of Archytas (A13), the text from which Fragment 3 derives was at least one source for this section of the *Politics*.

There are some interesting features of the vocabulary of lines 8–10. πένητες and πλούσιοι are standard in these contexts, but the juxtapositions of πένητες with δυνάμενοι and πλούσιοι with δεόμενοι seem to have no exact parallel. The use of δεόμενοι to refer to "the poor" or the "needy" is not prominent in either Plato or Aristotle but does occur at Isocrates *Arch.* 67.6. οἱ δυνάμενοι is found as early as Euripides (*Or.* 889) and Thucydides (VI. 39 etc. – see Lintott 1982: 92–93 and 121, n. 18). Its use in Thucydides in the speech of Athenagoras at Syracuse is particularly striking, since this same passage is important in the development of the concept of τὸ ἴσον (the equal or fair), which is also a central theme here in Fragment 3 of Archytas. δυνάμενοι thus appears to be an important part of the vocabulary that was used in late fifth-century political debates. This is supported by the similar use of it in Democritus Fragment 255, which may be the best parallel for Archytas Fragment 3. Democritus argues that "when those who are able venture to help the 'have-nots' . . . the citizens are in concord and there are countless other goods" (ὅταν οἱ δυνάμενοι τοῖς μὴ ἔχουσι καὶ προτελεῖν τολμέωσι . . . τοὺς πολιήτας ὁμονόους εἶναι καὶ ἄλλα ἀγαθά. ἅσσα οὐδεὶς ἂν δύναιτο καταλέξαι).

It is thus clear that Democritus and Aristotle are in agreement with Archytas regarding the need for the wealthy to make contributions to the needy in order to maintain concord in the state. How exactly does Archytas think that calculation will foster this practice? There are at least two different problems that need to be addressed in order for such a policy to go into effect. As Aristotle notes at *Politics* 1318b1, it is difficult enough to discover the truth about equality and justice but even harder to persuade those who can get more than others to heed what is discovered to be fair. Is Archytas saying that calculation is valuable primarily for its help in determining what is fair for the rich to contribute to the poor, or is it valuable also for its ability to persuade the rich and the poor to implement what is determined to be fair? Lines 8–10 are too compressed to provide a definitive answer to this question. Certainly it would seem plausible that calculation was involved in determining the amount that the rich should give to the poor. The rhetoric of the sentence, however, places the emphasis not so much on this role of calculation as on its persuasive power. The point is that calculation makes both parties "trust" or "be confident" (πιστεύοντες) that they will have what is fair. It appears then that in Fragment 3 Archytas is praising calculation on much the same grounds that he praises the science of number in Fragment 4, for its ability to provide concrete and effective demonstrations of its points. Rather than just suggesting a vague obligation of the rich to give to the poor, calculation shows what resources are necessary to keep the poor from the abject poverty that leads to discord and also demonstrates the resources which are available to the wealthy. It provides the hard figures that convince both sides of the justice of the general policy.

10 τὸ ἴσον – See the note on ἰσότας in line 7 above. The manuscripts of Stobaeus read τὸ ἴσον rather than τὸ ἴσον, which is more typical in prose.

10–11 κανὼν δὲ καὶ κωλυτήρ . . . – The understood subject in this last sentence of the fragment is λογισμός, which has been the central focus since its introduction in line 6. The τούτῳ and the διὰ τοῦτον in lines 7–8 both refer to it. κανών δὲ καὶ κωλυτήρ are in agreement with this understood subject, and we should follow Blass in introducing the participle ἐὼν into the text, since the apposition without the participle is too abrupt.

The most common literal meaning for κανών is carpenter's straight edge or rule, and it is often paired with στάθμη as the "rule and line" which allow the craftsman to do good work (e.g. Xen. *Aeges.* 10.2). It is also used to refer to a number of other straight rods such as the staves or handle on a shield, a weaver's rod, the beam of a balance, and eventually to the monochord which was used in musical experiments (cf. the *Sectio Canonis*). κανών also has a metaphorical sense of "rule" or "standard." At the beginning of Euripides' *Electra*, the old farmer says that, if someone thinks that he is crazy for taking a young girl as his wife and never touching her, "let him know that he is measuring by the wicked standards (πονηροῖς κανόσιν) of his mind, being wicked himself" (52, cf. *Hecuba* 602 and Arist. *EN* 1113a33). Archytas is clearly using κανών in this metaphorical sense of "standard." The pairing of "standard" (κανών) with "hindrance" (or "preventer" κωλυτήρ) may be a purposeful deviation from the more typical pairing of κανών with another word which is a close synonym (i.e. μέτρον [as in Aristotle] or στάθμη), in order to emphasize its surprising role as a hindrance. Each of its two roles are treated in turn in the rest of the sentence. The clause beginning τοὺς μὲν ἐπισταμένους describes *logismos* as a standard, to which those who can calculate make appeal (ὅταν ἐπ' αὐτὸν ἔλθωντι), while the clause beginning τοὺς δὲ μὴ ἐπισταμένους explains the role of *logismos* in hindering those acting unjustly (κωλυτὴρ τῶν ἀδικούντων).

κανών does appear in several contexts in later Greek philosophy. *Canonic* became Epicurus' name for epistemology and κανών comes to be used almost interchangeably with the central Hellenistic concept of a κριτήριον of truth or "means of discrimination" of truth (Long and Sedley 1987: 1.88). κανών also appears in some of the pseudo-Pythagorean writers including pseudo-Archytas. At the end of Περὶ τῶν καθόλου λόγων (Thesleff 1965: 31.33), pseudo-Archytas says that "man is the κανών . . . καὶ στάθμα of true knowledge" (cf. Thesleff 1965: 37.18). Aresas in *On the Nature of Man* (Thesleff 1965: 48.22) says that the nature of man is the κανών of law and justice (cf. Metopos, Thesleff 1965: 119.25; pseudo-Philolaus Fr. 11: Thesleff 164.30; Arius Didymus in Stobaeus II. 7.20.93). None of these usages show particular affinity, however, to what we find in Fragment 3 of Archytas, and there are at least as good parallels to Archytas' use of κανών in technical and philosophical treatises of the fifth and fourth centuries.

Democritus, in the generation before Archytas, seems to have anticipated the Epicurean use of κανών to some extent. He uses it in an epistemological context in Fragment B6 and, even more significantly, in the list of Democritus' works are three books with the title Περὶ λογικῶν ἢ Κανών (D.L. ιχ. 47). Sextus (ΥΙΙ. 138) confirms the epistemological content of this work when he reports that it was ἐν τοῖς Κανόσι that Democritus distinguished between genuine and bastard knowledge (cf. Sextus ΥΙΙΙ. 327). Thus, it would appear that the title referred to "standards" of truth and that the work examined the types of knowledge open to human beings. Moreover, in the generation before Democritus and two generations before Archytas, the sculptor Polyclitus entitled his treatise on sculpture the Κανών. His statue, the Doryphorus, was probably created to illustrate his theory of sculpture and was called the Κανών as well. Polyclitus seems to have used κανών in the sense of a standard or guideline which all sculpture was to follow and which was expressed in terms of numerical ratios (Huffman 2002a). Archytas' description of calculation (λογισμός) as both a standard and also the basis of human inquiry (lines 3–4) combines Polyclitus' emphasis on the normative role of number and Democritus' interest in an epistemological standard.

The word paired with κανών, κωλυτήρ, is at first sight more problematic for someone of Archytas' date. It occurs only three other times in Greek literature, and all of these uses are late (Porph. *Philosophy from Oracles* 121.8, Iamb. *in Nic.* 52.17, and Hesychius 4823). It is true, however, that a number of nouns ending in -τηρ are alternate formations for the more common ending in -της. Thus for example κριτήρ appears as a less common alternative to κριτής (LSJ s.v.). In the case of κωλυτήρ, the form κωλυτής is both more common at all times and does occur fairly commonly in the fifth century. It is used with γίγνομαι where "to become a preventer" is the equivalent of "to prevent" (D. *De Corona* 72.6; Th. ΥΙΙΙ. 86.5.1). Given our meager knowledge of Archytas' dialect, it seems best then to accept κωλυτήρ as simply an alternative formation for the noun κωλυτής. This suggestion gains support from the fact that Archytas' fellow Tarentine, Aristoxenus, uses the form θεραπευτήρ rather than θεραπευτής (A9).

10–14 κανὼν δὲ καὶ κωλυτὴρ τῶν ἀδικούντων. . . ἐκώλυσεν ἀδικῆ-σαι – In these lines, Archytas turns from the role of calculation in establishing a just framework for society, which produces concord in the state, to its role in dealing with those who are nonetheless tempted to act unjustly. Most commentators have found the syntax and meaning of this sentence obscure (e.g. DK ι. 438; Harvey 1965–66: 106). It is important to recognize that the focus is "those who are unjust" (τῶν ἀδικούντων) and that this genitive is governed by both of the preceding nouns. Calculation is both the "rule" (κανών) of the unjust, in that it keeps some of those disposed to injustice from crossing the line into actual injustice, and "what prevents" (κωλυτήρ) others from persevering in the injustice they have already carried out. The μέν and δέ clauses are constructed in a closely parallel fashion, and it is the recognition of this parallelism that is the key to interpreting the sentence. Both clauses refer to people who are disposed to injustice. In the μέν clause we consider those who know how to calculate and in the δέ clause those who do not.

The unjust who know how to calculate are unjust in that they desire to commit injustice, but calculation stops them before they actually commit injustice (πρὶν ἀδικεῖν ἔπαυσε). The words ὅταν ἐπ᾽ αὐτὸν ἔλθωντι describe the would-be unjust as resorting to calculation as a standard before they act; αὐτόν refers to λογισμός, as is suggested by the close parallel in Plato's *Euthyphro* (7b), where Socrates says that, if they had a dispute about numbers, they would "resort to calculation" (ἐπὶ λογισμὸν ἐλθόντες). How then does resorting to calculation lead them to avoid acting unjustly? We are told that calculation persuades them that they will not be able to go undetected (οὐ δυνασοῦνται λαθεῖν). It is initially puzzling how the specifically mathematical calculation, which Archytas has emphasized up to this point, would help in such persuasion. When weighing whether we could get away with a crime, we might take into consideration the circumstances in which we would commit the crime (e.g. whether it would be dark, whether other people would be around, whether the police were efficient in catching criminals) but such considerations seem hard to quantify. We might rationally calculate about such considerations, but it is hard to see how specifically mathematical calculation would be important. In the modern world, we might imagine someone consulting crime statistics which suggested that the government was efficient in catching malefactors and hence deciding that the odds were against escaping detection, but we know of no such statistics in the ancient world. I would suggest instead that Archytas is not referring to the likelihood of detection of the action but rather the likelihood of the action being recognized as unjust or not. We should understand the remark in the context of an ancient court; the key point is the clarity with which calculation is supposed to show what is just. The potential malefactor realizes, thanks to calculation, that the rights and wrongs of the issue have the clarity of $2 + 2 = 4$ and that accordingly the chance of escaping detection by claiming in court that a given action is not unjust are nil.

Let us now turn to the second division of the unjust, those who cannot calculate. For this group, calculation serves not as a standard, which they consult in order to decide what to do, but rather as something which hinders them in their injustice. Three points of parallelism between this clause and the preceding one help to clarify the meaning. First, Archytas emphasizes that calculation stops the first group before they commit injustice. This surely suggests that the second group actually do go on to commit an injustice. Since they cannot calculate, they cannot appeal to calculation as a guide, which shows them the hopelessness of escaping detection, and accordingly they do act. In this case, then, calculation does not prevent injustice but instead keeps someone who has committed an injustice from continuing to act unjustly.

How does calculation hinder the unjust in this case? Archytas says that calculation "makes clear that they are unjust ἐν αὐτῷ." The meaning of the obscure phrase ἐν αὐτῷ is clarified by a second parallelism with the preceding clause: like ἐπ' αὐτόν in the previous line, ἐν αὐτῷ refers to calculation. The force of the preposition ἐν is a little ambiguous. It could have its common meaning "in the presence of" and, in the legal context, the point would be that the unjust are shown to be unjust before the tribunal of calculation (for such a use of ἐν see Pl. *Grg.* 464d). It seems more likely, however, that ἐν is being used instrumentally. Such usage is particularly common with verbs of showing (LSJ s.v. III) such as δηλόω, which Archytas uses here (see esp. Xen. *Cyr.* 8.7.3 and Th. VII. 11). Having made clear "in (i.e. by) calculation" that they are acting unjustly, calculation hinders them from committing injustice.

The third point of parallelism with the first clause is that it is the clarity of arithmetical calculation which is crucial in its ability to hinder injustice. The clarity which made the potential malefactors see that they would be unable to escape detection similarly reveals the actual injustice of the second group. Calculation shows clearly to judge and jury that the unjust have in fact been unjust, it is what convicts them and sets their penalty. In one sense then, it is this conviction and its attendant penalty that hinder the unjust person from going on to commit other injustices. It may also be true that, once the calculation is explained to the offender, he too will come to see his injustice. In this case he will move from the class of those who do not know how to calculate to the class of those who do, and he will then be prevented from future injustice by his new found ability to use calculation as a standard, which stops him before he actually commits the injustice. In an earlier article (2002b: 266), I argued that those who were unable to calculate might be prevented from committing injustice by the rest of society, who, once this deficiency was revealed in someone, removed such a person from the society (e.g. by death, imprisonment, exile), but this view seems less plausible to me now.

Archytas' distinction between calculation as the standard and the hindrance of the unjust is similar enough to Aristotle's distinction between distributive and corrective justice to lead us to inquire whether Archytas in some sense anticipated Aristotle. After close examination of Fragment 3, it does not appear, however, that Archytas is working with Aristotle's distinction. To begin with, in both of its roles (i.e. as a standard and as a hindrance) calculation is corrective for Archytas. In the one case it corrects the unjust desires of the individual before actual injustice occurs and in the other case it prevents further injustice after the individual has committed an injustice. Moreover, in Aristotle distributive justice is tied to the geometric mean and corrective justice to the arithmetic mean. No such neat correlation between the two means and two types of justice appears in Archytas. As a standard, calculation could involve employment of either the geometric or the arithmetic mean; the mean employed would depend on whether the situation involved distribution of goods, which would suggest the geometric mean, or the adherence to the terms of a contract or to rules governing political decisions, which might assume arithmetical equality and hence the arithmetic mean. Similarly, in its role as hindering further injustice calculation could use either the arithmetic or the geometric mean to reveal the injustice, depending on the nature of the circumstances. Aristotle's distinction is better understood as a later development of Archytas' initial insight into the importance of calculation and proportion in establishing justice.

Finally it is important to note that Archytas' view of justice is to be distinguished from the view of justice assigned by Aristotle to the Pythagoreans. Aristotle reports that the Pythagoreans "defined justice as simply suffering reciprocally with another" (*EN* 1132b21). This appears to mean that the Pythagoreans subscribed to the doctrine of an eye for an eye and a tooth for a tooth. Aristotle goes on to argue that this view of justice fits neither with distributive nor corrective justice. It is Aristotle's practice elsewhere to distinguish between Archytas and those he calls Pythagoreans (see A13), so he is not likely to be assigning the definition of justice as suffering reciprocally to Archytas here. Indeed, Fragment 3 with its vision of the rich giving to the poor is clearly at odds with such a definition of justice. In such redistributions of wealth, rich and poor do not suffer reciprocally. The poor gain and the rich lose. Archytas argues that both rich and poor nonetheless have reason to think that they have received what is fair, but this is because of an appeal to a principle of proportion which is at odds with simple reciprocal suffering.

11 λογίζεσθαι – Pflugk's correction of the manuscript reading, ὀργίζεσθαι, is about as certain as such a correction can be. ὀργίζεσθαι. makes no sense with τοὺς . . . ἐπισταμένους ("those knowing how to be angry"). Gesner tried to save the manuscript reading by inserting the genitive article thus giving τῶ ὀργίζεσθαι, which would presumably be taken as a genitive of separation with ἔπαυσε ("prevented them from anger before committing injustice"). A reference to anger, however, is not at all motivated by the context, whereas we do need a clear reference to the activity of λογισμός in this last sentence in order to complete the sense. λογίζεσθαι admirably fills this role. The corruption can be explained on the assumption that the first two letters of λογίζεσθαι became transposed in the course of transmission, giving the nonsense form ὀλγίζεσθαι, which was then corrected by a scribe to ὀργίζεσθαι.

CHAPTER IV

Fragment 4

Stobaeus 1, Proem 4 (p. 18.8 Wachsmuth)

Ἐκ τῶν Ἀρχύτου Διατριβῶν

καὶ δοκεῖ ἁ λογιστικὰ ποτὶ τὰν σοφίαν τῶν μὲν ἀλλᾶν τεχνῶν καὶ πολὺ 1
διαφέρειν, ἀτὰρ καὶ τᾶς γεωμετρικᾶς ἐναργεστέρω πραγματεύεσθαι 2
ἃ θέλει. καὶ ἃ ἐκλείπει αὖ ἁ γεωμετρία, καὶ ἀποδείξιας ἁ λογιστικὰ 3
ἐπιτελεῖ καὶ ὅμως, εἰ μὲν εἰδέων τεὰ πραγματεία, καὶ τὰ περὶ τοῖς εἴδεσιν. 4

1 δοκεῖ] F δοκέει Wachsmuth τὰν σοφίαν] Diels τὰν ἄλλαν σοφίαν F τῶν μὲν ἀλλᾶν τεχνῶν] Diels τῶν μὲν ἄλλων τεχνῶν F del. Meineke τὰν μὲν ἀλλᾶν τεχνᾶν Orelli καὶ²] F κἄπ Wachsmuth κατὰ Iacobs 2 διαφέρειν] F διαφέρεν Blass τᾶς γεωμετρικᾶς] Heeren τὰς γεωμετρικὰς F τᾶς γαμετρικᾶς Meineke ἐναργεστέρω] F ἐναργεστέρως Mullach 3 post θέλει <ἀποδείκνυσι γὰρ ἁ γαμετρία ἃ ἐκλείποντι ταὶ ἄλλαι τέχναι> Diels καὶ ἃ] F καὶ ἃς Meineke καθ' ἃ Heeren αὖ] F γὰρ Heeren ἁ γεωμετρία καὶ] F ἁ γαμετρικὰ Meineke ἁ γεωμετρία τὰς Heeren ἀποδείξιας] Meineke ἀπόδειξις F 4 ἐπιτελεῖ] F ἐπετελέει Meineke ἐπιτελέν Blass ὅμως εἰ μὲν] Diels ὅμως εἰ μὲν F ὅμως, αἱ μὴν Meineke ὁμοῦ ἐντι μὲν Heeren τεὰ] Diels τε ἁ F ἐντὶ Meineke ἐντὶ ἁ Wachsmuth τὰ περὶ τοῖς εἴδεσιν] F τῶν περὶ τὰ εἴδη Heeren τὰ ἐπὶ τοῖς εἴδεσιν <πραγματεύεται> Meineke τὰ περὶ τοῖς εἰδέεσσι <περιλαμβάνεν> Blass

From the Discourses (Diatribes) of Archytas:

Logistic seems to be far superior indeed to the other arts in regard to wisdom and in particular to deal with what it wishes more concretely (clearly) than geometry. Again in those respects in which geometry is deficient, logistic puts demonstrations into effect (completes proofs) and equally, if there is any investigation of shapes, [logistic puts demonstrations into effect (completes proofs)] with respect to what concerns shapes as well.

Note: The translation of this fragment is problematic. I give the translation that seems most probable to me, but provide an alternative translation for key phrases in parenthesis. For the issues involved see the detailed commentary and the section on the importance of the fragment.

Authenticity

Of the fragments that have generally been regarded as authentic, this is the fragment about the authenticity of which it is hardest to be confident. It is not so much that there is anything obviously suspect about the fragment as that it is simply too short to be certain that we can identify the conceptual world in which it is working. Fragment 4 was accepted by DK because it appeared to deal with technical mathematics, and most modern scholars have followed their lead. There are problems, however. The use of technical mathematical content as a criterion for authenticity is itself problematic (see the essay on authenticity) and it is far from clear that Fragment 4 comes from a technical work on mathematics (see the discussion of the importance of the fragment below). It is identified as coming from a book whose title, *Diatribai*, suggests that it had an ethical focus (see below).

Burkert raised doubts about the authenticity of the fragment precisely on the basis of the understanding of mathematics which it employs and the details of its language (1972a: 220–21, n. 14). Nonetheless, neither of the concerns that he raises is convincing. The reference to εἰδέων πραγματεία is not a suspect allusion to Plato's theory of forms but rather an allusion to the shapes which are the subject matter of geometry. Similarly, the assertion of the superiority of logistic to geometry need not be the mathematically nonsensical (and therefore suspect) assertion that Archytas could deal with irrational numbers arithmetically and not geometrically. Several plausible explanations of the superiority, which fit with what we know of Archytas' work in mathematics, have been proposed. Indeed, there is no smoking gun in the concepts and language of the fragment, nothing that cries "forgery."

Nonetheless several scholars have expressed unease about the authenticity of Fragment 4 (Mueller 1992b: 90, n. 12), some pointing to supposed similarities to treatises among the pseudo-Pythagorean writings (Gottschalk 1983: 92). Gottschalk (1982: 91) regards the use of the term λογιστική as suspicious and suggests that, since Fragment 4 seems to focus on σοφία, it might have come from the spurious Περὶ σοφίας (Thesleff 1965: 43 ff.). Closer examination, however, suggests that the use of λογιστική is, in fact, one of the best arguments for the authenticity of the fragment. Logistic is a term prominently used by Plato, and in the *Republic* it seems to be the term of choice to indicate the science of number rather than arithmetic, just as it is in Fragment 4 of Archytas. Plato's usage, however, does not suggest that this is all his own invention and it looks as if he is relying at least in part on terminology current in his day, especially in passages such as *Theaetetus* 145a, where he describes Theodorus in a general and non-technical passage as λογιστικός (see the commentary below). Aristotle abandoned the term λογιστική, and, most strikingly of all, it appears nowhere in the pseudo-Pythagorean writings. In the treatise *On Wisdom* by "Periktione," which is closely related if not the same as *On Wisdom* by "Archytas," it is ἀριθμητικά and not λογιστικά which is used for the science of number (Thesleff 146.7 and 146.16; so also in ps.-Archytas *Cathol.* 6.14). There are some texts in the later mathematical tradition which use λογιστική, but they are closely tied to commentary on Plato, and the term is not used in the Neopythagorean tradition, e.g. Nicomachus (for more details see the commentary on λογιστική). Thus the appearance of λογιστικά in Fragment 4 makes more sense, if the fragment were written by Plato's contemporary Archytas than if it is a later forgery.

None of the remaining features of Fragment 4 suggest any particular connection to the pseudo-Pythagorean tradition. The treatises *On Wisdom* by "Archytas" and "Periktione" show strong similarities to Aristotle's discussion of wisdom (= metaphysics or first philosophy) in the *Metaphysics* (see especially 982a ff., 1003a ff., and 1061b18 ff.). The brevity of Fragment 4 does make it hard to be sure that it does not come from a similar context. Fragment 4's assertion that logistic is superior to geometry is paralleled by Aristotle's assertion that arithmetic is more exact than geometry (*Metaph.* 982a28). On the other hand, there is the important difference that Fragment 4 uses logistic rather than Aristotle's term, arithmetic, which would be surprising in a forger following Aristotle. In addition, the reasons that Fragment 4 gives for the superiority of logistic do not parallel anything said by Aristotle in the *Metaphysics* (see further below). There is also a similarity between Fragment 4 and a passage in praise of the study of number in Plato's *Laws* (747a–b), but, while the Platonic passage provides an instructive parallel for what Archytas is doing in Fragment 4 (see below), none of the details of the Platonic passage are reproduced in Fragment 4, as we would expect if a forger were using the Platonic passage. There is enough uncertainty about exactly what Fragment 4 is saying about the superiority of logistic that it would be rash to conclude that it is impossible that the text went on to make points similar to those made in Aristotle, Plato and the pseudo-Archytan *On Wisdom*. As it stands, however, there is nothing overtly suspicious about Fragment 4 and the use of λογιστική suggests that it should be assigned to Archytas.

Context

Fragment 4 is preserved in the proem of Stobaeus' (fifth century AD) collection, in four books, of excerpts of poetry and prose designed for the edification of his son. Most of the proem has been lost and we know of it only from a description by Photius (Wachsmuth 13). It seems to have consisted of a section devoted to passages praising philosophy and a section which dealt with the various schools of philosophy. At the end there were collected excerpts on geometry, music and arithmetic. Of all of this, the only part that survives is the section entitled *On Arithmetic* (Περὶ Ἀριθμητικῆς), which consists of ten excerpts of which Fragment 4 is the fourth. It is thus clear that Stobaeus interpreted the central concept in Fragment 4, logistic, as what was commonly called arithmetic elsewhere. The excerpts in Stobaeus begin with a quotation from Aeschylus' *Prometheus Bound* (454–59). There are two pseudo-Pythagorean texts, "Philolaus" Fr. 11 (Huffman 1993: 347–50) and "Butheros" (Thesleff 1965: 59). There is an excerpt from Aristoxenus and most interesting of all, a passage from Plato's *Laws* (747a–b), which bears some similarity in content to Fragment 4 (see further below). Archytas is grouped with the other "Pythagoreans" Philolaus and Butheros, but there does not seem to be any particular significance to the order.

Title of the work from which Fragment 4 comes

The lemma in Stobaeus identifies Fragment 4 as from the *Discourses* of Archytas. The word that I have just translated "Discourses" (διατριβαί) raises some controversial questions. First, it is important to emphasize that we have no way of knowing whether this title goes back to Archytas himself, in the early fourth century BC, or, if it does not, when it arose in the 900-year period between Archytas and Stobaeus in the fifth century AD. Second, it is also unclear what connection, if any, the title of Archytas' book has with the later genre known as the diatribe. Some scholars, indeed, deny that there was any unified genre to which the name diatribe applied (e.g. Jocelyn 1982 and 1983). The genre is defined by its defenders along the following lines: "A Graeco-Roman form of moralizing lecture characterized by a conversational style with abundant rhetorical figures, anecdotes, examples, and at least some hint of dialogue or reference to an imagined opponent" (Wallach 1997: 181; see also Moles 1996). Good examples of practitioners of the genre are Musonius Rufus (AD 30–100) and Epictetus (AD 50–130). The genre is sometimes thought to have begun as early as the sophist Bion in the third century BC (D.L. II. 77; see Usener 1887: lxix). It almost always has a connection to oral presentation and can indeed be characterized as the pagan equivalent of a sermon. It is important to distinguish, however, between the diatribe as a literary genre and the book title "Diatribe." It is far from clear that the title always indicates that the book belonged to the literary genre, and this is especially true when talking of books as early as the fourth century BC. In order to understand the possible meanings of the book title, "Diatribe," it is necessary to look first at the common uses of the word and then at examples of the book title.

διατριβή basically means "something that one spends time on" so it can be translated "amusement" or "pastime" and in some cases it has a clearly negative sense of "waste of time" or "delay". It also has a serious sense of "occupation" or "study" and can be as broad as "way of life" or refer to the place in which one passes one's time ("haunt," Pl. *Euthphr.* 2a). In philosophical contexts, it develops a series of more specialized meanings focused around the quintessential philosophical activities of "discourse" and "teaching." In the *Apology*, Socrates says that the Athenians have not been able to endure τὰς ἐμὰς διατριβὰς καὶ τοὺς λόγους. LSJ suggests that διατριβάς should be translated "discourses" here; the Athenians could not tolerate his "discourses and arguments." It is true that διατριβή could be even more general and just refer to Socrates' "pursuits," but in his case those pursuits were primarily his discourses with individuals in Athens (for further passages of this sort see Jocelyn 1982: 4). At D.L. III. 8 we are told that Praxiphanes (late fourth to mid third century BC) wrote up a διατριβή of Plato and Isocrates about poets, which occurred in a country setting, where Isocrates was being entertained by Plato. In this case again we seem to have a "discourse" or "dialogue" between Plato and Isocrates.

Diogenes Laertius provides the best evidence for Διατριβαί as a title for a book. There are nine examples (II. 77, II. 84, II. 85, VII. 34, VII. 36, VII. 163 [2], VII. 175, VII. 178). The titles are ascribed mostly to authors in the Stoic school but also to the Socratic Aristippus and Bion, a sophist with connections to the Cynics. These treatises thus date to the late fourth and third centuries BC, with the exception of Aristippus, who is the earliest and was active in the later fifth and first half of the fourth centuries. The title does not appear in DK as the title for the work of any Presocratic, nor in the Pythagorean tradition (Iamblichus, Porphyry, D.L. Book VIII), nor in Thesleff's collection of the pseudo-Pythagorean writings. The exact connotation of the title remains somewhat elusive. This is strikingly illustrated by the astonishing variety of translations for the identical book title employed in the Loeb translation of Diogenes Laertius: "Interludes" of Zeno of Citium (VII. 34) and his disciple Persaeus (VII. 36), "Dissertations on Philosophy" and "Dissertations on Love" by another of Zeno's pupils, Ariston (VII. 163), two books of "Lectures" by Cleanthes (VII. 175), and five "Lectures on Heraclitus" by Sphaerus (VII. 178), the "Lectures" of Bion (II. 77), six books of "Essays" of Aristippus (II. 84, II. 85). Nothing in the contexts (indeed, there is often no context but simply a bare title in a list of works) justifies such a variation in translation.

Admittedly, we are seriously hampered in understanding the meaning of the title "diatribes" by the fact that none of these works from the fourth

and third centuries BC have survived. The fact that the title is used in two
instances in Diogenes Laertius with a genitive or an adjective which defines
the subject matter suggests that it refers to a form which can be employed to
treat different subject matters (D.L. VII. 163 "Discourses on Wisdom" and
"Erotic Discourses"; see Gottschalk 1983 and Jocelyn 1983). Indeed, even
when used without a defining adjective, it is hard to see to what the title can
refer except to a form, however fluid the definition of that form. "Essay"
is an attractive translation, because of its generality; it simply indicates the
focused attention of the author to a given topic. As we have seen, however,
διατριβή does not have quite such a general meaning. It is so often used in
contexts which imply oral presentation that "discourse" is a better choice.
The uses of διατριβή in philosophical contexts, which I have discussed
above, suggest that the form indicated by the title *Diatribai* was based on
the oral discourse or discussion of a specific issue by a philosopher and
his associates. A diatribe is thus less formal than a treatise. The translation
"Discourse" has the added advantage of referring to either an oral or a
written presentation in English just as διατριβή does in Greek. The book
title then indicates that we are dealing with a written form, which bears some
of the characteristics of an oral presentation on a given topic, although we
do not have to suppose, of course, that the written treatise is necessarily any
sort of a transcription of an oral presentation, which might be suggested
by the translation "lecture." "Dissertation" in modern English suggests
something too massive.

The *Diatribes* of Musonius Rufus and Epictetus in the first centuries AD
are clearly discourses on specifically ethical topics. Does this ethical focus
also apply to earlier works with the title *Diatribai*? Such a focus does also
seem to be present in most of the books bearing the title from the fourth
and third centuries BC. Thus, Aristippus' emphasis was almost exclusively
on ethics so that his *Discourses* are likely to have been ethical. Theopompus
indicates that they highlighted Socrates and hence presumably his discussions on ethics (*FGrH* 259). Theopompus also indicates that Aristippus'
contemporaries Bryson and Antisthenes wrote books entitled *Diatribai*.
These books also are likely to have been concerned with moral philosophy, since they focused on Socrates. Zeno's *Discourses* and thus perhaps
Persaeus' are said to have dealt with love (D.L. VII. 34). One set of Ariston's
discourses are specifically labeled *Discourses on Love* and the others *Discourses
on Wisdom* (VII. 163), which suggests a broadly ethical focus. Similarly the
content of Bion's *Discourses* had to do with the relation between wealth and
virtue (D.L. II. 77). We have no indication of the content of Cleanthes'
Discourses but they do appear in the context of ethical treatises in the list

of his works (D.L. VII. 175). The five books of *Discourses on Heraclitus* by Sphaerus clearly could be on something other than ethical topics, and they appear in the list of his works at the division between physical and ethical works. Certainty is particularly hard to achieve here, since this part of the list of Sphaerus' books could be understood as two titles, one *On Heraclitus* and another *Five Books of Discourses* (see Jocelyn 1983). Thus, anytime that we can be relatively sure of the content of a book entitled *Diatribai*, that content is ethical, although there are a few cases where we cannot be sure what the content was.

What conclusions can we draw for the interpretation of Fragment 4 of Archytas and for the nature of the book from which Fragment 4 derives, on the basis of the title *Diatribai*? If the title goes back to Archytas himself, Archytas' book along with that of his contemporary Aristippus are the earliest examples of works with this title. Since these are early examples and since the term *diatribe* in itself can refer to anything one spends time on, it is possible that the title simply has the same connotations as the English "discourse," which suggests a connection to an oral presentation but nothing further about the content. The fact remains that the example of Aristippus, whose focus appears to have been exclusively ethical, the application of the term to Socrates' activities in the *Apology* and the almost universal later tradition indicate that a book with such a title should deal with a topic in ethics. At first sight, however, Fragment 4 appears to be either from a work in technical mathematics or from a discussion of the hierarchy of the sciences. Certainly it is in the context of such a work that the fragment has almost universally been interpreted. This conflict between the title and apparent content of Fragment 4 exists whether the title goes back to Archytas himself or was assigned at a later date. In order for a later commentator to give the work such a title, something about the content of the work from which Fragment 4 came must have suggested that it had a moral purpose.

There seem to be three possible solutions. First, we could regard the treatise as dealing with technical mathematics and the title as simply the result of an error. Neither Archytas nor any later commentator ever consciously gave such a title to the work from which Fragment 4 came; the title came to be assigned to it by a mechanical error of some sort (miscopying or misremembering). Second, Fragment 4 does come from a work on technical mathematics, but our limited evidence, particularly for the early period, is misleading, and the title *Diatribes* does not indicate a focus on ethics. Third, despite initial appearances, Fragment 4 did come from a work, whose primary purpose was ethical and the title is thus appropriate. Certainly Fragment 3 suggests that Archytas did deal with the relation between mathematics and ethics, and the presentation of Archytas in Aristoxenus' life suggests that he did in fact give discourses on moral issues such as pleasure (A9). The obscurities of Greek book titles prevent us from being certain that a book entitled *Diatribes* must have consisted of discourses on moral topics (see Jocelyn 1983). Nonetheless, the preponderance of evidence pointing in this direction makes it at least reasonable to see if Fragment 4 can be understood as part of a work whose goal was primarily ethical (see below).

Importance of the fragment
The lack of a broader context and uncertainties concerning the text produce more problems for understanding Fragment 4 than any other fragment of Archytas. The fragment admits of two main lines of interpretation. First, it can be regarded as part of a technical discussion of the mathematical sciences, which is attempting to describe a hierarchy of sciences *qua* sciences, at least partially in terms of their ability to give proofs. Second, it can be regarded as part of a discussion of the relative contributions of the various sciences to human wisdom as a whole and in particular to our ability to live a good life. Neither the context nor the text is sufficiently clear to rule out either of these interpretations, but I will argue that peculiarities of the vocabulary of Fragment 4 and its connection to Fragment 3 make the second line of interpretation more likely.

The first line of interpretation views Archytas as doing something like what Aristotle does in the first book of the *Posterior Analytics* (see especially 78b34 ff.) and elsewhere (e.g. *Physics* 194a7), i.e. establishing a hierarchy of sciences (see Barnes 1994: 158–62; McKirahan 1978; Lloyd 1979: 119). Aristotle in turn relies on Plato's earlier account of the sciences in the *Philebus* (55c–59b) and *Republic* VII. There has not been much commentary on Fragment 4 but what there is all seems to follow this line of interpretation. There are indeed *prima facie* reasons for thinking that the fragment comes from the context of a technical discussion of the nature of the mathematical sciences: (1) two mathematical sciences are named (λογιστικά and γεωμετρικά) and compared with each other and other unnamed sciences (τῶν μὲν ἀλλᾶν τεχνῶν); (2) they are apparently compared in terms of their ability to complete proofs (ἀποδείξιας). Archytas has provided a brief discussion of the relation between the sciences in the introduction to his work on music (Fr. 1) and can be seen as going into the problem in more detail here. Further, an interest in proof fits perfectly with Archytas' famous proofs in number theory and stereometry (A14 and A19 – see

Burnyeat 2004). On this line of interpretation, the problem then becomes to determine the basis for Archytas' assertion of the superiority of logistic over geometry. Logistic is Archytas' term for the science of number (see further in the commentary on λογιστικά below). Fragment 4 asserts both a general superiority of logistic over geometry, i.e. that it deals with what it wishes "more clearly" or "more concretely" (ἐναργεστέρω) than geometry, and a more specific superiority, i.e. that in areas where geometry is deficient, logistic completes demonstrations or proofs. There is some parallel for the general superiority of the science of number over geometry in Aristotle's assertion that "arithmetic is more exact than geometry" (*Metaph.* 982a28). Aristotle bases this assertion on arithmetic's reliance on fewer principles than geometry, however, and, as we will see, Archytas gives a different argument.

Most of the scholarly focus has been on what to make of the assertion that logistic completes proofs where geometry is deficient. Burkert argues that "the assertion [of Fragment 4] that λογιστικά helps where γαμετρία fails is nonsensical mathematically" and accordingly concludes that Fragment 4 is spurious (1972a: 220, n. 14; van der Waerden regards the fragment as genuine but as an example of Archytas' "weak logic" [1947–49: 150]). Burkert's point is that Archytas could not determine a value for the cube root of two arithmetically, but his famous solution to the problem of doubling the cube provides a way of determining it geometrically. It is certainly true that, looked at from a certain perspective, Archytas could do things with geometry, which he could not do with logistic. The problem is in determining whether that is indeed the perspective of Archytas and what the perspective of Fragment 4 is. Certainly there is nothing to indicate that Fragment 4 is specifically arguing that logistic can deal with irrational numbers while geometry cannot.

Several ingenious suggestions have been put forth to explain why Archytas might have thought that logistic could solve problems which geometry could not. Knorr turns Burkert's point on its head by arguing that arithmetic/logistic is in fact required to recognize incommensurability, since incommensurability arises when two magnitudes "have not to one another the ratio which a number has to a number" (Euclid x. 7). "The analysis of certain classes of problems in geometry, e.g. the construction of irrational lines, can only be completed by means of arithmetic [i.e. logistic] principles" (1975: 311). Ian Mueller has suggested another interpretation of Fragment 4 according to which the point is not that "logistic establishes results in cases with which geometry cannot deal" but rather that "logistic yields true results where geometry yields false ones" (1992b: 90, n. 12). His example is Archytas' proof that a superparticular ratio cannot be divided in half and hence that there is no such thing as a half tone in music (A19). Here an arithmetical proof leads to the truth, whereas a geometrical representation of intervals as lines would suggest that there was always a half tone. An even closer fit to the language of Fragment 4 is achieved by the interpretation of Myles Burnyeat (2004). Burnyeat points out that the classic proof of the incommensurability of the side and the diagonal of a square depends on the impossibility of the same *number* being both odd and even (Euclid, *Elements* x, Appendix 27; cf. Arist. *APr.* 41a26–27). Thus, what appears to be a proof in geometry, involving the side and diagonal of the square, is in fact carried out by appeal to principles of logistic, odd and even numbers. Burnyeat connects the proof even more tightly to Archytas, by pointing out that it goes out of its way to rule out the possibility of the ratio between the diagonal and the side being one, a move that would be necessary for Archytas, since he regarded one as both even and odd (A21).

The suggestions of Knorr, Mueller and Burnyeat are enough to show, *contra* Burkert and van der Waerden, that there are intelligible ways of understanding how Archytas could say in Fragment 4 that logistic completes proofs where geometry is deficient. Given the brevity of Fragment 4, it is impossible, however, to be certain that Archytas had any of these proofs specifically in mind. Further, while these suggestions provide examples of cases in which logistic might supply the deficiencies of geometry, they do not explain Archytas' more general assertion that logistic deals with whatever problems it wishes more clearly than geometry. Archytas seems to be arguing that logistic is in some sense always superior to geometry, as well as being able to deal with certain specific problems for which geometry is inadequate. Burkert again suggests that the assertion of the general superiority of number theory over geometry shows the spuriousness of Fragment 4, since it reflects the point of view of Plato's late doctrine of ideal numbers with its derivation sequence, in which numbers are primary in comparison to geometrical magnitudes (1972a: 220–21, n. 14). There is, however, nothing in Fragment 4 to suggest that it is talking about a derivation sequence or ideal numbers. Burkert's suggestion is thus possible but hardly necessary. What are we, then, to make of the general superiority of logistic to geometry? It is time to turn from reading Fragment 4 as a discussion of technical mathematics to a second quite different approach.

If Archytas were simply asserting that logistic is superior to all the other sciences as sciences, the addition of the qualification "with regard to wisdom" (ποτὶ τὰν σοφίαν) would be puzzling and superfluous. The bare statement that logistic far exceeded the other sciences would in itself clearly indicate that logistic was superior as a science. Paying attention to this significant qualification is the key to the second reading of the fragment. While σοφία can refer to expertise in a specific technical field, it also and more commonly refers to the highest sort of human intellectual excellence, to wisdom (see the detailed commentary). Of course wisdom is open to different descriptions. Plato and Aristotle agree that it deals with the highest things. Aristotle, however, regards it as going beyond the specifically human good and hence as not always of practical benefit (*Metaph.* 982a4 ff.; *EN* 1141a16), while for Plato it is the intellectual virtue of the guardians which allows the city to be well governed (*R.* 428b ff.). Given Archytas' preeminence as a ruler in Tarentum, we would not be surprised if he sided with Plato on this point and regarded wisdom as not just knowledge of the highest things but also the knowledge that allows us to live a good life. Can any sense be made of the claim that logistic surpasses the other sciences in providing us with this sort of wisdom? Fragment 3 of Archytas suggests that there can.

Fragment 3 is crucial because its hero is λογισμός, which has undeniable connections to the hero of Fragment 4, λογιστική. It is natural then to connect Fragment 3, which can well be described as a hymn to λογισμός in terms of its contributions to human society, to Fragment 4 and its praise of λογιστική as far surpassing all other sciences. λογιστική is a science of numbers that lays particular emphasis on their quantitative relations to one another (see the detailed commentary). λογισμός does not refer to a science but rather to the general human capability for rational calculation. It need not refer to a specifically numerical calculation, but it often does and clearly carries that connotation in Archytas (see the commentary on Fragment 3). The natural suggestion would then be that logistic was viewed as the science of number which underlies the practical application of mathematical calculation (λογισμός) to human life. The second part of Fragment 3 argues that such calculation is the basis of all human society. Therefore, I suggest that, in Fragment 4, it is this sort of wisdom in which logistic far surpasses the other sciences. It is the wisdom that allows us to live a good life. λογιστική is the most important of the sciences precisely because it deals with the relations between numbers, relations that will also turn out to be crucial to the functioning of the state. Justice is an other-regarding virtue, and Archytas seems to have thought that this relation needs to be stated numerically. It is through such a statement that the rich and poor can live together, each seeing that he has what is fair. That concord (ὁμόνοια) is a crucial factor in society is, of course, a central doctrine of Plato's *Republic* (351d etc.). Temperance is defined in terms of concord (ὁμόνοια 432a) and justice in terms of harmony (ἁρμονία 443d–e). It is also clear that Plato regarded this concord as to some extent based on strict numerical calculations. One need only think of the famous nuptial number (546b) or the calculation that determines how many times more pleasurable the life of the philosopher king is than the life of the tyrant (729 times more pleasurable to be precise – 587e). Plato may well owe the emphasis on the importance of number in structuring the ideal state to Archytas, although he and Archytas disagree on the precise role of number in the state (see the overview of Archytas' philosophy).

Thus Fragment 4 asserts that it is specifically in wisdom that logistic far exceeds the other sciences, and Fragment 3 shows precisely how calculation (λογισμός), which is based on the science of logistic and connected to it etymologically, leads to a wise ordering of human life. Is it possible to make sense of the rest of Fragment 4 and in particular of the contrast between logistic and geometry in light of this understanding of the focus of Fragment 4? It is here that Archytas' predecessor Philolaus becomes important. As I have argued in the overview of Archytas' philosophy, Philolaus regards geometry as the "mother-city" of the sciences in that our first experience of the world is in terms of the geometry of limiters and unlimiteds and as a result geometry is the first science to be developed, but he, nonetheless, argues that it is through number that we gain real understanding of things. We do not have direct evidence that Archytas accepted the metaphysical system of Philolaus, although Archytas' theory of definition looks as if it is based on Philolaus' basic principles, limiters and unlimiteds (see A22). The relation between geometry and the science of number, which I have suggested for Philolaus, does, however, help to make sense of the rest of Fragment 4 of Archytas and in particular of his comparison between logistic and geometry. Archytas first says that calculation seems "to deal with what it wishes more vividly [or "more concretely" see below] than geometry." In the area of the human relations that are the foundation of the state, calculation does indeed excel over geometry. Geometry can help us to understand general relationships among parts, but it does not specify the exact relationships; unlike calculation it does not specify "how much," e.g. it does not give us a just tax rate. A geometrical conclusion still does not provide the *harmonia*, the number in which Philolaus was interested and which he thought to be the basis of knowledge. Archytas seems to agree that calculation is clearer in that it gives us this relevant number.

Crucial support for this reading of the superiority of calculation over geometry is provided by Archytas' use of the adverb ἐναργεστέρω. The fundamental meaning of the adjective ἐναργής is "visible, palpable, in bodily form." If we take this adjective in this fundamental sense,

Archytas is saying that calculation puts into bodily form, i.e. makes palpable and visible, what geometry leaves undetermined. Thus the adjective which Archytas uses to support the superiority of logistic over geometry highlights the ability of logistic to provide concrete results in opposition to the generality of the conclusions of geometry. To forestall objections I should emphasize that, although ἐναργής has its primary application to the sensible realm, it can be applied metaphorically to the intelligible realm and refer to intelligible "vividness" or "clarity" (see the detailed commentary). Indeed it is one of Plato's goals in the *Republic* to show that intelligible reality is, in the most important sense, more "manifest" than sensible reality. But that is Plato and not Archytas, and we have Plato's own testimony that it was in the sensible world that Archytas looked for numbers (*R.* 531c) and Aristotle's testimony that for the Pythagoreans there was no other realm besides the physical (*Metaph.* 990a4). In a certain sense then Archytas is valuing just the opposite of what Plato values. He learned from Philolaus that for something to be embodied in the physical order of the world it must have a number and that we know such things insofar as we know their number. On this reading of Fragment 4, then, we can explain what its reading as technical mathematics could not, Archytas' assertion of the general superiority of logistic over geometry. Logistic helps us to go beyond the limiters and unlimiteds of geometry, in order to determine the numbers that govern concrete particulars.

Archytas, however, is not done yet. He goes on to show two ways in which calculation deals with things in a more concrete way than geometry. Archytas' first point is that there are areas of human wisdom in which geometry is deficient and where calculation can provide demonstrations. I suggest that Archytas presents several such cases in Fragment 3. In fact, the fragment consists of a list of areas in which calculation can help and in which geometry can do little. Thus, geometry cannot help us in dealings with one another such as contracts, nor can it help the rich and poor to see that they are getting what is fair, nor finally can it serve as the "standard of what is unjust and a check against those acting unjustly." In each of these areas it is precise calculation that convinces us of what is fair, not generalized relations of magnitudes. We can imagine a number of other areas in the political and ethical sphere in which this would hold true.

It is important to note exactly what Archytas says that logistic can do and that geometry cannot in these cases. The usual translation has been that "logistic completes proofs" (ἀποδείξιας ἁ λογιστικὰ ἐπιτελεῖ) where geometry is deficient and some examples of what this might mean have been given above. Here again, however, it is important to look closely at Archytas' language. While the verb ἐπιτελέω can mean simply "complete," there is no exact parallel for the expression ἀποδείξιας . . . ἐπιτελεῖ, and ἐπιτελέω itself often implies that something expressed in word or in thought (e.g. an order or a plan) is "put into effect" (see the detailed commentary). If the verb is understood in this way, Archytas' point is not that logistic completes proofs where geometry cannot but that logistic can make demonstrations have effect where geometry cannot. Logistic can produce demonstrations that lead people to act on them in the ordering of the state and their lives. This meaning of the verb fits nicely with the use of the adverb ἐναργεστέρω in Archytas' description of logistic's general superiority over geometry. Logistic deals with what it wishes "more concretely" than geometry, because it specifies the numerical relations by which limiters and unlimiteds are combined in particular things. One example of the effectiveness of this concrete specificity of logistic is its ability to produce an effective demonstration of the proper roles of rich and poor in the state. On this reading of the fragment ἀποδείξιας refers not to a formal proof, but rather to a persuasive demonstration of a looser sort (see the detailed commentary on ἀποδείξιας).

This brings us to the problematic appearance of "forms" at the end of the fragment. The reading of the fragment that I have proposed can make very good sense of these forms. So far we have been dealing with areas in which geometry would not be expected to shine, in areas precisely where geometry is deficient. But if we now turn to the part of the physical world to which geometry would seem to apply most of all, to physical forms or shapes (this is my suggested translation of εἴδη, the same meaning that appears in Archytas' contemporary Democritus), surely we would expect that here geometry would surpass calculation. Archytas asserts, however, that, even in the case of physical forms, calculation can put demonstrations into effect where geometry cannot. His point may be clarified by considering a famous sentence in which the Argive sculptor, Polyclitus, asserts that "the good comes to be, just barely, through many numbers" (DK40 B2; see the note on κανών in Fr. 3, line 10). What is important for our purposes is that, while Polyclitus certainly made use of geometry in constructing this statue, he does not say that his Doryphorus came to be through many angles and lines but rather that it came to be "through many numbers" (on this fragment of Polyclitus see Huffman 2002a). A statue arises with difficulty through the use of numerical ratios and calculations just as a good state, according to Archytas, will arise through ratios and calculations. Polyclitus is no Pythagorean, but his experience as a sculptor illustrates Archytas' point. Even in the case of physical forms, it is not geometry that ultimately demonstrates to us what to do but rather number. True to his Pythagorean predecessor Philolaus, Archytas argues that the geometry of limiters and unlimiteds must ultimately be held together in a numerical harmony, and it is logistic that is the study of such numerical relations.

A passage in Plato's *Laws* provides a striking parallel for the sort of reading of Fragment 4 that I have just proposed. Stobaeus, in fact, quotes this section of the *Laws* (747a–b) in the same subject heading as and just shortly after Fragment 4. In this section of the *Laws*, the Athenian stranger has just described the division of the land of the ideal state into twelve sections and 5,040 allotments of land. He stops to recognize that conditions may never be such that the ideal arrangements which they are discussing can be carried out in fact but argues that the ideal pattern should be set out, nonetheless. He says that fabricators of even the most trivial object should make it in every way consistent with itself; none of the implements which the citizens possess should be without measure (ἄμετρον 746e). The following passage then emphasizes the value of the divisions and variations of number (τὰς τῶν ἀριθμῶν διανομὰς καὶ ποικίλσεις) in ways that are very reminiscent of Fragment 4 of Archytas. First, as in Archytas 4, the study of number is said not to have value just for the domain of numbers but to be useful in all the other mathematical sciences as well (geometry, music, astronomy). Geometry is not singled out as it is in Fragment 4, and there is no mention of demonstrations or proofs, but the study of number is clearly stated to be helpful (χρησίμους) to plane and solid geometry (ὅσα ἐν μήκεσι καὶ ἐν βάθεσι ποικίλματα). Plato does not explicitly say that the study of number far excels all the other mathematical sciences, but its usefulness to each of the sciences implies as much. Second, just as Archytas said that logistic was preeminent for its contributions not just to mathematical sciences narrowly conceived but especially to the wisdom that allows us to live a good life, Plato asserts that no subject of study has as much power in relation to economics, to politics, and to all the arts as the study of numbers (ἡ περὶ τοὺς ἀριθμοὺς διατριβή). He asserts that the lawgiver must look to the science of number and command the citizens to deviate as little as possible from "this organized numerical system" (τούτων [sc. ἀριθμῶν] . . . συντάξεως). Fragment 4 of Archytas and this passage of the *Laws* are different enough in vocabulary and the specifics of the argument that neither can be supposed to have been composed with the other as a model, but the outlook in the two passages is very much of a piece.

Fragment 4, then, turns out to be a protreptic for the study of logistic, which appeals to the value of logistic for attaining wisdom, i.e. the knowledge of the highest things, which allows us to order ourselves and the state well. This reading of the fragment goes a long way towards explaining the ancient tradition concerning the title of the work from which Fragment 4 is drawn, the *Diatribes* or *Discourses*. As we have seen, the best evidence suggests that this title should lead us to expect a practical discourse on an ethical topic, the pagan equivalent of a sermon (see the discussion of the title above). Fragment 4 is thus part of Archytas' sermon on the value of the science of logistic for the good life.

Detailed commentary

Line 1   λογιστικά – What exactly does Archytas mean by this term? The evidence presented below will show that it is Archytas' term for the science of number; its use, rather than ἀριθμητική, to designate that science puts the emphasis on the study of relative quantity, i.e. ratio and proportion, rather than the classification of types of number, with which ἀριθμητική was concerned. The earliest usages of λογιστική (τέχνη), apart from this usage in Archytas, are to be found in the dialogues of Plato. Indeed the use of λογιστική is largely limited to Plato and commentators on Plato, so it is appropriate to look at Plato's usage in some detail. In Plato, λογιστική is closely connected to ἀριθμητική. In *Gorgias* Plato connects but also makes a careful distinction between these two sciences. They are similar in that both of them are concerned with the same thing, the odd and the even (451c; for ἀριθμητική, see also *Theaet.* 198a). They are distinguished in that ἀριθμητική is concerned with odd and even, without reference to any specific quantity ("however many each may chance to be" ὅσα ἂν ἑκάτερα τυγχάνῃ ὄντα 451b.). At 453e2 ἀριθμητική is described as teaching "everything that pertains to number" (ὅσα ἐστὶ τὰ τοῦ ἀριθμοῦ tr. Zeyl). Finally at 453e7 ἀριθμητική is said to belong to the branch of instructive persuasion that deals with "the extent of even and odd" (περὶ τὸ ἄρτιόν τε καὶ περιττὸν ὅσον ἐστίν tr. Zeyl). Mueller (1992b: 91) has defended Lamb's translation of this last passage, "the amount of an odd or even number" (1925), as part of his argument that ἀριθμητική is basically counting rather than number theory. The two earlier passages in the *Gorgias*, however, say nothing about ἀριθμητική dealing with quantity, and 451b states that quantity is irrelevant. In each of these cases ὅσα indicates the extent of the field of ἀριθμητική rather than that it deals with quantity, so that Dodds (1959: 198–99, 205) and Zeyl (1987) are right to read ὅσον in this fashion at 453e7.

This interpretation of ἀριθμητική is further supported by Plato's complementary definition of λογιστική. λογιστική is explicitly said to consider quantity (πλῆθος); it considers "what amount the odd and even have both in themselves and in respect to one another" (καὶ πρὸς αὑτὰ καὶ πρὸς ἄλληλα πῶς ἔχει πλήθους 451c). An identical definition of λογιστική is given at *Charmides* 166a. Thus ἀριθμητική is something like number theory and investigates and classifies different types of numbers, beginning with the basic types, odd and even. The fact that ἀριθμητική is usually designated as concerned with "the odd and the even" rather than simply number indicates its focus on types of number rather than just counting. The classification of different types of odd numbers (prime, composite, etc.) and even numbers (even-times even, odd-times even, even-times odd) such as we find later in Nicomachus' *Introduction to Arithmetic* (I. 8–13) would seem to be examples of this sort of ἀριθμητική. ἀριθμητική thus does not deal with numbers *qua* specific quantities but rather *qua* types of number. It is, for example, concerned with defining prime numbers but has no particular interest in, to use the language of *Gorgias* 451b, "however many each [prime number] may chance to be" (e.g. 7).

λογιστική, on the other hand, does investigate what amount a number has both in itself and in respect to other numbers. There is a practical logistic that corresponds to "computation" or what we commonly mean by "arithmetic." At *Hippias Minor* 366c the multiplication of three times seven hundred is given as an example of the art of λογιστική. It is a mistake to understand λογιστική in Plato as simply practical computation, however, or as dealing with "numbered things" rather than numbers themselves. This latter conception of λογιστική appears in the later Greek tradition (see Geminus in Procl. *In Eucl.* 38.1 ff.; Hero *Def.* 135.5, 138.5; scholia in Plato *Charm.* 165e; Olympiod. *In Gorg.* 450b p. 31.4). The error of ascribing this later conception to Plato (as is done by e.g. Heath 1921: 14–15) has been repeatedly corrected (see especially Klein 1968; Burkert 1972a: 447, n. 119; Fowler 1987: 110–11). The logistic which Plato is defining in parallel to arithmetic in the *Gorgias* is a theoretical logistic which "arises from practical logistic when its practical applications are neglected and its presuppositions are pursued for its own sake" (Klein 1968: 23). This theoretical logistic "raises to an explicit science that knowledge of relations among numbers which, albeit implicitly, precedes, and indeed must precede, all calculation" (Klein 1968: 23). An example of one part of this sort of study of number might be the study of various types of means or proportions, which is also found in Nicomachus' *Introduction to Arithmetic* (II. 21 ff.). Such means are defined precisely in terms of relations of numbers to one another (e.g. a geometric proportion exists whenever of three terms as the first is to the second so is the second to the third, e.g. 8:4 :: 4:2).

That Plato did not limit λογιστική to practical calculation or "numbered things" is clear not just from the abstract formulation of its definition in parallel with ἀριθμητική in the *Gorgias* but also from Plato's later dialogues.

In the *Statesman* (259e) λογιστική is regarded as a theoretical rather than a practical art. At *Philebus* 56d a distinction is made between the ἀριθμητική of the many and the ἀριθμητική of the philosopher. Socrates makes a parallel distinction between two sorts of λογιστική at 56e. Plato provides the most extended treatment of λογιστική in Book VII of the *Republic*, where he sets out the propaideutic studies for his guardians. All of these studies have a practical side, but it is as theoretical studies, as studies that will turn the soul from the world of becoming to the world of being (521d), that Plato is most interested in them. Thus, while the normal connotation of λογιστική may have been something like our "arithmetic" or "computation," as is suggested by the *Hippias Minor* passage, it is important not to conclude that it was a purely practical art in contrast to ἀριθμητική, which dealt with number theory. Plato clearly thinks that there is a theoretical λογιστική which should be about non-sensible entities as much as ἀριθμητική.

Mueller has suggested that, in *Republic* VII, "Plato propounds a notion of 'pure' counting and calculating, but not one of pure 'theory of numbers'"(1992b: 93). This conclusion is partly based on a different reading of the passages on ἀριθμητική and λογιστική in the *Gorgias* (see above). Mueller's reading of the *Republic* seems to me to be problematic, however, in that it is hard to see what content this pure counting and calculating would have other than recognizing that you are dealing with abstract rather than concrete units. If this is all that theoretical ἀριθμητική and λογιστική amount to, why would Plato glorify them as one of the four propaideutic studies to which the guardians are supposed to devote ten years from ages 20 to 30? Indeed, Mueller himself recognizes that the apprehension of the abstract character of arithmetical units "will presumably facilitate the recognition of general features of numbers and perhaps the formulation of general laws" (1992b: 93). Mueller is right to say that "Plato does not go into this aspect of the study of abstract logistic," but it seems to me that there can be no doubt that Plato is calling for just such an abstract logistic.

No distinction is made between ἀριθμητική and λογιστική in this section of the *Republic*, both being seen as concerned with number and identified as the first of the propaideutic studies before introducing geometry as the second (526c). This combination of ἀριθμητική and λογιστική into one discipline is not very surprising in light of what we have seen in the *Gorgias*. In the *Gorgias* Plato had already emphasized that both dealt with the same subject, the odd and the even. Moreover, although they are distinguished by the way in which they deal with the odd and the even, λογιστική, as the discussion of the quantitative relations between numbers, is based on the study of different kinds of numbers by ἀριθμητική

(Klein 1968: 24). Taken together they constitute a full science of number. This explains the fact that, after introducing both ἀριθμητική and λογιστική at 525a–b, in the following description of the first propaideutic study, ἀριθμητική drops out and only one term, λογιστική, is used (cf. the *Statesman*, where the discussion of λογιστική at 259e seems to refer back to ἀριθμητική at 258d). Why was λογιστική chosen to designate the science of number rather than ἀριθμητική? Part of the answer may come from the immediate context. Plato starts with the practical value of computation for war (ἕνεκα πολέμου 525c) before turning to its true value in turning the soul and also emphasizes that people who are naturally good at computation are quick in all their studies (526b). Neither of these points is obviously true of number theory (ἀριθμητική). Perhaps more important is that λογιστική is chosen because it is, as it were, the crowning achievement of the study of number, since it presupposes ἀριθμητική. Aristotle, on the other hand, never refers to λογιστική and usually uses ἀριθμητική as his word for the science of number (e.g. *APo.* 75a39 etc.; at *APo.* 88b11 Aristotle does use λογισμῶν in parallel with γεωμετρίας which may indicate that he too could use a term stressing calculation to identify the science of number).

Does this analysis of Platonic usage help us to understand the use of λογιστική in Fragment 4 of Archytas? First, the evidence suggests that Archytas, like Plato and in contrast to Aristotle, used the term λογιστική rather than ἀριθμητική to designate the entire science of numbers. In Fragment 1, Archytas gives what appears to be a canonical list of four sciences (the list that is later known as the *quadrivium*). Some of the sciences are given an abstract name and others are described in terms of their subject matter. Thus, Archytas uses the terms "geometry" and "music" but identifies one of the other two sciences as concerned with "the speed of the stars and their risings and settings" (astronomy) and the other as concerned with "numbers." There is no suggestion here that there is any more than the one science of number, which is one of the four canonical sciences. Fragment 1 does not give a name to this science but, when λογιστικά is contrasted with γεωμετρικά and other sciences (τέχναι) in Fragment 4, the obvious conclusion is that λογιστικά is the science of numbers to which Archytas refers in Fragment 1. Archytas' choice of λογιστικά rather than ἀριθμητικά as the name for the science makes sense in light of Fragment 3's hymn to the value of λογισμός in establishing a state. λογιστικά, as the study of the relative quantity of numbers, is crucial for Archytas in determining a fair distribution of goods and power in the state. It seems plausible that Archytas might have defined λογιστική along the lines of

Plato's definition in the *Gorgias* and *Charmides* and saw it as building on ἀριθμητική in the same way that Plato did. Indeed, it is an intriguing suggestion that Plato in fact got the definition from Archytas, who was after all much more of a mathematician than Plato. There is some indication in Plato himself that λογιστική as the title for the science of numbers is independent of Plato. Thus at *Theaetetus* 145a, when Socrates gets Theaetetus' agreement that Theodorus is γεωμετρικός, ἀστρονομικός, λογιστικός and μουσικός, it seems implausible to assume that Plato is using λογιστικός in a technical Platonic sense rather than using the common currency among the mathematicians of the day (see also *Euthy.* 290c).

Archytas' pairing of λογιστικά with γεωμετρικά and other sciences in Fragment 4 suggests that he is thinking of a science and not just a practical skill of calculation. We must be careful, however, not to assume that he made the distinction between theoretical and practical λογιστική in the same way that Plato did. In particular, there is no reason to assign Platonic metaphysics to Archytas and to assume that he like Plato made a distinction between the intelligible and sensible worlds. Indeed, Plato may be directing his argument for that distinction in *Republic* VII against Archytas and the Pythagoreans (see the commentary on A15 and the overview of Archytas' philosophy). Fragment 2 of Archytas with its definitions of means in terms of the relative quantities of terms may be an example of Archytan λογιστικά, although the fragment itself appears to come from a work on music, in which logistic is applied to music.

ποτί – This is the Doric form for πρός.

σοφίαν – The manuscript reading of this passage is ποτὶ τὰν ἄλλαν σοφίαν τῶν μὲν ἄλλων τεχνῶν. Diels' text, which I follow, eliminates the first ἄλλαν and replaces the ἄλλων of the manuscripts with the Doric ἀλλᾶν. The problem with ἄλλαν is that it is hard to see what sense it makes. The passage would be translated "Calculation is far superior indeed to the other sciences in the rest of wisdom." What can be meant by "the rest of wisdom"? Usually the contrast would be between one branch of knowledge and "the rest of wisdom" but there is nothing to indicate what this branch would be. Admittedly we do not have the rest of the context for the fragment, but, given that the remainder of the first line of the fragment makes the contrast between "the other sciences" and geometry, it is hard to see how another contrast between one wisdom and "the rest of wisdom" could also fit in here. The manuscript reading can be plausibly explained as the result of a misunderstanding by copyists of an original Doric genitive (ἀλλᾶν τεχνῶν). A copyist might well have written ἄλλων as a gloss next to it. A later copyist confronted with the two forms ἀλλᾶν and ἄλλων might well have thought that the first was an accusative that went with σοφίαν earlier in the sentence and moved it there while keeping ἄλλων with τεχνῶν.

Why does Archytas say that it is in regard to σοφία that calculation is far superior to the other sciences? What does he mean by σοφία? σοφία can refer either to a specific "craft" or "skill" or to a broader intellectual ability, in which case it is often translated "wisdom" (Guthrie 1969: 27–34, Lesher 1992: 55 n. 1). At *EN* 1141a12 Aristotle makes this distinction, when he says that in one sense σοφία signifies excellence in an art but that, on the other hand, we think that some people are "wise" (σοφούς) in general (ὅλως) and not in part or in some other way. In this latter sense he says that σοφία is the most exact (ἀκριβεστάτη) of the sciences. In Aristotle's technical terminology, this most exact wisdom is a combination of understanding (νοῦς) and scientific knowledge (ἐπιστήμη). He adds that the knowledge in question is of the highest things rather than just of human things. Thus, Thales and Anaxagoras are called wise because they know marvelous things, even if they do not know what is practically good for human beings. Plato is similar to Aristotle in distinguishing a wisdom of the city as a whole, the wisdom of the guardians, from the many varieties of knowledge in the city (e.g. carpentry or farming; *R.* 428d ff.). For Plato, however, this wisdom does have to do with the practical concerns of how the city will conduct itself best both in itself and in regard to others (428d). Both Plato and Aristotle, then, use σοφία to refer to an exalted comprehensive intellectual virtue but differ in how that virtue is described. I have argued in the discussion of "The importance of the fragment" above that Archytas is using σοφία in this broader sense.

καὶ πολύ – With πολύ, καί "conveys a sense of climax, and denotes that something is not only true, but true to a marked degree" (Denniston 1959: 318). See, e.g. Pl. *R.* 562c.

1–2 μὲν . . . ἀτάρ – Denniston (1959: 54) says that this combination may, "like μὲν . . . δέ, denote either strong opposition, or little more than mere addition, or anything between the two." He classes Archytas' usage as an example of the weaker adversative force and compares Pl. *R.* 367e. This passage in the *Republic* does seem to provide a particularly good parallel for Archytas Fragment 4, since both passages have the pattern μὲν . . . ἀτάρ (. . .) καί. In the *Republic* Socrates is commenting that he had often in the past admired Glaucon and Adeimantus and that now on this particular occasion especially admired them. So in Archytas Fragment 4 the point is that calculation is far superior to the other sciences in general, and, in the particular case of geometry, it treats whatever matters it wishes to deal with more clearly than geometry.

2 ἐναργεστέρω – This is the manuscript reading, but this form for the comparative adverb of ἐναργής is unparalleled. It could be understood as parallel to formations such as ἐγγυτέρω for the comparative adverb of ἐγγύς. Mullach corrected to ἐναργεστέρως, but this form only appears four times and all in authors of the second century AD or later (e.g. Aristid., *Rh.* 1.10.1; Origen, *Cels.* 4.89.4) and is thus little improvement over the manuscript reading. It seems best, then, to accept the manuscript reading, perhaps as a Doric formation.

The fundamental meaning of the adjective ἐναργής is "visible, palpable, in bodily form" (LSJ). This emphasis on the immediate perceptible physical manifestation of something is present in Homer's use of the adjective to describe the gods appearing in their own form (*Il.* xx. 131) but also in Epicurus' usage of ἐνάργεια, some five hundred years later, to describe the "self-evidence" of sensations (see Long and Sedley 1987: 1. 88 for texts). Plato's usage also shows that the normal application of ἐναργής is to the sensible world. In the account of the divided line in Book vi of the *Republic*, Plato makes clear that in ordinary usage it is the objects in the second section of the line, the objects of the sensible world, that are esteemed as clear (ἐναργέσι δεδοξασμένοις) in comparison to the shadows and reflections in the lowest division of the line (511a). It is true that, although ἐναργής has its primary application to the sensible realm, it can be applied metaphorically to the intelligible realm and refer to intelligible "vividness" or "clarity" (see e.g. *Republic* 484c, where Plato refers to the "vivid pattern" [tr. Shorey ἐναργές . . . παράδειγμα] of truth in the soul). Indeed it is one of Plato's goals in the *Republic* to show that intelligible reality is, in the most important sense, more "manifest" than sensible reality. There are thus a number of places in which ἐναργής means simply "clear" or "distinct" without particular reference to a physical manifestation of any sort. Nonetheless, there is often, even in these cases, some residual reminder of the connection to the physical world and to the "vividness" of a sensible particular. Thus Aristotle says that "by nature the syllogism by means of the middle is prior and more knowable, but the syllogism by induction is more vivid (ἐναργέστερος) to us" (*APr.* 68b36). It would be possible to give the translation "syllogism by induction is clearer to us" but the reason that it is clearer is precisely that it starts with concrete perceptible particulars. Thus, when Archytas says that logistic deals with things in a more ἐναργής fashion than geometry, it might be that all that is meant is that it is "clearer," but it is more likely that Archytas means that logistic deals with things "more concretely" and "more vividly," in a way that evokes the visible and palpable (see the section on the importance of the fragment above).

πραγματεύεσθαι – With the accusative case πραγματεύομαι primarily means "occupy oneself with," "be engaged in," "treat," "deal with," or "investigate" a given subject matter (e.g. Pl. *Prt.* 361d, Pl. *Hp. Ma.* 304c). At *Metaphysics* 989b30 ff., Aristotle notes that, although the Pythagoreans use principles that are more abstruse than the rest of the *physiologoi*, since those principles are derived from mathematics rather than the natural world, nonetheless everything that they discuss and investigate (πραγματεύονται) concerns nature. Here in Fragment 4, Archytas' expression "deals with what it wishes" (πραγματεύεσθαι ἃ θέλει) states the application of logistic in the broadest possible way. Archytas is concerned not just with how logistic deals with its own proper subject matter, but with how it deals with any problem to which it chooses to apply itself.

3 ἃ ἐκλείπει – If ἐκλείπει is used transitively, ἃ is the direct object and refers to things that geometry "leaves out." If ἐκλείπει is used intransitively, ἃ is used adverbially as "those respects in which" geometry "is deficient." The use of ἐπιτελεῖ ("to complete" or "to finish") in the second part of the sentence suggests that calculation is completing something that geometry started but in which it was deficient rather than that calculation supplies something that geometry left out. Thus ἐπιτελεῖ supports the second alternative, i.e. that ἃ is adverbial. The syntax of the second part of the sentence also suggests that ἃ is adverbial: ἐπιτελεῖ has a direct object (ἀποδείξιας) so that we cannot understand ἃ ἐκλείπει . . . ἃ γεωμετρία as an object in this part of the sentence and must take it adverbially. A good parallel for this intransitive use of ἐκλείπω, although with the preposition περί rather than an adverbial accusative, is found in the *Politics* (1286a37), where Aristotle refers to matters "concerning which law must of necessity be deficient" (περὶ ὧν ἐκλείπειν ἀναγκαῖον αὐτόν [sc. νόμον]). For the combination ἐκλείπειν/ἐπιτελεῖν there is a sort of parallel at Aristotle *Rhetoric* 1371b4 and b25 where he talks of "supplying the deficiencies of our neighbors" (τὸ τὰ ἐλλιπῆ ἐπιτελεῖν). ἐλλείπω has a very similar meaning to ἐκλείπω, and there is an adjective ἐκλιπής that is less common than ἐλλιπής.

αὖ – αὖ basically means "again" and can be used either with δέ or in place of δέ to mean "on the other hand" (LSJ s.v.). The combination καί . . . αὖ functions here in Archytas very much like καί . . . δέ: the καί denotes that something is being added and the αὖ indicates that what is added is distinct from what precedes (Denniston 1959: 199). καί . . . αὖ is used to introduce another distinct way in which calculation surpasses geometry. Logistic treats whatever it deals with more clearly than geometry (even when geometry succeeds) and again (αὖ) in those respects where geometry is lacking, i.e. those areas in which geometry does not succeed, calculation is able to provide demonstrations. Looked at as a whole the sentence has the pattern of μέν . . . δέ . . . δέ used to list three different cases, but ἀτὰρ καί is used instead of δέ in one case and καί . . . αὖ is used instead of δέ in the other case.

Diels supposed that there was a lacuna after θέλει and the motivation for this supposition and for the supplement that he provides in his apparatus appears to be, in large part, the desire for something to contrast with αὖ. Thus, with Diels' supplement the passage would be translated "<For geometry gives proofs where the other sciences fail> and where geometry in turn (αὖ) fails, calculation also accomplishes proofs." This does give a neat sequence of thought, but, since the manuscript text also produces good sense, there is no need to suppose a lacuna.

ἀποδείξιας – The Attic accusative plural for iota-stem nouns would be -εις and this is what is found in most authors. Outside of Attic the accusative plural would be either ἀποδείξις (long final iota) or ἀποδείξιας. In the case of Fragment 4, the manuscripts give the former but accented incorrectly (ἀπόδειξις), and Meineke, followed by Wachsmuth and Diels, corrects to ἀποδείξιας. This seems justified by the fact that Archimedes, who like Archytas is from western Greece, uses ἀποδείξιας (e.g. *Spir.* 2.8.3). Note, however, that Heiberg's apparatus shows confusion about the form in the manuscripts.

The basic meaning of ἀπόδειξις is "a showing forth," "a making known," or "a display." It can thus refer to the "display" of valiant deeds (e.g. Hdt. 1. 207) or the "publication" of the research of Herodotus (proem). Closely related to this usage is the meaning "exposition" or "account." Thus Thucydides gives an "exposition" of how the Athenian empire came to be (1. 97.2.7). Finally, ἀπόδειξις can refer to a "demonstration" or "proof" of a given thesis, but there is a very wide range of conceptions of what counts as a demonstration or proof. Aristotle comes to define the term quite precisely as a deduction (συλλογισμός) which proceeds from premises that are true and primary (*Top.* 100a27), but not all authors are so precise. In the fifth and early part of the fourth centuries what counts as a demonstration is quite fluid even in philosophical authors (see Lloyd 1979: 102–22). In *On Fleshes* a demonstration that the moist part of the body is hot consists of showing that, if we cut the body, hot blood flows out and that the blood remains liquid as long as it is hot (9.14).

In a number of places Plato distinguishes between cogent proofs and those that rely just on probability (e.g. *Tht.* 162e). From those very passages, however, it is clear that ἀπόδειξις could be used either of a rigorous proof or of a demonstration based on probability and that this was true not just in philosophical arguments but also in mathematics (*Phd.* 92d). In Fragment 4, we might suppose that, since Archytas is discussing sciences such as geometry and logistic, ἀπόδειξις must be used in the sense of formal proof. This is a possibility, but we cannot be sure even in this case exactly what degree of formal rigor Archytas implied by the term. Certainly there is no hint of Aristotle's definition of demonstration here. Nor does Archytas use vocabulary that would be appropriate for making Plato's distinction between cogent and merely probable demonstrations. Moreover, given the lack of a clear context for Fragment 4, it is quite possible that ἀπόδειξις does not refer to a formal proof at all but to a less precisely defined demonstration such as that which Pericles provided in order to convince the Athenians that they would win the war (Thuc. II. 13.95). That Archytas is using ἀπόδειξις in this more general way is supported by his claim that logistic treats matters more vividly than geometry when it comes to making wise decisions.

4 ἐπιτελεῖ – ἐπιτελέω most commonly means "to carry out" or "to put into effect" something that exists only in thought or in word. Thus it is used of "carrying out" commands (Hdt. I. 115) or assigned tasks (Hdt. I. 126), "fulfilling" oracles or visions (Hdt. I. 13), "completing" something that was promised, or "putting into effect" a design (Thuc. I. 70; Pl. *Rep.* 442b) or purpose (Isoc. II. 38; Pl. *Gorg.* 491b). Similarly, it can also refer to paying in full what is owed or to discharging a religious duty. As a technical term in Aristotle, it is used of a syllogism "made perfect" by reduction to the first figure (*APr.* 28a). This process of perfecting a deduction involves inserting additional steps between premises and conclusion in order to make the necessity of the conclusion obvious (Smith 1995: 36–38). This usage seems connected to the others by its emphasis on making obvious what was only suggested before.

The question of the meaning of ἐπιτελέω in Archytas is complicated by its use with ἀποδείξιας as a direct object. There is no parallel for this combination of ἐπιτελέω with ἀποδείξιας. The normal use of ἐπιτελέω would suggest that Archytas was talking about "putting demonstrations into effect." On this reading, logistic is superior to geometry not in providing proofs or demonstrations but rather in making those demonstrations have effect. I have adopted this interpretation in my account of the importance of the fragment. On the other hand we might suppose that Archytas means that logistic completes proofs where geometry cannot. We might understand this to mean (1) that geometry makes some progress on proofs which logistic then has to complete, or (2) that logistic is able to accomplish a proposed demonstration when geometry cannot make any progress on it at all.

ὁμῶς – Accented in this way the word means "equally." It is overwhelmingly a poetic word and very rarely found in prose. It never occurs in Aristotle and only occurs in Plato in quotations from Homer. Of the few parallels in prose the most intriguing are in Iamblichus. The word appears twice in Iamblichus and both of those usages come from the same passage of *On the Pythagorean Life* (138.5 and 138.11). One of these has the same combination, καὶ ὁμῶς, that appears in Archytas Fragment 4. Dillon and Hershbell comment that this passage seems to come from Aristoxenus (1991: 157 n. 6). Aristoxenus would provide a perfect parallel in that he, like Archytas, comes from Tarentum and wrote in the fourth century BC.

Given the rarity of the word in prose, one might prefer ὅμως. ὅμως, "nevertheless," is much more common in prose and, since it is derived from ὁμῶς, often has a closely connected meaning. In Archytas the point seems to be that logistic puts demonstrations into effect where geometry is deficient and, if the investigation concerns shapes (where geometry would normally be thought to excel), logistic "equally" ("in this case as well") or "nevertheless" puts demonstrations into effect. In sense ὅμως/ὁμῶς is reinforced by καί ("also") before τὰ περὶ τοῖς εἴδεσιν. The position of ὅμως/ὁμῶς before the if-clause appears to be an example of prolepsis to emphasize the fact that logistic is "equally" or "nevertheless" superior, even where geometry is strongest. The meaning is thus essentially the same whether we read ὁμῶς or ὅμως but, especially in light of the possible parallels in Aristoxenus, it seems better to read ὁμῶς.

εἰδέων – This is the most problematic word in the fragment. Burkert takes it as a reference to Platonic forms and thus as a clear indication that the fragment is a forgery. There are, however, numerous other possible references for it besides Platonic forms. For the various possibilities (form, shape, kind, class, type, nature) see Huffman 1993: 184 ff. The word appears in Archytas' predecessor Philolaus in the sense of "kinds" when he refers to the two proper kinds of number, odd and even (Fr. 5 ἴδια εἴδη – see Huffman 1993: 184 ff.). Democritus used the closely related term ἰδέα, which is also used for Platonic forms, to refer to his atoms, in which context it is to be translated "shapes" (B167, B6, A57 – see Guthrie 1965: 395, n. 2). Among the titles of Democritus' works is one given variously as Περὶ ἰδεῶν

(Sext. VII. 137) or Περὶ εἰδῶν (Thphr. *Sens.* 51). These books were clearly not about Platonic forms but were instead about his atoms with their unlimited number of shapes.

The exact meaning of εἶδος in Fragment 4 remains uncertain since the fragment is so short. Nothing in the context, however, suggests that we are dealing with Platonic forms. This is in contrast to passages in the pseudepigrapha assigned to Archytas where all the marks of the Platonic theory of forms are present (e.g. Thesleff 38.14 ff. – τὰ μετέχοντα τῶν εἰδέων . . . νοατὰ δὲ αὐτὰ τὰ εἴδεα . . . αὐτὸς ὁ κύκλος). In Archytas Fragment 4, on the other hand, given that εἶδος occurs in the context of a comparison of logistic with geometry, it seems most plausible to take it as a reference to the shapes or figures with which geometry deals. The structure of the sentence in which εἰδέων and εἴδεσιν appear, in fact, suggests that geometry particularly focuses on εἶδος and that it is thus surprising that logistic "nevertheless" (see the commentary on ὁμῶς, this line) surpasses it in dealing with εἴδη. This structure makes perfect sense if εἶδος is taken to mean "shape," which is indeed the preeminent concern of geometry.

τεά – The manuscript reading is τε ά, but it is hard to see what force τε can have. Diels emends the text to τεά, the Doric/Ionic form of τις. The corruption is very easy palaeographically and understandable given the rarity of the Doric form, but most of the examples of this word are in cases other than the nominative. Emendations to ἐντί or ἐντὶ ά are less probable palaeographically.

πραγματεία – This word often occurs with a possessive genitive in the sense of "business of x" or "the occupation of x." So at Pl. *Tht.* 161e we have ἡ τοῦ διαλέγεσθαι πραγματεία "the business of dialectic." It also is used, however, with or without an objective genitive to refer to the "treatment" or "investigation" of a subject. Thus geometry is defined as ἡ τοῦ ἐπιπέδου πραγματεία "the investigation of plane surfaces" (Pl. *R.* 528d; cf. Arist. *EN* 1103b26 and *Top.* 100a18). This seems to be the usage here in Archytas Fr. 4. πραγματεία picks up on πραγματεύεσθαι in line 2.

καὶ τὰ περὶ τοῖς εἴδεσιν – Most editors have supposed that the fragment breaks off here, before the sentence which began with καὶ ἃ ἐκλείπει in line 3 is finished. Diels makes no suggestion as to how the sentence might have been completed. Meineke suggested adding πραγματεύεται and Blass περιλαμβάνεν (an infinitive dependent on δοκεῖ in Blass' emendation of the sentence), with each of which logistic is presumably to be understood as the subject and τὰ περὶ τοῖς εἴδεσιν as the object. These supplements yield the meaning that, if an investigation of shapes is involved, logistic "deals with" or "includes" the "things concerned with shapes." I suggest that the sentence can be understood without any supplement. τὰ περὶ τοῖς εἴδεσιν is parallel to ἃ (ἐκλείπει) at the beginning of the sentence. Thus it is an accusative adverbial to ἀποδείξιας . . . ἐπιτελεῖ as was ἃ ἐκλείπει: if the investigation concerns shapes, logistic also (puts demonstrations into effect) with respect to what concerns shapes. The syntax of this sentence understood in this way is not easy, but it makes the best sense of a difficult problem.

PART THREE

Genuine testimonia

CHAPTER I

Testimonia for Archytas' life, writings and reception

A1 Diogenes Laertius, *Lives of the Philosophers* VIII. 79–83

[cf. Pseudo-Hesychii Milesii *De Viris Illustribus* and *Magnum Excerptum*, Marcovich 1999: II. 100. 1–8; II. 313. 15–20]

Ἀρχύτας Μνησαγόρου Ταραντῖνος, ὡς δὲ Ἀριστόξενος, Ἑστιαίου,   1
Πυθαγορικὸς καὶ αὐτός. οὗτός ἐστιν ὁ Πλάτωνα ῥυσάμενος δι' ἐπισ-   2
τολῆς παρὰ Διονυσίου μέλλοντα ἀναιρεῖσθαι. ἐθαυμάζετο δὲ καὶ   3
παρὰ τοῖς πολλοῖς ἐπὶ πάσῃ ἀρετῇ· καὶ δὴ ἑπτάκις τῶν πολιτῶν   4
ἐστρατήγησε, τῶν ἄλλων μὴ πλέον ἐνιαυτοῦ στρατηγούντων διὰ τὸ   5
κωλύειν τὸν νόμον. πρὸς τοῦτον καὶ Πλάτων γέγραφεν ἐπιστολὰς δύο,   6
ἐπειδήπερ αὐτῷ πρότερος γεγράφει τοῦτον τὸν τρόπον. [A spurious   7
letter of Archytas and Plato's response follows: Thesleff 46.1–7 and Plato,   8
Ep. xii]   9
Γεγόνασι δ' Ἀρχῦται τέτταρες· πρῶτος αὐτὸς οὗτος, δεύτερος   10
Μυτιληναῖος, μουσικός, τρίτος Περὶ γεωργίας συγγεγραφώς, τέταρτος   11
ἐπιγραμματοποιός. ἔνιοι καὶ πέμπτον, ἀρχιτέκτονά φασιν, οὗ φέρε-   12
ται βιβλίον Περὶ μηχανῆς, ἀρχὴν ἔχον ταύτην· "τάδε παρὰ Τεύκρου   13
Καρχηδονίου διήκουσα." περὶ δὲ τοῦ μουσικοῦ φέρεται καὶ τόδε, ὡς   14
ὀνειδιζόμενος ἐπὶ τῷ μὴ ἐξακούεσθαι εἴποι· "τὸ γὰρ ὄργανον ὑπὲρ   15
ἐμοῦ διαγωνιζόμενον λαλεῖ."   16
Τὸν δὲ Πυθαγορικὸν Ἀριστόξενός φησι μηδέποτε στρατηγοῦντα   17
ἡττηθῆναι· φθονούμενον δ' ἅπαξ ἐκχωρῆσαι τῆς στρατηγίας, καὶ τοὺς   18
αὐτίκα ληφθῆναι.   19
Οὗτος πρῶτος τὰ μηχανικὰ ταῖς μαθηματικαῖς προσχρησά-   20
μενος ἀρχαῖς μεθώδευσε καὶ πρῶτος κίνησιν ὀργανικὴν διαγράμ-   21
ματι γεωμετρικῷ προσήγαγε, διὰ τῆς τομῆς τοῦ ἡμικυλίνδρου δύο   22

7 γεγράφει] P¹ γέγραφε BD ἔγραψε FP⁴ ἐγεγράφει Stephanus, Long   11 μουσικός] om.
F   12 ἐπιγραμματοποιός] BP ἐπιγραμματικός F   13 παρά] P⁵ Frob. περὶ
BP¹FD   14 καὶ τόδε] om. F   15 τῷ] PD τὸ BF   19 ληφθῆναι] λειφθῆναι
B²P¹Q   20 μαθηματικαῖς] Kuehn μηχανικαῖς BPFD

μέσας ἀνὰ λόγον λαβεῖν ζητῶν εἰς τὸν τοῦ κύβου διπλασιασμόν. 23
κἂν γεωμετρίᾳ πρῶτος <τὴν τῶν> κύβων <αὔξην> εὗρεν, ὥς φησι 24
Πλάτων ἐν Πολιτείᾳ. 25

24 κἂν] Roeper² (51), Cobet, Diels   καὶ BPFD   <τὴν τῶν> κύβων <αὔξην>] scripsi, cf. Plato, *R.* 528b   κύβον BPD   κύβην F   κύβου διπλασιασμὸν Meibom   εὗρεν] εὗξεν Wil.

Archytas of Tarentum, the son of Mnesagoras or, according to Aristoxenus, of Hestiaios, was also himself a Pythagorean. He is the one who rescued Plato by means of a letter, when he was about to be killed by Dionysius. He was also admired among the multitude for every virtue. Indeed, he served as general (*stratēgos*) of his fellow citizens seven times, although others served no more than a year because the law prevented it. Plato has also written two letters to him, since Archytas had written to him first in the following fashion [There follows a spurious letter of Archytas to Plato and Plato's response. See Thesleff 46.1–7 and Plato, *Ep.* xii].

There have been four men with the name Archytas: First, this man himself, second a man from Mytilene who was a musician, third the author of *On Agriculture*, fourth, a writer of epigrams. Some say that there was also a fifth, an architect, whose book *On Mechanism* has been preserved. It has the following beginning, "I heard the following from Teucer of Carthage." Concerning the musician, the following story has also been preserved, that, when he was reproached because he could not be heard, he said, "yes, for my instrument speaks for me in the competition."

Aristoxenus says that the Pythagorean was never defeated when he was *stratēgos* but that, once, he withdrew from the office, because his success was begrudged by others, and the Tarentines were immediately captured.

He was the first to systematize mechanics by using mathematical first principles, and he was the first to apply the motion appropriate to instruments to a geometrical proof, seeking to find two mean proportionals by cutting the semicylinder, in order to duplicate the cube. And in geometry he was the first to discover the dimension of the cube [i.e. solid geometry], to use Plato's language in the *Republic*.

A1a Athenaeus Mechanicus, *On War Machines* 5.1
(Schneider 1912: 10)

τουτὶ γὰρ ἄν τις <εἰς> πραγμάτων λόγον ὠφεληθεὶς ἀπέλθοι, 1
ἐπιμελῶς ἐπιστήσας ἑαυτόν, ἐκ τοῦ Δελφικοῦ ἐκείνου παραγγέλματος 2

1 <εἰς>] Byz. paraphrase 201.16   ἀπέλθοι] Wescher   ἀπέλθοιεν codd.

ἢ ἐκ τῶν Στράτωνος καὶ Ἑστιαίου καὶ Ἀρχύτου καὶ Ἀριστοτέλους καὶ 3
τῶν ἄλλων τῶν παραπλήσια ἐκείνοις γεγραφότων. νεωτέροις μὲν γὰρ 4
φιλομαθοῦσιν οὐκ ἄχρηστα εἴη <πρὸς ἕξιν> τοῦ στοιχειωθῆναι· τοῖς 5
δὲ βουλομένοις ἤδη τι πράττειν μακρὰν παντελῶς ἂν εἴη καὶ ἀπηρτη- 6
μένα τῆς πραγματικῆς θεωρίας.   7

3 <μᾶλλον> ἢ] Nitsche Ἑστιαίου] Wescher ἐστίου M ἐστίου PV **3–4** ἐκ τῶν
Στράτωνος καὶ Ἑστιαίου καὶ Ἀρχύτου καὶ Ἀριστοτέλους καὶ τῶν ἄλλων τῶν παραπλήσια] ἐκ
τῶν Φιλολάου καὶ Ἀριστοτέλους Ἰσοκράτους τε καὶ Ἀριστοφάνους καὶ Ἀπολλωνίου καὶ τῶν
παραπλήσια Byz. 202.1 **5** <πρὸς ἕξιν>] Byz. 202.3 **6** μακρὰν] M ἢ μακρὰν PV
ἀπηρτημένα] cod. Lugdun. Vossianus 7 ἀπηρτισμένα MPV

Someone who has given it careful attention would receive more benefit,
for the purpose of writing a practical treatise [sc. on mechanics], from
that Delphic precept than from the writings of Strato, Hestiaeus, Archytas,
Aristotle and the others who have written treatises similar to theirs. For
young people eager to learn, these treatises are not without use for gaining
instruction in basic principles. For those who are at the point of wanting
to do something, however, they are utterly removed and separated from
practical considerations.

A1b Vitruvius, *On Architecture* I. 1.17

Quibus vero natura tantum tribuit sollertiae, acuminis, memoriae, ut
possint geometriam, astrologiam, musicen ceterasque disciplinas penitus
habere notas, praetereunt officia architectorum et efficiuntur mathematici.
Itaque faciliter contra eas disciplinas disputare possunt, quod pluribus telis
disciplinarum sunt armati. Hi autem inveniuntur raro, ut aliquando fuerunt
Aristarchus Samius, Philolaus et Archytas Tarentini, Apollonius Pergaeus,
Eratosthenes Cyrenaeus, Archimedes et Scopinas ab Syracusis, qui multas res organicas, gnomonicas numero naturalibusque rationibus inventas
atque explicatas posteris reliquerunt.

Those on whom nature has bestowed such great intellectual resources,
acuteness and powers of memory, that they are able to have profound
knowledge of geometry, astronomy, music and other disciplines, go beyond
the duties of an architect and become mathematicians. Accordingly they
are able to engage in discussions in these disciplines with ease, since they
have been armed with the very many weapons provided by the disciplines.
These individuals are rarely found, however, such as once were Aristarchus
of Samos, Philolaus and Archytas of Tarentum, Apollonius of Perga, Eratosthenes of Cyrene, Archimedes and Scopinas from Syracuse, who left to

posterity many mechanical devices and sundials, which were discovered and explained by means of mathematics and natural science.

A1c Plutarch, *Precepts of Statecraft* 821b–c

ἄνθρωπον δ' ἀνθρώπῳ χειροήθη καὶ πρᾶον ἑκουσίως οὐδὲν ἀλλ' ἢ πίστις εὐνοίας καὶ καλοκαγαθίας δόξα καὶ δικαιοσύνης παρίστησιν. ᾗ καὶ Δημοσθένης ὀρθῶς μέγιστον ἀποφαίνεται πρὸς τοὺς τυράννους φυλακτήριον ἀπιστίαν ταῖς πόλεσι· τοῦτο γὰρ μάλιστα τῆς ψυχῆς τὸ μέρος, ᾧ πιστεύομεν, ἁλώσιμόν ἐστιν. ὥσπερ οὖν τῆς Κασάνδρας ἀδοξούσης ἀνόνητος ἦν ἡ μαντικὴ τοῖς πολίταις . . . οὕτως ἡ πρὸς Ἀρχύταν πίστις καὶ πρὸς Βάττον εὔνοια τῶν πολιτῶν μεγάλα τοὺς χρωμένους αὐτοῖς διὰ τὴν δόξαν ὠφέλησε.

Nothing else makes one man manageable by and willingly gentle to another man than trust in his good will and belief in his nobility and justice. Thus, Demosthenes correctly asserts that the greatest protection for city-states against tyranny is distrust. For the part of the soul with which we trust is especially easy to take captive. Therefore, just as the prophetic ability of Cassandra gave no profit to the citizens, because she was not respected . . . so the trust of the citizens with regard to Archytas and their good will towards Battus greatly benefitted those who employed them on account of their reputation.

A1d Aelian, *Historical Miscellany* VII. 14

τί δέ; οὐκ ἦσαν καὶ οἱ φιλόσοφοι τὰ πολέμια ἀγαθοί; ἐμοὶ μὲν δοκοῦσιν, εἴ γε Ἀρχύταν μὲν εἵλοντο ἑξάκις στρατηγὸν Ταραντῖνοι, Μέλισσος δὲ ἐναυάρχησε . . .

What, were not the philosophers also good in military matters? It seems so to me, if indeed the Tarentines chose Archytas *stratēgos* six times, and Melissus served as an admiral . . .

A1e Themistius, *Orations* 17 (215c5 Hardouin; 308: 14–16 Schenkl–Downey)

ἐῶ δὲ Πιττακὸν καὶ Βίαντα καὶ Κλεόβουλον, ἐῶ δὲ Ἀρχύταν τὸν Ταραντῖνον, οἳ πλείοσι πράγμασιν ὡμίλησαν ἢ συγγράμμασι.

I pass over Pittacus, Bias and Cleobulus, I pass over Archytas of Tarentum, men who busied themselves more with public affairs than treatises.

A1f Synesius, *On the Gift of the Astrolabe* II. 5 ff. (308c, Terzaghi 1944: 134, 7–16)

Ἰταλία μὲν γὰρ πάλαι τοὺς αὐτοὺς ἔχουσα Πυθαγόρου τε ἀκουστὰς καὶ τῶν πόλεων ἁρμοστάς, Ἑλλὰς ἡ μεγάλη προσηγορεύετο, καὶ μάλα ἐν δίκῃ, παρ' οἷς Χαρώνδας μὲν ἐνομοθέτει καὶ Ζάλευκος, ἐστρατήγουν δὲ Ἀρχῦται τε καὶ Φιλόλαοι, ὁ δὲ ἀστρονομικώτατος Τίμαιος ἐπολιάρχει τε καὶ ἐπρέσβευε καὶ τἆλλα ἐπολιτεύετο, παρ' οὗ καὶ Πλάτων ἡμῖν περὶ κόσμου φύσεως διαλέγεται. ταῦτ' ἄρα μέχρις ἐνάτης ἀπὸ Πυθαγόρου γενεᾶς τὰ κοινὰ πιστευθέντες, εὐδαίμονα τὴν Ἰταλίαν ἐτήρησαν.

For, in antiquity, Italy, since it contained in the same people both students of Pythagoras and governors of their cities, was called great Greece. This was very proper, since Charondas and Zaleucus gave laws for them and Archytases and Philolauses served as generals, and that most astronomical man, Timaeus, ruled his city, had the highest rank and in other ways participated in the government of the state. It is from the mouth of this man that Plato discourses about the nature of the cosmos for us. These men were trusted with public affairs up to the ninth generation from Pythagoras, and they guarded the prosperity of Italy.

A1g Theophylactus of Ohrid, *Letters* 127.48–51 (Gautier 1986: 573. 48 ff.)

πῶς δ' ἂν στρατιωτικὴν καὶ γεωμετρικὴν εἰς ταὐτὸ συνήγαγε καὶ συνῆψε τὰ μακροῖς θριγγίοις ἔκπαλαι διειργόμενα μετ' Ἀρχύταν, μετὰ Φιλόλαον, μετὰ τὸν Αἴλιον Ἀδριανόν, μετὰ τὸν ἔκπτωτον ἡμῖν Ἰουλιανόν;

How could he have united military science and geometry and joined together things that had been long separated by great walls, following on Archytas, Philolaus, Aelius Hadrianus, and Julian the apostate?

A2 *Suda* 4121

Ἀρχύτας Ταραντῖνος, Ἑστιαίου υἱὸς ἢ Μνησάρχου ἢ Μνασαγέτου ἢ Μνασαγόρου, φιλόσοφος Πυθαγορικός. οὗτος Πλάτωνα ἔσωσε μὴ φονευθῆναι ὑπὸ Διονυσίου τοῦ τυράννου. τοῦ κοινοῦ δὲ τῶν

Ἰταλιωτῶν προέστη, στρατηγὸς αἱρεθεὶς αὐτοκράτωρ ὑπὸ τῶν πολιτῶν καὶ τῶν περὶ ἐκεῖνον τὸν τόπον Ἑλλήνων. ἅμα δὲ καὶ φιλοσοφίαν ἐκπαιδεύων μαθητάς τ᾽ ἐνδόξους ἔσχε καὶ βιβλία συνέγραψε πολλά. τοῦτον φανερῶς γενέσθαι διδάσκαλον Ἐμπεδοκλέους. καὶ παροιμία "Ἀρχύτου πλαταγή·" ὅτι Ἀρχύτας πλαταγὴν εὗρεν, ἥτις ἐστὶν εἶδος ὀργάνου ἦχον καὶ ψόφον ἀποτελοῦντος. ὁ δὲ πλαταγὴν χαλκευσάμενος ἐπλατάγει.

Archytas of Tarentum, son of Hestiaios or Mnesarchos or Mnasagetes or Mnasagoras, a Pythagorean philosopher. He saved Plato from being murdered by Dionysius the tyrant. He was the leader of the Italian league and was chosen general with special powers by the citizens and the Greeks in that region. At the same time also, as a teacher of philosophy, he both had students of high reputation and also wrote many books. [They say] that he was manifestly the teacher of Empedocles. And there is the proverb, "a clapper of Archytas," because Archytas invented a clapper, which is a kind of instrument that produces a resounding noise. And he having forged a clapper from bronze was making it clap. [This last sentence is probably a reference to Heracles, who used a clapper to scare away the birds from the Stymphalian Lake. See A.R. II. 1055.]

A3 Horace, *Odes* I. 28

Te maris et terrae numeroque carentis harenae	1
mensorem cohibent, Archyta,	2
pulveris exigui prope litus parva Matinum	3
munera, nec quicquam tibi prodest	4
aërias temptasse domos animoque rotundum	5
percurrisse polum morituro.	6
occidit et Pelopis genitor, conviva deorum,	7
Tithonusque remotus in auras,	8
et Iovis arcanis Minos admissus, habentque	9
Tartara Panthoiden iterum Orco	10
demissum, quamvis clipeo Troiana refixo	11
tempora testatus nihil ultra	12
nervos atque cutem morti concesserat atrae,	13
iudice te non sordidus auctor	14
naturae verique. sed omnis una manet nox	15
et calcanda semel via leti.	16

dant alios Furiae torvo spectacula Marti; 17
  exitio est avidum mare nautis; 18
mixta senum ac iuvenum densentur funera; nullum 19
  saeva caput Proserpina fugit. 20

me quoque devexi rapidus comes Orionis 21
  Illyricis Notus obruit undis. 22
at tu, nauta, vagae ne parce malignus harenae 23
  ossibus et capiti inhumato 24

particulam dare: sic, quodcumque minabitur Eurus 25
  fluctibus Hesperiis, Venusinae 26
plectantur silvae te sospite, multaque merces 27
  unde potest tibi defluat aequo 28

ab Iove Neptunoque sacri custode Tarenti. 29
  neglegis immeritis nocituram 30
postmodo te natis fraudem committere? fors et 31
  debita iura vicesque superbae 32

te maneant ipsum: precibus non linquar inultis, 33
  teque piacula nulla resolvent. 34
quamquam festinas, non est mora longa; licebit 35
  iniecto ter pulvere curras. 36

A small amount of dust offered as meager funeral rites confines you near the Matine shore, Archytas, you who measured the sea and the earth and sands without number. Nor is it any use to you to have investigated the heavenly realms and to have traversed the rounded sky with a mind that was going to die. The father of Pelops, who shared in the banquets of the gods, also died, as did Tithonus, who was taken away into the winds, and Minos, although he was admitted to the secrets of Jupiter. Tartarus holds the son of Panthous, who was sent down to Orcus a second time, although by taking down the shield he invoked the Trojan age to show that nothing beyond sinews and skin had yielded to black death. He who, by your judgment, was no mean authority on nature and truth. But one night waits for all of us and the path of death must be trod once and for all. The Furies give some men over to the spectacles of grim Mars. The sea is eager for the death of sailors. The funerals of young and old are crowded together in confusion; savage Persephone avoids no one. Me too the south wind, rushing companion of the setting of Orion, has overwhelmed in the Illyrian waves. But you, sailor, don't be spiteful and omit to give a grain of the shifting sands to my unburied head and bones: If you do this, however the east wind may threaten you in western seas, may you be safe, although Venusian woods are buffeted, and may a great reward flow down for you from all possible sources, from favoring Jupiter and from Neptune, the protector of holy Tarentum. Do you not care that you are committing a crime, which will afterwards harm your descendants, who do not deserve it? It may be that just requests ungranted and haughty requital await even you. I will not be left behind with curses unfulfilled, and no rites of expiation will absolve you. Although you are in a hurry, the delay is not long; throw three handfuls of dust on me and you can hurry on.

A3a Scholia to Horace (ps.-Acron, Keller 1902)

105. 9–16   Haec ode ex prosopopeia formata est; inducitur enim corpus naufragi Architae Tarentini ad litus expulsum conqueri de iniuria sua et a praetereuntibus petere sepulturam. Qui Archyta Pythagoricus fuit, geometriae et asteroscopiae peritus. Pythagorici enim omnia numeris constare dicunt. Ad eius ergo solationem etiam famosos et diis oriundo coniunctos homines perisse commemorat. 105. 21–106.2   Prope latum parva Matinum munera] Matinus mons Apuliae est, iuxta quem Archita sepultus est, sive, ut quidam volunt, plana Calabriae . . . 107.20   iudice te] Hoc est: o Archita. 109. 1–2   At tu nauta] Hic quasi Architam ponit nautam precari, ne remaneat insepultus, sed iam harenam iniciat . . .

105. 9–16   In this ode the poet assumes a persona. For the corpse of the shipwrecked Archytas of Tarentum is presented to us cast out on the shore and complaining of the injustice done to it and seeking burial from those passing by. This Archytas was a Pythagorean, who was expert in geometry and astronomy. For the Pythagoreans say that all things consist of numbers. Therefore, in order to console him he enumerates men who have perished, although they were famous and joined to the gods by birth. 105.21–106.2 Near the Matine shore . . .] Matinus is a mountain in Apulia next to which Archytas was buried, or, as some wish it, a plain in Calabria . . . 107.20   In your judgment . . .] i.e. Archytas. 109.1–2   But you sailor . . .] Here it is as if he makes Archytas beg a sailor not to leave him unburied but to throw sand upon him.

A3b Scholia to Horace (Porphyrio, Holder 1894)

36.27–37.5 Haec ode prosopopoeia forma est. Inducitur enim corpus naufragi Archytae Tarentini in litus expulsum conqueri de iniuria sui et petere <a> praetereuntibus sepulturam. Hic autem Archytas Pythagoricus fuit <at>que merito geometriae peritus, quia Pythagorici omnia numeris constare credunt

Matinus mons sive promunturium est Apuliae, iuxta quem Archytas sepultus est.

38.4–6   At tu nauta vagae . . .] Ad praetereuntes nautas sermonem Archytam convertisse fingit.

36.27–37.5   In this ode the poet assumes a persona. For the corpse of the shipwrecked Archytas of Tarentum is presented to us, cast out on the shore, complaining of the injustice done to it and seeking burial from those passing by. This Archytas was a Pythagorean and appropriately expert in geometry, since the Pythagoreans believe that all things consist of numbers.

Matinus is a mountain or promontory in Apulia, next to which Archytas was buried.

38.4–6   But you sailor . . .] He [sc. Horace] contrives it that Archytas turns his address to passing sailors.

A3c Propertius, *Elegies* IV. 1.75–78

certa feram certis auctoribus, aut ego vates
    nescius aerata signa movere pila,
me creat Archytae suboles Babylonius Horops
    Horon, et a proavo ducta Conone domus.

I shall report sure things on sure authority, or I am a seer who does not know how to move the constellations on the bronze sphere. Horops of Babylon, shoot of Archytas, begot me, Horos, and my house is descended from Conon as a forefather.

A3d Diogenes Laertius, *Lives of the Philosophers* IV. 52 (= Bion Fr. 227, Lloyd-Jones and Parsons 1983: 86; Kindstrand Fr. 7)

εὐφυὴς γὰρ ἦν [sc. Βίων] καὶ παρῳδῆσαι· οἷά ἐστιν αὐτοῦ καὶ ταῦτα·   1
    ὦ πέπον Ἀρχύτα, ψαλληγενές, ὀλβιότυφε,   2
    τῆς ὑπάτης ἔριδος πάντων ἐμπειρότατ᾽ ἀνδρῶν   3
καὶ ὅλως καὶ μουσικὴν καὶ γεωμετρίαν διέπαιζεν.   4

---

2 ψαλληγενές] ψαλμηγενές Reiske

For he [i.e. Bion] was also clever at parody. These verses of his are an example:

> O dear Archytas, born for harp playing, happy in your conceit, most skilled of all men in the quarrel of the highest pitch.

And in general he made fun of both music and geometry.

A3e Christopher of Mytilene 122. 86–90 (Kurtz p. 85)

(Εἰς τὸν ἀράχνην)

> ὢ πῶς συνάπτει ταῖσδε ταῖς γραμμαῖς ἅμα
> καὶ ῥομβοειδὲς καὶ σκαληνὸν εὐτέχνως,
> οὐκ Ἀρχιμήδην οὔτε μὴν τὸν Ἀρχύταν
> ἑωρακώς που, τοὺς σοφοὺς γεωμέτρας,
> οὐ ταῖς ἐκείνων ἐντραφεὶς ὁμιλίαις . . .

(To the Spider)
Oh, how does he [sc. the spider] skillfully join with these lines at the same time both rhomboid and scalene figures, although never having seen anywhere Archimedes nor indeed Archytas, the wise geometers, nor having been brought up in their instruction . . .?

A3f John the Geometer

(J. P. Migne, *Patrologiae Cursus, series Graeca*, vol. 106: 919; cf. *Epigrammatum anthologia Palatina cum Planudeis et appendice nova*, vol. 3: Epigrammata demonstrativa 203 [ed. E. Cougny])

Εἰς τοὺς τρεῖς φιλοσόφους

> Τρεῖς σοφίης πολυΐστορος ἔκκριτοι ἀστέρες οἷοι
> ἐνθέμενοι βίβλοις ὄλβον ἀπειρέσιον·
> Ἀρχύτας ἦρξε, Πλάτων πλάτυνε· τέλος δ' ἐπὶ πᾶσιν,
> ὡς ἔτυχε κληθείς, θῆκεν Ἀριστοτέλης.

On the Three Philosophers
There are three lone stars of multifaceted wisdom, a select group, who stored up immense wealth in their books: Archytas was the architect, Plato gave it a broader platform and, in accordance with the name he chanced to have, Aristotle ended by summing the total.

A4 Strabo, *Geography* VI. 3.4 (C. 280)

ἴσχυσαν δέ ποτε οἱ Ταραντῖνοι καθ᾽ ὑπερβολήν, πολιτευόμενοι 1
δημοκρατικῶς. καὶ γὰρ ναυτικὸν ἐκέκτηντο μέγιστον τῶν ταύτῃ καὶ 2
πεζοὺς ἔστελλον τρισμυρίους, ἱππέας δὲ τρισχιλίους, ἱππακοντιστὰς 3
δὲ χιλίους. ἀπεδέξαντο δὲ καὶ τὴν Πυθαγόρειον φιλοσοφίαν, διαφερόν- 4
τως δ᾽ Ἀρχύτας ὃς καὶ προέστη τῆς πόλεως πολὺν χρόνον. ἐξίσχυσε 5
δ᾽ ἡ ὕστερον τρυφὴ διὰ τὴν εὐδαιμονίαν, ὥστε τὰς πανδήμους ἑορτὰς 6
πλείους ἄγεσθαι κατ᾽ ἔτος παρ᾽ αὐτοῖς ἢ τὰς ἡμέρας. ἐκ δὲ τούτου καὶ 7
χεῖρον ἐπολιτεύοντο. ἓν δὲ τῶν φαύλων πολιτευμάτων τεκμήριόν ἐστι 8
τὸ ξενικοῖς στρατηγοῖς χρῆσθαι· καὶ γὰρ τὸν Μολοττὸν Ἀλέξανδρον 9
μετεπέμψαντο ἐπὶ Μεσσαπίους καὶ Λευκανούς, καὶ ἔτι πρότερον Ἀρχί- 10
δαμον τὸν Ἀγησιλάου καὶ ὕστερον Κλεώνυμον καὶ Ἀγαθοκλέα, εἶτα 11
Πύρρον, ἡνίκα συνέστησαν πρὸς Ῥωμαίους. 12

3 ἱππακοντιστὰς] scripsi ἱππάρχους codd.

The Tarentines were once exceedingly powerful, when they had a democratic government. For they possessed the greatest fleet of those in the region
and sent to battle 30,000 footsoldiers, 3,000 cavalry, and 1,000 mounted
javelin throwers. They also adopted the Pythagorean philosophy, especially
Archytas, who was also the leader of the city for a long time. The luxury, which developed later because of their prosperity, prevailed to such
an extent that more city-wide festivals were conducted by them each year
than there were days in the year. As a result of this the government became
worse. One mark of their weak government is the use of foreign generals.
For, they called in Alexander the Molossian to fight against the Messapians
and Leucanians, and still earlier Archidamus the son of Agesilaus and after
that Cleonymos and Agathocles, and then Pyrrhus, when they formed an
alliance with him against the Romans.

A4a L. Annaeus Florus, *Epitome of Roman History* I. 13.2–3

Tarentus, Lacedaemoniorum opus, Calabriae quondam et Apuliae
totiusque Lucaniae caput, cum magnitudine et muris portuque nobilis,
tum mirabilis situ. Quippe in ipsis Hadriani maris faucibus posita in
omnis terras, Histriam, Illyricum, Epiron, Achaiam, Africam, Siciliam vela
dimittit.

Tarentum, foundation of the Lacedaemonians, once the capital of Calabria,
Apulia and all of Lucania, is both famous for its size, walls and port and
also remarkable for its situation. Indeed, situated at the very entrance to the

Adriatic sea, it sends forth ships into all lands, to Istria, Illyricum, Epirus, Achaea, Africa and Sicily.

A5 Plato, *Letter* VII

324a ὅτε γὰρ κατ' ἀρχὰς εἰς Συρακούσας ἐγὼ ἀφικόμην, σχεδὸν ἔτη τετταράκοντα γεγονώς . . . 326b–d ταύτην δὴ τὴν διάνοιαν ἔχων εἰς Ἰταλίαν τε καὶ Σικελίαν ἦλθον, ὅτε πρῶτον ἀφικόμην. ἐλθόντα δέ με ὁ ταύτῃ λεγόμενος αὖ βίος εὐδαίμων, Ἰταλιωτικῶν τε καὶ Συρακουσίων τραπεζῶν πλήρης, οὐδαμῇ οὐδαμῶς ἤρεσεν, . . . ταῦτα δὴ πρὸς τοῖς πρόσθε διανοούμενος, εἰς Συρακούσας διεπορεύθην . . .

338c–d ὅμως δ' οὖν ἀσφαλέστερόν μοι ἔδοξεν χαίρειν τότε γε πολλὰ 1
καὶ Δίωνα καὶ Διονύσιον ἐᾶν, καὶ ἀπηχθόμην ἀμφοῖν ἀποκρινάμενος 2
ὅτι γέρων τε εἴην καὶ κατὰ τὰς ὁμολογίας οὐδὲν γίγνοιτο τῶν τὰ νῦν 3
πραττομένων. ἔοικεν δὴ τὸ μετὰ τοῦτο Ἀρχύτης τε παρὰ Διονύσιον 4
[πρὶν] ἀφικέσθαι – ἐγὼ γὰρ πρὶν ἀπιέναι ξενίαν καὶ φιλίαν Ἀρχύτῃ 5
καὶ τοῖς ἐν Τάραντι καὶ Διονυσίῳ ποιήσας ἀπέπλεον – ἄλλοι τέ τινες ἐν 6
Συρακούσαις ἦσαν Δίωνός τε ἄττα διακηκοότες καὶ τούτων τινὲς ἄλλοι, 7
παρακουσμάτων τινῶν ἔμμεστοι τῶν κατὰ φιλοσοφίαν· οἳ δοκοῦσί μοι 8
Διονυσίῳ πειρᾶσθαι διαλέγεσθαι τῶν περὶ τὰ τοιαῦτα, ὡς Διονυσίου 9
πάντα διακηκοότος ὅσα διενοούμην ἐγώ. 10

5 πρὶν ἀφικέσθαι] AO   τὸ πρὶν ἀλλαχοῦ ὠβέλισται in marg. O   7 καὶ τούτων] in marg.
A³O² om. AO

339a–b ἔπεμψε μὲν γὰρ δὴ Διονύσιος τρίτον ἐπ' ἐμὲ τριήρη ῥᾳστώνης ἕνεκα τῆς πορείας, ἔπεμψεν δὲ Ἀρχέδημον, ὃν ἡγεῖτό με τῶν ἐν Σικελίᾳ περὶ πλείστου ποιεῖσθαι, τῶν Ἀρχύτῃ συγγεγονότων ἕνα, καὶ ἄλλους γνωρίμους τῶν ἐν Σικελίᾳ· οὗτοι δὲ ἡμῖν ἤγγελλον πάντες τὸν αὐτὸν λόγον, ὡς θαυμαστὸν ὅσον Διονύσιος ἐπιδεδωκὼς εἴη πρὸς φιλοσοφίαν.

339d–e ἐπιστολαὶ δὲ ἄλλαι ἐφοίτων παρά τε Ἀρχύτου καὶ τῶν ἐν 1
Τάραντι, τήν τε φιλοσοφίαν ἐγκωμιάζουσαι τὴν Διονυσίου, καὶ ὅτι, 2
ἂν μὴ ἀφίκωμαι νῦν, τὴν πρὸς Διονύσιον αὐτοῖς γενομένην φιλίαν δι' 3
ἐμοῦ, οὐ σμικρὰν οὖσαν πρὸς τὰ πολιτικά, παντάπασιν διαβαλοίην. 4
ταύτης δὴ τοιαύτης γενομένης ἐν τῷ τότε χρόνῳ τῆς μεταπέμψεως, 5
τῶν μὲν ἐκ Σικελίας τε καὶ Ἰταλίας ἑλκόντων, τῶν δὲ Ἀθήνηθεν ἀτεχ- 6
νῶς μετὰ δεήσεως οἷον ἐξωθούντων με, καὶ πάλιν ὁ λόγος ἧκεν ὁ 7

4 διαβαλοίην] Vind. 109   διαβαλλοίην AO

αὐτός, τὸ μὴ δεῖν προδοῦναι Δίωνα μηδὲ τοὺς ἐν Τάραντι ξένους τε καὶ 8
ἑταίρους . . . 340a πορεύομαι δὴ τῷ λογισμῷ τούτῳ κατακαλυψά- 9
μενος, πολλὰ δεδιὼς μαντευόμενός τε οὐ πάνυ καλῶς . . . 10

350a ᾤκουν δὴ τὸ μετὰ τοῦτο ἔξω τῆς ἀκροπόλεως ἐν τοῖς μισ- 1
θοφόροις· προσιόντες δέ μοι ἄλλοι τε καὶ οἱ τῶν ὑπηρεσιῶν ὄντες 2
Ἀθήνηθεν, ἐμοὶ πολῖται, ἀπήγγελλον ὅτι διαβεβλημένος εἴην ἐν τοῖς 3
πελτασταῖς καί μοί τινες ἀπειλοῖεν, εἴ που λήψονταί με, διαφθερεῖν. 4
μηχανῶμαι δή τινα τοιάνδε σωτηρίαν. πέμπω παρ᾽ Ἀρχύτην καὶ τοὺς 5
ἄλλους φίλους εἰς Τάραντα, φράζων ἐν οἷς ὢν τυγχάνω· οἱ δὲ πρόφασίν 6
τινα πρεσβείας πορισάμενοι παρὰ τῆς πόλεως πέμπουσιν τριακόν- 7
τορόν τε καὶ Λαμίσκον αὐτῶν ἕνα, ὃς ἐλθὼν ἐδεῖτο Διονυσίου περὶ ἐμοῦ, 8
λέγων ὅτι βουλοίμην ἀπιέναι, καὶ μηδαμῶς ἄλλως ποιεῖν. ὁ δὲ συν- 9
ωμολόγησεν καὶ ἀπέπεμψεν ἐφόδια δούς . . . ἐλθὼν δὲ εἰς Πελοπόννησον 10
εἰς Ὀλυμπίαν, Δίωνα καταλαβὼν θεωροῦντα, ἤγγελλον τὰ γεγονότα· 11

4 λήψονταί] ΑΟ λήψοιντο in marg. Ο² 8 καὶ Λαμίσκον] καὶ ** λαμίσκον Α καὶ
σαλαμίσκον Ο 11 ἤγγελλον τὰ] in marg. Α² om. Α

324a When I [i.e. Plato] originally arrived in Syracuse, being about forty years of age . . . [ca. 388/387]

326b–d I [Plato] went to Italy and Sicily holding this point of view [i.e. that there will be no end of evils until there are philosopher kings], when I first arrived. Upon my arrival, in turn, the life that is there called "happy," full as it is of Italian and Syracusan banquets, nowhere and in no way pleased me . . . with these reflections in addition to my earlier ones I made my way to Syracuse . . .

338c–d All the same, then, it seemed safer to me [Plato] to keep well clear of Dion and Dionysius, at least at that time, and both of them were angry with me, when I answered that I was an old man and that nothing of what was now being done was in accord with the agreements that had been made between us. After this then it seems both that Archytas came to Dionysius – for when I sailed away, I established hospitality and friendship between Archytas and the Tarentines, on the one hand, and Dionysius, on the other, before my departure – and also that there were some others at Syracuse, both those who had studied some with Dion and some others who were pupils of these pupils, who were filled full of certain second-hand philosophical notions. These, as I think, tried to discuss such matters with Dionysius, on the assumption that Dionysius had studied my whole philosophical system.

339a–b   On the third occasion, then, Dionysius sent a trireme to me [Plato], in order to make the journey easier, and he sent Archedemus, whom he thought that I valued most of those in Sicily and who was one of the associates of Archytas, and he sent others of my acquaintances in Sicily. All of these kept giving me that same report, that it was amazing how much Dionysius had progressed in philosophy.

339d–e   Other letters came regularly both from Archytas and also from those in Tarentum, giving a panegyric of the philosophy of Dionysius and saying that, if I [Plato] did not come now, I would entirely discredit the friendship which had arisen between them and Dionysius through my efforts, a friendship which was of no small political importance. When such a summons as this had come at that time, with those in Sicily and Italy pulling me, and those at Athens literally pushing me out, as it were, with entreaties, the same argument kept coming back, namely that I must not betray Dion and my guest-friends and associates in Tarentum . . . 340a Having deceived myself with such a line of reasoning, I made the journey with many fears and no very happy forebodings.

350a   Then, after this, I [Plato] lived outside the acropolis among the mercenaries. Amongst others, some servants, who were from Athens, fellow citizens of mine, coming up to me kept reporting that I had been slandered among the soldiers [*peltasts*] and that some of them were threatening to kill me, if they got hold of me. I contrived the following means of saving myself. I sent to Archytas and my other friends in Tarentum, explaining the situation in which I found myself. They, providing some excuse for an embassy from the city, sent a thirty-oared ship with Lamiscus, who was one of them. When he arrived, he entreated Dionysius about me, saying that I wanted to leave, and that he should in no way act contrary to this wish. Dionysius agreed and sent me off, having given me provisions for my trip. . . . Having arrived at Olympia in the Peloponnese, I found Dion attending the games and reported what had happened.

A5a1 Plutarch, *Dion*

18.5.4 . . . εὐθὺς ὥρμησεν ἐπὶ τὸν Πλάτωνα, καὶ πᾶσαν μηχανὴν αἴρων, συνέπεισε τοὺς περὶ Ἀρχύταν Πυθαγορικοὺς τῶν ὁμολογουμένων ἀναδόχους γενομένους καλεῖν Πλάτωνα· δι' ἐκείνου γὰρ αὐτοῖς ἐγεγόνει φιλία καὶ ξενία τὸ πρῶτον. οἱ δ' ἔπεμψαν Ἀρχέδημον παρ' αὐτόν·

20.1.1   ἐν τοιούτῳ δὲ κινδύνῳ γενομένου τοῦ Πλάτωνος οἱ περὶ Ἀρχύταν πυθόμενοι ταχὺ πέμπουσι πρεσβείαν καὶ τριακόντορον, ἀπαιτοῦντες τὸν ἄνδρα παρὰ Διονυσίου καὶ λέγοντες ὡς αὐτοὺς λαβὼν ἀναδόχους τῆς ἀσφαλείας πλεύσειεν εἰς Συρακούσας. ἀπολεγομένου δὲ τοῦ Διονυσίου τὴν ἔχθραν ἑστιάσεσι καὶ φιλοφροσύναις περὶ τὴν προπομπήν . . .

18.5.4 . . . he [sc. Dionysius] immediately began to pursue Plato eagerly, and, taking up every stratagem, persuaded Archytas and the Pythagoreans to become sureties for the agreements [sc. between Dionysius and Plato] and to summon Plato. For it was through Plato that the friendship and hospitality between them [sc. Dionysius and the Pythagoreans] had arisen in the first place. They sent Archedemus to him.

20.1.1 When Plato had become involved in such danger, Archytas and his followers, having learned of it, quickly sent an embassy on a thirty-oared ship, demanding that Dionysius give him up and saying that he [Plato] had sailed to Syracuse only after having taken them as sureties for his safety. Dionysius renounced his enmity by giving banquets for him and being solicitous about his journey . . .

A5a2 Aelius Aristides, *To Plato: In Defense of the Four* (section 232 Jebb, 377 Lenz and Behr 1978. Cf. the scholia ad loc., Dindorf III. 677)

ποῖα ἄττ᾽ ἀπέλαυσας τῶν τυράννων οὓς παιδεύειν προῃροῦ; . . . οὕτω μὲν ἐξ ἀρχῆς εἰρχθεὶς ἐτρέφου παρ᾽ ἐλπίδα καὶ παρ᾽ ἀξίαν ἅπασαν σεαυτοῦ, καὶ εἰ μή σε ἀνὴρ Ἰταλιώτης ἐξῃτήσατο τῶν Πυθαγορείων, ὥσπερ σὺ φῂς τὸν πρύτανιν, ὅτι ἡμῶν ἕνα μέλλοντα εἰς τὸ βάραθρον ἐμπεσεῖσθαι διεκώλυσεν [*Gorg.* 516e], κἂν αὐτὸς ἴσως εἰς τὰς λιθοτομίας ἐνέπεσες . . . νῦν δὲ Ἀρχύτας ἦν ὁ κωλύσας καὶ Διονύσιος Ἀρχύταν μὲν ἐπιστέλλοντα ᾐσχύνθη καὶ ἔδωκε τὴν χάριν, Πλάτωνα δὲ οὐκ ᾐσχύνετο, ᾧ συνῆν καὶ οὗ τοὺς καλοὺς ἐκείνους καὶ σεμνοὺς λόγους ἤκουσεν . . . [See also Georgius Gemistus Plethon, *E Didoro et Plutarcho* 19–20 for a summary of the story of Archytas' rescue of Plato based on Plutarch.]

What sort of benefit did you [Plato] receive from the tyrants whom you chose to educate? . . . From the beginning you were confined and treated contrary to your expectation and contrary to all your worth, and, if an Italian man, one of the Pythagoreans, had not demanded your release, just as you say that the chairman of the council [*prytanis*] prevented it, when one of us was about to be thrown into the pit for punishment [*Gorg.* 516e], so you yourself would have perhaps been thrown into the quarries . . . As it was, Archytas was the one who prevented it, and it was Archytas and his demands, before whom Dionysius felt shame and to whom he granted the favor, before Plato he did not feel shame, Plato with whom he had associated and from whom he had heard those fine and noble discourses . . .

A5b1 Cicero, *Republic* I.10.16

. . . audisse te credo, Tubero, Platonem Socrate mortuo primum in Aegyptum discendi causa, post in Italiam et in Siciliam contendisse, ut Pythagorae inventa perdisceret, eumque et cum Archyta Tarentino et cum Timaeo Locro multum fuisse et Philoleo commentarios esse nanctum . . .

. . . I believe that you have heard, Tubero, that, after Socrates had died, Plato first went to Egypt for the sake of learning and afterwards to Italy and Sicily, so that he might thoroughly learn the discoveries of Pythagoras, and that he spent much time with Archytas of Tarentum and Timaeus of Locri and obtained treatises from Philolaus . . .

A5b2 Cicero, *On Ends* V. 29.87

Nisi enim id faceret, cur Plato Aegyptum peragravit ut a sacerdotibus barbaris numeros et caelestia acciperet? cur post Tarentum ad Archytam? cur ad reliquos Pythagoreos, Echecratem, Timaeum, Arionem Locros, ut, cum Socratem expressisset, adiungeret Pythagoreorum disciplinam eaque, quae Socrates repudiabat addisceret?

For, if it did not do this [sc. if philosophy did not lead to happiness], why did Plato traverse the distance to Egypt in order to learn arithmetic and astronomy from the foreign priests? Why afterwards did he travel to Archytas in Tarentum? Why to the other Pythagoreans, Echecrates, Timaeus and Arion at Locri, so that, after he had given his portrait of Socrates, he might join to it the system of the Pythagoreans and learn in addition those things which Socrates repudiated.

A5b3 Cicero, *Tusculan Disputations* V. 23.64

Non ego iam cum huius [sc. Dionysii] vita . . . Platonis aut Archytae vitam   1
comparabo, doctorum hominum et plane sapientium . . .   2

1 architae] V

I will not compare with the life of this man [Dionysius I of Syracuse] . . .
the life of Plato or Archytas, learned and manifestly wise men . . .

A5b4 Philodemus, *History of Philosophers: Index of Members of the Academy* X. 5–11 (Dorandi 1991: 130)

Π]λάτων Σωκράτους γεγον[ὼς μαθ]ητὴς ἀπο[λ]ειφθε[ὶ]ς νεώ[τερος]
ἅ[τ᾿ ὢν] ἐτῶν [εἰ]κοσιεπτά, ἀπῆρεν εἰς [Σι]κελίαν καὶ Ἰταλίαν, εἰς τοὺς
Πυθαγ[ορ]ήους, οἷς συνγενόμενός τινα χρόνον συνέμειξ[εν Διο]νυσίῳ
τῷ πρεσβυτέρῳ [λεγομέ]νῳ·

Plato, who was a pupil of Socrates and who at rather a young age had been
left behind by him, since he was twenty-seven years old, departed to Sicily
and Italy to the Pythagoreans. He associated with them for some time and
then had dealings with Dionysius the elder.

A5b5 Cornelius Nepos, *Dion* 2.1–2

Quo fiebat ut uni huic [sc. Dioni] maxime indulgeret [sc. Dionysius I]
neque eum secus diligeret ac filium; qui quidem, cum Platonem Tarentum
venisse fama in Siciliam esset perlata, adulescenti negare non potuerit, quin
eum accerseret, cum Dion eius audiendi cupiditate flagraret. dedit ergo huic
veniam magnaque eum ambitione Syracusas perduxit.

So that it came about that he [sc. Dionysius I] was especially indulgent to
Dion and loved him like a son. Indeed, when report was brought to Sicily
that Plato had come to Tarentum, he was not able to deny the young man's
request to send for him, since Dion burned with the desire to hear him.
Therefore, he granted him the request and brought Plato to Syracuse with
great ostentation.

A5b6 Valerius Maximus, *Memorable Deeds and Sayings* VIII. 7. ext. 3

quo minus miror in Italiam transgressum ut ab Archyta Tarenti, a Timaeo
et Arione et Echecrate Locris, Pythagorae praecepta et instituta acciperet.

So much the less am I surprised that he [Plato] crossed over to Italy in
order to learn the precepts and doctrines of Pythagoras from Archytas at
Tarentum and Timaeus, Arion and Echecrates at Locri.

A5b7 Apuleius, *On Plato* I.3

sed posteaquam Socrates homines reliquit, quaesivit [sc. Plato], unde profi-
ceret, et ad Pythagorae disciplinam se contulit. quam etsi ratione diligenti
et magnifica instructam videbat, rerum tamen continentiam et castitatem

magis cupiebat imitari et, quod Pythagoreorum ingenium adiutum disciplinis aliis sentiebat, ad Theodorum Cyrenas, ut geometriam disceret, est pro-
fectus et astrologiam adusque Aegyptum ivit petitum, ut inde prophetarum
etiam ritus addisceret. et ad Italiam iterum venit et Pythagoreos Eurytum
Tarentinum et seniorem Archytam sectatus est.

After Socrates left the world of men, he [Plato] sought a way to continue to
progress in philosophy and resorted to the teaching of Pythagoras. Although
he perceived that it was ordered by an exacting and splendid system of
thought, he even more desired to imitate the self-control and integrity
of the Pythagorean life. Because he saw that the Pythagorean spirit was
aided by other studies, he set out to Theodorus at Cyrene in order to learn
geometry, and he went as far as Egypt to seek out knowledge of astronomy,
so that he also learned the rites of the prophets there. He also came a second
time to Italy and studied with the Pythagoreans Eurytus of Tarentum and
the older Archytas.

A5b8 Jerome, *Against Rufinus* III. 40 (cf. *Ep.* LIII. 1.2)

Nam post Academiam et innumerabiles discipulos, sentiens [sc. Plato] multum suae deesse doctrinae, venit ad Magnam Graeciam ibique ab Archyta
tarentino et Timaeo locrensi Pythagorae doctrinae eruditus, elegantiam et
leporem Socratis cum huius miscuit disciplinis . . .

For after [establishing] the Academy with its innumerable disciples, [Plato],
seeing that much was lacking from his learning, came to Magna Graecia
and, having been instructed there in the Pythagorean doctrine by Archytas
of Tarentum and Timaeus of Locri, he combined the elegance and charm
of Socrates with the teachings of Pythagoras . . .

A5b9 Olympiodorus, Commentary on the First Alcibiades of Plato 2. 86–93

μετὰ δὲ τὴν τελευτὴν Σωκράτους διδασκάλῳ πάλιν ἐχρήσατο [sc.   1
Πλάτων] Κρατύλῳ τῷ Ἡρακλειτείῳ, εἰς ὃν καὶ διάλογον ὁμώνυμον   2
ἐποίησεν, ἐπιγράψας Κρατύλος ἢ περὶ ὀρθότητος ὀνομάτων. μετὰ   3
τοῦτον δὲ πάλιν στέλλεται εἰς Ἰταλίαν καὶ διδασκαλεῖον εὑρὼν ἐκεῖ   4
τῶν Πυθαγορείων συνιστάμενον Ἀρχύταν πάλιν ἔσχε διδάσκαλον τὸν   5
Πυθαγόρειον· φέρεται δὲ αὐτοῦ καὶ διάλογος ὁ Φίληβος Πυθαγορείου   6
τινὸς ὁμώνυμος, ἔνθα καὶ Ἀρχύτου μέμνηται.   7

7 μέμνηται] om. M

After the death of Socrates, he [sc. Plato] in turn regarded Cratylus the Heraclitean as his teacher, for whom he composed a dialogue of the same name, having entitled it *Cratylus* or *Concerning Correctness of Names*. After this he in turn made a journey to Italy, and, having found a school of the Pythagoreans organized there, he in turn had Archytas the Pythagorean as a teacher. It is reported that his dialogue, *Philebus*, was named after a Pythagorean. Archytas is also mentioned there.

A5b10 Photius, *The Library* 249 (438b16 ff. Bekker)

ἀνεγνώσθη Πυθαγόρου βίος.

ὅτι ἔνατος ἀπὸ Πυθαγόρου διάδοχος γέγονε, φησί, Πλάτων, Ἀρχύτου τοῦ πρεσβυτέρου μαθητὴς γενόμενος, δέκατος δὲ Ἀριστοτέλης.

I read a life of Pythagoras.

He [i.e. the author] says that Plato is the ninth successor of Pythagoras, having become a pupil of Archytas the elder, and that Aristotle is the tenth.

A5b11 Photius, *The Library* 167 (114a15 ff. Bekker)

. . . παρατίθησιν . . . ὁ Ἰωάννης [sc. Στοβαῖος] ἔκ τε τῶν ἐκλογῶν καὶ τῶν ἀποφθεγμάτων καὶ τῶν ὑποθηκῶν δόξας τε καὶ χρήσεις καὶ χρείας. ἀγείρει δὲ ταύτας ἀπὸ μὲν φιλοσόφων, ἀπό τε Αἰσχίνου τοῦ Σωκρατικοῦ . . . καὶ Ἀρχύτου . . .

John [sc. Stobaeus] sets out opinions, examples, and maxims drawn from selections, apophthegms, and precepts. He collects these, on the one hand, from philosophers, from Aeschines the Socratic . . . and from Archytas . . .

A5b12 Tzetzes, *Letters* 75 (Leone 1972: 110. 22)

Ἀρχύτᾳ δὲ τῷ Πυθαγορείῳ τῷ ἐκ τῆς Τάραντός ποι ἐντυχὼν [sc. ὁ ναύαρχος] τοῦτον [sc. Πλάτωνα] ἀπεμπολεῖ, ἐξ οὗπερ ὁ Πλάτων τὴν Πυθαγορικὴν φιλοσοφίαν ὠφέλητο, δεσπότῃ τε τῷ αὐτῷ καὶ διδασκάλῳ χρησάμενος.

He [sc. the admiral to whom Dionysius I had given Plato], meeting some-where with Archytas the Pythagorean from Tarentum, sold him [sc. Plato]. This was the very man from whom Plato, by treating the same man both as a slave treats his master and also as a student his teacher, had gained the benefit of the Pythagorean philosophy.

A5b13 Tzetzes, *Histories* x. 988–92 (Leone 1968: 429)

ἐκ Πώλιδος ναυάρχου μὲν τῷ γένει Σπαρτιάτου
Πλάτωνα τὸν φιλόσοφον ὠνήσατο Ἀρχύτας
φιλόσοφος καὶ οὗτος μέν, ἀλλ᾽ ἐκ Πυθαγορείων.
δοῦλον δὲ σχὼν ἐδίδαξε καὶ τὴν φιλοσοφίαν
αὐτῷ τὴν Πυθαγόρειον. . . .

Archytas bought the philosopher Plato from the admiral Polis, a Spartan. Archytas was also a philosopher but from the Pythagorean school. After he acquired Plato as a slave, he also taught the Pythagorean philosophy to him.

A5c1 [Demosthenes] lxi, *Erotic Oration* 44

νόμιζε δὲ πᾶσαν μὲν τὴν φιλοσοφίαν μεγάλα τοὺς χρωμένους ὠφελεῖν,   1
πολὺ δὲ μάλιστα τὴν περὶ τὰς πράξεις καὶ τοὺς πολιτικοὺς λόγους   2
ἐπιστήμην . . . γνοίης δ᾽ ἂν ἐξ ἄλλων τε πολλῶν, καὶ παραθεωρήσας   3
τοὺς πρὸ σαυτοῦ γεγενημένους ἐνδόξους ἄνδρας. τοῦτο μὲν Περικ-   4
λέα . . . ἀκούσει πλησιάσαντ᾽ Ἀναξαγόρᾳ τῷ Κλαζομενίῳ καὶ   5
μαθητὴν ἐκείνου γενόμενον ταύτης τῆς δυνάμεως μετασχόντα· τοῦτο   6
δ᾽ Ἀλκιβιάδην εὑρήσεις . . . ἀπὸ δὲ τῆς Σωκράτους ὁμιλίας πολλὰ   7
μὲν ἐπανορθωθέντα τοῦ βίου. . . . εἰ δὲ δεῖ μὴ παλαιὰ λέγοντας δια-   8
τρίβειν, ἔχοντας ὑπογυιοτέροις παραδείγμασι χρῆσθαι, τοῦτο μὲν   9
Τιμόθεον . . . ἐξ ὧν Ἰσοκράτει συνδιατρίψας ἔπραξεν, μεγίστης δόξης   10
καὶ πλείστων τιμῶν εὑρήσεις ἀξιωθέντα· τοῦτο δ᾽ Ἀρχύταν τὴν Ταραν-   11
τίνων πόλιν οὕτω καλῶς καὶ φιλανθρώπως διοικήσαντα [καὶ] κύριον   12
αὐτῆς καταστάντα ὥστ᾽ εἰς ἅπαντας τὴν ἐκείνου μνήμην διενεγκεῖν·   13
ὃς ἐν ἀρχῇ καταφρονούμενος ἐκ τοῦ Πλάτωνι πλησιάσαι τοσαύτην   14
ἔλαβεν ἐπίδοσιν.   15

12 καὶ] del. Wolf.

Acknowledge that all of philosophy gives great benefits to those who employ it, but that the knowledge which concerns actions and political issues is most especially beneficial. . . . You may recognize this both from many other indications and especially by considering the men who have become famous before your time. There is Pericles . . . who you will hear acquired his power after having associated with Anaxagoras of Clazomenae and having become his pupil. There is Alcibiades whom you will discover . . . to have corrected many aspects of his life from his association with Socrates . . . If we should not spend time speaking about ancient history, when we are able to use more recent examples, there is Timotheus . . . whom you will find to have been deemed worthy of the greatest reputation and very many honors as a result of what he did after he spent time with Isocrates. There is Archytas, who was established as ruler of Tarentum, and managed the city so well and humanely that mention of him has been spread abroad to all peoples. Archytas, although despised in the beginning, made such great progress after his association with Plato.

A5c2 Cicero, *On the Orator* III. 34.138–139.14

Quid Pericles? . . . At hunc . . . docuerat . . . Clazomenius ille Anaxagoras, vir summus in maximarum rerum scientia: itaque hic doctrina, consilio, eloquentia excellens quadraginta annis praefuit Athenis . . . Quid Critias, quid Alcibiades? . . . nonne Socraticis erant disputationibus eruditi? Quis Dionem Syracusium doctrinis omnibus expolivit? non Plato? atque eum idem ille non linguae solum verum etiam animi ac virtutis magister ad liberandam patriam impulit, instruxit, armavit. Aliisne igitur artibus . . . instituit . . . Isocrates . . . Timotheum . . . Lysis . . . Epaminondam . . .? aut Xenophon Agesilaum? aut Philolaus Archytam Tarentinum? aut ipse Pythagoras totam illam veterem Italiae Graeciam quae quondam Magna vocitata est?

What of Pericles? . . . Anaxagoras of Clazomenae, a man preeminent in the knowledge of the greatest sciences, had taught him . . . , and therefore this man, who excelled in learning, judgment and eloquence led Athens for forty years . . . What of Critias? What of Alcibiades? . . . had they not been instructed by discussions with Socrates? Who adorned the Syracusan Dion with every branch of learning? Was it not Plato? Did not that same man, a teacher not only of eloquence but of the mind and virtue, impel, prepare and arm Dion to free his fatherland? With what other arts, therefore, . . . did Isocrates train Timotheus . . . Lysis Epaminondas . . . Xenophon Agesilaus or Philolaus Archytas of Tarentum? Or Pythagoras himself that entire ancient Greek part of Italy, which was once called Magna Graecia?

A5c3 Philodemus, *History of Philosophers: Index of Members of the Academy PHerc.* 1021, V. 32–VI. 12, Dorandi 1991: 134–35

(cf. *PHerc.* 164, Fr. 12.5, Dorandi 1991: 178 and Theon of Smyrna's *Life of Plato* as reported in Ibn al-Qifṭī, *Taʾrīḫ al-ḥukamâ*, ed. Julius Lippert, Leipzig 1903: 24, 2–8. See Gaiser 1988: 439)

Πλάτωνος μ[αθητα]ὶ ἦσ[α]ν. . . . Ἀρχύτας Ταραν[τῖ]νος . . .

The pupils of Plato were . . . Archytas of Tarentum . . .

A5c4 Plutarch, *On the Education of Children* 8b

πειρατέον οὖν εἰς δύναμιν καὶ τὰ κοινὰ πράττειν καὶ τῆς φιλοσοφίας ἀντιλαμβάνεσθαι κατὰ τὸ παρεῖκον τῶν καιρῶν. οὕτως ἐπολιτεύσατο Περικλῆς, οὕτως Ἀρχύτας ὁ Ταραντῖνος, οὕτω Δίων ὁ Συρακόσιος, οὕτως Ἐπαμεινώνδας ὁ Θηβαῖος . . .

We must try, insofar as we are able, both to engage in public life and also to take part in philosophy to the degree that circumstances permit. So Pericles served the city-state, so Archytas of Tarentum, so Dion of Syracuse, so Epaminondas of Thebes . . .

A5c5 Aelian, *Historical Miscellany* III.17

ἐπολιτεύσαντο οὖν καὶ φιλόσοφοι ἢ αὐτὸ τοῦτο μόνον τὴν διάνοιαν   1
ἀγαθοὶ γενόμενοι ἐφ᾽ ἡσυχίας κατεβίωσαν . . . Ταραντίνοις δὲ ἐγένετο   2
ἀγαθὸν Ἀρχύτας, Σόλων δὲ Ἀθηναίοις.   3

1 ἢ] μηδ᾽ He. ἢ <οὐ> Sch. <μᾶλλον> ἢ Wilson   2 sigl. interrog. post κατεβίωσαν interpunxit Kor.

Philosophers also took part in the government of their city-states rather than just living a quiet life after having attained excellence in intellect alone . . . Archytas proved to be of benefit to the Tarentines and Solon to the Athenians.

A6 Proclus, *Commentary on Book One of Euclid's Elements* Prologue 11. 66.4–18 (Friedlein)

ἐφ᾽ οἷς Ἱπποκράτης ὁ Χῖος ὁ τὸν τοῦ μηνίσκου τετραγωνισμὸν εὑρών, καὶ Θεόδωρος ὁ Κυρηναῖος ἐγένοντο περὶ γεωμετρίαν ἐπιφανεῖς, πρῶτος γὰρ ὁ Ἱπποκράτης τῶν μνημονευομένων καὶ στοιχεῖα συνέγραψεν. Πλάτων δ᾽ ἐπὶ τούτοις γενόμενος . . . ἐν δὲ τούτῳ τῷ χρόνῳ καὶ Λεωδάμας ὁ Θάσιος ἦν καὶ Ἀρχύτας ὁ Ταραντῖνος καὶ Θεαίτητος ὁ Ἀθηναῖος, παρ᾽ ὧν ἐπηυξήθη τὰ θεωρήματα καὶ προῆλθεν εἰς ἐπιστημονικωτέραν σύστασιν.

After these men, Hippocrates of Chios, who discovered the quadrature of the lunes, and Theodorus of Cyrene became distinguished in the field of geometry. For, Hippocrates is also the first person who is mentioned as having composed an Elements. Plato [came] after these men . . . At this time lived Leodamas of Thasos, Archytas of Tarentum and Theaetetus of Athens, by all of whom the theorems were increased in number and brought into a more scientific order.

A6a Heron, *Definitions* 136.1 (Heiberg IV. 108)

εὕρηται ἡ γεωμετρία πρῶτον μὲν ἐκ τῶν Αἰγυπτίων, ἤγαγε δὲ εἰς
τοὺς Ἕλληνας Θαλῆς. μετὰ δὲ τὸν Θαλῆν Μαμέρτιος ... καὶ Ἱππίας ...
καὶ μετὰ ταῦτα ὁ Πυθαγόρας ... μετὰ τοῦτον Ἀναξαγόρας καὶ ὁ
Πλάτων καὶ Οἰνοπίδης ... καὶ Θεόδωρος ... καὶ Ἱπποκράτης πρὸ
τοῦ Πλάτωνος. μετὰ ταῦτα καὶ Λεωδάμας ὁ Θάσιος καὶ Ἀρχύτας ὁ
Ταραντῖνος καὶ Θεαίτητος ὁ Ἀθηναῖος, Εὔδοξος ὁ Κνίδιος ... οὐ πολὺ
δὲ τούτων νεώτερός ἐστιν ὁ Εὐκλείδης ...

Geometry was first discovered by the Egyptians. Thales brought it to the
Greeks. After Thales (was) Mamertios . . . and Hippias . . . and after
these Pythagoras . . . after him Anaxagoras and Plato and Oinopides . . .
and Theodorus . . . and Hippocrates was before Plato. After these (were)
Leodamas of Thasos, Archytas of Tarentum, Theaetetus of Athens, and
Eudoxus of Cnidus . . . Not much younger than these is Euclid . . .

A6b Iamblichus, *On the Pythagorean Life* (Deubner 1937)

104 καὶ γὰρ οἱ ἐκ τοῦ διδασκαλείου τούτου, μάλιστα δὲ οἱ παλαιό- 1
τατοι καὶ αὐτῷ συγχρονίσαντες καὶ μαθητεύσαντες τῷ Πυθαγόρᾳ 2
πρεσβύτῃ νέοι, Φιλόλαός τε καὶ Εὔρυτος καὶ Χαρώνδας καὶ Ζάλευκος 3
καὶ Βρύσων, Ἀρχύτας τε ὁ πρεσβύτερος καὶ Ἀρισταῖος καὶ Λῦσις 4
καὶ Ἐμπεδοκλῆς καὶ Ζάμολξις καὶ Ἐπιμενίδης καὶ Μίλων, Λεύκιπ- 5
πός τε καὶ Ἀλκμαίων καὶ Ἵππασος καὶ Θυμαρίδας καὶ οἱ κατ' αὐτοὺς 6
ἅπαντες, πλῆθος ἐλλογίμων καὶ ὑπερφυῶν ἀνδρῶν ... 127 καὶ 7
ταῦτα πρὸς ἐκεῖνον εἰπεῖν [sc. πρὸς Ἀριστόξενον τὸν Διονύσιον cf. 8
VP 234] καὶ τὰ περὶ Φιντίαν καὶ Δάμωνα, περί τε Πλάτωνος καὶ 9
Ἀρχύτου, καὶ τὰ περὶ Κλεινίαν καὶ Πρῶρον. 250 οἱ δὲ λοιποὶ τῶν 10
Πυθαγορείων ἀπέστησαν τῆς Ἰταλίας πλὴν Ἀρχύτου τοῦ Ταραντίνου· 11
266 ζηλωτὰς δὲ γράφει [sc. Διόδωρος ὁ Ἀσπένδιος] γενέσθαι τῶν 12
ἀνδρῶν περὶ μὲν Ἡράκλειαν Κλεινίαν καὶ Φιλόλαον, <ἐν> Μεταπον- 13
τίῳ δὲ Θεωρίδην <καὶ> Εὔρυτον, ἐν Τάραντι δὲ Ἀρχύταν. 267 14
Ταραντῖνοι: Φιλόλαος, Εὔρυτος, Ἀρχύτας, Θεόδωρος, Ἀρίστιππος ... 15

11 Ἀρχύτου] Ἀρχίππου Fr. Beckmann   12 γράφει] Cobet γράφειν codd.   13 <ἐν>]
Arcerius   14 Θεωρίδην] Θεαρίδαν Cobet <καὶ>] Küster

104 For indeed, those from this school, especially the members of greatest antiquity, both contemporaries of Pythagoras and also those who as
young men studied with him in his old age [are]: Philolaus, Eurytus,
Charondas, Zaleucus, Bryson, Archytas the elder, Aristaeus, Lysis, Empedocles, Zamolxis, Epimenides, Milo, Leucippus, Alcmaeon, Hippasus,

Thymaridas, and all those associated with them, a multitude of distinguished and extraordinary men.

127 And he told these stories to that man [sc. Dionysius II told these things to Aristoxenus. See *On the Pythagorean Life* 234.]: the story about Phintias and Damon, about Plato and Archytas and the story about Cleinias and Prorus.

250 [After the attacks on the Pythagorean societies in the fifth century] The rest of the Pythagoreans left Italy, except for Archytas of Tarentum

266 He [sc. Diodorus of Aspendus] writes that, in Heracleia, Cleinias and Philolaus were followers of these men [sc. the Pythagoreans], in Metapontum, Theorides and Eurytus and in Tarentum, Archytas.

267 From Tarentum: Philolaus, Eurytus, Archytas, Theodorus, Aristippus . . .

A6c Diogenes Laertius, *Lives of the Philosophers* VIII. 86

Οὗτος [sc. Εὔδοξος] τὰ μὲν γεωμετρικὰ Ἀρχύτα διήκουσε . . .

This man [i.e. Eudoxus] learned geometry from Archytas.

A6d Eunapius, *Lives of the Sophists* 23. 1.8 (500; Giangrande 1956: 91–92)

. . . ἐντεῦθεν ἀφῆκεν [sc. Χρυσάνθιος] αὐτὸν ἐπὶ θεῶν γνῶσιν, καὶ σοφίαν ἧς Πυθαγόρας τε ἐφρόντιζε καὶ ὅσοι Πυθαγόραν ἐζήλωσαν, Ἀρχύτας τε ὁ παλαιός, καὶ ὁ ἐκ Τυάνων Ἀπολλώνιος, καὶ οἱ προσκυνήσαντες Ἀπολλώνιον, οἵτινες σῶμά τε ἔδοξαν ἔχειν καὶ εἶναι ἄνθρωποι.

. . . next he [sc. Chrysanthius] devoted himself to inquiry about the gods and the wisdom to which Pythagoras gave his attention as did those who emulated him, Archytas of old and Apollonius of Tyana and those who worshiped Apollonius, all those who only seemed to have a body and to be men.

A6e Eusebius, *Against Hierocles* XI (Kayser 1870: 380.5 ff.)

τίς δὴ οὖν τούτων σύνεσίν τε καὶ φοίτησιν εἰς διαλέξεις θεῶν ὁρωμένων καὶ οὐχ ὁρωμένων αὐτός τε ὡς ἀπὸ Πυθαγόρου μαθὼν εἰδέναι, διδάσκεσθαί τε ἑτέρους ἐπηγγέλλετο; καὶ μὴν οὐδ' ὁ

περιβόητος Πλάτων, πάντων γε μᾶλλον τῆς Πυθαγόρου κεκοιν-
ωνηκὼς φιλοσοφίας, οὔτ᾽ Ἀρχύτας, οὔτ᾽ αὐτὸς ἐκεῖνος ὁ τὰς Πυθαγόρου
γραφῇ παραδοὺς ὁμιλίας Φιλόλαος, . . . ἐπὶ τοιαύτῃ τινὶ ἐσεμνύναντο
σοφίᾳ.

Who, then, of these men proclaimed both that he himself, having learned it
from Pythagoras, had wisdom about the gods, both those that are seen and
those that are unseen, and knew how to frequent their discourses, and also
that he taught this to others? Indeed, not even Plato, about whom people
talk so much and who shared in the philosophy of Pythagoras more than
anyone, nor Archytas, nor that man himself who committed the teachings
of Pythagoras to writing, Philolaus, . . . boasted of such wisdom.

A6f Psellus, *Short History* 100. 5–11 (Aerts 1990: 88)

Λέων ὁ υἱὸς βασιλείου ὁ σοφὸς τὰ πολλά. Λέων ὁ βασιλεὺς σοφίας
ἐκτόπως γέγον<εν> ἐραστής, οὐ μόνον τῆς κοινῆς ταύτης καὶ νενομισ-
μένης, ἣν Πλάτων ἐξῆρε καὶ Ἀριστοτέλης <ἐξήνεγκεν> ἐν πολλοῖς
γε βιβλίοις ὕστερον ἀκριβώσας, ἀλλὰ καὶ τῆς ἀπορρητοτέρας, ἧς
Πυθαγόρας ἦρξε καὶ Ἀρχύτας ἐζήλωσε διὰ κρυφίων τινῶν δυνάμεων
καὶ ἐπῳδῶν ἐπιρρήτων κινοῦντες, ὅ φασι, τὰ ἀκίνητα καὶ τὰ μέλλοντα
καταμαντευόμενοι.

Leo, the son of Basilius, the wise for the most part. The emperor Leo
[sc. Leo VII, "The Wise," AD 867–86] became an extraordinary lover of
wisdom, not only of that wisdom which is commonly accepted, which Plato
exalted and which Aristotle later developed, having set it out accurately in
many books, but also the more secret wisdom, which Pythagoras began and
which Archytas pursued, both of them, through certain occult powers and
contemptible spells, disturbing what is not to be disturbed, as the proverb
has it, and foretelling the future.

A6g Gregory of Corinth, *On Dialects*, preface
(pp. 1–7 Schaefer 1811)

ἰδού σοι καὶ τὰς διαλέκτους ἐγχειρίζω . . . περὶ ὧν ὅτε Φιλόπονος
Ἰωάννης ἐφιλοπόνησε, καὶ Τρύφων ὁ γραμματικός, καὶ ἄλλοι πολ-
λοί. . . . αὐτοὶ τοίνυν Ἀττικῆς μὲν φράσεως κανόνα τὸν κωμικὸν
Ἀριστοφάνην προθέμενοι, καὶ Θουκυδίδην τὸν συγγραφέα, καὶ
[Δημοσθένην τὸν] ῥήτορα, Ἰάδος δὲ Ἱπποκράτην τὸν Ἴωνα, καὶ τὸν
Ἁλικαρνασέα Ἡρόδοτον, Δωρίδος δὲ τὸν Ταραντῖνον Ἀρχύταν, καὶ

Θεόκριτον τὸν τὰ βουκολικὰ συγγραψάμενον, καὶ τῆς Αἰολίδος Ἀλκαῖον, ἴσως ἂν περὶ τῶν διαλέκτων ἱκανῶς διαλάβοιμεν.

Here, I entrust to you the dialects . . . concerning which John Philoponus labored, and Tryphon the grammarian and many others . . . If we ourselves then set up as a standard of the Attic dialect the comic writer Aristophanes, the historian Thucydides and the orator Demosthenes, of the Ionic dialect Hippocrates the Ionian and Herodotus of Halicarnassus, of the Doric dialect the Tarentine Archytas and Theocritus who composed pastoral poetry, and of the Aeolic dialect Alcaeus, perhaps we would give a sufficient treatment of the dialects.

B5 Theon of Smyrna, *Mathematics Useful for Reading Plato* 106. 7–11 (Hiller 1878)

ἡ μέντοι δεκὰς πάντα περαίνει τὸν ἀριθμόν, ἐμπεριέχουσα πᾶσαν φύσιν ἐντὸς αὑτῆς, ἀρτίου τε καὶ περιττοῦ κινουμένου τε καὶ ἀκινήτου ἀγαθοῦ τε καὶ κακοῦ· περὶ ἧς καὶ Ἀρχύτας ἐν τῷ Περὶ τῆς δεκάδος καὶ Φιλόλαος ἐν τῷ Περὶ φύσιος πολλὰ διεξίασιν.

The decad marks the limit of all number, encompassing all nature within itself, both even and odd, both moving and unmoved, both good and bad; concerning which [sc. the decad] both Archytas in *On the Decad* and also Philolaus in *On Nature* expound many things.

B5a Jerome, *Letter* XLIX (XLVIII) 19. 4–5 (Hilberg 1910: 384.10 ff.)

scilicet nunc enumerandum mihi est, qui ecclesiasticorum de inpari numero disputaverint: Clemens, Hippolytus. . . . an forsitan Pythagoram et Archytan Tarentinum et Publium Scipionem in sexto τῆς πολιτείας de inpari numero proferam disputantes? et si hos audire noluerint obtrectatores mei, grammaticorum scholas eis faciam conclamare: numero deus inpare gaudet [Verg., *Ecl.* VIII.75].

I must now enumerate those ecclesiastical writers who have discussed odd numbers: Clement, Hippolytus . . . Or perhaps I should cite the discussions of odd numbers by Pythagoras, or by Archytas of Tarentum, or by Publius Scipio in the sixth book of *The Republic* [sc. of Cicero]. If my detractors are not willing to listen to these authorities, I will make the grammar schools shout: "God delights in odd numbers" [Vergil, *Eclogues* VIII. 75].

B6 Athenaeus, *The Sophists at Dinner* IV.184e (Kaibel 1887)

Ἀριστόξενος δὲ καὶ Ἐπαμινώνδαν τὸν Θηβαῖον αὐλεῖν μαθεῖν παρὰ Ὀλυμπιοδώρῳ καὶ Ὀρθαγόρᾳ. καὶ τῶν Πυθαγορικῶν δὲ πολλοὶ τὴν αὐλητικὴν ἤσκησαν, ὡς Εὐφράνωρ τε καὶ Ἀρχύτας Φιλόλαός τε ἄλλοι τε οὐκ ὀλίγοι. ὁ δ' Εὐφράνωρ καὶ σύγγραμμα περὶ αὐλῶν κατέλιπεν· ὁμοίως δὲ καὶ ὁ Ἀρχύτας.

And Aristoxenus says that Epaminondas the Theban learned to play the aulos from Olympiodorus and Orthagoras. Indeed many of the Pythagoreans practiced playing the aulos, as did Euphranor, Archytas, Philolaus and not a few others. Euphranor has, in fact, left behind a treatise on auloi, likewise also Archytas.

B7 Vitruvius, *On Architecture* VII. Preface 14

Non minus de machinationibus [conscripserunt], uti Diades, Archytas, Archimedes, Ctesibios, Nymphodorus, Philo Byzantius . . .

Others have written about machines: Diades, Archytas, Archimedes, Ctesibios, Nymphodorus, Philo of Byzantium . . .

B8 Varro, *On Agriculture* I. 1. 8

Qui Graece scripserunt [sc. de agri cultura] dispersim alius de alia re, sunt plus quinquaginta. Hi sunt . . . de philosophis Democritus physicus, Xenophon Socraticus, Aristoteles et Theophrastus peripatetici, Archytas Pythagoreus . . .

There are more than fifty people who have written various treatises [sc. on agriculture] in Greek, one about one aspect, another about another. They are . . . of the philosophers, Democritus the writer on nature, Xenophon the Socratic, Aristotle and Theophrastus the Peripatetics, Archytas the Pythagorean . . .

B8a Columella, *On Agriculture* I. 1. 7

Magna porro et Graecorum turba est de rusticis rebus praecipiens, cuius princeps . . . Hesiodus Boeotius. Magis deinde eam iuvere fontibus orti sapientiae Democritus Abderites, Socraticus Xenophon, Tarentinus Archytas, Peripatetici magister ac discipulus Aristoteles cum Theophrasto.

There is, moreover, also a great throng of Greeks who give advice about agriculture, the first of them Hesiod of Boeotia . . . Then the subject was further advanced by those who have arisen from the fonts of wisdom: Democritus of Abdera, Xenophon the Socratic, Archytas of Tarentum, the Peripatetics Aristotle and Theophrastus, master and pupil.

B8b Pliny, *Natural History* I.8c; I.14c; I.15c; I.17.c; I.18.c

Ex auctoribus:. . . . externis: . . . Archyta

I. 10c Ex auctoribus: . . . externis: . . . Archyta Tarentino

Authorities:. . . . foreign authorities: . . . Archytas

I. 10c Authorities: . . . foreign authorities: . . . Archytas of Tarentum

CHAPTER II

Moral philosophy and character

A7 Iamblichus, *On the Pythagorean Life* 197–98 = Aristoxenus Fr. 30 (= 49) Wehrli

(197) λέγεται δὲ καὶ τάδε περὶ τῶν Πυθαγορείων, ὡς οὔτε οἰκέτην 1
ἐκόλασεν οὐθεὶς αὐτῶν ὑπὸ ὀργῆς ἐχόμενος οὔτε τῶν ἐλευθέρων 2
ἐνουθέτησέ τινα, ἀλλὰ ἀνέμενεν ἕκαστος τὴν τῆς διανοίας ἀποκατάσ- 3
τασιν (ἐκάλουν δὲ τὸ νουθετεῖν πεδαρτᾶν)· ἐποιοῦντο γὰρ τὴν ἀνα- 4
μονὴν σιωπῇ χρώμενοι καὶ ἡσυχίᾳ. Σπίνθαρος γοῦν διηγεῖτο πολ- 5
λάκις περὶ Ἀρχύτου <τοῦ> Ταραντίνου, ὅτι διὰ χρόνου τινὸς εἰς ἀγρὸν 6
ἀφικόμενος, ἐκ στρατιᾶς νεωστὶ παραγεγονώς, ἣν ἐστρατεύσατο ἡ 7
πόλις εἰς Μεσσαπίους, ὡς εἶδε τόν τε ἐπίτροπον καὶ τοὺς ἄλλους 8
οἰκέτας οὐκ εὖ τῶν περὶ τὴν γεωργίαν ἐπιμελείας πεποιημένους, 9
ἀλλὰ μεγάλῃ τινὶ κεχρημένους ὀλιγωρίας ὑπερβολῇ, ὀργισθείς τε καὶ 10
ἀγανακτήσας οὕτως ὡς ἂν ἐκεῖνος, εἶπεν, ὡς ἔοικε, πρὸς τοὺς οἰκέτας, 11
ὅτι εὐτυχοῦσιν, ὅτι αὐτοῖς ὤργισται· εἰ γὰρ μὴ τοῦτο συμβεβηκὸς 12
ἦν, οὐκ ἄν ποτε αὐτοὺς ἀθῴους γενέσθαι τηλικαῦτα ἡμαρτηκότας. 13
(198) ἔφη δὲ λέγεσθαι καὶ περὶ Κλεινίου τοιαῦτά τινα· καὶ γὰρ ἐκεῖνον 14
ἀναβάλλεσθαι πάσας νουθετήσεις τε καὶ κολάσεις εἰς τὴν τῆς διανοίας 15
ἀποκατάστασιν. 16

---

4 πεδαρτᾶν] Hemsterhusius   παιδαρτᾶν codd.   **5** γάρ] δὲ Rohde   ἀναμονήν] codd.
ἀναβολήν Cobet   **6** <τοῦ>] Cobet   **7** ἐκ] Scaliger   καὶ F   στρατιᾶς] στρατείας Mahne
8 Μεσσαπίους] Cobet   μεσανίους F   μεσηνίους C   **9** ἐπιμελείας] ἐπιμέλειαν Wakefield

The following things are also said about the Pythagoreans: no one of them either punished a slave, when held by anger, or corrected any free person, but each of them waited until their capacity for rational thought was reestablished (they called correction "retuning"). For they observed silence and calm while they waited. At least Spintharus often told the story about Archytas of Tarentum that, when he arrived at his farm after some time, having recently come from a campaign, which the city mounted against the Messapians, he saw that his steward and the other slaves had not given proper care to the farming, but had shown very extreme negligence. Although he was angry and vexed, in the way that he could be, he said, as it seems, to the slaves, that they were lucky that he was angry with them. For, if this had not happened, they would never have gone unpunished, when they had committed such great wrongs. He [Spintharus?] said that some such things were also reported about Cleinias. For (he said) that man also put off all correction and punishment, until his capacity for rational thought was restored.

Related Texts

Text A. Diodorus Siculus X. 7.4 (1st century BC), preserved in Constantius VII Porphyrogenitus, *De Sententiis* 294 (10th century AD)

ὅτι φασὶ τὸν Ταραντῖνον Ἀρχύταν τὸν ὄντα Πυθαγόρειον ἐπὶ μεγάλοις ἀδικήμασιν οἰκέταις ὀργισθῆναι, καὶ κατεξαναστάντα τοῦ πάθους εἰπεῖν, ὡς οὐκ ἂν ἐγενήθησαν ἀθῷοι τηλικαῦτα ἁμαρτήσαντες, εἰ μὴ ἔτυχεν ὀργιζόμενος.

They say that Archytas of Tarentum, who was a Pythagorean, became angry with his slaves over great wrongs, and, when he had recovered from his emotion, said that they would not have been unpunished, having committed such great wrongs, if he had not happened to get angry.

Text B. Plutarch, *On the Education of Children* 14. 10d (ca. AD 50–ca. AD 120)

ἀδελφὰ τούτοις καὶ σύζυγα φανήσονται πεποιηκότες Ἀρχύτας ὁ Ταραντῖνος καὶ Πλάτων. ὁ μὲν γὰρ ἐπανελθὼν ἀπὸ πολέμου (στρατηγῶν δ᾽ ἐτύγχανε) <τὴν> γῆν καταλαβὼν κεχερσωμένην, τὸν ἐπίτροπον καλέσας αὐτῆς "ὤμωξας ἄν" ἔφησεν "εἰ μὴ λίαν ὠργιζόμην." Πλάτων δὲ δούλῳ λίχνῳ καὶ βδελυρῷ θυμωθείς, τὸν τῆς ἀδελφῆς υἱὸν Σπεύσιππον καλέσας "τοῦτον," ἔφησεν ἀπελθών, "κρότησον· ἐγὼ γὰρ πάνυ θυμοῦμαι."

Archytas of Tarentum and Plato will be seen to have done things related and connected to these. For the one, having returned from war (he happened to be general) and having found his land made barren, summoned the steward in charge of it and said, "You would have wailed, if I were not so angry." And Plato, having become angry with a gluttonous and impudent slave, summoned his sister's son, Speusippus, and said as he went away, "Beat this fellow for I am too angry."

Text C. Plutarch, *On the Delays of Divine Vengeance* 5. 551a
(ca. AD 50–ca. AD 120)

ὅθεν ἡμεροῦνται καὶ τοῖς ἀνθρωπίνοις παραδείγμασιν, ἀκούοντες ὡς
Πλάτων τε τὴν βακτηρίαν ἀνατεινάμενος τῷ παιδὶ πολὺν ἔστη χρόνον,
ὡς αὐτὸς ἔφη, τὸν θυμὸν κολάζων, καὶ Ἀρχύτας, οἰκετῶν τινα πλημ-
μέλειαν ἐν ἀγρῷ καὶ ἀταξίαν καταμαθών, εἶτα ἑαυτοῦ συναισθανόμενος
ἐμπαθέστερον ἔχοντος καὶ τραχύτερον πρὸς αὐτούς, οὐδὲν ἐποίησεν
ἀλλ᾽ ἢ τοσοῦτον ἀπιών, "εὐτυχεῖτε," εἶπεν, "ὅτι ὀργίζομαι ὑμῖν."

Whence people are made gentle even by human examples, hearing both
that, upon raising his staff to strike the slave, Plato remained motionless for
a long time chastising his own anger, as he himself said, and that Archytas,
having learnt of some misconduct and indiscipline of slaves on his farm
and then being conscious that he was too impassioned and harsh towards
them, did nothing more than say as he left, "You are lucky that I am angry
with you."

For a similar version see Proclus, *On Providence* 54 (in the Latin of William
of Moerbeke).

Text D. Cicero, *Tusculan Disputations* IV. 36.78 (1st century BC)

ex quo illud laudatur Archytae, qui cum vilico factus esset iratior, "quo te
modo," inquit, "accepissem, nisi iratus essem!"

For which reason that saying of Archytas is praised, who, when he had
become too angry with his steward, said, "How I would have dealt with
you, if I were not angry!"

Text E. Cicero, *On the Republic* I. 38.59 (1st century BC)

(SCIPIO) "Quid? tum, cum tu es iratus, permittis illi iracundiae domina-
tum animi tui?"
(LAELIUS) "Non mehercule," inquit, "sed imitor Archytam illum Tarentinum, qui cum ad villam venisset et omnia aliter offendisset ac iusserat,
'A te infelicem,' inquit vilico, 'quem necassem iam verberibus, nisi iratus
essem.'"
"Optime," inquit Scipio. "ergo Archytas iracundiam videlicet dissiden-
tem a ratione seditionem quandam animi esse iure ducebat, atque eam
consilio sedari volebat."

(SCIPIO) "What? When you are angry, do you relinquish control of your
mind to that anger?"

(Laelius) "No, by god," he said "but I imitate the famous Archytas of Tarentum, who, when he had come to his estate and had found that none of his commands had been followed, said to his steward, 'I would have beaten you to death by now, you wretch, if I were not angry.'"

"Excellent," said Scipio, "It is clear, therefore, that Archytas correctly regarded anger, when it is at variance with reason, as a kind of rebellion in the mind and wanted it to be restrained by deliberation."

Text F. Valerius Maximus, *Memorable Deeds and Sayings* IV. 1. ext. 1 (1st century AD)

Tarentinus Archytas, dum se Pythagorae praeceptis Metaponti penitus immergit, magno labore longoque tempore solidum opus doctrinae complexus, postquam in patriam revertit ac rura sua revisere coepit, animadvertit neglegentia vilici corrupta et perdita intuensque male meritum "sumpsissem," inquit "a te supplicium, nisi tibi iratus essem": maluit enim impunitum dimittere quam propter iram iusto gravius punire.

Nimis liberalis Archytae moderatio, temperatior Platonis: nam cum adversus delictum servi vehementius exarsisset, veritus ne ipse vindictae modum dispicere non posset, Speusippo amico castigationis arbitrium mandavit . . .

Archytas of Tarentum immersed himself completely in the teachings of Pythagoras at Metapontum and with great and long labor embraced the complete course of training. After he returned to his fatherland and began to review his estates, he became aware that they had gone to wrack and ruin by the negligence of his steward. Looking at the culprit he said, "I would have punished you, if I were not angry with you." For he preferred to let him go unpunished rather than, because of his anger, to punish him more severely than was just.

The moderation of Archytas was too generous, that of Plato more temperate. For, when he had become too violently angry in response to the offense of a slave, fearing lest he himself not be able to discern the proper amount of punishment, he entrusted the determination of the punishment to his friend Speusippus . . .

Text G. Lactantius, *On the Anger of God* 18.4 (ca. AD 240–ca. AD 320)

Laudatur Archytas Tarentinus, qui cum in agro corrupta esse omnia comperisset vilici sui culpa, "miserum te," inquit, "quem iam verberibus necassem, nisi iratus essem." unicum hoc exemplum temperantiae putant, sed auctoritate ducti non vident quam inepta et locutus fuerit et fecerit . . . si enim senserint servi dominum suum saevire cum non irascitur, tum parcere cum irascitur, non peccabunt utique leviter, ne verberentur, sed quantum poterunt gravissime, ut stomachum perversi hominis incitent atque impune discedant.

Archytas of Tarentum is praised because, when he had found out that everything on his farm had been ruined by the fault of his steward, he said, "I would have beat you to death by now, you wretch, if I were not angry." People think that this is a singular example of self-control, but led astray by authority they do not see how foolish was both what he said and did. . . . For, if servants perceive that their master is severe when he is not angry, but spares them when he is angry, they will certainly not commit minor sins, lest they be beaten, but will commit sins as serious as possible, so that they might arouse the anger of the misguided man and go unpunished.

Text H. St. Jerome, *Letter* 79.9 (ca. AD 347–420)

et illud Archytae Tarentini ad vilicum neglegentem: "iam te verberibus enecassem, nisi iratus essem."

There are also the famous words of Archytas of Tarentum to his negligent steward: "I would have beaten you to death by now, if I were not angry."

Authenticity
Similar anecdotes were also told about Plato and Pythagoras' wife, Theano (Proclus, *De Prov.* 54). Riginos provides a complete listing of such anecdotes concerning Plato (1976: 155–56). Only one of these (Riginos 113C) really has the same form as the anecdote concerning Archytas, and this version is cited only in a few sources (Seneca assigns it to Socrates, *De Ira* 1.15). The authority of Aristoxenus' father Spintharus, who is earlier than any source connecting Plato with the anecdote, suggests that the anecdote was originally told about Archytas and only later transferred to Plato (cf. Dillon and Hershbell 1991: 203). On the problems concerning the authenticity of anecdotes see the introductory essay on authenticity.

Context in Iamblichus and Iamblichus' use of Aristoxenus as a source
Testimonium A7 is drawn from Chapter 31 of Iamblichus' *On the Pythagorean Life*. This chapter is devoted to the Pythagorean practice of the virtue of temperance. Iamblichus appears to start using Aristoxenus

as a source at the beginning of section 196, since he there switches to Aristoxenus' practice of referring to Pythagoreans rather than Pythagoras (Dillon and Hershbell 1991: 203). Section 197 begins with a general assertion that no Pythagoreans punished or admonished in anger. Archytas is then cited as an example. Cleinias is given as a second example, at the beginning of section 198, which concludes by stating that the Pythagoreans avoided lamentation, tears and emotions that produce disagreements.

Although he is never mentioned by name, Aristoxenus is probably the source for the entire passage from 196–98, which forms a coherent whole. One sentence in 198 is quoted virtually *verbatim* later in Iamblichus (*VP* 234) and is there explicitly said to be from Aristoxenus. The anecdote about Archytas in 197 is reported on the authority of Aristoxenus' father Spintharus, who is likely to have been one of Aristoxenus' major sources for the *Life of Archytas*. It is explicitly reported that Spintharus served as a source for Aristoxenus' *Life of Socrates* (Aristox. Fr. 54a Wehrli). Because of the parallel with section 234, which comes from Aristoxenus' *On the Pythagorean Life*, it is most reasonable to conclude that sections 196–98 of Iamblichus are close to what appeared in that work. As Wehrli argues, however, it is likely that the anecdote about Archytas was also used in Aristoxenus' *Life of Archytas* (1945: 56).

Importance of the testimonium

The basic point of this anecdote about Archytas and the similar ones about Plato is that one should never punish in anger (D.L. VIII. 20 has Pythagoras himself make the point). The exact grounds on which this admonition is made are not usually spelled out. We might suppose that the fundamental principle is that we should not let our emotions, rather than our reason, guide our actions. This is the central point of Archytas' speech against pleasure in A9a. Applied to the specific circumstances of punishing when controlled by anger, the point would be that, if we punish in anger, we will punish unjustly. This in turn could be judged morally problematic for two different reasons: (1) the person punished will suffer unjustly, (2) the person punishing will act unjustly and hence harm his own soul. Although the anecdotes all make the same basic point, there are important differences between the way the point is developed in the cases of Archytas and Plato.

The anecdote featuring Archytas is the most paradoxical. Archytas was so concerned about not acting in anger that he let his steward and slaves go completely unpunished, even though they were deserving of great punishment. The startling fact that the slaves escape all punishment is precisely what makes this version so memorable. The dour Lactantius (Text G) complains about this feature of the anecdote; although Archytas' action is usually regarded as a singular act of self-control, it is, in fact, very foolish (see also Text F). The slaves will be encouraged to commit the most outrageous acts in order to enrage their master and hence avoid punishment. This version of the anecdote is also assigned to Plato by a few late sources (Riginos 1976: 113C, p. 156), but there can be little doubt that it was originally told of Archytas and only later attached to Plato. The confusion in part arose, undoubtedly, because the anecdotes about Archytas and Plato were often presented as a pair by ancient authors (e.g. Texts B, C and F above).

Two other anecdotes about Plato develop the point differently. The first (Riginos 1976: 113A, p. 155) is less paradoxical than the story about Archytas (and hence approved by Lactantius!). Plato, because he has become angry, does not punish the slave himself. Nonetheless, the slave does get his just punishment, since Plato asks someone else, who is not emotionally involved (e.g. Speusippus or Xenocrates), to carry out the punishment. The second anecdote shifts the focus from the punishment of the slave to the correction of the person who has become angry. It is unclear if the slave receives any punishment. Plato stays his hand, when it is raised to strike, and keeps it there for some time, so that a puzzled bystander asks what he is doing, and Plato responds that he is chastising his own anger. The emphasis is on punishing the internal injustice of acting in anger rather than on correcting the external injustice of the slave.

If we look a little more carefully at the anecdote about Archytas, it is striking that its central paradox, i.e. the failure to punish the slaves at all, is in tension with the context in which it is quoted. Aristoxenus, both before and after the anecdote, indicates that, while the Pythagorean practice was not to punish in anger, punishment was exacted after the capability for rational thought had been restored. It is also suggested that, while waiting for reason to be restored to its commanding role, the Pythagoreans observed silence and calm (lines 3–4). This is in contrast to Archytas' actions, since he is usually presented as saying, in the heat of his anger, something like, "I would have punished you, if I were not angry." Diodorus alone (Text A) presents Archytas as waiting until he had recovered from his anger before speaking at all. It is more likely that this is a revision on Diodorus' part, in order to make the anecdote square with Pythagorean practice as attested elsewhere, than that the rest of the tradition preserves an erroneous version of the anecdote, which is in tension with usual Pythagorean practice (*pace* De Vogel 1966: 161–62). Aristoxenus' version emphasizes the severity of the neglect of the estate by the slaves and the length of time Archytas has been away in the service of Tarentum, in order to make intelligible the violence of his anger, which in turn leads him to speak.

The tension between the general point about Pythagoreanism, which Aristoxenus is developing, and the story about Archytas, which he uses as an example suggests that the story was not invented by Aristoxenus in order to illustrate his point but derived from an independent tradition. Surely Aristoxenus would have made Archytas illustrate his point more exactly, if he were creating the anecdote out of whole cloth. His appeal to Spintharus as the source of the story is thus not a fiction to lend credibility to something that is Aristoxenus' own invention but is rather a legitimate citation of his source. Aristoxenus cites the anecdote because it is memorable and conforms to his basic point, although it does not perfectly fit his purposes.

Wehrli took this testimonium to contain the essence of Aristoxenus' presentation of Archytas: he was the model of Pythagorean self-control. This characterization of Archytas is then to be set in contrast to Aristoxenus' emphasis on Socrates' lack of self-control in the *Life of Socrates* (1945: 64). It is true that, in the anecdote, Archytas has the self-control to keep from punishing his steward and servants in anger. He is not, however, presented as the ideal model of calm and self-control. Archytas does allow himself to get so angry that he cannot allow himself to punish his slaves. Even more significantly, Aristoxenus notes that Archytas was prone to such anger (see οὕτως ὡς ἂν ἐκεῖνος in line 11). Archytas is being portrayed in a positive light, but Aristoxenus shows him to be a fallible human being rather than just a moral exemplum.

Detailed commentary

Line 4 πεδαρτᾶν – πεδά is Doric for μετά. In compound verb forms it most commonly expresses "change" in condition. πεδαρτάω is reasonably explained as the Doric equivalent for μεθαρμόζω, which means "to make a change" and, as a technical term in music, "to change the mode" (Iamb. *VP* 25.113). The musical connotation may be the reason for the Pythagoreans' adoption of πεδαρτάω as a technical term for "to correct" or "to admonish." An English equivalent would be "change of tuning" or "retuning." Empedocles' tuning his lyre to a different mode, in order to stop a youth from killing a judge, is a graphic example of such "retuning" (*VP* 25.113). The verb occurs in only two places, both times as a Pythagorean technical term, here and at D.L. VIII. 20. In both cases it was corrupted in the manuscripts because the prefix πεδα- was not understood. The manuscripts of Iamblichus have παιδαρτᾶν, which is unparalleled but is a clear attempt to interpret the term for "to correct" as built on the root meaning "child" (παιδ), while manuscripts of Diogenes Laertius have the nonsensical πελαργᾶν (cf. the *Suda*). The corresponding noun is found twice in the plural (πεδαρτάσεις) in Iamblichus' *On the Pythagorean Life*. In one case (*VP* 33.231) the correct form is preserved by the manuscripts, but, in the other, the form has been corrupted to παιδαρτάσεις (*VP* 22.101).

5 ἀναμονήν – This word for "delay" is rare and only used by authors of the second century AD or later. Accordingly, Cobet suggested ἀναβολήν and was followed by Nauck. ἀναβολή is used with the meaning "delay" by authors of the fifth and fourth centuries BC and hence might be more appropriate to Aristoxenus. The verb ἀνέμενεν is used two lines before this, which might suggest the noun form ἀναμονήν to a copyist who was familiar with the later noun form.

6–7 διὰ χρόνου τινὸς – DK (1. 471.14, note) says that τινός is the addition of Iamblichus, presumably because the simple expression διὰ χρόνου is more common. The expression διὰ χρόνου is more common in all periods, however, and there is no real reason to suppose that τινός belongs to Iamblichus rather than Aristoxenus. A search of the TLG reveals only six parallels for the phrase διὰ χρόνου τινός, see e.g. Plu. *Nic.* XI. 1.3.

7 στρατιᾶς – The form στρατείας would be more usual for the meaning "campaign," which is required here, but στρατιά is on occasion used with this meaning (see LSJ s.v. II).

8 Μεσσαπίους – This is Cobet's correction for the μεσανίους of the manuscripts. The Messapii were the inhabitants of the heel of Italy and hence bordered on Tarentum. Together with the Daunians and Peucetii they made up the people known as the Iapygians. They were allied with Athens against Sparta in the Peloponnesian War (Thuc. VII. 33) and were in constant conflict with Tarentum (Sparta's colony) in the fifth century (e.g. Hdt. VII. 170; see further in the introduction on Archytas' life). Ribezzo (1951: 13 ff.) argues that we should accept the manuscript reading as a reference to a war against a city Mesania (Mesagne).

9 ἐπιμελείας – The singular may be more common, but the plural with the meaning to take "pains" is also found (e.g. Xen. *Cyr.* I. 6.4).

11 οὕτως ὡς ἂν ἐκεῖνος – Dillon and Hershbell (1991) translate "Though he was angry and annoyed as one like him could be . . ." but ἐκεῖνος does not usually pick out a kind of person but rather a specific person, in this case Archytas. Clark (1989) translates "he was *as* enraged and furious *as* he could be," but in the English idiom this conveys the idea that he was enraged to the extreme degree, for which meaning we would have expected some sort of superlative in Greek. The Greek phrase rather suggests that we are describing the characteristic behavior of a specific person, Archytas. Aristoxenus is making the point that Archytas was angry and vexed in the way that he could (in certain circumstances) be. Thus, there is the suggestion here that Archytas was of a somewhat irascible temper. A similar phrase is used to describe the tyrant Phalaris at *VP* 31.216: "he uttered blasphemies against the gods τοιαύτας οἵας ἂν ἐκεῖνος εἶπεν (such as he would [typically] utter)." This parallel suggests that in line 11 it is an indicative form of the verb that is to be understood with ἐκεῖνος and that the construction is the "past potential" (Smyth 1956: 1784). De Vogel (1966: 161) translates "in so far as that was possible for him" (see also Timpanaro Cardini 1962: 285, "per quanto la sua natura lo consentiva"), which is an attempt to do away with the implication that Archytas was irascible and even that he got very angry in this case. This interpretation goes contrary to the clear structure of the anecdote and the almost universal understanding of it in the ancient tradition, which emphasizes Archytas' extreme anger. For the meaning "insofar as," moreover, we would expect a construction with ὅσος (e.g. καθ' ὅσον, ἐς ὅσον or ἐφ' ὅσον, see Pl. *Ti.* 51b).

ὡς ἔοικε – Diels (DK I. 471, note) suggests that in light of Diodorus' version of the story (Text A), in which Archytas does not speak until he has recovered from his anger, we might expect that something like ὡς ἔληγε [sc. τῆς ὀργῆς], "when he had ceased [from his anger]," should be read instead of ὡς ἔοικε. There is, however, a parallel for this use of ὡς ἔοικε = "as they say," at *VP* 126 (72.11 Deubner), and Diodorus elsewhere presents material from Aristoxenus in heavily modified form (von Fritz 1940: 22–26), so that it is doubtful that he is preserving the original version rather than Iamblichus, who often seems to quote Aristoxenus.

14 ἔφη – Spintharus was the last source mentioned (line 4), and he is most likely to be the subject of ἔφη. Since Cleinias is also said to be from Tarentum (Iamb. *VP* 239), it would not be surprising, if Spintharus has special information about him as well as about Archytas. On the other hand, given that Iamblichus is clearly quoting Aristoxenus throughout this passage, it is not impossible that he is being careless and intends Aristoxenus to be the subject.

Κλεινίου – In Athenaeus (624a; cf. Ael. *VH* XIII. 23) Cleinias soothes his anger by playing the lyre.

A7a Cicero, *Laelius On Friendship* XXIII. 88

Verum ergo illud est, quod a Tarentino Archyta, ut opinor, dici solitum   1
nostros senes commemorare audivi, ab aliis senibus auditum: "Si quis in   2
caelum ascendisset, naturamque mundi et pulchritudinem siderum per-   3
spexisset, insuavem illam admirationem ei fore; quae iucundissima fuisset,   4
si aliquem cui narraret habuisset." Sic natura solitarium nihil amat sem-   5
perque ad aliquod tamquam adminiculum adnititur, quod in amicissimo   6
quoque dulcissimum est.   7

5   si aliquem] nisi aliquem M   nisi aliqui B

Therefore, those words are true which I have heard our elders mention were
habitually said by Archytas of Tarentum, if I am not mistaken, and which
they heard from their elders: "If someone should ascend into the heavens
and gain insight into the nature of the universe and the beauty of the stars,
his wonder at those things would be without pleasure, although it would
be most pleasant, if he should have someone to whom to describe it." To
such a degree does [human] nature love nothing solitary and always lean,
as it were, on some support, and the most pleasant support is found in the
best friend.

Authenticity

The saying that Cicero here ascribes to Archytas appears nowhere else in the
ancient tradition, and Cicero does not give his source. It is therefore very
hard to determine to what extent the saying might reflect anything that
Archytas actually said or wrote. There is no evidence, however, that Cicero
invented such anecdotes. Assuming then that Cicero did have an authority
for this saying of Archytas, the most likely source is Aristoxenus' *Life of
Archytas*, which Cicero appears to use elsewhere (A7, A9a). Aristoxenus
favored the use of such anecdotes as we find in A7a (see A7 and A9). The
portrayal of Archytas as an investigator of the heavens finds its best parallel
in one of Horace's odes (1. 28) published some twenty years after Cicero's
De Amicitia. Archytas is there portrayed, in a way very reminiscent of A7a,
as having "investigated the heavenly abodes and traversed the round vault
of the sky with the mind" (A3).

   In the case of A9a, Cicero constructed a quite elaborate explanation of
how the Cato of his dialogue, *De Senectute*, came to have heard the anecdote
about Archytas. In A7a, Cicero is clearly following the same procedure, in
that he has his character Laelius mention an oral tradition for an anecdote
that Cicero himself derived from a written source. Here in the *De Amicitia*,

however, Cicero just gives the bare outlines of an oral tradition, according to which Laelius heard the story from his elders, who in turn heard it from their elders. There are none of the circumstantial details which Cicero provides in the *De Senectute*, and we are not told how Laelius had access to oral traditions from Tarentum. De Vogel does not notice Cicero's connections to Aristoxenus' *Life of Archytas* and implausibly supposes that Cicero is drawing on local Tarentine oral tradition (1966: 30). If Aristoxenus is the source, A7a may be expected to reflect accurately Archytas' general outlook (see the introductory essay on authenticity).

Context

Cicero's treatise on friendship is presented in the form of a speech by Gaius Laelius and set in 129 BC. In section 86 Laelius asserts that friendship is the one thing in human life which is recognized as advantageous by everyone. Someone can be found who despises everything else that is usually thought valuable – riches, political honors, even virtue – but no one despises friendship. Those devoted to public life, to private business, to science and philosophy, even those devoted to sensual pleasure all agree that, without friendship, there is no life at all. By questionable reasoning, Laelius even argues that a misanthrope like Timon requires someone before whom he might pour out his abuse. Laelius then asks us to imagine someone provided by a god with every material good but deprived of all human society, and argues that there would be no one able to endure such a life nor anyone for whom solitude would not take away the enjoyment of every pleasure. It is at this point that Laelius introduces the words attributed to Archytas. After the reference to Archytas, Laelius sums up the point by asserting that human nature does not like what is solitary and always leans on the support which a friend can provide best.

Immediately before Archytas is introduced, we are asked to consider an imaginary person, who is provided by some god with all material wants but who is isolated from society. Archytas' words apply to the sort of person who in real life might most approach such a life, a *physiologos*, one who investigates the nature of the universe. Such a life seems to be most free of the necessity of external support (Arist. *EN* 1177a27 ff.), but already in section 86 Laelius has pointed out that even such scientists (*ei qui rerum cognitione doctrinaque delectantur*) think that life without friendship is no life. Cicero introduces Archytas' words to show that even that activity which appears most self-sufficient, intellectual achievement, will produce no pleasure, unless we have someone to whom we can tell our discovery.

Importance of the testimonium

This anecdote is important for what it reveals both about the general focus of Archytas' philosophy and also about his views on two specific topics: pleasure and friendship. Archytas here recognizes the importance of intellectual pleasures in stark contrast to his criticism of bodily pleasures in A9a. It is striking that these intellectual pleasures are specifically those of a *physiologos*, one who is devoted to understanding the nature of the universe, who focused especially on the heavens and the stars. Other fragments and testimonia show that Archytas was indeed particularly interested in three of the sciences of the *quadrivium* (logistic [Fr. 2, Fr. 4, A19], geometry [A14–A15] and especially music [Fr. 1, A16 etc.]) as well as other less-prominent sciences such as optics and biology (A25 and A23a). Elsewhere, however, we have little evidence for Archytas' work specifically in astronomy and cosmology, so that it is remarkable that such fields are here presented as providing the highest of intellectual pleasures. Eudemus' report, according to which Archytas attempted to prove that the cosmos was unlimited, by imagining someone standing at the supposed limit of the universe (A24), does, however, accord very well with Archytas' ascent to the heavens here in A7a. The combination of A24 and A7a may then be responsible for Horace's and Propertius' portrayal of Archytas as the master astronomer (see the introduction on the reception of Archytas in Rome).

The main point of the testimonium, however, is that a cosmologist only derives the great pleasure inherent in the investigation of the heavens, if he has someone to whom he can describe what he has discovered. Cicero emphasizes that Archytas made this point repeatedly (*solitum*, line 1). Perhaps we should suppose that Aristoxenus presented the anecdote as Archytas' response to those who would stubbornly argue that a person who contemplates the nature of the universe is self-sufficient and does not require human society in order to be happy. Several passages in Aristotle's *Nicomachean Ethics* show that fourth-century philosophers debated both whether friends were necessary for happiness and also whether the life of solitary contemplation was sufficient for happiness. At 1169b18 Aristotle argues that, "No one would choose to have all good things on the condition that he must enjoy them alone, for human beings are by nature social and such as to live with others." This argument is very close to what Cicero has Laelius say at *De Amicitia* 87, in introducing A7a. It is not impossible that Cicero is directly dependent on Aristotle here (cf. Powell 1990: 19).

Aristotle and Archytas are clearly in general agreement on the necessity of friends. When Aristotle says at 1172a2 that "Whatever pursuit it is which constitutes existence for a man or on account of which he chooses to live, he wants to spend life in that pursuit with friends," the study of the natural world would clearly be included in these pursuits. On the other hand, there is nothing in Aristotle that directly corresponds to the anecdote about Archytas, i.e. the *physiologos* ascending into the heavens is not given as an example of someone in need of friends. Thus, if Aristotle knows of the anecdote concerning Archytas, he does not choose to mention it, and Cicero cannot have derived the anecdote from Aristotle. Indeed, Aristotle seems to back away slightly from the necessity of friendship in Book 10 of the *Nicomachean Ethics*, when at 1177a35 he says that "The wise man can contemplate by himself and the more so the wiser he is; perhaps he will study better if he has fellow workers, but he is nevertheless the most self-sufficient of all men." Archytas' comments in A7a could be understood as a response to someone who was trying to emphasize the self-sufficiency of the wise man as Aristotle does here.

Friendship is a prominent topic in ancient accounts of Pythagoreanism, but it is impossible to tell to what extent, if any, Archytas drew on earlier Pythagorean teaching on the topic. Iamblichus treats the topic extensively in his treatise *On the Pythagorean Life* (229–40), but the anecdote concerning Archytas is not reported. Iamblichus' primary source for this section is Aristoxenus' *On the Pythagorean Way of Life*, to which he explicitly refers in section 233. Aristoxenus is particularly cited for the story of those most famous of all Pythagorean friends, Damon and Phintias. There is no mention of Archytas in these chapters of Iamblichus on friendship. In an earlier passage (127) Iamblichus appears to refer again to Aristoxenus' account of Pythagorean friends (the passage is corrupt; see Dillon and Hershbell 1991: 149). This time, however, Archytas and Plato are included as Pythagorean friends (A6b), along with Damon and Phintias and Cleinias and Prorus. Thus, we might wonder whether Aristoxenus had Archytas deliver the words on friendship in A7a to Plato. It should be remembered, however, that the nature of the relationship between Archytas and Plato is problematic (see the introduction on Plato and Archytas).

Detailed commentary

Lines 2–5 si quis . . . habuisset – This is a future less vivid condition in which the perfect subjunctives in the protases have been changed to pluperfect subjunctives, because of the indirect statement. We might have expected the accusative and infinitive construction, *quam iucundissimam fore*, in line 4 rather than *quae . . . fuisset*. Nauck took the subjunctive to indicate that these are the words of Laelius rather than Archytas. Reid shows, however, that Cicero's usage in such relative clauses admits of either the infinitive or the subjunctive construction (1897: 113).

3 caelum ascendisset – For this phrase and image see Cic. *Dom.* 75.4 and Horace, *Carm*, I. 28, line 5.
naturamque mundi – For this phrase see Cic. *N.D.* II. 84; II. 58.
pulchritudinem siderum – For a similar phrase see Cic. *N.D.* II. 15.

6 adminiculum – This word is often used of vine props but also of other sorts of support (see the commentary on Archytas A25, line 8 and e.g. Cic. *N.D.* II. 47.20). Seyffert and Müller 1965: 508–09 discuss the usage in some detail but rely on the earlier view that derived the word from *ad-manus* rather than the current view which derives it from the same root as *moenia* and *munio* (OLD). It is striking that this not terribly common word is also used by Apuleius in describing Archytas' theory of vision. For Archytas the visual ray is derived from our eyes alone "without any external support" (*sine ullo foris amminiculo* – A25, line 8). In A7a the word is not assigned to Archytas but is instead put in the mouth of Laelius, as he sums up the point of Archytas' words. It is possible, however, that the word or its Greek equivalent (ἀντέρεισμα? see A25) was used by Archytas in Cicero's source (probably Aristoxenus) and that Cicero wrote the sentence he puts in Laelius' mouth under the influence of a fuller version of the anecdote concerning Archytas.

A8 Athenaeus, *Sophists at Dinner* XII, 519b

καὶ Ἀθηνόδωρος δὲ ἐν τῷ περὶ Σπουδῆς καὶ Παιδιᾶς Ἀρχύταν φησὶ τὸν   1
Ταραντῖνον πολιτικὸν ἅμα καὶ φιλόσοφον γενόμενον πλείστους οἰκέτας   2
ἔχοντα αἰεὶ τούτ<ων τοῖς παιδί>οις παρὰ τὴν δίαιταν ἀφιεμένοις εἰς τὸ   3
συμπόσιον ἥδεσθαι. ἀλλ' οἱ Συβαρῖται ἔχαιρον τοῖς Μελιταίοις κυνιδ-   4
ίοις καὶ ἀνθρώποις οὐκ ἀνθρώποις.   5

1 Παιδιᾶς] Musurus   παιδείας Α   Ἀρχύταν] Ἀρχύτην Α   Ἀρχύτας CE (in a different construction)   3 τούτ<ων τοῖς παιδί>οις] Casaubon (see Aelian below)   3–4 ἀφιεμένοις εἰς τὸ συμπόσιον] ἀφικνουμένοις C (epitome)

Athenodorus, in his book *On Seriousness and Play*, says that Archytas of Tarentum, who became both a statesman and a philosopher and who had a very great number of slaves, always took delight in <the children of> these slaves, when, as a part of his routine, they were let loose into his dinner parties. The Sybarites, on the contrary, enjoyed Melitaean miniature dogs and human beings who were less than human.

Aelian, *Historical Miscellany* XII.15

ἀλλὰ καὶ Ἀρχύτας ὁ Ταραντῖνος, πολιτικός τε καὶ φιλόσοφος ἀνὴρ   1
γενόμενος, πολλοὺς ἔχων οἰκέτας, τοῖς αὐτῶν παιδίοις πάνυ σφόδρα   2
ἐτέρπετο μετὰ τῶν οἰκοτρίβων παίζων· μάλιστα δὲ ἐφίλει τέρπεσθαι   3
αὐτοῖς ἐν τοῖς συμποσίοις.   4

Even Archytas of Tarentum, who became both statesman and philosopher, took exceeding delight in the children of his many slaves and played games with those who were born in the house; he was especially wont to delight in their presence at his dinner parties.

Authenticity

Since this testimonium is not likely to be based on anything written by Archytas himself but derives from the anecdotal tradition, it is very hard to know what, if anything, reliable it tells us about Archytas. If it goes back to Aristoxenus' *Life of Archytas* (see below), then we might suppose that its portrayal of Archytas has at its core something historical or that it is at least based on a common fourth-century view of Archytas. This supposition is supported by Aristotle's evidence for Archytas' fondness for children (A10).

Context

Both Athenaeus and Aelian appear to derive this anecdote from the treatise *On Seriousness and Play* by the Stoic Athenodorus of Tarsus, son of Sandon. Athenaeus explicitly identifies Athenodorus as his source. The anecdote appears in Book XII of Athenaeus' *Deipnosophistae* (ca. AD 200), which is devoted to "those who became notorious for their luxury" (509e). The latter part of Book XII focuses on the luxury of individuals and includes another testimonium of Archytas (A9). The first part of the book (up to 528e), in which A8 appears, deals with the luxury of nations and peoples. In the pages immediately preceding A8, Athenaeus has been discussing the notorious luxury of the Sybarites. At 518f he says that on account of their luxurious habits they kept deformed human beings and lap-dogs, which accompanied them even to the gymnasia. This leads Athenaeus to tell the story of Massinissa, king of the Mauretanians, who responded to men who wanted to buy up large numbers of monkeys for pets with the retort, "Do not your women beget children?" Massinissa's fondness for children is then recounted. The poet Eubulus is then quoted, "For how much better it is that a human being raise a human being . . . than a goose . . . sparrow or monkey." It is at this point that Athenaeus quotes the anecdote about Archytas. As Athenaeus' summarizing remarks show, he quotes the anecdote in order to show that the statesman and philosopher Archytas (rightly) takes his delight in human children, while the Sybarites, corrupted by their luxury, delight in lap-dogs and deformed human beings instead. Archytas, uncorrupted by luxury, takes natural human pleasure in children, in contrast to the perverted pleasures of the Sybarites.

The anecdote has a quite different context in Aelian. Aelian's *Historical Miscellany* is "a miscellaneous collection of anecdotes and historical material," which "was put together in the early third century" AD, probably after the publication of the *Deipnosophistae* (Wilson 1997: 1, 6, 10–11). Chapter 15 of Book XII is a series of four brief anecdotes in which Heracles, Socrates, Agesilaus and finally Archytas are given as examples of adults who like to play with children. The whole chapter is likely to go back to Athenodorus (Hense 1907). Thus, although elsewhere Aelian appears to rely heavily on Athenaeus (Wilson 1997: 10–11), in this case they both appear to be drawing on a common source, Athenodorus. The point of the four anecdotes in Chapter 12 of Aelian, of which A8 is the last, is stated in the first anecdote about Heracles: great men need to play games in order to relax from their labors.

It is likely that this theme originates in Athenodorus, who was a Stoic philosopher, friend of Cicero and court philosopher of Augustus. Athenodorus is one of the major sources for Seneca's *On Tranquility of Mind* (Philippson, *RE*: suppl. 5, 47–55). At 17.4 Seneca asserts that "the mind must not be kept invariably at the same tension but must be diverted to play" and then cites as evidence the anecdote about Socrates playing with children, which Aelian draws from Athenodorus. It seems very likely that Seneca is not borrowing just the anecdote but also Athenodorus' reason for quoting it, since the reason Seneca gives matches the reason given in the anecdote about Heracles, which Aelian draws from Athenodorus. Thus, in both Aelian and Athenodorus the anecdote concerning Archytas is told in order to show that even a great statesman and philosopher rests his mind from more serious pursuits by play with children.

Can we trace the anecdote back beyond Athenodorus in the first century BC? We have no evidence to allow us to do so, but there is also no obvious reason to regard it as completely the invention of the later tradition. It is striking that Athenodorus did most of his work in Rome at about the same time that Cicero, Horace and Propertius all show interest in anecdotes about Archytas and is hence part of the renaissance of interest in Archytas during that period. It is a reasonable guess that Aristoxenus' *Life of Archytas* was the ultimate source for Athenodorus as it appears to have been for Cicero (A9a) and later for Athenaeus (A9).

Importance of the testimonium

The presentation of Archytas in this testimonium coheres well with other testimonia regarding him. It is emphasized that he was both a statesman and a philosopher (as in A1; see also Aelian *VH*, III. 17.6; VII. 14.2) and that he had a great number of slaves (as in A7). The particular focus of this testimonium is his delight in playing with his slaves' children, who were raised in the house (see A10). Aelian presents him as quite generally liking to play with the children but also highlights the only manifestation of this fondness that Athenaeus mentions: his having them let loose at dinner parties (*symposia*). The details are not given, but we are to imagine, surely, that he enjoyed giving them food and drink from the table as well as joking and playing with them.

It might be that we are to view this anecdote in light of Archytas' pronouncements on pleasure elsewhere. He expounds the dangers of bodily pleasure in A9a, but A7a shows that he valued the pleasures associated with intellectual inquiry. A8 may then be presenting yet another sort of pleasure which we should welcome, natural human enjoyment in our young. In Athenaeus this natural pleasure is contrasted with the unnatural pleasure of the Sybarites in miniature dogs and dwarves, which arises from their excessive luxury. It is just possible that A8 was introduced to develop this theme in Aristoxenus as well, since we know that, in his *Life of Archytas*, Aristoxenus presents a speech by Polyarchus, in which he describes the refinements of luxury to which people are driven by their desire for new pleasures (A9). If so, Athenaeus' source, Athenodorus, may have emphasized not just that great men need to rest by playing with children but followed Aristoxenus is emphasizing that the pleasure taken in such play is natural in contrast to the perverted pleasures spawned by luxury.

Detailed commentary

Athenaeus, line 3 τούτ<ων τοῖς παιδί>οις – Something like this correction of Casaubon must be read in order to introduce a reference to children. Aelian's version of the anecdote makes clear that it was the children of the slaves rather than the slaves themselves in whom Archytas took delight. A reference to children is also required by the context in Athenaeus, where the immediately preceding anecdote about Massinissa and the quotation from Eubulus (τρέφειν ἄνθρωπον . . . ἄνθρωπον) both refer to children.

3 παρὰ τὴν δίαιταν – The two basic meanings of δίαιτα are "way of living" and "dwelling" or "room." LSJ lists this passage under the first meaning and says that it should be interpreted as "at table." No justification is given for this interpretation, and it appears to be simply what was judged to be an appropriate meaning from the context. Gulick's translation of the passage in the Loeb, "when he was at meals," appears to follow LSJ. The expression "at table" is a bit redundant, given Athenaeus' reference to "dinner parties" at the end of the sentence, and the epitome keeps just παρὰ τὴν δίαιταν and eliminates εἰς τὸ συμπόσιον. Aelian's version of the story refers just to the symposium and has no analogue to παρὰ τὴν δίαιταν. It is not easy to find an exact parallel for the phrase παρὰ τὴν δίαιταν. A search of the TLG disk turns up only three other occurrences. One is a discussion of an etymology in Plutarch, which does not provide a real parallel (*Lyc.* XII. 1.7). The other two come from late medical treatises (Aet. II. 103.3; Dsc., *Mat. Med.* IV. 173.3.2) and refer to the application of a treatment παρὰ τὴν δίαιταν, where it must mean something like "in accordance with the regimen" or "in addition to the regimen." A passage in Plutarch sheds most light on the phrase, although it is not an exact parallel. In the treatise *Advice About Keeping Well*, wine is praised as the best of drinks provided that it is mixed with water and that pure water is taken between drinks of the wine and water mixture. We are then (132b) advised to accustom ourselves to drink two or three cups of water παρὰ τὴν καθ' ἡμέραν δίαιταν, which, in context, clearly means "in our daily routine." The interpretation of δίαιταν as "routine" is supported by the emphasis in the passage on the necessity of "accustoming" (ἐθιστέον) ourselves to drinking water and making it "habitual" (συνήθη). In light of this parallel, it is better to interpret the passage in Athenaeus as saying that Archytas not only delighted in children on the occasions when they were let loose at his dinner parties but also had them brought to his parties "as part of his routine."

4 τοῖς Μελιταίοις κυνιδίοις – These were popular lap-dogs (see e.g. Thphr. *Char.* 21.9 and Arist. *HA* 612b10). Pliny says that they came from the island of Melite (Meleda) off Dalmatia. Melite was also the name for Malta, however, and Strabo (VI. 2.11) says that the dogs came from there. See further Forster's (1927) note on Arist. *Prob.* 892a20.

5 ἀνθρώποις οὐκ ἀνθρώποις – This is a reference to the Sybarites' use of dwarves and other odd looking human beings as "ornaments" in their luxurious lifestyle. See Gulick's (1933) note on 519f.

Aelian, line 3 οἰκοτρίβων – The ancient lexicographers explain this as the Attic term for οἰκογενής, a slave born in the house. See also e.g. Luc. *Apol.* II.23.

A10 Aristotle, *Politics* VIII. 6 (1340b25–31; see also A1, A2 and B7)

ἅμα δὲ καὶ δεῖ τοὺς παῖδας ἔχειν τινὰ διατριβήν, καὶ τὴν Ἀρχύτου 1
πλαταγὴν οἴεσθαι γενέσθαι καλῶς, ἣν διδόασι τοῖς παιδίοις ὅπως 2
χρώμενοι ταύτῃ μηδὲν καταγνύωσι τῶν κατὰ τὴν οἰκίαν· οὐ γὰρ δύν- 3
αται τὸ νέον ἡσυχάζειν. αὕτη μὲν οὖν ἐστι τοῖς νηπίοις ἁρμόττουσα 4
τῶν παιδίων, ἡ δὲ παιδεία πλαταγὴ τοῖς μείζοσι τῶν νέων. 5

1 ἀρχύτα M^s P^1 Anchytae Guil. 2 γίνεσθαι P^1 Γ 4 ἁρμόττουσα τοῖς νηπίοις Π^1
5 παιδίων] P^1 παιδικῶν π^3 παιδιῶν cet.

At the same time it is also necessary that children have something to keep them busy and to think that the clapper of Archytas was a good invention, which they give to children, so that, since they are busy with this, they do not break anything in the house. For, the young cannot stay still. This clapper then is appropriate for younger children, but education is a clapper for older children.

Text A. *Corpus Paroemiographorum Graecorum* (Leutsch and Schneidewin) I. 213 (= Diogenianus II. 98.1; identical to CPG II. 615.6–9 = Michael Apostolius XIV.37.1)

Ἀρχύτου πλαταγή· ἐπὶ τῶν ἡσυχάζειν οὐ δυναμένων· ὁ γὰρ Ἀρχύτας τέκτων ὢν ἐπενόησε πλαταγήν, ἣν ἐδίδοσαν τοῖς παιδίοις, ἵνα μηδὲν τῶν κατὰ οἰκίαν σκευῶν διασαλεύσωσιν.

A clapper of Archytas: Applied to those who are not able to keep still. For, Archytas, being a carpenter, contrived a clapper, which they gave to children so that they would not upset any of the furnishings of the house.

Authenticity

The primary question is whether the clapper of Archytas, to which Aristotle refers in the *Politics*, is the work of Archytas the philosopher or of another Archytas, who was a carpenter, as is suggested by Text A. All other references to Archytas in Aristotle are to the philosopher, and we know that Aristotle wrote books on the philosophy of Archytas (see A13). We might then suppose that it would be very surprising if Aristotle were referring to a different Archytas here in the *Politics*, without giving any explicit indication to that effect. This argument would carry considerable force, if Aristotle were discussing a philosophical position in the *Politics*. Since the context is child-rearing and children's toys, however, it is quite possible that Aristotle would have assumed that such a context made clear to his readers that he was not talking about the philosopher but rather about a craftsman of the same name, who was famous for a clapper. Similarities in language make clear that the paroemiographical tradition represented in Text A ultimately derives from Aristotle (ἣν διδόασι/ἐδίδοσαν τοῖς παιδίοις ... τῶν κατὰ <τὴν> οἰκίαν), but it is perfectly possible that someone in the later tradition felt it necessary to explicitly label the Archytas in question as a carpenter rather than a philosopher, although Aristotle had not done so. Perhaps at a later date, the clapper was less well known, while Archytas had become famous in philosophical circles, and a commentator wanted to make clear that the clapper was not the work of the philosopher. In A1 Diogenes Laertius indicates that there was in circulation a treatise *On Mechanism* by another Archytas, an architect, and the tradition in Text A may represent someone's decision that this (ἀρχι)τέκτων was more likely to be the creator of the clapper.

Two pieces of evidence perhaps give a slight presumption in favor of regarding the clapper as the work of the philosopher, however. First, the anecdotes in A8 portray Archytas as exceptionally fond of children so that his invention of a clapper to keep them entertained would be in character. Second, Fragment 1 shows that Archytas was interested in the general phenomenon of percussion and the sounds that result from collisions of bodies. In that fragment he also mentions the bull-roarer, which is sometimes listed along with the clapper as a child's toy (see below). If the clapper is the invention of Archytas the philosopher, it hardly follows from the creation of a children's toy that he wrote an entire treatise *On Mechanism*. The work *On Mechanism* alluded to in A1 and B7 is more plausibly identified as the work of a separate Archytas, given what Diogenes Laertius says in A1.

Context

In Book VIII, Chapter 6 of the *Politics*, Aristotle is asking whether it is a good idea for the young to learn music by actually performing it themselves. He argues that the young must have some training in music in order to be good judges of it. In Testimonium A10, he then makes the additional point that education in general and hence learning to play musical instruments in particular keeps the young busy and out of mischief. The clapper of Archytas is introduced as an example of a toy which keeps very young children occupied so that they do not ruin the furnishings of the house. Education is presented as playing the same role for older children which the clapper plays for younger children, i.e. it keeps them busy and out of trouble.

Importance of the testimonium

There are two main questions regarding the content of Testimonium A10. First, what is the function of the "clapper of Archytas"? Second, what is the exact nature of this clapper? Regarding the first question, the testimonium presents us with Aristotle's account of the clapper's value, without indicating whether Archytas had precisely this purpose in mind when designing it. Frank is mistaken to ascribe Aristotle's reasoning explicitly to Archytas (1923: 339), but in the absence of any other evidence it is not implausible to assume that Archytas had a similar purpose. Aristotle's explanation rests on the assumption that the young are not able to keep still (see also Plut. *Mor.* 714e) and need something to keep them occupied lest they cause destruction. This applies to older children for whom education serves as a "clapper" to keep them occupied, but for younger children toys are needed. Since the children envisioned by Aristotle are capable of destroying the furnishings of the house, they must be older than infants. The clapper is then probably not comparable to a modern baby's rattle, which is usually associated with infants who are not yet or just barely walking. The clapper of Archytas seems designed to entertain a toddler (ages 2–4?), who can move about the house causing destruction and thus needs something to distract it. Plato too recognizes that the young are unable to keep body or voice quiet but regards these movements and cries as the raw material from which song and dance are developed (*Lg.* 653d–e). Nothing in Aristotle's report, however, suggests that he regarded the clapper of Archytas as playing a role in musical education or as a musical instrument, as some scholars have suggested (Brumbaugh 1966: 30; Trendall and Cambitoglou 1978: 315). The toy and musical education play a similar role in keeping young minds occupied, but this does not make the toy a musical instrument. The clapper of Archytas evidently became proverbial (Text A). To say that someone needs a "clapper of Archytas" suggests that she is not able to keep still.

No ancient source provides a description of the clapper of Archytas so that we must try to determine its nature by indirect means. Linguistic evidence suggests that πλαταγή is better translated "clapper" than "rattle," which has been the translation commonly used. The verb πλαταγέω, which is cognate with the noun πλαταγή, is used to refer to the clapping of hands (Theoc. 8.88) or the striking of the breast with the palm or fist in lamentation (Bion 1.4). This suggests that the "clapper" was a toy which produced noise by having two objects clapping together. Mathiesen's hypothesis that the πλαταγή was similar to "the modern castanets, which consist of a single castanet mounted on either side of a flat stick," thus seems quite plausible

(1999: 172). The suggestion is also supported by the gloss of πλαταγή with κρόταλον, which was a sort of clapper larger than modern castanets and perhaps similar to slapsticks (e.g. *Et. Mag.* 674.37; so also in the scholia to A.R. II. 1055). On *krotala* see Barker 1984: 17; Mathiesen 1999: 163 ff. and West 1992: 122 ff.

The other major text in which a πλαταγή is mentioned is Apollonius Rhodius' *Argonautica* II. 1055, where Heracles is described as shaking (τινάσσων) a bronze πλαταγή in order to scare away the Stymphalian birds. The scholion on this line of Apollonius tells us that the term πλαταγή was used in the fifth century, before Archytas, by the mythographers Hellanicus (*FGrH* 104) and Pherecydes of Athens (*FGrH* 72), in their descriptions of Heracles (See also D.S. IV. 13.2). According to some versions, the πλαταγή was made by Hephaestus and given to Heracles by Athena, but Hellanicus said that Heracles made it himself. What joins Archytas' πλαταγή to that of Heracles is the racket that it made. Such a noisemaker is precisely the thing not just to frighten away man-eating birds but also to make a child feel as if he is being naughty enough that he does not need to do damage to the house. It is striking that Archytas' fellow Tarentine, the poet Leonidas (*AP* VI. 309), writing about a century after Archytas, describes the πλαταγή along with a ball, dice and a bull-roarer as toys of youth (κουροσύνης παίγνια). Again there is an emphasis on the noise it makes, since it is described as "clapping well" (εὐκρόταλον). In Leonidas' poem the πλαταγή is made of wood (πυξινέην), and this may well be true of Archytas' πλαταγή as well. Plutarch also joins the clapper with the ball as children's toys (*Mor.* 714e).

Some scholars have wanted to identify Archytas' clapper with a ladder-shaped object, which appears in numerous Apulian vase paintings in the fourth century BC (e.g. Smith 1976: 129–32; Keuls 1979). The object appears in the context of musical instruments, and one vase has recently been identified in which the instrument appears to be played by plucking the rungs (for an illustration see Mathiesen 1999: 281). The case for connecting this instrument with Archytas' clapper (i.e. both come from Apulia in the fourth century) was never strong. It was always a difficulty that the ladder-shaped object was not presented in the context of children or toys, which is surely what we would expect, if it were Archytas' (or Leondias') clapper. It would also be surprising that a recent invention such as the clapper should find its way so quickly into the iconography of Apulian funerary ritual. Further scholarship has shown, moreover, that the ladder-shaped instrument depicted on Apulian vases had a forerunner, which has been found in graves in southern Italy dating to 500 years earlier. This instrument is also depicted on a Phoenician or Syrian box of the eighth century and may appear on fifth-century bone tablets from Olbia associated with Orphic ritual (West 1992: 126–27; West 1983: 17–19). This seriously undercuts the main argument for associating the instrument on the vases with Archytas' clapper, the supposed coincidence of Archytas' invention with the appearance of the object on the vases. We will now have to suppose that Archytas reinvented or modified a much earlier musical instrument and that the reinvention led to its prominence.

The instrument found in the graves had wooden rungs wrapped with delicate coils of bronze wire. As West suggests, these coils could have tinkled, if the instrument was shaken or if the player plucked at the rungs (Keuls 1979: 477, n. 12 and Mathiesen 1999: 280–82 also argue that the instrument was plucked). If the instrument on the vases was indeed of this construction and played in this way, it is quite implausible that it was Archytas' πλαταγή. The object on the vases would not clap as its name suggests it should, would be difficult for a child to play, and would not appear to make the raucous sort of noise required both by Heracles and young children. West (1992: 127–28) identifies it not with Archytas' clapper but with the *psithyrā* described by Pollux. Even if the instrument on the vases is not to be identified with the similar instruments from the graves (those in the graves are apparently smaller; see Mathiesen 1999: 282, n. 275), the method of playing the instrument depicted on the vases (i.e. plucking or striking the rungs) does not fit Archytas' "clapper," which is compared to *krotala*.

One final way to associate Archytas' clapper with the ladder-like object on the vases is to argue that the object on the vases is not primarily a musical instrument but rather part of the apparatus of Orphic initiations. This is contradicted by the vases mentioned above, where it clearly is a musical instrument. Orphic ritual did make use of toys, which were connected to the toys with which the infant Dionysus was playing, when attacked by the Titans. Commonly included among these toys are a ball, knucklebones and a bull-roarer (West 1983: 154 ff.). Archytas' clapper, however, is never mentioned in the written accounts of such Orphic toys. Smith argues, nonetheless, that Archytas' clapper, "the national toy," could not be left out in depictions of such toys on vases made in Archytas' native Apulia (1976: 146–47). He also makes much of Archytas' mention in Fragment 1 of the bull-roarer's use in initiations, but it is surely a gross overinterpretation of that passage to conclude that "Archytas frequented the *teletē*" (1976: 134). Fragment 1 allows us to conclude nothing more than that Archytas knew that the bull-roarer was used in initiations. Leonidas of Tarentum does include the clapper on his list of toys along with the ball, bull-roarer and knucklebones, but no Orphic connections are suggested in the poem. Sometimes toys are just toys. Aristotle suggests nothing about a cultic use for Archytas' toy. It is surely at least somewhat odd, moreover, to suppose that the infant Dionysus was playing with a toy that everyone knew had just been invented by Archytas.

A9 Athenaeus, *Sophists at Dinner* XII. 545a
(Aristoxenus Fr. 50, Wehrli)

Ἀριστόξενος δ᾽ ὁ μουσικὸς ἐν τῷ Ἀρχύτα Βίῳ ἀφι<κέσθαι φ>ησὶ παρὰ   1
Διονυσίου τοῦ νεωτέρου πρεσβευτὰς πρὸς τὴν Ταραντίνων πόλιν,   2
ἐν οἷς εἶναι καὶ Πολύαρχον τὸν ἡδυπαθῆ ἐπικαλούμενον, ἄνδρα περὶ   3
τὰς σωματικὰς ἡδονὰς ἐσπουδακότα καὶ οὐ μόνον τῷ ἔργῳ ἀλλὰ   4
καὶ τῷ λόγῳ. ὄντα δὲ γνώριμον τῷ Ἀρχύτᾳ καὶ φιλοσοφίας οὐ   5
παντελῶς ἀλλότριον ἀπαντᾶν εἰς τὰ τεμένη καὶ συμπεριπατεῖν τοῖς   6
περὶ τὸν Ἀρχύταν ἀκροώμενον τῶν λόγων. ἐμπεσούσης δέ ποτε   7
ἀπορίας καὶ σκέψεως περί τε τῶν ἐπιθυμιῶν καὶ τὸ σύνολον περὶ τῶν   8
σωματικῶν ἡδονῶν ἔφη ὁ Πολύαρχος· "ἐμοὶ μέν, ὦ ἄνδρες, πολλάκις   9
ἤδη πέφηνεν ἐπισκοποῦντι κομιδῇ <ἄτοπον> τὸ τῶν ἀρετῶν τούτων   10
κατασκεύασμα καὶ πολὺ τῆς φύσεως ἀφεστηκὸς εἶναι. ἡ γὰρ φύσις   11
ὅταν φθέγγηται τὴν ἑαυτῆς φωνήν, ἀκολουθεῖν κελεύει ταῖς ἡδον-   12
αῖς καὶ τοῦτό φησιν εἶναι νοῦν ἔχοντος. τὸ δὲ ἀντιτείνειν καὶ κατα-   13
δουλοῦσθαι τὰς ἐπιθυμίας οὔτ᾽ ἔμφρονος οὔτε εὐτυχοῦς οὔτε ξυνιέντος   14
εἶναι τίς ποτε ἐστὶν ἡ τῆς ἀνθρωπίνης φύσεως σύστασις. τεκμήριον   15
δ᾽ ἰσχυρὸν εἶναι τὸ πάντας ἀνθρώπους, ὅταν ἐξουσίας ἐπιλάβωνται   16
μέγεθος ἀξιόχρεων ἐχούσης, ἐπὶ τὰς σωματικὰς ἡδονὰς καταφέρεσθαι   17
καὶ τοῦτο νομίζειν τέλος εἶναι τῆς ἐξουσίας, τὰ δὲ ἄλλα πάντα σχεδὸν   18
ἁπλῶς εἰπεῖν ἐν παρέργου τίθεσθαι χώρᾳ. προφέρειν δ᾽ ἔξεστι νῦν μὲν   19
τοὺς Περσῶν βασιλεῖς [νῦν δὲ] καὶ εἴ τίς που τυραννίδος ἀξιολόγου   20
κύριος ὢν τυγχάνει. πρότερον δὲ τούς τε Λυδῶν καὶ τοὺς Μήδων   21
καὶ ἔτι ἀνώτερον καὶ τοὺς Σύρων· οἷς οὐδὲν γένος ἡδονῆς ἀζήτητον   22
γενέσθαι, ἀλλὰ καὶ δῶρα παρὰ τοῖς Πέρσαις προκεῖσθαι λέγεται τοῖς   23
δυναμένοις ἐξευρίσκειν καινὴν ἡδονήν· καὶ μάλα ὀρθῶς. ταχὺ γὰρ ἡ   24
ἀνθρωπίνη φύσις ἐμπίπλαται τῶν χρονιζουσῶν ἡδονῶν, κἂν ὦσιν   25
σφόδρα διηκριβωμέναι· ὥστε ἐπεὶ μεγάλην ἔχει δύναμιν ἡ καινότης   26

---

1 ἀρχύται A   ἀφι<κέσθαι φ>ησὶ] Casaubon   ἀφίησι A   10 <ἄτοπον>] Capps   <κενόν> Wilam.   13 εἶναι] Casaubon   εἰδέναι A   19 παρέργου] Kaibel   παρέργῳ ACE παρέργων Meineke   20 [νῦν δὲ]] del. Schweighauser   21 τοὺς Μήδων] Kaibel   τῶν Μήδων AE   23 λέγεται] A   om. CE

πρὸς τὸ μείζω φανῆναι τὴν ἡδονήν, οὐκ ὀλιγωρητέον [οὖν], ἀλλὰ 27
πολλὴν ἐπιμέλειαν αὐτῆς ποιητέον. διὰ ταύτην δὲ τὴν αἰτίαν πολλὰ 28
μὲν ἐξευρεθῆναι βρωμάτων εἴδη, πολλὰ δὲ πεμμάτων, πολλὰ δὲ θυμι- 29
αμάτων καὶ μύρων, πολλὰ δὲ ἱματίων καὶ στρωμάτων καὶ ποτηρίων 30
καὶ τῶν ἄλλων σκευῶν· πάντα γὰρ δὴ ταῦτα συμβάλλεσθαί τινας 31
ἡδονάς, ὅταν ᾖ ἡ ὑποκειμένη ὕλη τῶν θαυμαζομένων ὑπὸ τῆς ἀνθρω- 32
πίνης φύσεως· ὃ δὴ πεπονθέναι δοκεῖ ὅ τε χρυσὸς καὶ ἄργυρος καὶ τὰ 33
πολλὰ τῶν εὐοφθάλμων τε καὶ σπανίων, ὅσα καὶ κατὰ τὰς ἀπεργα- 34
ζομένας τέχνας διηκριβωμένα φαίνεται." 35
    Εἰπὼν δὲ τούτοις ἑξῆς τὰ περὶ τῆς θεραπείας τῆς τοῦ Περσῶν 36
βασιλέως, οἵους καὶ ὅσους ἔχει θεραπευτῆρας, καὶ περὶ τῆς τῶν 37
ἀφροδισίων αὐτοῦ χρήσεως καὶ τῆς περὶ τὸν χρῶτα αὐτοῦ ὀδμῆς 38
καὶ τῆς εὐμορφίας καὶ τῆς ὁμιλίας καὶ περὶ τῶν θεωρημάτων καὶ τῶν 39
ἀκροαμάτων, εὐδαιμονέστατον ἔφηκρῖναι τῶν νῦν τὸν τῶν Περσῶν 40
βασιλέα. "πλεῖσται γάρ εἰσιν αὐτῷ καὶ τελειόταται παρεσκευασμέναι 41
ἡδοναί. δεύτερον δέ," φησί "τὸν ἡμέτερον τύραννον θείη τις ἂν καίπερ 42
πολὺ λειπόμενον. ἐκείνῳ μὲν γὰρ ἥ τε Ἀσία ὅλη χορηγεῖ . . . τὸ δὲ 43
Διονυσίου χορηγεῖον παντελῶς ἂν εὐτελές τι φανείη πρὸς ἐκεῖνο συγ- 44
κρινόμενον. ὅτι μὲν οὖν περιμάχητός ἐστιν ὁ τοιοῦτος βίος φανερὸν 45
ἐκ τῶν συμβεβηκότων. Σύρους μὲν γὰρ Μῆδοι μετὰ τῶν μεγίστων 46
κινδύνων ἀφείλαντο τὴν βασιλείαν οὐκ ἄλλου τινὸς ἕνεκα ἢ τοῦ κυριεῦ- 47
σαι τῆς Σύρων ἐξουσίας, Μήδους δὲ Πέρσαι διὰ τὴν αὐτὴν αἰτίαν. αὕτη 48
δ᾽ ἐστὶν ἡ τῶν σωματικῶν ἡδονῶν ἀπόλαυσις. οἱ δὲ νομοθέται ὁμαλίζειν 49
βουληθέντες τὸ τῶν ἀνθρώπων γένος καὶ μηδένα τῶν πολιτῶν τρυφᾶν, 50
ἀνακῦψαι πεποιήκασι τὸ τῶν ἀρετῶν εἶδος· καὶ ἔγραψαν νόμους περὶ 51
συναλλαγμάτων καὶ τῶν ἄλλων [καὶ] ὅσα ἐδόκει πρὸς τὴν πολιτικὴν 52
κοινωνίαν ἀναγκαῖα εἶναι καὶ δὴ καὶ περὶ ἐσθῆτος καὶ τῆς λοιπῆς 53
διαίτης, ὅπως ᾖ ὁμαλής. πολεμούντων οὖν τῶν νομοθετῶν τῷ τῆς 54
πλεονεξίας γένει πρῶτον μὲν ὁ περὶ τὴν δικαιοσύνην ἔπαινος ηὐξήθη, 55
καί πού τις καὶ ποιητὴς ἐφθέγξατο· 56

δικαιοσύνας τὸ χρύσεον πρόσωπον. 57

καὶ πάλιν· 58

τὸ χρύσεον ὄμμα τὸ τᾶς Δίκας. 59

ἀπεθεώθη δὲ καὶ αὐτὸ τὸ τῆς Δίκης ὄνομα, ὥστε παρ᾽ ἐνίοις καὶ 6c
βωμοὺς καὶ θυσίας γίνεσθαι Δίκῃ. μετὰ ταύτην δὲ καὶ Σωφροσύνη καὶ 6ı

---

27 [οὖν]] del. Meineke   **30** ποτηρίων] CE   ποτηρίων δὴ A   ποτηρίων δὲ Kaibel
40 ἔφη κρῖναι] A   κρίνει CE   **42** ἡμέτερον] Musurus   ὑμέτερον A   **43** lacunam
indic. Casaubon   **47** ἀφείλαντο] A   ἀφείλοντο Kaibel   **52** [καὶ]] del.
Schweighauser   **59** τᾶς] τὰς A and Stob. *Ecl.* ı. 3. 37   **61–2** σωφροσύνη καὶ ἐγκράτεια]

Ἐγκράτεια ἐπεισεκώμασαν καὶ πλεονεξίαν ἐκάλεσαν τὴν ἐν ἀπολαύσ- 62
εσιν ὑπεροχήν· ὥστε τὸν πειθαρχοῦντα τοῖς νόμοις καὶ τῇ τῶν πολλῶν 63
φήμῃ μετριάζειν περὶ τὰς σωματικὰς ἡδονάς." 64

Cobet -ην . . . -αν codd.   **62** ἐπεισεκώμασαν] ACE ἐπεισεκόμισαν Dalechamp
ἐνεκωμίασαν Gulick   **63** τὸν πειθαρχοῦντα] E τῶν πειθαρχούντων C τὸν πιθαρχοῦντα
A

Aristoxenus, the writer on music, in his life of Archytas says that ambassadors from Dionysius the Younger came to the city of Tarentum, among whom was Polyarchus, nicknamed "the voluptuary," a man most zealous about the bodily pleasures not only in his actions but also in his discourse. Since he was an acquaintance of Archytas and not a complete stranger to philosophy, he presented himself at the sacred precincts, walked about with Archytas and his followers and listened to the discourses. Once, when the question for discussion and investigation concerned the appetites and in general the bodily pleasures, Polyarchus said, "It has often before appeared to me, gentlemen, as I examined the matter, that the contrivance of these virtues is quite absurd and far removed from nature. For, nature, whenever it speaks with its own voice, commands us to follow pleasures and says that this is the course of a sensible man. But to resist and enslave the appetites belongs neither to one who is intelligent nor to one who is fortunate nor to one who understands the constitution of human nature. A strong sign of this is the fact that all men, whenever they lay hold of a power that has sufficient magnitude, are carried towards bodily pleasures and think that this is the goal of their power and, to speak plainly, put pretty much everything else in a subordinate position. At the present time one can cite the Persian kings and anyone who happens to have become somewhere a tyrant that is worthy of mention. In earlier times there were the kings of Lydia and of the Medes and still earlier also the kings of the Assyrians. There was no type of pleasure that these kings did not pursue; indeed it is said that rewards were established for those who were able to discover a new pleasure, and rightly so. For human nature quickly gets its fill of pleasures which are repeated often, even if they have been excessively refined. So that, since novelty has great power to make pleasure appear greater, it must not be neglected but much attention must be paid to it. It is for this reason that many kinds of food, pastry, incense and perfume have been invented, and many kinds of clothes, rugs, wine cups and other furnishings. For, indeed, all of these things contribute some pleasure, whenever the material of which they are made belongs to those things admired by human nature. Certainly this seems to be the case with gold and silver and most of the things that please the eye and are rare, as many of them indeed as appear to be carefully wrought in accordance with the arts that perfect them."

When, following upon these things, he had spoken of the service given to the Persian king, of the type and number of his servants, of his practices regarding sexual pleasure, the fragrance of his flesh, the beauty of his form, the society he enjoyed, and the entertainments of sight and sound, he said that he judged the king of Persia to be the happiest man of that time. "For the greatest number and the most complete pleasures have been provided for him. In second place," he said, "someone might put our tyrant, although he is far behind. For both the whole of Asia pays for the former's enjoyment and . . . and the revenue of Dionysius would appear to be utterly trifling in comparison. Well then, that such a life is fought over is clear from what has happened in the past. For the Medes took for themselves the empire of the Assyrians, undergoing the greatest dangers, for no other reason than to become master of the power of the Assyrians, and the Persians took the empire of the Medes for the same reason. Such are the advantages of the bodily pleasures. But the lawgivers, wishing that human beings be reduced to one level and that no individual citizen live in luxury, have caused the class of virtues to rear its head. And they wrote laws about our dealings with one another and about as many other things as seemed to be necessary for political union and in particular about dress and the rest of our lifestyle so that it would be uniform. Therefore, since the lawgivers were at war with the clan of those who wanted more than their share, first the praise of justice was magnified and I suppose that some poet spoke of "the golden face of Justice" and again of "the golden eye of Justice." And then even the very name of Justice was deified, so that altars and sacrifices to Justice appeared among some peoples. After this Temperance and Self-control joined the revel and gave the name of greed to any preeminence in enjoyment, so that it is the one who is obedient to the laws and the voice of the multitude that is moderate in bodily pleasures."

Authenticity

For the reasons given in the introductory essays on authenticity and on Archytas' life, I think it not implausible that Aristoxenus preserves the general tenor of the arguments of both Polyarchus and Archytas (A9a). At the other extreme there is the possibility that Aristoxenus constructed the anecdote in the way that Plato constructed dialogues so that the meeting between Polyarchus and Archytas may have no historical basis and the views on pleasure assigned to Archytas might reflect a legendary Archytas of Aristoxenus' own invention. The parallel for the later type of construction would be Heraclides' story of the meeting between Leon of Phlius and Pythagoras that is designed to show Pythagoras as the inventor of the word philosophy (Fr. 44). Burkert has shown that this story is not historically accurate, since the conception of philosophy that it embodies seems to have been first developed by Plato over 100 years after the time of Pythagoras (1960). The motive for constructing such an anecdote is to assign an important advance in philosophy to the person in question, in this case Pythagoras.

It does not seem possible, however, to understand Aristoxenus' presentation of the meeting between Polyarchus and Archytas in this way. First, if we were to suppose that this confrontation was fabricated as the original on which Plato's portrayal of Callicles' discussion with Socrates in the *Gorgias* is based and thus intended to glorify the Pythagoreans (Wehrli 1945: 64), insuperable difficulties arise. Aristoxenus clearly sets the meeting of Polyarchus and Archytas in the reign of Dionysius the Younger (367–357 BC) some twenty years after the usual date of composition of Plato's *Gorgias* and some forty years after the supposed meeting of Socrates and Callicles in the dialogue. Thus, Polyarchus' speech and Archytas' response are not presented as the precursors of Plato's dialogue and Socrates' meeting with Callicles but rather as occurring considerably later. It thus becomes very hard to see how the anecdote can in any way glorify Archytas at Plato's expense. Indeed, if there were a strong similarity to Plato, it would just make Archytas look like a later imitator. Close examination of Archytas' response to Polyarchus shows that it is not just a rehash of Platonic and Aristotelian ideas and in fact contains a unique twist that is quite plausibly Archytas' own contribution (see A9a). Thus, while certainty is impossible, it seems most likely that what Aristoxenus presents is based on an oral tradition of a meeting between Polyarchus and Archytas. The main lines of the argument are likely to be historically accurate, although the speeches are largely Aristoxenus' creation.

Context in Athenaeus
Athenaeus' *Deipnosophistai* ("The Sophists at Dinner") was written at the end of the second century AD. It is structured as a symposium with a large number of guests but is largely a collection of excerpts from ancient authors on topics related to symposia. This passage from Aristoxenus' *Life of Archytas* comes from Book 12, which is introduced as devoted to "those who have become notorious for their luxury" (509d). The first part of Book 12 deals with the luxury of nations and cities, but, at 528e, the focus switches to the luxury of individuals. At 544a Athenaeus remarks that whole schools of philosophers have made the pursuit of luxury the goal of life and begins by discussing Aristippus and the Cyrenaics. Aristoxenus' account of Polyarchus is the next example. Athenaeus then goes on to discuss further

figures who made a philosophical defence of pleasure, notably Speusippus and Epicurus.

There is no reason to doubt that what Athenaeus presents here as from Aristoxenus' *Life of Archytas*, in fact, has its origin there. Examples of Athenaeus' quotations from authors we can check suggest that he quotes reasonably accurately but can abridge the quotations (e.g. 527c where Plato *Epist.* 326b ff. is quoted and 527d–e where *R.* 404d is quoted accurately but without the responses of the interlocutor and with minor changes). He quotes some passages in indirect discourse making appropriate changes but also summarizing and abridging in some cases (e.g. 541f where Diod. XI. 25 is quoted in indirect discourse and the last line in Athenaeus summarizes three or four lines in Diodorus). It certainly does not appear that Athenaeus is likely to introduce new material of his own.

In light of these examples the following observations can be made about the passage from Aristoxenus' *Life of Archytas*. Lines 1–9 reported largely in indirect discourse after φησί in line 1 are likely to reflect Aristoxenus' words fairly accurately with the appropriate changes made for indirect discourse. Since the speech assigned to Polyarchus beginning at line 9 starts with a reference to "these virtues," while no virtues have been mentioned in the preceding lines, it is possible that Athenaeus has abridged here in a way that omitted a reference to virtues in Aristoxenus. The distinctive features of the language in the first nine lines, however, such as Polyarchus' nickname, go back to Aristoxenus. The speech assigned to Polyarchus in lines 9–35 once again all seems likely to go back to Aristoxenus with perhaps some minor abridgement. Lines 36–41, which switch from the direct speech of Polyarchus to a summary of what he said, are more difficult to interpret. Is this a case of Athenaeus condensing and summarizing Aristoxenus or did Aristoxenus himself present this section in summary form? Certainty is impossible, but it seems hard to imagine how Aristoxenus could present any great elaboration on the materials in lines 36–41 or what purpose it would serve so that the indirect summarizing style of lines 36–41 may well be his. The direct speech of Polyarchus from line 41 to the end at line 64 once again seems likely to be largely Aristoxenus with the possibility of some abridgement. It is less clear whether Polyarchus' speech ended here in Aristoxenus. The last line is a possible ending but seems a little bit abrupt. One might expect a return to an assertion of the primacy of pleasure.

The argument of Polyarchus

Polyarchus starts with a condemnation of the traditional system of virtues as "far removed from what is natural." He will return to these unnatural virtues and their origin at the end of his speech, but the bulk of the first part of his speech concentrates on what nature calls for when she "speaks in her own voice," i.e. the pursuit of bodily pleasures. Polyarchus may mean that the study of the natural world as a whole suggests that pleasure is the proper goal, but the specific reference to the composition of human nature suggests that it is mainly human nature of which he is thinking. In some cases he refers simply to "pleasures," but his speech is introduced by a reference to specifically bodily pleasures (line 9) and the last two words of his speech are once again "bodily pleasures," so that there is little doubt that bodily pleasures are meant throughout. Polyarchus introduces a slightly paradoxical twist by emphasizing that the pursuit of such pleasures is, in fact, the mark of the sensible (νοῦν ἔχοντος) and prudent (ἔμφρων) as well as the fortunate man, of the man who understands the composition of human nature (lines 14–15). Polyarchus is asking us not to picture a crazed voluptuary but rather someone who calculates rationally that the pursuit of pleasure is the proper course in human life and who can pursue pleasure as part of a rational plan. This emphasis on the rational pursuit of pleasure is important, since Archytas' response attacks the possibility of just such a life of pleasure.

At line 15 Polyarchus turns to the arguments for his assertion that nature calls on us to pursue pleasure. The primary argument is that all men, once they gain any remarkable power, are borne toward the bodily pleasures and think that the pursuit of such pleasure is the goal of their power. There are two slightly different strands to this argument. First, Polyarchus is asserting that once humans get sufficient power they are naturally impelled toward bodily pleasures. This is a sort of "is to ought" argument. At the same time, the point is made that people who get such power also judge (νομίζειν) that the pursuit of bodily pleasure is the goal, so that once again Polyarchus emphasizes that the pursuit of pleasure is a rational choice. The kings of the Persians, Lydians, Medes and Assyrians are all cited as evidence, but it is the Persian king who is the primary example in the following passage. The thesis that pleasure is the central goal is then further supported by the observation that no sort of pleasure was left unexplored and that the Persians even offered rewards for the discovery of new pleasures. This continual search for new pleasures is based on a subsidiary point, that human nature becomes quickly sated with the same pleasure and that novelty has great power to increase pleasure. Polyarchus then lists the ways in which this search for novelty has led to the elaboration of pleasures through the creation of new kinds of food, incense, perfume, clothing, etc. Aristoxenus then reports that Polyarchus went on to describe the sexual practices of the Persian king, the company he kept and his various entertainments, before giving the final judgment that the Persian king was the happiest man of the day and that the tyrant of his own city of Syracuse was a distant second. As further evidence that such a life of pleasure is the goal of human action he cites the risks undertaken by the Medes to conquer the Assyrian empire, and by the Persians to take over the empire of the Medes in turn. Polyarchus rounds out this section of his argument with the exclamation that "such are the advantages of the bodily pleasures" (48–49).

At this point Polyarchus concludes by returning to the unnatural virtues that he mentioned at the beginning of his speech. They are stated to be the creation of lawgivers who wanted to keep all humanity at one level and allow no one to live in luxury. Such leveling in lifestyle is thought to be necessary to preserve political community (κοινωνία). As a result of their attempts at leveling, the lawgivers are at war with all attempts to gain more than one's share (πλεονεξία) and therefore introduce and literally deify virtues such as justice, temperance and self-control. Once again Polyarchus uses paradoxical language by suggesting that it is virtues like temperance and self-control that are the out-of-control revelers (ἐπεισεκώμασαν 62). They give the name of greedy to anyone who is exceptional in his enjoyments, while moderation in bodily pleasures is, in reality, only obedience to custom and to the voice of the masses.

This defense of *pleonexia* and the pursuit of pleasure by Polyarchus has been little studied (e.g. Gosling and Taylor 1982 make no mention of it) and what study there has been has quickly concluded that it is largely derived from Plato: Aristoxenus constructed the speech by plundering Plato's presentation of Callicles in the *Gorgias* for the greater glory of the Pythagoreans (Wehrli 1945: 64). It is therefore necessary to examine in some detail the relation between Polyarchus' argument and both earlier and contemporary defenses of *pleonexia*. Five conclusions emerge from such an examination. First, there is indeed a clear similarity between Polyarchus' arguments and the arguments of Callicles in the *Gorgias* and Thrasymachus in *Republic* I. Callicles appeals to what "nature herself reveals" (ἡ . . . φύσις αὐτὴ ἀποφαίνει, *Gorg.* 483d) just as Polyarchus champions what "nature commands when she speaks in her own voice" (11–12). Both regard the goal of life to be pleasure and both say that it is only the laws and not nature that fight against having more than one's share (πλεονεξία, *Gorg.* 483c). Just as Thrasymachus regards acting justly as simply yielding to the will of those who have political power (*R.* 343c), so Polyarchus says that the ones who are called moderate in bodily pleasures are just those who are obedient to the laws and the voice of the multitude (63–64).

A second conclusion, however, is that the constellation of ideas shared by Polyarchus and the Platonic Callicles and Thrasymachus is also found in passages in Aristophanes, Thucydides and Antiphon, which similarly make the case for following nature rather than conventional law and for rejecting temperance and pursuing *pleonexia*. Thus, in the *Clouds* (1075–78) the Weaker Argument praises what is necessary by nature (τὰς τῆς φύσεως ἀνάγκας), giving sexual pleasure as an example, and urges Pheidippides to obey his nature (χρῶ τῇ φύσει). The Weaker Argument also attacks temperance as producing no good (1061) and goes on to characterize laws as simply the expression of the will of those who have political power (1400 ff.). Similar themes are developed in Antiphon 44. Thucydides refers to a necessary law of nature to rule wherever one can (ὑπὸ φύσεως ἀναγκαίας, οὗ ἂν κρατῇ, ἄρχειν, v. 105) and says that the principle that the weaker be controlled by the stronger (τὸν ἥσσω ὑπὸ τοῦ δυνατωτέρου κατείργεσθαι) is in accord with human nature (ἀνθρωπείου τρόπου, I. 76). The language in these passages of Thucydides is as close to Plato's *Gorgias* (cf. 483d δίκαιόν ἐστι . . . πλέον ἔχειν . . . τὸν δυνατώτερον τοῦ ἀδυνατωτέρου/ τὸν κρείττω τοῦ ἥττονος ἄρχειν) as anything in Polyarchus' speech, yet no one would suppose that Plato is plundering Thucydides. Heinimann (1945: 145, n. 68) suggested that the similarities between Plato, the *Clouds*, Aristoxenus' presentation of Polyarchus' speech and other fourth-century accounts of pleasure are to be explained by assuming an early sophistic treatise as a common source. It is unnecessary and implausible to posit a single written source on which all the later presentations draw, however. All of these texts are better understood as largely independent representations of a thought pattern that was prominent in the late fifth and fourth centuries.

Third, while it is plausible enough that Aristoxenus was familiar with Plato's *Gorgias* and *Republic*, there is no indication that he composed the speech of Polyarchus with those texts in front of him or prominently in mind. What is conspicuously lacking in Polyarchus' speech are the specific trademarks of Plato's Thrasymachus and Callicles. Polyarchus does not call justice "the advantage of the stronger" or "another's good" as Thrasymachus does. Indeed justice, although present, is not the central focus at all. Similarly Polyarchus says nothing of the superior man who is so important to Callicles' view (483c) and who has often been compared with Nietzsche's superman. The contrast between the better and stronger man (βελτίονός τε καὶ κρείττονος) and the worse and weaker man (χειρόνων τε καὶ ἡττόνων, *Gorgias* 484c etc.) simply is not to be found in Polyarchus' speech. Yet, if Aristoxenus were using the *Gorgias* and *Republic* I as his models, it is just such central concepts that we would expect to appear. Indeed, the central focus of Polyarchus' speech is quite different from those of Callicles and Thrasymachus. Although pleasure does become a central topic in the discussion between Callicles and Socrates in the *Gorgias*, both Callicles and Thrasymachus make their case for *pleonexia* primarily in terms of who should have power in the state. Polyarchus' speech, on the other hand, is focused on arguments to show that pleasure is the goal of all our actions.

There was, in fact, a large body of literature devoted to the topic of pleasure later than Plato among Aristoxenus' immediate predecessors and contemporaries. A fourth conclusion is that the speech of Polyarchus is best understood as arising in the context of this literature. Aristotle reports Eudoxus' argument that pleasure is the good because all creatures, both rational and irrational, seek to obtain it (*EN* 1172b9). Polyarchus' argument can be seen as a refinement of this basic point, which focuses just on rational creatures, i.e. human beings, and examines those human beings who appear to be most free to pursue what they really want, i.e. tyrants with absolute power. There are other similar developments of Eudoxus' argument. In the same Book 12 of the *Deipnosophistai* from which A9 is derived, Athenaeus quotes passages from works entitled *On Pleasure* by both Theophrastus (511c) and Heraclides of Pontus (512a etc.). Only fragments of these works survive and they have been little studied. Gosling and Taylor dismiss them without discussion as providing ". . . no evidence of any development of the theoretical treatment of the topic, consisting as they do mostly of picturesque anecdotes . . ." (1982: 345). A passage from Heraclides' *On Pleasure* parallels Polyarchus' argument in stressing that tyrants and kings, who have experienced all the good things in life and have the power to choose whichever they want, value pleasure above all other things (Athenaeus 512a). At this point, however, the two arguments diverge. Heraclides goes on to explore the reason why tyrants and kings put such value on pleasure and concludes that it is because the enjoyment of pleasure makes human nature "more great-souled" (μεγαλοψυχοτέρας). There is no trace of this development in Aristoxenus, who instead has Polyarchus give further empirical support for the conclusion that kings value pleasure above all else by detailing their unending search for novelty in pleasure.

A fifth and final conclusion is that there are original and striking features of the language of the Polyarchus passage, which clearly suggest that Aristoxenus is giving us his own unique presentation of the argument for *pleonexia*. This originality of presentation is likely to be due partly to Aristoxenus' own invention and partly to the traditions concerning the life of Archytas on which he drew. First there is the character of Polyarchus himself and his unique epithet, "the voluptuary" (ὁ ἡδυπαθής). It is possible that Polyarchus is the complete invention of Aristoxenus, but it seems more likely to me that he is an historical figure and that his nickname is historical as well. The setting in Tarentum and the references to the tyranny of Dionysius II are also to be derived from the historical tradition. On the other hand, we must surely suppose that the specific formulation of the argument is due to Aristoxenus. One of the most original things about that formulation is the description of the lawgivers as "leveling" society (ὁμαλίζειν, line 49) and as trying to make the way of life "uniform" (ὁμαλής, line 54), a description which finds no parallel in Plato or other early developments of the nature/convention dichotomy (see the commentary on lines 49–55). If we should wonder why Aristoxenus developed the argument in this way, a clear and striking answer is available. Polyarchus' speech is constructed specifically as a challenge to Archytas, who is known to have advocated policies directed at diminishing the differences between rich and poor and to that extent leveling society. Thus, in Fragment 3 (lines 9–10), Archytas argues that the rich should give to the poor, and Aristotle (*Pol.* 1320b12) confirms that the Tarentines of his day made property common for the use of the needy. Other features of Polyarchus' language also suggest that Aristoxenus may have written the speech with specific passages of Archytas in mind (see the commentary on lines 51–53).

The figure of Polyarchus is thus Aristoxenus' own contribution to the series of powerful advocates of *pleonexia* which appear in fifth- and fourth-century Greek literature ranging from Thucydides' Athenians at Melos, to Aristophanes' "Weaker Argument" to Plato's Callicles and Thrasymachus. Aristoxenus' Polyarchus is just as original and as powerful as any of these other figures. What is remarkable is that Polyarchus is presented in such a favorable light (Momigliano 1993: 76). Aristoxenus does not go out of his way to blacken his character, and he is allowed to develop an effective argument for his position. Archytas' response is, in fact, not as impressive, although we only have it in Cicero's version (see A9a) and not in the original words of Aristoxenus. It may be, however, that Aristoxenus' *Life of Archytas* was less an exercise in hagiography and more an account of the controversies of the day than is usually assumed (for further discussion of A9, A9a and Fr. 3, see Huffman 2002b).

Detailed commentary

1–2 παρὰ Διονυσίου τοῦ νεωτέρου πρεσβυτὰς πρὸς τὴν Ταραν-τίνων πόλιν – Since Dionysius the Younger was tyrant of Syracuse from 367–357, the embassy to Tarentum, of which Polyarchus was a member, and Polyarchus' meeting with Archytas are imagined as occurring during these

years. There is no indication in A9 that Archytas was one of the leaders of
Tarentum at this time, although nothing said rules this out. It is not in his
official capacity as ambassador that Polyarchus visits with Archytas. The
implication is rather that, although the occasion for his visit to Tarentum
was the embassy from Dionysius II to Tarentum, Polyarchus, of his own
accord and separately from the other members of the embassy, went to the
sacred precincts where Archytas and his followers met in order to engage
in philosophical discussion.

3 Πολύαρχον – This is the only extant reference to Polyarchus of Syracuse
in Greek literature. A full corpus search of the TLG disk reveals twenty-six
occurrences of the name Polyarchus but none refer to a person matching
Aristoxenus' description.

ἡδυπαθῆ – There seems to be no other example of an individual receiv-
ing the epithet ὁ ἡδυπαθής, the "high-liver" or "the voluptuary." The
noun ἡδυπάθεια, "luxurious living," is not uncommon and was used as
the title of a work by Polyarchus' fellow Sicilian, Archestratus of Gela (cf.
Athenaeus 4e), ca. 350 BC, which is very close in date to the supposed meeting of Archytas and Polyarchus. Archestratus' work is in hexameters and
is described as a 'culinary tour of the mediterranean' (*OCD*). The adjective ἡδυπαθής appears in the comic writer Antiphanes (Fr. 91 = Athenaeus
526d), who was active between 400 and 350, in a description of a throng of
Ionians as "delicate" (ἁβρός) and "on pleasure bent" (ἡδυπαθής tr. Loeb).

5 γνώριμον – This adjective implies that Polyarchus was an acquaintance
of Archytas without suggesting any closer connection of friendship. See e.g.
Pl. *R.* 376a.

6 τὰ τεμένη – Aristoxenus makes clear that Archytas and his associates
met in various sacred precincts (τεμένη) in Tarentum in order to walk and
carry on philosophical discussions. A τέμενος is a piece of land cut off (cf.
τέμνω) and dedicated to a god or a hero (see Burkert 1985: 84 ff.). The limits
of the precinct can be marked either simply by boundary stones or by a wall.
At the entrance to the *temenos* were found water basins for purification. Its
most essential element was an altar where sacrifices were carried out, but
a temple could also be included. A *temenos* could be dedicated to several
gods and have several altars. One of its main functions was to serve as the
location for dedications to the god, including statuary.

Pausanias' usage of τέμενος and related terms in his travel guide to the
monuments of Greece (*Description of Greece*, ca. AD 150) helps to further clarify matters. The περίβολος, "enclosure," is used very similarly to τέμενος
but focuses more on the boundary, often indicating the boundary wall

(e.g. VII. 30.2), while τέμενος refers to the land enclosed (Jones 1918: I. xxvi). "Sanctuary" (ἱερόν) is also a close synonym to τέμενος but focuses more on the sacred nature of the site rather than simply indicating a geographical precinct. The two terms are used almost synonymously at VIII. 34.1. Pausanias' usage makes clear that τεμένη varied widely in size, contents and use. In some instances he describes what seems to be a quite small precinct dedicated to a hero (I. 18.2.2; I. 37.2.2). At the other extreme the entire sacred precinct of Apollo at Delphi, including the temple, treasuries etc., is described as a *temenos* (x. 9.3.1). In his description of the *temenos* of Itonian Athena, Pausanias mentions that it was used as a meeting place for the general assembly of Boeotia (IX. 34.1).

The various sacred precincts or sanctuaries in Tarentum would thus provide pleasant and uncrowded places for Archytas and his associates to meet. There is no implication that any religious scruple led to their meeting in "holy ground." I have not been able to find any other passage in which philosophers are described as meeting in places specifically described as τεμένη. It is true, however, that in Athens, Plato and his followers met in an area dedicated to the hero Academus and Aristotle and his followers met in a precinct dedicated to Apollo Lykeios. Plato's and Aristotle's schools are associated with the gymnasia built in these precincts, which came to be called the Academy and the Lyceum. A scholion to Demosthenes *Oration* XXIV. 114 emphasizes, however, that these gymnasia were (or were part of) sanctuaries (see Lynch 1972: 9). The scholion uses the term *hiera* for sanctuary, which emphasizes the sacred nature of the precinct, but it appears perfectly plausible that these precincts could also be described as *temenē*. It would appear then that Archytas is following the same practice as his contemporary Plato in meeting in the confines of a sacred precinct in order to carry out philosophical discussions. Such sanctuaries had also been used earlier by Socrates and the sophists for philosophical discussions and instruction (Lynch 1972: 32 ff.). There may also be earlier Pythagorean precedent for meeting in the sacred precincts. Iamblichus describes Pythagoras, upon his arrival in Croton, as giving a discourse to the boys of the town in the sanctuary (ἱερῷ) of Pythian Apollo and to the women in the sanctuary of Hera. He also describes Pythagoras and his associates taking their morning walks in sanctuaries (ἱερά) and groves because of the calm and later meeting in sanctuaries (ἱεροῖς) for instruction and lessons (*VP* 96; see Por. *VP* 32).

συμπεριπατεῖν – See Pl. *Prt.* 314e.

6–9 συμπεριπατεῖν . . . ἡδονῶν – These lines provide a precious and somewhat surprising glimpse into how Archytas practiced philosophy. It is commonly assumed that the practice of philosophy in the Pythagorean brotherhoods was quite different from what went on in the Academy and Lyceum. Lynch, for example, regards Pythagorean teaching as (1) closed to anyone who has not gone through a rigorous and secret initiation (2) strictly sectarian, presenting only the Pythagorean line on any issue (3) authoritarian, involving no discussion and embodying the *ipse dixit* mentality. Lynch relies primarily on a passage from the *Life of Plato* (61) attributed to Olympiodorus, which contrasts Plato's practice with that of the Pythagoreans. This view could also be supported from passages in Iamblichus' *Life of Pythagoras*. There are of course problems with the reliability of these sources, given their late date. Even more problematic is the tendency to treat all Pythagoreans at all times as following the same practices.

Aristoxenus is just about as reliable a source for Archytas as we are likely to get, although he, of course, had his own agenda. What is striking about Aristoxenus' presentation of Polyarchus' meeting with Archytas is that it contradicts the traditional picture of Pythagorean teaching on every point. First, although he is described as an acquaintance of Archytas, Polyarchus is not in any obvious sense an initiate into Pythagoreanism nor are Archytas' meetings with his associates presented as closed or secret. It is clearly public knowledge where Archytas meets with his followers, and Polyarchus simply shows up at the sanctuary in order to join the discussion. Second, the discussion is not strictly sectarian or just a presentation of the party line. Bodily pleasure is treated as a topic for discussion and investigation, and Polyarchus' very un-Pythagorean speech praising such pleasure is a clearly accepted part of the discussion. It follows that the method of instruction does not follow the *ipse dixit* format but involves give and take between the members of the discussion. Aristoxenus' presentation suggests that the discussion involved relatively long speeches by participants such as Polyarchus and Archytas, rather than the question and answer method used by Socrates in many Platonic dialogues. Aristoxenus' presentation of Archytas' "school" thus makes it look very much like the Academy as described by Lynch. One might wonder whether Aristoxenus is simply imposing educational practices found in the Academy or Lyceum on his account of Archytas, if Aristoxenus were not in such a good position to know what Archytas' practice actually was. Aristoxenus was raised in the Tarentum of Archytas, started out as a Pythagorean himself, and is, in all probability, writing only twenty or thirty years after the death of Archytas.

10 κομιδῇ – This adverb is most common with adjectives and should thus be taken with <ἄτοπον> ("quite absurd") rather than with ἐπισκοποῦντι.

32 ἡ ὑποκειμένη ὕλη – Aristoxenus shows his Aristotelian training with this collocation (see e.g. *EN* 1094b12; *Metaph.* 988a12). The phrase here refers to the material out of which a given object is made. The point is that not only the function of a given object contributes to luxurious living but also the material from which that object is made, if it is such as to excite human wonder. A gold drinking cup generates more pleasure than a pottery one.

37 θεραπευτῆρας – It is interesting that Aristoxenus uses the form θεραπευτήρ rather than θεραπευτής, since his fellow Tarentine, Archytas, uses κωλυτήρ rather than κωλυτής in Fragment 3, line 11.

43–45 ἐκείνῳ μὲν γὰρ ἥ τε Ἀσία ὅλη χορηγεῖ . . . , τὸ δὲ Διονυσίου χορηγεῖον παντελῶς ἂν εὐτελές τι φανείη πρὸς ἐκεῖνο συγκρινόμενον – The appearance of τε in the manuscripts suggests that a few words specifying another source of income for the Persian king have fallen out of the text.

48–49 αὕτη δ᾽ ἐστὶν ἡ τῶν σωματικῶν ἡδονῶν ἀπόλαυσις – αὕτη is best understood not as looking back to αἰτίαν but rather forward to ἀπόλαυσις. On this reading αὕτη is equivalent to τοιαύτη (see LSJ οὗτος c III), and the sentence becomes a concluding comment on the whole preceding discussion of the pursuit of pleasure by the Lydians, Medes, Assyrians and Persians: "such are the advantages of the bodily pleasures." In the Loeb, αὕτη is taken as referring back to αἰτίαν and further explicating the immediately preceding words (διὰ τὴν αὐτὴν αἰτίαν): "for the same motive, and the motive here is the enjoyment of pleasure" (tr. Gulick). The problem is that, in lines 47–48, we have already been given the reason why the Medes underwent the greatest dangers in obtaining the Assyrian empire, i.e. "to become master of the power of the Assyrians" (οὐκ ἄλλου τινὸς ἕνεκα ἢ τοῦ κυριεῦσαι τῆς Σύρων ἐξουσίας). It seems natural then that, in the parallel clause describing the Persians' conquest of the Medes (line 48), "the same cause" should be the one mentioned in the first part of the sentence, "to become master of the power of the Medes." There is thus no need for αὕτη to explain what "the same reason" is, it is the reason already given in the first part of the sentence.

49 ὁμαλίζειν – The image of "leveling" all human beings and making the lifestyle of each person "on a level" with others (see line 54) is unique to Polyarchus' presentation of the case for *pleonexia*. The verb ὁμαλίζειν does not appear in Plato's presentation of Callicles or Thrasymachus or indeed anywhere in Plato. Aristotle does use the verb a few times to refer to attempts, such as that of Phaleas, to equalize property in the state

(*Pol.* 1266b3). Since Archytas is likely to have favored some sort of at least limited redistribution of wealth from rich to poor (Fr. 3, lines 9–10), it is likely that Polyarchus' argument against leveling is designed specifically with Archytas' policies in mind.

51 ἀνακῦψαι – This verb means either "to lift the head up" (cf. Pl. *R.* 529d of lifting the head to look at decorations on a ceiling) or "to lift the head out of" (usually out of water, cf. Pl. *Phd.* 109d–e) or "to pop up" or "emerge." Plato memorably uses it of Protagoras popping up out of the ground as far as the neck in the midst of the discussion in the *Theaetetus* (171d). It seems likely that we are to understand the lawgivers as causing the class of virtues to "pop up" or "rear its head" above the plane to which they (the lawgivers) have leveled (ὁμαλίζειν, line 49) the human race. The point is that virtues are exalted rather than human beings.

51–53 . . . νόμους περὶ συναλλαγμάτων καὶ τῶν ἄλλων ὅσα ἐδόκει πρὸς τὴν πολιτικὴν κοινωνίαν ἀναγκαῖα εἶναι – The connection between νόμους περὶ συναλλαγμάτων and κοινωνίαν in this passage is reminiscent of the connection between ὁμόνοια and the συναλλάγματα achieved by calculation in Fragment 3 of Archytas.

54–55 τῷ τῆς πλεονεξίας γένει – The supporters of πλεονεξία are presented as an aristocratic clan against whom the lawgivers are battling. This continues the imagery introduced with the "human clan" which the lawgivers level and put under the class of virtues in lines 50–51.

57–59 δικαιοσύνας τὸ χρύσεον πρόσωπον . . . τὸ χρύσεον ὄμμα τὸ τᾶς Δίκας – These are quotations from Euripides' *Melanippe* (*TGF* p. 512) and Sophocles' *Locrian Ajax* (*TGF* p. 133), respectively.

62 ἐπεισεκώμασαν – We should accept this striking expression, preserved in all the manuscripts ("they joined the revel") rather than the more pedestrian emendation, ἐπεισεκόμισαν ("they introduced"). Since ἐπεισεκώμασαν is used intransitively elsewhere, we need to follow Cobet and read the nominatives Σωφροσύνη καὶ Ἐγκράτεια rather than the accusatives found in the manuscripts. The accusatives may have been mistakenly introduced after the immediately preceding accusative, ταύτην. It is a fine touch to have Polyarchus personify Temperance and Self-control (as Justice was personified by the poets) and paradoxically present them as out-of-control revelers. Plato uses the verb ἐπεισκωμάζω twice, once of a disorderly crowd of arguments (*Tht.* 184a) and once of pretenders to philosophy who have besmirched its name (*R.* 500b).

A9a Cicero, *Cato the Elder on Old Age* (12. 39–41)

39 Sequitur tertia vituperatio senectutis, quod eam carere dicunt volup- 1
tatibus. o praeclarum munus aetatis, siquidem id aufert a nobis quod est 2
in adulescentia vitiosissimum! accipite enim, optimi adulescentes, veterem 3
orationem Archytae Tarentini, magni in primis et praeclari viri, quae mihi 4
tradita est cum essem adulescens Tarenti cum Q. Maximo. nullam cap- 5
italiorem pestem quam voluptatem corporis hominibus dicebat a natura 6
datam, cuius voluptatis avidae libidines temere et ecfrenate ad potiundum 7
incitarentur. 8

40 Hinc patriae proditiones, hinc rerum publicarum eversiones, hinc 9
cum hostibus clandestina colloquia nasci, nullum denique scelus, nullum 10
malum facinus esse, ad quod suscipiendum non libido voluptatis impelleret; 11
stupra vero et adulteria et omne tale flagitium nullis excitari aliis illece- 12
bris nisi voluptatis; cumque homini sive natura sive quis deus nihil mente 13
praestabilius dedisset, huic divino muneri ac dono nihil tam esse inimicum 14
quam voluptatem. 15

41 Nec enim libidine dominante temperantiae locum esse, neque 16
omnino in voluptatis regno virtutem posse consistere. quod quo magis 17
intellegi posset, fingere animo iubebat tanta incitatum aliquem voluptate 18
corporis quanta percipi posset maxima: nemini censebat fore dubium quin 19
tamdiu, dum ita gauderet, nihil agitare mente, nihil ratione, nihil cogita- 20
tione consequi posset. quocirca nihil esse tam detestabile tamque pestiferum 21
quam voluptatem, siquidem ea cum maior esset atque longinquior, omne 22
animi lumen exstingueret. haec cum C. Pontio Samnite, patre eius a quo 23
Caudino proelio Sp. Postumius T. Veturius consules superati sunt, locu- 24
tum Archytam, Nearchus Tarentinus hospes noster, qui in amicitia populi 25
Romani permanserat, se a maioribus natu accepisse dicebat, cum quidem ei 26
sermoni interfuisset Plato Atheniensis, quem Tarentum venisse L. Camillo 27
Ap. Claudio consulibus reperio. 28

For a full apparatus and discussion of the text see Powell 1988. Portions of the text are also preserved in the ancient grammarians: **7–8**   avidae . . . incitarentur] Charisius (198 Keil);   **10–11** nullum denique . . . impelleret] Nonius (309 Mercier);   **12–17**   stupra vero . . . posse consistere] Lactantius *Inst. Div.* vi. 20.4–5 (see Powell 1988). There is also a literal translation of the entire *De Senectute* into Greek by Theodore of Gaza (fifteenth century AD – see Salanitro 1987).

39   There follows the third censure of old age, that they say it is bereft of pleasures. O great service of old age, if indeed it takes away from us what is the greatest defect of youth. For listen, most excellent young men, to an ancient discourse of Archytas of Tarentum, a particularly great and outstanding man, which was handed down to me, since as a young man

I was with Q. Maximus at Tarentum. Archytas used to say that no more deadly curse had been given to men by nature than bodily pleasure, since, eager for this pleasure, our lusts spur themselves on blindly and without restraint to possess it.

40   From this source are born betrayal of the fatherland, from this the overthrow of the state, from this secret conversations with the enemy. To sum up, there is no crime, no evil deed which the lust for pleasure does not drive us to undertake. Debauchery, indeed, and adultery and all such shameful behavior are aroused by no other allurements than those of pleasure. And, although nothing more excellent has been given to man than intellect, whether it be by nature or by some god, there is nothing so opposed to this divine benefaction and gift than pleasure.

41   For, neither is there a place for self-control where lust is master, nor is virtue able to gain any foothold under the tyranny of pleasure. In order to make this better understood, he used to tell people to picture someone spurred on by the greatest bodily pleasure that can be perceived. He was of the opinion that no one would have any doubt that, so long as he was enjoying himself in this way, he would not be able to think about anything, to achieve anything by calculation, anything by deliberation. Wherefore, nothing is so detestable and so pernicious as pleasure, since indeed it, when very intense and prolonged, extinguishes all the light of the soul. Nearchus of Tarentum, my host, who had persevered in his friendship to the Roman people, said that he had heard from his elders that Archytas said these things in the presence of C. Pontius the Samnite, the father of that one by whom the consuls Spurius Postumius and T. Veturius were defeated in the battle of the Caudine Forks. Indeed he said that Plato the Athenian had been present at the conversation, whom I discover to have come to Tarentum in the consulship of L. Camillus and Ap. Claudius.

Authenticity and Cicero's source
Aristoxenus of Tarentum, in his *Life of Archytas*, also presented a speech of Archytas attacking pleasure. The section of the *Life of Archytas* containing Archytas' speech has not survived, but we know that the speech existed. A speech of one Polyarchus of Syracuse identifying pleasure as the proper goal of our life, expressly identified as from the *Life of Archytas* and said to have been delivered in a discussion of pleasure with Archytas has been preserved (see A9). There would be no reason for Aristoxenus to include this speech of Polyarchus in a *Life of Archytas*, unless he also gave Archytas' response. Most scholars have assumed that the speech against pleasure which Cicero presents in the *De Senectute* must be based on Aristoxenus, although

they recognize that Cicero considerably reworked the speech (e.g. DK 1. 424; Wehrli 1945: 65; Burkert 1961: 239). Such a view has a great deal of plausibility. Granted that Aristoxenus did present a speech by Archytas on pleasure, it is far simpler to assume that Cicero is drawing on this speech than to arbitrarily posit an otherwise unattested second speech by Archytas on pleasure from which Cicero draws. How many different speeches by Archytas attacking bodily pleasure are we to suppose were preserved in the tradition? If we argue that Cicero invented the speech himself, it then seems a remarkable coincidence that he should have put it into the mouth of Archytas, rather than assigning it to a number of other philosophers or even to Cato himself.

Powell, in his excellent edition of *De Senectute*, argues, however, that we should be skeptical both about the content of Archytas' speech and about whether or not Aristoxenus is Cicero's source (1988: 183–84). Powell argues that the content of Archytas' speech can be found in other passages in Cicero and is all ultimately derived from Plato or his followers. There is nothing in the speech that can be identified as distinctively Archytan. This suggests that Cicero himself might have composed the speech based on texts of Plato. Powell recognizes, however, that Aristoxenus elsewhere tries to undercut the originality of Plato and that he might thus be responsible for composing for Archytas a speech on pleasure, which is full of Platonic ideas, in order to suggest that Archytas was the originator of these ideas. On this latter reading, Aristoxenus might still be Cicero's source. Powell is skeptical, however. He argues that it is nothing more than a guess that Aristoxenus is Cicero's source. The only known connection between Cicero and Aristoxenus is that they both present a speech of Archytas on pleasure, and the setting for the speech is described quite differently in the two authors.

Powell's skepticism is misplaced on both points, however. The central argument of Archytas' speech in Cicero is not Platonic; there is independent evidence suggesting that Archytas originated the argument himself. It is also very probable that Cicero is relying directly on Aristoxenus. To begin with the second point, the connections between Cicero and Aristoxenus are closer than Powell recognizes. This is shown both by features internal to Archytas' speech in Cicero and by external evidence for Cicero's knowledge of Aristoxenus. First, Archytas' speech in Cicero has close connections to what we would have expected from Archytas' response to Polyarchus in Aristoxenus. We should not overlook an obvious point of similarity between Cicero and Aristoxenus: in both, Archytas' views on pleasure were presented in the form of a speech rather than as deriving from a written text. In Aristoxenus Archytas' views were presented in a speech in response to Polyarchus. Cicero clearly refers to a speech (*orationem*, line 4) given by Archytas in the presence of Plato and C. Pontius, and he implies that the speech was handed down through oral tradition. Powell oddly says that "there is nothing in Cicero's wording here to imply that Archytas' speech was not envisaged as being handed down in writing" (1988: 184). If Cicero is assuming a written tradition, why does he emphasize Cato's actual visit to Tarentum and that Nearchus was Cato's host? Cato could have had access to a book by Nearchus independent of a visit to Tarentum or to staying with Nearchus. Again, Nearchus is said to have received the information that C. Pontius and Plato were present at the speech from "his elders," and both this and the fact that the verb used here for "receive" (*accepisse*) is the same that Cato uses when he begins his oral presentation of Archytas' speech (*accipite . . . optimi adulescentes*) clearly suggest an oral tradition.

The content of the speech in Cicero is also in accord with what we would expect to have been in the speech in Aristoxenus. Archytas' speech in Cicero specifically attacks pleasures of the body (6 *voluptatem corporis*, 18–19 *voluptate corporis*), rather than attacking the body in general (including its fears and imaginings etc. as well as pleasures), as Plato does in the *Phaedo* (66b ff.). This connects what is found in Cicero with the speech of Polyarchus in Aristoxenus' *Life of Archytas*, since Polyarchus is precisely making the case for bodily pleasure (σωματικὰς ἡδονάς, A9, line 4 etc.). Again, Polyarchus is arguing that the life of pleasure is the rational choice (see A9, lines 13–15), and Cicero's Archytas is making the point that there is nothing more hostile to reason than pleasure (lines 14–15). Finally, Polyarchus argues that people pursue political power in order to gain pleasure (A9, line 15 ff.), and Cicero's Archytas may be pointing out the self-defeating nature of coupling pleasure with political power, by emphasizing the disastrous consequences for the state which result from the pursuit of pleasure (lines 9–10). Thus, Archytas' speech in Cicero works very well as a specific response to Polyarchus and is not a general attack on the body such as is found e.g. in Plato's *Phaedo*.

There is also considerable external evidence that Cicero knew of Aristoxenus' work in general and his *Life of Archytas* in particular. Eight passages from Cicero are listed in Wehrli's collection of Aristoxenus' fragments (this number does not include A9a, which Wehrli regards as derived from Aristoxenus but does not quote, because he thinks that Cicero only followed the original in general outlines 1945: 65). Cicero mentions Aristoxenus as a great teacher and musician and also for his views on the soul (*Ep. Ad Att.* VIII. 4.1; *De Or.* III. 33.132; *De fin.* V. 18.49; *Tusc.* I. 22.51, I. 11.24, I. 10.19, I. 18.41). In addition, while there is no direct evidence for Cicero's having read treatises by Aristoxenus, we have explicit evidence that Cicero read treatises by Dicaearchus (*Ep. ad Att.* XIII. 32 – Dicaearchus' *Letter to Aristoxenus* is mentioned), who was a contemporary of Aristoxenus and fellow member of the Lyceum. Thus, Cicero read works of the provenance of the fourth-century Peripatetic school.

Moreover, Cicero seems to have had considerable information about the life of Archytas. He quotes two further anecdotes about him (*Laelius* 88, *Tusc.* IV. 78, *Rep.* I. 59) and is as willing to talk of the life of Archytas as the life of Plato (*Tusc.* V. 64). Yet, the only life of Archytas which we know is that of Aristoxenus. Most significantly of all, one of the anecdotes, the story of Archytas' refusal to punish his servants when angry, which is cited twice by Cicero (*Tusc.* IV. 78, *Rep.* I. 59), is almost certainly from Aristoxenus (see A7). One final piece of evidence connecting Cicero to Aristoxenus is the fact that, in his famous debunking of the connection between Numa and Pythagoras at *Rep.* II. 28, Cicero relies on the tradition that Pythagoras came to southern Italy in 532. Aristoxenus seems to be the source of this dating, although he undoubtedly gave the date not in his *Life of Archytas* but rather in one of his other works on the Pythagoreans (Fr. 16, Wehrli; see Burkert 1972a: 110). One can only conclude from this evidence that Cicero is either using Aristoxenus' *Life of Archytas* and his other writings on the Pythagoreans directly, or that he is using other sources which relied on Aristoxenus heavily.

Cicero is not the only Roman author in the first century BC who mentions Archytas. There appears to be a renaissance of interest in him (see my introductory essay on Archytas' life). Burkert has argued that this may represent a conscious attempt by first-century Romans to claim Pythagoreanism as a native Italian philosophy (1961; see also Powell 1995: 11 ff.). Where did they get their information about Archytas? Since we know of no other life of Archytas in antiquity, it is surely tempting to suppose that Aristoxenus' *Life of Archytas* played a major role here. Suetonius, writing at the beginning of the second century AD, regarded Aristoxenus as the foremost biographer of the Greeks (St. Jerome, *De Viris Illustribus* [praefatio]; see Momigliano 1993: 73). Thus both the internal characteristics of Archytas' speech in Cicero and the external evidence for Cicero's knowledge of Aristoxenus' work show that Powell has understated the evidence for a connection between Cicero and Aristoxenus.

Nor is the content of Archytas' speech in Cicero all derived from Plato or his followers. To be sure, Powell is right to point out that the similarities between what we find in Archytas' speech in *De Senectute* and Cicero's early work *Hortensius* (Fr. 84) are indeed striking (note especially the use of the word *illecebrae* and the sentence *quis enim, cum utatur voluptate ea qua nulla possit maior esse, attendere animum, inire rationes, cogitare omnino quidquam potest?*), but this does not show that Cicero composed the speech from Platonic ideas. If Cicero knew of Archytas' speech from Aristoxenus, he could perfectly well have used ideas from it in the *Hortensius* without citing the source and still, in the *De Senectute*, explicitly mention Archytas. Further, while much of what Archytas says against bodily pleasure in Cicero has, unsurprisingly, a general similarity to what is said in the long tradition of attacks on bodily pleasure (including Plato's), there is no direct parallel to either Plato's or Aristotle's developed theory of pleasure, and the central idea of Archytas' speech can quite plausibly be assigned to Archytas himself (see below). The most reasonable explanation of what we find in Cicero is that he is drawing on Aristoxenus' presentation of Archytas' speech in response to Polyarchus.

Cicero's usual treatment of his sources suggests that we would not expect him to give a literal translation of Aristoxenus but rather adapt the original for his own purposes. At the same time he tends to maintain the substance of the original (Powell 1988: 111–13). It hence seems likely that the main points in Cicero's presentation of Archytas' speech go back to Aristoxenus. Cicero was then presented with the problem of integrating this speech of Archytas into the literary context of the *De Senectute*. Cicero's particular problem was to explain how his speaker, Cato, had access to Archytas' speech. To assert that Cato had knowledge of the speech from his reading of a second-tier Peripatetic such as Aristoxenus, would make Cato out to be more of a scholar of Greek philosophy than his Roman audience would be willing to accept; we know that Cicero was concerned lest Cato seem too learned (*Sen.* 3). The natural solution to the problem is to exploit Cato's historical connection to Archytas' home city of Tarentum, or to invent such a connection (Powell, 1988: 274–75, thinks that the connection is historical but provides bibliography for other views). Cicero thus constructs an oral tradition about Archytas' speech that reaches from the time of Archytas' prominence in Tarentum, in the middle of the fourth century, down to Nearchus, who served as Cato's host on his visit to Tarentum as a soldier in 209. It seems best to follow Powell in regarding Nearchus as a historical figure (1988: 182–83, 187), but there is no reason to follow Salmon (1967: 120–21) in ascribing a written work to Nearchus on which Cicero drew. There is simply no evidence for this work.

Cicero then constructs the circumstances in which Archytas delivered his speech in order to emphasize two points, which are revealed by other passages to have been dear to Cicero's heart. First, he makes Plato a member of

Archytas' audience, in order to stress Plato's dependence on the Pythagoreans. Cicero underlines this same point at *Rep.* I. 16, where he again has Plato
visit Archytas. Second, he makes the Samnite C. Pontius Archytas' other
auditor. He thus displays the influence of Pythagoreanism on the Italian
peoples as he does elsewhere (*Laelius* 13, *Tusc.* IV. 2–3), making Pythagoreanism a sort of native Italian philosophy. There is a tradition of Pontius'
great wisdom (cf. Livy IX. 1) which is independent of Cicero, but it might
be Cicero's innovation to explain this as the result of contact with Archytas.
Thus, the circumstantial details that Cicero provides for Archytas' delivery
of his speech against pleasure and for Cato's knowledge of that speech all
derive, as we would expect, from Cicero's purposes in the *De Senectute* itself,
but the core of the speech itself goes back to Aristoxenus.

It is instructive to compare Cicero's practice here with a passage in
Plutarch's *Life of Cato* (2.3). Plutarch describes Cato's trip to Tarentum
and meeting with Nearchus in a way that clearly shows his dependence
on Cicero's *De Senectute* (Powell 1988: 182). When Plutarch turns to the
account of the speech on pleasure, however, he makes some very interesting
changes. First, he makes no mention of Archytas and assigns the speech to
Nearchus himself, whom he calls a Pythagorean, although Cicero does not.
Second, he describes Nearchus as using language "which Plato also used."
Thus, by replacing Archytas with the unknown and much later Nearchus,
Plutarch has done the opposite of Cicero: he has made Plato the central
figure upon whom later Pythagoreans are shown to depend. Third, while
Plutarch's assertion that pleasure is "the greatest incentive to evil" does
match what Archytas says in Cicero, Plutarch completely omits the main
argument of Archytas' speech in Cicero and replaces it with an argument
not found in Cicero but clearly taken from Plato's *Phaedo*. There is nothing
in Plutarch about Archytas' thought experiment, according to which we
imagine someone enjoying the greatest possible pleasure. Instead, Plutarch
reports that Nearchus called the body the chief detriment to the soul and
said that the soul can only be freed and purified from contamination of the
body by those reasonings which most separate the soul from bodily sensations. Nearchus is here made to mirror the argument in Plato's *Phaedo*
(64c ff.), which is directed not just at pleasure but at the body as a whole
and which urges us to prepare for death by trying to separate the soul
from the body. Plutarch is a Platonist and knows his Plato very well. What
he has done is to deny Cicero's implicit claim that Plato was dependent
on the Pythagoreans and to replace Archytas' argument against pleasure,
which he knew was not in Plato, with the strongest Platonic denuncia-
tion of pleasure and the body. Far from finding Archytas' argument to be

simply derived from Plato, Plutarch has to replace what he finds in Cicero, which accurately preserves Archytas' argument, with the real Plato of the *Phaedo*.

Cicero's explicit dating of Archytas' speech to 349, by mentioning the consuls for that year, is puzzling. Aristoxenus presents Polyarchus as coming from the court of Dionysius the Younger so that Archytas' speech would thus naturally fall in the years 367–357, when Dionysius was in power. As we have seen, however, Cicero is not likely to be bound by what Aristoxenus says for circumstantial details. Cicero's date can be explained in two ways. Either Cicero knew of a tradition assigning a visit of Plato to Italy to 349 or Cicero himself introduced the date for his own literary purposes. Cicero also mentions a visit of Plato to Archytas in *De Republica* I. 16 (A5bi). No precise date is given, but it is certainly implied that the visit is earlier than 349, since it is tied to Plato's travels after the death of Socrates. Münzer (1905: 54) suggested that, in the interval between the *De Republica* (54–51) and the *De Senectute* (44), Atticus published his *Liber Annalis* and that Cicero got the precise dating of 349 for Plato's visit from Atticus. Others have suggested that Atticus' dating may ultimately rely on Varro (Fantham 1981: 7, 11). That Cicero drew on Atticus or some other tradition for the date of 349 is also supported by Cicero's use of the verb *reperio* (line 28), which suggests some investigation (Powell 1988: 279). Powell points out that Aulus Gellius (*NA* 17.21) records a visit of Plato to Italy between 354 and 338 and suggests that this refers to the same tradition that appears in Cicero. Gellius, however, says that Plato went to Sicily rather than Italy and says that the visit was to Dionysius the Younger. The testimony of Gellius is thus internally contradictory, since Dionysius left power in 357. Whether Cicero is relying on an earlier tradition or not, most scholars have doubted the plausibility of such a visit, since Plato would have been 78 or 79 years old at this date (see Gudeman 1913 for an explanation of how the date could have arisen in error). The second possibility is that Cicero himself introduced the date of 349. He knew that Plato had visited Sicily and southern Italy several times and while leaving the exact date vague in the *De Republica* assigned a visit to 349 in the *De Senectute* in order to make plausible the presence of C. Pontius the Elder, who is likely to have been born around 380 and who thus would been in more of a position to appreciate Archytas' speech in 349 than the 360s.

De Vogel (1966: 141, 176–77) argues that Cicero's whole account is based on local Tarentine oral tradition. Such a scenario has great *prima facie* improbability, given the three hundred years between Archytas and Cicero. Even more importantly, she takes no account of Cicero's clear artistic purposes, which I have sketched above, and makes no mention of Aristoxenus' *Life of Archytas*. Cicero's report of the circumstances in which Archytas delivered his speech is a product of his literary goals in the *De Senectute* and cannot be treated as evidence for Archytas' life. The speech which he assigns to Archytas, however, is likely to be based on the speech of Archytas against pleasure in Aristoxenus' *Life of Archytas*.

Context
In the *De Senectute* Cicero puts his defense of old age in the mouth of Cato the Elder (3). Cato is envisaged as conversing with Laelius and Scipio Aemelianus in the year AD 150, when Cato was appropriately 84 years old, just one year before his death. Towards the beginning of *De Senectute*, Cato had identified four reasons why old age is thought to be miserable (15). His strategy is to consider each of these reasons in turn and ultimately to show that they are mistaken. The speech of Archytas on pleasure is presented at the beginning of the discussion of the third reason for condemning old age, i.e. that it is bereft of sensual pleasures. After presenting Archytas' speech on pleasure, Cato/Cicero says (42) that he has cited the speech to show that we should, in fact, be grateful to old age, since "it brings it about that we do not want to do what we ought not." Archytas' speech is taken to show that pleasure hinders our reason (*impedit . . . consilium*) and has "no fellowship with virtue." Cicero thus agrees that old age is lacking in the pleasures of the body but thinks that, in light of the dangers of such pleasures outlined by Archytas, we should be grateful that old age lacks them. He will go on to argue that some pleasures still remain for old people (44).

The structure and content of Archytas' speech on pleasure
It is important to recognize that Archytas' speech is specifically directed against bodily pleasure rather than pleasure in general or the body in general (*voluptatem corporis*, line 6; *voluptate corporis*, lines 18–19). The structure of the speech is as follows:

1. A succinct statement of the dangers of bodily pleasure: it causes us to act blindly and without restraint (*temere et ecfrenate*).
2. Examples of the evils to which we are driven by pleasure:
   (a) Betrayal and overthrow of the state
   (b) Sexual crimes: debauchery and adultery
3. There is nothing so opposed to the best part of us, i.e. intellect, than pleasure.
   (a) Political analogies: where lust is master there is no place for self-control. Virtue cannot live under the tyranny of pleasure.

(b) A thought experiment to show that pleasure is opposed to intellect: if we imagine someone under the influence of the greatest pleasure, there is no doubt that, in such a state, he would not be able to consider anything with his mind or achieve anything by calculation or deliberation. Therefore, nothing is so pernicious as pleasure, since extreme and prolonged pleasure extinguishes the light of the soul.

The central assumption of the speech is that it is reason or intellect which should govern our lives along with the self-control necessary to follow the dictates of reason. Lust for pleasure lacks both the intelligent planning of reason and the restraint of self-control and thus acts "blindly and without restraint." Cicero's/Aristoxenus' presentation shows close connections to Archytas' description of calculation (λογισμός) in Fragment 3, which suggests that Aristoxenus may have composed the speech by paying close attention to what Archytas had written. Under the influence of pleasure, we act blindly and heedlessly (*temere*) of calculation as the standard (κανών) which should guide our behavior and also unrestrained (*ecfrenate*) by calculation as what prevents (κωλυτήρ) us from acting unjustly (Huffman 2002b: 267). The political analogies that Cicero develops next make clear that the central issue is not whether bodily pleasures are in some sense good, but whether they should be the ruling factor in the soul and whether virtue can have any role where pleasure is the controlling goal. This emphasis makes sense as a response to Polyarchus, who celebrates bodily pleasure precisely as the goal of all our power (τέλος . . . τῆς ἐξουσίας, A9, line 18), while everything else is subordinate to this goal (τὰ δὲ ἄλλα πάντα σχεδὸν ἁπλῶς εἰπεῖν ἐν παρέργου τίθεσθαι χώρᾳ, lines 18–19).

The problem with bodily pleasure is not just that the pursuit of it might, in some cases, be in conflict with reason but that, in itself, bodily pleasure is totally antithetical to reason and thought. Someone in the throes of the most intense pleasure is completely unable to reason. Thus to a proponent of a hedonistic calculus Archytas might reply that, in its purest and most intense form, bodily pleasure negates the possibility for calculation. Archytas argues that it is precisely calculation, in a strongly mathematical sense, that is the basis of the good life both for the individual and the state (see Fr. 3). It is tempting to see Cicero's use of *ratione* in line 20 as a reflection of Archytas' emphasis on λογισμός (Fr. 3) and λογιστικά (Fr. 4). Bodily pleasure cannot be the goal of rational calculation, precisely because the more successful we are in achieving pleasure the less able we are to calculate; try constructing a harmonic proportion in the midst of orgasm. This argument once again makes excellent sense as a response to Polyarchus, who repeatedly maintains that the life of pleasure is the rational choice (νοῦν ἔχοντος . . . ἔμφρονος . . . ξυνιέντος, A9 lines 13–14). Nothing in Archytas' argument suggests that more moderate bodily pleasures could not play a role in life, as long as they are guided by reason, nor that bodily pleasures are the only kind of pleasure. That Archytas did recognize and value some non-bodily pleasures is clear from Testimonium A7a.

Among the negative effects of pleasure Cicero's Archytas particularly emphasizes those involving danger to the state (lines 9–10). Is this likely to have been Archytas' own emphasis or is this the good Republican Cicero speaking? Certainty on this issue is impossible. Polyarchus does stress that political power is pursued for the sake of pleasure and bolsters his case with multiple examples of such power (A9 15–22, 45–48). Archytas could be responding that making pleasure the goal of life paradoxically undercuts the political power that had been sought for the sake of pleasure. Moreover, Fragment 3 of Archytas focuses on the state and the dangers of *pleonexia* for it, so that it would not be surprising if Archytas had put his emphasis on the threat to the state posed by the pursuit of pleasure in his response to Polyarchus.

As I will show in the following section, Aristotle refers to Archytas' central argument against pleasure at *EN* 1152b16–18. Aristotle responds to the argument at 1153a20–23. His response depends on distinguishing the proper pleasures of a given activity from those that belong to some other activity. Thus, the pleasures of intellectual activity do not impede intellectual activity, although pleasures foreign to the intellect, such as bodily pleasures, would impede intellectual activity. Accordingly, it is to be expected that the pleasures of one sphere would impede the activities of another, and this does not show that all pleasure is bad. In fact, the pleasures associated with intellectual activity help us to think better. Since Archytas was clearly arguing only that bodily pleasures impede intellectual activity, Aristotle's response does not really address Archytas' point and, in fact, seems to concede it. Aristotle's response would only have force against someone who maintained that only bodily pleasures existed and who denied that pleasures were good on this basis.

The originality of Archytas' argument and its relation to Plato and Aristotle
If, as I have argued above, Cicero's account of Archytas' views on pleasure is based on Aristoxenus' *Life of Archytas*, we can be fairly confident that at least the core of what Cicero ascribes to Archytas is based on reliable evidence for what Archytas actually believed. It is, of course, still possible that Aristoxenus did not give a historically accurate presentation of Archytas' views on pleasure but rather a view colored by Aristoxenus' knowledge of

ideas in the Academy and the Lyceum. It is, in fact, a common view to think that Aristoxenus assigned views colored by Academic and Peripatetic ideas to Pythagoreans in his *Pythagorean Sayings* (Burkert 1972a: 107–08), and Wehrli regards the *Life of Archytas* as an attempt to glorify Archytas at the expense of Plato (1945: 64–65). Polyarchus' speech on pleasure does not seem to fit this description, however (see the commentary on A9), and in the case of Archytas' views on pleasure there seems even less reason to think that any such adulteration of his views is going on. Certainly Archytas' attack on bodily pleasure as presented in Cicero has nothing in common with Aristotle's subtle view of pleasure in the *Nicomachean Ethics* nor with the related theory of pleasure found in the Peripatetic *Magna Moralia*. There are general similarities to what is found in Plato's early work on pleasure, particularly the *Phaedo*, but no trace of the mature Platonic theory of pleasure found in the *Philebus*.

The primary similarity to the *Phaedo* is the idea that bodily pleasure impedes thought. Thus, at 66c Socrates says that the body "Fills us with lusts and desires and fears and imaginings of all sorts and with a great deal of nonsense so that, as the saying goes, we are really and truly never able to think of anything at all because of it" (after Gallop 1975). When the details of the *Phaedo* and the Archytas passage in *De Senectute* are considered, however, it is not very plausible to think that Aristoxenus based his account of Archytas' speech on what he found in Plato. The *Phaedo* focuses more generally on the contrast between body and soul, and pleasure is treated as only one way in which the body corrupts the soul, whereas in Archytas it is only bodily pleasure that is at issue with no mention of "fears and imaginings." Moreover, none of the Platonic emphasis on the philosopher's "preparation for death" (64a) and the separation of soul from body (67a) is found in Archytas. Most importantly, the really distinctive feature of Archytas' speech, the argument that the man in the throes of the most intense pleasure is unable to reason, is not paralleled in Plato.

The passage of the *Phaedo* quoted above bemoans the various interruptions that arise from the concerns of the body and regards the lusts, desires, fears and fantasies of the body as hardly allowing us to think at all, but we are not asked to imagine someone undergoing the most extreme of pleasures and to consider whether such an individual could think rationally. Some have tried to find a parallel for Archytas' thought experiment in the *Philebus*. When Socrates asks Philebus whether he would lack anything if he lived his whole life enjoying the greatest pleasures (21a, cited by Powell 1988: 186), however, the point is not that intense pleasure makes reasoning impossible, as in Archytas, but rather that the continuous enjoyment of great pleasures is not sufficient for a good life and that we need intelligence and thought in addition. Later in the *Philebus* at 63d, the extreme pleasures (by which primarily bodily pleasures seem to be meant) are rejected by intelligence and mind as "putting impediments in our way" (ἐμποδίσματα), but once again, while this passage agrees with the general point of Archytas' speech, it is missing the distinctive Archytan twist. There is no discussion of Archytas' man in the state of maximum pleasure in Plato and no use of Plato's personification and interrogation of intelligence (63c) in Archytas.

There is a very close parallel in Aristotle for the main argument of Archytas' speech. The parallel is not to Aristotle's own views on pleasure, however, but rather to one of the arguments against pleasure as a good, which Aristotle ascribes to his predecessors in Book VII of the *Nicomachean Ethics*. There is good reason to think that this predecessor was precisely Archytas. Aristotle presents several reasons why people have thought that pleasure was not a good; the fourth of these is that "the pleasures are an impediment to thought and the greater our enjoyment of pleasure the greater the impediment, e.g. sexual pleasure, for they say that no one is able to think of anything in the midst of it" (1152b16). Most commentators on the *Nicomachean Ethics* have not attempted to identify the origin of this argument (e.g. Stewart 1892, Joachim 1955, Irwin 1985, Ackrill 1973, Gosling and Taylor 1982). The remainder have concluded that Aristotle is referring to Plato or a reading of Plato under the influence of Speusippus (Burnet 1900, Gauthier and Jolif 1970, and Diès 1959: LXIV). In his commentary on this passage of the *Nicomachean Ethics*, Burnet argued that "This really comes from Plato . . . The similarity of language is too striking to be accidental . . ." (1900: 331). The similarities in language that Burnet notes are (1) between Plato's description of the body as ἐμπόδιον to the acquisition of φρόνησις at *Phaedo* 65a (see also *Phlb.* 63d) and Aristotle's description of pleasure as ἐμπόδιον τῷ φρονεῖν at 1152b16, and (2) between Aristotle's statement regarding sexual pleasure that "no one would be able to think of anything in the midst of it" (οὐδένα γὰρ ἂν δύνασθαι νοῆσαί τι ἐν αὐτῇ) and Plato's assertion about the body that, as the saying goes, "we are never able to think of anything on account of it" (ὑπ᾽ αὐτοῦ οὐδὲ φρονῆσαι ἡμῖν ἐγγίγνεται οὐδέποτε οὐδέν, 66c). These similarities are undeniable; Aristotle is clearly thinking in part of Plato, when presenting the argument against pleasure at 1152b16–18.

This is not the end of the matter, however. The focus of the commentators has been on Aristotle's first and last words, on the assertion that pleasure is an impediment to thought and that we are not able to think anything on account of it. The intervening words, which make the point that the more extreme the pleasure is the more it is an impediment, and which give sexual pleasure as an example of the most extreme pleasure, in which we are not able to think anything, have almost universally escaped the attention of scholars. Once Archytas' speech on pleasure is put next to the passage in the *Nicomachean Ethics*, however, it appears much more likely that, while the general idea of bodily pleasure as impeding thought may be common to Plato, Archytas and indeed a broader tradition (cf. the common saying that Plato quotes), Aristotle is drawing specifically on Archytas' argument as reported by his pupil Aristoxenus.

Aristotle like Archytas singles out a particularly extreme pleasure and argues that thought is not possible during such a pleasure. The emphasis on someone experiencing the extreme degree of pleasure is the crucial similarity. It is true that Aristotle specifically mentions sexual pleasure, whereas Archytas just refers to the greatest bodily pleasure that can be conceived. Sexual orgasm, however, would be likely to garner most people's vote as the greatest bodily pleasure, and it is likely that this is what Archytas had in mind. Moreover, a few lines earlier, Archytas had particularly singled out debauchery and adultery (line 12, *stupra vero et adulteria*) as set in motion by pleasure, and it is quite possible that Cicero has left vague what was an explicit reference to sexual pleasure in Aristoxenus' version. Cicero does have some tendency to "tone down" Greek anecdotes in the interests of decorum (see Powell 1988: 113, 116 and esp. 199). There is little doubt, then, that in *EN* 1152b16–18 Aristotle is thinking of the argument against pleasure as an impediment to thought in the form of Archytas' peculiar thought experiment, what might be called "the argument from orgasm" (Ostwald 1962: 204, n. 67 and Lieberg 1958: 75 also noticed the connection as apparently did DK I. 424.9–10, although the reference to *EN* VII. 12 seems to be a mistake for VII. 11. We need not assume, as Dirlmeier [1967: 498] does, that Aristotle has to be referring either to Plato or to Archytas to the exclusion of the other. He is referring to the general argument according to which pleasure impedes the soul but clearly is also familiar with Archytas' peculiar take on that argument). Indeed, a thought experiment of this sort seems very typical of Archytas, who, in order to prove that the cosmos is unlimited, is famous for asking us to imagine someone standing at the edge of the universe (A24).

If Aristotle had mentioned Archytas by name, we might suppose that Aristoxenus constructed a speech on pleasure based on this reference in Aristotle, but, since Aristotle does not identify his source, it seems most likely that the similarity between Aristoxenus' Archytas and Aristotle is to be explained by the fact that Aristotle is referring to the anecdote about Archytas and Polyarchus, whether he derived it from Aristoxenus himself or whether both Aristotle and Aristoxenus drew on a common source. The negative effects of pleasure mentioned by Archytas have general parallels with the tradition that sees pleasure as the root of all evil (Powell 1988: 185 on *hinc nasci*), and the claim that reason is a divine gift is similarly paralleled (Powell 1988: 185 on *cumque . . . dedisset*). Likewise the image of pleasure as a tyrant is common (Powell 1988: 186). These traditions are so widespread, however, and the similarities so general that it is impossible to use them to either impugn or authenticate the content of Archytas' speech as belonging to the historical Archytas. It is the trademark "thought experiment," that makes the presentation of pleasure in Archytas' speech distinctive.

Detailed commentary
For a thorough treatment see the excellent commentary on the *De Senectute* by J. G. F. Powell (1988). See especially his defense of the historical accuracy of Cicero's presentation of Cato and his visit to Tarentum on pp. 274–75.

Line 7 cuius voluptatis – This could depend on *potiundum* "to obtain which pleasure voracious desires were brought into play in defiance of prudence and restraint." It is more likely that it depends on *avidae* and that the object of *potiundum* is implied (so Powell).

A11 Aelian, *Historical Miscellany* XIV. 19

Ἀρχύτας τά τε ἄλλα ἦν σώφρων καὶ οὖν καὶ τὰ ἄκοσμα ἐφυλάττετο τῶν 1
ὀνομάτων, ἐπεὶ δέ ποτε ἐβιάζετό τι εἰπεῖν τῶν ἀπρεπῶν, οὐκ ἐξενικήθη, 2
ἀλλ' ἐσιώπησε μὲν αὐτό, ἐπέγραψε δὲ κατὰ τοῦ τοίχου, δείξας μὲν ὃ 3
εἰπεῖν ἐβιάζετο, οὐ μὴν βιασθεὶς εἰπεῖν. 4

4 εἰπεῖν (post βιασθεὶς)] V εἶπε x

Archytas was both temperate in other respects, and he was even on his guard against offensive language. Once, when he was about to be forced to say something unseemly, he was not overcome but, instead of speaking it, wrote it down on the wall, thus having shown what he was being forced to say but not having been forced to say it.

Authenticity
Since we have no indication of Aelian's source for this anecdote, there is no way to determine if it is connected to anything that Archytas actually

said or did. The portrayal of Archytas' self-control here is reminiscent of his control of his anger in an anecdote derived from Aristoxenus' *Life of Archytas* (A7). We might thus guess that this anecdote too is derived from Aristoxenus and has the same likelihood of being authentic as other sections of the *Life of Archytas* (see the introductory essay on authenticity).

Context
This anecdote concerning Archytas has no obvious connection with either the preceding or the following paragraph in Aelian. This is not surprising, in that one of the essential features of Aelian's *Historical Miscellany* is precisely its variety and apparently haphazard order. It is of some interest that the succeeding anecdote focuses on Sybaris, since Archytas' actions are compared with those of the Sybarites elsewhere (A8). In this case there is no explicit connection drawn between Archytas and the slave from Sybaris described in xiv. 20, but it is true that the slave certainly does not possess Archytas' temperance, since after chastising his young charge for picking up a fig from the street, he eats it himself.

Importance of the testimonium
This anecdote primarily provides an illustration of Archytas' temperance or self control (σώφρων, line 1). Specifically, it shows how steadfastly he was on his guard against saying anything unseemly (τὰ ἄκοσμα . . . τῶν ὀνομάτων, τι . . . τῶν ἀπρεπῶν). What exactly would count as an "unseemly" utterance is left unclear. Such language probably included calling fellow citizens names which were regarded as libellous. We do not know anything about Tarentine law in this area, but in Athenian law such expressions were "father-beater," "mother-beater," or even "murderer." A law first passed by Solon, which still existed in the fourth century, forbade speaking evil of the dead (MacDowell 1978: 126–29). Simple swear words and obscenities as well as particular subject matters were probably also excluded as in themselves "unseemly."

Why should Archytas feel obliged to avoid unseemly language? The anecdote does not answer this question directly, and it is helpful to examine other prohibitions against shameful speech contemporary with and prior to Archytas. Herodotus tells us that the Persians were not allowed to speak about what they were not allowed to do, but he does not give the justification for this practice (i. 138). Xenophon similarly portrays the Persian nobles as neither saying nor doing shameful things but suggests that part of the motivation for such behavior was the desire that their children neither see nor hear anything shameful (*Cyr.* vii. 5.86). Protection of children is the primary motivation for both Plato's and Aristotle's prohibitions on shameful language. Plato argues that the young are trained better by example than by admonition, so that the young must not observe their elders either doing or saying anything shameful (*Lg.* 729b). The most detailed discussion of shameful talk is found in Book VII, Chapter 17 of Aristotle's *Politics* (1336b3–8). Aristotle argues that someone who lightly says something shameful will also carry out similar actions. This argument leads him to ban shameful language particularly among the young but also among all the citizens lest the young see or hear them. Plutarch (*Moralia* 9f) appears to ban foul language among the young on the same grounds as Aristotle and quotes a saying of Democritus ("A word is a deed's shadow" = DK68 B145) in support of the prohibition. Aristotle also argues that the young should not be exposed to indecent pictures or stories. Adults are allowed to see such representations, including comedies which must include shameful language, because they are protected by their education. Aristotle is probably not saying that talking about father-beating makes you go out and beat your father so much as arguing that, if we are in the habit of breaking the societal prohibition against unseemly words, we may also be inclined to break prohibitions against unseemly actions (Kraut 1997: 162). Children might be particularly inclined to do so, since they have not yet firmly habituated themselves against shameful actions.

Nothing in the anecdote about Archytas suggests a concern with children. We might suppose that the point is still that shameful speech can lead to shameful action except that Archytas does end up writing out the shameful words, which at first sight might seem to be just as likely to lead to shameful action as speaking them. The emphasis is not so much on actually saying the unseemly language as on resisting the compulsion to say it. The imperfect ἐβιάζετο indicates the attempt to make him say it without indicating that he actually said it. What was the source of the compulsion? Presumably we are to suppose that it is Archytas' own emotions. This scenario would be similar to that of A7, where Archytas is driven by his anger to want to punish his slaves but restrains himself from punishing in anger. Similarly, here in A11, he is not overcome by his anger (οὐκ ἐξενικήθη) and exerts his self-control to refrain from cursing.

The surprising feature of the anecdote is that he instead writes the unseemly language on a wall. This is puzzling in several ways. Why a wall rather than, say, a wax tablet? Perhaps the idea is that he had nothing else at hand and so he picked up a sharp object and wrote on the nearest surface in order to vent his anger (cf. the graffiti on the walls at Pompeii). From a philosophical point of view he seems to have won a very minor victory, first because he should not have allowed himself to be overcome by anger under any circumstances and secondly because it seems only marginally better to express something unseemly in writing than in speech. The point of the anecdote, at least from Aelian's point of view, might simply be humor. We are to imagine Archytas, red in the face, restraining himself from swearing aloud but writing "f***, f***, f***" on the wall instead. The humor is highlighted by the play in language: "having shown what he was being forced to say, but not having been forced to say it" (δείξας μὲν ὃ εἰπεῖν ἐβιάζετο, οὐ μὴν βιασθεὶς εἰπεῖν). Understood in this way the anecdote fits the characterization of Archytas in A7 as prone to anger yet willing to go to absurd extremes rather than express it.

We might construct a more philosophically interesting interpretation of the anecdote, by recognizing that the act of actually writing out the offensive language is considerably less spontaneous than blurting out the swear word. Writing is thus more an act of reason than swearing aloud, which could simply be an expression of emotion (I owe this suggestion to Noah Lemos). The point would be not that offensive language is, in itself, to be avoided but rather that the act of swearing is bad, because it is an action governed by emotion. On this reading Archytas has been largely successful; he has not been forced by his emotions to say something offensive, and his written obscenities are not problematic, because they are mediated by reason. The writing on the wall then shows to others what he was tempted to say in his moment of fury but also illustrates the victory of his reason by its written rather than oral form.

AIIa Aelian, *Historical Miscellany* X. 12

Ἀρχύτας ἔλεγεν· "ὥσπερ ἔργον ἐστὶν ἰχθὺν εὑρεῖν ἄκανθαν μὴ ἔχοντα,   1
οὕτω καὶ ἄνθρωπον μὴ κεκτημένον τι δολερὸν καὶ ἀκανθῶδες."   2

1 ἰχθὺν εὑρεῖν] VΦ   εὑρεῖν ἰχθύν x   ἄκανθαν] om. V

Archytas used to say, "Just as it is difficult to find a fish which does not have bones, so also it is difficult to find a man who does not possess some treacherous and prickly characteristic."

Authenticity
It is puzzling that DK do not include this apophthegm among their testimonia for Archytas, along with other material from Aelian (A8, A11). Certainly it is much more similar to other anecdotes that they do accept (e.g. A8, A11),

including those that with certainty go back to Aristoxenus (A7, A9), than it is to anything in the pseudo-Archytan texts collected by Thesleff. Perhaps the objection was that A11a is not just an anecdote but purports to quote Archytas' own words. The quotation is not presented as something Archytas wrote, however, in contrast, e.g., to the suspect quotation that Philostratus gives from Archytas' supposed treatise on the education of children (*VA* vi. 31 = Thesleff 47.19–22). It is also short and of just the pithy nature that we would expect in the anecdotal tradition arising from Aristoxenus. Thus, there does not seem to be adequate reason for supposing it to be a later forgery. See the introductory essay on authenticity for a discussion of the general problems with anecdotes.

Context
As is the case with A11, this anecdote has no obvious connection to the material which precedes or follows it in Aelian. Aelian presents his material in a manner that emphasizes variety rather than order.

Importance of the testimonium
The same Archytas who saw an altar as analogous to an arbitrator and who used analogy in formulating definitions (A12 and A22) might have drawn this analogy between fish and people. Just as it is difficult to eat a fish without finding a troublesome bone, which might choke us (see the amusing story in Plutarch described below), so it is difficult to find a person who does not have some treacherous characteristic, which can stick in our craw and cause us trouble. Archytas, in light of his political career, may have been all too familiar with the potential for treachery among his associates.

Detailed commentary
Line 1 ἄκανθαν – This refers to the material from which fish bones are made, which is treated by Aristotle as analogous to bone in mammals (*HA* 486b20). It could be used to refer to fish bones in general or to a single fish bone. Plutarch tells an amusing story of the sophist Niger, who, although choking on a fish bone, kept speaking so as not to appear to yield to a rival (*Mor.* 131a–b).

CHAPTER III

Geometry: The duplication of the cube

A14 Eutocius, *Commentary on Archimedes' On the Sphere and Cylinder* II (III. 84.12–88.2 Heiberg/Stamatis)

(See also the *Verba Filiorum* of the Banu Musa, Clagett 1964: 334–41)

ἡ Ἀρχύτου εὕρησις, ὡς Εὔδημος ἱστορεῖ   1

Ἔστωσαν αἱ δοθεῖσαι δύο εὐθεῖαι αἱ ΑΔ, Γ. δεῖ δὴ τῶν ΑΔ, Γ δύο μέσας   2
ἀνάλογον εὑρεῖν. γεγράφθω περὶ τὴν μείζονα τὴν ΑΔ κύκλος ὁ ΑΒΔΖ,   3
καὶ τῇ Γ ἴσῃ ἐνηρμόσθω ἡ ΑΒ, καὶ ἐκβληθεῖσα συμπιπτέτω τῇ ἀπὸ τοῦ   4
Δ ἐφαπτομένῃ τοῦ κύκλου κατὰ τὸ Π. παρὰ δὲ τὴν ΠΔΟ ἤχθω ἡ ΒΕΖ,   5
καὶ νενοήσθω ἡμικυλίνδριον ὀρθὸν ἐπὶ τοῦ ΑΒΔ ἡμικυκλίου, ἐπὶ δὲ τῆς   6
ΑΔ ἡμικύκλιον ὀρθὸν ἐν τῷ τοῦ ἡμικυλινδρίου παραλληλογράμμῳ   7
κείμενον. τοῦτο δὴ τὸ ἡμικύκλιον περιαγόμενον ὡς ἀπὸ τοῦ Δ ἐπὶ   8
τὸ Β μένοντος τοῦ Α πέρατος τῆς διαμέτρου τεμεῖ τὴν κυλινδρικὴν   9
ἐπιφάνειαν ἐν τῇ περιαγωγῇ καὶ γράψει ἐν αὐτῇ γραμμήν τινα. πάλιν   10
δέ, ἐὰν τῆς ΑΔ μενούσης τὸ ΑΠΔ τρίγωνον περιενεχθῇ τὴν ἐναντίαν   11
τῷ ἡμικυκλίῳ κίνησιν, κωνικὴν ποιήσει ἐπιφάνειαν τῇ ΑΠ εὐθείᾳ, ἣ δὴ 12
περιαγομένη συμβαλεῖ τῇ κυλινδρικῇ γραμμῇ κατά τι σημεῖον· ἅμα δὲ   13
καὶ τὸ Β περιγράψει ἡμικύκλιον ἐν τῇ τοῦ κώνου ἐπιφανείᾳ. ἐχέτω δὴ   14
θέσιν κατὰ τὸν τόπον τῆς συμπτώσεως τῶν γραμμῶν τὸ μὲν κινούμενον   15
ἡμικύκλιον ὡς τὴν τοῦ ΔΚΑ τὸ δὲ ἀντιπεριαγόμενον τρίγωνον τὴν τοῦ   16
ΔΛΑ, τὸ δὲ τῆς εἰρημένης συμπτώσεως σημεῖον ἔστω τὸ Κ· ἔστω δὲ   17
καὶ τὸ διὰ τοῦ Β γραφόμενον ἡμικύκλιον τὸ ΒΜΖ, κοινὴ δὲ αὐτοῦ τομὴ   18
καὶ τοῦ ΒΔΖΑ κύκλου ἔστω ἡ ΒΖ, καὶ ἀπὸ τοῦ Κ ἐπὶ τὸ τοῦ ΒΔΑ   19
ἡμικυκλίου ἐπίπεδον κάθετος ἤχθω· πεσεῖται δὴ ἐπὶ τὴν τοῦ κύκλου   20
περιφέρειαν διὰ τὸ ὀρθὸν ἑστάναι τὸν κύλινδρον. πιπτέτω καὶ ἔστω ἡ   21
ΚΙ, καὶ ἡ ἀπὸ τοῦ Ι ἐπὶ τὸ Α ἐπιζευχθεῖσα συμβαλέτω τῇ ΒΖ κατὰ τὸ Θ, 22

---

1 Ἀρχύτου] A   ἀρχίτου E   εὕρησις] A   εὕρεσις G   **2** ΑΔ (prior)] e corr. B   ΑΒ Α   ΑΔ
(alter)] B   ΑΒ Α   **4** τῇ (alter)] mg. G   την Α   **12** τῇ ΑΠ εὐθείᾳ] Basil.   της ΑΠ ευθειας
ΑΒ

ἡ δὲ ΑΛ τῷ ΒΜΖ ἡμικυκλίῳ κατὰ τὸ Μ, ἐπεζεύχθωσαν δὲ καὶ αἱ ΚΔ, ΜΙ, 23
ΜΘ. ἐπεὶ οὖν ἑκάτερον τῶν ΔΚΑ, ΒΜΖ ἡμικυκλίων ὀρθόν ἐστι πρὸς τὸ 24
ὑποκείμενον ἐπίπεδον, καὶ ἡ κοινὴ ἄρα αὐτῶν τομὴ ἡ ΜΘ πρὸς ὀρθάς 25
ἐστι τῷ τοῦ κύκλου ἐπιπέδῳ· ὥστε καὶ πρὸς τὴν ΒΖ ὀρθή ἐστιν ἡ ΜΘ. 26
τὸ ἄρα ὑπὸ τῶν ΒΘΖ, τουτέστι τὸ ὑπὸ ΑΘΙ, ἴσον ἐστὶ τῷ ἀπὸ ΜΘ. 27
ὅμοιον ἄρα ἐστὶ τὸ ΑΜΙ τρίγωνον ἑκατέρῳ τῶν ΜΙΘ, ΜΑΘ· καὶ ὀρθὴ 28
ἡ ὑπὸ ΙΜΑ. ἔστιν δὲ καὶ ἡ ὑπὸ ΔΚΑ ὀρθή. παράλληλοι ἄρα εἰσὶν αἱ 29
ΚΔ, ΜΙ, καὶ ἔσται ἀνάλογον, ὡς ἡ ΔΑ πρὸς ΑΚ, τουτέστιν ἡ ΚΑ πρὸς 30
ΑΙ, οὕτως ἡ ΙΑ πρὸς ΑΜ, διὰ τὴν ὁμοιότητα τῶν τριγώνων. τέσσαρες 31
ἄρα αἱ ΔΑ, ΑΚ, ΑΙ, ΑΜ ἑξῆς ἀνάλογόν εἰσιν. καί ἐστιν ἡ ΑΜ ἴση τῇ 32
Γ, ἐπεὶ καὶ τῇ ΑΒ. δύο ἄρα δοθεισῶν τῶν ΑΔ, Γ δύο μέσαι ἀνάλογον 33
ηὕρηνται αἱ ΑΚ, ΑΙ. 34

27 Β(Θ)Ζ] Stamatis Θ(Θ)ΒΖ ΑΒ tb tz Β² ΑΘΙ] Stamatis Θ(Θ)ΑΙ ΑΒ ta ti Β²

The Solution of Archytas, as Eudemus reports it.

Let the two given straight lines be ΑΔ and Γ. It is then necessary to find two mean proportionals of ΑΔ and Γ. Let the circle ΑΒΔΖ be drawn around the greater ΑΔ, let ΑΒ, equal to Γ, be fit into (the circle) and being extended let it meet the line, which is tangent to the circle and drawn from Δ, at Π. Let line ΒΕΖ be drawn parallel to ΠΔΟ, and let a right semicylinder be conceived on the semicircle ΑΒΔ, and on ΑΔ a semicircle at right angles lying in the rectangle of the semicylinder. When this semicircle is rotated from Δ to Β, while the endpoint Α of the diameter remains fixed, it will cut the cylindrical surface in its rotation and will describe a line on it. And again, if, while ΑΔ remains fixed, the triangle ΑΠΔ is rotated in an opposite motion to that of the semicircle, it will make the surface of a cone with the line ΑΠ, which as it is rotated will meet the line on the cylinder in a point. At the same time the point Β will also describe a semicircle on the surface of the cone. Let the moving semicircle have as its position ΔΚΑ at the place where the lines meet, and let the triangle being rotated in the opposite direction have as its place ΔΛΑ, and let the point of intersection described above be Κ. Let the semicircle described by Β be ΒΜΖ, and let the line of intersection between it and the circle ΒΔΖΑ be ΒΖ. And let a perpendicular be drawn from Κ to the plane of the semicircle ΒΔΑ. It will fall on the circumference of the circle, because the cylinder is a right cylinder. Let it be dropped and let it be line ΚΙ, and let the line which connects Ι to Α meet the line ΒΖ in Θ, and the line ΑΛ meet the semicircle ΒΜΖ at Μ. Let ΚΔ, ΜΙ, and ΜΘ be connected.

Since each of the semicircles ΔΚΑ and ΒΜΖ are at right angles to the plane that lies under them, therefore their line of intersection ΜΘ is also perpendicular to the plane of the circle, so that ΜΘ is also perpendicular to ΒΖ. Therefore the rectangle formed by ΘΒ and ΘΖ, that is the rectangle formed by ΘΑ and ΘΙ, is equal to the square formed by ΜΘ. The triangle ΑΜΙ is therefore similar to each of the triangles ΜΙΘ and ΜΑΘ. And the angle ΙΜΑ is right. But the angle ΔΚΑ is also right. The lines ΚΔ and ΜΙ are therefore parallel and there will be a proportion: as ΔΑ is to ΑΚ, that is as ΚΑ is to ΑΙ, so ΙΑ is to ΑΜ on account of the similarity of the triangles. The four lines ΔΑ, ΑΚ, ΑΙ, ΑΜ are therefore in continued proportion. And ΑΜ is equal to Γ, since it is also equal to ΑΒ. Therefore of the two given lines ΑΔ and Γ two mean proportionals have been found, ΑΚ and ΑΙ.

A14a Proclus, *Commentary on Plato's Timaeus* 32a–b (II. 33.29–34.4 Diehl)

πῶς μὲν οὖν δύο δοθεισῶν εὐθειῶν δυνατὸν δύο μέσας ἀνὰ λόγον λαβεῖν, ἡμεῖς ἐπὶ τέλει τῆς πραγματείας εὑρόντες τὴν Ἀρχύτειον δεῖξιν ἀναγράψομεν, ταύτην ἐκλεξάμενοι μᾶλλον ἢ τὴν Μεναίχμου, διότι ταῖς κωνικαῖς ἐκεῖνος χρῆται γραμμαῖς, καὶ τὴν Ἐρατοσθένους ὡσαύτως, διότι κανόνος χρῆται παραθέσει.

How, then, it is possible to find two mean proportionals of two given straight lines, I will record at the end of my work, since I have found the demonstration of Archytas. I picked this demonstration rather than that of Menaechmus, because he uses conic sections and similarly rather than the solution of Eratosthenes since he uses a ruler laid alongside.

Authenticity

A14 is generally recognized to be based on genuine work of Archytas, although it has certainly been reworked by Eudemus and Eutocius (see below). It is impossible to imagine a forger, who could develop such a sophisticated construction and who, if he did, would then ascribe it to Archytas. The only plausible scenario according to which we could see A14 as not authentic, would be to regard it as the work of another mathematician, which was mistakenly ascribed to Archytas. This is unlikely. We have strong evidence that the solution was regarded as Archytas' already in the fourth and third centuries BC. Eutocius assigns the construction to Archytas on the authority of Eudemus, which means that it was ascribed to Archytas already in the second half of the fourth century shortly after his death, and

Eratosthenes, in the third century, makes reference to Archytas' distinctive construction with a semicylinder (A15).

Context

Archytas' solution to the problem of the duplication of the cube is preserved by Eutocius of Ascalon, who was active in Alexandria in the first half of the sixth century AD (Bulmer-Thomas 1971a). Eutocius was the student of Ammonius and perhaps his successor as head of the Alexandrian school (Westerink 1961: 129). The only works of Eutocius that survive are his commentaries on mathematical works. He wrote commentaries on three mathematical works of Archimedes and on the first four books of the *Conics* of Apollonius. Eutocius does not seem to have made any original contribution to mathematics. In the commentary on Archimedes' *On the Sphere and Cylinder* II, however, he preserves a series of previous solutions to the problem of the duplication of the cube, including that of Archytas.

The first proposition of Book II of Archimedes' work is "Given a cone or cylinder, to find a sphere equal to the cone or cylinder." Archimedes shows that this can be reduced to the problem of finding two mean proportionals. However, in the synthesis, Archimedes simply asserts "Between the two straight lines, let the two mean proportionals be found," without giving any indication as to how this can be done. Eutocius comments (66.8 ff.) that he cannot find any solution written by Archimedes himself but that he "has encountered the writings of many famous men which address the problem." He notes that he will not give the solution of Eudoxus, since it has a mathematical mistake that is not worthy of such a great mathematician and since it is in conflict with the preface which is attached to it. But, he continues, "in order that the thought of those who have come before us be made manifest, the manner of the solution of each one will also be written here." He then lists the solutions in the following order: Plato, Hero, Philo of Byzantium, Apollonius, Diocles, Pappus, Sporus, Menaechmus, Archytas, Eratosthenes and Nicomedes. There is no obvious system to this order. Proclus (A14a), in the century before Eutocius, as part of his commentary on Plato's reference to the two mean proportionals at *Timaeus* 32a–b, says that he will provide Archytas' solution in an appendix of mathematics relevant to the *Timaeus* (now lost, see II. 76.22). He indicates that he has selected Archytas' solution over those of Menaechmus and Eratosthenes. The rationale for his choice is not clear, but his mention of Eratosthenes' use of a ruler perhaps suggests that he prefers the more theoretical solution of Archytas (Sturm 1895: 32; see A15). At any rate, it is clear that a number of the solutions which Eutocius quotes were available to Proclus in the previous century. In some cases Eutocius specifies the book of the given author, in which he found the solution, in other cases he specifies no source. In the case of Archytas alone, he indicates that he has the solution at second hand, saying that it is the solution of Archytas "according to Eudemus."

Eudemus of Rhodes was a student of Aristotle who was active in the second half of the fourth century BC. He is one of the most important sources for the history of Greek mathematics, because he wrote the first and perhaps only histories of arithmetic, geometry and astronomy (see Zhmud 2002). In the preface to his commentary on Archimedes' *Measurement of the Circle,* Eutocius clearly includes himself among "those who have examined Eudemus' *History of Geometry*" (p. 228 Heiberg = Eud. Fr. 139). Moreover, later in the sixth century AD, Simplicius provides a long quotation from the *History of Geometry* (Eud. Fr. 140), gives several quotes from the *History of Astronomy* and frequently quotes from Eudemus' *Physics* (Zhmud 2002: 264, n. 3). It is always possible that Eutocius just means that he has examined extracts from the *History of Geometry*, although that is not what he says, and that Simplicius also knew of Eudemus' work on geometry only through excerpts in other authors. Given the evidence we have, however, it seems better to follow Zhmud in concluding that Eutocius and Simplicius used Eudemus' *History of Geometry* directly, and hypercritical to conclude with Tannery (followed by Knorr 1989: 126 n. 124) that Eutocius only knew of Eudemus' work through Sporus' *Keria*.

Archytas' solution to the duplication of the cube is also preserved, although not under his name, in an Arabic treatise of the ninth century AD. This treatise was the work of three brothers, the sons of Mūsā ibn Shākir, who were thus known as the Banū (i.e. sons of) Mūsā. They were celebrated mathematicians working in Baghdad. The treatise was translated into Latin by Gerard of Cremona in the middle of the twelfth century with the title *Verba filiorum Moysi filii Sekir, i.e. Maumeti, Hameti, Hasen,* or just *Verba filiorum,* "The Words of the Sons." Clagett (1964) provides a Latin text along with variant readings from the Arabic text, which survives in an edition by al-Ṭūsī (thirteenth century). It appears that al-Ṭūsī was an intrusive editor and that the text translated by Gerard provides a better picture of the original (Clagett 1964: 233). Gerard's translation meant that Archytas' solution to the duplication was influential in the geometry of the thirteenth century in the west (Clagett 1964: 224–25).

Archytas' solution appears as the sixteenth proposition in the *Verba filiorum.* The Banū Mūsā say nothing about Archytas or Eudemus and instead identify the solution as coming from "one of the ancients called Menelaus, who wrote a *Book of Geometry*" (Clagett 1964: 336–37). This is Menelaus of Alexandria who was active at the end of the first century AD. He was known to Plutarch and was depicted as present at the conversation in *The Face on the Moon* and called "the mathematician" (930a). Three of his books are extant but only in Arabic translation. His *Elements of Geometry* in three books, to which the Banū Mūsā refer, is not extant but is referred to in other Arabic sources (Clagett 1964: 365). It is not clear whether Menelaus presented the solution as his own or whether he attributed it to Archytas (or someone else) and the attribution dropped out in the Arabic tradition.

Knorr (1989: 100 ff.) has carried out a very thorough comparison of Archytas' proof as it appears in Eutocius and as it appears in the Banū Mūsā. The version in the Banū Mūsā adds nothing to our basic understanding of the proof and in fact omits a crucial passage, while being less clear than the version of Eutocius in several places. The two versions are, nonetheless, very close in their ordering of the construction and show a number of textual parallels as well. Knorr concludes that the versions derive from a common source but not from the same immediate source. There is indeed no evidence that Eutocius knew of Menelaus. The obvious conclusion is that Eutocius is drawing directly on Eudemus, while the Banū Mūsā draw on Menelaus, who ultimately will have taken his version from Eudemus as well. The activity of Menelaus and perhaps other intermediary sources and the translation into Arabic will account for the differences between the two versions. Knorr prefers to follow Tannery's conclusion that Eutocius knew of Eudemus only through Sporus (1989: 126 n. 124). He notes, however, that the superior conciseness of Eutocius' version may reflect Eudemus more closely, since Eudemus had a reputation for such brevity and that the general agreement between the two versions suggests that Eutocius' version represents Eudemus' version fairly accurately.

One interesting point about the context of Archytas' proof in the Banū Mūsā has not been sufficiently appreciated. Immediately following Archytas' solution, the Banū Mūsā present the solution which Eutocius hands down as belonging to Plato (on this solution see the commentary on A15). The Banū Mūsā, however, do not mention Plato and introduce the solution by saying that the demonstration of Menelaus (i.e. Archytas) which they have just given, while theoretically correct (*certa . . . in mente*), "is very difficult to follow (*difficilis valde per inquisitionem*) and by means of it [actually] to place two quantities between two quantities . . ." (tr. Clagett 1964: 341). Clagett's translation of the Arabic is even more emphatic: "And since the things which Menelaus used – even if they are true – are either not possible to execute or are very difficult, we have accordingly sought an easier method." Thus the Banū Mūsā appear to present "Plato's" solution as their own. Most strikingly they make the same complaint about Archytas' solution that Eratosthenes makes in A15: it is hard to contrive (δυσμήχανα) or even impossible to put in practice (χειρουργῆσαι δὲ καὶ εἰς χρείαν πεσεῖν μὴ δύνασθαι). Just like Eratosthenes they have a more practical solution to present. Rather than presenting Eratosthenes' device, however, they present the device ascribed elsewhere to Plato.

It seems very unlikely that this similarity between Eratosthenes and the Banū Mūsā is coincidental. The remarks of the Banū Mūsā here are clearly drawing on the Greek tradition just as the two solutions they present draw on the Greek tradition. What is most striking though is that "Plato's" solution should be presented as the more practical alternative to Archytas'. If these two solutions were in fact paired with one another in the tradition, it is possible that the second more practical solution, which was in origin a reaction to Archytas' very abstract solution, became known as Archytas' as well and that this is what gave rise to the story of Plato's attack on Archytas for producing a solution which used an instrument (A15a and A15b). The more practical solution would then be labeled in a marginal comment as "not according to Plato," a comment which could easily have been corrupted to the "according to Plato" which we find in Eutocius (see the commentary on A15).

If we return now to Eutocius' version of Archytas' solution, it is important to consider to what extent that version represents anything that Archytas, or even Eudemus, actually wrote. As Knorr notes, "Eutocius is a mathematical commentator, not an archivist." His practice elsewhere shows that he would be likely to remove odd dialect forms and anachronistic usage for the sake of clarity (see his treatment of what was probably an original text of Archimedes in his commentary on *On the Sphere and Cylinder* II 4), and there are indeed expressions in his presentation of Archytas' solutions that are characteristic of Eutocius (Knorr 1989: 100–01). Some of the language is not characteristic of Eutocius (Knorr 1989: 100–01), however, and this along with the basic similarity between his presentation and that of the Banū Mūsā suggests that he is following Eudemus' text in its basic structure and in a few places perhaps even in its language. A comparison of Eutocius' text of Eudemus in A14 with Eudemus' account of Hippocrates' quadrature of lunes, which is preserved by Simplicius (Eudemus Fr. 140), shows, however, that Eutocius' text lacks some of the archaic features that are characteristic of Eudemus and that Eutocius' text of Eudemus has thus been modernized either by Eutocius himself or in the transmission (Neuenschwander 1974; Knorr 1989: 100).

What about Eudemus himself? Simplicius emphasizes Eudemus'
penchant for brevity and clarity (Eud. Frs. 140, 149), and it thus seems
probable that Eudemus did away with the Doric dialect, which must have
stood in Archytas' original, and regularized some of the anachronistic features of Archytas' language. Zhmud points out that Eudemus does, in the
case of Thales, comment on the quality of proofs and on archaic terminology (Procl. *In Euc.* 250; Eud. Fr. 135. See Zhmud 2002: 295), so that we
might have expected something of the sort in his treatment of Archytas,
but no trace of such comments survives in Eutocius' version. Thus it seems
very problematic to assign any of the specific language or phrasing in A14 to
Archytas himself. On the other hand, it is plausible that the basic conception and structure of the proof reflect Archytas' original fairly well. Given
the complexity of the proof, it is probable that Eudemus was relying on
a written text of Archytas, but it is not possible to determine in which
work of Archytas his solution to the duplication of the cube might have
appeared. No list of Archytas' works has survived, and the duplication of
the cube is obviously unlikely to have come from the *Harmonics* (from
which Fragments 1 and 2 derive). To judge by the surviving fragments of
On Sciences (Fr. 3) and *Discourses* (Fr. 4), these works were too general to
have contained the very technical solution to the duplication of the cube.
We might expect that A14 would have appeared in an *Elements of Geometry*,
but we have no evidence for such a work by Archytas.

Analysis of Archytas' solution
There have been a number of insightful examinations of Archytas' solution.
In terms of mathematical sophistication, the most helpful are Knorr 1986:
50–52 and van der Waerden 1963: 150–52. See also Knorr 1989: 100–10,
Heath 1921: 246–49, Freeman 1946: 236–37 and Thomas 1939: 1. 284–89.
My goal is to present an account of the solution which will be intelligible
to classicists and historians of philosophy and which can serve as a basis
for discussion of the basic mathematical and philosophical issues raised by
the proof. In what follows I will as a matter of convenience often talk as if
the proof were completely the work of Archytas, but as my remarks above
indicate, it is undoubtedly the case that most of the language does not go
back to Archytas.

   Archytas begins with a clear statement of what is to be done, i.e. given
two straight lines to find two mean proportionals between them (the exact
formulation may be Eutocius', see Knorr 1989: 100). Thus, if AΔ and Γ
are the two given lines, we need to find the mean proportionals x and y
so that Γ:x :: x:y :: y:AΔ. There is no mention of the relevance of finding

these mean proportionals to the problem of the duplication of the cube. We are told by other sources (see A15 and Procl. *In Euc.* 213), however, that Hippocrates of Chios, who was active in the second half of the fifth century, reduced the problem of doubling the volume of a cube to the problem of finding two mean proportionals.

We do not know how Hippocrates came to see that the problem of the duplication of the cube could be reduced to the problem of finding the two mean proportionals in continued proportion (see below on the connection between Plato's *Meno* and the duplication of the cube). The truth of his insight can be illustrated in the following way. If we take Γ to be the side of the original cube and make $A\Delta$ a side twice as long, a cube constructed with $A\Delta$ as its side will have a volume not twice that of the original cube but eight times as great, since the doubling of the one side will have to be multiplied by itself twice, in order to get the volume of the cube ($2 \times 2 \times 2 = 8$). If, however, we find the two mean proportionals in continued proportion between the original side Γ and a side twice as long, $A\Delta$, the cube built on the first of these mean proportionals will be double the volume of the original cube. For, suppose the two mean proportionals to be found so that $\Gamma{:}x :: x{:}y :: y{:}A\Delta$. Since all three terms are equal to $\Gamma{:}x$, if we set them all equal to $\Gamma{:}x$, multiplied together they are equal to $\Gamma^3{:}x^3$. However, if we carry out the multiplication using all the terms of proportion, $\Gamma{:}x$ times $x{:}y$ will give $\Gamma{:}y$, and $\Gamma{:}y$ times the last term, $y{:}A\Delta$, will give $\Gamma{:}A\Delta$. Thus, $\Gamma^3{:}x^3$ will equal $\Gamma{:}A\Delta$. But $A\Delta$ was twice Γ so x^3 will be the cube twice as large as the original cube Γ^3. Archytas makes no allusion to Hippocrates' work, and he does not even formulate the problem specifically in terms of the duplication of the cube, since his solution applies no matter what ratio exists between $A\Delta$ and Γ, although his formulation of course does apply to the case where $A\Delta$ is twice Γ. His statement of the problem shows, however, that he is starting where Hippocrates left off, and the tradition about the Delian problem (A15) makes it probable that he was interested in the more general problem of finding the two mean proportionals, because of the particular problem of the duplication of the cube.

The first two thirds of the proof (lines 2–24) is devoted to the construction that produces the two mean proportional lines. The last third of the proof (lines 24–34) consists of a demonstration showing that the lines constructed are in fact the two mean proportionals which we were seeking. In the first part of the proof, Archytas assumes a number of geometrical constructions which appear later in Euclid's *Elements* either as postulates (e.g. Euc. I. Post. I, to draw a straight line from any point to any point) or as having been rigorously demonstrated (e.g. Euc. I. 31, to draw a line parallel to a given line through a given point). There is, however, no explicit allusion anywhere in the construction to postulates or to previously established constructions or proofs. We have no way of knowing what sort of elements of geometry, if any, Archytas was drawing on. I have included references to relevant parts of Euclid's *Elements* to aid in understanding of the proof, but do not intend these references to suggest anything about what elements, if any, Archytas had access to (refer to Fig. A14 for the following discussion). Archytas starts his proof by drawing a circle around the line AΔ as a diameter (Euc. I. Post. 3) and fitting line AB, equal to line Γ, as chord into this circle (Archytas' word ἐνηρμόσθω matches Euclid's ἐναρμόσαι at IV. 1). Line AB is then extended (Euc. I. Post. 2) until it meets the tangent of the circle, which is drawn from Δ, at point Π. Line BEZ is drawn parallel to the line tangent to the circle at Δ, i.e. line ΠΔΟ (Euc. I. 31).

At this point Archytas asks us to conceive (νενοήσθω) a right semicylinder on the semicircle ABΔ and a right semicircle lying in the rectangle of the semicylinder. Archytas' language asking us to "conceive" these figures is paralleled in several places in Euclid, most notably XII. 14, line 9 and XII. 15, line 23, where we are asked to conceive a cylinder on a given base with a given axis. The semicylinder is right in that the parallelogram which would be rotated in order to produce it (Euc. XI. Def. 21) has right angles. One side of this parallelogram is equal to the radius of the circle ABΔZ. The semicircle is right in that it is conceived to be at right angles to the plane of the circle ABΔZ. This semicircle is conceived to be on line AΔ, the diameter of the circle ABΔZ, and hence to be in the plane which constitutes the flat side of the semicylinder. Note that the parallelogram which constitutes this flat side is not the same as the parallelogram which would be used to generate the semicylinder, but is instead twice the width of the generating parallelogram.

Archytas then says that, if the semicircle is rotated from Δ toward B around point A, which remains fixed, it will cut the surface of the semicylinder as it is rotated and will draw a line on the surface of the semicylinder. Since the diameter of the semicircle (AΔ) is twice the length of the radius of the cylinder (EB), the semicircle will indeed cut the surface of the semicylinder as it is rotated. As it begins to rotate from Δ toward B, the end of the semicircle will stick out beyond the surface of the semicylinder at an height close to the plane of the circle ABΔZ, but, as the semicircle rotates further, it will extend more and more beyond the surface of the semicylinder, and the point at which it cuts the surface of the semicylinder will be higher and higher above the plane of ABΔZ. Thus the successive points at which the semicircle cuts the surface of the semicylinder will form a curve, which rises from Δ higher and higher on the surface of the semicylinder, until, if we continued the rotation of the semicircle, its maximum height would be the radius of the semicircle, before the line began to curve back down, getting lower and lower until it reached point A.

It is interesting that point Δ is conceived of as rotating with the semicircle rather than having a fixed position as the end of the diameter AΔ, so that there are two points which have the same label, Δ, in the construction, which is unusual (Netz 1999: 70 n. 3). The unusual nature of this practice may suggest that we are dealing with something that goes back to Archytas himself. Van der Waerden sees it as an indication of Archytas' kinematic way of thinking in which Δ "is not a definite point in space, but a moving point" (1963: 150 n. 2). Some commentators have labeled the moving point Δ′ in order to avoid confusion, but I don't think that any serious confusion arises. Archytas' usage may in the end be a practical expedient; by keeping Δ as the end point of the diameter of the rotating semicircle, Archytas makes clear that this length is the same as the original length AΔ, which was one of the lines between which the two mean proportionals are to be found.

In the next stage of the proof, the original line AΔ remains fixed and the triangle AΠΔ is rotated in a motion opposite that of the semicircle (a motion that will lead it to meet the rotating semicircle, i.e. the triangle is rotated up out of the plane of the circle ABΔZ); the line AΠ will create the surface of a cone. Euclid will later define a cone in very similar terms as the figure produced when one of the sides around the right angle in a right-angled triangle remains fixed, while the other is carried round and restored to the same position (XI. Def. 18). The vertex of Archytas' cone would be A and the base would be in a plane at right angles to the plane of the circle ABΔZ. Archytas does not generate the whole cone, but simply says that line AΠ will create the surface of a cone as it is rotated. As it rotates line AΠ will also cut the surface of the semicylinder in a curve that starts at point B and ascends higher and higher to the right on the surface of the semicylinder, until, if the rotation continued, it would reach a height above the plane of ABΔZ that is equal to ΔΠ. Archytas next points out that, as AΠ rotates (and the curve which it traces on the surface of the semicylinder ascends to the right) it will at some point intersect the curve which was drawn on the surface of the semicylinder by the rotation of the semicircle. In addition, as line AΠ is rotated, point B, which is on that line, will describe a semicircle on the surface of the cone.

Archytas then defines the rotating semicircle, at the point at which the two lines on the surface of the semicylinder meet, as AKΔ and the triangle, which rotates in the opposite direction, at the same point of intersection as ΔΛΑ. The point on the surface of the semicylinder at which the lines meet is called K. K is in fact the crucial point in the whole construction, as we will see shortly, but Archytas needs to finish a few features of the construction. He first labels the semicircle, which is described by B as line ΑΠ rotates, as BMZ and says "let the line which cuts circle BΔZA and which is shared with BΔZA be BZ." Van der Waerden complains (1963: 151) that this last remark is superfluous and emphasizes that it must be part of Archytas' original proof and is not to be attributed to Eudemus. This is in accord with van der Waerden's view that Archytas has an unusually prolix style. In my opinion this view is without good foundation (see the commentary on A19). In the case of A14, it is true that Archytas does not need to declare by fiat (ἔστω) that the line of intersection is line BZ, since this fact follows from the way in which semicircle BMZ is defined and the way in which BZ was defined earlier in the proof. Even if this one statement is granted as unnecessary, it would hardly seem true, however, to characterize the proof as a whole as prolix. Moreover, it may even be that this remark in line 19 is simply designed to draw attention to a certain relationship that results from the construction. If Archytas had written ἐστί rather than ἔστω, the remark would serve this function very well.

Archytas continues the construction by dropping a perpendicular from point K to the plane of the circle ABΔZ (Euc. XI. 11). He points out that, since the semicylinder was conceived to be a right semicylinder, the perpendicular will fall on the perimeter of the circle on which the cylinder stands (Archytas here switches to talking of the cylinder to which the semicylinder belongs). Since K is on the surface of the semicylinder, and since the semicylinder is right, that is its surface rises at a right angle to the semicircle which is its base, the perpendicular which is dropped will be on that surface and meet the semicircle which is the base of the semicylinder on its periphery. The perpendicular is labeled KI, point I is connected to point A by a straight line, and the point at which AI crosses BZ is labeled Θ. The point at which line AΛ intersects semicircle BMZ is labeled M. The construction is then completed by drawing lines KΔ, MI, and MΘ.

The construction complete, Archytas will now focus on the triangles AKΔ, AIK, AMI, and AΘM, which have been generated, and will show that these are similar triangles and that accordingly the sides opposite the right angle in each triangle are proportional, so that AΔ:AK :: AK:AI :: AI:AM. But, since AM is equal to AB (point M is the position of B on the semicircle BMZ, when line AΠ rotates up to position AΛ) and AB was made equal to the original line Γ, we have found the two mean proportionals AK and AI between the two original lines AΔ and Γ, for which we were looking. We can see, then, that the crucial step in the construction was the determination of point K, the intersection point of the two curves on the surface of the semicylinder, which in turn determines point I. Eratosthenes talks of the "cylinder or semicylinder of Archytas" (A15 lines 24 and 50) as a shorthand way of referring to the solution as a whole, and it is clear that the solution was famous under this description. This shorthand reflects the central importance of the determination of point K on the surface of the semicylinder.

Archytas begins his work with the triangles by establishing that line MΘ is perpendicular to line BZ. This follows from the fact that semicircles AKΔ and BMZ are at right angles to the plane of the circle ABΔZ, so that their line of intersection, MΘ, must also be perpendicular to that plane (Euc. XI. 19). Since BZ was constructed in the plane of the circle ABΔZ, it follows that MΘ is also perpendicular to BZ (Euc. XI. Def. 3). Archytas now asserts that the square formed by MΘ is equal to the rectangle BΘ, ΘZ. This can be most clearly seen, if we imagine the semicircle BMZ completed into a full circle and the line MΘ extended to the opposite side of the circle. Since the extended line MΘ and the line BZ are two straight lines that cut each other in a circle, the rectangle contained by BΘ, ΘZ will be equal to the square on MΘ (MΘ × MΘ – Euc. III. 35). But the rectangle BΘ, ΘZ is also equal to the rectangle AΘ, ΘI, because the lines AI and BZ are two straight lines that cut each other in the circle ABΔZ. Thus, the square on MΘ will also be equal to the rectangle on AΘ, ΘI. Archytas next concludes that the triangle AMI is similar to the triangles MΘI and AΘM, which in turn allows him to draw the crucial conclusion that AMI is a right angle, since that angle corresponds to the angles AΘM and MΘI in the similar triangles.

How does he get to the conclusion that the triangles AMI, MΘI, and AΘM are similar? Archytas does not spell out the reasoning that leads him to this conclusion, but the procedure that he is likely to have followed is indicated by the two points that he established immediately before the assertion of the similarity of these triangles: (1) that MΘ is perpendicular to AI, so that the angles AΘM and MΘI are both right (2) the square on MΘ is equal to the rectangle AΘ, ΘI, so that AΘ is to MΘ as MΘ is to ΘI. This means that the triangles MΘI and AΘM have one angle equal and the sides around that angle proportional and precisely these facts allow us to conclude that these two triangles will be equiangular (Euc. VI. 6). But in equiangular triangles the sides about the equal angles can be shown to be proportional (Euc. vi. 4). Thus the two triangles are similar since similar triangles "are such as have their angles severally equal and the sides about the equal angles proportional" (Euc. vi. Def. 1). Once we have shown that the triangles MΘI and AΘM are similar, we can also show that triangle AMI is similar to each of them. From the similarity just established between the two triangles we know that angles AMΘ and MIΘ are equal, as are angles MAΘ and ΘMI. The large triangle AMI will share the angle MAΘ with the smaller triangle MAΘ and the angle AMΘ in the smaller triangle has been shown to be equal to MIΘ which is an angle in the larger triangle AMI. Thus the large triangle AMI and the smaller triangle MAΘ have two angles equal and thus must be equiangular and hence similar. In the same way we can show that triangles AMI and MΘI are similar. Thus the corresponding angles AΘM, MΘI and AMI in the three triangles are all right angles.

Since Archytas has established that angle AMI is a right angle and angle AKΔ is a right angle, because it is the angle in a semicircle (Euc. iii. 31), he can conclude that MI is parallel to KΔ (Euc. i. 27). At this point Archytas can show that he has constructed a series of right-angled triangles, where a perpendicular has been dropped from the right angle to the base so that the triangles adjoining this perpendicular are similar both to each other and to the whole triangle (Euc. vi. 8). Thus, in triangle AKΔ, a perpendicular has been dropped from the right angle AKΔ, so that the triangles AIK and KIΔ which adjoin the perpendicular are similar to each other and to the whole triangle AKΔ. Archytas is interested in the similarity of the large triangle AKΔ to the triangle AIK, which in turn allows him to conclude that the sides around the equal angle KAΔ are proportional, so that AΔ:AK :: AK:AI (Euc. vi. Def. 1). Then we consider the right triangle AIK, in which the perpendicular has been dropped to M. In this case the similar triangles of interest are AIK and AMI, so that the sides around the equal angle KAI are proportional, so that AK:AI :: AI:AM. Combining the two proportions Archytas can thus get the continued proportion AΔ:AK :: AK:AI :: AI:AM. But since AM is equal to AB, which was made equal to one of the original lines, namely Γ, and since AΔ is the other original line, AK and AI are the two mean proportionals between the given lines.

Archytas' solution is remarkable in a number of ways. Above all it is the first solution we know of, and likely to be the first solution ever, to the problem of finding two mean proportionals in continued proportion between two given lines. This in itself is enough to ensure Archytas a significant place in the history of Greek mathematics. Archytas' solution is also the earliest pieces of solid geometry that we possess. Although it

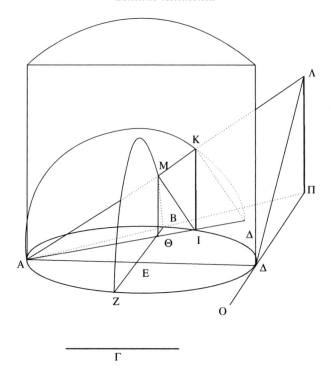

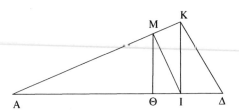

AΔ:AK :: AK:AI : : AI:AM

Figure A14

was later mistakenly thought to have been criticized by Plato for being too mechanical (i.e. too connected to the physical world – see the commentary on A15), it is in fact just the opposite, dazzlingly abstract, and calls on us to perform great feats of mathematical imagination. Eratosthenes rightly saw that this was a solution that was highly abstract and, to pun on his description, "hardly mechanical" (δυσμήχανα – "hard to put into effect," A15 line 50, see also lines 25–27).

At the level of general mathematical knowledge and mathematical rigor, Archytas' solution is strikingly similar to what we find in the work of his predecessor, Hippocrates of Chios, who was active ca. 430 BC. Hippocrates' work on the quadrature of lunes shows "a clear grasp of deductive argument" (Lloyd 1987a: 75, n. 96), and the same can certainly be said of Archytas' duplication of the cube as described above. Archytas' solution also assumes a considerable body of geometrical knowledge and that body of knowledge is similar to what Hippocrates assumes. Hippocrates' quadrature of lunes employs theorems later found in Books I, II, III, IV and VI of Euclid's *Elements* (Lloyd 1979: 109; Bulmer-Thomas 1971b: 414–15). Archytas' solution does not rely on exactly the same geometrical theorems as Hippocrates, since it is a response to a different problem than Hippocrates was addressing, but Archytas presupposes the same type of material. First, he uses basic postulates and theorems of plane geometry, such as Euclid will present in Book I of the *Elements* (e.g. Euc. I. Posts. 1–3; Euc. I. 27 and 31), and theorems of the geometry of the circle, which Euclid presents in Books III and IV (e.g. Euc. III. 31 and 35). Second, he relies on the geometry of similar rectilinear figures, which appears in Book VI of Euclid (e.g. VI. def. I; VI. 4, 6, and 8) but which is already attested in Aristotle's *Posterior Analytics* (99a13). Archytas, not surprisingly, also relies on definitions and propositions dealing with solid geometry which Euclid will collect in Book XI (e.g. XI. def. 3; XI. 11 and 19), and to which Hippocrates does not appeal, since his work on lunes is not a problem in solid geometry. It is true, however, that Archytas' doubling of the cube is based on Hippocrates' reduction of the problem to finding two mean proportionals, so that Archytas' work in solid geometry is building on Hippocrates here as well. Archytas' duplication of the cube as reported by Eudemus is thus very much in accord both with the standards of rigor and also with the geometrical knowledge which we find in his predecessor Hippocrates, while also extending that rigor and knowledge into the field of solid geometry.

Archytas' use of material later found in Euclid does not ensure that he had himself written an *Elements of Geometry*, which had anything like the structure we find later in Euclid, or that he could appeal to a work of this sort written by anyone else. We do not know in exactly what state the elements of geometry were in Archytas' time. Proclus, following Eudemus, tells us that Hippocrates of Chios was the first to write on elements (στοιχεῖα, Procl. *In Euc.* 66), but we have no fragments of that work. The ascription of a work on elements of geometry to Hippocrates does at a minimum indicate that he had some interests in the starting points of mathematics and made some distinction between more or less fundamental principles (Lloyd 1979: 112; 1987a: 75, n. 96). At the same time, we have little direct evidence indicating how Hippocrates might have conceptualized the starting points of mathematics or whether he distinguished between different sorts of starting points, as Euclid distinguished between definitions, postulates and common notions. Lloyd has pointed to the importance of the use of the word "starting point" (ἀρχή) at the beginning of Eudemus' account of Hippocrates' quadrature of lunes, as preserved in Simplicius. Eudemus says that Hippocrates "made his starting point and set out as the first of his theorems useful for his quadratures, that similar segments of circles have the same ratios as the squares on their bases. And this he proved by showing that the squares on the diameters have the same ratios as the circles" (tr. Lloyd 1979: 109). Here the starting point is not a definition, postulate or common notion but rather a geometrical theorem (that similar segments of circles have the same ratios as the squares on their bases), which itself depends on another proposition. At one extreme, then, we might conclude that for Hippocrates "elements" were just theorems which were important for a given demonstration and that his work on elements looked little like Euclid and contained no definitions, postulates and common notions.

There are difficulties with this extreme position, however. First, it is far from certain that the use of "starting point" in this passage of Eudemus does in fact go back to Hippocrates and that the usage tells us anything about Hippocrates' conception of elements. Second, if the usage does go back to Hippocrates, the theorem in question, as Lloyd argues (1979: 112) can only be called a starting point relative to a specific set of demonstrations, i.e. Hippocrates' demonstrations of the quadrature of lunes. It is perfectly possible, however, that Hippocrates used the term "starting point" in both a relative and an absolute way. He could consistently regard a given theorem as the "starting point" for a set of demonstrations, such as those dealing with the quadrature of lunes, while still recognizing that the theorem is not a basic starting point for the whole of geometry, such as the definitions and postulates employed by Euclid. Menaechmus, in the middle of the fourth century, made something like this distinction between two different senses of the term "element" (Proclus, *In Eucl.* 72–73), but we need not suppose that he invented the distinction. That Hippocrates might have been working with such a distinction gains some support from the observation that the use of "starting point" reported by Eudemus, if it is indeed Hippocrates' usage, is cited not from an *Elements* but from the quadrature of lunes. It is possible and even likely that the quadrature of lunes was an independent work and not part of Hippocrates' work on elements, since the study of lunes, while interesting in itself, does not make much contribution to the rest of geometry and hence does not appear in Euclid's *Elements* (Bulmer-Thomas 1971b: 416; Tannery 1912: I. 354–58). Thus, the concept of the starting point which appears at the beginning of the work on lunes may be quite different than that used in Hippocrates' work on elements. Thus, the meager evidence that we have for Hippocrates' understanding of elements might indicate only that he recognized some theorems as more fundamental than others for a given demonstration, but that evidence does not rule out his having a more complicated understanding of elements.

Hippocrates' work on elements was not the final but only the first word on the subject. Leon, who belonged to the generation after Archytas, produced an improved elements as did Theudius at about the same time or a little later (Proclus, *In Eucl.* 66–67). The evidence clearly suggests, as Lloyd has rightly emphasized, that it is only with Aristotle that we get a fully developed theory of demonstration. In the first half of the fourth century agreement had not been reached either on the types of starting points that were necessary for mathematics or on specific definitions, postulates or common notions (1979: 112–15), but the issue of what counted as elements of geometry was, nonetheless, as Eudemus' evidence shows, a central concern and elements of some sort were being produced. Archytas' solution to the duplication of the cube was thus developed against the background of a considerable body of geometrical knowledge but in an environment in which there was a degree of flux as to how that knowledge was organized. His solution would only have force, however, if he and his readers felt confidence in the geometry which he assumes. Without some sort of shared assumptions about what had been established in geometry, all of Archytas' rigor would have no point. It thus seems very likely that he appealed to some sort of elements, even if those elements did not look exactly like what we find in Euclid. Eudemus reports that Archytas was one of the geometers who both increased the number of theorems and contributed to the more intelligible ordering of them (A6); it seems very probable that the duplication was one of the theorems to which Eudemus was referring. What contribution Archytas made to the ordering of theorems is less clear. We might suppose that it was precisely in the area of solid geometry that he contributed not only new theorems but also an arrangement of those theorems. Plato's criticism of Archytas in *Republic* VII, however, suggests that Plato, at least, did not think that Archytas had produced a successful elements of stereometry (see A15 and the overview of Archytas' philosophy). It is perhaps more likely that he arrived at his own ordering of part of the geometrical knowledge of his day precisely in order to support his remarkable duplication of the cube and thus produced a modification of the parts of Hippocrates' work on elements, which dealt with the material in Euclid 1–4 and 6.

Plato's Meno *and Archytas' solution to the duplication of the cube*
It has long been recognized that the problem of doubling the cube is connected to the simpler problem of doubling a square, which is the focus of the conversation between Socrates and the slave in Plato's *Meno* (82b9–85b7). This can be most easily seen by looking at the problem in terms of finding mean proportionals. If we can find a mean proportional between the given length, a, and double that length so that a:x :: x:2a, the square on x will be double the square on a. We can see this easily by recognizing that, if we multiply a:x by x:2a, this is the same as multiplying a:x by itself, since a:x is equal to x:2a. If we then multiply a:x by itself we get $a^2:x^2$ but this will be equal to the product of a:x and x:2a, which is ax:2ax which reduces to a:2a. Thus $a^2:x^2$ is equal to a:2a, and thus the square on x is double the square on a. Heath argues that "it may then have been the connexion between the doubling of the square and the finding of one mean proportional which suggested the reduction of the doubling of the cube to the problem of finding *two mean proportionals* between two unequal straight lines" (Heath 1953: cxxiv). Hippocrates of Chios made this reduction in the second half of the fifth century (see the beginning of the analysis of Archytas' solution above), so that the solution to the doubling of the square certainly antedates this reduction by Hippocrates.

Thus the problem which Socrates presents to the slave was not a novelty either at the time of composition of the *Meno* (380s) or at the dramatic date of the dialogue (402? Bluck 1964: 120). It is important to note that Plato does not present the problem of doubling the square in the terms in which it is most easily connected to the duplication of the cube, i.e. in terms of finding mean proportionals. Instead he uses a geometrical construction without mentioning the theory of proportions. There is thus nothing on the surface of the text in the *Meno* that suggests any connection to the duplication of the cube or to Archytas. If the *Meno* was written after Plato's first visit to Sicily and southern Italy, it is quite plausible to suppose that the interest in mathematics displayed in the *Meno* and subsequent dialogues was spurred by Plato's contact with Archytas (Vlastos 1991: 128 ff.). There is not adequate evidence, however, to make any more specific connection between Archytas and the mathematics of the *Meno*. Brown's argument (1967: 77 ff.) that there is a strong connection between the slave-boy passage in the *Meno* and Archytas rests on a very questionable reading of the *Meno*, according to which Plato is in fact criticizing the geometrical solution to the duplication of the square, and on parallels between testimony for Archytas and the *Meno* which are too general to produce conviction.

A15 Eutocius, *Commentary on Archimedes' On the Sphere and Cylinder* II (III. 88.3–96.27 Heiberg/Stamatis)

ὡς Ἐρατοσθένης   1

Βασιλεῖ Πτολεμαίῳ Ἐρατοσθένης χαίρειν.   2
   τῶν ἀρχαίων τινὰ τραγῳδοποιῶν φασιν εἰσαγαγεῖν τὸν Μίνω   3
τῷ Γλαύκῳ κατασκευάζοντα τάφον, πυθόμενον δέ, ὅτι πανταχοῦ   4
ἑκατόμπεδος εἴη, εἰπεῖν·   5

μικρὸν γ᾽ ἔλεξας βασιλικοῦ σηκὸν τάφου·   6
διπλάσιος ἔστω· τοῦ καλοῦ δὲ μὴ σφαλεὶς   7
δίπλαζ᾽ ἕκαστον κῶλον ἐν τάχει τάφου.   8

ἐδόκει δὲ διημαρτηκέναι. τῶν γὰρ πλευρῶν διπλασιασθεισῶν τὸ μὲν   9
ἐπίπεδον γίνεται τετραπλάσιον, τὸ δὲ στερεὸν ὀκταπλάσιον. ἐζητεῖτο   10
δὲ καὶ παρὰ τοῖς γεωμέτραις, τίνα ἄν τις τρόπον τὸ δοθὲν στερεὸν   11
διαμένον ἐν τῷ αὐτῷ σχήματι διπλασιάσειεν. καὶ ἐκαλεῖτο τὸ τοιοῦτον   12
πρόβλημα κύβου διπλασιασμός· ὑποθέμενοι γὰρ κύβον ἐζήτουν τοῦ-   13
τον διπλασιάσαι. πάντων δὲ διαπορούντων ἐπὶ πολὺν χρόνον πρῶτος   14
Ἱπποκράτης ὁ Χῖος ἐπενόησεν, ὅτι, ἐὰν εὑρεθῇ δύο εὐθειῶν γραμμῶν,   15
ὧν ἡ μείζων τῆς ἐλάσσονός ἐστι διπλασία, δύο μέσας ἀνάλογον λαβεῖν   16
ἐν συνεχεῖ ἀναλογίᾳ, διπλασιασθήσεται ὁ κύβος, ὥστε τὸ ἀπόρημα   17
αὐτοῦεἰς ἕτερον οὐκ ἔλασσον ἀπόρημα κατέστρεφεν. μετὰ χρόνον δὲ   18
τινάς φασιν Δηλίους ἐπιβαλλομένους κατὰ χρησμὸν διπλασιάσαι τινὰ   19
τῶν βωμῶν ἐμπεσεῖν εἰς τὸ αὐτὸ ἀπόρημα, διαπεμψαμένους δὲ τοὺς   20
παρὰ τῷ Πλάτωνι ἐν Ἀκαδημίᾳ γεωμέτρας ἀξιοῦν αὐτοῖς εὑρεῖν τὸ   21
ζητούμενον. τῶν δὲ φιλοπόνως ἐπιδιδόντων ἑαυτοὺς καὶ ζητούντων   22
δύο τῶν δοθεισῶν δύο μέσας λαβεῖν Ἀρχύτας μὲν ὁ Ταραντῖνος λέγε-   23
ται διὰ τῶν ἡμικυλίνδρων εὑρηκέναι, Εὔδοξος δὲ διὰ τῶν καλουμένων   24
καμπύλων γραμμῶν. συμβέβηκε δὲ πᾶσιν αὐτοῖς ἀποδεικτικῶς   25
γεγραφέναι, χειρουργῆσαι δὲ καὶ εἰς χρείαν πεσεῖν μὴ δύνασθαι πλὴν   26

---

7 διπλάσιος] Valckenaer   διπλασιον Α   τοῦ καλοῦ δὲ] Nauck   του δε του καλου ΑΒ
κύβου mg. G²   τοῦ κύβου δὲ Valckenaer   σφαλεὶς] e corr. Ε   σφαλης ΑΒ   **8** δίπλαζ᾽]
Nauck   διπλασιαζ᾽ Α   **9** δὲ] autem supra scr. Β²   om. ΑΒ   **11** δὲ] Hiller   δη ΑΒ
18 αὐτοῦ] ΑΒ   αὐτῷ Bernhardy   **20** διαπεμψαμένους] D²   διαμεμψαμενους ΑΒ   **22**
ἑαυτοὺς] se ipsos Β   ἑαυτοις Α

ἐπὶ βραχύ τι τὸν Μέναιχμον καὶ ταῦτα δυσχερῶς. ἐπινενόηται δέ τις 27
ὑφ' ἡμῶν ὀργανικὴ λῆψις ῥαδία, δι' ἧς εὑρήσομεν δύο τῶν δοθεισῶν 28
οὐ μόνον δύο μέσας, ἀλλ' ὅσας ἄν τις ἐπιτάξῃ. τούτου δὲ εὑρισκομένου 29
δυνησόμεθα καθόλου τὸ δοθὲν στερεὸν παραλληλογράμμοις περιεχό- 30
μενον εἰς κύβον καθιστάναι ἢ ἐξ ἑτέρου εἰς ἕτερον μετασχηματίζειν, 31
καὶ ὅμοιον ποιεῖν καὶ ἐπαύξειν διατηροῦντας τὴν ὁμοιότητα, ὥστε 32
καὶ βωμοὺς καὶ ναούς... τὴν δὲ ἀπόδειξιν καὶ τὴν κατασκευὴν τοῦ 33
λεχθέντος ὀργάνου ὑπογέγραφά σοι. 34
   δεδόσθωσαν δύο ἄνισοι εὐθεῖαι... 35
   ταῦτα οὖν ἐπὶ τῶν γεωμετρουμένων ἐπιφανειῶν ἀποδέδεικται. ἵνα 36
δὲ καὶ ὀργανικῶς δυνώμεθα τὰς δύο μέσας λαμβάνειν, διαπήγνυται 37
πλινθίον ξύλινον ἢ ἐλεφάντινον ἢ χαλκοῦν... 38
ἐν δὲ τῷ ἀναθήματι τὸ μὲν ὀργανικὸν χαλκοῦν ἐστιν καὶ καθήρμοσται 39
ὑπ' αὐτὴν τὴν στεφάνην τῆς στήλης προσμεμολυβδοχοημένον, ὑπ' 40
αὐτοῦ δὲ ἡ ἀπόδειξις συντομώτερον φραζομένη καὶ τὸ σχῆμα, μετ' 41
αὐτὸ δὲ ἐπίγραμμα. ὑπογεγράφθω οὖν σοι καὶ ταῦτα, ἵνα ἔχῃς καὶ ὡς 42
ἐν τῷ ἀναθήματι... 43

εἰ κύβον ἐξ ὀλίγου διπλήσιον, ὦγαθέ, τεύχειν 44
φράζεαι ἢ στερεὴν πᾶσαν ἐς ἄλλο φύσιν 45
εὖ μεταμορφῶσαι, τόδε τοι πάρα, κἂν σύ γε μάνδρην 46
ἢ σιρὸν ἢ κοίλου φρείατος εὐρὺ κύτος 47
τῇδ' ἀναμετρήσαιο, μέσας ὅτε τέρμασιν ἄκροις 48
συνδρομάδας δισσῶν ἐντὸς ἕλῃς κανόνων. 49
μηδὲ σύ γ' Ἀρχύτεω δυσμήχανα ἔργα κυλίνδρων 50
μηδὲ Μεναιχμείους κωνοτομεῖν τριάδας 51
διζήσῃ, μηδ' εἴ τι θεουδέος Εὐδόξοιο 52
καμπύλον ἐγ γραμμαῖς εἶδος ἀναγράφεται. 53
τοῖσδε γὰρ ἐν πινάκεσσι μεσόγραφα μυρία τεύχοις 54
ῥεῖά κεν ἐκ παύρου πυθμένος ἀρχόμενος. 55
εὐαίων, Πτολεμαῖε, πατὴρ ὅτι παιδὶ συνηβῶν 56
πάνθ', ὅσα καὶ Μούσαις καὶ βασιλεῦσι φίλα, 57
αὐτὸς ἐδωρήσω· τὸ δ' ἐς ὕστερον, οὐράνιε Ζεῦ, 58
καὶ σκήπτρων ἐκ σῆς ἀντιάσειε χερός. 59
καὶ τὰ μὲν ὡς τελέοιτο, λέγοι δέ τις ἄνθεμα λεύσσων 60
τοῦ Κυρηναίου τοῦτ' Ἐρατοσθένεος. 61

27 βραχύ τι] Basil. βραχυτητι AB τὸν Μέναιχμον] Stamatis τοῦ Μενεχμου AB 40 προσμεμολυβδοχοημένον] Dressler προς μεμολυβδοχημενω A 45 ἢ] Jacobs την A καὶ Heiberg 47 σιρὸν] Fell σειρον A 51 citat Proclus _In Eucl._ III.23 Μεναιχμείους] Wilamowitz, Stamatis Μενεχμειους A Μεναιχμίους Proclus 52 διζήσῃ] Wilamowitz διζηαι A 53 ἐγ γραμμαῖς] A ἐν γραμμαῖς GH 54 γὰρ] Wilamowitz δε A

[Given two straight lines, how to find two mean proportionals in continued   62
proportion] according to Eratosthenes.   63

Eratosthenes to King Ptolemy, greetings,   64
   They say that one of the ancient tragedians portrayed Minos constructing   65
a tomb for Glaucus, and that, when he learned that it was a hundred feet   66
on each side, he said,   67

> Small indeed is the tomb you have spoken of for a royal burial.
> Let it be double! While not destroying its beauty,
> quickly double each side of the tomb.

But he was considered to have made a mistake. For when the sides are
doubled, a surface is increased four-fold and a solid is increased eight-
fold. But geometers also sought in what manner someone could double a
given solid, while it continued in the same shape. And this sort of problem
was called the duplication of the cube. For having posited a cube, they
sought to double it. After everyone had been in perplexity for a long time,
Hippocrates of Chios first conceived that, if a way can be found to get two
mean proportionals in continued proportion between two straight lines,
of which the greater is double the lesser, the cube will be doubled. As a
result he transformed his problem into another no less difficult problem.
Some time later they say that some Delians, devoting themselves to doubling one of their altars in accordance with an oracle, fell into the same
difficulty. They sent to the geometers associated with Plato in the Academy
and expected them to find that which they sought. After these geometers
devoted themselves industriously to seeking to determine the two means
of the two given lines, Archytas of Tarentum is said to have discovered
them through the semicylinders, and Eudoxus through the so-called bent
lines. But it has turned out that they all have written in the form of a
geometrical demonstration and that they cannot build what they describe
or descend to practice, except to some small extent Menaechmus and that
only with difficulty. But I have contrived an easy approach, by means of
an instrument, through which I will find not only two means of the two
given lines, but however many someone demands. With this discovery we
will be able in general to transform any given solid, which is bounded by
parallelograms, into a cube, or to change it from one shape to another, and
to make a similar solid and to augment the solid while preserving similarity,
so as [to make] both altars and temples . . . I have written out for you below
the mathematical demonstration and the construction of the instrument
which I have described.
   Let two unequal straight lines be given . . .

This, then, is the demonstration on geometrical surfaces. But in order that we also be able to determine the two means with an instrument, a frame is fashioned out of wood, or ivory, or bronze . . .

On the votive monument the instrument is bronze and it has been attached with lead right under the crown of the column. Under it is the demonstration, phrased more concisely, and the diagram, and after it there is an epigram. Let these things also be written out for you below, so that you might also have them as they are on the votive monument . . .

[The following is the epigram, with which the letter concludes.] If your purpose is to produce a cube double the size from one too small, my friend, or to change properly any solid nature into another, this is your instrument, and you could measure in this way a cattle-fold, or a pit for corn, or the broad hollow of a well cavity, by taking means which run together with the extreme terms within twin rulers. Don't seek out the deeds of the cylinders of Archytas, which are hard to put into effect, nor to produce the triadic conic sections of Menaechmus, nor if any bent shape of lines is described by god-fearing Eudoxus. For with these plates of mine, you would easily produce myriads of means, although beginning from a small foundation. O Ptolemy, O fortunate father, that enjoying youth with your son, you yourself gave him all the things that are dear both to the Muses and to kings; and in the future, heavenly Zeus, may he receive the scepter from your hand. May these things come to pass in this way, and may anyone who sees this dedication say, this is the offering of Eratosthenes of Cyrene.

A15a Plutarch, *Table Talk* VIII. 2.1, 718e (Hubert 1971: 261.27–262.13)

πᾶσι μὲν οὖν τοῖς καλουμένοις μαθήμασιν, ὥσπερ ἀστραβέσι καὶ λείοις   1
κατόπτροις, ἐμφαίνεται τῆς τῶν νοητῶν ἀληθείας ἴχνη καὶ εἴδωλα·   2
μάλιστα δὲ γεωμετρία κατὰ τὸν Φιλόλαον ἀρχὴ καὶ μητρόπολις οὖσα   3
τῶν ἄλλων ἐπανάγει καὶ στρέφει τὴν διάνοιαν, οἷον ἐκκαθαιρομένην   4
καὶ ἀπολυομένην ἀτρέμα τῆς αἰσθήσεως, διὸ καὶ Πλάτων αὐτὸς ἐμέμψ-   5
ατο τοὺς περὶ Εὔδοξον καὶ Ἀρχύταν καὶ Μέναιχμον εἰς ὀργανικὰς καὶ   6
μηχανικὰς κατασκευὰς τὸν τοῦ στερεοῦ διπλασιασμὸν ἀπάγειν ἐπι-   7
χειροῦντας, ὥσπερ πειρωμένους δίχα λόγου δύο μέσας ἀνὰ λόγον,   8
ᾗ παρείκοι, λαβεῖν· ἀπόλλυσθαι γὰρ οὕτω καὶ διαφθείρεσθαι τὸ   9

3 δὲ] Ald. δὴ codd. Φιλόλαον] Hu. φίλαον T Φίλωνα edd. inde ab Ald.   **8** ὥσπερ] Turn. ὅπερ codd. ὥσπερ . . . λαβεῖν] del. Wy. δίχα λόγου] Wil. διαλόγου T δι᾽ ἀλόγου Holwerda ἀνὰ λόγον] Madvig ἀνάλογον codd.   **9** ᾗ] Herw. μὴ codd.

γεωμετρίας ἀγαθὸν αὖθις ἐπὶ τὰ αἰσθητὰ παλινδρομούσης καὶ μὴ 10
φερομένης ἄνω μηδ᾽ ἀντιλαμβανομένης τῶν ἀιδίων καὶ ἀσωμάτων 11
εἰκόνων, πρὸς αἷσπερ ὢν ὁ θεὸς ἀεὶ θεός ἐστιν. 12

12 αἷσπερ] Bern   οἷσπερ T, Plato, *Phaedr.* 249c   θεῖός ἐστιν Platonis codd.

Now in all the so-called sciences, just as in undistorted and smooth mirrors,
traces and images of the truth of intelligible things appear. But geometry,
being, according to Philolaus, the source and mother-city of the rest of the
sciences, especially leads upward and turns the intellect, purified, as it were,
and gently freed from sense-perception. For this reason Plato himself also
reproached Eudoxus, Archytas, Menaechmus and their followers for trying
to lead away the problem of the duplication of a solid into constructions
that use instruments and that are mechanical, just as if they were trying to
obtain the two mean proportionals apart from reason, in whatever way it
was practicable. For its good was ruined and destroyed, when geometry ran
back again to the sensibles and was not borne upwards and did not lay hold
of the eternal and incorporeal images, in relation to which God is always
God.

A15b Plutarch, *Marcellus* xiv. 5–6 (Ziegler 1994: 123. 6–22)

τὴν γὰρ ἀγαπωμένην ταύτην καὶ περιβόητον ὀργανικὴν ἤρξαντο 1
μὲν κινεῖν οἱ περὶ Εὔδοξον καὶ Ἀρχύταν, ποικίλλοντες τῷ γλαφυρῷ 2
γεωμετρίαν, καὶ λογικῆς καὶ γραμμικῆς ἀποδείξεως οὐκ εὐποροῦντα 3
προβλήματα δι᾽ αἰσθητῶν καὶ ὀργανικῶν παραδειγμάτων ὑπερείδον- 4
τες, ὡς τὸ περὶ δύο μέσας ἀνὰ λόγον πρόβλημα καὶ στοιχεῖον ἐπὶ 5
πολλὰ τῶν γραφομένων ἀναγκαῖον εἰς ὀργανικὰς ἐξῆγον ἀμφότεροι 6
κατασκευάς, μεσογράφους τινὰς ἀπὸ καμπύλων γραμμῶν καὶ τμημά- 7
των μεθαρμόζοντες· ἐπεὶ δὲ Πλάτων ἠγανάκτησε καὶ διετείνατο πρὸς 8
αὐτούς, ὡς ἀπολλύντας καὶ διαφθείροντας τὸ γεωμετρίας ἀγαθόν, ἀπὸ 9
τῶν ἀσωμάτων καὶ νοητῶν ἀποδιδρασκούσης ἐπὶ τὰ αἰσθητά, καὶ 10
προσχρωμένης αὖθις αὖ σώμασι πολλῆς καὶ φορτικῆς βαναυσουργίας 11
δεομένοις, οὕτω διεκρίθη γεωμετρίας ἐκπεσοῦσα μηχανική, καὶ περιορ- 12
ωμένη πολὺν χρόνον ὑπὸ φιλοσοφίας, μία τῶν στρατιωτίδων τεχνῶν 13
ἐγεγόνει. 14

2 Εὔδοξον] δέξιον L¹   δώξιον P   3 γραμμικῆς] Valckenaer   πραγματικῆς codd.
4–5 ὑπερείδοντες] Xylander   ὑπεριδόντες codd.   5 ἀνὰ λόγον] Bryan   ἀνάλωτον
L¹KP   ἄλογον QL²   7 μεσολάβους Amyot   γραμμῶν] Coraes   γραμμάτων codd.
11 αὖ] om. P   11 βαναυσουργίας] em. anon.   βαναύσου ἀργίας codd.
12 δεομένοις]δεομένης QL²

Eudoxus and Archytas and their followers began to set in motion this prized and famous science of mechanics, by embellishing geometry with its subtlety, and, in the case of problems which did not admit of logical and geometrical demonstration, by using sensible and mechanical models as supports. Thus, they both employed mechanical constructions for the problem of the two mean proportionals, which is a necessary element in many geometrical figures, adapting to their purposes certain mean lines from bent lines and sections. But, when Plato was upset and maintained against them that they were destroying and ruining the value of geometry, since it had fled from the incorporeal and intelligible to the sensible, using again physical objects which required much common handicraft, the science of mechanics was driven out and separated from geometry, and being disregarded for a long time by philosophy, became one of the military arts.

A15c Vitruvius, *On Architecure* IX. Prologue 13–14 (Krohn 1912: 199. 13–27)

Transferatur mens ad Archytae Tarentini et Eratosthenis Cyrenaei cogitata;   1
hi enim multa et grata a mathematicis rebus hominibus invenerunt. Itaque   2
cum in ceteris inventionibus fuerint grati, in eius rei concitationibus   3
maxime sunt suspecti. Alius enim alia ratione explicaverunt, quod Delo   4
imperaverat responsis Apollo, uti arae eius, quantum haberent pedum   5
quadratorum, id duplicarentur, et ita fore uti, qui essent in ea insula, tunc   6
religione liberarentur.   7

    Itaque Archytas cylindrorum descriptionibus, Eratosthenes organica   8
mesolabi ratione idem explicaverunt. Cum haec sint tam magnis doc-   9
trinarum iucunditatibus animadversa et cogamur naturaliter invention-   10
ibus singularum rerum considerantes effectus moveri, multas res attendens   11
admiror etiam Democriti de rerum natura volumina . . .   12

3 concitationibus] x cogitationibus Rodum   4 explicaverunt] rec. explicarentur x   5
imperaverat] S^c impetraverat x   6 fore uti] Rodum forenti HS forent hi EG

Let us turn our attention to the thoughts of Archytas of Tarentum and Eratosthenes of Cyrene. For these men have discovered many pleasing things for humanity by means of mathematics. Therefore, although they have been popular for other discoveries, they have been especially admired for the stimulation that they have provided in this area. For they each in their own way accomplished that which Apollo had commanded in his response to the Delians, that the number of cubic feet in his altar be doubled, and thus it would come about that those on the island would then be freed from their religious duty.

So Archytas by means of diagrams of cylinders and Eratosthenes by a method that employed the mesolab as an instrument solved the same problem. Although these things are apprehended with the very great pleasure which attends such learning, and we are naturally compelled to be moved by the discovery of remarkable things, as we consider what has been accomplished, after a wide survey, I also admire the books of Democritus on the nature of things . . .

Text A. Theon of Smyrna, *Mathematics useful for reading Plato* (p. 2. 3–15 Hiller 1878)

Ἐρατοσθένης μὲν γὰρ ἐν τῷ ἐπιγραφομένῳ Πλατωνικῷ φησιν ὅτι, Δηλίοις τοῦ θεοῦ χρήσαντος ἐπὶ ἀπαλλαγῇ λοιμοῦ βωμὸν τοῦ ὄντος διπλασίονα κατασκευάσαι, πολλὴν ἀρχιτέκτοσιν ἐμπεσεῖν ἀπορίαν ζητοῦσιν ὅπως χρὴ στερεὸν στερεοῦ γενέσθαι διπλάσιον, ἀφικέσθαι τε πευσομένους περὶ τούτου Πλάτωνος, τὸν δὲ φάναι αὐτοῖς, ὡς ἄρα οὐ διπλασίου βωμοῦ ὁ θεὸς δεόμενος τοῦτο Δηλίοις ἐμαντεύσατο, προφέρων δὲ καὶ ὀνειδίζων τοῖς Ἕλλησιν ἀμελοῦσι μαθημάτων καὶ γεωμετρίας ὠλιγωρηκόσιν.

Eratosthenes, in the work entitled *Platonicus*, says that, when the god had ordered the Delians, in an oracle, to construct an altar double the existing one, in order to escape from a plague, great perplexity fell on the builders as to how a solid should become the double of another solid, and they came to ask Plato about this, and he said to them, that the god did not give this oracle to the Delians because he wanted an altar twice the size, but in order to bring forward as a reproach to the Greeks that they pay no attention to mathematics and have neglected geometry.

Text B. Plutarch, *The E at Delphi* 6, 386d–f (Patton 1929: vi. 5–18)

ταῦτα τοῦ Νικάνδρου διελθόντος, οἶσθα γὰρ δὴ Θέωνα τὸν 1
ἑταῖρον, ἤρετο τὸν Ἀμμώνιον εἰ διαλεκτικῇ παρρησίας μέτεστιν 2
οὕτω περιυβρισμένη <καὶ κακῶς> ἀκηκουίᾳ· τοῦ δ' Ἀμμωνίου λέγειν 3
παρακελευομένου καὶ βοηθεῖν, "ἀλλ' ὅτι μέν," ἔφη, "διαλεκτικώτα- 4
τος ὁ θεός ἐστιν, οἱ πολλοὶ τῶν χρησμῶν δηλοῦσιν· τοῦ γὰρ αὐτοῦ 5
δήπουθέν ἐστι καὶ λύειν καὶ ποιεῖν ἀμφιβολίας. ἔτι δ', ὥσπερ Πλάτων 6

3 περιυβρισμένως Babbitt <καὶ κακῶς>] Blass ἀκηκουίᾳ] om Πx

ἔλεγε, χρησμοῦ δοθέντος ὅπως τὸν ἐν Δήλῳ βωμὸν διπλασιάσωσιν, 7
ὃ τῆς ἄκρας ἕξεως περὶ γεωμετρίαν ἔργον ἐστίν, οὐ τοῦτο προστάτ- 8
τειν τὸν θεὸν ἀλλὰ γεωμετρεῖν διακελεύεσθαι τοῖς Ἕλλησιν· οὕτως ἄρα 9
χρησμοὺς ἀμφιβόλους ἐκφέρων ὁ θεὸς αὔξει καὶ συνίστησι διαλεκτικὴν 10
ὡς ἀναγκαίαν τοῖς μέλλουσιν ὀρθῶς αὐτοῦ συνήσειν. 11

After Nicander had gone through these things, my friend Theon, whom you know, asked Ammonius if logic had a right to speak, since it had been treated so insultingly and spoken ill of. When Ammonius encouraged him to speak and to come to its aid, he said "that God is most skilled in logic, many of his oracles make clear. For I suppose that it belongs to the same person both to create and to resolve ambiguities. Moreover, as Plato said, when an oracle had been given commanding that they double the altar in Delos, which is a task involving the highest geometrical ability, that it was not this that the God was ordering but that he was commanding the Greeks to practice geometry, in the same way, by putting forth ambiguous oracles, the god is extolling and establishing logic as necessary for those who are going to understand him correctly."

Text C. Plutarch, *On the Sign of Socrates* 7, 579b–d
(Patton 1929: III. 469–70)

... κομιζομένοις ἡμῖν ἀπ᾽ Αἰγύπτου περὶ Καρίαν Δηλίων τινὲς ἀπήντη- 1
σαν δεόμενοι Πλάτωνος ὡς γεωμετρικοῦ λῦσαι χρησμὸν αὐτοῖς ἄτο- 2
πον ὑπὸ τοῦ θεοῦ προβεβλημένον. ἦν δ᾽ ὁ χρησμὸς Δηλίοις καὶ τοῖς 3
ἄλλοις Ἕλλησι παῦλαν τῶν παρόντων κακῶν ἔσεσθαι διπλασιάσασι 4
τὸν ἐν Δήλῳ βωμόν. οὔτε δὲ τὴν διάνοιαν ἐκεῖνοι συμβάλλειν δυνά- 5
μενοι καὶ περὶ τὴν τοῦ βωμοῦ κατασκευὴν γελοῖα πάσχοντες (ἑκάστης 6
γὰρ τῶν τεσσάρων πλευρῶν διπλασιαζομένης ἔλαθον τῇ αὐξήσει 7
τόπον στερεὸν ὀκταπλάσιον ἀπεργασάμενοι δι᾽ ἀπειρίαν ἀναλογίας 8
ἣν τὸ μήκει διπλάσιον παρέχεται) Πλάτωνα τῆς ἀπορίας ἐπεκαλοῦντο 9
βοηθόν. ὁ δὲ τοῦ Αἰγυπτίου μνησθεὶς προσπαίζειν ἔφη τὸν θεὸν 10
Ἕλλησιν ὀλιγωροῦσι παιδείας οἷον ἐφυβρίζοντα τὴν ἀμαθίαν ἡμῶν 11
καὶ κελεύοντα γεωμετρίας ἅπτεσθαι μὴ παρέργως· οὐ γάρ τοι φαύλης 12
οὐδ᾽ ἀμβλὺ διανοίας ὁρώσης ἄκρως δὲ τὰς γραμμὰς ἠσκημένης ἔργον 13
εἶναι [καὶ] δυεῖν μέσων ἀνάλογον λῆψιν, ᾗ μόνη διπλασιάζεται σχῆμα 14
κυβικοῦ σώματος ἐκ πάσης ὁμοίως αὐξόμενον διαστάσεως. τοῦτο μὲν 15
οὖν Εὔδοξον αὐτοῖς τὸν Κνίδιον ἢ τὸν Κυζικηνὸν Ἑλίκωνα συντελέσειν· 16

---

3 δ᾽ ὁ] Kronenberg   δὲ codd.   **9** ἦν τὸ] Hartman   ἢ τῷ codd.   **14** del. Wyttenbach
μέσων] Ald.²   μέσον codd.

μὴ τοῦτο δ' οἴεσθαι χρῆναι ποθεῖν τὸν θεὸν ἀλλὰ προστάσσειν Ἕλλησι 17
πᾶσι πολέμου καὶ κακῶν μεθεμένους Μούσαις ὁμιλεῖν καὶ διὰ λόγων 18
καὶ μαθημάτων τὰ πάθη καταπραΰνοντας ἀβλαβῶς καὶ ὠφελίμως 19
ἀλλήλοις συμφέρεσθαι 20

17 δ' οἴεσθαι] Reiske δεῖσθαι codd.

... some of the Delians met us in the region of Caria, as we were journeying from Egypt and asked Plato, as a geometer, to solve the strange oracle which had been posed to them by the god. The oracle said that there would be a cessation of their present evils for the Delians and the other Greeks, when they had doubled the altar on Delos. But they, not able to understand what was meant and having made fools of themselves in regard to the construction of the altar (for they unwittingly produced a solid eight times as great, when each of the four sides was doubled, because of their inexperience with the proportion which the double length creates), called upon Plato as an ally in their perplexity. Plato, remembering the Egyptian, said that the god was mocking the Greeks for neglecting education, as it were insulting our ignorance and commanding us to pursue geometry in no cursory fashion. For he said that the grasp of the two mean proportionals, by which alone a body with the shape of a cube is doubled, while being augmented in the same way in each dimension, was the task of no mean or dim sighted intelligence but of one trained to the highest degree in geometry. This, he said that Eudoxus of Cnidos or Helicon of Cyzicus would accomplish for them. But he said that they were not to think that this was what the god desired but rather that he was ordering all the Greeks, having laid aside war and evils, to consort with the Muses and, allaying their passions through discourse and study of mathematics, to associate without doing harm to one another but rather benefit.

Summary of other texts
Valerius Maximus, *On Memorable Deeds and Sayings* VIII. 12. ext. 1. Plato refers those trying to consult with him about the altar to Euclid!!!

Philoponus, *On the Posterior Analytics* (*CAG* XIII.3. 102.12–22). The Delians unsuccessfully try to escape the plague by placing a second altar, identical to the original altar, on the original altar. Plato tells them that the god is chiding them for neglecting geometry and explains that doubling the cube requires finding two mean proportionals. He poses the problem to his pupils. Philoponus reports that "some" of them "have written about the discovery of these things."

Asclepius of Tralles, *On Nicomachus' Introduction to Arithmetic* 11.17.8–15
(61 Taran). The Delians make an altar four times as big. Plato's response is
similar to that in Philoponus. Asclepius says that some solved the problem
with lines and some with cones (Eudoxus and Menaechmus?). "Each one
simply solved it as he hit upon it. For it is a very difficult problem."

Anonymous Prolegomena to Platonic Philosophy 5. 15–24 (11 Westerink). Plato
is said to have discovered the mean proportional! Here the plague strikes
the Athenians (!), who consult Delphi. The Athenians put one cube on top
of another, as the Delians did in Philoponus. Plato tells them that the god
is not asking them to double the cube "in an everyday way" (ἰδιωτικῶς)
but by finding "a mean proportional."

Contents and contexts
(The best discussions of the problems surrounding Eratosthenes' account
of the Delian problem are found in Cambiano 1998, Knorr 1986, Knorr
1989, Sturm 1895, Wilamowitz 1894, and Wolfer 1954). The testimonia in
A15 provide the purported historical setting and intellectual context for
Archytas' solution to the problem of the duplication of the cube, which is
presented in A14. The immediate cause of Archytas' work on this problem
is said to be an oracle given to the inhabitants of the island of Delos and
instructing them to double the size of an altar. The testimonia also suggest,
however, that the problem had arisen much earlier and, already in the fifth
century, had been reduced by Hippocrates of Chios to the problem of
finding two mean proportionals between two given lines. It is indeed in
terms of these two mean proportionals that Archytas addresses the problem
in A14. In addition to providing this historical setting for Archytas' work,
the testimonia provide a series of reactions to that work, beginning with the
reaction of Archytas' contemporary Plato, which, if genuine, would reflect
the intellectual context in which Archytas' solution arose, and continuing
with the reactions of Eratosthenes in the third century BC and Vitruvius
in the first century BC. This contextualizing of Archytas' discovery is just
a part of a wider story focusing on the Delian problem, of which Plato
is the focus. If we are to come to an understanding of these accounts of
Archytas, it is necessary to reconstruct the over-arching Platonic story, at
least in outline (see Texts A–C and the summary of other texts above; see
further Riginos 1976: 141–46 for discussion of these texts and references to
Arabic texts).

It is probable, but not certain, that all surviving accounts of the Delian
problem go back to Eratosthenes' *Platonicus*, which was written in the

third century BC. Theon of Smyrna (second century AD), at the beginning of his handbook entitled *Mathematics Useful for Reading Plato*, identifies Eratosthenes as his source for the story (Text A above), and we know of no earlier account than Eratosthenes'. To the issue of what sources Eratosthenes might have used we will return below. Since Theon is the only author to refer to the *Platonicus* by name (Text A), it is reasonable to begin reconstructing what Eratosthenes said from Theon's account. According to Theon, the Delians were beset by a plague and consulted the oracle of Apollo as to how to escape it. The oracle tells them to double the size of a given altar, and, when the builders are perplexed as to how to accomplish this, the Delians consult Plato. The point of the story is Plato's response. In accordance with a typical literary pattern regarding oracles, the literal meaning is rejected for an interpretation with wider implications. Plato says that the god is not interested in having an altar that is twice the size but is reproaching the Greeks for not having paid enough attention to mathematics and for neglecting geometry. This fits Theon's purposes at the beginning of his treatise, where he is emphasizing the importance of mathematics to Plato and thus the importance of Theon's own book in understanding Plato.

The precise meaning of Plato's answer is made a little clearer in two further versions of the story found in Plutarch (Texts B and C), which are probably also based on Eratosthenes, since the core of what they say coheres closely with what is found in Theon. First, these texts emphasize that the problem of doubling the altar is a task of great geometrical complexity and that the apparently obvious solutions had been tried by the Delians without success, so that Plato's point is sharpened. The god is not calling for any passing knowledge of geometry but for serious dedication to the study of it. Second, the texts downplay even more the importance of the particular problem of doubling the altar; Plato tells the Delians that Eudoxus or Helicon can solve the problem for them, but insists that it is not this that the god wants. It is the serious pursuit of geometry and mathematics in general that the god is commanding for all Greeks. So far Texts B and C agree with each other and with Theon's version. In Text C, however, the Delian story has been tied to a story of Plato's visit to Egypt and elaborated in new ways for this context. Thus, Plato's assertion, in Text C, that mathematics is to be pursued in order to direct the energies of the Greeks away from war, appears to arise from the new context and is unlikely to go back to Eratosthenes.

The other texts summarized after Text C show further variations in the story arising from the different purposes for which the story was used and from the inevitable fluidity of such a tradition. Since the focus of the story

is really Plato, it is not surprising that in some versions the Delians are
replaced by Plato's fellow Athenians as those suffering from the plague, nor
that Plato is further glorified by the absurd assertion that he was the first
to discover the mean proportionals. There is some variation also in the
account of how the Delians went wrong in their initial attempts to satisfy
the oracle. Instead of producing a cube that was eight times the desired
size, an error that parallels the slave's error in his attempt to double the
square in Plato's *Meno*, the Delians simply make another altar identical
to the original altar and put it on top of the original. In some cases the
story is changed beyond all historical verisimilitude as when Plato refers
those wanting to double the altar to Euclid, who was active fifty years after
Plato's death. Here Euclid, who was more famous in the later tradition, may
have replaced Eudoxus. Despite these later variations, the broad outlines
of Eratosthenes' presentation of the Delian problem in the *Platonicus* are
clear from Texts A–C: the Delians, suffering from a plague, are told by an
oracle to double a certain altar. After their initial attempts fail, they consult
Plato. Plato interprets the injunction to double the size of the altar as an
exhortation to the Greeks to pursue advanced geometry in general and
criticizes others for focusing instead on the particular problem.

  The *Platonicus* was not the only text in which Eratosthenes discussed the
Delian problem. Eutocius of Ascalon (early 500s AD), in his commentary on
Book II of Archimedes' *On the Sphere and Cylinder*, provides an invaluable
collection of solutions to the Delian problem (see A14). Eutocius presents
Eratosthenes' own solution to the Delian problem, in the form of a letter
from Eratosthenes to Ptolemy Euergetes, king of Egypt (A15). The letter
purports to have been written to accompany a votive offering dedicated by
Eratosthenes, in thanksgiving for his discovery of an instrument which can
be used to determine the two means (the mesolab or "mean getter"), which
are necessary to solve the Delian problem. A model of the instrument was
attached to the votive offering, which took the form of a column, and a brief
mathematical account of the solution and a poem concerning the solution
and addressed to Ptolemy were inscribed on the column. The votive offering
has not survived. There are good contemporary parallels for such offerings,
however (Fraser 1972: I. 412–13). They served both to advertise the scientific
achievement of their dedicator and to honor the person to whom they were
dedicated, in this case Ptolemy. The letter preserved by Eutocius ends by
quoting the mathematical proof and epigram, which were inscribed on the
offering, but also provides a preface, which includes: (1) further background
to the Delian problem, (2) an account of the virtues of Eratosthenes' own
solution, (3) a more detailed account of the proof, (4) a brief account of

the practicalities of constructing the instrument, (5) a brief account of the votive offering.

Wilamowitz argued that the account of the solution and the poem which were inscribed on the votive offering and which are preserved at the end of the letter, are likely to be genuine but that the rest of the letter is a later composition derived from the inscription on the monument and from Eratosthenes' *Platonicus* (1962: 54–55). Wilamowitz's judgment has been accepted for a long time, and it is still probably the case that the majority of scholars follow Wilamowitz, in regarding the letter as spurious (see e.g. Fraser 1972: 1. 410ff.). Some of the arguments recently advanced by Knorr, however, suggest that the letter may be authentic after all (1986: 18 ff.; 1989: 131 ff.; Zhmud 1998: 216 accepts Knorr's defense of authenticity). There is nothing mathematically anachronistic in the letter. It is true that Pappus (fl. AD 320), two centuries before Eutocius, describes Eratosthenes' instrument in quite different terms, among other things using triangles rather than the parallelograms used in the letter. But it is quite possible that there were different versions of the instrument and that Eutocius and Pappus made different selections from the descriptions available for it in the tradition. Eutocius' version in fact corresponds better to what is said in the material inscribed on the votive offering, which Wilamowitz accepts as authentic (Knorr 1986: 19; 1989: 132–34).

Wilamowitz argued that, if Ptolemy had the votive offering, he would have no need for the letter (1962: 52; Fraser 1972: 1. 412). This is very unconvincing. It is far from clear that the votive monument would in fact reside in a location where the king would have easy access to it or where the inscription would be easy to read. The letter, by including the text of the inscription, provides the king with an easily legible version of what is inscribed there, which can always be at hand and is easily portable. The introductory material on the history of the Delian problem is also appropriate, since the brief material inscribed on the monument would hardly make clear to the king the significance of what Eratosthenes had achieved. Moreover, it is far from clear that such a letter is intended just for the king's eyes. It may also have been intended as a method of publication of Eratosthenes' discovery. The monument can hardly be reproduced to be disseminated to others as the letter can.

Wilamowitz's strongest arguments against authenticity were based on the failure of the letter, as a literary composition, to conform to the style of such letters in the third century BC (1962: 53 ff.). It is true that the letter is relatively plain in style and certainly we cannot use the banality of style as "the strongest indication of the letter's authenticity" as Knorr does (1986: 19).

The assumption that a forger would not be banal but would let his "imagination run" is belied by the large number of very banal forgeries in the Pythagorean tradition (Thesleff 1965 *passim*). But as Knorr points out there is not really that much difference between Eratosthenes' letter and, for example, Archimedes' *Sand Reckoner*, which has the form of a letter to king Gelon (1986: 20). Knorr's attempt to show that the use of second-person address (to Ptolemy and Gelon respectively) in the letters is equally sparing (1986: 43 n. 22; 12 uses in 43 pages for Archimedes and 3 in 5 for Eratosthenes) is misleading, since the *Sand Reckoner* has a much longer technical section, in which such addresses would not be expected. If we compare just the parts of the compositions in which second-person address would be expected, it is clear that it is more frequent in Archimedes (12 uses in about 4 pages as compared to 3 uses in about 4 pages). Nonetheless, both letters start with very plain addresses to the king and have a similar structure. While Archimedes does use second-person address more frequently than Eratosthenes, in the appropriate parts of the letter, it must be remembered that Eratosthenes' letter is very brief, and that he does address Ptolemy in the second person in the logical places (in the first line, in line 34 to mark the transition from the introductory account of the Delian problem to the demonstration of his own solution, in line 42 before the quotation of the inscription on the monument). Again the letter only appears to end abruptly if one does not recognize that the closing poem, with its address to Ptolemy, is intended to serve as the conclusion to the letter. I would agree, however, that the introduction of the monument in line 39 of the letter is somewhat abrupt. Nonetheless, the onus of proof is on those who would reject the letter, and, while certainty is not possible, I regard it as similar enough to letters such as that in the *Sand Reckoner* in order to be regarded as authentic. However, even should Wilamowitz's conclusion be accepted, it is important to note that he argues (1962: 54–55) that the content of the letter is almost totally based on Eratosthenes' work (either the inscription on the monument or the *Platonicus*) and can thus be used judiciously as further evidence for the content of the *Platonicus*.

The letter (Testimonium A15) differs in emphasis from the story we have so far derived from the *Platonicus*, but, although several scholars have argued that the two sources are contradictory (Wolfer 1954: 8 ff.; Knorr 1986: 22), they are, in fact, generally consistent with one another. The letter pushes the problem of the duplication of the cube back before the time of Plato into the fifth century. Three lines from an unidentified tragedian are cited in order to illustrate Minos' mistaken attempt to double the size of the tomb of Glaucus by doubling its side. Hippocrates of Chios (second half of the fifth century) is said to have reduced the problem of doubling the cube to the problem of finding two mean proportionals between two straight lines, of which the greater is double the lesser (see further on A14). This earlier history of the problem is in no way inconsistent with the story in the *Platonicus*, as has sometimes been suggested (e.g. Wolfer 1954: 8), since nothing in what Theon says of the *Platonicus* (Text A) suggests that the Delians at the time of Plato were the first to raise the problem. Indeed, the letter does not even claim that the problem first arose with the tragedy in which Minos appears. In the letter the practical problem confronting the Delians can be seen as stirring new interest in an old problem and as supplying the renewed interest which leads to a solution. Plutarch's presentation of Plato as recognizing that the problem requires "the highest geometrical ability" (Text B) might suggest a Plato who knew the history of the problem, and this Plato's assertion that the Greeks neglect geometry would have even more force, if the problem had been around for a long time, but was still not solved. If Plutarch's presentation reflects the *Platonicus* here, then the *Platonicus* may assume the earlier history of the story as outlined in Eratosthenes' letter.

In contrast to the *Platonicus*, there is no mention of Plato's interpretation of the oracle in the letter, or of his disagreement with those who thought that the god wanted only a solution to the particular problem. Instead the emphasis is on the actual solutions that emerged. It is here that Archytas enters Eratosthenes' story for the first time, since his is the first of three solutions mentioned (along with the solutions of Eudoxus and Menaechmus, who belong to the next two generations). This emphasis on actual solutions is perfectly intelligible in terms of Eratosthenes' goal in the letter and in the concluding epigram: to present and glorify his own solution to the problem. The most striking thing about Eratosthenes' letter (and the body of the letter is in close agreement with the concluding epigram on this point) is the way in which he characterizes the solutions of Archytas, Eudoxus and Menaechmus in contrast to his own. He complains that their solutions are all presented in the form of a geometrical demonstration (ἀποδεικτικῶς γεγραφέναι) and that their methods cannot be put into actual practice (χειρουργῆσαι δὲ καὶ εἰς χρείαν πεσεῖν μὴ δύνασθαι), except to a small extent the solution of Menaechmus. The epigram warns the reader not to "seek out the deeds of the cylinders of Archytas, which are hard to put into effect" (δυσμήχανα). On the other hand, Eratosthenes himself has devised an "easy approach" and developed an instrument which allows the practical determination not only of the two means but however many someone demands. He goes on to specify a number of the practical applications in both the letter and epigram: the construction of altars, temples, cattle-folds, and catapults. Eratosthenes certainly appears to be right in his characterization of the earlier solutions. Archytas' solution, as presented in A14, while a geometrical tour de force, does not provide an easy way for someone, who is building something (e.g. a catapult), to determine the actual values of the two mean proportionals necessary to double the size of what is being constructed. The same is true of Menaechmus' solution. Eudoxus' solution has not survived.

It is important to note here that, in the account of the solutions proposed by others, the body of the letter is more precise than the epigram and could not be derived from the epigram alone. In the epigram, Eratosthenes talks of the cylinders of Archytas whereas the body of the letter refers to the semicylinder that Archytas actually uses in his proof. Similarly the author of the body of the letter seems to know enough of Menaechmus' solution to concede that it could to some extent have practical application. This is easy enough to explain, if Eratosthenes is the author of both the letter as a whole and the epigram, since he is clearly more concerned with economy of expression in the epigram. If we suppose a different author for the letter, that author must have consulted the actual solutions of Archytas and Menaechmus in some form and cannot be relying just on the epigram. Knorr (1986: 21), while in general arguing that the letter was written by Eratosthenes, suggests that at least one line is interpolated. He argues that, since Eratosthenes' description of Archytas' solution suggests that he had access to that solution it is odd for him to adopt a tentative tone concerning Archytas' method: "Archytas of Tarentum is said to have discovered them through semicylinders . . ." (lines 23–24). But the use of λέγεται ("is said") need not suggest any doubt on Eratosthenes' part as to Archytas' method. Eratosthenes is simply indicating that he is working from a set of solutions handed down by the tradition rather than from an original treatise of Archytas (Sturm 1895: 27 suggests that it indicates that he is working from Eudemus). So far as I can see, then, the whole of the letter is most reasonably assigned to one author, and Eratosthenes remains the most likely author.

Once again I would argue that there is nothing in Eratosthenes' presentation of either the earlier solutions or his own solution, which is in conflict with the core account of the Delian problem in the *Platonicus* as I have reconstructed it above. But what are we to make of this "history" of the problem of the duplication of the cube according to Eratosthenes? Some scholars regard virtually the whole story as the invention of Eratosthenes himself. Perhaps the most extreme in this regard is Sachs, who treats even Hippocrates' reduction of the problem as due to Eratosthenes (1917: 150) and will only allow that Archytas' solution is independent of Eratosthenes, since Eutocius cites Eudemus as his source. It is true that we do not have any direct evidence for the story of the Delian problem before Eratosthenes. Some have seen direct allusions to the problem in Plato (*R.* 528b3) and Aristotle (*APo.* 75b13–14; Philoponus ad loc. *CAG* XIII. 3: 102.12), but both allusions are doubtful (Sachs 1917: 151–53; Heath 1949: 46). On the other hand, the account of stereometry in Book VII of the *Republic* shows that Plato was very concerned about the state of work in solid geometry, in which area the duplication of the cube is an important problem. Moreover, the passage on stereometry is full of references that reek of a contemporary controversy (e.g. the pride of those who pursue stereometry, but the undoubted charm of their results). Whether or not it is the Delian story that lies behind all of this, some story does. Closer analysis of the *Republic* passage below will show that the Delian story, in fact, fits very well. It is certainly true that biography and history are created in the later tradition on the basis of passages in the dialogues (Zhmud 1998: 243). But, in cases such as the passage on stereometry in the *Republic* and the Delian story, there is no overwhelming evidence to show that we should prefer to explain the Delian story as the creation of early members of the Academy who were attempting to explain the *Republic* passage, especially when they will have been in the position to know what story did lie behind that passage.

Of course the story of the Delian problem bears some of the signs of a literary composition, particularly in the divergent interpretations of the oracle. Nonetheless, there is nothing incredible in the story (Wilamowitz 1962: 48: "Die Geschichte kann sehr gut wahr sein"). Certainly the Delians could have had a plague and would have naturally consulted the oracle. A response concerning building an altar also seems plausible. We know for a fact that mathematicians associated with Plato dealt with the problem (Archytas on the authority of Eudemus, Eudoxus, Menaechmus). It is true that some of these mathematicians, and in particular Archytas, are not likely to have actually worked in the Academy (Zhmud 1998: 225 ff.). But Eratosthenes' account of the Delian problem need not be read as saying that Archytas was in the Academy; one version has the Delians sending just to Plato, who could have told Archytas about the problem (Text A). Even Eratosthenes' letter (Testimonium A15), which talks about the Delians sending to "the geometers at Plato's side in the Academy," need not be read so strictly as to mean that all the mathematicians associated with Plato were literally in the Academy (Sturm 1895: 27). It need only mean that the Delians received help from geometers who were known to Plato, who of course is thought of as being in the Academy.

That the problem of the duplication of solids should first arise as a practical one having to do with an altar or a tomb, and that the search for the solution to the problem should continue to receive impetus from practical difficulties is perfectly believable (Sturm 1895: 11). None of this is to deny that the problem will also have had a separate life among mathematicians. Discovery that the duplication of a square involves finding one mean proportional probably led Hippocrates to his reduction of the duplication of the cube to finding two mean proportionals (see the commentary on A14) and mathematicians will have been dealing with the problem in these terms for some time before the Delians' specific problem. There is no reason to suppose that the origin and development of the problem had to lie either solely in external stimuli or solely in developments internal to mathematics as Knorr does (1986: 24). It is most likely that the problem had stimulus both from developments internal to and external to mathematics.

Many scholars have seen in Eratosthenes' account of the Delian problem a set of connected contradictions, to which I have not yet alluded (Wolfer 1954). At this point I have attempted to reconstruct Eratosthenes' account of the problem as it appeared in his *Platonicus*, on the basis of the only source who directly refers to the *Platonicus*, Theon (Text A), and two passages in Plutarch that cohere closely with what is said in Theon (Texts B and C). I also hope to have shown that this version in the *Platonicus* is consistent with Eratosthenes' other presentation of the Delian problem in his letter to Ptolemy, although the latter has a different emphasis. It is in this letter that Archytas first entered the story (Testimonium A15). Archytas also makes his appearance in two other versions of the story in Plutarch (15a and 15b), and it is here that problems arise.

These versions emphasize Plato's surprising interpretation of the oracle, by focusing on the tension between that interpretation and the work of Archytas, Eudoxus and Menaechmus. These testimonia are clearly part of the tradition going back to Eratosthenes in that the primary emphasis is again on the difference between the three geometers, who see the oracle as commanding the solution of one particular problem, and Plato, who argues that the god is interested in the broader good which the pursuit of geometry provides. There is also a development in these texts, however, which is not likely to go back to Eratosthenes. The dispute is spelt out (in terms familiar from *Republic* VII) as a contrast between those who apply mathematics to the sensible realm, and those like Plato for whom the goal of mathematics is to lead us to the intelligible realm. Plato has a more specific description of how the geometers rely on the physical rather than the intelligible, namely that they employ constructions which use physical instruments and are mechanical. In Testimonium 15b this split between Plato and Archytas et al. is used as a sort of etiological myth in order to explain the separation of the science of mechanics from geometry.

This emphasis on the mechanical and practical nature of the solutions of Archytas, Eudoxus and Menaechmus is in direct contradiction to Eratosthenes' letter to Ptolemy and his epigram, in which the solutions of these geometers are criticized for being too theoretical and not admitting of practical application. In order to see this contradiction clearly it is important to look carefully at the language of both Eratosthenes and Plutarch. One might try to avoid the contradiction by suggesting that Eratosthenes' description of Archytas' solution as δυσμήχανα means that Eratosthenes thought that the solution was indeed mechanical (-μήχανα) but a very difficult (δυσ-) mechanical solution. This will not work, however, since Eratosthenes has made clear earlier in his letter (lines 25–26) what he means by calling the solution δυσμήχανα. The problem with Archytas' solution is that it is just a geometric demonstration (ἀποδεικτικῶς γεγραφέναι) and that it is not just difficult but *impossible* to build or to put into practice (χειρουργῆσαι δὲ καὶ εἰς χρείαν πεσεῖν μὴ δύνασθαι). Eratosthenes is saying that Archytas' geometrical demonstration does not help one to devise an instrument (ὀργανική A15, line 28) which will allow one to determine the two means easily (ῥᾳδία, ῥεῖα A15, lines 28 and 55), in order to deal with building altars, temples, cattle folds, corn pits and wells (A15 lines 33 and 46–47). Eratosthenes is presenting to Ptolemy just such an instrument which will easily determine the means. In calling the deeds of Archytas' cylinders δυσμήχανα Eratosthenes means not that the cylinders are part of a mechanical construction, although a difficult one, but rather that the cylinders are part of a geometrical construction that is hard or even impossible to put into effect.

Plutarch, on the other hand, clearly portrays Archytas as employing just the sort of practical mechanical instruments (ὀργανικὰς καὶ μηχανικὰς κατασκευὰς A15a, lines 6–7) which Eratosthenes declares inconsistent with Archytas' solution and which Eratosthenes himself claims to have been the first to invent. Again we need to look at Plutarch's language carefully to see what he is saying. When he asserts that Archytas employed ὀργανικὰς καὶ μηχανικὰς κατασκευάς (A15a, lines 6–7, A15b, lines 6–7) there is some ambiguity, since the term κατασκευάς could refer either to the physical construction of an instrument or to a geometrical construction which Plutarch is labeling mechanical. That Plutarch is not referring to a geometrical construction, however, is first of all suggested by his insistence that Archytas was appealing to what is sensible (αἰσθητά A15a, line 10; A15b, line 4) rather than to the intelligible. We might still think that Plutarch was just suggesting that, in doing his geometrical demonstration, Archytas appealed to sensible diagrams or visual aids, such as a physical cylinder. At A15b, lines 11–12 Plutarch makes clear, however, that when he describes Archytas as running from the intelligible to the sensible he means that he used "physical objects which required much common handicraft" (σώμασι πολλῆς καὶ φορτικῆς βαναυσουργίας δεομένοις). This language makes clear that he is not thinking of a diagram or a simple visual aid but an actual instrument that required a great deal of handicraft to construct. When Plutarch refers to Archytas' mechanical models and mechanical constructions he is referring to exactly the same sort of instrument that Eratosthenes claims to have been the first to invent and which Eratosthenes explicitly denies to Archytas. (Cambiano [1998: 296] also notes the contradiction between Plutarch and Eratosthenes and argues that Plutarch is ascribing a mesolab like that invented by Eratosthenes to Archytas.)

But there is a yet greater paradox to come. For among the solutions to the problem preserved by Eutocius we find not just the solutions of Archytas (A14) and Menaechmus, which are very theoretical and correspond to Eratosthenes' description of them in the letter, but also a solution attributed to Plato himself. Moreover, it is not in the solutions of Archytas and Menaechmus that an instrument is employed in order to find the two means but rather in this solution of Plato! Most scholars have rejected this ascription to Plato, since it appears only in Eutocius and since Eratosthenes would surely have said something about a Platonic solution in his account of the Delian problem in the *Platonicus* or his letter and epigram, if he had known of a Platonic solution (e.g. Heath 1921: 255; Thomas 1939: 262–63; Knorr 1986: 57–59). Ian Mueller, on the other hand has recently suggested (1992c: 174) that we should accept the ascription, since it is harder to explain how a mistaken ascription could have come about than to explain how the (false) story of Plato's criticism of Archytas et al. might have arisen. But to accept that Plato solved the problem by relying on a physical instrument not only makes it hard to understand Eratosthenes' silence on Plato's solution, it also runs the risk of making Plato seriously contradict the principle, clearly enunciated in *Republic* VII, that mathematics should lead us away from the physical to the intelligible. We might be able to imagine scenarios in which Plato presents the physical solution only to reject it (Sturm 1895: 54), but to present such a solution at all seems to seriously muddy the point about the true value of mathematics, which Plato works hard to establish in *Republic* VII.

We do not in fact have to choose between Plato's criticism of Archytas for employing instruments in Plutarch and the ascription of the use of an instrument to Plato himself in Eutocius. Both traditions are likely to be erroneous. It is not, in fact, hard to explain how the type of solution which Plato rejected came to be assigned to him. For the solution assigned to Plato is not just problematic in some features; it is an example of what he warns against in *Republic* VII and embodies precisely what he is said to criticize in Archytas' solution. Its ascription to Plato may be an example of what is known in textual criticism as a polar error: a reading is often replaced by its opposite (Kopff 1975; Briggs 1983; Davies 1990). This can be a result of simple carelessness but can also result from a common trick that our mind plays on us, where we write the opposite of what we mean. Thus a solution to the Delian problem, which used an instrument, was initially identified either in the text or in the margin of a text as "not as Plato" (would have us solve the problem), and at some point in the transmission the "not" disappears, either by simple carelessness or by a polar error, and the solution becomes "as Plato" (ὡς Πλάτων in Eutocius 56.13). To whom does this solution belong if not Plato? I don't think that the evidence allows us to decide that question (Knorr 1986: 59–61 suggests Eudoxus; for the possibility that it might even have been assigned to Archytas see my comments on the context of A14), but I will say more about the date of the solution below. Another explanation of "Plato's" solution has recently been suggested by Netz (2003).

What are we to make of the blatant contradiction between Plato's criticism of Archytas' solution for being too mechanical and practical in Plutarch, and Eratosthenes' clear assertion that Archytas' solution was too theoretical and of no practical application, an assertion that is borne out by Archytas' actual solution? It is here that scholars have employed their greatest ingenuity. The most pervasive explanation has been to argue that the apparent contradiction can be solved by recognizing that Eratosthenes' *Platonicus* was in fact a dialogue and that this literary form would allow Eratosthenes to assign conflicting solutions to the same person (van der Waerden 1963: 161; Wolfer 1954: 12 ff.; Sachs 1917: 150). For example (see Wolfer 1954: 18), he might first have presented the mechanical solutions of Archytas et al. and then Plato's criticisms of these solutions, perhaps accompanied by Plato's own practical solution ("A practical solution is not hard! Here is one I dashed off"), to be followed by the "correct" theoretical solutions of Archytas, Eudoxus and Menaechmus (the first and third of which are preserved in Eutocius). There are, however, important problems with this solution.

First, it is not very satisfying as a solution, since it serves as a *deus ex machina* for any apparent contradictions in the tradition regarding the *Platonicus*. We could thus argue that the tradition which says that the plague arose in Athens rather than Delos is not, as it almost certainly is, a later simplification of the story, but is also based in the *Platonicus*, since someone in the dialogue could have said "didn't the Athenians come to you once when there was a plague . . ." only to be corrected by Plato who said "it was the Delians." Second, in its most extreme form, this interpretation of the *Platonicus* turns it implausibly into one of the great intellectual tours de force of ancient literature. For, according to Sachs, Eratosthenes would have been responsible not only for devising the Delian story, he will have invented Hippocrates' role in the earlier history of the problem and will have developed both the mechanical and the theoretical solutions to the problem which are assigned to Menaechmus, Eudoxus and Plato (1917: 150). Thus what was recognized as one of the more difficult early geometrical problems gets a raft of solutions from Eratosthenes alone.

Furthermore, while it is possible that the *Platonicus* was a dialogue (the *Suda* says that Eratosthenes' wrote many dialogues), this is far from certain. Theon, who is the only person who refers to it, does not call it a dialogue and none of the material which he derives from it is in dialogue form. Wolfer (1954: 14 ff.) has provided the only real argument that the *Platonicus* might be a dialogue by pointing out that a doctrine which Theon assigns to Eratosthenes is assigned to Plato by Pappus. This could be explained, as Wolfer does, by supposing that the doctrine was put into Plato's mouth by Eratosthenes in the *Platonicus*, so that different authors can quote it as Plato or as Eratosthenes, just as Aristotle will refer to a view as belonging to Socrates, when he means the Socrates of Plato's dialogues. But this is not the only or even the most likely way to explain the conflict between Theon and Pappus. The doxographical tradition is littered with contradictory ascriptions of doctrines. Given the evidence we have, it is best to admit that we have no basis on which to decide what form the *Platonicus* took (Solmsen 1942: 193 n. 3).

A slightly different approach in dealing with the contradictions in the tradition about Eratosthenes' account of the Delian problem is simply to say that the accounts differ because they occur in works of different genres, the *Platonicus* being assumed to be a literary work as opposed to the letter which is more historical (Knorr 1986: 22). Eratosthenes is referring to the same solutions of Archytas et al. in both the *Platonicus* and the letter (i.e. the solutions preserved by Eutocius). In the letter, however, he emphasizes the theoretical aspect of the solutions of the other geometers in contrast to his own more practical solution, while in the *Platonicus* it might have been his goal to emphasize the mechanical aspects of their solutions in contrast to Plato. But it remains difficult to see what is mechanical about the solutions of Archytas and Menaechmus, which have been preserved (see further below).

All of these attempts to reconcile the supposed content of the *Platonicus* with Eratosthenes' epigram and letter fail to note that the anti-mechanical version of the story in Plutarch simply cannot have been present in the *Platonicus*, because that version is not just in tension with what we find in the epigram and letter but completely undercuts their entire thrust. The clear implication of both the epigram and the letter is that Eratosthenes is claiming to present the first practically useful solution to the problem of the duplication of the cube. He gives the history of the problem, lists the solutions of Archytas, Eudoxus and Menaechmus but finds all of them too abstract and is emphatic that they are very difficult or impossible to put into practice. Thus the practicality of the solutions is a central focus of Eratosthenes here, and he is claiming the first practical solution for himself. The central point of both Eratosthenes' epigram and his letter would be completely undercut, if Archytas, Eudoxus and Menaechmus had already produced solutions that dealt with the problem in a mechanical fashion using instruments, which is precisely what Eratosthenes is claiming to be the first to do. His point would be similarly completely undercut if Plato had already proposed the instrument ascribed to him by Eutocius. Either Eratosthenes did not know of the "Platonic" solution, or more probably, that solution and its ascription to Plato both arose after Eratosthenes.

Some have suggested that it is incredible that a practical solution to the problem had not been achieved before Eratosthenes and that Eratosthenes must be covering up earlier solutions (Sturm 1895: 56). We have no reason to suspect such an extreme case of bad faith on Eratosthenes' part, how-ever, nor to believe that other mathematicians of the time could be fooled by such a cover up. It is always possible to rely on the supposed dialogue form or literary genre of the *Platonicus* to devise some scenario which allows Eratosthenes' assertions in his epigram and letter to still make sense. But the natural thing to do, if he knew of Plato's complaint about the mechanical solutions of Archytas and his successors or had invented the complaint and the solutions himself, would be to emphasize his own genuinely practical solution in contrast to the solutions supposed practical by Plato. There is no trace of such an approach. But all of these contortions are in fact unnec-essary. There is a much easier explanation at hand. We have already seen that the story of the Delian problem goes through all sorts of developments in the tradition which are unlikely to go back to the *Platonicus*. Moreover, as we have seen, Theon's version, which is likely to be the most reliable, and the other versions in Plutarch which are closely tied to Theon's version say nothing of the anti-mechanical version of the story. For this reason it seems best to regard Plato's attack on Archytas for being too mechanical as a development of the later tradition (Riginos 1976: 146, followed by Zhmud 1998: 217 n. 19, thinks Plutarch is the originator, but for reasons different than those I have developed above). This same development may be present in Vitruvius (Testimonium 15c). Here Archytas and Eratosthenes are lumped together as great practical benefactors of humanity and the distinction that Eratosthenes tried to make between his practical solution and Archytas' more abstract one is obscured.

The Hellenistic period saw great progress in the mechanical arts and the question of the relation between abstract mathematics and practical utility emerges as a central theme (see the presentation of Archimedes in Plutarch's *Life of Marcellus*, from which Testimonium A15b derives). It makes a great deal of sense that, in the wake of this growth of the field of mechanics, the story of the solution to the Delian problem, which is central to the field of mechanics (Pappus 1028.18–21 puts the finding of the two mean proportionals second in his list of the most important theorems in mechanics), should be developed as a founding myth for the science of mechanics. Since Archytas was the first to develop a solution to that problem, even though it was resolutely abstract and not mechanical, and perhaps because he did develop a mechanical device (the mechanical dove in A10a), he was a logical choice to be the hero of the founding myth. Diogenes Laertius, in his life of Archytas (A1), has taken over the myth from Plutarch or Plutarch's source, although his presentation also shows that it was in regard to the mathematical foundations of mechanics that Archytas had made his contribution (see the overview of Archytas' philosophy).

In conclusion, I would suggest that the version of the duplication of the cube, which Eratosthenes knew, contained the following elements: (1) the early history of the problem which led to Hippocrates of Chios' reduction of the problem to the determination of two mean proportionals, (2) the story of the oracle given to the Delians which raised the difficulty again and led to the consultation with Plato and geometers associated with him, (3) Plato's interpretation of the oracle as an exhortation to all Greeks to pursue advanced geometry, (4) Plato's criticism of Archytas and other geometers for focusing on the specific problem rather than on the pursuit of geometry in general and thus not recognizing the true value of geometry. Eratosthenes is also familiar with the solutions to the problem developed by Archytas, Eudoxus and Menaechmus, but it seems unlikely that he knew of the solution later attributed to Plato. Points 2–4 are likely to have been in the *Platonicus*. Point 1 is found only in the letter and might have been omitted from the *Platonicus* because of Eratosthenes' particular goals in that work but, given the meager state of our knowledge, certainty is impossible.

Eratosthenes' account of the Delian problem and Republic VII
(The best account of the stereometry passage in *Republic* VII is Sachs 1917.) Scholars have naturally wanted to see a connection between Eratosthenes' account of the Delian problem and Plato's remarks in *Republic* VII on the sciences in general and on stereometry in particular. For example, Riginos (1976: 146) suggests that Plutarch fabricated Plato's complaints about the early solutions to the Delian problem from Plato's comments on the strangely physical nature of the language used by geometry at *Republic* 527 a–b. Adam, in his commentary on the discussion of stereometry in *Republic* VII (1929: II. 120 ff.), suggests that the Delian problem and in particular the solution of Eudoxus, may have been the general background to Plato's comments. Nonetheless, it is the case both that a number of the proposed connections are mistaken and also that it has not been fully appreciated how close the connection really is between Plato's account of stereometry (*Republic* 528a–d) and Eratosthenes' account of the Delian problem. In order to understand the nature of the connection, it is necessary to look at Plato's presentation of stereometry in *Republic* VII in some detail.

At 527c Glaucon and Socrates have agreed that geometry is the second of the studies (following arithmetic/logistic), which the young guardians should pursue, in order to turn their souls from the sensible to the intelligible world. When Socrates suggests that astronomy is the third such science, Glaucon readily agrees, but on the grounds that astronomy is useful for farming, navigation and the military art. Socrates chides him for being too concerned about the conception of utility held by the multitude and suggests that they need to retrace their steps a bit. They need to look at a discipline whose benefits are not familiar to the public at large, because the discipline is not generally recognized to exist. The discussion of stereometry then begins by emphasizing the importance of taking the mathematical sciences in sequence: "just now we did not correctly (ὀρθῶς) take what comes next (τὸ ἑξῆς) after geometry" (528a6–7). After plane surfaces (ἐπίπεδον), with which geometry deals, we then went directly to the discussion of the revolutions of solids (στερεόν), astronomy, without having first discussed solids themselves (αὐτὸ καθ' αὑτό, 528a9–b1). The correct procedure is to take things in order, after the second dimension (αὔξην), it is correct to take the third.

Plato's next words are controversial and crucial. He says that this (τοῦτο = taking the third dimension in order) "is concerned with the dimension of cubes and everything having depth" (περὶ τὴν τῶν κύβων αὔξην καὶ τὸ βάθους μετέχον). It is important to note that the expression τὴν τῶν κύβων αὔξην cannot be taken as a literal reference to the Delian problem and translated as "the duplication of the cube" or "the increase (in size) of the cube." In addition to the convincing arguments of Sachs based on Greek usage (1917: 151–53), the immediate context in the *Republic* shows that αὔξην cannot mean "increase in size." In the immediately preceding sentence αὔξην is used with the adjectives "second" and "third" and accordingly must have the sense "dimension." Furthermore τὴν τῶν κύβων αὔξην is immediately glossed with the words "everything having depth" (τὸ βάθους μετέχον), so that we must surely translate the preceding words as "the dimension of cubes." Moreover, in what follows Socrates is not talking of a solution to a problem but about the discovery of a science (Sachs 1917: 153). It may nonetheless be the case that Plato chose to identify the third dimension as that of cubes because of the importance of the problem of the duplication of the cube and that his audience will naturally have thought of the problem as well. As Adam points out, "the most famous stereometrical problem of Plato's time was the . . . duplication of the cube, and it is highly probable that he had this question in mind when he wrote the present chapter" (1929: II. 120).

Glaucon's response to Socrates' introduction of the study of mathematical solids is of the utmost interest. He admits the logic of Socrates' proposal that consideration of the third dimension should follow that of the second. But, he continues, "this (discipline) does not yet seem to have been invented (εὑρῆσθαι)" (528b4–5). This latter statement is puzzling at first sight and often misunderstood and mistranslated. We have already seen that one of the central problems in the study of three-dimensional bodies, the duplication of the cube, goes well back into the fifth century. Hippocrates of Chios may well have completed his reduction of the problem to finding two mean proportionals before the dramatic date (422) let alone the date of composition of the *Republic* (mid 370s?). Theaetetus, who died in 369, is known to have completed his constructions of the five regular solids during the first thirty years of the fourth century and Archytas is likely to have completed his solution to the duplication of the cube in that period as well. How then can Glaucon say that the study of mathematical solids has not yet been invented?

We cannot dismiss the remark as a misunderstanding that Plato puts in Glaucon's mouth, although Plato does assign Glaucon some crude misunderstandings elsewhere (e.g. 529a ff.). In the discussion following Glaucon's assertion, Socrates confirms Glaucon's assessment by asserting that those investigating problems in solid geometry will be unable to invent the discipline (Socrates repeats Glaucon's word: εὕροιεν, 528b7), until a director is found, and that investigations in this area are currently a joke (γελοίως ἔχει, 528d9). Some conclude that Plato must be having Socrates and Glaucon describe the situation at the dramatic date of the dialogue, which would at least be before the work of Archytas and Theaetetus (e.g. Taylor 1928: 5). Socrates' account of harmonics a few pages later in the *Republic*, however, fits Archytas' scalar divisions very well (see A16) and he may even quote from Archytas' book (see Fr. 1), all of which suggests that Socrates' remarks on the state of the *mathēmata* apply to the time of composition of the dialogue, since Archytas is unlikely to have completed his work before 400. Further, in the rest of the passage on stereometry, as we will see below, Socrates gives the clear impression that he is referring to actual disputes in the study of stereometry and van der Waerden has a point when he asks "Is it conceivable that Plato, for the sake of the historical accuracy of the picture, would have spoken so caustically about an undesirable state of affairs which had existed fifty years earlier and which had been improved long since?" (1963: 139; see also Sachs 1917: 155–56).

It seems better, then, to take Socrates' and Glaucon's remarks as applying to the state of stereometry in the mid 370s when Plato was writing the *Republic*. We are still left with the apparent contradiction between Glaucon's words and the work in stereometry that Archytas and Theaetetus were doing. Sachs supposes that stereometry was still not developed at this time and takes Glaucon's remark as an indication that Theaetetus' work was completed after the composition of the *Republic* (1917: 159–60). She has to suppose, implausibly, that Hippocrates' work was the invention of Eratosthenes in his dialogue the *Platonicus* (see above), and she simply does not explain how Glaucon can ignore Archytas' solution to the problem of the duplication of the cube. Other answers fare worse. Van der Waerden proposes that Glaucon cannot be talking of solid geometry in general but only of the specific problem of the duplication of the cube, and that Archytas' solution had not appeared yet. We have seen, however, that Socrates has referred precisely to the general subject matter of "the third dimension" and does not refer directly to the duplication of the cube. Fowler follows a similar tactic of trying to argue that Socrates is not talking about, what he clearly is talking about, solid geometry as a whole (1987: 118). We would appear to be at an impasse, but perhaps we have misunderstood what Glaucon is saying.

The key to dealing with the apparent contradiction between Glaucon's words and what we know of the history of solid geometry is to recognize that the same tension exists in the *Republic* passage on stereometry itself. The assertion that "these things have not yet been invented" grows ever more problematic as the passage continues. For, we discover that there are people who are currently investigating these matters and who have investigated them in the past (528b7–8). Plato is clearly quite familiar with the work of these investigators, since Socrates is able to characterize them as arrogant (μεγαλοφρονούμενοι, 528c1). Things get worse, since we discover that not only are people investigating this non-existent subject matter, but, despite considerable difficulties, they are making progress and understanding of the subject is advancing (αὐξάνεται, 528c7) and finally that, in light of the charm of the subject matter, it is not surprising that these discoveries have come to light. This last passage is often translated as suggesting just the possibility of development in the field ("it would not surprise us if the truth about them were to be made apparent" Shorey 1935). There are serious grammatical problems for such a translation, however, and, as Wilamowitz argues, φανῆναι emphasizes that results have actually been achieved: stereometry is presented as "a field of research in which the first steps have been taken" (Sachs 1917: 157–58). Clearly we need to look at Glaucon's initial assertion more carefully.

In light of the whole passage, Glaucon must mean that it is the *discipline* of stereometry as such, which does not exist. This is in fact the reading which makes most sense in the context of *Republic* VII as a whole. Socrates and Glaucon are looking for appropriate disciplines of study, not just possible areas of inquiry, and all the other examples that they come up with, arithmetic, geometry, astronomy and music are coherent disciplines. Archytas Fr. 1, to which Plato alludes in the discussion of harmonics a few pages later, identifies just this *quadrivium*. If you asked someone whether they understood the terms geometry or arithmetic, they would know what you meant, but they would be puzzled by the idea that the study of mathematical solids is a separate discipline. Indeed, as the stereometry passage makes clear, there was no name for such a discipline and the word stereometry is not used by Plato here. It appears for the first time in the *Epinomis* (990d). Socrates' jump from geometry to astronomy is meant to highlight the fact that problems in stereometry, such as the duplication of the cube, were regarded as problems in geometry and not treated as forming a discipline of their own. It is clearly assumed, however, that there has been a considerable amount of interesting geometrical work done on solids. There are demonstrations and proofs regarding solids, which have a charm and beauty (528c7–d1), but they have not been integrated into a coherent science.

This lack of coherent organization is underlined by Plato's call for a director (ἐπιστάτης) of such studies and by his characterization of those investigating the area as "arrogant." These investigators produce insights that are brilliant in their own right but they are not willing to submit those insights to an overall discipline. At 528b7 Socrates repeats Glaucon's word "invent" (εὕροιεν), precisely to make the point that it is the lack of a central organizing principle that can combine the brilliant insights of the arrogant individuals, which prevents stereometry from being "invented." The same point, stated in slightly different terms, concludes the section on stereometry. Socrates says that they had initially passed over the study of the third dimension, because the investigation of it was in a laughable state (528d9); people are investigating problems having to do with the third dimension, but such investigations have not been connected to one another coherently enough in order to be regarded as a separate discipline. We should translate Glaucon's remark not as saying that solid geometry has not been "investigated," the passage itself shows that there has been a great deal of investigation. Plato is telling us that, despite all this investigation, the separate discipline of solid geometry has not yet been "invented" (a similar view was reached by Heiberg; see Sachs 1917: 146 n. 1).

If this is what Plato is likely to have meant, it seems to me that Glaucon's remark could certainly apply to the date of composition of the *Republic* in the mid 370s. Plato's remarks reflect the division of mathematics presented in Archytas Fr. 1, which cannot be much earlier that 400 BC, and where there is no trace of a discipline of stereometry to go along with the *quadrivium* of arithmetic, geometry, astronomy and music. Archytas' solution to the problem of the duplication of the cube was probably complete by 375 but would not, in itself, constitute the establishment of a discipline. Theaetetus was the first to complete constructions of all the five regular solids, but, as Sachs suggests, this could have been done in the 370s, after the composition of the *Republic* but before his death in 369. We also have no way of being certain whether Plato would regard Theaetetus' constructions as constituting the sort of overall organization which should characterize a discipline of stereometry or as further brilliant individual achievements lacking integration into a whole. In fact, the first scholium to Euclid's treatment of the regular solids in Book XIII of the *Elements* (Heiberg p. 654) says that, while Theaetetus added the constructions of the oktahedron and the icosohedron to the three solids discovered earlier, the book bears Euclid's name because "he imposed on it the order of elements" (τὸ στοιχειῶδη τάξιν ἐπιτεθεικέναι, see Burkert 1972a: 443 n. 100). This comment cannot be pressed too hard, but it suggests that what Plato was calling for regarding stereometry in Book VII of the *Republic* might not have been accomplished until Euclid.

It has been a common amusement for scholars to try and divine exactly whom Plato had in mind, when he called for a director of stereometry. Some have thought of Plato himself (Sachs 1917: 156), and there are a variety of other candidates (see Adam 1929: II. 123–24, who nominates Eudoxus). It may be however that the question is misguided. Plato rather suggests that he knows of no such person than that he has someone up his sleeve. His solution in fact appears to be that the *polis* as a whole, presumably the *polis* that he is sketching in the *Republic*, should play the role: "If the *polis* as a whole should join in superintending these studies and hold them in honor, these (specialists) would take advice and being subjected to continuous and strenuous study the true nature of these things would become clear" (528c2–4). Adam (1929) argues that ξυνεπιστατοῖ means that the city is to cooperate with the director, and to be sure we cannot imagine every member of the society functioning as a director. The suggestion still seems to be, however, that the directorship of this area be institutionalized and be of the city as a whole, in the sense that some group of guardians or the guardians as a whole would play the role. At any rate, this role for the city does undercut any suggestion that Plato had a particular person in mind.

This shift of focus from the individual to the state brings us to what is arguably Plato's central point in the whole passage on stereometry, the deplorable neglect of stereometry by the Greeks in general. At 528b6 Socrates says that there are two reasons why the discipline of stereometry has not yet been invented. The first reason is that "no *polis* holds it in honor" (cf. its lack of esteem by the multitude at 528c4–5). Socrates' second reason is the point developed in detail above, the arrogance of those who pursue problems in the area and the consequent need for some sort of central authority to guide them. One final aspect of the deficiency of the current investigators needs to be brought out, however. Socrates says that they hinder the development of the field because they don't understand the *logos*, the reason or account, with respect to which this field is useful (528c5–6). They pursue problems dealing with three-dimensional figures, but do not understand the value of the discipline of stereometry as a whole. This point is made even more forcefully at *Euthydemus* 290c. In this passage Plato is talking about mathematicians in general rather than stereometers in particular. Clinias asserts with Socrates' approval that mathematicians only know how to hunt out diagrams (i.e. solve problems). Like the stereometers in the *Republic* they do not themselves know how to use the solutions that they hunt out (χρῆσθαι αὐτοὶ αὐτοῖς οὐκ ἐπιστάμενοι) and therefore they hand over their discoveries to the dialecticians, if they are not completely senseless.

It is now time to return to Eratosthenes' account of the Delian problem. I submit that the two central points in Eratosthenes' presentation are the same two points that have emerged from close examination of Plato's presentation of stereometry in *Republic* VII. In Eratosthenes, *Plato's* interpretation of the oracle given to the Delians as commanding not the construction of an altar of double the size but rather as reproaching the Greeks for paying no attention to mathematics and for neglecting geometry, is exactly the message that Socrates is presenting about every *polis'* neglect of stereometry at *Republic* 528a ff. There is a difference of course, in that, in Eratosthenes, Plato is talking about mathematics and geometry in general, while in the *Republic* Socrates makes the point solely in terms of stereometry. This generalization of the more specific point in the *Republic* is not surprising, in light of the fact that stereometry for the most part never did emerge from the shadow of geometry in order to be regarded as an independent discipline (e.g. Plato himself treats plane and solid geometry as part of one discipline at *Laws* 817e. Aristotle mentions stereometry only once at *APo.* 78b38. Nicomachus, *Ar.* I. 3 uses the quadrivium as given by Archytas. Proclus, *In Euc.* 39 ff. reports Geminus' classification, in which stereometry is a division of geometry. Mueller 1992b: 86 n. 1 even suggests that Plato did not really intend for there to be a separate discipline of stereometry but was artificially highlighting the backward state of this aspect of geometry).

Plato's complaint about the practitioners of stereometry is also very similar in the two sources. In Eratosthenes, Plato's complaint is that it is the specific proof that they think is important rather than the pursuit of the subject matter as a whole (Texts A and B) and they are said to pursue it apart from reason (δίχα λόγου, Testimonium A15a). So in the *Republic* investigators in the field are said not to understand the reason (λόγον οὐκ ἐχόντων) in terms of which this subject matter as a whole is valuable. In both Eratosthenes' account of the Delian problem and in *Republic* VII, Plato concedes that those who work in this area do solve important problems. Surely in the *Republic* Plato must be thinking at least in part of Archytas' and perhaps Eudoxus' solution to the problem of the duplication of the cube as well as, perhaps, Theaetetus' constructions of the five regular solids.

It seems to me that the similarities between *Republic* VII 528a–d and Eratosthenes' account of the Delian problem are so great that we must suppose a strong connection between them. There are two ways to explain the striking similarity. First, we could suppose that Eratosthenes or his source invented the account of the Delian problem on the basis of what Plato wrote in the *Republic*. There are some problems for this approach in that there is nothing in the *Republic* to suggest the Delian connection, nor indeed the mention by name of any of the geometers who solved the Delian problem. Nonetheless, it remains a possibility that Eratosthenes or his source is trying to attach some names and a context to Plato's allusions in 528a–d.

On the other hand, in the *Republic*, Plato is clearly alluding to some specifics in the history of the development of the study of solids. It is very unlikely that he is inventing the state of stereometry which he is describing. His comments on the state of contemporary harmonics a few pages later in the *Republic* are clearly connected to his analysis of the actual state of the discipline and involve a similar criticism of the experts in the field. Thus, some historical circumstance has raised the issue of the neglect of stereometry, and it is clear that Plato has had some dispute with the arrogant practitioners of the field, who do not understand its true value. It seems to me just as plausible that some version of the Delian story underlies Plato's comments in *Republic* VII as that the Delian story is a later invention based on the *Republic*. Indeed, because of the doubts raised above about the second scenario, I think that it is more likely that Eratosthenes is preserving an independent account of the events that led to Plato's remarks in the *Republic*. It is of course quite likely that, even if Eratosthenes' account is based on some historical events, those events have been shaped in various ways by Eratosthenes and his predecessors, but the parallels with the *Republic* can serve as some guide as to what the historical kernel is likely to be. The presentation in the *Republic* certainly supports the conclusion that I have suggested above, that Plato's attack on mechanical solutions to the Delian problem and solutions that use instruments (Testimonia 15a and 15b) is likely to have entered the tradition after Eratosthenes. There is no trace of the antimechanical theme in the *Republic* account of stereometry. What problem, then, if any, would Plato have had with Archytas' solution to the problem of the duplication of the cube?

Plato's criticism of Archytas' proof

Scholars have traditionally explained Plato's criticism of Archytas' solution to the problem of the duplication of the cube in light of Testimonia 15a and 15b: Archytas' solution was flawed in that it employed constructions that were mechanical and that used instruments. As I have just shown, however, this feature of Testimonia A15a and A15b is not paralleled in the *Republic* account of stereometry and is not found in the earliest evidence for Eratosthenes' *Platonicus* and is thus likely to have entered the tradition after Eratosthenes. Further support for this understanding of the tradition is provided by an examination of Archytas' solution (A14). For the criticisms ascribed to Plato in A15a and A15b simply do not apply to that solution. There is no trace of the physical instrument of which Plutarch complains in Archytas' solution.

Is it possible that Plutarch misunderstood the criticism of Archytas and that there is some other sense in which Archytas' solution is mechanical? What is meant by the term mechanical and mechanics in the ancient world? For the solution to be mechanical in the primary sense, and in the sense that would bother Plato, it should rely on an appeal to the sensible world and to the motion of physical bodies. Thus, when defining mechanics Pappus (*Collection* VIII. 1, 1022.7–9), writing in the fourth century AD, says that it deals with "the doctrine of nature concerning the material of the elements in the cosmos" (τῆς περὶ τὴν ὕλην τῶν ἐν τῷ κόσμῳ στοιχείων φυσιολογίας) and in particular deals with "the stability and motion of bodies" (στάσεως . . . καὶ φορᾶς σωμάτων). As Cuomo puts it "According to Pappus' first, and probably foremost, definition, mechanics is in particular an inquiry into the movement, rest and local motion of bodies in the universe. It studies the causes of phenomena that happen according to nature . . . and also determines the occurrence of phenomena that go against nature . . . It thus has both a productive part – it acts on nature – and a cognitive one – it aims to understand nature" (2000: 104). A similar characterization of mechanics can be found already in Aristotle. In the *Posterior Analytics* he ranges mechanics under geometry in one place (76a34) and under stereometry in another (78b37), as being a subordinate science, which studies the physical facts about bodies as opposed to the science to which it is subordinate, which studies "the reason" (78b38). In the pseudo-Aristotelian *Mechanical Problems*, problems of mechanics are said to share in both mathematical and physical speculations, and the first of the problems discussed are those involving the lever (847a–b). If Archytas' solution made appeal to machines such as the lever or to the motion of physical bodies, Plato would clearly want to criticize it on the grounds that it focused our attention on the physical realm rather than turning our minds toward the intelligible, which is the true function of mathematics.

Archytas' solution not only does not appeal to the motion of physical bodies, however; it could not be carried out by using them, as Eratosthenes later commented (see above). The crucial point K in Archytas' construction (see A14) is determined as the intersection of two curves on the surface of a semicylinder, one curve produced by the rotation of a semicircle and the other by a rotation of a triangle around one of its sides. For these curves to be generated and the intersection to occur, the cone, semicircle and triangle must be able to pass through one another, which is clearly impossible on the assumption that they are solid bodies. Archytas' solution only works if we are dealing with intelligible rather than physical entities. It makes no use of mechanics according to the definitions of that term most commonly used in antiquity.

Pappus does recognize that there is a theoretical part of mechanics which is composed in part by geometry, and indeed some of the propositions he presents in his mechanics are almost completely geometrical (see e.g. Cuomo 2000: 110–12). As Cuomo shows, Pappus often first examines "the mathematical structure" of a given problem but then "transports it to a more real situation, adding flesh to the basic skeleton" (2000: 116). In a sense, then, one could argue that Archytas' purely geometrical solution is still something that could appear in a treatise on mechanics, because it embodies the mathematical structure of the problem. To say that the sort of mathematics we see in Archytas could appear in a treatise on mechanics, however, is not to say that it is therefore mechanical in any distinctive sense. It is to say that it is geometrical and that geometry has a role to play in mechanics. For Archytas' solution to be called mechanical there should be evidence that it was linked to the physical world, that there was flesh put on its mathematical bones. If it had such a connection, then Plato could complain that it directed the mind to the sensible rather than the intelligible. Once again, however, there is no evidence for such linkage to the physical world. As we have seen, Eratosthenes explicitly says that flesh *cannot* be put on these bones. Although Pappus does not refer to Archytas' solution *per se*, he rejects Menaechmus' solution in terms of conic sections, which Eratosthenes pairs with Archytas' as too theoretical, in favor of a solution employing a moving ruler. In the case of the duplication of the cube, Pappus found that "geometrical procedures [were] . . . not viable and solutions must be found with the help of instruments" (Cuomo 2000: 119), so that Pappus too implicitly suggests that Archytas' solution is not a suitable mechanical solution.

As a final attempt to save the testimony in A15a and A15b as genuinely Platonic and as reasonably applying to Archytas' solution, some scholars have supposed that what Plato is objecting to is Archytas' use of motion of geometrical figures (Knorr 1986: 22; Brown 1967: 84). The solution does involve a semicircle rotating around a point at one end of its diameter and a triangle rotating around one of its sides. Ancient definitions of mechanics such as those found in Pappus always refer to the motion of physical bodies, but is the motion even of geometrical entities such as semicircles and triangles enough to make Archytas' proof objectionably mechanical in Plato's eyes? Motion in itself does not cause any problem for Plato's conception of the mathematical sciences in *Republic* VII and it is in fact the proper subject of at least one of them. Astronomy and harmonics are both explicitly said to deal with motion (φορά 530d, 529d), and it is because they both deal with different sorts of motion (visible and audible respectively) that Plato calls them "related" sciences. It is true that Plato famously argues that the proper astronomer should "let be the things in the heavens" and thus not focus on the motion of the visible heavens. Yet motion has not been banished from Plato's ideal astronomy, which will study "the movements . . . of real speed and real slowness in true number and in all true figures both in relation to one another and as vehicles of the things they carry and contain" (529d tr. Shorey). This is a notoriously difficult passage (see Mourelatos 1980: 34–36 for an overview of various interpretations). We might suppose that "real speed" and "real slowness" are Forms and that Plato was not thinking of any objects that move. On the other hand, his reference to the "movements" (φοράς), in the plural, and to the objects (plural) which are carried in those motions (τὰ ἐνόντα φέρει) suggest that Plato envisages some sort of motion of intelligible entities in the proper study of astronomy. Again, we might suppose that Plato, while accepting motion in astronomy, thinks that it is out of place in stereometry. As we have seen, when Plato introduces stereometry he says that the proper sequence is to study solids in themselves, before studying solids in motion. Thus, he might think that all problems and proofs in stereometry should be achieved without motion and that motion only properly enters with astronomy, but this will not work either. For, even if we suppose that Plato thinks it illegitimate to use motion of solids in doing stereometry, Archytas does not in fact have any moving solids in his solution. Solids are generated, or rather are potentially generated (since no complete cone is in fact generated in the proof and we are simply asked to conceive of a semicylinder on a given semicircle with no account of how it is generated), by the movement of plane figures (e.g. a triangle), but no geometrical solids move.

It was, in fact, typical to define solid figures in terms of the rotation of two dimensional figures, as is clear from Euclid's definitions of the sphere, the cone and the cylinder (XI. Def. 14, 18, 21). We might suppose that this is just the work of decadent geometers, whom Plato would condemn. At *Republic* 527a, Plato has told us, however, what he thinks of the tendency of geometers to talk as if action is actually going on in their proofs. When they talk as if they are actually squaring, applying, or adding objects, their language is in one sense ludicrous (γελοίως), since the study of geometry is not pursued in order to do anything physical but rather for the sake of knowledge. But Plato recognizes that such language is also necessary (ἀναγκαίως), since geometers have no other language with which to describe what they are doing (Burnyeat 2000: 42 says that Plato is not criticizing but placing mathematics; see Shorey 1935: II. 170 n. b, and Cherniss 1951: 424 for parallel uses of ἀναγκαίως). Archytas' solution in A14 involves much such language. Circles are drawn, lines extended, perpendiculars dropped. When we are told that the semicircle is "led around" (περιαγόμενον, line 8) or the triangle is "borne around" (περιενεχθῇ, line 11), this is just the necessary geometrical vocabulary rearing its head again and does not differ in essence from the language in line 5, where we are told that a line should be led alongside (παρά . . . ἤχθω) another line (i.e. drawn parallel). The vocabulary of motion is part and parcel of geometric constructions; Archytas' solution differs only in having two dimensional figures move as well as lines. After the construction is complete and Archytas considers the crucial point K, which determines the two mean proportionals, he treats the problem in a completely static fashion in terms of the position of the semicircle and the triangle at the point of intersection of the curves that they draw (ἐχέτω . . . θέσιν).

Euthydemus 290c can further help us to understand how Plato might have regarded Archytas' use of motion in his solution to the problem of finding the two mean proportionals. In the _Euthydemus_ the point is that the mathematicians do not really make the diagrams which they use (οὐ γὰρ ποιοῦσι τὰ διαγράμματα), they instead discover the ones that really are (τὰ ὄντα ἀνευρίσκουσιν). The point seems to be the same as in the _Republic_: despite all their talk of action, mathematicians are in fact not dealing with the physical but rather the intelligible realm. Mathematical constructions have an heuristic value, and we seem compelled to use them to talk of intelligible relations for want of a better vocabulary. Archytas talks as if he is constructing something by rotating his triangles and semicircles, but in the end he is simply discovering a series of relationships that properly belong in the intelligible realm and which are in no way generated by his proof. Archytas' solution is subject to the same _caveats_ as Plato would apply to all mathematics. There is nothing in it to call for any special complaint on Plato's part.

The tradition which has Plato damn Archytas' solution for using an instrument or being mechanical is itself triply damned: there is no evidence of such a condemnation in the *Republic* passage on stereometry, there is no evidence for such a condemnation in Eratosthenes' account of the Delian problem, and there is nothing in Archytas' proof which would justify such a criticism. In an important sense Archytas' solution seems to be the sort of solution that Plato would welcome. If one tries to construct a physical model as an aid to understanding the intersection of the two curves on the surface of the semicylinder, frustration is the inevitable result. Knorr thinks that Archytas' solution retains "vestiges of an underlying practical procedure" (1989: 110). His claim that Eratosthenes says only that Archytas' solution is "hard" but not "impossible" to put into effect, however, overlooks Eratosthenes' letter where it is said to be impossible (line 26 μὴ δύνασθαι). Knorr's reconstruction of how Archytas' method might admit of a simple mechanical execution (1989: 109 ff.) is ingenious, but his conclusion that Archytas' solution bears vestiges of such a practical approach is unconvincing and in clear conflict with Eratosthenes' presentation which resolutely emphasizes the abstract nature of Archytas' approach. We should recognize that Archytas' solution in fact demands what Plato calls for in all mathematical sciences, that we turn away from the physical world and carry out an heroic effort of abstract thought in order to mentally envision the intersection of the two curves on the surface of the semicylinder.

Nonetheless, both the passage on stereometry in the *Republic* and Eratosthenes' version of the Delian story do suggest that Plato was critical of the stereometry of his day and of the solutions to the problem of the duplication of the cube. If there is nothing in Archytas' solution that should cause him to pause, what could have been the problem? Of course Plato will be critical of Archytas, if he does not recognize that mathematics is ultimately valuable only insofar as it directs the mind away from the sensible to the intelligible and prepares us for the study of dialectic. Since there is no evidence that Archytas accepted the intelligible/sensible distinction or that he regarded dialectic as the highest science, he, like many mathematicians, will be the subject of Platonic criticism on these grounds. This then is a complaint about all mathematicians from the Platonic point of view. Why are stereometry and Archytas singled out for criticism?

Plato complains both in the *Republic* and in Eratosthenes' account that Greek cities do not pay enough attention to stereometry/mathematics. It is not implausible to suggest that Plato was chastising Archytas as a prominent political figure in the city of Tarentum and as a prominent geometer for not taking the lead in the promotion of stereometry and not bringing it about that at least the city of Tarentum held the discipline in honor.

Socrates' second explanation for the state of stereometry is the arrogance of its practitioners and the lack of a director to guide studies in the area. Since it is quite possible that Plato already knew of Archytas' solution to the doubling of the cube, when he wrote this passage in the *Republic*, it is perhaps more likely that he sees Archytas as one of the arrogant individuals pursuing isolated problems in stereometry than that Plato envisages him as the potential director. It could, however, be precisely a call for Archytas to abandon his arrogance and become the director. Both of these potential criticisms of Archytas leave the central problem untouched, however. What is it that the attentions of a Greek city-state and of a director are supposed to do for stereometry? They are supposed to encourage more work in the area but to what end? What is it precisely that constitutes the laughable state of stereometry?

The analysis of the passage on stereometry in the *Republic*, which I have given above, suggests that the problem was not anything internal to individual theorems in solid geometry such as Archytas' solution to the duplication of the cube but was rather an external problem, which related to how the theorem fit into, or rather did not fit into, a larger mathematical structure. While there were established disciplines of arithmetic and geometry, there was no such discipline of stereometry. I would suggest that Plato regarded Archytas' duplication as one of the charming accomplishments of the stereometers of his day to which he refers at 528c. Both in the *Republic* and in the tradition going back to Eratosthenes, what is emphasized is that these stereometers do not understand the true value of their charming proofs: in the language of the *Republic* "they do not have an account of in what respect they are useful" (528c), in the language of the Delian story they do not understand what the oracle is really calling for and produce solutions "apart from reason" (Text A and Testimonium 15a). Thus there was a scattering of proofs, which, while gems in themselves, had not been integrated with one another in a way that would create the discipline of "stereometry."

Plato's complaint here seems to be parallel in important ways to his complaint about Pythagorean (= Archytan) harmonics at *Republic* 531a ff. (see the commentary on A16). Socrates remarks that the Pythagoreans make the mistake of focusing their attention on audible concords. Glaucon jumps to the conclusion that he is referring to theorists who tried to build an harmonics on a purely empirical basis and tried to identify solely by hearing and "torturing of strings" the least interval as a unit of measurement. Socrates corrects Glaucon. The Pythagoreans are not so bad. They rightly base their harmonics on non-sensible entities, numbers, but go astray by seeking the numbers only in the heard harmonies. He calls on them instead to forget about the harmonies we hear and ascend to problems and consider which numbers are concordant and which not and why. So Archytas' harmonics ends up by giving a mathematical account of actual musical practice, while Plato is calling for a science of the harmony of number that stays inside the mathematical realm. The goal is to arrive at a discipline of concordant numbers based on a set of basic principles and proofs. The exact nature of this science is still up for debate, some think of something like the *Sectio Canonis* (Mueller 1980: 112), others of the structure of the world soul in the *Timaeus* (Burnyeat 2000: 47 ff.).

In a similar way, then, we would be as mistaken about Pythagorean stereometry as Glaucon initially was about Pythagorean harmonics, to think that Archytas' stereometry is defective in that it is based on mechanical motion or the use of physical instruments. Archytas is resolutely abstract in his use of geometry. But just as in the case of harmonics, all of this admirable abstraction is pointed in the wrong direction; it is directed at problems suggested by this world, by problems such as doubling the size of an altar. As Eratosthenes' letter and later treatises on mechanics make clear, there are a very wide range of practical problems to which solid geometry in general and the problem of the duplication of the cube in particular can be applied, from the building of temples, altars and statues to the construction of war machines, wells, and automata. To forestall misunderstanding, I must emphasize again that the complaint is not that Archytas gave a purely practical solution to the Delian problem but rather that he gave a properly mathematical solution, but to a problem the origin of which was in the physical world. Even this would not be problematic, if Archytas and other stereometers had gone further to attempt to study all the basic three-dimensional bodies and their relations to one another, just as Plato's harmonic theorists are supposed to study what numbers are concordant and why. Archytas, however, thinks that he is done, according to Plato, when he solves the Delian problem. Stereometry is not a discipline, because its practitioners think that the god just wants them to solve individual problems suggested by the physical world rather than constructing an elements of stereometry. They don't understand what stereometry is good for, i.e. an understanding of the nature of and relation between solid bodies at a completely abstract level.

If this is Plato's criticism of Archytas and other stereometers of the day, we are not in a position to determine how justified it is. Our knowledge of systems of elements in Greek geometry before the time of Euclid is very meager. In the commentary on A14, I have discussed some of the problems concerning the nature of early Greek work on the elements of geometry, including the first such work by Hippocrates of Chios. Since Eudemus tells us that Archytas is one of the people who helped bring the theorems of geometry into a more scientific order (A6), i.e. that one of his important contributions was precisely to the systematization of geometry, it might seem perverse to suppose that Plato was criticizing him for what was in fact one of his strengths. If Archytas had constructed at least a rudimentary elements of geometry that allowed him to produce a proof in stereometry such as the duplication of the cube, don't we and Plato have to admit that he has developed a rudimentary stereometry as well? It must be remembered, however, that Plato is not talking about geometry here, which he does seem to think is a properly constituted discipline, but specifically about stereometry. It seems quite possible that, however advanced Archytas was in elementalizing geometry, he had not recognized that there was a distinct discipline of stereometry to pursue. Plato, however, was in a minority in thinking that there should be a discipline of stereometry apart from geometry. As I have shown above, later philosophers and mathematicians starting with Aristotle did not recognize a distinct discipline. Archytas may even have been aware that Plato supposed there to be a separate discipline of stereometry and may have consciously rejected such a view.

The debate between Plato and Archytas which I have reconstructed in the last paragraph is of course very speculative. Leaving aside the speculative details of that reconstruction, however, I have argued that it is likely that Plato's criticism of the stereometers of his day in the *Republic*, a criticism which I take to be reflected in the later tradition about the Delian problem, focuses precisely on the issue of what it means to properly constitute a mathematical discipline. Lloyd has very persuasively argued that the first half of the fourth century was a time in which there was considerable debate both about what types of principles should be used in an elements of mathematics and also about specific definitions of key concepts and that Aristotle was the first to reach a clear conception of demonstrative science (1979: 111–15). My argument is that Plato's comments on stereometry in the *Republic* are important evidence for that debate. If Plato is arguing that there should be a separate science of stereometry, then it is quite plausible that he thinks that there are a set of distinctive starting points for such a discipline such as the definitions which Euclid prefaces to Book xi of the *Elements* and that the director of stereometry would push his researchers to come up with such definitions. He says nothing directly about such starting points for stereometry, however. If the analogy that I have drawn between Plato's vision of the ideal science of harmonics and his vision of the science of stereometry has any validity, it would appear that Plato's central point was that the focus needed to be on the geometrical solids themselves and their interrelations with one another. Such a focus would lead to an ordering of theorems such as we find in Euclid xiii, where each of the five regular solids is constructed and their interrelations explored.

In the end Plato is complaining precisely about a stereometry that is "externalist," in that its development is being guided by issues external to the discipline itself rather than its own internal logic. It may well be that it was the desire to find a more concrete explanation for Plato's critique of stereometry and an explanation that could point to some feature internal to the proposed solutions to the problem of the duplication of the cube, which led to the elaboration of the Delian story that we find in Plutarch. Such an elaboration might naturally have arisen after Eratosthenes' pointed emphasis on providing an instrument, which could be used in practice in order to determine the two means. The dissatisfaction with such practical solutions by later-day Platonists such as Plutarch would have been a natural stimulus for reading the same dissatisfaction back into Plato's quite different malaise about earlier solutions to the problem. Then, in the ultimate twist in this strange history, a marginal comment denoting a solution as precisely not as Plato would have wanted is corrupted to say that this was a solution as Plato wanted it, so that the solution is interpreted as Plato's own and the name of its original author is lost. Thus, Archytas' solution to the problem of the duplication of the cube is much more Platonic than what the tradition assigns to Plato himself. In Plato's eyes, however, Archytas in his duplication of the cube, just as in his divisions of the tetrachord, while employing proper mathematical form, fails to see the real good to which his work can be put, the establishment of a science of harmonious numbers in the one case and the establishment of the science of geometrical solids in the other.

CHAPTER IV

Music

A16 Ptolemy, *Harmonics* I. 13–14 (Düring 1930: 30–32; cf. II. 14, Düring 1930: 70–73)

See Boethius, *De Institutione Musica* v. 17–18 and Porphyry, *On Ptolemy's Harmonics* I. 13–14 (Düring 1932: 138–42, cf. 136.13)

ιγ΄. Περὶ τῆς κατὰ Ἀρχύταν τῶν γενῶν καὶ τῶν τετραχόρδων διαιρέσεως

Οὗτος μὲν οὖν κἀνταῦθα φαίνεται μηδέν τι τοῦ λόγου φροντίσας, ἀλλὰ τοῖς μεταξὺ μόνοις τῶν φθόγγων διορίσας τὰ γένη καὶ μὴ ταῖς αὐτῶν πρὸς ἀλλήλους ὑπεροχαῖς, τὰ μὲν αἴτια τῶν διαφορῶν ὡς ἀναίτια καὶ τὸ μηθὲν καὶ πέρατα μόνον παραλιπών, τοῖς δὲ ἀσωμά- τοις καὶ κενοῖς προσάψας τὰς παραβολάς. διὰ τοῦτο δὲ οὐδὲν αὐτῷ μέλει δίχα διαιροῦντι σχεδὸν πανταχῇ τὰς ἐμμελείας, τῶν ἐπιμορίων αὐτῶν μηδαμῶς τὸ τοιοῦτον ἐπιδεχομένων. Ἀρχύτας δὲ ὁ Ταραν- τῖνος μάλιστα τῶν Πυθαγορείων ἐπιμεληθεὶς μουσικῆς πειρᾶται μὲν τὸ κατὰ τὸν λόγον ἀκόλουθον διασῴζειν, οὐκ ἐν ταῖς συμφωνίαις μόνον, ἀλλὰ καὶ ταῖς τῶν τετραχόρδων διαιρέσεσιν, ὡς οἰκείου τῇ φύσει τῶν ἐμμελῶν ὄντος τοῦ συμμέτρου τῶν ὑπεροχῶν. ταύτῃ δ' ὅμως τῇ προθέσει χρησάμενος εἰς ἔνια μὲν καὶ τέλεον αὐτῆς φαίνεται δια- μαρτάνων, ἐν δὲ τοῖς πλείστοις τοῦ μὲν τοιούτου περικρατῶν, ἀπᾴδων δὲ σαφῶς τῶν ἄντικρυς ἤδη ταῖς αἰσθήσεσιν ὡμολογημένων, ὡς αὐτίκα εἰσόμεθα ἐκ τῆς κατ' αὐτὸν τῶν τετραχόρδων διαιρέσεως. τρία μὲν τοί- νυν οὗτος ὑφίσταται γένη, τό τε ἐναρμόνιον καὶ τὸ χρωματικὸν καὶ τὸ διατονικόν· ἑκάστου δὲ αὐτῶν ποιεῖται τὴν διαίρεσιν οὕτως. τὸν μὲν γὰρ ἑπόμενον λόγον ἐπὶ τῶν τρίων γενῶν τὸν αὐτὸν ὑφίσταται καὶ ἐπὶ κζ΄, τὸν δὲ μέσον ἐπὶ μὲν τοῦ ἐναρμονίου ἐπὶ λέ, ἐπὶ δὲ τοῦ διατονικοῦ ἐπὶ ζ΄, ὥστε καὶ τὸν ἡγούμενον τοῦ μὲν ἐναρμονίου γένους συνάγεσθαι

3 διαστήμασι add. post φθόγγων e P^{par} fg ss. A   4 αὐτῶν] αὐταῖς g   5 παραλιπών mgA παραλαμβάνων f ss. V¹ παρέλιπε P^{par}   6 δέ] om. fg   8 αὐτῶν] MWEg λόγων αὐτῶν V   λόγων fA e P^{par} irrepsit   17–19 ὑφίσταται (bis)] MWEfg ὑφιστᾷ WⁿA ὑφίστησι V ss. GAγρ cf. Düring p. 29:16, 68:17

ἐπὶ δ̄, τοῦ δὲ διατονικοῦ ἐπὶ η̄· τὸν δὲ ἐν τῷ χρωματικῷ γένει δεύτερον 22
ἀπὸ τοῦ ὀξυτάτου φθόγγου λαμβάνει διὰ τοῦ τὴν αὐτὴν θέσιν ἔχον- 23
τος ἐν τῷ διατονικῷ. φησὶ γὰρ λόγον ἔχειν τὸν ἐν τῷ χρωματικῷ 24
δεύτερον ἀπὸ τοῦ ὀξυτάτου πρὸς τὸν ὅμοιον τὸν ἐν τῷ διατονικῷ τὸν 25
τῶν σνϛ̄ πρὸς τὰ σμγ̄. συνίσταται δὴ τὰ τοιαῦτα τετράχορδα κατὰ 26
τοὺς ἐκκειμένους λόγους ἐν πρώτοις ἀριθμοῖς τούτοις. ἐὰν γὰρ τοὺς μὲν 27
ὀξυτάτους τῶν τετραχόρδων ὑποστησώμεθα αϕιβ̄, τοὺς δὲ βαρυτά- 28
τους κατὰ τὸν ἐπίτριτον λόγον τῶν αὐτῶν βιϛ̄, ταῦτα μὲν ποιήσει τὸν 29
ἐπὶ κζ̄ πρὸς τὰ α⅃μδ̄ καὶ τοσούτων ἔσονται πάλιν ἐν τοῖς τρισὶ γένεσιν 30
οἱ δεύτεροι ἀπὸ τῶν βαρυτάτων. τῶν δ᾽ ἀπὸ τοῦ ὀξυτάτου δευτέρων 31
ὁ μὲν τοῦ ἐναρμονίου γένους ἔσται αωϙ̄. ταῦτα γὰρ πρὸς μὲν τὰ α⅃μδ̄ 32
ποιεῖ τὸν ἐπὶ λε̄ λόγον, πρὸς δὲ τὰ αϕιβ̄ τὸν ἐπὶ δ̄· ὁ δὲ τοῦ διατονικοῦ 33
γένους τῶν αὐτῶν ἔσται αψᾱ. καὶ ταῦτα γὰρ πρὸς μὲν τὰ α⅃μδ̄ τὸν 34
ἐπὶ ζ̄ ποιεῖ λόγον, πρὸς δὲ τὰ αϕιβ̄ τὸν ἐπὶ η̄· ὁ δὲ τοῦ χρωματικοῦ καὶ 35
αὐτὸς ἔσται τῶν αὐτῶν αψϙβ̄ · ταῦτα γὰρ λόγον ἔχει πρὸς τὰ αψᾱ 36
ὃν τὰ σνϛ̄ πρὸς τὰ σμγ̄. ὑπογέγραπται δὲ καὶ ἡ τούτων τῶν ἀριθμῶν 37
ἔκθεσις ἔχουσα οὕτως. 38

ἐναρμόνιον		χρωματικόν		διατονικόν	
αϕιβ̄	1512	αϕιβ̄	1512	αϕιβ̄	1512
ἐπὶ δ̄	5/4		32/27	ἐπὶ η̄	9/8
αωϙ̄	1890	αψϙβ̄	1792	αψᾱ	1701
ἐπὶ λε̄	36/35		243/224	ἐπὶ ζ̄	8/7
α⅃μδ̄	1944	α⅃μδ̄	1944	α⅃μδ̄	1944
ἐπὶ κζ̄	28/27	ἐπὶ κζ̄	28/27	ἐπὶ κζ̄	28/27
βιϛ̄	2016	βιϛ̄	2016	βιϛ̄	2016

ιδ̄. Ἀπόδειξις τοῦ μηδετέραν τῶν διαιρέσεων σῴζειν τὸ τῷ ὄντι ἐμμελές. 39

Παρὰ μὲν δὴ τὴν πρόθεσιν ὡς ἔφαμεν αὐτῷ συνεστάθη τὸ χρωματικὸν 40
τετράχορδον – ὁ γὰρ τῶν αψϙβ̄ ἀριθμὸς οὔτε πρὸς τὸν τῶν αϕιβ̄ 41
ποιεῖ λόγον ἐπιμόριον, οὔτε πρὸς τὸν τῶν α⅃μδ̄ – παρὰ δὲ τὴν ἀπὸ 42
τῆς αἰσθήσεως ἐνάργειαν τό τε χρωματικὸν καὶ τὸ ἐναρμόνιον. τὸν 43

25 τόν³] om. f　**26** συνίσταται] συνίστησι ss. G　τρία add. ante τετράχορδα f ss. AV¹
29–30 τόν add. post ἐπὶ κζ̄ m sed eras. W　**35** τά om. W add. W¹　**41–42** τόν] τήν bis
F　**42** τῶν om. V

τε γὰρ ἑπόμενον λόγον τοῦ συνήθους χρωματικοῦ μείζονα καταλαμ- 44
βάνομεν τοῦ ἐπὶ κζ καὶ τὸν ἐν τῷ ἐναρμονίῳ πάλιν ἑπόμενον τῶν ἐν 45
τοῖς ἄλλοις γένεσιν ὁμοίων ἐλάττονα πολλῷ φαινόμενον ἴσον αὐτοῖς 46
ὑποτίθεται, καὶ πρὸς τούτοις ἐλάττονα αὐτοῦ τὸν μέσον ἐν ἐπὶ λέ λόγῳ 47
τιθέμενος, ἐκμελοῦς ἄντικρυς τοῦ τοιούτου πανταχῇ γινομένου, καθ᾽ ὃ 48
τὸ πρὸς τῷ βαρυτάτῳ μέγεθος τοῦ μέσου συνίσταται μεῖζον. ταῦτα 49
μὲν δὴ δοκεῖ τῷ λογικῷ κριτηρίῳ περιποιῆσαι τὴν διαβολήν, ὅτι κατὰ 50
τοὺς ἐκτιθεμένους λόγους ὑπὸ τῶν προϊσταμένων αὐτοῦ γινομένης 51
τῆς τοῦ κανόνος κατατομῆς οὐ διασῴζεται τὸ ἐμμελές. οἱ γὰρ πλεῖστοι 52
τῶν τε προκειμένων καὶ τῶν τοῖς ἄλλοις σχεδὸν ἅπασι διαπεπλασ- 53
μένων οὐκ ἐφαρμόζουσι τοῖς ὁμολογουμένοις ἤθεσιν. ἔοικε δὲ καὶ τὸ 54
πλῆθος τῶν γενῶν κατὰ μὲν τὸν Ἀρχύταν ἐνδεῖν τοῦ μετρίου, μὴ μόνον 55
αὐτοῦ τὸ ἐναρμόνιον ἀλλὰ καὶ τό τε χρωματικὸν καὶ τὸ διατονικὸν 56
ἑκάτερον μονοειδὲς ὑποθεμένου, κατὰ δὲ τὸν Ἀριστόξενον ὑπερβάλλειν 57
μὲν ἐπὶ τοῦ χρωματικοῦ, τῶν τε τοῦ μαλακοῦ καὶ τοῦ ἡμιολίου διέσεων 58
εἰκοστῷ καὶ τετάρτῳ μέρει τόνου διαφερουσῶν, ὡς μηδεμίαν ἀξιό- 59
λογον ταῖς αἰσθήσεσιν ἐμποιεῖν παραλλαγήν, ἐνδεῖν δὲ ἐπὶ τοῦ δια- 60
τονικοῦ, πλειόνων φαινομένων σαφῶς τῶν μελῳδουμένων, ὡς ἐκ τῶν 61
αὐτίκα ἐπιδειχθησομένων ἐξέσται σκοπεῖν . . . 62

53 λόγων add. post προκειμένων e P^{par} f ss. g　　**54** ἐν ταῖς μελῳδίαις add. post. ἤθεσιν
e P^{par} f　ἐν μελῳδίαις ss. Eg　　**56** αὐτοῦ]αὐτό f　　**56** τό add. ante χρωματικόν M
59 διαφερουσῶν τόνου g　　**61** ὡς] om. m add. $W^I V^I E^I$

13　Concerning the division of the genera and of the tetrachords according
to Archytas.

　So then, he [Aristoxenus], also in this case, manifestly paid no attention
to reason, but distinguished the genera by what lies between the notes alone
and not by the excesses of the notes in comparison with one another, and
left to one side the causes of their differences as no causes and as nothing
and as mere limits, but made their comparison depend on what is bod-
iless and void. Because of this, he, without concern, divides in half the
melodic distances in nearly every case, although those of them that are
epimoric in no way admit of such a thing. But Archytas of Tarentum, who
engaged in the study of music most of all the Pythagoreans, does attempt
to preserve what follows in accord with reason, not only in the concords
but also in the divisions of the tetrachord, on the grounds that having
an excess that is a common measure is proper to the nature of what is
melodic. Nevertheless, while having employed this principle, in some cases
it is clear that he completely strays from it. In the majority of cases he does
have full mastery of such a principle yet clearly is at variance with what

is immediately and obviously accepted by the senses, as we will shortly see from his division of the tetrachords. So then, he posits three genera, the enharmonic, the chromatic and the diatonic. He makes the division of each of them as follows. He lays down the "following ratio" as the same in each of the three genera, i.e. 28:27, but as the middle in the enharmonic 36:35, in the diatonic 8:7, so that the "leading ratio" of the enharmonic genus is calculated to be 5:4, and of the diatonic 9:8. The second note from the highest in the chromatic genus he gets through the note having the same position in the diatonic. For he says that the second note from the highest in the chromatic has a ratio to the similar note in the diatonic of 256:243. According to the ratios that have been set out, such tetrachords are constituted in their lowest terms in the following numbers. For if we posit 1,512 as the highest note in the tetrachords, and, in accord with the ratio 4:3 to these same notes, the lowest as 2,016, this latter term will make the ratio 28:27 to 1,944 and the second notes from the lowest in the three genera will again be of this quantity. Of the second notes from the highest, that in the enharmonic genus will be 1,890. For this makes the ratio 36:35 in relation to 1,944, and the ratio 5:4 in relation to 1,512. The note in the diatonic genus that belongs to this same class will be 1,701. For this makes the ratio 8:7 in relation to 1,944, and the ratio 9:8 in relation to 1,512. The note in the chromatic genus that belongs to this same class will itself be 1,792; for this has a ratio to 1,701 which 256 has to 243. The table of these numbers arranged in this way is written below.

Enharmonic	Chromatic	Diatonic
1512	1512	1512
5/4	32/27	9/8
1890	1792	1701
36/35	243/224	8/7
1944	1944	1944
28/27	28/27	28/27
2016	2016	2016

14 Demonstration that neither of the divisions [i.e. those proposed by Aristoxenus and by Archytas] preserves what is truly melodic.

On the one hand, then, as we said, the chromatic tetrachord was constructed contrary to his principle – for the number 1,792 makes an epimoric ratio neither with the number 1,512 nor with the number 1,944. On the other hand, both the chromatic and the enharmonic were constructed contrary to what is obvious from perception. For we take the "following" ratio of the customary chromatic genus as greater than 28:27. Again, the "following" ratio in the enharmonic genus, although it is manifestly much smaller than the similar ratios in the other genera, he supposes to be equal to them, while in addition making the middle ratio less than it, in the ratio 36:35, although such a thing turns out to be obviously unmelodic in every case, when the magnitude next to the lowest note is made greater than the middle. These things, then, seem to provide a point of attack against the criterion of reason, because, when the division of the canon is carried out in accordance with the ratios set out by his proposals, what is melodic is not preserved. For both the majority of the ratios set out above and also of those concocted by nearly all the others do not agree with the accepted characteristics. It also seems that the number of genera in Archytas' system falls short of what is fitting, since he not only supposes that the enharmonic, but also both the chromatic and the diatonic each have one form. But in Aristoxenus' system, the number is excessive in the chromatic, since the dieses of the soft and hemiolic differ by a twenty-fourth part of a tone, so as to make no noticeable difference to the senses, but deficient in the diatonic, since it is clear that those that are sung are more numerous, as it will be possible to see from the things that are going to be demonstrated shortly . . .

Authenticity

Scholars have almost universally regarded A16 as based on genuine work of Archytas, in large part because of the technical nature of the testimonium, with its intricate set of ratios. As Burkert says, "no forger works out complicated calculations like those in A16" (1972a: 220 n. 14). It is important to note in addition, since a forged work like that ascribed to Timaeus Locrus also contains complex mathematics, that the ratios of A16, unlike those of Timaeus Locrus, do not correspond to anything in the Platonic tradition. Thus, the supposed forger could not have the motivation of showing Archytas to have anticipated Plato nor the model of the *Timaeus* for developing the set of ratios found in A16. A final strong argument for the authenticity of the material in A16 is Winnington-Ingram's demonstration (1932) that each of the sets of ratios found in A16 and the technical features of their construction (e.g. the importance of the ratio 7:6) correspond to actual musical practices of Archytas' time as attested by Aristoxenus. It is highly implausible that a forger would be so accurate as to develop a set of ratios based on very technical features of the musical practice of Archytas' day. Clearly what we have is a record of Archytas' own subtle attempt to give a mathematical account of important features of the music of his day.

Context in Ptolemy

The testimony about Archytas' music theory, which appears in A16, comes from Chapters 13 and 14 of Book 1 of Ptolemy's *Harmonics*. This is the Ptolemy who is most famous for the astronomical system set out in the *Almagest*. He was active in the middle of the second century AD, some 500 years after the death of Archytas. We are in a much better position to understand his *Harmonics,* as a result of the annotated translation by Andrew Barker (1989: 270–391). Translations from the *Harmonics* in the following paragraphs are from Barker. In order to understand Ptolemy's account of Archytas, it is important to see its context in the wider theory of harmonics that Ptolemy develops in Book 1.

Ptolemy begins his work by defining harmonics as knowledge of the distinctions related to high and low pitch in sound. He then develops a subtle theory, in which both the senses and reason serve as the criteria of the content of this knowledge, although not in the same way. The senses first present to reason the distinctions in pitch that they have grasped in outline. Reason, with the aid of instruments, such as a string stretched over a ruler, or *kanōn*, then produces distinctions that are more accurate. The results of reason, however, are then confirmed by the senses. So the ultimate aim of the student of harmonics is to preserve "the rational postulates of the *kanōn*" while not conflicting with the perceptions that most people have. In accordance with their use of these two criteria (reason and perception), Ptolemy divides his predecessors in the study of harmonics into two camps, the Pythagoreans and the Aristoxenians. He regards both of them as mistaken, although his own position is much closer to that of the Pythagoreans. He criticizes the Pythagoreans for proceeding too much in accord with abstract reason and not following the senses, even where everyone must do so, and the Aristoxenians for following nothing but the "irrational exercise of perception" (Chapter 2).

After developing an acoustic theory to explain differences in pitch (Chapters 3–4), Ptolemy turns to a discussion of the Pythagorean approach to the concords (Chapter 5). He accepts the Pythagorean practice of assigning equal numbers to equal tones. He also adopts the ratios of numbers that they assign to the concords of the octave (2:1), fifth (3:2) and fourth (4:3). It is important to note that he does not single out any specific Pythagoreans in this passage. In setting out the Pythagorean position he starts by referring to "leaders of the school" and later in the chapter says that "they argue to the same conclusion in a more geometrical way." This last more geometrical presentation is in fact drawn from the *Sectio Canonis* ascribed to Euclid, although Ptolemy himself does not identify the source of the material. In Chapter 6, Ptolemy turns to his critique of the Pythagorean position. His major criticism in this area concerns the Pythagorean rejection of the interval of the octave + a fourth as a concord, even though perception indicates that this interval is a concord. They reject it, because the ratio that corresponds to it (8:3) does not fit their stipulation that all concords must be either epimoric or multiple ratios. (Epimoric ratios are those in which the difference between the two terms of the ratio is an integral part of the smaller term, e.g. in the ratio 12:9, the difference between the two terms, 3, is an integral part of the smaller term 9, i.e. it divides into 9 with no remainder. All ratios of the form (n + 1):n, which are particularly important in music theory, will thus be epimoric except 2:1, where the difference between the terms, 1, is not a part of the lesser term but equal to the whole of it. Multiple ratios are those that have the form (mn):n, e.g. 2:1, 4:1.) He also criticizes the Pythagoreans for arbitrarily selecting only certain epimoric and multiple ratios as corresponding to concords and rejecting others, such as 5:4 and 5:1.

In Chapters 7 and 8, Ptolemy gives his own account of how the concords should be defined and then demonstrates the truth of his position, by the use of the single-stringed *kanōn*. Chapters 9–11 serve as a critique of various aspects of the Aristoxenian way of dealing with the concords. In particular Ptolemy criticizes the Aristoxenians for ignoring the notes themselves, whose relations are what are concordant and discordant, and focusing instead on the "empty" distance between the notes.

At the beginning of Chapter 12, Ptolemy marks a change of topic. He says that he has completed his account of "the greater differences between notes," and will now turn to discuss the "smaller ones," that result when the fourth is divided into three ratios. These further divisions of the fourth admit of some variety. He identifies three basic kinds or genera of divisions of the fourth: the enharmonic, chromatic and diatonic. In the case of these genera of the tetrachord, Ptolemy starts by setting out Aristoxenus' view rather than the Pythagoreans. This takes the rest of Chapter 12. Chapter 13 begins with a brief criticism of the system of Aristoxenus, which has just been set out. The rest of the chapter contains Archytas' account of the ratios in the three genera of the tetrachord. Chapter 14 provides a critique of both of the systems, that of Archytas first and then that of Aristoxenus. Finally, in the last two chapters of Book I, Ptolemy presents his own account of the divisions of the tetrachord by genera. Thus, Archytas and his ratios serve as the Pythagorean account of the division of the tetrachord, which is set in contrast to Aristoxenus' account. Ptolemy is critical of both accounts, just as he was critical of the basic positions of both the Pythagoreans and Aristoxenians in Chapter 2.

Archytas' ratios for the three genera of the tetrachord are repeated by Ptolemy, in Chapter 14 of Book II of the *Harmonics*. In this chapter, the ratios in each of the three genera according to Archytas, Aristoxenus, Eratosthenes, Didymus and Ptolemy himself are set out in table form. Since the ratios are identical to those found here in Book I, Chapter 13 and are simply listed with no additional commentary, I have not printed the text of Chapter 14, Book II.

Boethius' translation

Boethius' *De Institutione Musica* v. 17–18 is a translation/paraphrase of Book I. 13–14 of Ptolemy's *Harmonics*. For the general characteristics of Boethius' translations see the commentary on A19. In the specific case of Ptolemy I. 13–14, Boethius presents Ptolemy's text more concisely rather than expanding upon it. In some cases he even leaves out significant material. He adds little or nothing new; there is no sign that he is using any source other than Ptolemy to elucidate Archytas' divisions of the tetrachord. Accordingly, I have not thought it worthwhile to present the text of Boethius here. There is, however, one point that is worth noting. Boethius repeats Ptolemy's complaint that hearing tells us that the lowest interval in the usual chromatic genus is much larger than the corresponding interval in Archytas' division. Ptolemy does not specify what the size of this interval is in the usual chromatic genus, but Boethius says that the ratio was 22:21 in comparison to Archytas' 28:27. This is the only place where Boethius makes a significant addition to what we find in Ptolemy. Bower (1989: 178) says that "Boethius' source for this ratio is unknown." But 22:21 is a ratio used by Ptolemy in his own division of the chromatic tetrachord in the very next chapter, so that it is likely that Boethius got the ratio from Ptolemy. Porphyry (141.7) also reports this same ratio in his commentary on this passage of Ptolemy.

Porphyry's commentary on Ptolemy

In many places in his commentary, Porphyry supplies texts and information that are not provided by Ptolemy (e.g. see Archytas A17). In the case of Ptolemy's discussion of Archytas' divisions of the tetrachord in A16, however, there is no indication that Porphyry has consulted any other source. In his commentary on these two chapters of Ptolemy (Düring 1932: 138–42), Porphyry follows Ptolemy's text very closely. In the introductory comments that lead up to the presentation of Archytas' ratios, he simply quotes Ptolemy, while inserting a few explanatory words and phrases. Accordingly, I have not provided the text of Porphyry's commentary on this section of Ptolemy.

Archytas' division of the tetrachord in the three genera
At first sight the ratios that Archytas presents as determining the structure of the tetrachord in the three genera seem forbidding indeed. Many commentators, starting with Plato and Ptolemy, have been very critical of Archytas' procedure. Nonetheless, the initial puzzle that the ratios provide has elicited some brilliant scholarship (most notably by Tannery, Winnington-Ingram and Barker), which has solved a number of the most prominent difficulties in understanding Archytas' work in this area. My account will, accordingly, rely heavily on the work of these and other scholars. There do remain a couple of unsolved difficulties on specific points, which I will address below. The major outstanding problem is that no clear consensus has emerged on the nature of Archytas' goals in this area and on his success in achieving them. Burkert is the most negative about Archytas' achievement, concluding that ". . . some observed facts and some speculative *a priori* postulates are manipulated in a logical way, but do not coalesce into a complete system" (1972a: 386; on Burkert's analysis see my overview of Archytas' philosophy). At the other extreme is Barker, who concludes that ". . . Archytas' analysis is a triumphant fusion of attentive observation, metaphysical commitment and mathematical ingenuity" (1989: 52). My own analysis suggests that Barker's general assessment of Archytas is closer to the truth, but I will differ from Barker on two important points.

Before turning to detailed analysis of Archytas' ratios, it is necessary briefly to provide some general background on the area of Greek music theory in which Archytas is working (for a fuller account of these matters see Barker [1989: 11–13]). The most fundamental musical interval is of course the octave, which is in turn composed of the fourth and the fifth. Traditionally the lowest note in the octave is known as *hypatē* and the highest as *nētē* (see the figure which follows). The note that is a fourth up from *hypatē* is known as *mesē* and it is a fifth from *mesē* up to *nētē*. Typically the octave was viewed as composed of two fourths joined in the middle by a whole tone. When constructing scales, the Greeks usually worked with a span of two octaves, but, for purposes of simplicity, I will deal with just a single octave here. From *hypatē* to *mesē* is a fourth. A note known as *paramesē* ("next to *mesē*") is a tone above *mesē*, and then the interval from *paramesē* to *nētē* is another fourth. The variety in Greek music is produced by differing divisions of the two fourths that make up the octave. Although the outside notes of these fourths are fixed (*hypatē*, *mesē*, *paramesē*, *nētē*), two movable notes are inserted between them. If we focus on the lower of these two fourths, the highest movable note is known as *lichanos* and the lowest is *parhypatē* ("next to *hypatē*"). The position of *lichanos* was in practice found in three basic ranges of positions, one range centers upon a *lichanos* which is two tones below *mesē*, another upon a *lichanos* which is one tone below, and another upon a *lichanos* which is between one and two tones below. Divisions of the fourth that put *lichanos* in the first range are said to belong to the enharmonic genus, in the second range to the diatonic genus, and in the third range to the chromatic genus. There is also variation as to where the second movable note, *parhypatē*, is placed, but it is the position of *lichanos* that generally determines to which of the three genera the scale is thought to belong. The upper tetrachord in the octave is divided in the same way as the lower tetrachord, the movable notes being known as *tritē* and *paranētē* in ascending order. Music theorists and practical musicians would differ as to how they divided the tetrachord in each genus. Archytas' ratios provide his specifications of where the *lichanos* and *parhypatē* should be inserted in the enharmonic, chromatic, and diatonic tetrachord.

The octave divided into two disjunct tetrachords

Nētē
Paranētē
                        Tetrachord (4:3)
Tritē
Paramesē
                        Tone (9:8)   Octave
Mesē
Lichanos
                        Tetrachord (4:3)
Parhypatē
Hypatē

We are now in a position to discuss Archytas' divisions of the tetrachord in each of the three genera. The following chart gives the ratios that correspond to the intervals in the lower tetrachord. The same ratios also apply to the intervals of the upper tetrachord. Several things are immediately striking about these ratios: (1) The lowest interval is the same in all three genera; (2) seven, but only seven, of the nine ratios are superparticular; (3) the diatonic tetrachord differs from the division of the diatonic which is implied by Fr. 6a of Philolaus, Archytas' predecessor, and found in Plato's *Timaeus* (9:8, 9:8, and 256:243).

	Enharmonic	Chromatic	Diatonic
Mesē			
	5:4	32:27	9:8
Lichanos			
	36:35	243:224	8:7
Parhypatē			
	28:27	28:27	28:27
Hypatē			

Modern scholarship has made important strides in explicating these unusual ratios. Yet, as we will see shortly, the significance of one of the most striking results of modern scholarship on Archytas' divisions of the tetrachord has not been fully appreciated. Winnington-Ingram concludes his important article, "Aristoxenus and the Intervals of Greek Music," with the words ". . . the chief service of Aristoxenus' account of the genera seems, on examination, to be the confirmation of Archytas" (1932: 208). What has been "confirmed" is the crucial discovery of modern scholarship that Archytas' scalar divisions are based on actual Greek musical practice of his day. Each of Archytas' three scalar divisions corresponds to one mentioned by Aristoxenus, writing in the generation after Archytas died. Aristoxenus does not regard all three as the "proper" divisions, but there can be no doubt that he found all three in the music of his day. For example, in the case of the enharmonic genus he champions a *lichanos* that is a ditone down from *mesē*. He comments, however, that "those who are used only to the style of composition at present in vogue rule out the ditone *lichanos*, since most people nowadays use higher ones. The reason is their endless pursuit of sweetness" (23 tr. Barker). A little later he suggests that the *lichanos* is either a ditone or less by "some extremely small amount" (28). This exactly describes Archytas' enharmonic *lichanos* (5:4 = 80:64) which is smaller than the ditone (81:64) by a very small amount (1:64). It is important to stress that Aristoxenus does not ascribe this slightly higher *lichanos* to abstract theorists but presents it as the current vogue of musical practice pursued not because of theoretical principles but because it is sweeter to the sense of hearing. The scale that accords with Archytas' diatonic tetrachord is mentioned by Aristoxenus in passing as an example of the case where the middle interval in the tetrachord is larger than the highest interval. In this case Aristoxenus regards the resulting division of the tetrachord as "melodically proper" (27) and Ptolemy attests to its widespread practical use (Winnington-Ingram [1932: 196, 202]). Aristoxenus also refers to a division of the chromatic tetrachord that corresponds to Archytas' as a division that is perceived as melodic (52 – Winnington-Ingram [1932: 203]).

Winnington-Ingram has yet more evidence that ties Archytas to musical practice. One of the most singular features of Archytas' ratios, the fact that the lowest interval of the tetrachord is the same for all three genera (28:27), is paralleled by the fact that Greek notation for *parhypatē* (the note next to the lowest) is also the same in all three genera. The most natural explanation of this parallel is that there was a time when it was the custom for all three genera to have an identical lowest interval and that Archytas' ratios are a representation of such practice. Burkert suggests that Archytas was blindly following the notation that was common to the three genera in defiance of the ear and musical practice. This suggestion, however, is based on Ptolemy's mistaken complaint that Archytas' ratio for the lowest interval in the tetrachord contradicts the senses (1972a: 385). Winnington-Ingram's comparisons with Aristoxenus, who wrote in the latter part of the fourth century BC, show that Archytas' theory was closely tied to the practice of the fourth century. Ptolemy, on the other hand, is writing some 500 years later, and it is surely right to follow Winnington-Ingram and conclude that "the criticisms of Ptolemy arise in part from Ptolemy's ignorance" of much earlier musical practice (1932: 207). It was this musical practice that led both to the notation and to Archytas' common *parhypatē*.

There is yet one more strong piece of evidence to tie Archytas, *pace* Ptolemy and Burkert, to the musical practice of his day. Several sources, most notably a fragment of Euripides' play *Orestes*, suggest that in the late fifth century an interval comparable to a minor third and corresponding to the ratio 7:6 was very important (Winnington-Ingram 1932: 205ff.; Düring 1934: 251ff.). This ratio does not directly appear in the ratios given by Archytas, but its importance in fact explains Archytas' use of the ratio 28:27 for the lowest interval in all three genera. If one starts from *mesē*, the top note of the lower tetrachord, and goes up an interval of 7:6, the note thus arrived at (*tritē*) will form exactly Archytas' interval 28:27 with the lowest note in the upper tetrachord (*paramesē*). It would thus appear that the importance of the minor third (7:6) in musical practice was such that it was built into all three genera, and Archytas' ratios reflect this fact by making the lowest interval in the tetrachord 28:27 in all genera.

What has not been sufficiently appreciated is that Winnington-Ingram's demonstration of Archytas' close connection to the musical practice of the day confirms and is confirmed by Socrates' famous comment at *Republic* 531c that the Pythagoreans who study music "seek the numbers in these heard concords" and do not ascend to problems. This remark in the *Republic*, like other similar remarks by Plato on contemporary and pre-ceding thinkers, has been open to a wide range of interpretations. Barker (1994: 133), for example, has argued that the remark is intended to be true of Pythagoreanism of the dramatic date of the *Republic* in the late fifth cen-tury rather than the Pythagoreans who were Plato's contemporaries at the time of the writing of the *Republic* (ca. 380). Such questions are impossible to answer with certainty. However, since Plato may well be quoting from Archytas Fragment 1 when introducing the Pythagoreans in this passage (530d), the most likely answer is that he is referring to the Pythagoreans who were his contemporaries and most notably, Archytas. Moreover, the Archytas that emerges from Winnington-Ingram's study exactly fits Plato's description. He is someone who is focused on explaining the concords that he hears in the musical practice of his day, for it is in these terms that the ratios which appear in his division of the tetrachords in each of the three genera make sense, especially the uniformity of the lowest interval.

Now any rational explanation of musical practice will have to consist of more than a simple description of what occurs and will go on to ground practice in a consistent set of theoretical principles. The central questions then become what those principles are and how they are related both to one another and to the phenomena. It seems likely that Archytas is attempting such an explanation, but there is no direct evidence as to what explanatory principles he used and scholars have accordingly disagreed in reconstruct-ing them. Ptolemy thinks he knows what principles Archytas was following but argues that he failed to apply them consistently. According to Ptolemy, Archytas thought that "having an excess that is a common measure is proper to the nature of what is melodic" and this is equivalent to saying that melodic intervals must be intervals that correspond to superparticular ratios or to the multiple ratio 2:1 (see the commentary on lines 11–12 below). A similar principle, that concordant intervals must correspond to superparticular or multiple ratios, is regarded as a hallmark of Pythagorean harmonics in the later tradition. Ptolemy assigns it to the Pythagoreans in general in Book 1,

Chapter 5, and it is clearly stated in the preface to the *Sectio Canonis* ascribed to Euclid. The principle does not appear to have been extended to melodic intervals by Archytas' Pythagorean predecessor, Philolaus, who accepted a diatonic tetrachord made up of two whole tones, each of which is a superparticular ratio 9:8, and the so-called leimma, whose 256:243 ratio is decidedly neither superparticular nor multiple (Fragment 6a; see Huffman 1993: 145ff.). Accordingly, some scholars, on the basis of Ptolemy's testimony that Archytas did apply the principle to melodic intervals, have also suggested that Archytas was in fact the first to have done so (Barker 1994: 129). There are very good reasons, however, for thinking that, despite Ptolemy's testimony, Archytas did not follow the principle at all.

First, as I show in the commentary below, it is not at all clear on what basis Ptolemy assigns the principle to Archytas. Perhaps he had seen a direct statement of it in a text of Archytas. There is nothing in the context, however, to indicate that Ptolemy is relying on a text of Archytas at this point. This leaves open the possibility that Ptolemy ascribes the principle to Archytas on the basis of something like the following grounds: (1) since Archytas is "the Pythagorean most engaged in the study of music," he must have followed the principle of superparticular and multiple ratios in regard to concords that is central to Pythagorean harmonics in the later tradition. (2) Since seven of the nine ratios in his account of the tetrachords are in fact superparticular, he must have been aiming to apply the principle to melodic intervals as well. The combination of these two grounds may have had such force for Ptolemy that he, as a matter of course, assumed that Archytas adopted the principle.

Burkert has pointed to Archytas A19 as support for Ptolemy's ascription of the principle to Archytas (1972a: 385). In that testimonium Archytas gives a proof that there is no geometric mean between numbers in superparticular ratio. Burkert is certainly right that the proof shows that the superparticular ratio "played an essential part in his music theory," since the ratio is only important there. Superparticular ratios, however, will have played an important role in any theory that treated intervals as ratios, since the fifth and fourth are both superparticular. What precise role superparticular ratios played in the theory is not shown by Archytas' proof. Indeed, since the fourth and fifth are superparticular ratios, the proof that they cannot be divided in half by a geometric mean and thus must be divided by the arithmetic and harmonic mean instead would quite naturally be motivated by reflection on Philolaus' harmonic scheme where these facts, if not their proof, are obvious. This proof in no way entails that every melodic interval must be superparticular and, as we have seen, Philolaus' diatonic scale would certainly not suggest this principle. So Archytas' proof in A19 provides no support for the idea that he adopted the principle that all melodic intervals must be superparticular or multiple.

There are two major problems with accepting that Archytas built his harmonics on this principle. First, as Ptolemy points out, he fails miserably in following it. It is not just that two of the ratios in Archytas' chromatic tetrachord are not superparticular or multiple (32:27 and 243:224), but, more importantly, that it is not at all hard to come up with a chromatic tetrachord that does not break the principle (Barker 1989: 49). Ptolemy, Eratosthenes and Didymus all present divisions of the chromatic tetrachord that consist only of superparticular ratios (Ptolemy, *Harmonics*, II. 14). Burkert, who believes that Archytas was striving for superparticular ratios, suggests that he may have come up with the ratios by a trial and error manipulation of numbers that was completely divorced from musical practice (1972a: 389 n. 17). This position is hardly tenable, in light of Winnington-Ingram's demonstration that Archytas is tied closely to actual musical practice. Burkert's ingenious reconstruction of Archytas' procedure in fact provides a *reductio ad absurdum* of the thesis that Archytas was striving for superparticular ratios. Burkert supposes that Archytas started from the embarrassing diatonic of Philolaus with its 256:243 leimma and, instead of keeping the top two intervals in the tetrachord both at 9:8, tried changing one slightly to 8:7 and found, to his delight, that the last interval then turns out to be superparticular as well (28:27). So much for the unbearable leimma! Again in the enharmonic he fiddled with the unsatisfactory top interval of a ditone (81:64), which was favored by Aristoxenus, and changed it slightly to 80:64 = 5:4. If he borrowed the 28:27 ratio for the lowest interval from the diatonic, this would leave the perfectly satisfactory 36:35 for the middle interval. Burkert then says that, if he turned to the chromatic scale and knew of a ratio of 32:27 for the top interval (from practice?), it was now "not so easy" to change this to the superparticular ratios 35:30 = 7:6 or 30:25 = 6:5. But why is this not so easy? If he takes the closest of these to the interval of 32:27 with which he started, i.e. the ratio 30:25 = 6:5, and again takes the lowest interval as 28:27, the middle interval is magically again a superparticular (15:14), and he has achieved his goal. What is produced is Ptolemy's "soft chromatic." It is surely incredible to think that Archytas would not hesitate to change 81:64 to 80:64 in the enharmonic genus, but would suddenly flinch at changing 32:27 to 30:25 in the chromatic and instead keep a set of ratios that are directly in conflict with his supposed central principle that all ratios must be superparticular. If Archytas were in the business of trial and error manipulation of ratios in order to fit preconceived principles, he would have had no problem coming up with a chromatic tetrachord that fit his principles. The fact that his chromatic genus does not fit such principles is very strong evidence that he was not manipulating ratios in abstraction from actual music and that he was not attempting to follow the principle that all melodic intervals must be superparticular or multiple.

There is yet another strong piece of evidence that Archytas was not employing the principle that all ratios corresponding to melodic intervals must be superparticular or multiple. Barker tries to save this principle for Archytas by cleverly pointing out that, while two of the ratios in the chromatic genus are not superparticular, Archytas could have derived all of his ratios, including these, by movements up and down the scale through intervals whose ratios are solely superparticular (1989: 47). There is once again evidence, however, that Archytas cannot have been applying even this principle, i.e. that coherent scalar systems are those in which the notes are *constructed* by the application of superparticular ratios. The one place in which Ptolemy explicitly indicates that he is following Archytas closely, A16, lines 24–26 ("he says"), shows Archytas calculating the top interval in the chromatic scale not by the application of superparticular ratios but by determining the chromatic *lichanos* as lower than the diatonic *lichanos* by the decidedly non-superparticular ratio of the leimma (256:243). The evidence is thus strong that Archytas was not employing the principle that the ratios for all melodic intervals must be superparticular or multiple, even in the weakened sense that Barker proposes.

How then should we understand what Archytas is doing, if he is not governed by this principle? It is clear that he is studying the musical practice of his day, but is he applying any coherent set of principles in order to explain that practice? In trying to answer this question it is important to recognize that the mathematical relationships between the ratios of Archytas' three genera cannot in themselves reveal Archytas' approach. Archytas could have come to these ratios in a number of different ways (Vogel's detailed consideration of Archytas' ratios [1963, see esp. pp. 47–57] is undercut by a failure to realize this). In order to determine the procedure Archytas actually followed we must not just look at the numbers in the abstract but also look closely at three other types of evidence: (1) what Ptolemy tells us about the numbers, (2) the other testimonia and fragments concerning Archytas' music theory, (3) the music theory of his predecessor, Philolaus.

A reasonable first step would be to assume that he started with what Philolaus knew. His familiarity with the musical structure that Philolaus presents in Fragment 6a, the so-called Pythagorean diatonic, is assured by his reference to its characteristic interval of the leimma (256:243) as attested by Ptolemy in lines 24–26 of A16. Philolaus already makes clear that the octave is not divided in half but is made up of the unequal intervals of the fourth and the fifth. In addition Fragment 6a of Philolaus follows the tuning procedure known as the "method of concordance" (Barker 1989: 49–50) to construct a whole tone as the difference between the fourth and the fifth and as having the ratio 9:8. If we go up a fourth from *hypatē* to *mesē* and then up a fifth, we will reach the octave at *nētē*. But if we reverse the procedure and come down a fourth from *nētē*, the difference between this note, known as *paramesē* (although Philolaus calls its *tritē* following earlier musical practice), and *mesē* is the difference between the fourth and the fifth, since the interval between *mesē* and *nētē* was a fifth. By subtraction of the ratio corresponding to the fourth (4:3) from the ratio corresponding to the fifth (3:2) this interval, the whole tone, is seen to be 9:8. This same procedure of "subtracting a fourth from a fifth" can be used to divide up the octave and the fifth and the fourth by intervals of a tone. As Philolaus recognizes, the tone does not go equally into any of these intervals: the fourth is two whole tones plus a left-over (leimma = 256:243), the fifth is three tones and a leimma, and the whole octave is thus five tones and two leimmata. As Barker points out, the Pythagorean diatonic scale that results from this practice, in which the tetrachord has the structure, in descending order, of 9:8, 9:8, 256:243, may well not have been used in actual music but is rather "a mathematical representation of the basic tuning procedure" (1989: 51). Philolaus in Fragment 6a and Plato in the *Timaeus* seem to have regarded this mathematical system as fundamental in the ordering of the cosmos and show no desire to go on to examine the use to which it was put by practicing musicians in devising the scales used in actual music. Archytas, however, is interested in studying the mathematics of music in itself and thus goes on to examine the diatonic scale that is found in actual practice and the enharmonic and chromatic genera as well.

It is plausible that Archytas started this more detailed pursuit of the mathematics of music by examining the division of the octave in Philolaus. That in fact he did so is indicated by the definitions of the three means (arithmetic, geometric, harmonic) which we find in Fragment 2 of Archytas. Philolaus' procedure showed that the octave cannot be divided in half. The unequal division of the octave into the fourth and the fifth turns out to be equivalent to inserting the arithmetic and harmonic mean into the ratio that corresponds to the octave (if we take the ratio of the octave to be 12:6 [= 2:1], 9 is the arithmetic mean and 8 is the harmonic mean, and 12:9 = 4:3 [the fourth] and 12:8 = 3:2 [the fifth]). Archytas is thus able to describe the basic division of the octave in terms of these two means. He does not, however, rest content with the brute fact that the octave cannot be divided in half, or the fact that the same is true of the fifth and fourth, but instead develops the proof found in A19 to show that no superparticular ratio can be divided in half (i.e. divided by a geometric mean). It is this emphasis on precise definition and on rigorous proof that reveals Archytas as a mathematician.

Now Archytas is in a position to go beyond Philolaus in the analysis of music, just as he has in mathematical rigor. Another important insight of modern scholarship, first developed by Tannery (1912: III. 105) and followed by most subsequent scholars (van der Waerden 1943: 185; Vogel 1963: 50; Barker 1989: 48–49), is that Archytas turned to the most important intervals after the octave, the fourth and the fifth, and divided them by inserting the harmonic and arithmetic mean, just as was done in the case of the octave. In the case of the fourth, the arithmetic mean between 4 and 3 will turn out to be 7/6 (if we take 4/3 = 24/18, clearly 21/18 = 7/6 is the arithmetic mean, differing by 3/18 from each extreme). The harmonic mean will be 8/7 (if we take 28/21 = 4/3, then 24/21 = 8/7 will be the harmonic mean in that it differs from 28/21 by 4/21 which is 1/7 of 28/21 and it differs from 21/21 by 3/21 which is 1/7 of 21/21). In the case of the fifth, the arithmetic mean between 3 and 2 will be 5/4 and the harmonic mean will be 6/5. Thus by taking the harmonic and arithmetic means of the octave, fourth and fifth along with the octave itself and the whole tone we produce the orderly sequence of numbers 1/2, 2/3, 3/4, 4/5, 5/6, 6/7, 7/8, 8/9. This might seem to be purely an exercise in arithmetic. What connection is there to practical music?

Now Barker has pointed out that Archytas and others could not have measured intervals precisely enough in practical terms to make fine distinctions such as that between the interval 81:64, which Aristoxenus favored for the top interval in the enharmonic tetrachord, and 80:64 = 5:4, which Aristoxenus attests that most musicians used and which Archytas accepts in his division. How then could they have known which heard interval corresponded to which ratio? Barker's brilliant suggestion is that they did so by watching the practice of tuning according to the "method of concordance" (1989: 50). Archytas may well have seen musicians use this method to tune down two tones from *mesē* in the enharmonic tetrachord, but then noticed that they were not satisfied with this tone and tightened the string just slightly to produce the more pleasing tone of a major third. So this tone must have a slightly smaller ratio than that of the ditone, which can be precisely calculated at 81:64 (9:8 × 9:8) from the method of concordance. If Archytas had observed this, he will have been struck with a remarkable parallel to his work on means. The arithmetic mean in the fifth $80/64 = 5/4$ is just slightly smaller than the ditone. Thus, actual musical practice seems, in the case of the further divisions of the fifth and fourth, as in the case of the original division of the octave, to correspond to the mathematical process of finding harmonic and arithmetic means.

This correspondence between mathematics and practical music in determining the upper interval of the enharmonic tetrachord is strikingly confirmed by the tuning process used to find the interval of the minor third between *mesē* and *tritē* which, as was shown above, played an important part in the music of Archytas' time. As Barker again shows, if Archytas saw a musician tune down a ditone from *nētē* to *tritē* by the method of concordance and then, in this case, loosen the string a little more in order to attain the interval of the minor third with *mesē*, this will suggest that *tritē* is a little more than two tones ($9{:}8 \times 9{:}8$) down from *nētē*, and a natural suggestion would be that it was therefore $9{:}8 \times 8{:}7$. Once again remarkable things follow from this suggestion. The remaining interval in the fifth from *nētē* to *mesē* can be calculated to be $7{:}6$ ($3{:}2/[9{:}8 \times 8{:}7]$). Thus, the minor third which was so important in the music of Archytas' time turns out to correspond to the ratio $7{:}6$ (one of the ratios that Archytas reached by taking arithmetic and harmonic means within the fourth and fifth). The ratio of $28{:}27$, which is the lowest interval in all three genera can then be calculated as a by-product of the tuning that was used to get the minor third. Since the interval between *mesē* and *paramesē* is fixed at a tone ($9{:}8$), and the whole interval between *mesē* and *tritē* is now known to be $7{:}6$, the interval between *tritē* and *paramesē* can be calculated to be $28{:}27$ (subtraction of ratios is equivalent to division of fractions, $7{:}6/9{:}8 = 56{:}54 = 28{:}27$).

Since we now have two of the ratios in the enharmonic tetrachord, the highest interval of $5{:}4$ and the lowest of $28{:}27$, the final ratio can be calculated giving $36{:}35$. In the case of the diatonic it seems very likely that Archytas would have accepted the whole tone as the top interval as suggested by Philolaus' scale and indeed by musical practice, so that taking its top interval to be $9{:}8$ and its bottom as $28{:}27$, the final interval can be calculated as $8{:}7$. But now we must confront the most puzzling aspect of Archytas' ratios, his division of the chromatic tetrachord. The lowest interval is $28{:}27$ as in all the other genera, but what are we to make of the strange ratios of $243{:}224$ and $32{:}27$ for the two upper intervals? They are clearly not intervals derived from the division of the fourth, fifth, or octave by harmonic and arithmetic means. The crucial thing is to recognize that these ratios are similar in an important way to the ratio $28{:}27$ for the lowest interval in all three genera. That ratio, as we have just seen is not important in itself and is clearly the result of calculation and not any actual measurement. In a similar way the ratios 243:224 and 32:27 are not important in themselves but reached as the by-product of another procedure.

What is this procedure? It is striking but not often noticed that it is exactly here that Ptolemy reports what Archytas "said" in answer (A16, 24–26). The procedure is to take the chromatic *lichanos* at a ratio of 256:243 greater than the diatonic *lichanos*. But this may just seem to remove the mystery a step further. What is the method in this madness? If we accept Barker's thesis, as we have so far, that Archytas' numbers make sense in light of a tuning using the method of concordance which corresponds to the scale of Philolaus, then we should not be too puzzled. For, as we have seen, the ratio 256:243 makes sense precisely in that tuning as the interval left after two whole tones have been cut off from a fourth. We have to remember that Archytas is trying to account for actual tunings of his day and that the ratios for his chromatic tetrachord do correspond to a tetrachord that is attested by Aristoxenus. Just as in the case of the enharmonic *lichanos* of 5:4 and the common *tritē* in all genera of 28:27 Archytas' initial motivation for pursuing this division of the chromatic tetrachord is that he sees it in practice. The question for Archytas is how this tuning fits with the ratios he has determined by the use of the harmonic and arithmetic mean and by observing the use of the method of concordance. In Archytas' chromatic tetrachord, the interval from *hypatē* to *lichanos* is a tone ($28:27 \times 243:224 = 9:8$). Thus he may have seen musicians use the method of concordance to achieve the interval of a tone from *hypatē* to *lichanos* in the chromatic tuning. Since he has already fixed the lowest interval in the tetrachord as 28:27, the chromatic tetrachord is now determined as 28:27 and then 243:224 (the amount necessary to make up the rest of the tone to *lichanos*) and then 32:27 (the amount necessary to complete the fourth to *nētē*). But how are we to fit this into a coherent pattern with the other two genera and how does this correspond to Archytas' explanation of the chromatic tetrachord as given by Ptolemy?

The central feature of the method of concordance as represented in Philolaus' scale, the Pythagorean diatonic, is that the primary intervals of the octave, fourth and fifth are measured by the whole tone 9:8 and, since the whole tone does not go evenly into these intervals, a remainder of 256:243. By this method of measurement, the fourth is two whole tones and one remainder. When Archytas looked at the three genera of musical practice, what will have struck him is that, since they all have the same lowest interval, the difference between the genera can be viewed as determined by the size of the top interval in the tetrachord (*nētē* to *paranētē* or *mesē* to *lichanos*). In the case of the enharmonic the top interval is very close to two whole tones which would leave the leimma for the rest of the interval. In the case of the diatonic the top interval is a tone which leaves, by Philolaus' method of measurement, one tone and the leimma for the rest of the interval. When Archytas says that the top interval of the chromatic is a leimma larger than the corresponding interval in the diatonic, what he is saying is that, in terms of the units of measure in Philolaus' scale and thus the method of concordance, the chromatic is midway between the diatonic and enharmonic. The top interval in the diatonic is one tone, the top interval in the enharmonic is close to two tones, so we can intelligibly regard the top interval in the chromatic as a tone plus the only smaller measure available, the leimma.

	Enharmonic	Chromatic	Diatonic
Mesē to *Lichanos*	2 tones (approx) (80:64)	1 tone + leimma	1 tone
Lichanos to *hypatē* (the *puknon*)	leimma (approx)	1 tone	1 tone + leimma

It is true that the top interval in the chromatic is not a mean between the diatonic and chromatic in any strict mathematical sense. Archytas can, nonetheless, see it as having an intelligible relationship to the intervals in the other genera when viewed in terms of the units of Philolaus' scale. It is not just any old interval but an interval that can be expressed precisely in terms of the whole tone and the leimma.

Thus, Burkert (1972a: 384–85) was right to point out that Archytas' ratios cannot have been determined by precise measurement, as Frank had suggested (1923: 266), but had to be the result of calculation. He was wrong, however, to conclude that these calculations were divorced from musical practice and based solely on abstract principles such as the desire for superparticular ratios. The calculations that lead to the ratios are motivated by the study of musical practice. But it is not just the brute fact of the ratios in the three genera that Archytas gets from practice. As Barker has shown, he must have observed the method of tuning through concordance and it was relationships derived from that practice, not abstract number games, which led to the calculation of the odd ratios such as 28:27, 32:27 and 243:224. Barker does not go all the way, however, to recognize that the later principle that all ratios in the division of the tetrachord must be superparticular or multiple has no role to play in Archytas. By the time of Ptolemy, all attention has become focused on the nature of the ratios themselves that make up the tetrachords. Thus to Ptolemy, Archytas' system looks like a puzzling failure; he almost gets them to be all superparticular but then falls short in the chromatic where appropriate superparticular ratios were easily at hand. Archytas simply does not fit into the dichotomy between Pythagoreans and Aristoxenians, in terms of which Ptolemy is trying to describe the history of harmonics.

He is a good Pythagorean in understanding musical intervals as corresponding to ratios of whole numbers, but his overall position in regard to the dichotomy between reason and the senses, which Ptolemy sets up, is less clear. He does not follow the next step of Ptolemy's later Pythagoreans in dictating that all intervals must correspond to superparticular or multiple ratios. Nonetheless it is reasonable to conclude, on the basis of Barker's arguments, that he did posit two further principles to govern the choice of "well-formed" tetrachords: (1) All intervals should be derivable either directly from the "method of concordance," of which Philolaus' system is a representation, or by intelligible deviations from it (Barker 1989: 50); (2) intelligible deviations are those deviations that rely on the division of the fifth and fourth by the harmonic and arithmetic means. All of his divisions of the tetrachords can be explained in terms of these principles. To this extent he does pursue the criterion of reason. It is important to note, however, that his three genera do not fall neatly out of the application of these two principles and are not dictated by them. We might see the ratios 7:6 and 5:4 as dictated by the application of the theory of means to the fourth and fifth, but, after the application of 7:6 has given the common *tritē* in all three genera, how are we to explain the fact that it is only in the enharmonic that the *lichanos* is 5:4? Why should this not apply in all cases as well, so that there will in effect be just one genus? The answer seems to be that there simply is more variety in actual music than that. There are three genera because the phenomena tell us there are. Here Archytas seems to be on the other side of the dichotomy and to be following the senses.

A final ray of light may be cast on Archytas by returning to Plato's criticism of Pythagorean harmonic theorists in the *Republic*. Socrates complains that "they seek the numbers in these heard harmonies and do not ascend to problems to consider which numbers are concordant and which not and why in each case" (531c). Barker argues that Plato's criticism does apply to Archytas, insofar as Archytas is directing his attention to the "heard harmonies" of actual practice. According to Barker, however, Archytas is not a reasonable target of Plato's complaint that the Pythagoreans do not ascend to problems and determine "which numbers are concordant and which are not," because Archytas' theory of means is an attempt to do just that (1989: 52). Barker is right to see that Archytas is trying to make musical practice intelligible and that he gives criteria in terms of which to determine which scalar divisions are well formed and which not. I do not think, however, that this is what Plato is asking for in the *Republic*, and in terms of what Plato is asking for, Archytas is a legitimate object of Plato's criticism in this latter case as well.

In this passage of the *Republic* harmonics is only valuable insofar as it turns our attention to purely abstract relations between numbers and thus turns us away from the physical world. Socrates is looking for studies that "draw the soul from the world of becoming to the world of being" (521d) and as a result is rejecting sciences as currently practiced. He is telling the harmonic theorist to "let be" the heard harmonies just as he has told the astronomer "to let be the things in the heavens" (530c). Once the phenomena have suggested the basic concordant ratios and their relation to one another and directed our attention to these relations, there is no immediate reason for the Platonic theorist to be interested in the variations on these basic principles that practicing musicians employ. Such knowledge might possibly be useful to the philosopher king on his return to the cave, but it is the ascent from the cave and not the return to it that is at issue in the passage of Book VII where Plato's criticism of Pythagorean harmonic theory appears. Plato wants the young philosophers to consider number sequences in themselves and determine principles of concordance in a way that is completely divorced from the senses. It is thus significant that in the *Timaeus*, when Plato presents the sequence of numbers in accordance with which the world soul is constructed, although we know that the sequence was in fact suggested by the "method of concordance" in practical music, nothing in Plato's presentation suggests its origin in heard harmonies. It is presented as an intelligible mathematical sequence in itself. The numbers found in Archytas' divisions of the tetrachord are not intelligible in themselves and require an appeal to heard harmonies.

Archytas, however, knows nothing of Plato's two worlds and the radical distinction between the intelligible and the visible. Archytas and his predecessor Philolaus, "discuss and busy themselves only with the natural world" (Aristotle, *Metaphysics* 989b34). Archytas is interested in the numbers by which phenomenal things are known (Philolaus, Fr. 4) and of which they give signs (Philolaus, Fr. 5). Archytas surpasses Philolaus in being able to describe a wider variety of musical practice in a way that is consistent with the application of the theory of the three means and the scalar theory of Philolaus. To the extent that musical practice can be described in this way, it is shown not to be completely arbitrary and to "have number" and hence be knowable. The numbers involved in the divisions of the tetrachord in each of the three genera are precisely numbers "in heard concords," however, and, from Plato's point of view, time spent on them represents a disastrous tarrying in the phenomenal realm.

Detailed commentary

Lines 8 ff. What is Ptolemy's source for the following information on Archytas likely to have been? At one extreme, Ptolemy might have had a copy of Archytas' treatise on harmonics in front of him and based his remarks on what he read there. This does not seem very plausible because, if he had such a treatise, it would seem very likely that Ptolemy would refer to such an important document at other points. Yet this is the only place in the *Harmonics* where Archytas is mentioned by name. Indeed, Barker (1994: 128) has suggested that the primary source of information on Archytas for both Porphyry and Ptolemy is Didymus. The question remains: what did Ptolemy find in Didymus? We might suppose that he found only a table of Archytas' ratios for the divisions of the tetrachord and that everything else in his report is his own commentary on those ratios. The use of φησί ("he says") in line 24 shows, however, that, on at least one point, Ptolemy thought he had Archytas' own account of his procedure. This then suggests that what Ptolemy found in Didymus was a section from Archytas' book, which included at least some narrative describing how the ratios were derived. Regrettably, this does not get us very far, since Didymus might have referred to just one line from Archytas, in order to explain the puzzling ratios in his chromatic tetrachord. So the most we can say with confidence is that the sentence beginning with "he said" in lines 24–26 is based on a text of Archytas. The rest of Ptolemy's comments in A16 seem to be his own analysis. Lines 8–16 (up to the sentence beginning with τρία) are clearly marked as Ptolemy's own introductory remarks by the concluding clause which refers to Archytas' divisions as what "we will shortly see." The summary of Archytas' divisions then extends from line 16 to line 26, with the last sentence clearly marked as directly based on something Archytas said. It seems most likely that lines 26–38 are then Ptolemy's recasting (cf. ἐάν . . . ὑποστησώμεθα "if we posit" in lines 27–28) of Archytas' ratios in terms of the least numbers in which they can all be expressed. Chapter 14 is clearly all analysis by Ptolemy.

9–12 The statement that Archytas "does attempt to preserve what follows in accord with reason" is clearly a judgment made by Ptolemy or his source rather than reflecting anything Archytas said, since the remark is framed in terms of the contrast between reason and perception as the criterion, which is the basis of Ptolemy's analysis of the development of harmonics. The point that Archytas followed reason not just in the case of the concords but also in terms of the division of the tetrachord might be seen as an historical comment, i.e. that Archytas was the first Pythagorean to give a mathematical analysis of the tetrachord (Barker 1989: 43 n. 62). It is certainly true that Archytas' predecessor, Philolaus, focuses on the octave, fourth and fifth and, while he does use the whole tone as a measure of each of these intervals, he does not explicitly address the question of the division of the tetrachord. Nonetheless, it seems more likely that the primary function of Ptolemy's comment is to structure his own work. He has earlier talked about the Pythagorean theory of the concords and now is making the transition to their theory of the division of the tetrachord.

11–12 Ptolemy's statement of the principle (πρόθεσις lines 12 and 40) that Archytas followed in his divisions of the tetrachord is crucial. The principle that "having an excess that is a common measure is proper to the nature of what is melodic" means that, in the ratios that govern the melodic intervals, the larger number should exceed the smaller by an amount that is a common measure of both numbers (e.g. in the ratio 9:6, 9 exceeds 6 by 3 which is a common measure of 9 and 6, i.e. it divides both 9 and 6 without remainder). This is another way of saying that melodic intervals should be superparticular ratios, since a ratio is superparticular "when the greater term contains the less once and some one part of the less, i.e. when the difference between the greater and the less is such as to be a factor of the less" (Theon 76.21), although one multiple ratio also fits the principle, 2:1. See further the commentary on A19.

On what basis does Ptolemy assign this principle to Archytas? Did Ptolemy, or his source, find an explicit statement of the principle in Archytas? In Chapters 5 and 6 of Book 1, Ptolemy discusses and criticizes in detail the principle that concords must correspond to superparticular ratios, assigning it to "the leaders of the school" (11.7 Düring, οἱ τῆς αἱρέσεως προστάντες). Since he calls Archytas the Pythagorean most engaged in the study of music, it seems likely that he is including him among these "leaders." Barker has indeed argued that a large part of Chapter 5 is drawn from Archytas (1994). I have shown above, however that there are good reasons for thinking that Archytas did not apply the principle to melodic intervals as Ptolemy suggests here. It is thus important to recognize that Ptolemy does not mark his statement of the principle as a quote from Archytas. The remark is in fact part of a sentence that is clearly formulated in terms of the problematic of the tradition later than Archytas and serves as part of Ptolemy's introduction to the material actually derived from Archytas.

12–16 Ptolemy here outlines his criticisms of Archytas' scalar divisions. He gives a more detailed explanation in Chapter 14. He criticizes Archytas for two basic failings: (1) he is not able to stick to the principle that ratios of melodic intervals should be superparticular ratios (two ratios in the chromatic genus are not superparticular); (2) although he does stick to the principle in the case of the other seven ratios, in several cases he does not produce ratios that agree with the accepted phenomena. I have commented further on the first criticism in my account of Archytas' scalar divisions above, but it is worth noting that the ratios themselves might have suggested to Ptolemy that Archytas was striving for superparticular ratios. Seven of nine are superparticular. This makes the two non-superparticular ratios in the chromatic genera stand out unpleasingly. Ptolemy or someone else in the tradition might have concluded, wrongly in my view but as Burkert does, that it could not be "a coincidence that in Archytas' table seven of nine proportions are superparticular" (1972a: 385). With regard to the second general criticism, that Archytas' ratios do not agree with accepted sense phenomena, Winnington-Ingram has shown that Ptolemy's comments may largely miss the point, because he does not take into consideration what was customary in the music of Archytas' day. "If we are to believe the evidence, he [Archytas] was making a genuine attempt to interpret the actual facts of music, and the criticisms of Ptolemy arise in part from Ptolemy's ignorance. Archytas is in a fair way towards being justified in every department" (1932: 207).

26–38 As I suggested above, these lines seem to be Ptolemy's own recasting of Archytas' ratios in terms of the least numbers in which they can all be expressed. Porphyry's commentary on the passage (Düring 139.27) shows how these least numbers were derived.

39–62 I have discussed Ptolemy's criticisms of Archytas in my account of Archytas' scalar divisions above. In lines 53–54, Archytas is grouped with "pretty nearly all the others" (i.e. Pythagoreans) as having provided an opening for an attack on reason as a criterion, because their ratios do not produce what is melodic when tested on the canon and do not accord with accepted scales. This statement exactly accords with the criticism of the Pythagoreans given already in Chapter 2. It is important to note that

Ptolemy's grouping of Archytas with "pretty nearly all the others" suggests that he knew of other divisions of the tetrachord by Pythagoreans, although he does not give them here. It may be that he is referring to Didymus and Eratosthenes, who, although not Pythagoreans in other senses, did practice ratio-based harmonics (I owe this suggestion to Andrew Barker). In lines 55–57 Ptolemy adds a final criticism that Archytas had too few genera, in that, while he correctly had only one enharmonic genus, he also had only one chromatic and one diatonic, whereas Ptolemy believed that there were two varieties of the chromatic and five of the diatonic.

A17 Porphyry, *On Ptolemy's Harmonics* I. 6 (Düring 1932: 107.15–108.21)

καὶ ἔτι τὸ τὴν ἐκλογὴν ἕως τοῦ τὰ ἀνόμοια [Ptolemy, *Harmonics* I. 6, Düring 1930: 14.1–14.10]

τῶν Πυθαγορικῶν τινες, ὡς Ἀρχύτας καὶ Δίδυμος ἱστοροῦσι, μετὰ τὸ   1
καταστήσασθαι τοὺς λόγους τῶν συμφωνιῶν συγκρίνοντες αὐτοὺς   2
πρὸς ἀλλήλους καὶ τοὺς συμφώνους μᾶλλον ἐπιδεικνύναι βουλόμενοι   3
τοιοῦτόν τι ἐποίουν. πρώτους λαβόντες ἀριθμούς, οὓς ἐκάλουν πυθμέ-   4
νας, τῶν τοὺς λόγους τῶν συμφωνιῶν ἀποτελούντων – τουτέστιν ἐν   5
οἷς ἐλαχίστοις ἀριθμοῖς αἱ συμφωνίαι ἀποτελοῦνται, ὡς λόγου χάριν   6
ἡ μὲν διὰ πασῶν ἐν πρώτοις θεωρεῖται ἀριθμοῖς τοῖς β΄ καὶ ά· πρῶτος   7
γὰρ διπλάσιος ὁ δύο τοῦ ἑνὸς καὶ πυθμὴν τῶν ἄλλων διπλασίων· ἡ   8
δὲ διὰ τεσσάρων ἐν ἐπιτρίτοις τοῖς τέσσαρσι καὶ τρισί· πρῶτος γὰρ   9
ἐπίτριτος καὶ πυθμὴν ὁ δ΄ τῶν γ΄. ὁ δὲ διὰ πέντε ἐν τρισὶ καὶ δύο· πρῶτος   10
γὰρ ἡμιόλιος καὶ πυθμὴν ὁ γ΄ τοῦ β΄ – τούτους οὖν τοὺς ἀριθμοὺς   11
ἀποδόντες ταῖς συμφωνίαις, ἐσκόπουν καθ᾽ ἕκαστον λόγον τῶν τοὺς   12
ὅρους περιεχόντων ἀριθμῶν, ἀφελόντες ἀφ᾽ ἑκατέρων τῶν ὅρων ἀνὰ   13
μονάδα, τοὺς ἀπολειπομένους ἀριθμοὺς μετὰ τὴν ἀφαίρεσιν, οἵτινες   14
εἶεν· οἷον τῶν β΄ <καὶ> ά, οἵπερ ἦσαν τῆς διὰ πασῶν, ἀφελόντες ἀνὰ   15
μονάδα, ἐσκόπουν τὸ καταλειπόμενον· ἦν δ᾽ ἕν· τῶν δὲ δ΄ καὶ γ΄, οἵτινες   16
ἦσαν τῆς διὰ τεσσάρων, ἀφελόντες ἀνὰ μονάδα εἶχον ἐκ μὲν οὖν τῶν   17
τεσσάρων ὑπολειπόμενον τὸν τρία, ἐκ δὲ τῶν τριῶν τὸν δύο· ὥστ᾽ ἀπὸ   18
συναμφοτέρων τῶν ὅρων μετὰ τὴν ἀφαίρεσιν τὸ ὑπολειπόμενον ἦν   19
πέντε. τῶν δὲ γ΄ καὶ β΄, οἵτινες ἦσαν τῆς διὰ πέντε, ἀφελόντες ἀνὰ μονάδα   20

---

5 τῶν συμφωνιῶν] G   συμφωνιῶν V¹⁸⁷   **6** αἱ] om. Düring   **8** πυθμήν] scripsi πυθμένος codd.   **10** ὁ δ΄ τῶν γ] G   ὁ δ΄ πρὸς τὸν γ ΄ V¹⁸⁷   **10–11** ὁ δὲ ... β] om. G, Düring   **12** ἀποδίδοντες V¹⁸⁷   **15** <καὶ>] Diels   **16** τὸ] G   τὸν V¹⁸⁷   ἕν] G   ἀεί V¹⁸⁷   τῆς] V¹⁸⁷   τῶν G   **17** τεσσάρων] G   πασῶν V¹⁸⁷   **20** τῆς] Düring   τῶν GV¹⁸⁷

εἶχον ἐκ μὲν τῶν τριῶν ὑπολειπόμενα δύο, ἐκ δὲ τῶν δύο ὑπολειπόμενον 21
ἕν, ὥστε τὸ συναμφότερον λειπόμενον εἶναι τρία. ἐκάλουν δὲ τὰς μὲν 22
ἀφαιρουμένας μονάδας ὅμοια, τὰ δὲ λειπόμενα μετὰ τὴν ἀφαίρεσιν ἀνό- 23
μοια· διὰ δύο αἰτίας, ὅτι ἐξ ἀμφοῖν τῶν ὅρων ὁμοία ἡ ἀφαίρεσις ἐγίνετο 24
καὶ ἴση· ἴση γὰρ ἡ μονὰς τῇ μονάδι· ὧν ἀφαιρουμένων ἐξ ἀνάγκης τὰ 25
ὑπολειπόμενα ἀνόμοια καὶ ἄνισα. ἐὰν γὰρ ἀπ' ἀνίσων ἴσα ἀφαιρεθῇ, 26
τὰ λοιπὰ ἔσται ἄνισα. οἱ δὲ πολλαπλάσιοι λόγοι καὶ ἐπιμόριοι, ἐν οἷς 27
θεωροῦνται αἱ συμφωνίαι, ἐν ἀνίσοις ὅροις ὑφεστήκασιν, ἀφ' ὧν ἴσων 28
ἀφαιρουμένων τὰ λοιπὰ πάντα ἄνισα. γίνεται οὖν τὰ ἀνόμοια τῶν 29
συμφωνιῶν συμμιγέντα· συμμίσγειν δὲ λέγουσιν οἱ Πυθαγόρειοι τὸ 30
ἕνα ἐξ ἀμφοτέρων ἀριθμὸν λαβεῖν. ἔσται οὖν τὰ ἀνόμοια συντεθέντα 31
καθ' ἑκάστην τῶν συμφωνιῶν τοιαῦτα· τῆς μὲν διὰ πασῶν ἕν, τῆς δὲ 32
διὰ τεσσάρων πέντε, τῆς δὲ διὰ πέντε τρία. ἐφ' ὧν δ' ἂν φασι τὰ ἀνό- 33
μοια ἐλάσσονα ᾖ, ἐκεῖνα τῶν ἄλλων εἰσὶ συμφωνότερα. σύμφωνον μέν 34
ἐστιν ἡ διὰ πασῶν, ὅτι ταύτης τὰ ἀνόμοια ἕν· μεθ' ἣν ἡ διὰ πέντε, ὅτι 35
ταύτης τὰ ἀνόμοια τρία· τελευταία δ' ἡ διὰ τεσσάρων, ὅτι ταύτης τὰ 36
ἀνόμοια πέντε. 37

22 ὥστε συναμφότερον <τὸ ὑπο>λειπόμενον ἦν Diels **28** ἀνίσοις] ἴσοις G **29**
πάντα] GV¹⁸⁷ πάντως Düring **30** συμμίσγειν] G συμμίγειν V¹⁸⁷ **31** ἀριθμόν]
GV¹⁸⁷ ἀριθμῶν p **34–35** ἐλάσσονα . . . ἀνόμοια] om. V¹⁸⁷ **34** εἰσί] ἐστί G (cf.
Düring)

"And still the selection," up to "the dissimilars" [Ptolemy, *Harmonics* 1. 6,
Düring 1930: 14.1–14.10]

   Some of the Pythagoreans, as Archytas and Didymus record, after establishing the ratios of the concords, compared them against one another, and,
wishing to show the ones that are more concordant, used to do something
such as the following. Having taken the first numbers (which they called
pythmenes ["bases"]), of those which produce the ratios of the concords (i.e.
the least numbers in which the concords are produced, as, for the sake of
example, the octave is seen first in the numbers 2 and 1. For two of one is the
first double and base of the other doubles. The fourth [is first seen] in four
and three; for four of three is the first epitritic and a base. The fifth [is first
seen] in three and two; for three of two is the first hemiolic and a base) –
having assigned these numbers to the concords, they were examining in
the case of each ratio of the numbers comprising the terms, having taken
one away from each term, what the remaining numbers were after the subtraction. For example, of 2 and 1, which were the numbers of the octave,
having taken away one from each, they examined what was left, and it was
one. Of 4 and 3, which were (the numbers) of the fourth, having taken

away one from each, they then had three left over from four, and two left over from three. So that from both terms added together what was left over after the subtraction was five. Of 3 and 2, which (were the numbers) of the fifth, having taken one away from each, they had two left over from three, and one left over from two, so that what was left over added together was three. They used to call the units which were subtracted "similars" and that which was left after the subtraction "dissimilars," for two reasons, because the subtraction from both the terms was similar and equal; for unit is equal to unit. If these things are subtracted, it is necessary that what remains be dissimilar and unequal. For if equals are subtracted from unequals, the remainders will be unequal. But multiple ratios and epimoric ratios, among which the concords are observed, are constituted by unequal terms, and if equals are taken away from these, the remainders will all be unequal. The "dissimilars" of the concords then arise when mingled. By "mingling" the Pythagoreans mean to derive one number from both the others. Therefore the "dissimilars" will be composed with regard to each of the concords as follows: of the octave, one; of the fourth, five, of the fifth, three. They say that, in whichever intervals the "dissimilars" are less, those intervals are more concordant than the others. The octave is concordant because "the dissimilars" of this are one; after this the fifth, because "the dissimilars" of this are three; the fourth is last because "the dissimilars" of this are five.

Authenticity

This testimonium does not purport to present a teaching of Archytas himself. The doctrine described in the testimonium is instead ascribed to "some Pythagoreans" and Archytas is presented as one of the sources of the information. There are thus two questions to consider regarding the authenticity of the testimonium: (1) Does the method for determining relative concordance, which is described in A17, go back to the early Pythagoreans of the fifth or early fourth century or is it a product of the later tradition? (2) If the method is early, is Archytas likely to have referred to it in his writings? In regard to the first question, the commentary below will show that there are connections between the technical terminology of A17 and Plato's description of the nuptial number in Book VIII of the *Republic* (546c). It will also be shown, however, that the mathematical content of A17 shows no connection to this passage of the *Republic*, so that A17 is very unlikely to reflect the work of a forger drawing on the Platonic passage. Plato's use of technical terminology that is similar to what is found in A17 is best explained as reflecting his attempt to use the high-flown vocabulary of contemporary Pythagorean arithmetic, and thus supports the early

Pythagorean provenance (early fourth century or earlier) of A17. Regarding the second point, there is other evidence that Archytas in fact made a practice of referring to the work of his predecessors or contemporaries (see the overview of Archytas' philosophy), so that we should believe Porphyry, when he says that Archytas reported the practice described in A17.

Context in Porphyry
The material in Testimonium A17 is part of Porphyry's commentary on Chapter 6 of Ptolemy's *Harmonics*, in which Ptolemy sets out his criticisms of Pythagorean harmonics. In particular Ptolemy points out two problems with the Pythagorean principle that all concordant intervals must correspond to a ratio that is either epimoric (i.e. superparticular, a ratio in which the difference between the terms is an integral part of the lesser term, e.g. 4/3) or multiple (mn:n, e.g. 3:1): (1) Some intervals which are obviously concordant according to our senses do not correspond to either an epimoric or multiple ratio (his example is the octave plus a fourth, which is quite plainly a concord yet has 8:3 as its ratio). (2) Only some epimoric and multiple ratios (e.g. 2:1, 4:3, 3:2, 3:1) correspond to intervals that we hear as concordant, while other such ratios do not (as examples he mentions 5:4 and 5:1, which are respectively epimoric and multiple yet excluded from the list of ratios associated with concords). The passage upon which Porphyry is commenting follows immediately on these examples and makes the further point that "they make their selection of the concords [from intervals with epimoric or multiple ratios] in whatever way suits their fancy" (tr. Barker). In this passage Ptolemy goes on to ridicule a Pythagorean method for determining the relative concordance of intervals. A17 is Porphyry's more detailed account of this "ridiculous" method.

How does Porphyry's presentation differ from the text of Ptolemy on which he is commenting? There is no significant difference in the basic method as described in Ptolemy and Porphyry, but Ptolemy describes the method in only three lines, before giving an initial criticism in another four lines. Porphyry is much more detailed, using thirty lines to comment on Ptolemy's three. Both Ptolemy and Porphyry assign the method in question to the Pythagoreans in general, but only Porphyry supplies the sources of his information about these Pythagoreans, i.e. Archytas and Didymus. Porphyry differs significantly, moreover, in providing and explaining the terminology actually used by the Pythagoreans in several places. He defines the terms *pythmenes* ("bases") and *summisgein* ("mingling") that are not even hinted at in Ptolemy. Porphyry also explains the Pythagorean "similars" and "dissimilars." Ptolemy does refer to the concepts of similarity and difference but slightly changes the Pythagorean usage and, most importantly, does not make clear that these words reflect Pythagorean usage rather than his own. Finally, Porphyry, as is his practice elsewhere, provides specific examples of the method as applied to the fourth, the fifth and the octave. These examples are welcome here, because Ptolemy's initial presentation of the method is abbreviated to the point of being cryptic, as Porphyry himself comments a few lines after the end of A17 (108. 28–9). Testimonium A17, then, provides both a very helpful explication of a compressed passage of Ptolemy and also important additional information on the source of the passage and the original terminology in which the method was expressed. Porphyry is thus here achieving two of the goals he sets for himself in the proem to his commentary: (1) To explain Ptolemy's compressed treatment of mathematical matters for readers without training in mathematics (3.18 ff.), (2) To give the sources of his information even where Ptolemy does not (5.8 ff.).

Immediately after A17 Porphyry connects the information that he has provided with the passage in Ptolemy upon which he is commenting: "these are the things of which Ptolemy spoke, when he alleged that the selection of the concords, 'according to whatever method they want', is ridiculous." Porphyry then explains that for Ptolemy it is not the Pythagorean view on the relative concordance of the octave, fourth and fifth that is ridiculous but rather the method they use to show which is more concordant. Porphyry then concludes his commentary on this section by agreeing with Ptolemy's criticisms of the Pythagoreans on this point (14. 6–10).

The ranking of concords: an overview of Testimonium A17
This testimonium presents a method for comparing concords with each other in order to determine which is more concordant. A ranking of concords in terms of relative concordance results. For the unidentified Pythagoreans of A17, who are the contemporaries or predecessors of Archytas, the octave is rated most concordant, followed by the fifth and the fourth. The ranking of concords is in fact common in the Pythagorean tradition and is in no way peculiar to the Pythagoreans who are the subject of Archytas' report in A17. None of the other methods of ranking, nor indeed any of the other rankings, exactly match A17, however.

Ptolemy himself, although he is very critical of the method in A17, presents a ranking of concords that is similar to the ranking in A17 (octave, fifth, fourth, but the double octave would be regarded as more concordant than the fifth; *Harmonics* I. 7; see Barker 1989: 272–73). There is an earlier attempt at explaining why the octave is the finest concord, in the Aristotelian *Problems* (XIX. 35; Barker 1989: 93). Perhaps most interesting are two rankings preserved in Boethius' *De Institutione Musica* (II. 18–20; cf. I. 32), one of which is ascribed to Nicomachus (AD 100) and a second to the early Pythagorean Hippasus. A certain Eubulides is mentioned along with Hippasus, but it appears more probable that he was a later writer who reported Hippasus' views than that he was an early Pythagorean (*Theol. Ar.* 52.9). It is very likely that Books I–IV of Boethius are translating and paraphrasing Nicomachus' lost *Introduction to Music*, so that all the material presented in Boethius ultimately goes back to that work of Nicomachus (see on A19). Boethius' report of Nicomachus' views is not completely consistent. At I. 32 Nicomachus is reported to have given the ranking octave (2:1), fifth (3:2), octave + fifth (3:1), fourth (4:3), double octave (4:1), while at II. 18 and II. 20 the ranking is octave (2:1), octave + fifth (3:1), double octave (4:1), fifth (3:2), fourth (4:3). Hippasus, who was probably active in the middle of the fifth century, is said (II. 19) to have given the following ranking: octave, fifth, octave + fifth, fourth, double octave.

Nothing is said explicitly about how the Pythagoreans of A17 ranked intervals other than the octave, fifth and fourth. All the methods agree in the ranking octave, fifth, fourth. If the method described in A17 is applied to the intervals found in the other rankings, the following sequence would result: octave ("dissimilars" = 1), octave + fifth (2), fifth (3) and double octave (3), fourth (5). This does not match any of the other rankings but comes closest to that of Nicomachus in II. 18 and 20, differing in that Nicomachus clearly ranks the double octave as more concordant than the fifth, whereas the method of A17 would make them equal. A17 seems to differ the most from the other early Pythagorean ranking, that of Hippasus. When we turn to the method used to arrive at the rankings, there is no parallel for the procedure used in A17. It is noteworthy that, while Boethius does translate/paraphrase Ptolemy, *Harmonics* I. 6, he does not include the passage in which Ptolemy criticizes the method described in A17 and shows no awareness of the material presented by Porphyry in A17 (*Inst. Mus.* V. 8–10).

Ptolemy is very critical of the method used to rank the concords in A17. That method takes the ratios of the concords in their lowest terms, subtracts one from each term, and then adds the remaining numbers. The lower the resulting number is (the "dissimilars"), the more concordant the interval is. So the octave has the ratio 2:1 in lowest terms, while the fifth has the ratio 3:2. If we subtract one from each of the terms in these ratios and then add the remainders, the octave has a dissimilars of 1 ($2 - 1 = 1$, $1 - 1 = 0$, $1 + 0 = 1$), while the fifth has a dissimilars of 3 ($3 - 1 = 2$, $2 - 1 = 1$, $2 + 1 = 3$). Since the "dissimilars" of the octave is smaller than the "dissimilars" of the fifth, the octave is more concordant than the fifth. Ptolemy's basic complaint is that this treats the musical intervals not as corresponding to ratios of numbers but rather to a single number. Thus the fifth is somehow made up of the addition of its two terms, after one has been subtracted from each. In reality, however, it is the ratio of 3:2 that constitutes the fifth and that ratio could just as easily be represented in the numbers 6:4 or 12:8. If we represented the ratios by any of these other pairs of numbers, the "dissimilars" number that resulted from the method of A17 would be different. We might defend the Pythagoreans of A17 by suggesting that they are trying to find common terms in which to compare the concords and that reducing each ratio to its lowest terms is not an implausible way of doing so; since they treat each of the ratios the same, there is a legitimate basis for comparison. Ptolemy goes on to suggest, however, that a more reasonable basis from which to compare the concords would be to express them in terms of a common denominator, e.g. 12:6, 9:6, 8:6, and then subtract 6 from each term as the "similar" factor. If this procedure is followed, however, a ranking which is exactly the reverse of the ranking in A17 results (fourth [dissimilar = 2], fifth [3], octave [6]). So, even if we grant that there is some sense to the Pythagorean practice of comparing the ratios in lowest terms, there is no clear evidence that this procedure is more appropriate than Ptolemy's suggestion, which gives the opposite results. Accordingly, the Pythagorean practice appears arbitrary and they seem to make their selection of concords "in whatever way they themselves fancy" (1. 6, Düring 14.1–2).

Barker (1989: 35 n. 29), while granting the mathematical absurdity of the procedure, suggests that it is not pointless. Some sense can be made of the method, if we assume that it is based on a physical model according to which sounds are produced by impacts on the air, with higher pitches resulting from a greater number of impacts. Thus, the two notes that form the interval of the fifth (A and B below) would be produced by three impacts and two impacts respectively, in the same period of time. If we assume that the first impact of each note occurs at the same time, the higher note will have to get in two more impacts and the lower one more impact before impacts again occur at the same time:

```
Note A    *        *              *        *
Note B    *                  *             *
```

The impacts that coincide would be the "similars" and the ones that did not would be the "dissimilars," so that, in the case of the fifth, the "dissimilars" would be three between each pair of coinciding impacts.

This is a very ingenious suggestion, but it is not clear that such a theory lies behind A17. As presented in Porphyry and Ptolemy, the method in A17 is purely arithmetical with no hint of an underlying acoustic theory. Barker seems to suggest that the term συμμίσγειν ("mingling" – see the commentary below) indicates such a theory. He says that the term is "probably intended within the context of a theory of concord as the 'blending' of two sounds" (1989: 35 n. 28) and goes on to suggest that, in the model he proposes, "impacts that coincide may be deemed to blend acoustically, and correspond to the similars." It is at this point that a difficulty arises. For the text of A17 connects "blending" or "mingling" not with the similars as one would expect, if the term had its origin in an acoustic theory (see Euclid *Sect. Can.* 149.18–20) but rather with the "dissimilars." It is the dissimilars that are said to arise from the mingling (lines 29–30 γίνεται οὖν τὰ ἀνόμοια τῶν συμφωνιῶν συμμιγέντα). Thus, the connection of the term "blending" with the dissimilars in fact argues against thinking that an acoustic theory is behind A17, and indeed "blending" is defined solely in arithmetical terms in A17 (see below).

The oddest feature of the procedure in A17 is not the feature of which Ptolemy complains: taking the ratios of the concords in lowest terms. This search for common terms in which to compare the concords is, as we have seen, understandable, if somewhat arbitrary. The real oddity of the procedure is the subtraction of one from each term of the ratios. Obviously this subtraction makes no difference whatsoever in the resulting ranking of concords, since the same amount is being subtracted in each case. It would have worked just as well to add the two terms in each ratio without any subtraction. This suggests that there were theoretical reasons for the subtraction of the "similars." One of the virtues of Barker's explanation is that it explains the subtraction of the similars as taking into account the notes that coincide according to an acoustic theory. As suggested above, however, other features of the passage suggest that there was no acoustic theory involved. As an alternative we might suppose that it seemed desirable that the "dissimilars" number for the octave be one, the number which above all suggests unity, in order to symbolize the special position of the octave. Without the subtraction, the "dissimilars" of the octave would have been three, but it appears that theoretical concerns enter at even a more basic level. The procedure in A17 assumes that ratios are combinations of "similars" and "dissimilars" so that, if the "similars" are subtracted, all that remains will be the "dissimilars." This understanding of the composition of ratios is parallel to what we find in Fragment 6 of Philolaus, who was active in the second half of the fifth century and is Archytas' reputed teacher. In Fragment 6,

Philolaus argues that the two types of basic principles from which the world arises, limiters and unlimiteds, cannot by themselves combine to form an ordered world. Limiters and unlimiteds cannot combine because they are dissimilar and while "similar things (τὰ ὁμοῖα) . . . did not in addition require any harmony" it is necessary that "things that are dissimilar (τὰ ἀνόμοια) . . . be bonded together by harmony, if they are going to be held in an order."

The connection between A17 and Fragment 6 of Philolaus is not just that we have exactly the same language of "similars" and "dissimilars." Indeed, similar (like) and dissimilar (unlike) are common concepts in Presocratic philosophy. Philolaus also connects these "similars" and "dissimilars" to the whole number ratios that correspond to the musical concords. In Fragment 6a, he goes on to describe the structure of the cosmos in terms of the octave, fourth and fifth. Now Philolaus does not explicitly tie the *harmonia* that holds limiters and unlimiteds together in the cosmos to similarity. The similars that he talks about directly are things that do not need to be harmonized, precisely because they are similar and of the same kind to begin with. Nonetheless, it seems very plausible to suppose that the process of fitting together the dissimilar things in the world, or the dissimilar numbers in a ratio, was thought of as establishing a bond of similarity between them. This understanding of the ratios corresponding to the musical concords as "dissimilars made similar" would seem to be exactly the theoretical assumption that underlies the procedure in A17, where "dissimilars" are determined by subtracting the "similars." So we can conjecture that Philolaus or others influenced by Philolaus are the Pythagoreans whose practice Archytas is reporting in A17. It is possible to imagine a number of contexts in which it would make perfect sense for Archytas to set out the views of his teacher or of those influenced by him, although we must recognize that there is no evidence that Archytas himself adopted these views. Plato's connection of similarity to concord and dissimilarity to discord in the *Timaeus* (80a) may also reflect in some way the Pythagorean concatenation of similars, dissimilars and concordance in A17, but it is hard to see any more specific relation between A17 and the *Timaeus*.

In the commentary that follows much of the attention will be focused on the terminology that is used by the Pythagoreans in A17. Before looking at the details of that terminology, it is important to emphasize one important conclusion that arises from close study of it. The terminology of A17 shows marked connections to Plato's famous discussion of the nuptial number in Book VIII of the *Republic* (546a ff.). This is the number that controls better and worse births for human beings and, in ignorance of which, the guardians allow improper births that lead to civil war and the dissolution of the ideal state. But the similarity between A17 and *Republic* 546a resides precisely in terminology; there is no connection in the actual mathematics of the two passages. As a result, there is little likelihood that A17 is based on a Pythagorean forgery inspired by the Platonic passage. What the similarity in terminology suggests rather is that Plato is using the technical Pythagorean terminology of his day to describe the nuptial number. In doing so he is following Muses who use the tragic and lofty tone of mock seriousness, as he says in his introductory comments (545e . . . τραγικῶς . . . ὡς δὴ σπουδῇ λεγούσας, ὑψηλολογουμένας . . .). Plato's goal is precisely to present the nuptial number in language that will sound technical and impressive to his audience. Thus, to give a small example, the passage that Grube/Reeve translate as ". . . four and three, married with five . . ." is much better rendered by Shorey as ". . . a basal four-thirds wedded to the pempad . . ." A17 shows us that contemporary Pythagorean arithmetic did indeed have high-flown diction worthy of a second-rate tragic poet. However much Plato does believe in the importance of the study of mathematics and of a cosmos ordered in accord with mathematical ratios, he is still able to laugh at the excesses of "some Pythagoreans."

Detailed commentary

Line 1 There is a problem with the punctuation of the first words. I have punctuated "Some of the Pythagoreans, as Archytas and Didymus report, . . ." In Düring's text the passage is punctuated "Some of the Pythagoreans, as Archytas and Didymus, report . . ." But this punctuation will simply not work with the syntax of the rest of the sentence, which would need to be in indirect statement after "report." It may well be that this is a simple typographical error, since Düring says nothing to justify the punctuation in his commentary. Both DK and Barker punctuate as I have.

Ptolemy does not identify his source for the Pythagorean practice which he is criticizing and Porphyry, as is his practice elsewhere and as is in accordance with his stated goal (5.8 ff.), here gives the sources that Ptolemy did not. The citation of the sources is puzzling and open to several interpretations, which have significant implications for what the testimonium tells us about Archytas. Porphyry names two sources, Archytas and Didymus. This Didymus lived in the first century AD (Barker 1989: 230) and wrote a book entitled *On the Difference Between Pythagorean and Aristoxenian Music Theory*. It is clear that Porphyry had a copy of this book, not just because he quotes from it elsewhere but also because he is able to assert, in the proem to his commentary, that Ptolemy copied this work in many places without citing his source (5.13–14). On the most straightforward reading, then, Porphyry is saying that he found the method of unnamed

Pythagoreans, which he details in A17, described in two different books, one by Didymus and one by Archytas.

It is far from clear, however, that Porphyry had Archytas' book. He does not, for example, appeal to such a book when commenting on Ptolemy's criticism of Archytas' discussion of the tetrachord in A16. Moreover, if he had Archytas' book there would be little reason for him to refer to Didymus, since Didymus' description of the Pythagorean practice would be likely to rely on the much earlier book of Archytas. Since Porphyry mentions both names, it may well be that he found the Pythagorean practice described in Didymus, but that Didymus associated the practice with Archytas in some way. Some have thought that Didymus must have ascribed the practice to Archytas himself (Burkert 1972a: 386; Mueller 1997: 289, without argument, treats A17 as reflecting Archytas' own views). This is simply not what Porphyry says, however. He does not ascribe the practice to "Archytas, as Didymus reports" but rather to "some Pythagoreans, as Archytas and Didymus report." The most reasonable conclusion is that Porphyry found in Didymus something such as the following: "Archytas reports that some of the Pythagoreans . . ." Or it may be that Didymus gave a direct quote from Archytas, in which he described the practices of his predecessors. There is other evidence that Archytas made a practice of reporting and commenting on the work of his predecessors and contemporaries (see my overview of Archytas' philosophy). The best parallel to A17 is Theophrastus, *Metaphysics* 6a where Archytas is given as the source for the story of the Pythagorean Eurytus' practice of setting out pebbles in order to determine the "number" of specific things in the world, such as man or horse. Thus, the most likely scenario is that Porphyry is relying on Didymus' account of what Archytas said about "some Pythagoreans."

4–5 πυθμένας – The basic meaning of πυθμήν is "base" (e.g. of a cup), "bottom" (e.g. of the sea), or the "stock" or "root" of a tree. In A17, however, it is used as a technical term in mathematics: the "base" or lowest number (or numbers) having a given mathematical property. As Porphyry goes on to explain, πυθμένες are, here in A17, specifically the ratios of the musical concords expressed in their lowest terms. Thus we could express such ratios in an unlimited number of forms, including e.g. 12:6 (octave), 12:9 (fourth), 12:8 (fifth). But the πυθμένες of these ratios, these ratios stated in lowest terms, are 2:1, 4:3, 3:2.

Porphyry will refer to the Pythagorean practice of using the πυθμένες in describing concords, as well as Ptolemy's disapproval of that practice, several times in the pages succeeding A17, but none of these passages add anything to the definition of πυθμένες which Porphyry has given in A17 (109.3; 112.12; 115.1). In later passages in his commentary on Ptolemy's *Harmonics*, Porphyry will himself use the term πυθμήν as "a given ratio in its least terms," even where he is not referring to the ancient Pythagoreans, so that it is clear that he found it a useful piece of terminology and not just an historical curiosity (130.9; 144.5; 148.5). The general definition of πυθμήν as "the lowest terms of a given ratio" is, in fact, common in the later Greek arithmetical tradition. Theon of Smyrna (80.15) gives such a description: "Of all the ratios described according to kind [e.g. sesquialter, sesquitertian etc.] those that are expressed in the lowest numbers and numbers prime to one another are called first of those having the same ratio in each case and are called *pythmenes* of the ratios of the same species." Nicomachus consistently uses πυθμήν in this way in his *Introduction to Arithmetic* (I. 19, II. 19) and sets out tables of ratios (I. 21) with the "root-forms" (πυθμένες) given first, e.g. 5:3 (πυθμήν), 10:6, 15:9, 20:12 etc. (D' Ooge et al. 1926: 216 n. 1).

This meaning of the term is not limited just to the early Pythagoreans and to the later arithmetical tradition, however, and it is so used already by Plato in the famous passage on the so-called nuptial number at *Republic* 546c. Although it is sometimes mistranslated, Plato's expression ἐπίτριτος πυθμήν clearly means "the epitritic ratio in its lowest terms" (i.e. 4:3; see Adam 1929: II. 276). The word is used in a different but related sense by Plato's nephew and successor as head of the Academy, Speusippus (Fr. 28 Tarán). The fragment is said to derive from a work entitled *On Pythagorean Numbers*, so we might expect it to reflect Pythagorean usage to some extent. In the passage in question, Speusippus is explaining the properties of the number ten. He says that ten is the πυθμήν of the larger numbers with one of these properties and has some perfection "as the first having this characteristic and the least of those having it." This latter phrase, as Tarán points out (1981: 279), defines what Speusippus means by a πυθμήν. In this case, then, we are dealing with a single number rather than a ratio, but the usage is clearly analogous to what we have seen in the passages dealing with ratios: a πυθμήν is the smallest number (or numbers) to exhibit a certain mathematical property and is thus the "foundation" of all the subsequent numbers which exhibit this property.

There is evidence for interest in finding *pythmenes* even prior to Plato and Speusippus, but this time from outside the field of mathematics. Diogenes Laertius (IX. 54) tells us that Protagoras was the first to divide discourse into four parts (wish, question, answer, command) and that he called these parts "*pythmenes* of discourse." Clearly Protagoras was trying to identify the "foundations" or "bases" from which all discourse can be derived. Whether or not Protagoras derived this usage of πυθμήν from its use in mathematics cannot be determined. At the least, however, it is clear that, starting in the second half of the fifth century, πυθμήν played an important role in the technical terminology of those who were trying to establish "the foundations" of a number of different disciplines.

Heath (1921: 115–16) drew attention to yet another sense of πυθμήν. The Christian author Hippolytus (AD 170–ca. 236), in his *Refutation of all Heresies* describes a method of foretelling the future called the Pythagorean calculus (Πυθαγορείῳ ψήφῳ IV. 13 ff.). Those who used this method claimed to predict the future by taking advantage of the fact that Greek letters were also used to express numbers, so that a Greek name could be reduced to a number. Hippolytus says that, in order to determine the number of a name, they made use of the principle of the *pythmēn*. In this case the *pythmēn* turns out to be the number of ones, tens, hundreds etc. So the *pythmēn* of 80 is 8 and the *pythmēn* of 700 is 7 etc. (the same meaning of *pythmēn* is found in the mathematician Apollonius of Perga [200 BC] but for purposes of calculation rather than foretelling the future [Heath 1921: 54–57]). Thus, in the Greek name Hektor (Ἕκτωρ), the letters stand for the numbers 5, 20, 300, 800, 100. If we take the *pythmēn* of each of these numbers, we get the series 5, 2, 3, 8, 1. These *pythmenes* are then added, giving the number 19 and the *pythmēn* of each of these numbers is taken giving 1 and 9. These *pythmenes* are added giving 10, the *pythmēn* of which is 1, which is thus the *pythmēn* for the name Hektor. Comparison of the *pythmenes* for two different names allowed one to decide which would be "victorious." It is not at all clear whether this practice goes back to the time of Archytas or whether it is from the Hellenistic period or later (Thesleff treats all such practices as late [1965: 243 ff.]). Nonetheless, the practice does show some similarity to the mathematical procedure described in A17. In each case the first step is to take a given set of numbers or a ratio and find its *pythmenes* or base forms. Then a mathematical operation is applied to these *pythmenes:* in A17 one is subtracted from each of the terms of the ratio and the remainders are added; in the Pythagorean calculus the *pythmenes* are added together and, if necessary, the *pythmenes* of this sum are taken until a number between 1 and 9 is reached. There are also some very significant differences: the meaning of "base number" or *pythmēn* is different in the two cases, and the goals of the process are radically different: foretelling the future and comparing musical concords for relative concordance.

The evidence is too incomplete to draw any sweeping conclusions. A17 appears to be the earliest testimony for a common practice in Pythagorean mathematics, which also spread beyond Pythagoreanism, according to which one was looking for the base form or *pythmēn* of a number or set of numbers. What it means to be a base differs with the context and we have seen three different senses (A17, Plato, Theon, Nicomachus; Speusippus; the Pythagorean calculus). It is then common to apply some arithmetical operations, most commonly simple addition, to these base numbers. The resulting numbers were then used for a variety of purposes from telling the future to determining relative musical concordance. A17 provides no evidence that Archytas himself followed these practices, nor does it tell us what he thought of them, but it does show that he knew of some of them among either his predecessors or his contemporaries.

7 The manuscripts read πρῶτος, a nominative case agreeing with διπλά-σιος and ὁ δύο τοῦ ἑνός but then read πυθμένος, a genitive agreeing with ἑνός. Thus, the ratio 2:1 is called the first double, but then the number one (and not the ratio 2:1) is said to be the foundation of the other doubles. In lines 9–10, however, when describing the ratio 4:3, both πρῶτος and πυθμήν are in the nominative agreeing with ὁ δ' τῶν γ'. Here the ratio 4:3 is more logically described as both the first example of the epitritic ratio and the foundation (of other epitritic ratios). In light of the construction in lines 9–10, I have replaced the πυθμένος in line 8 with πυθμήν, supposing that πυθμένος has been put into the genitive to agree with the nearby ἑνός by a careless copyist. Porphyry does go back and forth between regarding the ratio as a whole as a πυθμήν (144.15) and regarding the individual numbers in the ratio as each a πυθμήν and together as πυθμένες (lines 4–5 of A17). In the end, however, this fluidity of usage cannot satisfactorily solve the problem in line 8. Granted that one of the terms of a ratio can be called a πυθμήν, it is still nonsense to start by talking of the ratio 2:1 as the first double and then say that the number one alone is the foundation of the other doubles. It is more in accord with Porphyry's usage to talk of the numbers one and two as a πυθμένες of the ratio 2:1 (145.13, 148.5), or of the two together as each a πυθμήν of the ratio (149.6), than to refer to the number one alone as the foundation of the other doubles.

23–26 ὅμοια . . . ἀνόμοια (similars . . . dissimilars) – There is some awkwardness in the sequence of thought here. We are first told that the Pythagoreans gave the name "similars" to the units which were subtracted from the *pythmenes* of the concords and the name "dissimilars" to what was left after the subtraction. Then Porphyry, or his source, says that there are two reasons for these names. The first reason is stated clearly in a ὅτι clause and seems to explain the use of the term "similars": "because the subtraction from both terms was similar and equal. For unit is equal to unit." The second reason is much less clearly marked and grows out of the first. It seems to be contained in the next words, which explain why the remainders are "dissimilar": "If these [the units] are subtracted, it is necessary that what remains be dissimilar and unequal." This explanation is further justified by pointing out (1) that if equals are taken away from unequals the remainders will be unequal (cf. Euclid, *Elements*, Common Notion 5), and (2) that the ratios of the concords are all either multiple or superparticular and hence have terms that are unequal. The whole passage is awkward, because we at first expect two distinct reasons for the two names; what we get is one explanation for each name and these explanations arise because of the same basic principle: when equals are subtracted from unequals, the remainders are unequal. It would have been more felicitous, if Porphyry had simply said "they assigned these names for the following reason."

The more interesting question about these "similars" and "dissimilars" is their connection to Pythagorean thought of the fifth and fourth century and to Greek philosophy of that period in general. It is at first sight striking that, just as the term πυθμήν appeared in both A17 and Plato's account of the nuptial number, so also the "similars" (ὅμοια) and "dissimilars" (ἀνόμοια) in A17 seem to be echoed in Plato's phrase "making like and unlike" (546b14 – ὁμοιούντων τε καὶ ἀνομοιούντων; see Burkert 1972a: 386 n. 77). Nonetheless "like" and "unlike" are very common terms in Greek philosophy, and the most reasonable reading of the Platonic passage on the nuptial number, which is admittedly obscure, does not match up with the use of similars and dissimilars in A17. Adam (1929: II. 274) points out that there is evidence, in the later arithmetical tradition, that square numbers were known as ὅμοιοι and oblong numbers were known as ἀνόμοιοι (Iamblichus, *In Nic.* 82 ff.). Since Plato seems to be referring precisely to square and oblong numbers in his description of the nuptial number (546c ". . . the one the product of equal factors[τὴν μὲν ἴσην ἰσάκις] . . . the other of equal length one way but oblong [προμήκη]), it is reasonable to understand his words ὁμοιούντων τε καὶ ἀνομοιούντων, in light of what Iamblichus says, as meaning "producing squares and oblongs." On the other hand, no convincing connection can be made between what Iamblichus says and the procedure in A17. It simply isn't the case that similars and dissimilars in A17 are square and oblong numbers as they are in Iamblichus and Plato. It may be that the terms "like" and "unlike" had multiple applications in the mathematics of the period. The similarity between Plato and A17 appears not to be based on common mathematical procedures but rather on Plato's heaping up of current mathematical terminology for rhetorical effect. The "similars" and "dissimilars" of A17 show a more promising, but still speculative, connection with the usage of "similars" and "dissimilars" in Fragment 6 of Philolaus, Archytas' predecessor. See my comments in the overview of A17 above.

30 συμμίσγειν – This is the last piece of technical terminology that Porphyry ascribes to the Pythagoreans. It appears that strictly speaking the "dissimilars of the consonances" only arise after the "mingling" of the numbers which are left after the subtraction of one from both terms of the ratio. By "mingling," the Pythagoreans mean "obtaining one number from both the remaining numbers." As the examples show, what is meant is the addition of the remaining numbers (e.g. after 1 is subtracted from each of the terms of the ratio 3:2, which corresponds to the fifth, the remaining numbers 2 and 1 are then "mingled" to give one number, 3, which is "the dissimilars" of the interval of the fifth). There do not seem to be any parallels for συμμίσγειν meaning "to add" in a narrowly mathematical sense in the Greek arithmological tradition. Indeed, συμμίσγειν is not common in any sense in mathematical works. One of the rare exceptions is Nicomachus *Ar.* ii. 21.3 where a proportion is said to be a combination of ratios "so that this [a proportion] is 'composed' (συμμέμικται) of three terms at the least."

A18 Porphyry, *On Ptolemy's Harmonics* I. 6 (Düring 1932: 104. 4–16)

Τοιαύτης δὴ τυγχανούσης ἕως τοῦ καταλαμβανομένοις [Ptolemy, *Harmonics* I. 6, Düring 1930: 13.1–13.23]

ὃ λέγει τοιοῦτόν ἐστιν. οἱ ποιοῦντες τὴν διὰ πασῶν συμφωνίαν φθόγ- 1
γοι, οἷον ὑπάτη μέσων καὶ νήτη διεζευγμένων, ἀδιαφοροῦσι κατὰ τὴν 2
δύναμιν ἑνὸς φθόγγου· ὄντων γὰρ ἐναντίων δύναμίς ἐστιν ἡ αὐτὴ καὶ 3
οὕτως γ' ἀμφοῖν ὡς ἑνός. τοῦτο γάρ ἐστι τὸ δύο ἀδιαφορεῖν ἑνὸς κατὰ 4
δύναμιν, ὅταν ἐκ δυεῖν ἀποδίδωται δύναμις ὥσπερ ἀπὸ τοῦ ἑνός. διὸ 5
καὶ ἀντίφωνοι οἱ φθόγγοι λέγονται, ὡς ἀντίθεος ὁ ἰσόθεος καὶ ἀντιάν- 6
ειραι αἱ ἀμάζονες αἱ τῇ δυνάμει ἀνδράσιν ἰσούμεναι καίτοι οὖσαι 7
γυναῖκες. ἔλεγον δ' οἱ περὶ τὸν Ἀρχύταν ἑνὸς φθόγγου γίνεσθαι κατὰ 8
τὰς συμφωνίας τὴν ἀντίληψιν τῇ ἀκοῇ. καὶ συνεχώρει τοῦτο καὶ 9
Διονύσιος ἐπὶ τῆς διὰ πασῶν. 10

ἐπεὶ οὖν οἱ σύμφωνοι φθόγγοι τῆς διὰ πασῶν κατὰ δύναμιν ἑνὸς 11
φθόγγου ἀδιαφοροῦσιν, ὅταν ἄλλῃ τινὶ τῶν συμφωνίων προσλη- 12
φθῶσιν, ὡς εἷς συνάπτεται. 13

---

2 post μέσων add. καὶ νήτη μέσων V¹⁸⁷   **5** δυεῖν] G δυοῖν V¹⁸⁷ ἀποδίδωται] GV¹⁸⁷
ἀποδέδωται Düring   **6** ὁ] om. V¹⁸⁷   **9** συνεχώρει] GV¹⁸⁷ (cf. Düring) διονύσιος] G
ὁ δινύσιος V¹⁸⁷   **10** τῆς] V¹⁸⁷ τοῖς G   **11** ἐπεὶ . . . πασῶν] V¹⁸⁷ om. G, Düring
11–12 ἑνὸς φθόγγου] om. G   **12** ἄλλῃ τινὶ] G ἄλλο τι V¹⁸⁷

"This being," until "what is found." [Ptolemy, *Harmonics* I. 6, Düring 13.1–13.23]

What he means is this. The notes that make the concord of the octave, such as *hypatē mesōn* and *nētē diezeugmenōn*, do not differ in power from one note. For, although they are opposites, their power is the same and thus of both as of one. For it is "two not differing from one in power," whenever a power has been displayed by two just as from one. Wherefore the notes are also called *antiphōnoi*, as one equal to god is called *antitheos*, and the amazons are called *antianeirai* [antimen], since they are equal to men in power, although they are women. Archytas and his followers used to say that it is one note that hearing perceives in the case of concords. And Dionysius also conceded this in the case of the octave.

Since, then, the concordant notes of the octave do not differ from one note in power, whenever they are grasped with some other of the concords, they are conjoined as one note.

Authenticity
As the commentary below will show, the doctrine ascribed to Archytas and his followers in A18 is expressed largely in the language of later times. Nonetheless, there is nothing in the content of the doctrine that is suspicious, and it in fact shows connections to testimony for early Greek acoustic theory which is found in Aristotle and Nicomachus. A18 is thus likely to derive ultimately from Archytas' authentic work on music.

Context in Porphyry
The lemma that introduces this section of Porphyry's commentary is for page 13, lines 1–22 (Düring) of Ptolemy. In these lines Ptolemy points out that, since the Pythagoreans have adopted the postulate that all concords must have superparticular or multiple ratios (ratios in which the difference between the terms is an integral part of the lesser term or ratios of the form $(mn)/n$), the interval of an octave + a fourth is an embarrassment to them. For this interval is plainly concordant yet has a ratio, 8:3, which is neither superparticular nor multiple. Ptolemy then argues in detail that the octave + a fourth is a concord, on the grounds that the constituent notes of an octave do not differ from one note in power and that thus, when the octave is attached to another concord, such as a fourth, it keeps the form of the fourth, so that, if the fourth is concordant, so is the octave + a fourth.

Porphyry's commentary begins by explaining what Ptolemy means when he says that the notes defining an octave do not differ in power from one note. His explanation does not really add much to what Ptolemy has said but emphasizes that, while the notes are indeed different, it is in power that the two do not differ from one. Porphyry in fact treats the notes defining the octave not just as two notes that have one power but as opposites (ἐναντίων) that are one in power. He goes on to make an etymological point that these notes are called *antiphōnoi* ("sounding in answer"), where the prefix anti- stresses both their opposition and their equality. He then gives further examples of words with the prefix anti- that suggest equality in function coexisting with fundamental difference: *antitheos* can mean "equal to god" and the amazons are called *antianeirai* ("antimen"), because they are equal to men in power, although differing insofar as they are women. Porphyry then cites Archytas and his followers in order to support Ptolemy's point that the notes which form the octave are one in power. The emphatic position of ἑνὸς φθόγγου ("one note" line 8) stresses the point that, in the case of concords, we perceive one note. It thus appears that Porphyry is pursuing one of the main goals of his commentary here, i.e. to show the ancient precedent for Ptolemy's views (cf. 5.7 ff.). The structure of Porphyry's comment thus appears to be (1) a general statement of Ptolemy's point that the notes forming an octave are one in power but with an emphasis on the opposing nature of the notes, (2) an etymological digression that shows that the use of the term *antiphōnoi* for such notes illustrates this unity in opposition, (3) an appeal to Archytas and his followers to show that Ptolemy's general point explained in (1) had an ancient precedent.

Porphyry then adds that a certain Dionysius also conceded this point in the case of the octave. This Dionysius is probably the one described as "the musician" and as the author of a book *On Similarities* in an earlier passage in Porphyry (37.15). In the next paragraph (104.14), Porphyry goes on to Ptolemy's next major point, that when the octave is added to another concord it preserves the form of that concord. He begins by asserting that when the octave is added to some other concord, it is joined as one note. To whatever note of the two notes defining the octave, the higher or the lower, the concord is added it is joined as to one and the same note. Archytas and his followers, however, are only cited as precedent for the idea that the two notes defining the octave have one function (are perceived as one) and not for this further point that, when added to another concord, the octave preserves that concord, although this latter point seems to follow from the former.

The theory of concordance in A18
In Testimonium A18, Porphyry presents a brief paraphrase of the central thesis about concordance, which was put forth by Archytas and his followers.

Porphyry's own interpretation of this thesis provides the best place to start in understanding it. Porphyry clearly interprets what Archytas and his followers said as a parallel for Ptolemy's view that the notes that form the octave do not differ in power *from one note* (104.6–7). Thus in the paraphrase the emphatic first two words are "of one note." Porphyry's appeal to Archytas does not, however, function perfectly as a parallel for what Ptolemy is doing. Ptolemy is thinking only of the octave, when he says that its two notes do not differ from one note in power. The same would not be true of other concords such as the fifth or fourth, for then the double fifth and double fourth would be a concord, which Ptolemy does not accept. Ptolemy would not claim that the two notes defining a fifth have the same power. Porphyry's paraphrase of Archytas' view refers not just to the octave, however, but to concords in general. The paraphrase also makes no mention of the concept of a "power" (δύναμις; for this concept see Ptolemy II. 5 and Barker 1989: 325 n. 37, who translates the term as "function"). Matters become even more confused, because Porphyry expresses the view of Archytas and his followers in language that is used in a different context in Ptolemy. A few lines later in the passage upon which Porphyry is commenting, Ptolemy talks of "the same impression arising for the ears from the interval of the fourth + an octave and the interval of a fourth alone" (I. 6, Düring 13.14–15). Porphyry clearly borrows some of this phrasing in his paraphrase of Archytas' view, but Porphyry cannot intend to cite Archytas as a parallel for this point in Ptolemy. For at 13.14–15 Ptolemy is talking about the impression produced by the fourth in comparison with the impression produced by the fourth + an octave, whereas in the paraphrase of Archytas the impression is of just one note. In context, then, Porphyry's paraphrase of Archytas is intended to provide a parallel for Ptolemy's thesis that the notes of the octave do not differ from one note, but the paraphrase borrows language from a different context in Ptolemy.

The theory of Archytas that is presented in Porphyry's paraphrase in fact looks like a broad theory of concords and discords rather than a comment about the octave alone. Archytas' theory is that, in the case of concords such as the octave, fifth or fourth, the ear has the impression of a single note. Presumably in the case of discords the ear has the impression of more than one note, although that is not stated here. Barker notes that it was a commonplace of Greek music theory "that two notes in a concordant relation blend together to form a single, unified percept, whereas those in a discordant relation do not" (1989: 193 n. 7). He cites a number of texts which promulgate this view but only traces it back to Plato (1989: 409 n. 58). It is clear, however, that Archytas A18 (which Barker does not treat in his

book) is stating just such a view and is thus important as the earliest extant
statement of the view that, in the case of a concord, we perceive just one
note. A18 differs from other versions of this view by emphasizing the nature
of the impression that arises for the ear, i.e. that the ear has the impression
of one note, rather than the actual mixing of sounds. It is striking and
significant that the concord is described as a note (φθόγγου), whereas
most authors do not use the word note to describe the sound that arises
from two notes in a concord (Barker 1989: 233 n. 108). Plato, who will be
followed by most later thinkers, talks of the "blending" (ξυνεκεράσαντο)
of one sensation from high and low (*Timaeus* 80b; see also Aelianus in
Porphyry's commentary 35.27, where concordance is defined as a blending
(κρᾶσις) of two notes and Nic. *Harm.* 12, *Jan* 262.1, where concordant
notes are said to blend (ἐγκραθῶσιν) with one another to produce a single
form), whereas Archytas, as described by Porphyry, emphasizes that the ear
does not perceive any blending but has the impression of only one note.

Cherniss connected A18 with Aristotle *De Sensu* 448a ff. (1964: 217
n. 280). Aristotle discusses the theory of "some of those who write about
concords" that sounds do not arrive at the same time but only seem to do
so, because the intervening time is imperceptible. Aristotle himself rejects
such a view on the grounds that there is no such thing as an imperceptible
moment. Archytas, in at least some respects, could be very plausibly identified as one of the writers about concords to whom Aristotle is responding.
Archytas' acoustic theory in Fragment 1 does entail that higher pitched
sounds move more rapidly and thus reach the ears more quickly than lower
pitched sounds. Yet A18 suggests that Archytas thought that, in the case
of concords, the ear received the impression of one note rather than of
two, one higher and one lower. In order to explain how the ear had the
impression of just one note when the two notes that form the concord had
to reach the ears at different times, Archytas could well have appealed to
the sort of theory that Aristotle mentions: although the notes do reach the
ear at different times, the difference in time is imperceptible so that "the
impression of one note arises for the ears." Of course it is not just the fact
that the ear does not detect the difference in arrival time of the two notes
that produces a concord; Archytas must have argued that the notes will also
have to be of the proper sort so as to be heard as one rather than two, as a
concord rather than a discord. Without further evidence, however, we cannot with certainty identify Archytas with the writers on concords to whom
Aristotle is referring, because there are other ways to deal with the problem
of the different arrival times of high and low notes, and Archytas may have
used one of these. Plato, who adopts Archytas' view that notes of higher

pitch move more swiftly than those of lower pitch, explains concordance by imagining that the higher pitched note is slowed down after reaching us (by our perceptual apparatus?). As a result, when the lower pitched note arrives, it has a similar speed to that of the higher pitched note, and hence we perceive a concord (*Tim.* 80a; see Barker 1989: 62 n. 31). It is perfectly possible that Archytas had such an explanation of concordance and that Plato is following him in this as he does in his explanation of high and low pitch.

One final piece of evidence, however, suggests that Archytas and Plato may have disagreed on this point and that Archytas is after all one of Aristotle's "writers on concords." In his *De Institutione Musica* (1. 31) Boethius ascribes a view of concordance to Nicomachus which has strong similarities to the view that Aristotle attacks. This view of concordance is not found in Nicomachus' extant *Handbook of Music*. Boethius, however, is in all probability paraphrasing Nicomachus' lost *Introduction to Music* in the first books of his *De Institutione Musica* (Bower 1989: xxiv ff.), so that the view that Boethius ascribes to Nicomachus is likely to have been set out in the lost *Introduction to Music*. Nicomachus is not an original musical theorist, and it is thus very unlikely that he originated the view of concordance ascribed to him in Boethius. Moreover, since the view is so close to the one described by Aristotle, as I will show below, we have good reason to suppose that Nicomachus derives it from an author who dates before Aristotle. The author cannot be Plato, because the theory is adopted by Nicomachus as an alternative to Plato's; Archytas thus becomes a very plausible candidate as the originator of this theory, especially since Nicomachus refers to Archytas elsewhere and thus clearly knew his work (*Ar.* 1. 3.4).

In Chapter 30 of Book 1 of *De Institutione Musica*, Boethius describes Plato's theory of consonance as presented in the *Timaeus*. Chapter 31 then begins with an account of Nicomachus' criticisms of Plato's view followed by Nicomachus' own explanation of consonance. This sequence might suggest that the view of concordance ascribed to Nicomachus was developed in response to Plato and that it thus must have been developed after the *Timaeus*. If this were so, Archytas would not be a very likely candidate as originator of this theory. It is also possible, however, that the theory of consonance that Nicomachus adopts existed at the same time or before Plato's and that, while the criticisms of Plato are obviously post-Platonic and may belong to Nicomachus himself, the theory of concordance adopted by Nicomachus may have been developed independently of Plato. That this second scenario is the more likely is supported by the fact that the theory of concordance ascribed to Nicomachus in itself shows no signs of being developed in response to Plato, and Nicomachus' criticisms of Plato are in fact presented in a separate paragraph.

The theory of concordance which Boethius ascribes to Nicomachus emphasizes that a sound does not consist of one pulsation but rather a string that is struck "makes many sounds, striking the air again and again" (tr. Bower). Since the velocity of percussion is so great, however, one sound, "as it were, overcomes" the other and no interval of silence is perceived between the sounds, and it comes to the ears as if of one pitch. Each note is thus treated as in fact a series of percussions, and, if the percussions of the high note are commensurable with those with a low note, then they blend together and make one consonance of pitches. What connects this theory to the one Aristotle describes is the emphasis on the idea that no interval of silence is perceived between the sounds (*De Sensu* 448a22 ὁ χρόνος ἦ ἀναίσθητος, *Inst. Mus.* I. 31, p. 222. 7 *distantia non sentitur*), because of the rapidity of percussions. There is, however, an important difference in that, in Aristotle, the interval that is not perceived is that between the arrival of the faster high note and the slower low note, not the interval between the percussions that constitute each note. This difference may not be significant, however. The theory that Boethius ascribes to Nicomachus can account for the problem posed by the different speeds of high and low notes and their corresponding different arrival times. Both the high-pitched note and the low-pitched note are composed of multiple indistinguishable percussions. It may well be that the first percussions of the higher note reach us before any percussions of the lower note, but the speed of both notes' arrival may be such that we cannot distinguish between the different arrival times. Thus we still perceive the percussions of the higher pitched note as coexisting with those of the lower pitched, and, when these percussions are commensurable (i.e when their percussions have an appropriate ratio), they blend, so that we perceive one note.

The theory adopted by Nicomachus is connected to what we find in Archytas A18 in two ways: (1) In both cases there is a heavy emphasis on one note arising out of two (A18 ἑνὸς φθόγγου: *Inst. Mus.* I. 31, p. 222.8 *una vox*, 222.12 *unamque vocum . . . consonantiam*); (2) In both cases there is an emphasis on the idea that the single note is in fact an impression that occurs to the ear (A18 ἑνὸς φθόγγου γίνεσθαι . . . τὴν ἀντίληψιν τῇ ἀκοῇ, *Inst. Mus.* I. 31, p. 222.8 *quasi una vox auribus venit*), an impression that does not represent the physical phenomena in a completely accurate way (Barker points out to me that there are also some connections between Nicomachus' theory and the ideas of Heraclides described by Porphyry [*In Ptol.* 31. 6–21 = Barker 1989: 236]).

In conclusion, A18 establishes Archytas as the earliest thinker whom we know to have argued for the view, which was common later, that in the case of concords the ear perceives a single sound. Porphyry mistakenly associates this thesis with Ptolemy's idea that the notes forming the octave have the same power. The emphasis on what appears to the ear in Archytas' theory suggests that it may well be the theory that Nicomachus adopted in his lost *Introduction to Music* and also the theory that Aristotle attacks at *De Sensu* 448a. If so, we have yet another case in which a doctrine of Archytas, while sharing some features with a Platonic view, is nonetheless clearly not to be identified with it.

Detailed commentary

Line 8 ἔλεγον — At first sight this appears to introduce a quotation, but what follows is in indirect discourse and, as the commentary below shows, is formulated in language that cannot go back to Archytas. Porphyry is summarizing the view of Archytas and his followers, not quoting their formulation of it.

οἱ περὶ τὸν Ἀρχύταν — In the classical period the expression οἱ περὶ x or οἱ ἀμφὶ x usually means "x and his followers" (Kühner 1887 II. 1 403d; Cooper 1998: 1. 408 [50.5.6]), but some passages suggest that it can pick out the followers of x as distinct from x (e.g. Arist., *Pol.* 1314b25). In later Greek οἱ περὶ x comes to mean just "x," in many cases, and this practice may begin as early as Aristotle (see Bonitz 1955: 579a44). It can be very difficult to decide how to translate the phrase in a given instance, and there is considerable inconsistency among translators. In the Loeb translation of Diogenes Laertius, Hicks sometimes renders the phrase as "x" (e.g. I. 30.3; II. 77.4; II. 105.12) but sometimes as "x and his followers" (e.g. IV. 40.8; VII. 32.5; VII. 84.5) or sometimes just "the circle of x" (IV. 41.8) or "the followers of x" (VII. 64.2; VII. 68.8). In *The Hellenistic Philosophers*, Long and Sedley, with admirable consistency, usually translate the phrase as simply = "x," (e.g. VII. 64 = 33G), but at D.L. VII. 32 (= 67B) they render οἱ περὶ Κάσσιον as "the circle of Cassius."

There is nothing in the context of A18 to suggest that it is being used in the more unusual sense of "the followers of Archytas" in contrast to Archytas himself. It is thus most likely to mean "Archytas and his followers" or just "Archytas." It is not completely clear whether οἱ περὶ τὸν Ἀρχύταν is Porphyry's phrase or whether he has derived it from another source. Porphyry does not use the idiom elsewhere in his commentary on Ptolemy's *Harmonics*, but he does use it in other works (e.g. *In Cat.* 59.10). If Porphyry has taken over the phrase from someone else, Didymus is the most likely source, since he is the probable source for some of Porphyry's other reports on Archytas (see A17). The phrase may ultimately go back to even earlier sources, such as Aristotle's two books on Archytas or Aristoxenus' *Life of Archytas*. It appears in A15a, A9 and A19a of Archytas. A9 derives from Aristoxenus and the phrase there clearly means "Archytas and his followers."

9 ἀντίληψιν — In context this word means something like "(sense) impression." A literal translation would be "an impression of one note arises for the hearing in the case of concords." It is very doubtful that ἀντίληψις was used in this sense by Archytas and his contemporaries. The use of ἀντίληψις to mean "sense impression" cannot be convincingly paralleled in any Presocratic author, Plato, or Aristotle (Alcmaeon A10 is likely to be formulated in later terminology; in Democritus A37 = Aristotle Fr. 208 the reference, if it does go back to Democritus, is to atoms "catching hold of one another" rather than to a sense impression). LSJ indicates that the meaning "grasping with the mind" first appears in Epicurus (Fr. 250) and the Stoics (*SVF* II. 206), and the meaning "sense impression" seems to appear first in the Stoics (*SVF* II. 230). Closer examination of the usage of ἀντίληψις which is found in Ptolemy and Porphyry suggests that A18 is most likely to be Porphyry's recasting of an earlier Pythagorean idea in Ptolemy's language. The word appears with the meaning "sense impression" several times in both Ptolemy and Porphyry. More importantly, a construction with ἀντίληψις, which is very similar to the construction in A18, is found in the passage of Ptolemy upon which Porphyry is commenting (1. 6, Düring 13.14): τὴν αὐτὴν ἀντίληψιν γίνεσθαι ταῖς ἀκοαῖς. In both A18 and this passage of Ptolemy, we have ἀντίληψις in the accusative with γίνεσθαι and a form of ἀκοή in the dative. The remaining language of A18, like the construction with ἀντίληψις, is easily paralleled in Porphyry and Ptolemy (ἑνὸς φθόγγου, κατὰ τὰς συμφωνίας). Thus, A18 would appear to be a report of an earlier Pythagorean view which is expressed almost totally in the language of Porphyry's time.

A19 Boethius, *De Institutione Musica* III. 11 (Friedlein 1867: 285.7–286.19)

Demonstratio Archytae superparticularem in aequa dividi non posse, eiusque reprehensio.

Superparticularis proportio scindi in aequa medio proportionaliter inter- 1
posito numero non potest. Id vero posterius firmiter demonstrabitur. Quam 2

Inscript.] om. g eiusque reprehensio] om. k

enim demonstrationem ponit Archytas, nimium fluxa est. Haec vero est 3
huiusmodi. 4

Sit, inquit, superparticularis proportio · A · B ·, sumo in eadem proportione 5
minimos · C · DE ·. Quoniam igitur sunt minimi in eadem proportione · 6
C · DE· et sunt superparticulares, · DE · numerus · C · numerum parte 7
una sua eiusque transcendit. Sit haec · D ·. Dico quoniam · D · non erit 8
numerus, sed unitas. Si enim est numerus · D · et pars est eius, qui est · 9
DE ·, metitur · D · numerus · DE · numerum; quocirca et · E · numerum 10
metietur, quo fit, ut · C · quoque metiatur. Utrumque igitur · C · et · 11
DE · numeros metietur · D · numerus, quod est inpossibile. Qui enim 12
sunt minimi in eadem proportione quibuslibet aliis numeris, hi primi ad se 13
invicem sunt[, et solam differentiam retinent unitatem]. Unitas igitur est · 14
D ·. Igitur · DE · numerus · C · numerum unitate transcendit. Quocirca 15
nullus incidit medius numerus, qui eam proportionem aequaliter scindat. 16
Quo fit, ut nec inter eos, qui eandem his proportionem tenent, medius 17
possit numerus collocari, qui eandem proportionem aequaliter scindat. 18

Et secundum Archytae quidem rationem idcirco in superparticulari nul- 19
lus medius terminus cadit, qui aequaliter dividat proportionem, quoniam 20
minimi in eadem proportione sola differunt unitate, quasi vero [non] etiam 21
in multiplici proportione minimi eandem unitatis differentiam sortiantur, 22
cum plures videamus esse multiplices praeter eos, qui in radicibus collocati 23
sunt, inter quos medius terminus scindens aequaliter eandem proportionem 24
possit aptari. Sed haec, qui arithmeticos nostros diligenter inspexerit, faci- 25
lius intelligit. Addendum vero est, id ita evenire, ut Archytas putat, in sola 26
superparticulari proportione; non autem universaliter est dicendum. Nunc 27
ad sequentia convertamur. 28

7 superparticulares. DE numerus igitur . . . scribendum?   **14** et solam differentiam retinent
unitatem] del. Tannery   **21** non] delevi   **25** nostros] Bower (mss I, Q)   numeros
Friedlein

Archytas' proof that a superparticular ratio cannot be divided into equal
parts and a critique of it.

A superparticular ratio is not able to be divided into equal parts by a mean
proportional placed between. This indeed will be proved securely later. For
the proof which Archytas puts forth is too loose. At any rate, his proof is
of the following sort:

Let there be, he says, a superparticular ratio A:B. I take C:D + E as the least
numbers in the same ratio. Therefore, since C:D + E are the least numbers

in the same ratio and are superparticulars, the number D + E exceeds the number C by one of its own parts and by a part of C. Let this be D. I say that D will not be a number but a unit. For, if D is a number and is a part of D + E, the number D measures the number D + E, wherefore it will also measure the number E, by which it comes about that it also measures C. Therefore, the number D will measure both the numbers C and D + E, which is impossible. For those numbers which are the least in the same ratio to any other numbers whatever are prime to one another [and retain only the unit as a difference]. Therefore, D is a unit. Therefore, the number D + E exceeds the number C by a unit. Wherefore, no number falls in the middle which divides that ratio equally. By which it comes about that, in the case of those numbers which have the same ratio as these, it is also not possible that a number be placed in the middle, which divides the same proportion equally.

And indeed, according to the reasoning of Archytas, it is for this reason that no term, which equally divides the ratio, falls in the middle of a superparticular ratio, namely that the least numbers in the same ratio differ by a unit alone, as if indeed the least numbers in a multiple ratio [did not] also have allotted to them the same difference of a unit, although we see more multiple ratios besides those which are grounded in roots, in which a middle term can be fit, which divides the same proportion equally. But one who has examined my arithmetical books diligently understands this very easily. It must be added that it does turn out in the way Archytas thinks in the superparticular ratio alone; however, it must not be asserted universally. Now let us turn to what follows.

Authenticity

Since we are dealing with Boethius' Latin translation of a Greek original, it is obvious that this text cannot be treated as a literal fragment of Archytas. Further, Boethius is, in general, a careful translator but sees it as within his goals to expand and compress appropriately the text with which he is dealing (see below), so that it is possible that he has modified the text somewhat in translation. Again, the Greek text as it appeared in Boethius' source, Nicomachus (see below), had undoubtedly been the subject of glosses and commentary that may have led to changes in the text itself. Most scholars have seen little reason to doubt, however, that the Greek text which Boethius translates was ultimately based on authentic work of Archytas rather than on a forged text. Several features of the proof fit very well with what we do know about Archytas and the development of mathematics in the fourth century: (1) It is highly relevant to the well-attested interests of Archytas in music theory (Fr. 1, A16) and continued proportion (A14). (2) If the *Sectio Canonis* is by Euclid (ca. 300 BC), the proof in A19 must roughly date to the fourth century, during the first part of which Archytas was active (400–350), because it is quite similar to but not as developed as Proposition 3 of the *Sectio Canonis* (Barbera 1991 is skeptical of Euclidean authorship; Barker 1989: 190 accepts it). Most importantly, it is not very plausible to suppose that a forger would construct such a difficult mathematical proof on such a technical topic. As Tannery noted, "La particularité de cette proposition est une garantie évidente de son ancienneté" (1905: 246).

Boethius' source

Before it is possible to evaluate the source for this passage in Boethius' *De Institutione Musica*, it is necessary to examine the general characteristics of his mathematical works. These mathematical works are largely translations or paraphrases of earlier Greek works, along with further explanation and examples for clarification. In the case of his *De Institutione Arithmetica,* the Greek text that Boethius (AD 480–524) follows is Nicomachus' *Introduction to Arithmetic* (ca. AD 100), which is extant, so that, in this case, we can carefully study Boethius' practice in dealing with the text he translates. In the preface to his *De Institutione Arithmetica,* Boethius himself comments on his method (*Praef.* 4.27–5.4). He says that he adheres "to a rather strict rule of translation, but not slavishly to the precepts of another author" (tr. Bower 1989: xxv). When he diverges from the original, he says that he concentrates on the path not the footprints of the author. On matters that Nicomachus treated expansively, he has in some cases been brief and, on the other hand, where Nicomachus hurries through things, he has expanded. Study of Boethius' *De Institutione Arithmetica* generally confirms this description of his method. It appears that Boethius never added "anything essential, either original or derived from other sources, that departs from his model" and "there is little indication that Boethius used any other sources than the *Introduction* [of Nicomachus] itself" (F. E. Robbins in D'Ooge et al. 1926: 132). Boethius does leave some things out, e.g. Nicomachus' quotation of Archytas Fr. 1 in 1. 3, and adds an occasional chapter that is not found in Nicomachus. But, in general, he follows Nicomachus closely and in sequence. Two final peculiarities of his practice are worth emphasizing (Bower 1978: 4). First, when he quotes another author, the quotation is usually derived from Nicomachus. Second, apart from the reference to following Nicomachus in the preface, he never indicates that what he is doing is, in fact, translating Nicomachus' work.

What then can be said about Boethius' use of sources in his *De Institutione Musica*, in which Archytas' proof is quoted? What follows relies heavily on the conclusions of Bower (1978). The source for the first four books has not survived. The incomplete Book v is clearly based on Ptolemy's extant *Harmonics*, however, and shows the same practice as in the *De Institutione Arithmetica*: (a) Ptolemy, although quoted a couple of times, is never identified as Boethius' source, (b) the references to other authors which Boethius gives are mostly derived from Ptolemy (the reference to Aristoxenus and the Pythagoreans at v. 4 is the only apparent exception). There is a general consensus that in Books i–iii Boethius is translating and paraphrasing Nicomachus' lost *Introduction to Music* (Bower 1989: xxviii). Since Archytas' proof comes from Book iii and given Boethius' practice of drawing his references to other authors almost exclusively from the source he is translating, it is overwhelmingly likely that he drew Archytas' proof from Nicomachus' *Introduction to Music*.

There is often difficulty in determining which features of the text should be ascribed to Boethius and which to Nicomachus. It has sometimes been assumed that the critical remarks, which both precede and follow the proof, belong to Boethius. This is not certain, however. The "I" or "we" in Boethius can be a translation of Nicomachus' words, and thus the criticisms of Archytas' proofs may belong to Nicomachus and not Boethius (compare *De Inst. Arith.* ii. 42 [p. 138.12–15 Friedlein] with Nicomachus ii. 22 [p. 123. 14 ff. Hoche], and ii. 50 [p. 161.23 Friedlein] with ii. 27 [p. 138.5 ff. Hoche]; Burkert [1972a: 445–46] assumes that the critical remarks belong to Boethius' source.).

Context in Boethius/Nicomachus

Book iii of Boethius begins by arguing, against Aristoxenus, that a superparticular ratio, and hence the tone, cannot be divided into equal parts. The bald assertion that the tone cannot be divided into equal parts appeared already in Book i, Chapter 16, with a promise that the reason would be given later. Book iii fulfills this promise. Indeed, Book iii as a whole is devoted to the discussion of the parts of a tone. Thus, Archytas' demonstration, that a superparticular ratio cannot be divided into equal parts, fits well with the general subject matter of Book iii, in that it can be applied to the tone, which has the superparticular ratio 9:8, in order to show that it cannot be divided equally and hence that there is no true "semitone." Archytas' proof does not fit very well in its immediate context, however. Boethius has been discussing the division of the tone into two unequal parts, the larger is called the apotome and the smaller the minor semitone. The comma is defined as the difference between the apotome and the minor semitone. The tone can thus be said to consist of two minor semitones and a comma (III. 6). Chapter 10, which immediately precedes Archytas' proof, provides "one example for finding the minor semitone." At the end of this example, he points out that two semitones cannot fill a tone and that the interval of a comma remains. The comma is then identified as the smallest interval that the sense of hearing can grasp, and Boethius stresses the need to talk about it. He in fact goes on to do this in Chapter 12, but, before doing so, he abruptly says "but first let an appropriate beginning be taken from here" (*ac primum hinc conveniens sumatur initium*) and proceeds to give Archytas' proof in Chapter 11. After Archytas' proof and the criticism of it, he once again abruptly says, "let us now return to what follows" and returns to the discussion of the comma. This is all very puzzling indeed, because there is no obvious way in which Archytas' proof has anything to do with what Boethius goes on to say about the comma and the proof seems a very "*inconveniens*" preparation for Chapter 12. It must be admitted, however, that the structure of Book III is, on the whole, rather loose. Chapters 1–4 focus on criticism of Aristoxenus, ending with the point that six whole tones exceed the octave by a comma. Chapters 5–8, which discuss pseudo-Philolaus' division of the tone, are only loosely connected to the first four chapters with the words "Indeed, the Pythagorean Philolaus tried to divide the tone in another manner." Chapters 9–10 are again abruptly introduced with the words "But indeed, enough of these things," before turning to determinations of parts of the tone by use of consonances. Thus, it is clear that Boethius, or his model Nicomachus, did not have a tight sequence of topics, although the material was all generally related. Nonetheless, what is unusual about Archytas' proof is that it is not just loosely connected to what precedes and what follows but, in fact, interrupts the discussion about the comma and would fit much better with the refutation of Aristoxenus in Chapters 1–4. The attempt to label the proof as a "suitable introduction" looks like either Boethius' or Nicomachus' rather lame attempt to convince the reader that this proof, which is apparently included because of its intrinsic interest, belongs here rather than with the refutation of Aristoxenus in Chapters 1–4.

Context in Archytas

Boethius/Nicomachus gives no indication of the title of the book from which A19 derives. It seems not implausible that it came from the same work on harmonics of which Fragment 1 is the beginning and which may have included Fragment 2 and the account of the musical genera in A16.

Nature of the argument

It is widely recognized that this proof is very similar to Proposition 3 of Euclid's *Sectio Canonis*. The quality of Archytas' proof has, however, been open to a very wide range of assessments. Before turning to those assessments, it will be helpful to give a detailed commentary on the argument. I will reproduce Andrew Barker's translation of Proposition III of Euclid's *Sectio Canonis* (1989: 195) first, for purposes of comparison.

Euclid, Sectio Canonis

Proposition 3 – In the case of an epimoric interval, no mean number, neither one nor more than one, will fall within it proportionally

```
_____ B (12)

_____      C (9)

D__G_____ E (4)

      _____ F (3)
```

Let BC be an epimoric interval. Let DE and F be the smallest numbers in the same ratio as are B and C. These then are measured only by the unit as a common measure. Take away GE, which is equal to F. Since DE is the epimoric of F, the remainder DG is a common measure of DE and F. DG is therefore a unit. Therefore no mean will fall between DE and F. For the intervening number will be less than DE and greater than F, and will thus divide the unit, which is impossible. Therefore no mean will fall between DE and F. And however many means fall in proportion between the smallest numbers, there will fall in proportion exactly as many between any others which have the same ratio [Eucl. VIII.8]. But none will fall between DE and F; nor will one fall between B and C.

Archytas A19

1. "A superparticular ratio is not able to be divided into equal parts by a mean proportional placed between."

This sentence probably represents Archytas' statement of what is to be proved. That Boethius intended this as a translation of Archytas' words is indicated by the repetition between this statement and the chapter heading (if the chapter headings are the work of Boethius). Since the chapter heading already states the content of the proof, the only reason to repeat it in expanded form, as the first line of the chapter, is to provide a translation of Archytas' actual words. Boethius/Nicomachus then immediately breaks in, in order to comment that a better proof will be supplied later. We can only be sure that the translation is based on Archytas' own words, however, starting with the next step in the proof (line 5), which is introduced with "he says."

Even in the statement of what is to be proved there are important differences from the proof in the *Sectio*. First, in terminology (see Knorr 1975: 219), Euclid consistently talks of the mean "falling within" (ἐμπεσεῖται) both here and in the body of the proof, whereas Archytas describes the ratio as "divided" (*scindi* = a form of τέμνω?) both here and in several places in the proof, although other verbs in Boethius, such as *incidere, interponere,* and *collocari,* suggest that Archytas showed more variety of expression. Second, Euclid refers to an epimoric interval (διάστημα), while Archytas appears to have talked of an epimoric ratio (*proportio* = λόγος). Finally, Euclid's proof refers to one or more means, and is thus more general than Archytas' proof, which refers to only one mean (Knorr 1975: 220).

2. "Let there be, he says, a superparticular ratio A:B. I take C:D + E as the least numbers in the same ratio."

This is unproblematic except that some commentators (e.g Heath 1921: I. 90) describe the superparticular ratio (epimoric in Greek) as a ratio of the form $(n + 1)/n$. This cannot be what is literally meant by superparticular ratio in the first clause here, however, or in the corresponding first step of the *Sectio Canonis,* since $(n + 1)/n$ is already in lowest terms, while both Archytas and Euclid go on to reduce the superparticular ratio to its lowest terms (C:D + E). Archytas is following the ancient definitions of superparticular (see the next step below). Knorr's formulation, "$(A + B)/A$ where B is a proper divisor of A" (1975: 245, n. 1) follows the ancient definitions. Something like Euclid vii. 33, "Given as many numbers as we please, to find the least of those which have the same ratio with them," is assumed in this step by both the *Sectio* and Archytas.

3. "Therefore, since C:D + E are the least numbers in the same ratio and are superparticulars, the number D + E exceeds the number C by one of its own parts and by a part of C."

Archytas is appealing to something like the definition of superparticular that is found in Nicomachus, *Introduction to Arithmetic* I. 19: "the superparticular . . . is a number that contains within itself the whole of the number compared with it, and some one part of it besides." Theon's definition is even clearer: "It is the superparticular ratio, when the greater term contains the less once and some one part of the less, i.e. when the difference between the greater and the less is such as to be a factor of the less" (76.21). Note that both of these definitions and Archytas assume a definition of "part" such as we find at Euclid VII. Def. 3, where a part is a submultiple or a factor. The older commentators (e.g. Heath) describe such a part as an "aliquot part," which is defined as a part "contained in another and dividing it without remainder." Thus, 9:12 is a superparticular ratio because 12 exceeds 9 by 3, which is a factor of 9. In lowest terms 9:12 is 3:4, where 4 exceeds 3 by 1, which is a factor of 3. With these assumptions, Archytas' point is that, if C:D + E is superparticular, then, by definition, D + E will exceed C by a part (or factor) of C. It is also clear that, since by definition D + E is equal to C + a factor of C, the factor of C by which D + E exceeds C will also be a part of D + E.

Burkert (1972a: 445) argues that the words "are the least in the same ratio" appear to serve no function. The second part of the sentence follows from the fact that C:D + E is a superparticular ratio and has nothing to do with C and D + E being the least numbers in the ratio. On this reading, Archytas is careless here and unnecessarily repeats the fact established in the previous sentence, that C and D + E are the least numbers in the ratio. It is also possible, however, that Archytas is striving for formal correctness. The words "are the least in the same ratio" may be intended to pick up the point of the previous sentence and the continuation "and are superparticulars" may in fact hide an inference ("and are *therefore* superparticulars"). This is the point: If C:D + E is in the same ratio as A:B, and A:B are superparticulars, then C:D + E are superparticulars as well. It is just possible to see such a meaning in the text as printed, but it may be that the text should be emended. If we put a full stop after *superparticulares*, the sentence has this meaning with no emendation (*et sunt superparticulares* = "they are also superparticulars"). It seems quite plausible that in transmission the *et* was misunderstood as "and" rather than "also" and that a connective such as *igitur* then was dropped out of the next sentence. Archytas' precision here becomes more significant in light of Knorr's comment that both Archytas' proof and the proof in the *Sectio* have the formal flaw of assuming that the least terms of an epimoric ratio are also epimoric (1975: 218). While Archytas does not fully justify this step (Knorr suggests that a proof would follow from Euclid V. 17), we should see his words as a recognition that he is taking the step rather than follow Burkert in supposing them to be a mistaken repetition.

4. "Let this be D. I say that D will not be a number but a unit."

At this point it becomes clear that, in Archytas' proof, DE is not a line with end points D and E, which is what Euclid means by such a expression. Instead, DE in Archytas' proof means the quantity D + the quantity E.

It has often been assumed that this represents the practice of Archytas'
time which was later changed by Euclid (Knorr 1975: 221, van der Waerden
1947–49: 134, Tannery 1905: 249). As Burkert points out (1972a: 443 n. 94),
however, this practice should in fact be recognized as Boethius', since in
Boethius' translation of Proposition 3 of the *Sectio Canonis* (*Inst. Mus.* IV. 3)
he alters Euclid's usage and adopts the same usage as is found in the proof
assigned to Archytas. Boethius is "modernizing" the notation and it is
consequently impossible to be sure what notation Archytas used.

The distinction between a number and a unit is in accord with Euclid VII,
Definitions 1 and 2, where a unit is "that by virtue of which each of the
things that exist is called one" and a number is "a multitude composed on
units." Thus, for Euclid as well as Archytas, one is not a number. See Heath
1921: 69.

Quoniam, which usually means "because," is here used as "that," in
indirect statement after *dico*. It may represent a translation of the Greek
ὅτι, which has both the meanings "that" and "because" (Burkert 1972a: 445
n. 109).

5. "For, if D is a number and is a part of D + E, the number D measures
the number D + E . . ."

To measure a number means to divide it without remainder, so that it
follows directly from the fact that D is a part (see on 3 above) of D + E
that it measures D + E. Archytas is here beginning a *reductio* to show that
D is a unit, i.e. he has asserted that D is either a number or a unit and
now shows that, if we assume that it is a number, impossible consequences
result, and that therefore it must be a unit. Euclid diverges from Archytas
at this point and does not use a *reductio*. Burkert argues that Archytas' use
of the *reductio* is "basically superfluous repetition" (1972a: 445), which is
"made necessary by his view that one is not a number." As we have seen
above, however, Euclid shares Archytas' belief that one is not a number, so
that the *reductio* cannot be dictated by this belief.

6. ". . . wherefore it will also measure the number E, by which it comes
about that it also measures C."

Since D is a part of D + E (i.e. a factor of D + E), it must also be a part
of and hence measure E, which is what is left when D is subtracted from
D + E. For, if we take a factor of a number away from a number, the factor
will also be a factor of the remainder. But E is equal to C, so that D will
also measure C.

7. "Therefore, the number D will measure both the numbers C and D + E, which is impossible. For those numbers which are the least in the same ratio to any other numbers whatever are prime to one another [and retain only the unit as a difference]."

This is a direct application of Euclid VII. 22, "the least numbers of those which have the same ratio with them are prime to one another." The text in brackets above should be removed. It is not part of, nor implied by, Euclid VII. 22. Indeed, with the text in brackets the statement is clearly false (e.g. 3:1 are the least numbers in a given ratio and are prime to one another, but their difference is not a unit). Boethius' criticism of the proof focuses on just this point (line 21, *minimi in eadem proportione sola differunt unitate*). His final point (lines 26–28) is that the version of VII. 22 with the words in brackets does hold true for superparticular ratios but should not be asserted as a universal truth.

His earlier words (lines 20–26) are less clear. If we keep the manuscript text, he seems to be saying first that Archytas is acting "as if . . . the least terms in multiple proportion were also not allotted the same difference of unity" and then pointing out there are very many multiple ratios in which a middle term can be fit (e.g. 16:4 is in the ratio 4:1 and between 16 and 4 we can place the mean proportional 8 so that 16:8 is as 8:4). This is a puzzling argument that seems to say: although Archytas overlooks it, the least terms in multiple ratios also differ by 1 (in fact the only multiple ratio that differs by 1 in least terms is 2:1), which is then in conflict with the fact that many multiple ratios which are not in their least terms (*radicibus* – see below) can be divided by a mean proportional. This understanding of Boethius' words in lines 20–26 would indicate that Boethius himself is rather muddled about multiple proportions, in suggesting that many of them in least terms differ only by the unit. Worst of all, Boethius would directly contradict his own assertion in lines 26–28 that Archytas did apply the principle, that ratios in their lowest form differ by a unit, universally (i.e. to all types of proportion including the multiple proportion). I would accordingly suggest that the *non* in line 21 should be removed. Then in lines 21–25 Boethius is asserting that Archytas is acting as if the least numbers in multiple proportion also have the difference of a unit, which agrees with his assertion in lines 26–28 that Archytas applied the principle universally. On this reading, Boethius goes on to point out that many multiple ratios which are not in least terms can be divided by a mean proportional, although Archytas' assumption that in least terms they differ by a unit would make this impossible. The *non* would have come into the text through the work of a commentator or copyist, who was trying to make sense of this complicated criticism of Archytas and misunderstood the point, perhaps thinking of the fact that the multiple ratio 2:1 does have a difference of one. (In the passage discussed above, Boethius uses the phrase "multiple ratios besides those which are grounded in roots" (*radicibus* – line 23). These roots are the multiple ratios in their lowest terms 2:1, 3:1, etc. Nicomachus' term is πυθμένες (Burkert 1972a: 446). Knorr argues that roots (*radices*) refer to surds (1975: 222), but Boethius' use of the term elsewhere makes clear that it refers to ratios in their lowest terms. See *Inst. Arith.* I. 20 and *Nicom.* I. 21 and see *Inst. Mus.* II. 8 for a clear definition of *radices*.)

　　But let us turn from Boethius' criticism of the argument to the words that I think should be bracketed in his translation of the argument. Boethius clearly wrote the words in brackets, since they are the focus of his criticism, and he must have translated them from his Greek original (probably Nicomachus' *Introduction to Music*). Therefore, what reasonable grounds do we have for excluding them from the text of Archytas' proof? Burkert argues that "athetesis is no suitable way to get rid of the problem." To remove the words is "to create the illusion of a perfect mathematical clarity and obstruct our view of a mathematics still feeling its way along an uncertain path" (1972a: 446). Burkert is right that we run the danger of presenting a false picture of Archytas' mathematical sophistication, if we remove the words arbitrarily in order to free Archytas from Boethius' criticism. There are, however, more fundamental reasons for regarding the words as an interpolation than the problems raised by Boethius' remarks. Most importantly, keeping the words in the text makes nonsense of Archytas' *reductio* proof. If Archytas could assume the proposition in lines 12–14, including the words in brackets, then all that would have been necessary would have been to quote this full proposition at step 3 above and no *reductio* proof would have been needed. The crucial point that the difference between C and D + E is a unit would have been established. If we keep the bracketed words in the text, we must first assume that Archytas was sophisticated enough to construct a *reductio* proof and then unsophisticated enough to state, as the last step of the proof, a proposition, which is not only false but that completely obviates the need for the proof. I submit that it is much more plausible to assume that the words *et solam differentiam retinent unitatem* are a gloss on a difficult argument, which became incorporated into the text. The words are in fact a statement of the crucial point that both Archytas and Euclid are trying to establish at this stage of the argument and could well have been written in the margin by a commentator. The incorporation into the text must have occurred in the transmission of the Greek text that Boethius translates. (Tannery, without detailed explanation, also assumes

that the words were a gloss in the text that Boethius translated [1905: 248].
Burkert [1972a: 445 n. 113] oddly says that Tannery supposed that the words
in question were an interpolation by Boethius himself, but what Tannery
says is "Évidemment, Boethius n' avait pas sous les yeux un texte exempt
d' interpolations.")

In fact, all three logical possibilities for dealing with the inconsistency
between the bracketed words and the rest of the sentence are represented in
the scholarship. The first possibility is to keep the sentence as it is and see
the inconsistency as an indication of Archytas' confusion. This is Burkert's
approach, which must be rejected for the reasons that I have given above.
We then have the option of getting rid of one or the other of the conflicting
assertions. Knorr (1975: 218) sees the conflict but rejects the statement of
Euclid VII. 22 in the first part of the sentence as an interpolation, while
keeping the words in brackets. He does not recognize the other alternative
of eliminating the words that I have bracketed. One might concede that
it is just as likely that a commentator wrote a statement of VII. 22 in the
margin at this point as that a commentator wrote the bracketed words in
the margin. However, whereas the bracketed words can be inserted into
the text with, at most, the addition of an *et*, Knorr's suggestion requires
much more radical surgery on the text, a point that is obscured by the
fact that Knorr only discusses the interpolation in terms of the English
translation. In line 12 *qui* will have to be removed and *enim* moved later in
the sentence. Then in line 14 *igitur* will need to be inserted after *et*. Thus,
in terms of the mechanics of textual transmission, it is much less likely
that VII. 22 was inserted into the text than the words I have bracketed. The
even stronger reason for rejecting Knorr's suggestion is that it again makes
Archytas' *reductio* totally superfluous. In Knorr's version the sentence reads
"For they are the least in the same ratio and thus have unity as the sole
difference." If Archytas could conclude from the fact that C and DE are
the least in the same ratio that they have the unit as the sole difference,
then this should have been stated immediately after step two (where C and
D + E are said to be least in the same ratio) and no *reductio* is needed.
The only suggestion that both eliminates the incoherence in the sentence
in lines 12–14 and leaves a purpose for the *reductio* proof is to exclude the
words in brackets.

8. "Therefore D is a unit. Therefore the number D + E exceeds the number
C by a unit."

This is the end of the indirect proof. Step 4 asserts that D is either a
number or a unit. Steps 5–7 show that, if we assume that D is a number,
impossible results follow, so D must be a unit. Although many scholars,

starting with Tannery (1905: 247; cf. Barker 1989: 195; Barbera 1991: 58), have regarded both Archytas' proof and the *Sectio*'s proof as sound and essentially equivalent to each other, a number of others have suggested that Archytas' *reductio* argument shows him to be a confused and inferior thinker. Burkert (1972a: 445) calls the *reductio* "superfluous repetition" and van der Waerden (1963: 153) complains of Archytas' prolixity and says that "it looks as if he is afraid of stumbling on the slippery paths of logic."

In fact, there seems to be no reason to prefer one of these two forms of proof to the other (i.e. the *Sectio*'s direct proof and Archytas' *reductio*). They are simply two ways of making the same point (i.e. that DE exceeds C by a unit) and they rely on very similar assumptions. The *Sectio* (1) implicitly applies VII. 22 ("the least numbers of those which have the same ratio with them are prime to one another") and the definition of prime number ("that which is measured by an unit alone" VII. Def. 11) at the beginning, in order to show that the smallest numbers in the ratio only have the unit as a common measure; (2) then subtracts the smaller number from the larger (shorter line from the longer), in order to obtain the difference between the two; (3) then applies the definition of superparticular to show that this difference is a common measure; (4) concludes, by appealing to the first step, that the difference must be a unit. Archytas starts by applying the definition of the superparticular, in order to establish that the difference between the two least numbers in the ratio is a part of both of those numbers. This is equivalent to the *Sectio*'s use of the definition in step 3, except that Archytas states the point in terms of "parts," which suggests that he may have been working with a definition like Theon's quoted above, which differed from a definition in terms of common measure used by the *Sectio*. Archytas' first step also takes the place of step 2 in the *Sectio*, where the shorter line is subtracted from the longer. Next, Archytas sets up the *reductio*, in order to show that this difference is a unit. He then asserts that, if we assume that it is a number, then, since it has been shown to be a part of both the numbers in least ratio, it will measure both of them. In essence, a definition of "part" such as is found at Euclid VII. 3 ("A number is a part of a number, the less of the greater, when it measures the greater") is being applied here. This step can be seen as a restatement of the first step above but in terms of measuring, which is the proper terminology for the appeal to primes in the last step. The last step asserts that we have reached an impossible result by a direct quotation of Euclid VII. 22, and an implicit appeal to a definition of numbers prime to one another. The proof in the *Sectio* appealed to VII. 22 and the definition of prime numbers in its first step, but does not explicitly quote VII. 22 as Archytas does.

There is no reason to prefer one of these approaches to the other or to see either author as unnaturally afraid of the "slippery slopes of logic." Archytas in fact seems to be slightly more rigorous. Both authors appeal to essentially the same mathematical propositions and definitions in this section of the proof. Archytas does use one extra step that moves from the definition of superparticular in terms of parts to the definition of prime in terms of measuring. This might reflect a difference in the form of the definitions of these terms to which Archytas and the *Sectio* are respectively referring. It may well be, however, that the *Sectio* is eliding a step and that Archytas is being more rigorous. The same concern for rigor can be seen in Archytas' explicit quotation of the proposition equivalent to VII. 22.

9. "Wherefore, no number falls in the middle which divides that ratio equally."

Because the difference between C and D + E (i.e. D) is a unit, no other whole number can fall between C and D + E which would divide them ("for there is no integer intervening" Heath [1921: 215]). Whereas Archytas was somewhat fuller than the *Sectio Canonis* in his presentation of the argument in steps 3–7 above, he is briefer on this point. The *Sectio* more formally says that any intervening number would have to be more than C and less than D + E and thus divide the unit, which is impossible.

10. "By which it comes about that, in the case of those numbers which have the same ratio as these, it is also not possible that a number be placed in the middle which divides the same proportion equally."

This makes clear that the goal of the proof is to show that there is no mean proportional between numbers which are superparticular in the full sense of the definitions given by Nicomachus and Theon. In the case of numbers of the form $(n + 1)/n$ (e.g. 4:3), it might appear obvious that there could be no mean proportional and Euclid VII. 22 would do all of the work. In the case of numbers like 12:9, however, it is not clear at first sight that there is no mean proportional, and one of the proof's functions is to deal with such cases.

This final step relies on Euclid, *Elements* VIII. 8, which says that "If between two numbers there fall numbers in continued proportion with them, then however many numbers fall between them in continued proportion, so many will also fall in continued proportion between the numbers which have the same ratio with the original numbers." Even this proposition cannot be applied directly, because it assumes that there are some numbers that "fall between," whereas in this case there are none. An argument can be developed to show that we are dealing with a special case of VIII. 8 (Knorr 1975: 214). Hence we can conclude that, since C:D + E has no mean proportional, neither will A:B. The *Sectio Canonis* also makes use of Euclid VIII. 8 at this point without developing the special case. While the *Sectio* states this proposition clearly and then states the conclusion, Archytas gives the conclusion without formally stating anything like Euclid VIII. 8. The failure to state the needed proposition in full form suggests that Archytas did not know of a formal statement of it and that there was no equivalent to Book VIII of Euclid available to him. It may be that Archytas regarded the last step as obvious and did not see the need for a proposition like VIII. 8; what is "obvious" varies greatly with the context in which a mathematician is working. The *Sectio*'s improved proof is an improvement precisely because it recognizes that the step is not obvious and needs further justification.

Final assessment of the argument

Boethius' (or Nicomachus') criticism that Archytas' argument is "too loose" should not be taken as very damning, given that the argument that is preferred, the argument from the *Sectio Canonis* which Boethius translates at *Inst. Mus.* IV.2, is so similar to Archytas' proof. The latest analysis of the *Sectio Canonis* leaves the issue of date and authorship unsettled (Barbera 1991: 35–36), but if it is indeed by Euclid and hence was written around 300 BC (Barker 1989: 190), it is clear that Euclid's proof is derived from that of Archytas. Boethius' criticism of looseness is based on the words which I have bracketed in the text (line 14) and, once it is recognized that those words must be an interpolation in the text that Boethius translated, his criticism loses some of its force, although the weakness in the final step of Archytas' argument could justly be described as "looseness." Given the inability of Archytas to refer to something like Euclid VIII. 8 in the last step of the argument, we must also agree with Burkert (1972a: 446) that "the perfection of the Euclidean form had not yet been reached" and that the proof in the *Sectio* is an improvement on that of Archytas. This is not particularly surprising, given that Archytas was writing in the first half of the fourth century and Euclid 50–100 years later, at the end of a century full of important mathematical work by figures like Eudoxus. We should not follow Burkert, however, in describing the *Sectio*'s proof as "a basic improvement." The analysis of Archytas' argument that I have given above clearly shows that Burkert presents an unjustifiably negative assessment of Archytas' proof, the only significant weakness of which, relative to the proof in the *Sectio,* is the inability to appeal to something like Euclid VIII. 8.

What more general conclusions can we draw from A19 about Archytas' understanding of the nature of mathematical proof and about the state of development of the mathematics of his day? Burkert argues that to reconstruct the state of Greek arithmetic in Archytas' day by showing what propositions Archytas must have been presupposing in his proof illicitly assumes that "Archytas built up a complete theory of number, in accordance with the demands of Euclidean precision" (1972a: 444). This is a just warning. We should not introduce assumptions about Archytas' attitudes to mathematical precision into our analysis of the proof in A19 but should rather use A19 to determine what Archytas' attitudes were. However, we must not ignore what A19 does tell us. As Burkert himself recognizes, A19 presents a formal deductive proof: "the structure follows the conventional order: statement of what is 'given', statement of theorem, proof; and the method of proof is the *reductio ad absurdum*" (1972a: 443). Moreover, as I have shown above, Archytas, far from being repetitive and sloppy in the ways Burkert had supposed, shows great concern for rigor and precision. This level of attention to the demands of rigorous proof surely presupposes some sort of *Elements of Arithmetic*. Otherwise Archytas' proof becomes just a list of assertions for which no support can be given and why, in such circumstances, would he present all the other trappings of rigor? Of course it is impossible to prove that Archytas was appealing to a full deductive grounding for his proof, as long as we do not have direct evidence for an *Elements of Arithmetic* upon which he is drawing. Nonetheless, it is hypercritical to suppose that all the machinery of the deductive proof is deployed, including the explicit quotation of an auxiliary theorem, by someone who nonetheless did not understand the demands of a deductive system. We should be cautious of making too grand claims about the nature of the elements of arithmetic supposed by Archytas, but to deny that something like them existed is to ignore willfully the most obvious interpretation of A19.

The problem is that we have no way of knowing what level of development such an *Elements* had achieved nor who was responsible for it. On the one hand, it surely goes beyond our evidence to conclude with van der Waerden that the Seventh Book of Euclid's *Elements* had already been completed, in essentially the form in which we have it, by Archytas' Pythagorean predecessors (1963: 114–15). The fact that Book VII preserves some archaic features, as van der Waerden argues, cannot prove that the book, in precisely this form, existed before Archytas. There are simply too many different ways to explain its origin. Euclid may have contributed relatively little to its form, but it still could, in its present form, have been pulled together after Archytas (Knorr [1975: 244] argues that it is the work of Theaetetus). What seems undeniable is that the quotation of a proposition equivalent to VII. 22, along with the other implicit appeals to propositions (VII. 33) and definitions (superparticular ratio, prime number), in the context of a rigorous proof, implies the existence of an *Elements of Arithmetic*, whether it was the work of Archytas himself, or his predecessors, Pythagorean or otherwise.

Van der Waerden (1963: 152–55) advanced a view of Archytas' "style" and his contribution to fourth-century mathematics which has had considerable influence (e.g. Knorr 1975: 211–44, especially note 23). According to van der Waerden, Archytas' style is characterized by being unclear, prolix and illogical. Is he justified is describing Archytas' style in this way? He advances four pieces of evidence: (1) In Fragment 1, Archytas' writing style is unclear and prolix. (2) In Fragment 1, Archytas' theory of pitch is wrong and illogical. (3) The proof in A19 shows Archytas struggling with "the slippery paths of logic." (4) He makes an essential logical error in the foundations of his theory of music (this is a reference to the logical error in Proposition 11 of the *Sectio Canonis*; see van der Waerden 1943: 169). Point one is largely subjective and no extended discussion is given to support it. Moreover, I have shown that the text of Fragment 1 as printed in DK, which van der Waerden was using, is seriously defective and the corrected text may be less open to his charges. While it is certainly true that nothing in Fragment 1 suggests that Archytas had Plato's genius as a writer, there is no reason to see him as particularly unclear or prolix, especially in comparison with the later Presocratics, such as Anaxagoras and Democritus. Secondly, while Archytas is wrong in his theory of pitch, this is no basis on which to convict him of being an "illogical thinker." Most ancient writers were wrong in their accounts of the natural world. In this case Plato adopted the same view of pitch as Archytas, so the same argument would brand Plato as an illogical thinker. The third point is again subjective. Van der Waerden admits that there is no logical flaw in the proof in A19 but just asserts that "it looks as if he is afraid of stumbling." My analysis of A19 shows that Archytas was not preternaturally afraid of the paths of logic.

Van der Waerden's fourth point is the most problematic of all. There is an undeniable logical error in Proposition 11 of the *Sectio Canonis* (Barker 1981). There is no good reason, however, to think that the *Sectio Canonis* as a whole or this proposition in particular was the work of Archytas. Van der Waerden's argument for assigning the *Sectio* as a whole to Archytas is very tenuous. He argues that, since Proposition 3, which is a development of Archytas' proof in A19, is an important foundation for the rest of the work, we must conclude that the rest of the *Sectio* is the work of Archytas or his followers (1943: 169–70). This goes far beyond what we can prudently conclude on the basis of the evidence, i.e that the writer of the *Sectio* was clearly influenced by Archytas in Proposition 3. Certainly no ancient source ever ascribed the *Sectio* to Archytas. Moreover, the preponderance of evidence rather suggests that Archytas could not have been the author of the *Sectio*. While Proposition 3 and a passage in the preface to the *Sectio* do show similarities to Archytas A19 and Fr. 1 respectively, the theory of pitch developed in that same preface is significantly different from Archytas' theory in Fragment 1, and the analysis of the diatonic and enharmonic genera in the *Sectio* again are different from those of Archytas (A16; for further differences between Archytas and the *Sectio* see Bowen 1991b). Given these fundamental differences between Archytas and the *Sectio*, it is surely more reasonable to conclude that its author was not Archytas but rather someone else, probably Euclid, who drew on Archytas' writings in a few areas. We have no reliable basis on which to assign any parts of the *Sectio* to Archytas' influence besides Proposition 3 and a few sentences of the introduction.

It should thus be clear that van der Waerden's analysis of the "style" of Archytas has a very weak foundation. Yet that foundation is made to carry even more weight, for van der Waerden argues, largely on the basis of this analysis of Archytas' style, that Book VIII of the *Elements* also is the work of Archytas. His conclusions about Book VIII are (1) that it "is put together in a confused and disorderly manner," (2) that it is "as if the author were constantly fluttering about the problem," (3) that "there are extraordinary logical errors." Whether this analysis of Book VIII of Euclid's *Elements* is valid or not, these characteristics are hardly precise enough to allow ascription of the book to any specific author, let alone Archytas. Van der Waerden's subsidiary points are no stronger. His first point is that "the beginning of Book VIII is very closely related to Archytas' music theory, but this point in turn is based on van der Waerden's assertion that Archytas quotes VIII. 8 in A19. As we have seen above, however, this is precisely what Archytas does not do. He clearly needs something like VIII. 8 at the end of the proof but is unable to quote it, which suggests that it was not available to him. The second point, that VIII. 7 is equivalent to another proposition in the *Sectio*, relies again on the mistaken assumption that Archytas is the author of the *Sectio*. His third point is that Plato quotes a number of propositions and concepts from Book VIII and that, since Plato learned his theory of numbers from Archytas, Archytas must have written Book VIII. The second premise in this argument is very suspect. We have no convincing evidence that Plato learned his theory of numbers from Archytas (Knorr [1975: 89] argues that Theodorus was Plato's main teacher in this area).

Thus, van der Waerden's characterization of Archytas' work in mathematics as well as his ascription of Book VIII of Euclid's *Elements* and the *Sectio Canonis* to Archytas is based on very doubtful premises and inferences. It should therefore be rejected. Knorr's conclusion (1975: 244) that "the organization of Book VIII and the *Sectio Canonis* is the work of Archytas and his followers" seems to have been developed under the influence of van der Waerden, although he differs on some details. The only new argument that Knorr provides to show that Archytas is responsible for Book VIII and the *Sectio* is that, since Proclus associated Archytas with systematization of mathematical theorems, "we may accept that Archytas participated in this arithmetic work [i.e. *Elements* VIII]" (1975: 224). Obviously Proclus' remark does not help us identify any specific group of theorems as belonging to Archytas, however, and Knorr's conclusion that the theorems in question are in fact *Elements* Book VIII outruns the evidence.

The proof in A19 shows that Archytas understood the demands of a rigorous deductive proof and was not just "feeling his way." It is likely that Books VII and VIII of Euclid's *Elements* and Euclid's *Sectio Canonis* were the end result of much work throughout the fourth century and should not be assigned to Archytas or his predecessors. On the other hand, a collection of theorems and definitions that dealt with central ideas which are later found in Book VII of Euclid's *Elements*, even if in a somewhat different form than we find them in Euclid (see the overview of Archytas' philosophy), is clearly presupposed by Archytas' proof.

A19a Theon of Smyrna, *Mathematics Useful for Reading Plato* (Hiller 1878: 60.16–61.23)

τῶν δὲ φωνῶν αἱ μὲν ὀξεῖαι, αἱ δὲ βαρεῖαι, διὸ καὶ τῶν φθόγγων, <ὧν>   1
ὁ μὲν ὀξὺς ταχύς ἐστιν, ὁ δὲ βαρὺς βραδύς. εἰ γοῦν εἰς δύο ἰσοπαχεῖς   2
καὶ ἰσοκοίλους <καλάμους> τετρημένους εἰς σύριγγος τρόπον, ὧν τοῦ   3
ἑτέρου διπλάσιόν ἐστι τὸ μῆκος τοῦ ἑτέρου, ἐμφυσήσαι τις, ἀνακλᾶ-   4
ται τὸ πνεῦμα τὸ ἐκ τοῦ ἡμίσεος μήκους διπλασίῳ τάχει χρώμενον, καὶ   5
<γίνεται> συμφωνία ἡ διὰ πασῶν βαρέος μὲν φθόγγου τοῦ διὰ τοῦ μεί-   6
ζονος, ὀξέος δὲ τοῦ διὰ τοῦ ἐλάττονος. αἴτιον δὲ τάχος τε καὶ βραδυτὴς   7
τῆς φορᾶς. καὶ κατὰ τὰ ἀποστήματα δὲ τῶν ἐν τοῖς αὐλοῖς τρημάτων   8

1 <ὧν>] Hiller   3 <καλάμους>] scripsi <αὐλούς> Hiller   6 <γίνεται>] Hiller

τὰς συμφωνίας ἀπεδίδοσαν καὶ ἐπὶ ἑνός. διχῇ μὲν γὰρ διῃρημένου καὶ   9
τοῦ αὐλοῦ ὅλου ἐμφυσηθέντος ἐκ τοῦ κατὰ τὸ ἥμισυ τρήματος τὸ διὰ   10
πασῶν σύμφωνον ἀποτελεῖται. τριχῇ δὲ διαιρεθέντος καὶ τῶν μὲν δυεῖν   11
μερῶν ὄντων πρὸς τῇ γλωσσίδι, κάτω δὲ τοῦ ἑνός, καὶ τοῦ ὅλου συμ-   12
φυσηθέντος τοῖς δυσί, τὴν διὰ πέντε γενέσθαι συμφωνίαν. τεσσάρων   13
δὲ διαιρέσεων γενομένων, τριῶν μὲν ἄνω, κάτω δὲ μιᾶς, καὶ τῷ ὅλῳ   14
συμφυσηθέντων τῶν τριῶν γίνεται ἡ διὰ τεσσάρων.   15
   οἱ δὲ περὶ Εὔδοξον καὶ Ἀρχύταν τὸν λόγον τῶν συμφωνιῶν ἐν   16
ἀριθμοῖς ᾤοντο εἶναι, ὁμολογοῦντες καὶ αὐτοὶ ἐν κινήσεσιν εἶναι τοὺς   17
λόγους καὶ τὴν μὲν ταχεῖαν κίνησιν ὀξεῖαν εἶναι ἅτε πλήττουσαν   18
συνεχὲς καὶ ὠκύτερον κεντοῦσαν τὸν ἀέρα, τὴν δὲ βραδεῖαν βαρεῖαν   19
ἅτε νωθεστέραν οὖσαν.   20
   ταυτὶ μὲν περὶ τῆς εὑρέσεως τῶν συμφωνιῶν· ἐπανέλθωμεν δὲ ἐπὶ τὰ   21
ὑπὸ τοῦ Ἀδράστου παραδεδομένα.   22

13 συμφωνίαν] scr. aut συμβαίνει aut συμφωνίαν <συμβαίνει> Hiller

Some sounds are high pitched, and some low pitched, therefore the same is true of notes, of which the high pitched is fast, and the low pitched, slow. At least if one blows into two [reeds] of equal thickness and equal bore, drilled in the manner of a syrinx, of which the length of one is double the other, the breath is reflected from the half distance with double the speed, and the concord of the octave arises between the lower note, which passes through the greater distance, and the higher which passes through the lesser distance. The cause is the swiftness and slowness of the motion. And they displayed the concords even on one [reed], in accordance with the spacings of the finger-holes on *auloi*. For if one blows in the *aulos* divided in half and in the whole *aulos*, the concord of the octave is produced from the hole at the half way point. If it is divided in three parts, with two parts toward the mouthpiece and one part below, and the whole has been blown with the two parts, the concord of the fifth arises. And if a fourfold division has been made, three above and one below, and the three have been blown together with the whole, the fourth arises.

Eudoxus and Archytas and their followers thought that the ratio of concords was in numbers, agreeing themselves too that the ratios are in movements and that the swift movement is high pitched, since it strikes the air continuously and pricks the air more swiftly, but the slow is low-pitched, since it is more sluggish.

So much concerning the discovery of the concords. Let us go back to the things that have been handed down by Adrastus.

Authenticity

As I will argue below, this testimonium is ultimately derived from Fragment 1 of Archytas. Since Fragment 1 is authentic, it follows that the information presented in this testimonium is based on an authentic source, although this core of genuine tradition appears to have been reworked to a certain extent in the light of the later tradition.

Context

This testimonium comes from Theon of Smyrna's (fl. ca. AD 115–40) *Mathematics Useful for Reading Plato*. Theon evidently (1.15) provided introductions to all five mathematical sciences identified by Plato in the *Republic*, but all that survives are the sections on number theory, music (divided into sections on harmony that is perceptible in instruments and harmony that is intelligible in numbers [47.7–8]), and astronomy. Testimonium A19a comes from the section on "harmony as perceptible in instruments" (47.18–72.20), which is seen as a necessary propaideutic study for understanding "harmony as intelligible in numbers." Through most of this section, Theon is borrowing heavily from Adrastus' commentary on Plato's *Timaeus* (Barker 1989: 210, Theon 49.6; 61.19; 64.1). Adrastus, who was born in Aphrodisias, seems to have belonged to the generation just before Theon. The testimonium about Archytas, however, is not drawn from Adrastus, since, immediately after he gives that testimonium, Theon says that he is returning to "the things handed down by Adrastus." It is less clear exactly where Theon diverged from Adrastus' account (see Burkert 1972a: 377 n. 36).

Theon's discussion of the discovery of the ratios that correspond to the musical concords (56.9–61.18) ends with Testimonium A19a. There are several very corrupt passages in this material leading up to A19a, and it appears as if Theon is, in some cases, putting two accounts, which deal with the same material but which derive from different sources, side by side. In the first account (56.10–59.3), he identifies Pythagoras as the first to discover the ratios that correspond to the concords; lists the ratios and the corresponding concords; lists, without explanation, a series of ways in which Pythagoras supposedly discovered the ratios (e.g. strings, weights, wind instruments, vessels, discs); demonstrates how the ratios can be determined by using a string stretched over a ruler (a *kanōn*); and finally notes that the ratios for all the primary concords are contained in the Pythagorean *tetraktys* (the numbers 1–4).

From 59.4 to 60.11 Theon provides another account that overlaps considerably with the material just covered. "Some people" are said to derive the concords from weights, magnitudes, movements and numbers, and from vessels. Lasus and Hippasus are then introduced as having followed (?) speeds and slownesses of movements, but, after a corrupt passage, there is no mention of speeds and slownesses but instead an account of the use of vessels to demonstrate the ratios corresponding to the concords. Because of the corruption, it is not clear to whom this experiment with the vessels is attributed. The passage continues with an unnamed "he" who studied the ratios by using two strings rather than one string and ends with another reference to the use of weights and wind instruments.

After another lacuna, Theon says that another unnamed "he" gives a definition of a note as the incidence of the voice on a single pitch (see Barker 1989: 219 n. 41). It is at this point that the focus shifts to the explanation of high and low pitch, which provides the immediate context for Testimonium A19a. Taking the passage as a whole, the first two sections (56.10–59.3; 59.4–60.11) focus on the discovery of the ratios that govern the concords. There is repetition between the two passages, but the first mentions Pythagoras and emphasizes the experiment with the *kanōn*, while the second passage mentions Lasus and Hippasus and emphasizes the experiment with the vessels and the experiment with two strings. Although there was a brief allusion to speeds and slownesses of movement with reference to Lasus and Hippasus (59.9), this is left totally undeveloped, and the topic of high and low pitch is not really pursued until the passage at 60.16 ff., which leads into the reference to Archytas. In general terms, then, the passage suggests the same picture of the development of Pythagorean harmonics as that which derives from our primary sources for early Pythagoreanism, the fragments of Philolaus and Archytas Fragment 1: the ratios that governed the concords were known in the fifth century, but the theory of high and low pitch is developed later and is associated with Archytas. For further arguments that Archytas originated this theory of pitch see the commentary on Fragment 1.

Archytas' acoustic theory in Testimonium A19a

The acoustic theory that is assigned to Eudoxus and Archytas in this testimonium corresponds to the other evidence which we have for Archytas' theory and in particular to what is found in Fragment 1. It appears that this testimonium, including the material in lines 1–15 that precedes the explicit reference to Archytas in line 16, is ultimately based on Fragment 1, although the report has clearly been developed to reflect later work as well. Since the testimonium corresponds so well with the other evidence we have concerning Archytas, there is nothing left in it to assign to Eudoxus as his unique contribution. He seems to function simply as a follower of

Archytas, and perhaps was not even mentioned in the original version of the testimonium (see the note on line 16).

Testimonium A19a makes four basic assertions about Archytas' acoustic theory: (1) the ratio of the concords is in numbers; (2) the ratios are in motions; (3) swift motion is high pitched, because it strikes the air continuously and pricks the air quickly; (4) slow motion is low pitched, since it is more sluggish. The first assertion presumably means that the ratio of concords is in *whole* numbers. This thesis has been the central focus of the whole account of "the discovery of the concords" (line 21), which starts with Pythagoras himself at 56.9 and ends with Archytas, and it is explicitly mentioned in several different places (e.g. 58.14–15). Thus Archytas is being identified as adopting a common view rather than as an innovator on this point. There is no statement of this thesis in Fragment 1 of Archytas, but it is assumed in other testimonia such as A16, where Archytas sets out the ratios of the tetrachords in all three genera.

The second assertion, that the ratios are in motions, presumably means that the numbers which make up the ratios are, in some way, numbers of motions. This thesis is once again not explicitly stated in Fragment 1, but it is clearly implied by the central doctrine of pitch, which is given in assertions 3 and 4 above and which is also found in Fragment 1. If concords are determined by ratios of numbers (assertion 1, e.g. the octave by 2:1), and the difference between the higher and lower notes in a concord is defined in terms of speed of motion (assertions 3 and 4), then it appears to follow that these motions must be expressible in terms of numbers (assertion 2). It may be that Archytas argued explicitly for assertion 2 in the section of his *Harmonics* which immediately followed Fragment 1 (see the commentary on Fragment 1).

Assertions 3 and 4 correspond exactly to what is found in Fragment 1 of Archytas. Moreover the brief supporting arguments given for points 3 and 4 seem to originate in a reading of Fragment 1. The strongest point of connection is between Theon's use of the adjective νωθεστέραν ("sluggish," line 20) in the description of the slow motion that produces a low-pitched sound and Archytas' use of the adverb derived from the same adjective (νωθρῶς Fr. 1) to describe someone moving a stick "sluggishly" and producing a low-pitched sound. The adjective is rare. It appears nowhere else in Theon and only appears in Porphyry in his quotation of Fragment 1 of Archytas. Its appearance in this report of Theon strongly suggests that the report is ultimately based on Archytas Fragment 1. Theon's description of the swift motion as "striking (πλήττουσαν) the air continuously" reminds us of Archytas' emphasis on "impacts" (πληγαί) in Fragment 1 as well as his example of someone waving a stick back and forth; Theon's description of swift motion as pricking (κεντοῦσαν) the air might be inspired by Archytas' use of the image of missiles hurled through the air as a central analogy for the transmission of sound (Fr. 1).

Furthermore, the examples given in lines 1–15, in order to illustrate the thesis that swift motion is high pitched and slow motion is low pitched, even though they precede the explicit mention of Archytas, are closely tied to Fragment 1. In Fragment 1, two of Archytas' most prominent examples are the reed and the *aulos*, which are exactly the two examples found in these lines of Theon. These examples are relatively common in the later tradition as well, so that we might not think that there is a specific connection to Archytas, but some of the details suggest that Archytas is the ultimate source behind Theon's report. In both Theon and Archytas, it is the example of the octave alone that is illustrated with the two reeds, one of which is half of the other (ἐκ τοῦ ἡμίσεος μήκους Theon; τὸ ἥμισυ Archytas Fr. 1). The descriptions of the distances through which the breath has to travel are very similar in the two cases (τὸ πνεῦμα . . . τοῦ διὰ τοῦ μείζονος . . . τοῦ διὰ τοῦ ἐλάττονος, Theon; πνεῦμα διὰ μὲν τῷ μακρῷ . . . διὰ δὲ τῷ μείονος, Archytas).

On the other hand, Theon's presentation clearly reflects a later, more sophisticated, reworking of the material in Fragment 1. For example, Theon emphasizes the necessity of having reeds with equal bore, in order to carry out the experiment, a point on which Archytas is silent. Again, in discussing the *aulos*, Theon considers the case of each of the major concords and gives the specific arrangement of finger holes which produce the concords. In Fragment 1 Archytas simply uses the *aulos* to make the basic point that pitch depends on the speed of the motion and does not discuss specific concords or attempt to quantify the example in any way. In the end, it seems that lines 1–15 of Testimonium A19a, as well as lines 16–20, which are explicitly connected to Archytas, have Archytas Fragment 1 as their distant ancestor. Lines 16–20 are a reasonable summary of Archytas' acoustic theory as found in Fragment 1 and other testimonia but add little that is new.

Detailed commentary

Lines 2–3 ἰσοπαχεῖς καὶ ἰσοκοίλους – ἰσόκοιλος literally means "having an equal cavity," but in the context of a discussion of pipes, is best translated as "of equal bore." The word is rare, and its earliest occurrence is in Plutarch's treatise *On the Generation of the Soul in the Timaeus* (1021a), where it also refers to the use of pipes of equal bore. ἰσοπαχής is a more common word and seems to emphasize "equal thickness" of a solid body such as a string (Nicom. *Harm.* 6), but it can also be applied to something with a hollow center (e.g. a crayfish bowel at Arist. *HA* 527a7). In the context in Theon, its force does not seem to differ radically from ἰσόκοιλος. If it does not refer to the bores of two pipes as being of equal thickness, the only other possibility would seem to be a reference to the walls of the pipes as being of equal thickness, but the thickness of the walls is not relevant. It is perhaps best to understand the passage as first loosely asserting that the pipes are of equal thickness and then adding the unusual adjective ἰσόκοιλος to indicate more specifically that it is "the hollows" in the pipe, the bores, that are equal. It appears that Porphyry is drawing on Theon or the same tradition as Theon in his commentary on Ptolemy 1. 8. In this part of his commentary (119.13 ff.) he uses both of the adjectives used by Theon (ἰσοπαχεῖς καὶ ἰσοκοιλίους) and goes on to use other vocabulary that is similar to Theon's (e.g. εἰς συρίγγων τρόπον; γλωσσιδίων) in discussing the Pythagoreans' use of pipes to demonstrate the ratios of the concords.

3 <καλάμους> – The manuscripts of Theon have not preserved the noun that is modified by "of equal thickness and of equal bore" and "drilled in the fashion of a *syrinx*." Hiller supplied αὐλούς and refers to its use later in the passage (line 8 ἐν τοῖς αὐλοῖς). There are problems, however, with reading αὐλούς. In line 8 we are told that "they displayed the concords even on one (?) in accordance with the spacings of the finger-holes on *auloi*." Once again we are not told "on one what" they displayed the concords, but presumably it must be the same instrument of which two (line 2) were used in the preceding passage. It is, however, very unlikely that the instrument is the *aulos*, since it is being compared to an *aulos* ("in accordance with the spacings of the finger-holes on *auloi*"). The answer may be provided by the parallel passage in Porphyry, to which I refer at the end of the preceding note. Porphyry's description of the experiment is very similar to Theon's, but he says that is was carried out either on bronze *auloi* or on reeds, καλάμους (*In Ptol.* 119.14–15). Since Theon's account sets up a contrast between the *aulos* and some other instrument, it is reasonable to suggest that it is καλάμους rather than αὐλούς which has fallen out of the text in line 3. καλάμους also makes better sense with the expression "drilled in the fashion of a *syrinx*," since reeds were used in making the *syrinx* (Barker 1989: 42 n. 52).

4–5 ἀνακλᾶται – ἀνακλάω means "to bend back." Democritus used ἀνακλάω of an echo (Thphr. *Sens.* 53). I don't understand Barker's translation "burst out" (1989: 219). Since this example mentions two reeds, which are compared to a *syrinx*, we are probably to imagine someone blowing across the opening of two different reeds, one of which is twice the length of the other. This is the way in which a *syrinx* was usually played (Barker 1984: 16). In practice such tuning was done by filling the reeds to different lengths with wax (see the Aristotelian *Problems* xix. 23). The idea seems to be that the air enters the tube, and, being "bent back" by the wax, makes noise as it comes back out of the pipe. The breath that travels into and out of the tube half filled with wax produces a note that is an octave higher than the breath that travels the longer distance into and out of the tube that is twice as long. In lines 8–9 Theon says that the same thing can be shown on just one reed (ἐπὶ ἑνός), if the reed has holes drilled in the side of it like an *aulos* (κατὰ τὰ ἀποστήματα δὲ τῶν ἐν τοῖς αὐλοῖς τρημάτων). This sort of *syrinx* is described in the Aristotelian *Problems* (xix. 23 – see also Barker 1984: 16). Lines 9–15 then transfer the discussion from the reed to the *aulos* proper (line 10 τοῦ αὐλοῦ ὅλου ἐμφυσηθέντος).

16 οἱ δὲ περὶ Εὔδοξον καὶ Ἀρχύταν – "Eudoxus and Archytas and their followers." For this meaning of the phrase οἱ περί, see the commentary on A18, line 8. We have no other evidence for any writings on music by Eudoxus. Lasserre argues that the emphasis in the testimonium is on the role of numbers in defining the concords and suggests that the testimonium is thus more likely to refer to Eudoxus' development of Archytas' theory of means (Iamb. *In Nic.* 101) than to some, otherwise unattested, work on harmonics or acoustics (1966b: 176). It is not accurate, however, to say that the sole emphasis in the testimonium is on the role of numbers in the concords; there is also a clear emphasis on the acoustic thesis that the speed of a motion determines its pitch, and such a thesis would clearly belong in a work on acoustics. But there is no trace of such a work by Eudoxus. Since Diogenes Laertius tells us that Eudoxus was a pupil of Archytas, it is tempting to suppose that the original version of the testimony in A19a simply said "Archytas and his followers . . ." and that a later commentator wrote "Eudoxus" in the margin as an example of one of the followers of Archytas. Eudoxus' name then may have been incorporated into the text by later copyists.

17 ᾤοντο . . . ὁμολογοῦντες καὶ αὐτοί – It is tempting to suppose that the text is confused here. In the first part of the sentence Eudoxus and Archytas are said "to think" that the ratios of concords were in numbers. This is a common thesis that Theon has presented as going back to Pythagoras himself and is not unique to Eudoxus or Archytas. On the other hand

Eudoxus and Archytas are said "to agree" or "concede" that the ratios are in motions and that a swift motion is high pitched. It is just this thesis about pitch, however, that seems to belong to Archytas (see the commentary on Fragment 1). It would make much more sense, if ᾤοντο and ὁμολογοῦν-τες were reversed, so that Eudoxus and Archytas "while agreeing" that the ratios of the concords were in numbers "thought also themselves" (or "for their own part') that the numbers were in motions etc. This would also give a clear force to αὐτοί as identifying what they "themselves" contributed. Perhaps the two verbs could have been switched by a copyist, who was not proceeding word by word but read and then copied down larger parts of sentences, and who could accordingly have reversed the verbs in his mind.

A19b Quintilian, *Training in Oratory* I. 10. 17

Laudem adhuc dicere artis pulcherrimae videor, nondum eam tamen ora- 1
tori coniungere. Transeamus igitur id quoque, quod grammatice quon- 2
dam ac musice iunctae fuerunt: si quidem Archytas atque Evenus etiam 3
subiectam grammaticen musicae putaverunt, et eosdem utriusque rei prae- 4
ceptores fuisse cum Sophron ostendit, mimorum quidem scriptor, sed 5
quem Plato adeo probavit ut suppositos capiti libros eius cum moreretur 6
habuisse credatur, tum Eupolis, apud quem Prodamus et musicen et litteras 7
docet . . . 8

3   Evenus] B   ***nus A   Aristoxenus P   4   subiectam] subiunctam B²

Up to this point I appear to be delivering an encomium of a most glorious art [i.e. music] and nevertheless not yet to be connecting it to the orator. Let us, therefore, cover this point as well: grammar and music were once joined, seeing that Archytas and Evenus thought that grammar was even subordinate to music. That the same people were teachers of both subjects is shown not only by Sophron (who is admittedly a writer of mimes, but Plato admired him to such an extent that he is believed to have had Sophron's books under his pillow when he was dying) but also by Eupolis, in whose writings Prodamus teaches both music and letters . . .

Authenticity
This testimonium is so brief and general that it is very difficult to determine with certainty whether it is based on genuine tradition about Archytas or on something generated in the tradition of pseudo-Pythagorean writings. There is nothing in the content of the testimonium, however, that is in

conflict with the genuine writings of Archytas or that is problematic given Archytas' late fifth- and early fourth-century date.

Context
This testimonium comes from Book I, Chapter 10 of Quintilian's *Institutio Oratoria*. In Book I as a whole, Quintilian is discussing the education of a child, which is preliminary to study with a teacher of rhetoric. In Chapters 4–9, he discusses training in grammar (including literature) and in Chapter 10 turns to the other arts in which pupils ought to be educated: geometry, astronomy and music. Quintilian begins by praising the value of the study of music in sections 9–16, and, in section 17, he points out that the study of literature and the study of music were originally combined as a fundamental part of education by the Greeks. Archytas is then cited as having thought that grammar was even subordinate to music.

Detailed commentary
Line 3 Evenus – This is the reading of B, other manuscripts just have the last three letters of a name (*-nus*), and some give the name as Aristoxenus. Evenus is clearly the *lectio difficilior* and therefore to be preferred; Evenus was a somewhat obscure figure, while Aristoxenus is one of the most famous names in the area of ancient music and is also closely connected to Archytas, as the author of a *Life of Archytas*. Most editors accordingly read Evenus (e.g. Winterbottom, Radermacher), but Wehrli accepted the reading Aristoxenus and prints the testimonium as Fr. 72 of Aristoxenus (1945: 29, 70–71). Evenus of Paros was a sophist, who taught rhetoric around 400 BC and about whom we know very little. Socrates mentions his fee of five minae in the *Apology* (20b). Plato presents him as inquiring about Socrates' writing of poetry in prison (*Phaedo* 60d), and, in the *Phaedrus,* he is said to have written about the art of speaking (267a). Aristotle quotes several lines of his poetry (*Metaph.* 1015a29; *EN* 1152a31). Since he wrote about rhetoric, he might well have been mentioned in the sources upon which Quintilian drew, and it is not at all implausible that Evenus commented on the relation between grammar and music. It is less clear how he came to be connected with Archytas. Aristoxenus in his *Life of Archytas*, however, does present Archytas as confronting ideas associated with other sophists (A9), and it is possible that Aristoxenus also reported some contact between Archytas and Evenus.

4 subiectam grammaticen musicae ("grammar is subject to music") – It is difficult to be sure exactly what view is being ascribed to Archytas

here, because of the ambiguity of the term music. In the preceding pages
Quintilian has been treating music in two of its narrower senses as either
actual musical performance (Orpheus, I. 10.9) or as a branch of mathematics
(I. 10.12–13). On this understanding of music, Archytas would be asserting
that grammar is subject to the science of music, which he treats as one
of four basic sciences (along with astronomy, geometry and arithmetic)
in Fragment 1. Archytas may have thought that all human knowledge fell
under one of these four sciences and that grammar fell under music.

On the other hand, music can also be used as a very general term for all
education that is not physical education. Plato presents this as the traditional
understanding of music at *Republic* 376e, where he says that according to a
long tradition education consists in gymnastics for the body and in music
for the soul (Marrou 1956: 41). The term music here does include the narrow
sense of performance on instruments and with the voice but also includes
the study of literature and poetry, which Quintilian assigns to grammar. If
Archytas is talking about this broad conception of music, then all that is
being assigned to him is the traditional Greek view that music is the most
general term for the education of the soul and that grammar is of course a
part of this. This general sense of music is prominent in the examples which
follow the reference to Archytas in Quintilian. Eupolis is cited as presenting
the same people as teachers of grammar and music, and Aristophanes is said
to have presented children as having studied music from remote antiquity.
Since both of these authors belong to the fifth century, it is overwhelmingly
likely that what is meant is the traditional general understanding of music
alluded to by Plato. If we are to understand Archytas as using music in
this sense, it is more likely that the testimonium derives from something
like Aristoxenus' *Life of Archytas*, than from a technical treatise on music
in the narrower sense such as the *Harmonics*. In the end, since Quintilian
does not disambiguate the two senses of music (Colson 1924: 127 also sees
Quintilian as "confused" about the use of the term "music"), it is impossible
to be certain what view he or his source is assigning to Archytas.

4–5   eosdem . . . Sophron – There is again some ambiguity about what
Quintilian is assigning to Sophron. On one reading, Sophron showed that
"these same people" (i.e. Archytas and Evenus) were teachers of both grammar and music. On another reading, Sophron is making the more general
point that it is the same people (whoever they may be) who are teachers of
both arts. The passage is translated in the former way by Watson (1887),
and such a translation could be supported by the parallelism of the *cum . . .
tum* construction. Since, in the second part of the construction, Eupolis

is said to have named a specific person as a teacher of both arts, it might be natural to suppose that, in the first part of the construction, Sophron is not making an abstract point but rather the concrete point that Archytas and Evenus taught both subjects. On the other hand, for this translation we should have expected some word in the Latin corresponding to "these" in "these same people," and thus it is better to translate in the more general way "the same instructors were employed for the teaching of both" (Butler 1920). Whatever Quintilian intended here, it seems unlikely that Sophron, a contemporary of Socrates, portrayed Archytas in his mimes. Sophron comes from Syracuse, which is not far from Archytas' Tarentum, but Archytas would have been at most thirty when Sophron died (ca. 400 BC – see *RE*) and thus not likely to be famous enough to be portrayed on stage. Moreover, Sophron's mimes focused on stock characters rather than on satire of specific individuals.

A19c ps.-Plutarch, *On Music* 1147a

ἀλλὰ δὴ καὶ τὸ μέγιστον ὑμῖν, ὦ ἑταῖροι, καὶ μάλιστα σεμνοτάτην ἀπο-
φαῖνον μουσικὴν παραλέλειπται. τὴν γὰρ τῶν ὄντων φορὰν καὶ τὴν
τῶν ἀστέρων κίνησιν οἱ περὶ Πυθαγόραν καὶ Ἀρχύταν καὶ Πλάτωνα
καὶ οἱ λοιποὶ τῶν ἀρχαίων φιλοσόφων οὐκ ἄνευ μουσικῆς γίγνεσθαι
καὶ συνεστάναι ἔφασκον. πάντα γὰρ καθ᾽ ἁρμονίαν ὑπὸ τοῦ θεοῦ
κατεσκευάσθαι φασίν.

But indeed, my friends, the greatest indication that music is worthy of the utmost reverence has been omitted. For Pythagoras, Archytas, Plato and their associates as well as the rest of the ancient philosophers used to say that the motion of the universe and the movement of the stars did not arise and become organized without music. For, they say that all things were arranged by god in accordance with harmony.

Authenticity
There is nothing problematic about assigning these doctrines to Archytas. It is quite probable that he did believe that the universe was arranged according to harmony. There is specific evidence in the fragments of Philolaus for this thesis (e.g. Frs. 1, 6 and 6a). Since there is some indication that Archytas followed Philolaus in other respects, it would not be surprising if he also did so here (cf. A22). Fragment 1 of Archytas gives some indication that he accepted the doctrine of the music of the spheres, which is implied by this testimonium.

Context

The *De Musica* is not regarded by most scholars as a genuine work of Plutarch, although it probably dates to Plutarch's time in the first and second centuries AD (Barker 1984: 205). It has the form of a dialogue set at a symposium. The dialogue provides "an historical account of the origin of music, its progress, and its most famous practitioners" as well as "a discussion of the ends that it serves" (Einarson and De Lacy 1967: 345). Most of the material in the dialogue is drawn from fourth-century figures such as Plato and Aristoxenus. Testimonium A19c comes from the penultimate paragraph and makes the crowning point about the value of music: the whole universe is constructed in accordance with musical harmony.

Importance of the testimonium

The testimonium assigns to Archytas the view that the cosmos is structured according to the principles of musical harmony and thus by implication assigns to him the doctrine of the harmony of the spheres. Since there is no direct assertion of these views elsewhere in the fragments and testimonia of Archytas, this testimonium could be important direct confirmation of what we can conclude indirectly about Archytas' views on these issues (see on authenticity above). It is far from clear, however, that this testimonium is based on any texts of Archytas or on any detailed testimonia about his beliefs. Since Archytas is presented in a list of philosophers along with Pythagoras and Plato, it is quite possible that he is simply assumed to have the same views as others in the tradition, starting with Pythagoras, and that nothing in the testimonium is based on specific assertions of Archytas.

CHAPTER V

Metaphysics

A20 Theon of Smyrna, *Mathematics Useful for Reading Plato* (Hiller 1878: 20.19–20)

Ἀρχύτας δὲ καὶ Φιλόλαος ἀδιαφόρως τὸ ἓν καὶ μονάδα καλοῦσι καὶ τὴν μονάδα ἕν.

Archytas and Philolaus call the one also monad and the monad one, without making a distinction.

Authenticity
This testimonium is likely to represent the genuine views of Archytas, because its content differs from the Platonizing tendencies of the pseudo-Pythagorean tradition, in which the monad and the one are carefully distinguished (cf. ps.-Archytas at Thesleff 1965: 47.29–48.1: τὸ ἓν καὶ ἡ μονὰς συγγενῆ ἐόντα διαφέρει ἀλλάλων), and agrees instead with Aristotle's more reliable presentation of the early Pythagoreans (see below).

Context
In this section of *Mathematics Useful for Reading Plato*, Theon (fl. ca. AD 115–40) is presenting a series of views on the relationship between the monad and the one and the ways in which they serve as principles of number. At 19.14 ff., for example, he distinguishes the monad as the principle of "number," which is defined as quantity in the intelligible realm (e.g. the five itself), from the one as the principle of "the numerable," which is defined as quantity in the sensible realm (e.g. five horses). The monad is thus intelligible and indivisible, while the one is bodily and divisible. The general focus of the passage is a discussion of distinctions between the one and the monad as well as distinctions between different senses of each of these individual terms (e.g. the distinction between the monad and the first monad). In the midst of this discussion about the different senses of monad and one, Theon observes that "Archytas and Philolaus call the

one also monad and the monad one, without making any distinction."
The remark is not well integrated into the discussion and Theon does not
explain it further. It looks more like a parenthetical or marginal comment,
which has crept into the text.

Content of the testimonium

This testimonium has a significance that goes beyond the issue of terminology. As the context in Theon makes clear, the terminology ascribed to
Archytas and Philolaus may have important implications for their metaphysics. Distinctions between the one and the monad were developed precisely to distinguish between an intelligible and a sensible realm and the
principles of these realms. Such metaphysical distinctions go back to Plato
and the early Academy. One line of interpretation suggests that Speusippus distinguished the one, as his highest metaphysical principle, from the
monad as the first principle of numbers (Burkert 1972a: 231 relying on
Merlan 1953: 96–128, who argues that Iamblichus, *Comm. Math.* 17.15 is
derived from Speusippus; so also Dillon 1977: 15). Another line of interpretation suggests that Speusippus made no such distinction (Tarán 1981: 36,
86 ff.). In the later pseudo-Pythagorean tradition it is the monad that is the
highest principle, while the one is in the realm of numbers (Burkert 1972a:
57–58). Xenocrates seems to have called his highest principle the monad
rather than the one (Fr. 15). Plato's two highest principles were the one and
the indefinite dyad, but it is not clear whether he made any distinctions
between the one and the monad (Arist. *Metaph.* 987a29 ff.).

If Philolaus and Archytas had distinguished between the one and the
monad, this would clearly suggest a distinction between realms of being
of the sort which was evident in the early Academy. The lack of such a
terminological distinction does not, however, in itself prove that they did
not make the metaphysical distinction. The distinction could have been
developed in different terms. Nonetheless, the context in Theon implies
that he understood their failure to make any distinction between the one
and the monad as indicating that they also made no distinction between the
intelligible and sensible (see Burkert 1972a: 230–31). Such a metaphysical
position matches Aristotle's account of fifth-century Pythagoreanism, in
which Plato differs from the Pythagoreans by introducing separation (i.e.
of the sensible and intelligible, cf. *Metaph.* 987b26). Aristotle provides clear
support for Theon's testimony about terminology, when he reports that the
Pythagoreans called intelligence both monad and one (Fr. 203 = Alex. *in
Metaph.* 39.13–14). It thus seems certain that Philolaus and the fifth-century
Pythagoreans whom Aristotle is discussing did not distinguish between the

intelligible and sensible realms. Theon's report is crucial as indicating that Archytas followed the terminology and hence the metaphysical position of Philolaus on this point (Huffman 1993: 339–40).

In commenting on A20, Burkert follows this line of interpretation in arguing that Archytas stands with Philolaus "apart from the Platonizing line of interpretation" (1972a: 231), but he elsewhere seems to suggest that Archytas may have been the first Pythagorean to propose a derivation sequence, according to which the sensible world is derived from mathematical entities (1972a: 68–69). Burkert says that "what ontological status Archytas gave to the series point, line, plane, solid can hardly be determined," but for the derivation sequence to have any purpose, it must suppose a split between the sensible realm and a more fundamental level of being, from which the sensible realm is derived and in terms of which it is explained. To assign Archytas such a derivation sequence is thus to make him accept a distinction between the intelligible and sensible world and hence a "Platonist." The preponderance of evidence, however, suggests that Burkert was wrong to assign a derivation sequence to Archytas. That Archytas treated concrete compounds of limiters and unlimiteds as fundamental entities and did not believe in any realm beyond the sensible realm is supported not only by Theon's testimony here in A20 but also by his testimony in A21, by the definitions assigned to Archytas by Aristotle in A22 (see the commentary) and by Plato's criticisms of Archytas' stereometry and harmonics in the *Republic*, which complain of his seeking numbers in things rather than separating numbers from things and considering them in themselves.

A21 Theon of Smyrna, *Mathematics Useful for Reading Plato* (Hiller 1878: 22.5–10)

Ἀριστοτέλης δὲ ἐν τῷ Πυθαγορικῷ τὸ ἕν φησιν ἀμφοτέρων μετέχειν   1
τῆς φύσεως· ἀρτίῳ μὲν γὰρ προστεθὲν περιττὸν ποιεῖ, περιττῷ δὲ   2
ἄρτιον, ὃ οὐκ ἂν ἠδύνατο, εἰ μὴ ἀμφοῖν τοῖν φυσέοιν μετεῖχε· διὸ καὶ   3
ἀρτιοπέριττον καλεῖσθαι τὸ ἕν. συμφέρεται δὲ τούτοις καὶ Ἀρχύτας.   4

1 πυθαγορικῷ] ω corr. ex ων ut vid. A   3 φυσέοιν] mut. in φύσεοιν A

Aristotle, in his work on the Pythagoreans, says that the one participates in the nature of both [sc. the odd and the even]. For, when it is added to an even [number], it makes an odd, but when added to an odd, it makes an even, which it would not be able to do, unless it participated in both natures. Wherefore [he says] that the one is also called even-odd. Archytas is also in agreement with this.

Authenticity

There is no reason to doubt the authenticity of this testimony of Theon. It associates Archytas with fifth-century Pythagorean doctrine rather than making him adopt the later Platonic and Aristotelian views, which are typical of the pseudo-Archytan writings.

Context

This testimonium comes just a few pages after Testimonium A20 (p. 20.19). Theon completes the discussion of the one and the monad, in which A20 is embedded, at 21.19 and then begins a discussion of numbers, by dividing them into two types, odd and even (21.20–21). He next mentions the view of "some" that the monad is the first odd number and gives two arguments for this view: (1) The monad must be either even or odd, and it is not even, because what is even can be divided in half, and the monad cannot be divided at all; (2) When an even number is added to an even number, the resulting number is even but, when the monad is added to an even number, an odd number results. It is interesting that both of these arguments depend on the assumption that a number must be either even or odd, because the next view introduced, the view in Testimonium A21, to which Archytas is said to subscribe, is that the monad is both even and odd. Theon then presents what he seems to take to be the correct view, that the monad is the first form (ἰδέα) of the odd and the indefinite dyad is the first form of the even.

The last sentence of A21, which asserts that Archytas followed Aristotle's Pythagoreans in regarding the one as even-odd, appears to be a comment by Theon rather than anything Aristotle said (Burkert 1972a: 236 n. 236). It is presented in direct discourse rather than in indirect discourse depending on "Aristotle says," and Aristotle usually treats Archytas separately from the Pythagoreans (A13). Since the Pythagorean view reported by Aristotle in A21 is found in Fragment 5 of Philolaus, in joining Archytas to Aristotle's Pythagoreans here, Theon is in effect connecting Archytas to Philolaus, as he does just two pages earlier (20.19 = A20). It is impossible to know whether Theon connects Archytas to Philolaus on the basis of his own reading of texts of Archytas or whether he found the connection in some earlier source.

Content

This testimonium and testimonium A20 are crucial in showing that Archytas followed Philolaus and fifth-century Pythagoreanism on central points in metaphysics and number theory rather than participating in the

Platonic attempt to derive reality from the one and the indefinite dyad. A20 separates Archytas from the Platonizing trend by indicating that he did not make the kinds of terminological distinctions between the monad and the one, which were typical of the new Platonic derivation theories. A21 separates Archytas from Plato on the issue of the nature of the one. A21 tells us, on the authority of Aristotle, that the one was regarded as even-odd precisely because it could produce both odd and even numbers, when added to other numbers. This view of the one suggests that the number series is generated by the one being added to itself to produce two, with the successive numbers then being formed by simply adding one. Since it produces both even and odd numbers, the one is thus even-odd. This view is in stark contrast to the Platonic tradition. Our evidence for Plato's account of the origin of numbers is obscure on many points, but it is clear that he regarded both the one and the indefinite dyad as necessary to produce numbers and associated the one particularly with odd numbers (Arist. *Metaph.* 1084a36; Ross 1924: II. 451) and the dyad with even numbers (Annas 1976: 42 ff.). Speusippus (Fr. 28, see Tarán 1981: 276–77) and Xenocrates (Fr. 15) both regarded the one as odd. Testimonium A21 thus connects Archytas to fifth-century Pythagoreanism and distances him from the number theory and metaphysics of the late Plato and his immediate successors.

The argument given in A21 to support the thesis that the one is even-odd is problematic, since it is not just the one which produces an odd number, when added to an even, and an even number, when added to an odd; the same is true of any odd number. The argument would thus lead to the paradoxical conclusion that odd numbers are "even-odd." The one is the first number in the number sequence to produce both odd and even numbers by addition, however, and this fact may have led the Pythagoreans to regard it as the origin of evenness and oddness. Archytas may have defined the unit, which according to A20 is equivalent to the one, as "the starting point of number" (Arist. *Top.* 108b25; see A22). This definition is consistent with A21. The definition focuses on the necessity of specifying a unit before a number can be determined (i.e. we cannot count until we know what we are counting). Repeated applications of the unit then produce any given number, and hence, since some numbers are even and some odd, the unit must be even-odd. Evenness or oddness need not be mentioned in the definition of the one, since they are further attributes of the one, which are necessary to explain its ability to generate both odd and even numbers, rather than essential attributes. The one is most fundamentally "the starting point of number" not the starting point of a specific sort of number (i.e. odd or even number).

A21a Arnobius, *Adversus Nationes* II. 9 (Reifferscheid 1875: 54. 2–11)

quid? illa de rebus ab humana cognitione sepositis, quae conscribitis ipsi, 1
quae lectitatis, oculata vidistis inspectione et manibus tractata tenuistis? 2
nonne vestrum quicumque est huic vel illi credit auctoribus? non quod 3
sibi persuaserit quis verum dici ab altero velut quadam fidei astipula- 4
tione tutatur? qui cunctarum <rerum> originem <ignem> esse dicit aut 5
aquam, non Thaleti aut Heraclito credit? qui causam in numeris ponit, 6
non Pythagorae Samio, non Archytae? qui animam dividit et incorporales 7
constituit formas, non Platoni Socratico? 8

---

5 <rerum>] add. Hildebrandius   <ignem>] add. Hildebrandius   7 Archytae] Architae P

What about those things which you yourselves write or read concerning things which are removed from human investigation? Have you seen them and examined them with your eyes? Have you grasped hold of them and handled them with your hands? Does not each one of you put his faith in this or that authority? Is not that which someone persuades himself to be spoken truly by another preserved by a stipulation of faith, as it were? That person who says that the origin of all things is fire or water, does he not put his faith in Thales or Heraclitus? That person who makes numbers the cause, does he not put his faith in Pythagoras of Samos, does he not put it in Archytas? That person who divides the soul and establishes incorporeal forms, does he not put his faith in Plato the disciple of Socrates?

Context
Arnobius is a Christian apologist of the late third century AD. In this section of *Adversus Nationes*, Arnobius is arguing that those who attack Christianity because it rests on faith are inconsistent, since they rely on faith in many aspects of their lives. Pagans who adopt philosophical positions, for example, adopt them by putting their faith in the originator of the doctrine. So those who make fire or water the origin of all things put their faith in Heraclitus or Thales; those who make numbers the cause of things put their faith in Pythagoras or Archytas.

Authenticity and significance
This would be a valuable testimonium, if we could be sure that it was based on some assertion in a genuine writing of Archytas. The list of philosophers and their basic metaphysical theses presented by Arnobius suggests, however, that he is relying on a simple doxography and is not using original texts. The fact that Pythagoras is paired with Archytas suggests that we are

not getting testimony about the distinctive views of Archytas but rather that we are being given a statement of the general Pythagorean position with Pythagoras himself and Archytas given as examples of Pythagoreans. Aristotle presents fifth-century Pythagoreans as treating numbers as causes (*Metaph.* 985b24 ff.; 987b24). Although it is more usual for this view to be assigned to the Pythagoreans as a group than to Pythagoras himself, it seems quite possible that this doxography is based on Aristotle. The Platonizing view of Pythagoras, which assigns to him the monad and the indefinite dyad as basic principles, also describes him as regarding numbers as first principles (ἀρχάς, Diels 1879: 281b1). The doxography used by Arnobius could easily be based on this view as well. The view ascribed to Archytas in this testimonium may in some sense be correct; Archytas like Philolaus before him seems to think that it is through numbers that we gain accurate knowledge of things, and hence could say that numbers are principles of things (see the overview of Archytas' philosophy). On the other hand, there is no evidence that Archytas believed in any sort of derivation sequence according to which things derive from numbers as independently existing first principles (see A20 and A21). It is imprudent to put too much weight on this testimonium, since, for the reasons given above, it is doubtful that it is based on anything that Archytas wrote or said.

A22 Aristotle, *Metaphysics* VIII. 2 (1043a14–26)

[cf. Alexander, *In Metaph.*, *CAG* I. 550.37 ff. and Porphyry, *In Ptol.*, Düring 1932: II.24]

διὸ τῶν ὁριζομένων οἱ μὲν λέγοντες τί ἐστιν οἰκία, ὅτι λίθοι πλίνθοι 1
ξύλα, τὴν δυνάμει οἰκίαν λέγουσιν, ὕλη γὰρ ταῦτα· οἱ δὲ ἀγγεῖον 2
σκεπαστικὸν χρημάτων καὶ σωμάτων ἤ τι ἄλλο τοιοῦτον προτιθέν- 3
τες, τὴν ἐνέργειαν λέγουσιν· οἱ δ' ἄμφω ταῦτα συντιθέντες τὴν τρίτην 4
καὶ τὴν ἐκ τούτων οὐσίαν (ἔοικε γὰρ ὁ μὲν διὰ τῶν διαφορῶν λόγος 5
τοῦ εἴδους καὶ τῆς ἐνεργείας εἶναι, ὁ δ' ἐκ τῶν ἐνυπαρχόντων τῆς ὕλης 6
μᾶλλον). ὁμοίως δὲ καὶ οἵους Ἀρχύτας ἀπεδέχετο ὅρους· τοῦ συνάμφω 7
γάρ εἰσιν. οἷον τί ἐστι νηνεμία; ἠρεμία ἐν πλήθει ἀέρος· ὕλη μὲν γὰρ ὁ 8
ἀήρ, ἐνέργεια δὲ καὶ οὐσία ἡ ἠρεμία. τί ἐστι γαλήνη; ὁμαλότης θαλάτ- 9
της· τὸ μὲν ὑποκείμενον ὡς ὕλη ἡ θάλαττα, ἡ δὲ ἐνέργεια καὶ ἡ μορφὴ 10
ἡ ὁμαλότης. 11

2 τὴν] recc. Al. τῇ EJA^b 3–4 προτιθέντες] Ross προσθέντες codd. 4 ἐνέργειαν] ἐνεργείᾳ Bekker 7 οἵους] E²J²A^bAl. οὕς E¹J¹Γ 8 γὰρ (post μὲν)] A^bAl om. EJΓ

Wherefore, some of those who give definitions, when they say what a house is, say that it is stones, bricks, and wood and speak of the potential house, for these things are matter. Others, proposing that it is a receptacle that shelters property and people or some other such definition, speak of the actuality. Some, combining both of these, speak of the third substance that is composed out of these. (For the account by means of differentiae seems to be of the form and the actuality, but the account from those things which are present in it is rather of the matter.) Archytas also approved the same sort of definitions. For they are of both. For example, what is windlessness? Stillness in a quantity of air. For the air is matter, but the stillness is actuality and substance. What is calm-on-the-ocean? Levelness of sea. The sea is what underlies as matter. But the levelness is the actuality and form.

Authenticity
There can be no doubt about the authenticity of this testimony about Archytas provided by Aristotle. Aristotle is our most reliable source for early Pythagoreanism, and he wrote a work in three books on Archytas, so that he had clearly studied Archytas' views (A13).

Context and extent of the testimonium
This testimonium comes from Chapter 2 of Book Eta of Aristotle's *Metaphysics*. Chapter 1 of Book Eta starts with a summary of the discussion of substance in the preceding Book Zeta and ends with some concluding remarks on one of Aristotle's candidates for substance, matter. In Chapter 2, he turns to concluding remarks on that which is substance as actuality, i.e. form. Aristotle ends the chapter by distinguishing between definitions that are of the matter, definitions that are of the form and definitions that combine both and that thus speak of the third substance, the compound of matter and form. Archytas is introduced as an example of someone who approves the third sort of definition. There follows a single sentence that concludes the chapter by asserting that it is now clear what perceptible substance is, either as matter, or form, or the compound.

The most immediate question about this testimonium is its extent. What in Aristotle's account is to be ascribed to Archytas? At the least Aristotle would be simply making a brief factual observation that Archytas gave definitions that were of the third type, which involve both matter and form. This could be all that Aristotle is doing, but it leaves the reference to Archytas rather gratuitous. Why mention him at all? Thus it seems more likely that the examples of definitions that are given immediately after Archytas is mentioned (windlessness [νηνεμία] and calm-on-the-ocean [γαλήνη]) are drawn from Archytas. If this is the case, then Aristotle's mention of Archytas is very well motivated. Aristotle is not just making the point that "by the way Archytas made definitions like this." Instead he introduces Archytas in order to use some examples from Archytas that not only support his factual point about Archytas (i.e. that he approved this sort of definition) but also illustrate the main point about definition that Aristotle is making. This conclusion gets even stronger support from close examination of the definitions. These precise definitions appear nowhere else in Aristotle or in the ancient tradition. Aristotle does use windlessness and calm-on-the-ocean to make further points about definition in the *Topics*, but in those passages he does not give a precise definition and the definition implied is in terms of quiet (ἡσυχία, *Top.* 108b23, cf. 108a7), which does not appear in the definitions in the *Metaphysics*. It thus seems virtually certain that the definitions of νηνεμία as ἠρεμία ἐν πλήθει ἀέρος and γαλήνη as ὁμαλότης θαλάττης are Archytas' distinctive formulations.

We must be careful, however, to distinguish these definitions from Aristotle's analysis of them in the *Metaphysics*. That analysis is full of technical Aristotelian terminology and there is no evidence that Archytas used either that terminology or even precisely that analysis. To be sure Aristotle is here indicating that, in some sense, Archytas anticipated his distinction between form and matter and the same could be said for Plato (Burnyeat 2001: 95). Aristotle does not, however, assign the terminology of the *Metaphysics* (form and matter, actuality and potentiality, the distinction between three types of substance: form, matter and the composite) to Archytas. Nor is there any indication elsewhere in the authentic fragments and testimony that Archytas developed this terminology, although the later pseudo-Archytan treatises are full of it. We may well ask, then, what sort of metaphysical analysis and terminology Archytas did use, in order to arrive at these definitions, and it is to this question that I now turn.

Archytas' theory of definition

In order to understand the significance of Archytas' contribution to the theory of definition and the implications of that theory for his metaphysics, it is necessary first to look briefly at Aristotle's account of the history of definition before Archytas. Aristotle is, in general, quite critical of definitions given by philosophers prior to Socrates, whom he regards as an innovator in making definitions a central concern (*Metaph.* 1078b20 ff.). He briefly and dismissively alludes to definitions by Democritus (*Metaph.* 1078b21) and Empedocles (*PA* 642a14), but he does make some notable comments on the definitions of the Pythagoreans. The contrast between Aristotle's account

of the definitions of these fifth-century Pythagoreans and his account
of the definitions of Archytas provides a particularly striking example of
Aristotle's tendency to treat Archytas as a figure who is largely distinct from
other Pythagoreans. Aristotle makes no connection between Archytas' definitions and those of the earlier Pythagoreans, just as he wrote distinct
treatises on the Pythagoreans on the one hand and Archytas on the other
(A13). Moreover, he is critical of the definitions of the early Pythagoreans at the same time as he is complimentary about Archytas' definitions.
He clearly approves of the type of definition ascribed to Archytas here in
Metaphysics Eta; the sense of the passage at 1043a14–26 is that definitions
in terms of just the matter or of just the form are deficient in comparison
with definitions in terms of both matter and form, such as Archytas gives
(Bostock 1994: 259). That definitions in terms of form and matter are the
ideal sorts of definition is made even clearer a few pages later (*Metaph.*
1043b31, see Le Blond 1979: 66 n. 15). Aristotle explicitly praises Archytas as
"on target" (εὔστοχος), moreover, in a passage in the *Rhetoric*, which has
direct relevance to Archytas' definitions (A12).

Aristotle's account of the definitions of fifth-century Pythagoreans is
found primarily in two passages in the *Metaphysics* (987a20 ff. and 1078b21),
which can be supplemented by a passage from Alexander's commentary.
Alexander is likely, in turn, to be drawing on Aristotle's lost treatise on the
Pythagoreans (Fr. 203). Even before he deals explicitly with Pythagorean
definitions, Aristotle points out that their metaphysical system relies on the
belief that more similarities (ὁμοιώματα) can be found between numbers
and things than between things and material elements, such as fire, earth
and water. The Pythagoreans maintained that such and such a property of
number was analogous to justice, and such and such to soul, mind or opportunity (985b27 ff.). A little later, Aristotle makes clear that the Pythagoreans
used these similarities between things and numbers as the basis for definitions. Their procedure seems to have been as follows. They first looked for
the central characteristic of the thing to be defined, e.g. justice, mind or
marriage. They then looked to see where those characteristics are manifested
in numbers, and in particular where they are manifested first in the series
of numbers. The number which first manifests the property in question is
then said to define the thing in question ("they connected the accounts to
numbers" τοὺς λόγους εἰς τοὺς ἀριθμοὺς ἀνῆπτον *Metaph.* 1078b22–23;
cf. *Metaph.* 987a21, Fr. 203). For example, justice was thought to have the
character of reciprocity, i.e. a person who commits a wrong should suffer
the same thing that he has inflicted (an eye for an eye). This characteristic
of reciprocity was then found among numbers in square numbers, which

are described as equal times equal numbers (the name itself, τὸν ἰσάκις ἴσον ἀριθμόν, indicates that each of the components of the square number is "suffering" the same thing as the other, cf. Fr. 203, *MM.* 1182a14). The first number to manifest this quality, i.e. the first square number, is four, so that four was thought to define justice (Fr. 203). Similarly, marriage has the characteristic of being the union of male and female. In the realm of numbers, even numbers were considered female and odd numbers male, so that any number formed by the addition of an odd and an even number could be considered a combination of male and female. The first such number is five, so that five was said to define marriage. Similar lines of reasoning led the Pythagoreans to define opportunity as seven, opinion as two, mind and soul as one, and perhaps the whole as three (Arist. Fr. 203 and *Cael.* 268a).

Aristotle concludes that the Pythagoreans did indeed begin to discuss and define the form of things (περὶ τοῦ τί ἐστιν ἤρξαντο μὲν λέγειν καὶ ὁρίζεσθαι, *Metaph.* 987a21), but he is critical of these early Pythagorean definitions on several grounds. First, the Pythagoreans only attempted to define a fairly limited range of things (περί τινων ὀλίγων, 1078b22). Second, their definitions were superficial (ἐπιπολαίως 987a23). There seem to be several reasons for this second criticism. In the *Nicomachean Ethics*, Aristotle makes clear that the characteristic of justice upon which the Pythagoreans seize, reciprocity, is too simple to explain the phenomenon. There may be some cases in which it is just for the person who commits an injustice to suffer exactly what he has committed, but, in other cases, e.g. where the people involved are of different status, such a punishment would not be just (*EN* 1132b23 ff., cf. *MM.* 1194a28–1194b3). The biggest problem with the Pythagorean procedure, however, is in taking the number to which a given characteristic first applies, as defining the thing which has that characteristic. Two is the first number to be double another number, but this does not mean that two defines what it is to be double (987a25). Aristotle points out that this procedure could and did lead to one thing being many. We can see an example of what Aristotle means in the evidence provided by Alexander, which probably derives from Aristotle's treatise on the Pythagoreans (Fr. 203). The number seven is associated with opportunity and the sun, since it produces what is opportune (or seasonable), but also with the virgin goddess Athena, because seven is the first prime number, being neither generated by any number nor generating any other number in the decad. Thus one number, seven, does turn out to be many things, because it is both the first "virgin" number and the "seasonable" number as the seventh in the number series, as the sun is the seventh body in from the fixed stars (i.e. it comes after the fixed stars and five planets).

As we have seen, Aristotle clearly has a much higher opinion of Archytas' definitions than those of his Pythagorean and Presocratic predecessors. In what way are they an improvement? To begin with, Archytas' approach to definition appears to have been much more systematic. The Pythagoreans of the fifth century defined only a few important concepts such as justice, mind and soul. They were clearly not interested in definition in itself but rather in defining certain terms that were important in their philosophy for other reasons. The four things of which we can be sure Archytas offered definitions ("windlessness," and "calm-on-the-ocean" in A22 and "arbitrator" and "altar" in A12) are striking, precisely because they are not in themselves important philosophical concepts. The fact that Archytas should have offered definitions of them strongly suggests that he was interested in definition for its own sake. Archytas' definitions are also striking, in that they appear to abandon completely the Pythagorean attempt to define in terms of numbers. On the other hand, there is one important point of continuity with the earlier Pythagorean definitions. Archytas, like his predecessors, arrives at definitions by the use of similarity. Now, however, the similarity is not found between a property of things and a property of numbers. Archytas instead focuses on the relation between the two elements into which he analyzes each subject of definition and the similarity between that relation and other relations found in other subjects. In short, Archytas abandons the attempt to define things in terms of numbers but adopts another mathematical relationship as the foundation of definition, proportion.

In order to see how this is true, it is necessary to examine the two definitions ascribed to Archytas in *Metaphysics* Eta in some detail. νηνεμία (windlessness) and γαλήνη (calm-on-the-ocean) are at first sight very strange choices as subjects of definition. They appear both obscure and arbitrary. It is noteworthy, however, that Aristotle apparently felt them to be compelling examples, since he returns to them again in two different passages in the *Topics* (108a12, 108b25). The difficulty of translating the words into English illustrates one important characteristic that they share: they are both single words which obviously refer to a complex state of affairs, in contrast to single words such as air or fire, which might appear to pick out a simple substance. The use of a single word suggests that a unity is involved, but the meaning of the word suggests that it is a unity which admits of further analysis. Archytas offers an analysis of these apparently simple terms into two types of principles, which Aristotle identifies with his form and matter. νηνεμία is defined in terms of the material principle, air, and the formal principle, stillness, and γαλήνη in terms of the material principle, sea, and the formal principle, levelness. If the distinction in terms of matter (potentiality) and form (actuality) is Aristotelian, in what terms then did Archytas talk about the analysis he had carried out?

We simply don't have the evidence to determine with certainty either the reasoning that led Archytas to these sorts of definition or the terminology which he used in arriving at this analysis of things. However, it is easy to construct an account of his formulation of such definitions that both is in accord with his Pythagorean background and also shows his definitions to be independent of Aristotle's form-matter analysis. There is testimony that makes Archytas the pupil of the fifth–century Pythagorean Philolaus (A5c2). Even if Archytas was not the pupil of Philolaus, Philolaus was the most important Pythagorean of the fifth century, and Archytas was surely aware of his work. The central thesis of Philolaus' metaphysics is that the cosmos as a whole and all things in the cosmos are combinations of limiters and unlimiteds (Fr. 1). For Philolaus unlimiteds constitute continua, while limiters establish boundaries or limits in these continua (Huffman 1993: 47 ff.). Thus the fire which is at the center of Philolaus' astronomical system can be described in terms of an unlimited (the continuum of fire) and a limiter which determines the spatial location of that fire (the center), while a musical scale is a limited set of notes in a continuum of pitch. In Archytas' definitions, both air and sea are clear examples of what Philolaus meant by unlimiteds, things that are in themselves continua without further quantitative determination. Levelness would likewise seem to be an excellent example of one of Philolaus' limiters; it sets formal limits on the continuum constituted by the ocean, specifying that, in the case of γαλήνη, its surface remains all in one horizontal plane. Stillness is less obviously a limiter but can be seen as playing the same role with regard to air; it limits the air under consideration to a continuum that is not changing with regard to any plane.

Since Philolaus' thesis maintained that everything in the cosmos is a compound of limiter and unlimited, it would seem natural for him to be interested in definitions that involved both a limiter and an unlimited. It is striking, then, that there is no evidence that Philolaus himself produced definitions in terms of limiters and unlimiteds of the sort that I am suggesting for Archytas. Aristotle's evidence (Huffman 1993: 283 ff.) suggests that Philolaus gave the typical Pythagorean definitions in terms of number, which have been discussed above, and that he did so gains support from his assertion that all things are known through number (Fr. 4). It would appear, then, that, when Archytas abandoned Philolaus' attempt to give definitions in terms of numbers, he became free to recognize the usefulness of the distinction between limiters and unlimiteds for the purposes of a general theory of definition. I should stress that we have no direct evidence for Archytas' adoption of the metaphysics of limiters and unlimiteds, although he clearly ascribed to Philolaus' belief in an unlimited outside the cosmos (A24). Nonetheless, adoption of that metaphysics makes the most sense of the sorts of definitions which Aristotle ascribes to him in A22. It follows that Archytas' definitions are, as Aristotle indicates, closer to Aristotelian definitions in terms of form and matter than to definitions in terms of genus and species. Archytas is interested in studying things "in order to learn what their determinate and what their determinable elements are" (Le Blond 1979: 69).

The fact that the definitions of νηνεμία and γαλήνη are the sorts of definitions which Archytas "approved" certainly suggests that his basic entities are irreducible unities of limiters and unlimiteds. His definitions show him willing and able to make the distinction between limiters and unlimiteds but also as unwilling to accept the separate existence of limiters and unlimiteds, at least within the cosmos. It would appear that what is outside the cosmos is simply unlimited (A24). This metaphysics may then lie behind Archytas' approach to mathematics. His mathematics is not directed at a separable formal element as Plato's was, but is rather the mathematics of things. In the *Republic*, Plato seems to be referring to Archytas when he criticizes the Pythagoreans as looking for numbers in heard harmonies rather than ascending to study purely formal relations between numbers. Of course, it is clear that Archytas carried out proofs about numbers and mathematical figures abstracted from things (e.g. A14 and A19), but this says nothing about whether he thought that numbers or geometrical shapes had any existence separate from things. We do not know precisely how Archytas would describe the ontological status of the numbers and geometrical figures in his proofs, but his attitude to definition suggests that he would not have regarded them as ontologically separable from things. In this regard, Archytas seems to be following the emphatic rejection of separation, which Aristotle assigns to fifth-century Pythagoreans (*Metaph.* 987b28).

The examples of νηνεμία and γαλήνη also show that Archytas made important use of similarity in developing his definitions, and we have seen that in doing so, he is, to an extent, following the procedure of fifth-century Pythagoreans. Indeed, when Aristotle returns to these two examples in the *Topics*, without mentioning Archytas this time, it is precisely to stress the role of similarity in arriving at definitions (108b23, 108a7). The Aristotle of the *Topics* and Archytas appear to have had slightly different ideas on the precise role of similarity, however. Aristotle stresses that windlessness and calm-on-the-ocean are formally the same, they are both states of quiet (ἡσυχία 108b26). We might suppose that Archytas is making the same point, except that he does not define νηνεμία as ἡσυχία in the air and γαλήνη as ἡσυχία in the sea. In giving his definitions he uses not one limiter (rest) with two unlimiteds (sea and air) but rather two limiters (levelness and stillness). Not only that but the two limiters are not obviously identical to one another. This would be hard to explain, if his point were that the formal element is identical in the two cases. It appears that Archytas was not interested in the identity of the formal elements (limiters) but rather in the identity of the *relations between* limiter and unlimited in the cases of νηνεμία and γαλήνη. The point can be made clear with a mathematical example. It is true that the ratio 2:4 is equal to the ratio 8:16, but this in no way means that 2 is equal to 8. In the same way, the ratio ἠρεμία : πλῆθος ἀέρος is equal to the ratio ὁμαλότης : θάλαττα but this does not entail that ἠρεμία is the same as ὁμαλότης.

Understood in this way, these two definitions shed light on the passage in Aristotle's *Metaphysics* immediately preceding his allusion to Archytas' definitions. This passage has puzzled commentators (1043a12), by asserting that a different form is necessitated by a different matter (Bostock 1994: 258–59). Archytas agrees. Stillness in air and levelness in sea are not the same form but they are similar to one another. Different matters call for a different form in order to produce examples of quiet in each case. Thus, it is very clear why these examples would intrigue the Aristotle of the *Metaphysics*, even if they are in tension with the approach of the Aristotle of the *Topics*.

This interpretation of Archytas' theory of definition also fits two other Archytan definitions, which are preserved in Aristotle's *Rhetoric* (A12). Aristotle praises Archytas for his ability to see similarity even in things that differ greatly and gives as an example his assertion that an arbitrator and an altar are the same. The full definitions of arbitrator and altar are not given by Aristotle, but he gives the grounds upon which they were said to be the same: "one who has suffered an injustice takes refuge at both of them" (1412a 14–15). We might suppose that "place of refuge" is the formal element and is the same in each case. Thus, an altar might be defined as "stone in a certain arrangement, which serves as a refuge for one treated unjustly" and an arbitrator as "a person who serves as a refuge for one treated unjustly." Further consideration suggests, however, that Archytas may have had some-thing else in mind. It seems more likely that what he thought was the same was the relation between limiter and unlimited in the cases of the altar and the arbitrator. In the case of the altar the unlimited is the material altar made of stone and the limiter is the function of protecting the suppliant. In the case of the arbitrator the unlimited is the person, the material collection of flesh and bone, and the limiter is the function of deciding fairly between petitioners. The point is that just as the unlimiteds are different (stone in a certain shape as opposed to flesh and bone in a certain arrangement) so the limiters differ; protecting a suppliant from being taken away by his enemies is not the same as deciding between rival petitioners. What is "the same" is the relationship between limiter and unlimited in the two cases. Both the altar and the arbitrator provide a refuge for someone who is being treated unjustly, but they provide that refuge in quite different ways. Stated as a proportion the relation is as follows: protecting the suppliant against violence:the stone :: deciding fairly between rival petitioners:the person. In each case the limiter allows the unlimited to serve as a refuge for one who is treated unjustly.

If this reconstruction of Archytas' theory of definition is correct, he appears to have significantly expanded the notions of limiter and unlimited. In the definition of γαλήνη as levelness of the sea, both the limiter and the unlimited are easily understood in terms of a material continuum and a limitation of that continuum. When an arbitrator is defined as a person who provides refuge for one treated unjustly, by deciding fairly between rival petitioners, both the idea of an unlimited and the idea of a limiter have been significantly modified. The unlimited is no longer a relatively amorphous continuum such as the sea but is instead a person, who already is a compound of limiter (the shape and structure of a human body) and unlimited (flesh, bone, blood). The limiter is not a straightforward spatial or structural limit such as levelness but is instead a function which the person can fulfill. The relationship between limiter and unlimited in this case is something much more like a *qua* relation; an arbitrator is a person *qua* deciding between rival petitioners. In his "course" on definitions Archytas may well have begun with the examples of νηνεμία and γαλήνη, because they employ the analysis in terms of limiters and unlimiteds in a relatively intuitive way. He would then push his students to see that the same sort of analysis could be applied in situations where the conceptions of limiter and unlimited were less obviously spatial, such as the examples of the arbitrator and the altar. The same basic theory of definition is deployed in each case, however: things are defined in terms of an analysis into limiter and unlimited.

In Archytas' method, similarity serves as an heuristic device that helps us in developing definitions. It is clear from the *Topics* that Aristotle too thought of similarity as useful in formulating definitions (χρήσιμος πρὸς τοὺς ὁρισμοὺς ἡ τοῦ ὁμοίου θεωρία 108b24). As we have seen, it appears that Archytas understood this similarity as a similarity between relations and hence as a proportion. We do not have the original context in which Archytas employed similarity to generate definitions, but it is possible to construct a plausible line of thought. In essence Archytas' procedure treats the search for a definition as "solving" for a variable. Given that we see a basic similarity between νηνεμία and γαλήνη, if we have a definition for the latter as levelness of the sea we can then set up a proportion such that levelness : sea = x : air. We thus are led to try to think what limiter or formal element plays the same role in air as levelness does with sea. In the case of the altar and the arbitrator, we know the unlimited in each case but do not know the limiter in either case. We do know, however, that in each case the limiter allows the unlimited to serve as a refuge to someone treated unjustly, so that we can "solve" for the limiter in each case. It is as if we knew that x:4 = y:16 = 1:2. In this case we can solve the equation mathematically and conclude that x is 2 and y is 8.

Is there further testimony about Archytas' definitions in Aristotle?
There is reason to believe that Aristotle and Alexander may preserve even more definitions by Archytas, in passages where Archytas is not mentioned by name. Scholars have not commonly connected Aristotle's discussions of Archytas' definitions of νηνεμία and γαλήνη in the *Metaphysics* with his further discussion of the definitions of these terms in two passages of the *Topics* (108a12 and 108b25). In both of these passages, as well as in Alexander's commentary on *Topics* 108a7, other definitions are presented, although their author is not identified. Since we know from the *Metaphysics* that Archytas was responsible for the definitions of νηνεμία and γαλήνη, it is reasonable to wonder whether some of the other definitions which Aristotle presents in the *Topics* as parallel to the definitions of νηνεμία and γαλήνη should not also be ascribed to Archytas. Burnyeat (2001: 96 n. 18) has raised this question in particular with regard to the definitions of the unit and the point, which are presented in parallel to νηνεμία and γαλήνη at 108b25. Archytas is one of the foremost mathematicians of the time. When we are given definitions that we know are his, followed by definitions of such mathematical terms, it is natural to suspect that the definitions of point and unit also belong to him.

At 108b24, Aristotle asserts that the study of similarity is useful in forming definitions of things that differ greatly. He then gives two examples: (1) γαλήνη on the ocean and νηνεμία in the air are the same, since each is a state of quiet, (2) a point on a line and a unit in a number are the same, since each is a starting point (ἀρχή). He then suggests that we should assign the genus in the definitions to what is common in each case. According to Aristotle, this is just what "those who give definitions" (οἱ ὁριζόμενοι) in fact do, for they say "the unit is the starting point of number and the point is the starting point of a line" (τήν . . . μονάδα ἀρχὴν ἀριθμοῦ· τὴν στιγμὴν ἀρχὴν γραμμῆς). Are these Archytas' definitions of unit and point?

This passage of the *Topics* along with the definitions of the point and the unit have been claimed for Speusippus by Tarán (1981: 392 ff.) and earlier by Burkert (1972a: 67 n. 87; 69 n. 105), Cherniss (1944: 131 n. 82) and Stenzel (*RE* 1644). The case made for Speusippus by these scholars is quite plausible; it is particularly striking that Speusippus is reported by Aristotle to have said that "the point is such as the one" (*Metaph.* 1085a33), which would suggest that he set up an analogy between the one and the point. The evidence is, however, all circumstantial and there is no direct and explicit connection between Speusippus and this passage of the *Topics*. There are even some subtle differences in terminology. Thus, in the *Metaphysics* passage which refers directly to Speusippus, it is "the one" and not "the monad" (the word used in the *Topics*) that is said to be like the point.

A much stronger case can be made for Archytas. There are three direct and explicit connections between Archytas and this section of the *Topics*. First, in the *Metaphysics*, Aristotle explicitly identifies Archytas as someone who has given definitions of νηνεμία and γαλήνη, and we have no evidence that either Speusippus or any other Greek philosopher ever gave definitions of these terms (Plato mentions the pair at *Tht.* 153c but not in the context of definition). Moreover, although Aristotle does not repeat the precise Archytan definitions here in the *Topics*, what he presents looks very much like a recasting of Archytas' definitions in terms of his own theory of form and matter. Second, the *Topics* passage begins by asserting the value of the study of similarity particularly in situations "where things differ much" (καὶ ἐν τοῖς πολὺ διεστῶσι), but virtually the same phrase is used by Aristotle, when discussing Archytas' definitions of altar and arbitrator in the *Rhetoric* (1412a9 ff.) and praising him for being able to see similarity "even in things which differ greatly" (καὶ ἐν πολὺ διέχουσι). Finally, in the *Rhetoric* passage, Archytas is said to have asserted that an altar and an arbitrator are "the same" (ταὐτόν) and precisely this form of expression is used in the *Topics* passage both of the known Archytan definienda, νηνεμία and γαλήνη and of the point and the line; both pairs are said to be "the same" (ταὐτόν). Thus, the language and content of the two passages where Aristotle explicitly discusses Archytas show such remarkable similarities to this passage of the

Topics that we must consider it probable that the definitions of the unit and the point in this passage of the *Topics* also belong to Archytas. These definitions, therefore, bear careful examination.

That these should be Archytas' definitions of point and unit contradicts a common assumption (e.g. Heath 1925: 1. 155) that the Pythagoreans defined the point as "a unit having position" (μονὰς θέσιν ἔχουσα). Of course, even if we accepted that this was the common early Pythagorean definition of the point, it is perfectly possible that Archytas, here, as elsewhere, represents a further development in that tradition. It is far from clear, however, that the definition of the point as "a unit having position" should be ascribed to the Pythagoreans. It is the definition that Aristotle himself adopts, and he uses it in contexts that suggest that it is connected to the early Academy; nowhere does he ascribe this definition to the Pythagoreans, however (Burkert 1972a: 67). The sole basis on which this definition has been supposed to be Pythagorean is Proclus' ascription of it to them in his commentary on the first book of Euclid's *Elements* (95.21). The context in Proclus looks to be heavily contaminated with the later tradition according to which the Pythagoreans are assigned what are in fact derivation sequences of early Academic origin. Moreover, such a definition of the point will not work for the early Pythagoreans as Aristotle describes them, since they are supposed to believe in points which have magnitude, a view which is inconsistent with maintaining that they are simply units with position, which would have no magnitude (Burkert 1972a: 67).

There is one important piece of external evidence that provides at least partial support for assigning the definitions of the point as "the starting point of the line" and the unit as "the starting point of number" to Archytas. It is precisely these definitions that appear in Nicomachus' *Introduction to Arithmetic* (II. 7; see Heath 1921: 1. 69). Nicomachus' treatise is the most important extant treatise on arithmetic in the Pythagorean tradition, and that treatise features a prominent quotation from Archytas' *Harmonics* (Fr. 1), so that it would not be surprising, if Nicomachus also adopted Archytas' definitions of the point and unit, although he does not explicitly assign them to any particular thinker.

If we accept the hypothesis that the definitions of point and unit at *Topics* 108b24 belong to Archytas, how do they function in terms of the Archytan theory of definition outlined above? The proportion which is established is: point:line :: unit:number. It is important to note from the beginning that the terms "line" and "number" refer not to "unlimiteds" but rather to the specific number or line that results from the application of the limiters "point" and "unit" to unlimiteds. The similarity between the two relations is that just as the unit serves as the starting point of a number, in that, until a unit is specified, there can be no number, so the point is the starting point of a line in that, until a point in space is specified, there can be no line. These definitions of point and unit are very much in accord with Archytas' metaphysics. A number is a compound of the limiting unit and the unlimited countable, just as a line is a compound of the limiting point and unlimited extension in one dimension. Thus, numbers and lines would be basic entities for Archytas. They admit of analysis into limiters and unlimiteds, but those limiters and unlimiteds have no separate existence; points only exist as the limiting part in the analysis of a line, and units only exist as the limiting element in a number. It is tempting to suppose that Plato was taking an Archytan position of this sort, when he maintained that points were a geometrical fiction (Arist. *Metaph.* 992a20). Indeed, following the normal punctuation of this passage of the *Metaphysics* this is exactly what Aristotle says: "Plato struggled against this class (i.e. points) as being a geometrical fiction, and called it (i.e the point) the starting point of the line (ἀρχὴν γραμμῆς, see Heath 1949: 200 contra Ross 1924: I. 207).

This analysis of Archytas' definition of the point with its attendant thesis that the point is not ontologically separable from the line argues against attempts to make Archytas the author of the ontological derivation sequence whereby the line comes into being by the motion of the point, the surface by the motion of the line and the solid by the motion of a surface. If the point does not exist independently of the line, it can hardly bring the line into existence by moving. This derivation sequence is assigned to the Pythagoreans in the later tradition (e.g. S.E. *M.* x.278ff.), but Burkert has shown conclusively that it cannot be assigned to the Pythagoreans of the fifth century (1972a: 66 ff.). Aristotle mentions this derivation sequence only once in a polemic against Xenocrates, so that some have thought that it must be Xenocrates' own position (Guthrie 1962: 262 ff.). Others argue that the doctrine is Speusippus' (Tarán 1981: 363; Cherniss 1944: 396 n. 322). Burkert suggests that either Speusippus or Xenocrates may have taken the derivation sequence from Archytas, who by giving a "comprehensive treatment of geometrical magnitudes by the use of the idea of movement" may have gone further than "the older Pythagoreans" (1972a: 68–69).

It is true that, in the duplication of the cube, Archytas does use rotating plane figures, which by their rotation would create solid figures, although that is not Archytas' main interest and no actual solids are generated (A14). Similarly, Archytas' definition of the point could be understood to say that the point is the "starting point" of the line, in that it creates the line by its movement. Nothing necessitates this interpretation, however, and it is just as plausible that the point is the starting point just in that it determines an end point of a line. Moreover, as we have seen, Archytas' insistence on definitions that specify both the limiter and unlimited and the strong implication that limiters and unlimiteds do not have separate existence, argue that Archytas did not assign independent ontological status to the point.

There is one further passage of the *Topics* and the corresponding section of Alexander's commentary on the *Topics*, in which additional Archytan definitions may perhaps be found. At 108a7 Aristotle gives two further proportions in his discussion of definitions: knowledge:object of knowledge :: perception:object of perception; sight:eye :: reason:soul. It is harder to be confident that these proportions are Archytan, since they are the kind of thing that could have been developed by a number of philosophers (see e.g. Plato *Republic* 518c) and have no particular connection to Archytas' expertise in mathematics as did the definitions of point and unit. In his commentary on this passage of the *Topics*, Alexander mentions two further proportions (118. 13–19). He says that virtue and health are similar, in that virtue is the perfection of the soul just as health is the perfection of the body. Again this proportion is so pervasive in Greek thought and in particular in Plato that it is hard to regard it as peculiarly Archytan. Alexander's second example is more intriguing. He says that beauty and justice are the same, in that each resides in proportionate equality (ἐν ἰσότητι τῇ κατὰ ἀναλογίαν). Beauty is proportionate equality of the parts and limbs of the body, while justice is proportionate equality in distributions and transactions by administrators (ἐν διανομαῖς τε καὶ συναλλάγμασι τῶν νεμομένων). There is a specific connection to Archytas, since, in Fragment 3, Archytas does discuss the role of calculation in determining what is "equal" or fair in agreements (συναλλαγμάτων, the same word used by Alexander). It may well be then that Archytas compared justice in the state to beauty in the body, in terms of proportionate equality. If he did so, his conception of justice marks progress beyond the early Pythagorean definition. His definition takes into account any relevant differences between two individuals involved in a transaction, so that they each receive in proportion to what they deserve; the early Pythagoreans limited justice to simple reciprocity (see above).

Detailed commentary

Line 7   ἀπεδέχετο – It is hard to know what is implied by Aristotle's choice of this word. The basic meanings are "to accept," "to receive favorably" and "to approve." Aristotle uses the word in the *Nicomachean Ethics* in discussing the amount of exactness one should expect from conclusions in various disciplines before *accepting* them (e.g. 1094b23 ff.). So far as I can see, however, Aristotle never uses it elsewhere of a specific individual accepting a point of view. The word is frequently used in Plato to describe the give and *take* of dialectic (see *R.* 531e and Shorey's [1935] note ad loc.), and it is common in the Platonic dialogues (e.g. *Phlb.* 54a). There is an implication then that Archytas did not merely present some definitions but that he had standards for definition and that he accepted these specific definitions as meeting them. Given that a number of the testimonia about Archytas seem to have the form of a story or anecdote (e.g. A9, A24), it could be that Archytas' theory of definition was also presented in the form of a story, or at least in a dialectical structure of some sort, in which some definitions were rejected and others approved.

8 νηνεμία – νηνεμία is formed from the negative prefix νη- and ἄνεμος (wind) so that it means literally "windlessness". Socrates chides Cebes for fearing that his soul will blow away when it leaves the body, especially if he dies when a strong wind is blowing rather than when there is νηνεμία (*Phd.* 77c). Since absence of wind also produces calm at sea νηνεμία is often conjoined with γαλήνη (Hom. *Od.* v. 392, XII. 168–69; cf. Pl. *Tht.* 153c). It is intriguing that windlessness appears at *De Anima* 404a21, in Aristotle's report on the Pythagorean view of soul. He reports that some of them said that soul is the particles in the air or what makes those particles move. Aristotle comments that these particles came into the theory because they appear to be continuously moved even when there is total calm (νηνεμία).

ἠρεμία – ἠρεμία is not found in Plato but is Aristotle's standard word for rest as the opposite of motion (*Metaph.* 1068b24; *Cat.* 15b1 etc.). In the *Topics* Aristotle connects ἠρεμία with what is definite in contrast to motion and the indefinite (142a19). At *Topics* 128b he says that ἠρεμία always accompanies windlessness (νηνεμία) but that it is not the same as windlessness, so that it can be considered the genus, of which windlessness is part.

9 γαλήνη – γαλήνη refers specifically to calm or stillness of the sea. LSJ refer to *Topics* 108b in defining it. Other passages in Aristotle and in Homer show that it refers to the calm level sea, which is set in contrast to a sea that is rising in waves or swelling (κυμαίνω, κῦμα cf. Ar. *Mete.* 367b15; Hom. *Od.* v. 452, XII. 168).

ὁμαλότης – "Levelness," Tredennick; "Smoothness," Ross, Bostock. This may be the earliest extant use of this word, which appears eight times in Aristotle and ten times in Plato. ὁμαλότης does not appear in Aristotle's discussion of γαλήνη in the *Topics* (108a11, 108b25) so that here in the *Metaphysics*, where Archytas' name is mentioned, we seem to be getting Archytas' precise definition, whereas in the *Topics* Aristotle talks in terms of ἡσυχία which he wants to say is characteristic of both γαλήνη and νηνεμία (*Top.* 108b25).

ὁμαλότης may have a broader significance for Archytas than simply as a part of the definition of γαλήνη. Plato primarily contrasts ὁμαλότης with ἀνωμαλότης in defining the contrast between rest and motion in the discussion of the receptacle (*Ti.* 57e). Archytas' account of motion and rest is both connected to and contrasted with that of Plato by Eudemus (see A23), so that it is tempting to suppose that Archytas' definition of γαλήνη in terms of ὁμαλότης is in some way related to his account of motion. Both Plato and Aristotle use ὁμαλότης in a political context to refer to a state of society in which there is an equality of property (*Leg.* 918c3, *Pol.* 1266b16). The concept may have had an application in the political sphere for Archytas as well, and this would be in accord with his comments on the role of calculation in removing faction from the state (Fr. 3).

A12 Aristotle, *Rhetoric* III. 11 (1412a9–17)

δεῖ δὲ μεταφέρειν, καθάπερ εἴρηται πρότερον, ἀπὸ οἰκείων καὶ μὴ φαν- 1
ερῶν, οἷον καὶ ἐν φιλοσοφίᾳ τὸ ὅμοιον καὶ ἐν πολὺ διέχουσι θεωρεῖν 2
εὐστόχου, ὥσπερ Ἀρχύτας ἔφη ταὐτὸν εἶναι διαιτητὴν καὶ βωμόν· 3
ἐπ' ἄμφω γὰρ τὸν ἀδικούμενον καταφεύγειν. ἢ εἴ τις φαίη ἄγκυραν καὶ 4
κρεμάθραν τὸ αὐτὸ εἶναι· ἄμφω γὰρ ταὐτό τι, ἀλλὰ διαφέρει τῷ ἄνωθεν 5
καὶ κάτωθεν. καὶ τὸ ἀνωμαλίσθαι τὰς πόλεις ἐν πολὺ διέχουσιν ταὐτό, 6
ἐν ἐπιφανείᾳ καὶ δυνάμεσι τὸ ἴσον. 7

1 μὴ] om. ΘΠΓ   3 ἀρχύτης A   4 τὸν . . . καταφεύγειν] Kayser   τὸ ἀδικούμενον καταφεύγει codd.   5 κρεμάστραν ΘΠΣ   5 ταὐτό τι] ABCQΓ   ταὐτότητι DEYᵗZ τῷ] τὸ ΘΒΕ   6 ἀνωμαλίσθαι] ΘΠΓ   ἄνω μάλιστα εἶναι A   ὁμαλισθῆναι Vahlen ὡμαλίσθαι Freese   ἐν πολὺ] ΘΠΓ   ἐν πολὺν A

It is necessary to make metaphors, just as I have said before, from things that are related but not obviously related. So also in philosophy it is a characteristic of a person who is on the mark, to see what is similar even in things which differ greatly, just as Archytas said that an arbitrator and an altar are the same; for one who has suffered an injustice takes refuge at both of them. Or if someone should say that an anchor and a pot-hook are the same; for they are both the same sort of thing but differ by (hooking) from above or from below. And the same expression "cities are restored to equality" applies in situations that differ much, referring to equality in surface area or in political power.

Authenticity

There can be no reason to doubt the authenticity of this testimonium. Aristotle is our most reliable source for early Pythagoreanism and devoted a three-volume work to Archytas' philosophy (A13), upon which work this testimonium is likely to draw.

Context

This testimonium comes from the eleventh chapter of Book 3 of Aristotle's *Rhetoric*. In this section of the *Rhetoric*, Aristotle is explaining the principles from which clever sayings arise (τὰ ἀστεῖα cf. the beginning of Chapter 10). He has argued that such sayings arise from metaphors, among other things. In the immediate context of A12, he emphasizes a point about metaphors, which he has made elsewhere, that, although they should have some appropriateness, they must not be too obvious. In the succeeding paragraph, Aristotle emphasizes that the hearer should be surprised by the conclusion of the metaphor, so that he will feel that he has learned something. The skill of making a good metaphor is thus founded on the ability to see connections between things which are not obvious to most people yet which, once heard, are admitted to exist.

Content of the testimonium

DK include this testimonium, rather bizarrely, among the testimonia for Archytas' life, as if it referred to some specific incident in his career in Tarentum. Burkert seems to be influenced by this classification of the testimonium and suggests that it is "an apophthegm that is reminiscent of the acusmata," although he has no suggestion as to what it could mean in such a context (1972a: 236 n. 94). Careful study suggests, however, that these scholars have been on the wrong track and that it should instead be connected closely with Testimonium A22 and Archytas' procedure in giving definitions, which is discussed there. It is important to note that, in A12, Aristotle does not introduce Archytas as a maker of metaphors. Instead, Aristotle draws a parallel between people who make good metaphors and people who have the ability to recognize similarities in philosophy; it is only within the comparison to philosophy that Archytas is introduced. The ability to see such similarities produces a poet who is a master of metaphor (*Po.* 1459a7). What does the similar ability in a philosopher produce? At *Topics* 108b7 ff., the value of similarity in developing definitions is praised.

Aristotle echoes the language of the *Rhetoric*, when he says that consideration of similarity is useful with regard to definitions, in dealing with subjects which differ widely (ἐν τοῖς πολὺ διεστῶσι, cf. *Rh.* 1412a12 ἐν πολὺ διέχουσι). The examples that Aristotle goes on to give in the *Topics* are "windlessness" and "calm-at-sea." It can be no accident that it is precisely these terms, for which Aristotle reports Archytas' definitions in the *Metaphysics* (A22). Thus, while Testimonium A12 may not appear to teach us much of philosophical import on its surface (what do altars and arbitrators have to do with philosophy?), once we recognize its connection to Archytas' theory of definition, we can see why Aristotle explicitly describes what Archytas is doing in A12 as philosophy (see Lloyd 1996: 216–17). Aristotle is clearly praising Archytas for his natural gift at seeing the similarities which lead to good definitions. Archytas' claim that an arbitrator and an altar are the same and its relevance for his theory of definition are further discussed in the commentary on A22.

CHAPTER VI

Physics

A23 Eudemus, *Physics* Fr. 60 Wehrli = Simplicius, *In Aristotelis Phys.* III. 2 (*CAG* IX. 431.4–431.16)

καὶ ὅτι μὲν ὡς αἴτιον [sc. τῆς κινήσεως] τὴν ἀνισότητα ὁ Πλάτων εἶπε, 1
μετ᾽ ὀλίγον ἔσται δῆλον, ὅταν τὴν Πλάτωνος παραθῶμεν ῥῆσιν. νῦν 2
δὲ τοσοῦτον ἰστέον, ὅτι καὶ Εὔδημος πρὸ τοῦ Ἀλεξάνδρου ἱστορῶν 3
τὴν Πλάτωνος περὶ κινήσεως δόξαν καὶ ἀντιλέγων αὐτῇ τάδε γράφει· 4
"Πλάτων δὲ τὸ μέγα καὶ μικρὸν καὶ τὸ μὴ ὂν καὶ τὸ ἀνώμαλον καὶ ὅσα 5
τούτοις ἐπὶ ταὐτὸ φέρει τὴν κίνησιν λέγει. φαίνεται δὲ ἄτοπον αὐτὸ 6
τοῦτο τὴν κίνησιν λέγειν· παρούσης γὰρ δοκεῖ κινήσεως κινεῖσθαι τὸ ἐν 7
ᾧ. ἀνίσου δὲ ὄντος ἢ ἀνωμάλου προσαναγκάζειν ὅτι κινεῖται, γελοῖον· 8
βέλτιον γὰρ αἴτια λέγειν ταῦτα ὥσπερ Ἀρχύτας." καὶ μετ᾽ ὀλίγον "τὸ 9
δὲ ἀόριστόν, φησι, καλῶς ἐπὶ τὴν κίνησιν οἱ Πυθαγόρειοι καὶ ὁ Πλάτων 10
ἐπιφέρουσιν (οὐ γὰρ δὴ ἄλλος γε οὐδεὶς περὶ αὐτῆς εἴρηκεν)· ἀλλὰ γὰρ 11
ὁριστὴ οὐκ ἔστι καὶ τὸ ἀτελὲς δὴ καὶ τὸ μὴ ὄν· γίνεται γάρ, γινόμενον 12
δὲ οὐκ ἔστι." 13

9 αἴτια] αἴτιον F   ταῦτα] om. F   **11–12** ἀλλὰ γὰρ ὁριστὴ οὐκ ἔστι] Diels   ἀλλὰ γὰρ ὥρισται οὐκ ἔστι E   ἀλλὰ γὰρ ὥρισται καὶ οὐκ ἔστι F   οὐ γὰρ ὥρισται Aldina

That Plato spoke of inequality as a cause [of motion] will be clear shortly, when I quote the text of Plato. For now it is necessary to recognize this much, that Eudemus also, before Alexander, when examining Plato's theory of motion and arguing against it, writes as follows: "Plato says that motion is the great and the small and not-being and the uneven and as many things as have the same force as these. But it seems paradoxical to say that motion is just this. For, when motion is present, that in which it is present seems to be moved, but, when something is unequal or uneven, it is ridiculous to require in addition that it is moved. It is better to say that these are causes [of motion] just as Archytas does." And a little later "The Pythagoreans and Plato are right, he says, to apply the indefinite to motion (indeed no one else has spoken about it). For it is not definite and is the incomplete and what is not. For it [motion] comes to be, and, insofar as it is coming to be, it is not."

Authenticity

For several reasons, it seems very likely that A23 is based on the genuine beliefs of Archytas. First, the source of the information is excellent. Eudemus was active in the second half of the fourth century BC, before any of the pseudo-Archytan treatises were composed and undoubtedly knew Aristotle's special treatises on Archytas. Eudemus also had access to Archytas' solution to the duplication of the cube (A14). Second, A23 coheres well with other genuine fragments and testimonia of Archytas. Archytas' harmonic and acoustic theory, as developed in Fragment 1, show that he was centrally concerned with bodies in motion. Testimonium A23a, which is also based on an early Peripatetic source, provides further evidence of Archytas' interest in motion. It is true that Eudemus refers to Plato's doctrine of the great and the small, which has ties to the indefinite dyad, and it is one of the characteristics of the later pseudo-Pythagorean tradition to assign the doctrine of the one and the indefinite dyad to Pythagoras (Burkert 1972a: 57 ff.). In A23, however, Eudemus is not identifying Archytas with Plato and the doctrine of the indefinite dyad but rather distinguishing Archytas from Plato (see below), which again speaks for authenticity.

Context and extent of the testimonium

Eudemus' report on Archytas' account of motion is quoted in Simplicius' commentary on the first part of Book III, Chapter 2 of Aristotle's *Physics* (201b16–202a2). The context in Aristotle, Simplicius and Eudemus is complicated but important in order to understand the extent and the nature of the testimonium concerning Archytas. In Book III, Chapter 1 of the *Physics*, Aristotle gives his definition of motion: "the actuality of a potentiality, *qua* potentiality." He then defends this definition in Chapter 2, by examining what his predecessors have said about motion and showing the difficulties presented by their definitions. Aristotle does not appear to think that most of his predecessors have had anything to contribute to the definition of motion, since he considers only one previous definition. Moreover, Aristotle never explicitly names the authors of the definition which he does discuss. He refers only to an indefinite "some" who have said that motion is "difference," "inequality," and "non-being." Aristotle's objection to such definitions is that none of these things is necessarily moved (i.e. what is unequal is not *ipso facto* moved), nor is change necessarily into or out of these rather than their opposites (i.e. change is neither more likely to be into nor out of what is unequal than into or out of what is equal). According to Aristotle, such definitions arose because motion seems to be something indefinite and it is the principles of the second column (of the table of opposites) that are indefinite, because of their being privations. For motion is neither a substance nor a quality nor does it belong to any other of the categories. It would appear then that Aristotle views the three different definitions of motion as difference, inequality and non-being as equivalent, insofar as they are all motivated by an attempt to capture the indefinite nature of motion. His reference to the second column in the table of opposites (201b26 τῆς δὲ ἑτέρας συστοιχίας) makes it relatively clear that he at least has those Pythagoreans to whom he explicitly assigns the table at *Metaphysics* 986a22 in mind, although Aristotle himself uses the table on occasion and names no names here in the *Physics*.

In his commentary on Aristotle *Physics* III. 2, Simplicius makes frequent reference to Alexander's earlier commentary on the *Physics*, which has not survived. It is clear from these remarks that both he and Alexander understand the unnamed "some," with whose definition of motion Aristotle takes issue, to be the Pythagoreans and Plato. Simplicius begins his commentary on *Physics* III. 2 with an explanation of Aristotle's comment that motion came to be associated with difference, inequality and non-being, because these belong to "the second column." He explains Aristotle's comment in terms of the Pythagorean table of opposites. Simplicius quotes the whole table (429.8), saying that Aristotle reported it in another work (i.e. the *Metaphysics*). Motion does, in fact, appear in the second column of this table. At 430.4 Simplicius first brings Plato into the discussion by presenting a critique of Alexander's criticism of Plato's supposed definitions of motion as "difference" (430.4) and "non-being" (430.11). He gives several quotations from the *Sophist* (256d) in the discussion of the second definition. Simplicius concludes this section with Alexander's remark (430.34) that, if Plato and the Pythagoreans were saying that difference, inequality and non-being were the *causes* of motion [rather than identifying them with motion, which is what Aristotle took them to be doing and what Alexander has assumed], what they are saying may be possible, but nonetheless inadequate for an account of motion. For the cause is not the same as what is caused. If they said anything true in saying that motion was not being, they only gave an accidental quality of motion and did not state its essence.

It is after this remark of Alexander that the context quoted for Archytas A23 begins. Simplicius says that he will shortly show that Plato did indeed say that inequality was a cause of motion (he will fulfill this promise with a discussion of *Timaeus* 57e at 432.20). Before doing so, however, he says that we should note what Eudemus also said in his investigation of Plato's theory of motion as part of his criticism of Plato. Simplicius gives no indication that Alexander referred to Eudemus but rather seems to introduce Eudemus as a parallel to Alexander in his criticism of Plato. Simplicius is quoting Eudemus here precisely to show that Eudemus had to some extent anticipated Alexander's criticisms (note καὶ Εὔδημος and πρὸ τοῦ Ἀλεξάνδρου).

Eudemus attacks Plato on the same grounds as Aristotle did, i.e. for identifying motion with the unequal and other similar concepts. His list of things that Plato identified with motion only overlaps with Aristotle's in the cases of the unequal and non-being. Eudemus makes no mention of difference and instead refers to the great and the small and the uneven, which are not mentioned by Aristotle (Eudemus' account of Plato's view is in fact close to what is ascribed to Plato's pupil Hermodorus at Simplicius 247.33). Eudemus then introduces an alternative view according to which the unequal and the uneven rather than being identified with motion are instead causes of motion, a view which he says is better, but it is to Archytas that he assigns this view and not to Plato.

Simplicius breaks in at this point and indicates that he is skipping some material and then quotes four more lines, which come a little later in Eudemus. In these last four lines Eudemus says that the Pythagoreans and Plato are right to apply the label "indefinite" (ἀόριστον), to motion, although the text of the last two lines is problematic. Burkert (1972a: 47 n. 106) argues that this clearly refers back to the lines of Eudemus just quoted by Simplicius so that the reference to Pythagoreans must stand for Archytas. Burkert accordingly chastises DK for not including these last four lines in Testimonium A23. According to Burkert, Eudemus first distinguishes Archytas and Plato but later unites them, thus conforming to a pattern, which is especially common in the Academy of the later fourth century but which is also found in Peripatetics such as Theophrastus, according to which Plato and the Pythagoreans are identified (cf. 1972a: 62 n. 57). We have seen, however, that, in the broader context both in Aristotle and in Simplicius' commentary, it is the Pythagoreans of the table of opposites who are connected to the Platonic definitions of motion, because of the indefinite nature of the second column in the table. Eudemus generally follows Aristotle quite closely in his *Physics*, and it is not at all unlikely that he, like Aristotle, discussed the Pythagoreans of the table of opposites, in the material which has been left out by Simplicius. There is, moreover, no evidence to connect Archytas with the table of opposites; Burkert himself does not do so. This means that when Eudemus refers to the Pythagoreans and Plato agreeing in describing motion as indefinite, he is probably referring to the Pythagoreans who put forth the table of opposites and not Archytas. This makes more sense than Burkert's reading, which has Eudemus first say that Archytas did not identify motion with the unequal etc. and then turn around shortly thereafter and say that he did. It would, in fact, be very unusual for a Peripatetic such as Eudemus to identify Archytas with the Pythagoreans in the way that Burkert suggests. Aristotle did not include Archytas in his special treatises on the Pythagoreans and wrote separate treatises on Archytas (A13). Similarly, the references to Archytas elsewhere in Eudemus never identify him as a Pythagorean (A6, A14, A24). Thus, it seems more likely that Archytas is not to be identified with the Pythagoreans, whom Eudemus mentioned "a little later" in his commentary and that the views assigned to them are not evidence for Archytas' views.

After providing this quotation from Eudemus, Simplicius turns back to a direct account of Aristotle's criticism of the Platonic view. He will turn to the text of Plato's *Timaeus* at 432.20, and in the course of his discussion, he will again unite Plato and the Pythagoreans. At 433.13 he refers back to his quotation of Eudemus but only to praise Eudemus' summary of Aristotle's argument against Plato. There is no further reference to Archytas or his view of motion. It would appear that Simplicius quoted Eudemus' reference to Archytas only because it clearly showed that Eudemus (like Aristotle and Alexander) took Plato to be saying that motion was to be identified with inequality and unevenness. Simplicius is not interested in Archytas' view of motion for its own sake and says nothing more about Eudemus' discussion of it, if indeed Eudemus said anything further about it.

What does A23 tell us about Archytas' theory of motion?
The discussion of the context of A23, which I have just given, shows that what Eudemus is ascribing to Archytas is limited to the assertion that "these are causes [of motion]" in line 9. It is difficult to draw many conclusions about Archytas' theory of motion on the basis of such meager evidence. There are problems even in interpreting these few words. It is tolerably clear that Eudemus is asserting that, while Plato identified certain factors with motion, Archytas took a better approach by maintaining that these factors were not identical with motion but rather causes of motion. To which factors precisely did Archytas refer, i.e. precisely what is the reference of "these" in the assertion that "these are causes [of motion]"? We might take "these" to refer back to the entire list of factors which Plato is reported

to have identified with motion: the great and the small, not-being, the uneven, and "as many things as have the same force as these." This seems unlikely, however, for two reasons. First, the great and the small is identified as a distinctively Platonic doctrine by Aristotle (*Metaph.* 987b26), and we would thus not expect Archytas to have talked about it; similarly, Simplicius connects the reference to not-being with Plato's *Sophist* (256d). Second, in the sentence immediately preceding the reference to Archytas, Eudemus refers only to the unequal and uneven so that the most natural reference for "these" is the unequal and the uneven. Equality and inequality are in fact important concepts in other fragments and testimonia of Archytas (e.g. A23a, Fr. 2, Fr. 3); evenness and the process of leveling or making even (ὁμαλότης, ὁμαλίζειν) appear in A22 and A9 respectively. It seems reasonable to conclude, then, that Archytas might have said something like "inequality and unevenness are the causes of motion." What did he mean?

Eudemus' discussion of Plato's theory of motion here as well as Aristotle's similar discussion in *Physics* III.2 are problematic in a number of ways, and I cannot attempt a full discussion of Plato's theory of motion and Aristotle's criticism of it. It may, however, help in understanding what Archytas may have meant to give a brief picture of what Eudemus is saying about Plato. The Platonic view that Aristotle and Eudemus are attacking seems to be most clearly manifested in the discussion of the pre-cosmic motion of the receptacle in the *Timaeus*. At 52e the receptacle is described as filled with powers that are neither similar nor in equipoise (μήθ' ὁμοίων . . . μήτ' ἰσορρόπων). These powers are the powers of the elements earth, air, fire and water, traces of which are to be found in the receptacle before the universe came to be. As a result of the presence of these dissimilar and unevenly balanced powers, the receptacle as a whole is described as swaying unevenly. The adverb "uneven" (ἀνωμάλως) is derived from the adjective used to describe Plato's theory in Eudemus (ἀνωμάλου). It would appear that Eudemus and Aristotle read this passage of the *Timaeus* as identifying the state of "unevenness" of powers with the swaying motion of the receptacle. At 57e Plato returns to the topic of motion and asserts that "we must always place rest in uniformity and motion in non-uniformity" (tr. Cornford). The word translated as "non-uniformity" (ἀνωμαλότης) in this context picks up on the ἀνωμάλως used at 52e. The Greek at 57e is rather imprecise. The expression that Cornford translates literally as "place in" (ἐν . . . εἰς . . . τιθῶμεν) can more idiomatically be interpreted as "reckon among" or "consider as" (LSJ τίθημι B II. 3). For example, at *Republic* 475 Glaucon talks about "considering certain people as philosophers." Eudemus and Aristotle, then, seem to read *Timaeus* 57e as virtually a definition of motion: motion is to be "considered as" or "classified as" unevenness.

There is a testimonium in Aëtius (1. 23.1) which ascribes to Pythagoras and Plato a definition of motion as "a difference or otherness in matter" (διαφορά τις/διαφορότης ἢ ἑτερότης ἐν ὕλῃ). This definition works very well as a description of Plato's account of motion in the *Timaeus*. The "unevenness" or "non-uniformity" (ἀνωμαλότης) of the *Timaeus* is interpreted as "difference" or "otherness" and the receptacle is interpreted as a material principle. The context in Aëtius, however, suggests that the definition may in fact have been generated out of commentary on Aristotle's *Physics*. This is the first definition of motion given by Aëtius and it is immediately followed by Aristotle's definition, a sequence that mirrors Aristotle's consideration of only one earlier definition of motion as a precursor to his own. Moreover, the version of the Platonic/Pythagorean definition given in Stobaeus says that "motion is otherness in matter *qua matter*," which is obviously a formulation based on Aristotle's definition of motion as "the actuality of a potentiality *qua* potentiality" (*Ph.* 201b5) and once again suggests that the "Platonic/Pythagorean" definition is in fact constructed out of commentary on Aristotle. The coupling of Pythagoras with Plato here of course does not suggest that Pythagoras ever gave such a definition of motion. If the doxography is based on commentary on Aristotle's *Physics*, the general term Pythagoreans, which in context referred to the Pythagoreans of the table of opposites, has been replaced with Pythagoras.

There is much that remains obscure but this is a plausible account of how Aristotle, Eudemus and others came to read Plato as arguing that motion was to be defined in terms of "unevenness." As Simplicius points out, however, this is a one-sided reading of the Platonic texts, since Plato goes on at *Timaeus* 58a to say that "inequality is the cause of the non-uniform nature" (αἰτία δὲ ἡ ἀνισότης αὖ τῆς ἀνωμάλου φύσεως). So inequality, at least, is not identified with motion but rather specifically said to be the cause of the unevenness, which is identified with motion. This is not the place to decide whether Aristotle and Eudemus are being perverse in not distinguishing between "inequality" and "unevenness" as Plato appears to do here and in not recognizing that inequality is not identified with motion but is rather the cause of motion. It could be argued that Plato's presentation of motion in this whole section of the *Timaeus* is confused and contradictory. Aristotle and Eudemus act as if Plato has not, in fact, shown a clear distinction between inequality and unevenness and there seems to be some truth to this claim.

Regarding Archytas, however, Eudemus thinks that the case is clear. Inequality and unevenness are not identified with motion but are rather treated as causes of motion. The central difficulty in determining what Archytas may have meant is the lack of the specific Archytan context. We have seen that the Platonic doctrine is developed in the context of the doctrine of the receptacle in the *Timaeus*, and it would be rash in the extreme to assume that Archytas also adopted the receptacle. What can we conclude about Archytas' theory of motion? Three points emerge. First, the testimonium fits a pattern according to which Archytas is explicitly distinguished from Plato and adopts a position which is more congenial to Aristotle than the Platonic position (see the philosophical overview). Second, equality and evenness play a clear role in Archytas' discussion of the state in Fragment 3. That fragment suggests that equality leads to concord and therefore to stability, whereas the pursuit of inequality leads to strife and change. Again in Testimonium A9, Polyarchus describes the lawgivers as wishing to level or to make even (ὁμαλίζειν) the race of men. It seems not implausible to conclude that, both in nature and in the state, Archytas thought that equality and evenness produced stability and freedom from change, whereas inequality and unevenness produced change. Such a connection between natural and political philosophy is paralleled elsewhere in Archytas, particularly in the role he assigns to the science of logistic in both nature and the political sphere (see the philosophical overview). Third, we simply do not know enough about Archytas' account of the natural world to understand how he would flesh out the claim that inequality and unevenness cause motion in physical terms. It is striking, however, that one of the Archytan definitions which Aristotle discusses in the *Metaphysics* (A22) appeals precisely to the concept of evenness. Calm-on-the-ocean (γαλήνη) is defined as "evenness" or "levelness" of sea. The word used for "evenness" is ὁμαλότης, which is the positive form of the word used in A23 for "unevenness" (ἀνωμάλου) as the cause of motion. Thus, Archytas' definitions were consistent with his physical theory. We might wonder, however, whether Eudemus derived his account of Archytas' theory of motion precisely from these definitions. Whereas Plato identified motion with the condition (i.e. the unevenness) of the receptacle and hence with the material principle, Archytas, in his definitions, clearly identifies unevenness as a formal principle, which accordingly cannot be identical with what is moving, i.e. the sea, but must rather be the cause of the motion, as Eudemus suggests. See A23a and Bodnár 2004 for further discussion of Archytas' views on motion.

A23a [Aristotle], *Problems* xvi. 9 (915a25–32)

διὰ τί τὰ μόρια τῶν φυτῶν καὶ τῶν ζῴων, ὅσα μὴ ὀργανικά, πάντα 1
περιφερῆ, τῶν μὲν φυτῶν τὸ στέλεχος καὶ οἱ πτόρθοι, τῶν δὲ ζῴων 2
κνῆμαι, μηροί, βραχίονες, θώραξ· τρίγωνον δὲ οὐδὲ πολύγωνον οὔτε 3
ὅλον οὔτε μόριόν ἐστιν; πότερον, ὥσπερ Ἀρχύτας ἔλεγεν, διὰ τὸ ἐν τῇ 4
κινήσει τῇ φυσικῇ ἐνεῖναι τὴν τοῦ ἴσου ἀναλογίαν (κινεῖσθαι γὰρ ἀνάλ- 5
ογον πάντα), ταύτην δὲ μόνην εἰς αὐτὴν ἀνακάμπτειν, ὥστε κύκλους 6
ποιεῖν καὶ στρογγύλα, ὅταν ἐγγένηται; 7

3–4 οὔτε ὅλον] οὐ ὅλον A^P   **4** οὔτε μόριον] οὐδὲ μόριον Y^a X^a A^P   **6** αὐτὴν] αὐτὴν A^P

Why is it that the parts of plants and animals, which are not instrumental, are all rounded (of plants the stem and the shoots, of animals the calves, thighs, arms, and trunk), but neither the whole nor the part is triangular or polygonal? Is it, just as Archytas used to say, because the proportion of equality is present in natural motion (for he said that all things are moved in proportion), but this proportion alone bends back on itself, so as to make circles and curves, whenever it comes to be in something?

Authenticity

Diels did not include this testimonium in the early editions of *Die Fragmente der Vorsokratiker* but, on the basis of Frank's arguments (1923: 378 ff.), Kranz added it. There seems little reason to doubt its authenticity. It dates early in the tradition before the proliferation of Pythagorean forgeries, since the source is, in all likelihood, either Aristotle himself or an early Peripatetic (see below). Since it comes from the Peripatetic tradition, it is more likely to reflect Aristotle's sober evaluation of the Pythagoreans than the exaggerated praise found in the Academic tradition. Finally, the content shows no suspiciously Platonic or Aristotelian features. Indeed, much of the content is unparalleled, which makes it much more likely to reflect Archytas' actual work than a forgery of a later period designed to gain glory for Archytas. Such forgeries attempt to assign important Platonic and Aristotelian ideas to the Pythagoreans not obscure novelties.

Context

Testimonium A23a is Problem Nine in Book xvi of the *Problems* handed down under the name of Aristotle. Modern scholarship regards the surviving *Problems* as a compilation based primarily on Aristotle's lost *Problems*, Theophrastus and the Hippocratic corpus. The core of the collection seems to date to the middle of the third century BC, although some elements may be considerably later (Flashar 1983, Barker 1989: 85, Forster 1928). Flashar's study indicates that Book XVI does not show any language which is late or contrary to Aristotelian usage (1983: 347–56). A23a is thus likely to have been written by Aristotle or by a member of his school in the fifty or so years after Aristotle's death, although certainty is not possible.

Each of the books of the *Problems* is devoted to a different topic and has a heading specifying the topic. Book XVI is entitled "problems connected to inanimate objects" (ὅσα περὶ τὰ ἄψυχα), but the title is imprecise and the contents somewhat arbitrary (Flashar 1983: 579). Problem Nine itself does not fit the title, because it in fact concerns animate things (plants and animals) and thus would appear more appropriate to be included in the next book of the *Problems*. What does appear to connect Problem Nine to the rest of Book XVI is precisely the discussion of motion and in particular circular motion. Several of the early problems discuss circular motion and the motions of rotating cylinders and cones (3, 5, 6). Some scholars have supposed that Archytas wrote in a problem format (Krafft 1970: 150ff.) or that he lies behind other problems in Book XVI (Flashar 1983: 587). These conclusions far outrun our evidence, although A22 and A24 could be seen as having the form typical of problems. Book XVI may reflect the type of speculation on nature that arose in Archytas' time and in the following generation, but we cannot discern more precisely Archytas' role in developing the problem format or any of the specific problems in Book XVI beyond Problem Nine.

Extent of the testimonium
How much of Problem Nine should be attributed to Archytas? Most scholars seem to tacitly assume that the question about the parts of plants and animals in the first three lines, which is the focus of Problem Nine, was never raised or addressed by Archytas himself. There is, indeed, no other evidence that Archytas wrote anything about the parts of animals and plants. Lines 4–7, where Archytas is first mentioned, do not make any explicit reference to animals and plants or their parts. The author of the *Problems* may thus be saying not that Archytas said "plants and animals have curved parts because the proportion of equality is found in natural motion . . ." but rather that plants and animals have curved parts because, as Archytas said, "the proportion of equality is found in natural motion . . ." On the other hand, it has not been noticed that the vocabulary and the distinctions developed in the biological part of the testimonium (lines 1–4) are not on the whole in accord with the Aristotelian or Theophrastan usage which

we would expect from a Peripatetic author (see below). It thus seems quite possible that these lines are based on the thought of Archytas as well.

Significance of the testimonium

A23a is probably the most obscure of all the testimonia, because it uses technical terminology which is not paralleled elsewhere (e.g. "the proportion of equality") and makes connections between mathematics and motion which are also hard to parallel. As a result, there has been very little scholarly comment on A23a (see most recently Cambiano 1998: 322–23), and any attempt to explain the testimonium will be forced to rely on a considerable amount of conjecture. A23a is potentially quite important, since, along with A23, it provides evidence for Archytas' theory of motion. In addition to employing obscure terminology, however, both testimonia are quite brief and do not address Archytas' theory directly but only allude to it as part of a discussion of other issues (i.e. Plato's theory of motion in A23 and the shape of parts of plants and animals in A23a). It is impossible to provide a coherent and satisfying account of Archytas' theory of motion on the basis of such evidence. What I offer below is a very conjectural and partial account of some of the main points. The argumentation for this reconstruction is to be found in the detailed commentary below.

In A23a Archytas argues that non-instrumental parts of animals and plants (stem, shoots, calves, thighs, arms and trunk) are curved in shape, because they are produced by natural motion and that natural motion, in turn, is curved because it has the proportion of equality in it, which is the only proportion which "bends back on itself" and thus produces circles and curves, whenever it comes to be in something. The detailed notes below make the case for supposing that the terminology for the parts of plants and animals as well as the distinction between instrumental and non-instrumental parts belongs to Archytas rather than to the Peripatetic author of the *Problems*. The primary interest of the testimonium, however, is the theory of motion in terms of which Archytas explains the shape of the indicated parts of plants and animals. In A23 and A23a, Archytas seems to be making four main points about motion:

1. Motion is caused by inequality or unevenness (A23).
This point makes intuitive sense, in that we think of motion arising when an equilibrium is disturbed. If an equilibrium or state of equality persists, there is no motion. It is not clear, however, what is thought of as being equal or unequal. The point may have been quite general. Some sort of quantitative inequality was needed in order for motion to arise, e.g. the

force of human muscles must be greater than the resistance to movement of an object, if the object is to be moved. Archytas would differ from Plato, who may have simply identified the unevenness of the receptacle with its motion (see on A23), in recognizing that inequality does not guarantee movement. There might be other factors which would also be required, e.g. the human muscles would have to come in contact with the object in some way etc.

2. All things are moved in accordance with some proportion (A23a).
It would be most natural to take this point as a development from point 1. If motion arises from inequality, that inequality can be expressed as a ratio. Proportion could then be used to describe the way a motion develops over time, i.e. the proportion describes the relationship of successive stages of the same motion. Each stage of the motion can be analyzed into two components which move at right angles to one another. In modern terms, the object has one movement along the x axis and another movement along the y axis. Archytas probably conceived of the two component motions as motion along two sides of a rectangle (such an analysis of motion is suggested by the pseudo-Aristotelian *Mechanical Problems*. See the detailed commentary below and figures A23a(1) and A23a(2). These two components can be expressed as a ratio, which in turn is part of a proportion which defines the overall progress of the motion.

3. Different types of proportion will define different sorts of motion.
Archytas is here exhibiting what Aristotle recognized as a central feature of Pythagoreanism. He is explaining the world in terms of the similarity between the behavior of numbers (in this case the behavior of proportions) and the behavior of things (in this case the motion of things). His grand insight is that all motions in the world can be explained in terms of mathematical proportions. In a continued geometric proportion, there is no change in the ratio of each successive pair of terms (e.g. 4:2 :: 8:4 :: 16:8 etc.). This proportion is analogous to motion in a straight line, motion in which there is no change in the slope of the line as the motion progresses, i.e. motion along the diagonal of an ever increasing rectangle, whose sides are in the ratio of the given geometric sequence (See figure A23a(1)). There is evidence that another fourth-century Pythagorean, Caeneus (see the detailed commentary), who may have been influenced by Archytas, suggested that the motion of fire was to be explained in terms of a certain type of geometric proportion, the multiple proportion, in which succeeding terms are a given multiple of the preceding terms. Aristotle argued that fire had a natural motion upward. Caeneus, on the

other hand, focuses on the rapidity with which a fire spreads laterally (think of a forest fire). Just as a fire starts small but can quickly come to cover a large area, so a multiple proportion has terms that start small but quickly become great. In a continued multiple proportion where each term is four times the previous one, we can start with 2 and quickly reach terms in the hundreds (2:8 :: 8:32 :: 32:128 :: 128:512).

4. The proportion of equality (i.e. the arithmetic proportion) defines natural motion, which is curved (A23a).

The arithmetic proportion "bends back on itself" (A23a) in that its successive pairs of terms do not maintain the same ratio, as they do in the geometric proportion, but "turn back" to get progressively smaller (e.g. 2:1 > 3:2 > 4:3 > 5:4 etc.). Like the arithmetic proportion, natural motion turns back on itself and produces curves. It appears that Archytas takes it as a brute fact that natural motion is curved, giving the parts of plants and animals as examples. Once again, if we analyze motions as is suggested in the *Mechanical Problems*, each segment of motion according to an arithmetic proportion will be the diagonal of a rectangle, the sides of which are equal to the pair of terms in the arithmetic proportion (e.g. using the arithmetic proportion given above, in the first segment the motion will be along the diagonal of the rectangle with sides 2 and 1, in the next segment it will be along the diagonal of a rectangle with sides 3 and 2; see figure A23a(2)). This means that the slope of the line in the motion according to the arithmetic proportion will not stay the same, as it does in the case of a geometrical proportion, but will be constantly changing, and the resultant motion will be a curve (see figure A23a(3)). Such a curve will not in fact be part of a circle, but this might not have been clear to Archytas, and he might have assumed that some of the curves produced by arithmetic progressions were indeed parts of circles.

Archytas' theory of motion is a significant step beyond any treatment of motion either among the Presocratics in general, or among the Pythagoreans in particular. In the *Metaphysics*, Aristotle asserts that none of the Presocratics had given a thorough account of motion (985b19), although several had identified the source of motion as a cause (e.g. Empedocles identified Love and Strife as sources of motion). He particularly complains about the Pythagoreans' failure to explain how motion arises (990a8). When he turns to examine the precursors to his definition of motion in the *Physics* (201b16), he evidently can find only one previous definition, which the commentators ascribe to Plato and the Pythagoreans who developed the table of opposites (see A23). Archytas does not give a definition of motion, but he attempts to give a general theory of motion which (1) explains the cause of motion in terms of impersonal natural laws (inequality of forces rather than Love and Strife); (2) argues that all motions can be described mathematically in terms of different kinds of proportions; (3) connects specific kinds of motion with specific proportions (e.g. the geometric proportion describes motion in a straight line, while the arithmetic proportion describes curved motion). This theory contains fanciful elements and does not begin to answer all questions about the nature of motion, but it can be seen as a step towards a general theory. Certainly there is no trace of a theory of motion to be found in the fragments and testimonia of Archytas' predecessor in the Pythagorean tradition, Philolaus.

Archytas' theory also differs significantly from that of Plato. For Plato motion is a phenomenon of the sensible world and is thus at base disorderly. Plato has a tendency to identify motion with unevenness and inequality and to regard these in turn as indefinite and not definable in terms of number (see A23). The demiurge has to impose a mathematical order on this disorderly motion. The Pythagoreans of the table of opposites similarly regard motion as being essentially indefinite and associate it with characteristics of the "indefinite" column in the table of opposites. Archytas' point of view is quite different. Motion is not in its nature disorder. It does arise because of an inequality or an imbalance, but that inequality can be expressed in number, and motion always embodies some sort of proportion. Proportion describes the essential nature of the phenomena of the physical world and is not imposed from above.

Archytas occupies a sort of middle position between Plato and Aristotle. He does not make a split between a sensible and intelligible world, so that he does not have Plato's problems of accounting for the relationship between the disorderly motion of the receptacle and the orderly motion imposed by the demiurge. On the other hand, he describes the physical world largely in mathematical terms so that to Aristotle it is unclear how he can actually account for the physical nature of phenomena. Archytas, like Philolaus before him, however, finds an account of the world in terms of material principles inadequate. It is mathematical concepts that are the essence of the physical world not material stuffs. As Aristotle himself puts it in the *Metaphysics*, the Pythagoreans saw more similarities between things and numbers than between things and material principles such as earth, air, fire and water (*Metaph.* 985b27), and accordingly made numbers and not material elements the center of their account of the world. There is no doubt that they appealed to material principles as well (e.g. Archytas' definitions in A22 appeal to a "material" principle). They simply disagree with Aristotle on whether the world is more like a stuff or more like a number. Philolaus had been interested in how number and ratios accounted for the structure of the world, but that structure was largely viewed statically. Archytas takes a bold step further and accounts for another central feature of the world, its motion, in terms of mathematical proportion.

Frank's account of Archytas' theory of motion

Erich Frank argued that Archytas' treatment of motion was central to his achievement and indeed to his philosophy as a whole (1923: 124–34). Frank's account of Archytas' theory of motion is, however, radically different from the account that I have presented above. According to Frank motion was the essence of the corporeal world for Archytas, and motion indeed formed the matter of bodies. The problem with Frank's account is that it has very little basis in the surviving evidence. One would think that A23 and A23a, where Archytas' theory of motion is explicitly discussed, would be the basis of any account of Archytas' theory of motion. Frank argued that A23a was genuine (378 n. 365), leading to the inclusion of A23a in DK, but he makes essentially no use either of it or of A23 in developing his account of the role of motion in Archytas. There is nothing in A23 or A23a to suggest that Archytas regarded motion as the matter or essence of things. Indeed Archytas' assertion that "all things are moved in proportion" (A23a, lines 5–6) seems to patently assume that there are objects which undergo motion rather than that objects just are motions. Frank's evidence for assigning the view that matter is motion to Archytas is a report not about Archytas but rather about Pythagoras, which he arbitrarily transfers to Archytas (see the commentary on A13F).

Detailed commentary

Line 1   ὅσα μὴ ὀργανικά – The concept of instrumental parts of plants and animals, which is being employed here, is most puzzling, since it does not match the distinctions between types of parts found in Aristotle or Theophrastus. Here in A23a we do not know with what other types of parts "instrumental parts" are contrasted; we know only that stems and shoots of plants and calves, thighs, arms and trunks of animals are not regarded as instrumental parts. Aristotle divides the natural parts of animals into uniform (ὁμοιομερές) and non-uniform parts (e.g. *GA* 724b23) and often refers to the non-uniform parts as instrumental parts (e.g. *GA* 734b28; see Peck 1942: XVII ff.). Substances such as blood, semen, bile and flesh are regarded as uniform parts, while the non-uniform or instrumental parts include the head, the neck, the trunk, the two arms, and the two legs (*HA* 491a25 ff.; cf. *PA* 646b13). The problem is that the arms, trunk and legs are here labeled instrumental parts by Aristotle, whereas they are said not to be instrumental in A23a. Aristotle like A23a does treat the parts of plants as in some sense analogous to the parts of animals. At *De An.* 412b1 he describes plants as having organs and gives the leaves and the roots as examples.

Theophrastus also develops an analogy between the parts of plants and the parts of animals (*HP* 1. 1.9 ff.). The four major parts of the plant according to Theophrastus are the root, the stem, the branch and the twig. The Greek words used by Theophrastus do not match those used in A23a (see below), but the stem and the branch basically correspond to the stem and the shoot in A23a. The problem once again is that, while these parts are labeled "non-instrumental" in A23a, Theophrastus appears to regard them as instrumental. He contrasts the root and stem with "uniform" parts of plants such as bark. The part of the root or the stem of a plant is not called "root" or "stem" but rather "a part of a root," whereas a portion of a uniform part such as bark is simply called bark. He then says that the same distinction applies to non-uniform and uniform parts of an animal such as bone in contrast to an arm or a leg. Thus the stem of the plant is regarded as a non-uniform part of a plant in contrast to the bark which is a uniform (ὁμοιομερές) part, and these parts of the plant are in turn seen as analogous to the contrast in animals between the leg, which is non-uniform, and flesh, which is uniform. The non-uniform parts of both plants and animals seem to be regarded as "instrumental" just as they were in Aristotle (*HP* 1. 1.12).

The author of *Problems* XVI. 9 (A23a) was thus deploying a different distinction from those of Aristotle and Theophrastus. This author could be an innovative Peripatetic, but it is also possible that the distinction in fact belongs to Archytas and that the entirety of A23a reflects the work of Archytas and not just the reference to natural motion. If the author of A23a is deploying a different distinction between the instrumental and the non-instrumental, what is it? A hint is provided by a further division of instrumental parts (ὀργανικῶν) made by Theophrastus (*HP* 1. 1.12). He divides instrumental parts into those that are "of one form" (μονοειδῆ) and those that are "of many forms" (πολυειδῶν). Instrumental parts "of one form" (Hort 1916 confuses parts of one form, μονοειδῆ, with uniform parts, ὁμοιομερές) are parts such as the leg or arm, any part of which does not have a proper name but is simply called "part of an arm" (it is not clear what Theophrastus would say about a knee or an elbow, which do seem to be named parts of legs and arms). Instrumental parts "of many forms" are those parts such as the foot, the hand, or the head, whose parts do have names (e.g. toe, finger, nose or eye.). The author of A23a may then have had a similar distinction except that he reserved the term "instrumental parts" for parts such as the foot, the hand or the head, whose parts all have separate names, while regarding parts such as the leg or the arm as not properly instrumental, since none of their parts do have proper names.

The distinction in A23a would then be that instrumental parts, properly speaking, are those parts which are composed of instruments: the hand is composed of the fingers as instruments, the foot of toes, the head of eyes, ears, nose etc. The parts of the body listed in A23a are not properly instrumental because their parts are not instruments but rather "uniform parts"; the calf, the thigh, the arm, the trunk are all made up of bone, flesh, blood etc. It might be that there is a three-fold division into instrumental parts (e.g. hand), simple parts or limbs (arms, legs, trunk), and uniform parts (blood, flesh etc.). A23a would be arguing that all limbs are rounded in shape, whereas instrumental parts such as the hand or foot might in fact be closer to triangular or polygonal in shape. The head seems to be a problem, since it is clearly curved in shape. Moreover, the hand and the foot would seem to be just as natural as the arm or the leg so that, if curved shape is explained by natural motion being curved, then this ought to apply to the hand as well. In spite of these difficulties the basic observation might be that, looked at generally, both plants and animals seem to have main divisions or limbs which are rounded in shape, while in each case certain extremities, such as hands and feet in animals and leaves in plants, have shapes that can often be more naturally described as triangular or polygonal.

2 περιφερῆ – The adjective περιφερής has a range of meanings from "curved" or "rounded" to "circular" or "spherical," depending on the context in which it is used. It often serves as the opposite of εὐθύς (straight), e.g. Arist., *APo.* 73a39. At Arist., *Cael.* 298a7 it refers to a spherical shape (περιφερὲς ὂν τὸ σχῆμα τῆς γῆς). There has been controversy as to whether at *Phaedo* 108e the context suggests that Plato is describing the earth as merely curved in some sense or as properly spherical (see Gallop 1975: 223 for references), but in the *Timaeus* the term clearly means spherical (e.g. 44d4). Here in *Problems* XVI. 9, it seems best to use the translation "curved" or "round(ed)" (Forster 1984: 1424) rather than "circular" (Hett 1953: 359). Certainly the arms and legs cannot be taken to be literally circular. In the immediately following problem (XVI. 10, 915a33), it once again appears that the question must be "why are the extremities of things always rounded" (περιφερῆ) rather than "circular," for it might plausibly be suggested that extremities of things are usually curved, but it is implausible to suppose that extremities are always circular. Theophrastus does not accept the assertion of A23a that all stems of plants are rounded, since he regards the stems of the papyrus and the sari as triangular (*HP* IV. 8.3.7; IV. 8.5.6).

στέλεχος – The usage of this word to mean "stem" is decidedly atypical for a Peripatetic treatise. στέλεχος appears six times in Aristotle and over eighty times in Theophrastus. In these authors, however, it always seems to refer to the trunk of a tree, whereas here in A23a, where it is used of plants in general (φυτῶν), it must mean stem. Theophrastus' word for stem is καυλός (*HP* I. 1.9) and the trunk of a tree is viewed as a special type of καυλός, although it is true that Theophrastus uses the tree as the paradigm example of a plant (*HP* I. 12).

πτόρθοι – Paired with στέλεχος, this word seems to be a general word for all branches or shoots out from the main stem of a plant. Once again the usage is unusual for a Peripatetic treatise. πτόρθος is not a common word in general. It appears only once in all of Theophrastus and five times in Aristotle. The instances in Aristotle and a single instance in Plato point to a basic meaning of "shoots," i.e. new growth sent up from a seed, as opposed to roots, which are sent down into the earth (Arist. *GA* 741b37; Pl. *Prt.* 334b2). Other passages in Aristotle suggest that it refers to the opposite extremity of a plant from the root, i.e. the ends of the branches from which seeds are produced (*PA* 687a2). In its sole appearance in Theophrastus (*CP* v. 1.3), it is used as a synonym for the common terms κλῶνες and ἀκρεμόνες and refers to the extremities of the tree or plant (τὰ ἐσχατεύοντα τῶν δένδρων). Thus A23a uses πτόρθοι in a way that Theophrastus or Aristotle would understand, but it is not the word that is typical for branches or shoots in the Peripatetic tradition.

3 κνῆμαι, μηροί, βραχίονες, θώραξ – These are all the standard words used by Aristotle to refer to these parts of the body (lower leg, thigh, arm, trunk). κνήμη is often translated calf but is more properly the whole lower leg between the knee and the foot, while the calf (γαστροκνημία) is just the back part of the lower leg (*HA* 494a5). The relationship between the thigh and the lower leg is the subject of some of the *Problems* (v. 24 and 26, 883a30 and 883b14) and *Mechanical Problems* (30, 857b22).

3–4 οὔτε ὅλον οὔτε μόριον – These words make the point that it is not just the stem of a plant or the arm of an animal as a whole that is rounded but also that any segment of stem or arm, i.e. anything we would call "arm" rather than "flesh," is also rounded.

4–5 ἐν τῇ κινήσει τῇ φυσικῇ – What exactly is the conception of natural motion which is being ascribed to Archytas here and with what other sort(s) of motion did he set it in contrast? The concept of natural motion is not explicitly developed in the Presocratics or Plato but is central to Aristotle's account of the natural world. As Solmsen points out, the basic elements out of which Aristotle constructs the natural world are most of all distinguished by their natural motions. Natural movements are in a sense more basic than the elements, since "the existence of simple [natural] movements proves the existence of simple bodies [elements]" (*Cael.* 302b5, 304b20; see Solmsen 1960: 255). It is the existence of the circular motion of the heavens as a natural motion which leads Aristotle (*De Caelo* 268b11 ff.) to posit aether as a fifth element. For Aristotle, natural motions, the proper motions of the elements, are contrasted with motions imposed by force (βίᾳ) or contrary to nature (παρὰ φύσιν, *Cael.* 300a23).

Archytas' account of natural motion in A23a is different from the Aristotelian conception in several ways. First, for Archytas natural motion is apparently limited to circular or curved motion, while for Aristotle circular motion was only one of several natural motions. Second, whereas for Aristotle circular motion is the natural motion of the heavens, A23a suggests that Archytas recognized circular motion as a natural motion operative in plants and animals. Finally, while for Aristotle the explanatory principles of physics are and must be physical bodies, Archytas appears to make his ultimate explanatory principle mathematical in nature, i.e. the proportion of the equal. Aristotle would therefore have been critical of Archytas, as he was of Plato, for using a principle which properly belongs to mathematics to explain physical phenomena (*Cael.* 306a5 ff.; *APo.* 75a38 ff.).

Can we say anything else about Archytas' conception of natural motion? There is a tendency to assume that natural motion is the "best motion" in some sense and that circular motion is the highest form of this "best motion," but it is far from clear to what extent Archytas made these assumptions. It is true that in a report about the Pythagorean *acusmata*, which is likely to be based on Aristotle's lost work on the Pythagoreans and thus to be based on material that predates Archytas, there is the assertion that the sphere and the circle are the finest (κάλλιστον) of solid and plane figures respectively (D.L. viii. 34 ff. = DK i. 463.24). Since Philolaus, who was Archytas' predecessor and perhaps his teacher, also made his cosmos spherical (Fr. 7), it is sometimes assumed that Archytas is starting from a basic Pythagorean principle that the sphere and the circle are the best of shapes and thus that circular motion is the best of motions (Burkert 1972a: 169 n. 23). The importance of circular motion in the Pythagorean tradition is also indicated by the cyclical notion of time in the doctrine of eternal recurrence. Eudemus reports that certain unnamed Pythagoreans believed that "numerically the same things" come again (Simpl. *In Phys.* 732.26–733.1; cf. Por. *VP* 19 and Sorabji 1983: 182–83).

Even outside the Pythagorean tradition there is a prominent strain in Greek thought that regards circular motion as the primary motion and associates it with immortality and reason. Alcmaeon already associated the everlasting motion of the heavens with immortality (Arist. *De An.* 405a30), and his assertion that men die because they cannot join beginning to end ([Arist.], *Pr.* 916a24) seems to assume that immortality is associated with circular motion, which does join beginning to end (see Guthrie 1962: 350–57). Plato's proof of the immortality of the soul in the *Phaedrus* and his association of reason with circular motion (*Lg.* 898a, *Ti.* 40a) may both show the influence of Alcmaeon. There can be no doubt that for Plato circular motion is the noblest motion (see Solmsen 1960: 36–37). Aristotle arrives at the same conclusion, i.e. that circular movement is first in all respects, although by a different route, stressing that circular motion is the only continuous motion (*Physics* VIII. 260a20 ff.; Solmsen 1960: 235 ff.).

In light of all this evidence for the exalted place of circular motion, it is tempting to assume that Archytas too regards circular motion as the primary and highest sort of motion and that it is for this reason that he associates it with natural motion. Indeed, Flashar (1983: 587) has suggested that A23a must be supplemented by the immediately following passage in the *Problems* (Problem Ten) in order to grasp Archytas' full conception of natural motion. This problem asks why it is that things are always round at the edges. The answer is based on the twin assumptions (1) that nature always makes things as good and beautiful as possible from what is available, and (2) that this shape [the circle] is the most beautiful, since it is most like itself. To assign this problem and these assumptions to Archytas without further argument, however, is to beg the question about his attitude to natural motion and circular motion. Problem Ten also virtually quotes from the *Timaeus* (*Pr.* 915a35 τὸ αὐτὸ αὐτῷ ὁμοιότατον – *Ti.* 33b ὁμοιότατόν τε αὐτὸ ἑαυτῷ) and is thus clearly Platonic in outlook.

On the other hand, *Mechanical Problems*, which is generally regarded as a Peripatetic treatise of the fourth or third century BC and which shows some connections to Archytas (see below and Krafft 1970), takes a more neutral attitude towards nature. Nature does not always bring about what is best for us and is said often to act contrary to our advantage. Therefore we must use skill (*technē*) in order to overcome nature (847a ff.). *Mechanical Problems* does regard the circle as "most wonderful," because of the way in which it combines opposites (847b16 ff.), and uses the circle to explain other wonders, but most of these wonders are wonders of machines and not nature. *Mechanical Problems*, indeed, unlike Archytas, does not regard circular motion as natural motion but rather as a compound of a natural motion in the direction of the tangent and an unnatural motion towards the center (849a15 ff.). This among other reasons should make us hesitant to identify Archytas too closely with *Mechanical Problems*. Nonetheless, *Mechanical Problems* does show that natural motion did not necessarily carry with it the connotations of "the best motion" in technical writing of the fourth century.

We can take a further step in understanding Archytas' theory of natural motion by asking what other sort(s) of motion Archytas set in contrast to natural motion. The adjective "instrumental," which is used in A23a not to describe motion directly but rather to describe parts of animals, may provide a clue. As the commentary above has shown, the usage in the biological part of the problem does not in fact correspond very well with anything in Aristotle or Theophrastus, and it is thus reasonable to entertain the idea that the whole of *Problems* XVI. 9 is based on Archytas rather than just the answer. In the first part of the problem "instrumental parts" are those parts of an animal or plant which are composed of "instruments" and which in humans at least are those parts that we use to accomplish our purposive action, i.e. the head, the hands, and the feet. It would appear then that Archytas may be distinguishing between natural motion and instrumental motion. The point would be not that natural motion is curved and instrumental motion is not but rather that natural motion is always curved, whereas instrumental motion, motion used as a means by intelligence, need not be. The attitude here seems similar to *Mechanical Problems*, in that natural motion is not being privileged as the best sort of motion. Archytas is observing that nature left to itself produces curves and that these curves can be understood as manifesting "the proportion of equality". Instrumental motion on the other hand is the motion of skill, e.g. the motion of the hand. Such motion can be circular but need not be. Intelligence is free to use all sorts of proportion but nature has no such freedom.

That Archytas might be working with the distinction between natural and instrumental motion which I have just described receives some further confirmation from his optics as revealed in A25. We might suppose that vision is a natural activity and that it should thus involve circular motion rather than the linear motion which is in fact assumed in A25. The distinctive feature of Archytas' theory of vision, however, is that he relies solely on the visual ray which proceeds from the eye, in contrast to Plato who has the visual ray combine with a ray coming from the object of sight. Thus, in Archytas' theory, sight is a purely purposive activity and is accordingly a prime example of instrumental motion. It is in no way surprising then that the visual ray has the characteristics of linear rather than circular motion.

5 τὴν τοῦ ἴσου ἀναλογίαν – This is the most puzzling phrase in a puzzling testimonium. Many of the translators or commentators on the *Problems* (e.g. Forster and Flashar) have not even attempted to give an explanation of it (I discuss Hett's explanation at the end of this note). Burkert (1972a: 78 n. 156) suggests that "the proportion of equality" should be understood in a general sense as "the power of mathematics that governs the world." In A23a, however, the proportion of equality is contrasted with other sorts of proportion ("this proportion alone") so that it has to be a specific sort of proportion. Frank (1923: 378 n. 365) evidently takes "the proportion of the equal" to be "the ratio of the equal" (e.g. n:n), but he gives no argument for this suggestion, nor does he show how such an interpretation helps us to understand the testimonium. ἀναλογία does not, moreover, mean ratio.

In its broadest sense ἀναλογία refers to any similarity between two ratios so that A has a relation to B that is similar to the relation that C has to D. The evidence suggests, however, that "originally [only] the geometric proportion was called ἀναλογία, the others, the arithmetic, the harmonic, etc., means; but later usage . . . obliterated the distinction" (Heath 1925: II. 293). The early usage is to some extent reflected in Plato and Aristotle where ἀναλογία often just means "geometric proportion" (e.g. 2:4 :: 6:12). Thus, at *EN* 1131a31, Aristotle defines ἀναλογία as "equality of ratio," a definition that fits only the geometric proportion. The only other use of ἀναλογία in the *Problems* apart from A23a is an example of just such a use (910b36). It was, however, also applied to other sorts of proportion, and in Fragment 2 Archytas himself uses ἀναλογία of both the arithmetic and the harmonic proportion (see the commentary on Fragment 2, line 5 for a more detailed discussion of Greek usage of ἀναλογία). Here in A23a, the addition of the qualifying words "of the equal" (τοῦ ἴσου) might be taken, in light of Platonic and Aristotelian usage, to indicate that Archytas is referring not to the geometric proportion, which could be indicated by the simple ἀναλογία, but rather to some other type of proportion, which could be described as "the proportion of the equal," but this enigmatic expression requires further examination.

A complete corpus search of the TLG reveals no precise parallel for the expression, "the proportion of the equal." The only passage that is reasonably similar to A23a comes from the commentary on Book 5 of Aristotle's *Nicomachean Ethics* by the Byzantine writer of the twelfth century AD, Michael of Ephesus (for whom see Sorabji 1990b: 20–22; Mercken 1990: 429–36). The passage (*CAG* XXII. 3: 16.10) is commentary on *EN* 1130b28 and defines an arithmetic proportion: ἀναλογία οὖν ἀριθμητική ἐστιν ἡ ποσοῦ μὲν ἴσου ἐν ταῖς διαφοραῖς (cf. Nicom. *Ar.* II. 23.4). Since ἀναλογία is to be understood with ἡ, the latter phrase becomes ἡ ποσοῦ μὲν ἴσου ἐν ταῖς διαφοραῖς [ἀναλογία] ("the proportion of equal quantity in differences"), which is reasonably close to the ἡ τοῦ ἴσου ἀναλογία, which we find in Archytas A23a. Of course, Michael, writing some sixteen centuries later cannot serve as any sort of direct evidence for Archytas' usage. The passage does show, however, the thought process by which the arithmetic proportion could come to be known as "the proportion of the equal," i.e. in the arithmetic proportion there is an equal amount of difference between each term in the proportion (e.g. 2:4 :: 4:6 where 4 − 2 − 2 and 6 − 4 = 2).

At first sight, Fragment 2 of Archytas might seem to suggest a different interpretation of "the proportion of the equal." Archytas compares the arithmetic, geometric and harmonic proportions to one another in terms of a comparison of the ratio of the greater terms in each proportion with the ratio of the lesser terms in each proportion. In the arithmetic proportion, the ratio of the greater terms is less than that of the lesser terms (e.g. 12:9 < 9:6); in the geometric proportion, the ratio of the greater terms is equal to that of the lesser terms (e.g. 12:6 = 6:3); in the harmonic proportion, the ratio of the greater terms is greater than the ratio of the lesser terms (e.g. 12:8 > 8:6). We might then conclude that, since Archytas calls the ratio of the greater terms "equal" to the ratio of the lesser terms in the geometric proportion, Archytas might call the geometric proportion the "proportion of equality." We thus have two different ways of understanding what could be meant by "the proportion of equality." If we think in terms of the ratios between the two sets of terms in the proportion, then it is the geometric proportion, which is the proportion of equality, but, if we think in terms of the arithmetical difference between the two sets of terms, it is the arithmetic proportion, which is "the proportion of equality." Nicomachus (*Ar.* II. 23.4) makes the same point by saying that the arithmetic proportion partakes of equal quantity whereas the geometric proportion partakes of equal quality. The evidence for each interpretation is about equal. Fragment 2 argues to some extent for the geometric proportion, but it should be noted that Archytas does not explicitly call the geometric proportion the proportion of equality there. On the other hand, typical Greek usage would suggest that "the proportion of equality" must be some proportion other than the geometric proportion, which is usually indicated by the unadorned term ἀναλογία, and in this case the arithmetic proportion is the logical candidate.

Another approach to deciding whether the arithmetic or geometric proportion is meant by the proportion of equality is to see if either of these proportions can be regarded as "bending back on itself" and "producing circles and curves". It is hard to see how the geometric proportion could be said to bend back on itself, since the ratios in the proportion are equal to one another. It seems to repeat itself with ever increasing numbers rather than bend back or go back. On the other hand, it is a characteristic of an arithmetic progression that the ratio between the successive terms becomes smaller and smaller. The progression bends back on itself in that, rather than expanding to a greater and greater ratio, or even maintaining the same ratio, it turns back to smaller and smaller ratios. The first ratio in an extended arithmetic proportion is always the greatest and as the progression continues the ratios get closer and closer to 1:1 (e.g. 2:1, 3:2, 4:3, 5:4 etc.). In Fragment 2, Archytas himself drew attention to the fact that while the ratios in the geometric progression remained always the same and the ratios in the harmonic progression got larger as the terms increased, the ratios in the arithmetic progression got smaller as the terms increased. This interpretation of the arithmetic proportion turning back on itself gets further support, because this understanding of the arithmetic proportion can also be connected to circular motion.

The manner in which Archytas might have made such a connection is shown by passages in a treatise handed down under the name of Aristotle, *Mechanical Problems*. There is considerable doubt whether this is an authentic work of Aristotle (Krafft 1970 suggests that it is an early work of Aristotle). Most scholars make it, like the *Problems*, a work composed in the Peripatetic school in the fifty years or so after the death of Aristotle. It thus presents conceptions which were current in the hundred years or so after Archytas' death and may thus not be a bad indicator to possible approaches to explaining motion in Archytas' time as well. Indeed, it has been argued that the treatise is heavily indebted to a work on mechanics by Archytas (Krafft 1970). What follows may be taken as further evidence for Archytas' connection to the *Mechanical Problems*, but the evidence does not show that Archytas wrote a treatise specifically on mechanics as opposed to a more general account of the cosmos. Nor does the evidence admit of any stronger conclusion than that Archytas is one possible source for the *Mechanical Problems* or that the author of that treatise and Archytas had similar approaches to problems concerning motion.

At first sight it would appear that the *Mechanical Problems* cannot help to explain the connection between curved motion and arithmetic proportion, since neither arithmetic nor geometric proportion are mentioned in that treatise. The absence of these specific proportions and even ἀναλογία itself from the treatise is one of the reasons for doubting that the connections with Archytas can be very direct, since proportion is clearly crucial to Archytas' conception of movement (ἀνάλογον appears three times at 849b ff. but with no clear connection to Archytas). At *Mechanical Problems* 848b10, however, the principle is stated that "whenever a body is moved in two directions in a fixed ratio (ἐν λόγῳ τινί) it necessarily travels in a straight line, which is the diagonal of the figure which the lines arranged in this ratio describe" (tr. Hett). Thus, if a body's motion is analyzed into two components and it is conceived of as traveling e.g. four units on one axis and two units on another axis perpendicular to the first movement, its actual movement will be the diagonal of the rectangle whose sides are four and two respectively. Its movement will thus be on a straight line which is the diameter of a rectangle whose sides get larger and larger but always maintain the same ratio to one another. The interesting thing for our purposes is that, since the ratio of the sides stays the same as the rectangle increases in size (this is what it means to say it is moved "in fixed ratio"), the ratios of the sides of the ever larger rectangles will form a continued geometric proportion (e.g. 4:2 :: 8:4 :: 16:8 etc.; see figure A23a(1)). Thus, motion in a straight line can be connected to geometric proportion.

A little later in the *Mechanical Problems* at 848b31, a related principle is stated: "the body that travels in no constant ratio and in no fixed time will not make a straight line . . . So that if it moves in two directions with no fixed time it will be a curve (περιφερές)" (tr. Hett). This principle can be strikingly connected to the arithmetic proportion and hence to Archytas' connection between "the proportion of equality" and curved bodies. Note that both A23a and the *Mechanical Problems* use the same word περιφερές ("curved") to describe the result of the motion. As we have seen above, the ratio in the successive terms of the arithmetic proportion gets smaller and smaller as the proportion is continued and thus in a sense "turns back" on itself. It is also true, moreover, that the ratio of each successive pair of terms is constantly changing or, to use the language of the *Mechanical Problems*, a body traveling according to an arithmetic proportion would travel in no (constant) ratio (ἐν μηδενὶ λόγῳ, e.g. 2:1, 3:2, 4:3, 5:4 etc.).

The body traveling according to the arithmetic proportion would thus travel along the diagonal of rectangles whose sides are constantly changing in proportion. In the first segment of motion it would travel along the diagonal of a rectangle with sides 2 and 1 so that the slope of the line would be 2. In the second segment of the motion it would travel along the diagonal of a rectangle with sides 3 and 2 so that the slope of the line would be 1.5. Each successive segment of motion would thus be at a different slope (see figure A23a(2)). If these segements of motion are combined they will not produce a straight line, since they do not have the same slope, but rather a curved line (see figure A23a(3)). The curve produced will not be part of a circle but will approach the value 1 asymptotically. This might not have been clear to Archytas or he might have thought that the curve was close enough to being a part of a circle to describe the arithmetical proportion as "producing circles and curves." The addition of the qualification "in no (fixed) time," in the *Mechanical Problems*, might be intended to insure that the ratio is in fact constantly changing and that there is no period of time in which it remains fixed. If the ratio did remain fixed for a period of time, during that period of time the object would travel in a straight line, so that its overall movement would in fact be a sum of linear movements, whereas, in a curved movement, there are no linear movements.

The other main type of proportion known to Archytas, the harmonic proportion, will also have pairs of terms whose ratios are constantly changing and a body moving according to this proportion will also describe a curve. In this case, however, as Archytas points out in Fragment 2, the ratios will get greater as the proportion is continued (e.g. 8:6, 12:8 etc.; see further on Fr. 2). The difference between an object moving according to the arithmetic proportion and an object moving according to a harmonic proportion is that the former will "bend back on itself" to produce a tighter and tighter curve, whereas the latter will produce a curve that is continually opening out. Certainty is of course not possible where the evidence is so meager, but, with the help of these passages from the *Mechanical Problems*, we can construct a plausible case for arguing that by "the proportion of the equal" which "bends back on itself" and "creates circles and curves, whenever it comes to be in something" Archytas means the arithmetic proportion (Cambiano [1998: 322–23] also argues that "the proportion of the equal" is the arithmetic proportion but does not explain how it is connected to motion).

If we can use the *Mechanical Problems* in this way to explicate what Archytas is doing in A23a, it appears that he is both drawing an analogy between the way a proportion behaves and the way physical objects move (e.g. they both "bend back") and also attempting to describe physical motions in terms of precise mathematical ratios. This combination of seeing analogies between numbers and things and hoping that numbers can in fact give us knowledge of things is precisely what we find in Aristotle's descriptions of early Pythagoreanism and in Archytas' predecessor and possible teacher Philolaus. In the testimony of Aristotle and in Philolaus, however, the focus is on the similarities between individual numbers and things (e.g. four and justice) or on ratios as structural principles in the cosmos (Philolaus Fr. 6a). Archytas can then be seen as carrying the earlier Pythagorean program a step further by addressing the problem of motion and explaining it in terms of various sorts of continued proportion.

There is a striking parallel for Archytas' attempt to connect proportion with natural movement. Aristotle describes a certain Caeneus as arguing that fire consists in multiple proportion, on the grounds that both fire and this proportion spread quickly (*APo.* 77b41 ff.). "Multiple proportion" is usually, if a bit imprecisely, taken to mean geometric proportion. The geometric proportion is the only proportion that can be made up of ratios which are multiple and such multiples are the typical examples given for the geometric proportion (e.g. 1:2 :: 2:4 :: 4:8; or 1:3 :: 3:9 :: 9:27; see Nicom. *Ar.* II. 24.2), but a geometric proportion can also be made up of other than multiple ratios (Nicom. *Ar.* II. 24.4), so that a proportion consisting of multiple ratios is really just one type of geometric proportion. Caeneus' point is that the terms in such a geometric proportion increase in magnitude quickly as the proportion is extended (e.g. 1, 2, 4, 8, 16 . . .). The higher the multiple, the quicker the terms of the proportion grow (e.g. 1, 4, 16, 64, 256 . . .). The similarity to Archytas consists in the attempt to connect the behavior of a mathematical proportion to the behavior of some aspect of the natural world. For Archytas the natural motion which produces non-instrumental parts of plants and animals bends back to produce curves just as the terms of the arithmetic proportion bend back to smaller and smaller values. For Caeneus fire spreads rapidly, just as the value of the successive terms of a geometric proportion grows rapidly.

Unfortunately Caeneus is a bit of a mystery. Most references to Caeneus in Greek literature are to the figure in Greek myth, who was famous as one of the Lapiths, who fought against the Centaurs. Obviously Aristotle cannot be referring to the mythological figure. Philoponus, in his commentary on the *Posterior Analytics*, calls Caeneus a sophist with no further explanation (*CAG* XIII. 3: 159.46 and 160.3). Ross (1949: 548) notes that this looks like a guess and takes Caeneus to be the Lapith after all, but supposes him to be a character in a play of the same name by the comic poet Antiphanes, a contemporary of Aristotle (so also Barnes 1994: 153).

The only thing to suggest that Aristotle is referring to Caeneus as a character in the play, besides the fact that the Lapith is the most famous bearer of the name, is the rather tenuous point that Aristotle alludes to a line from this play elsewhere in his corpus. He in fact refers to the same line in three different places (*Rh.* 1407a17, 1413a1 and *Po.* 1457b21). He never, however, explicitly identifies the line as coming from Antiphanes or from the *Caeneus*. We are indebted to Athenaeus (x. 433c) for quoting the lines with explicit attribution to the *Caeneus* of Antiphanes (*PCG* ii. 369). In these lines Antiphanes ascribes the expression "the wine-bowl of Ares" to the poet Timotheus. All that we can conclude from Aristotles' quotation of this line is that he knew of the play *Caeneus* by Antiphanes. We in fact know nothing which would suggest that the Lapith in Antiphanes' play would have ever talked about geometric proportion, and it is *prima facie* improbable. Ross rests content with saying that "in burlesque all things are possible." Possible maybe but not probable. On the evidence given so far, it is better to follow Tredennick (1960: 82–83) in concluding that "Caeneus *may* be the Lapith in Antiphanes' play . . . but he may equally well have been a real person, though unknown to us."

There is, however, further evidence that has been neglected and which suggests that Caeneus was a writer of the fourth century. In Diogenes Laertius (iv. 2) the following report is given about Plato's successor Speusippus: "And according to Caeneus he was the first to reveal what Isocrates called the forbidden things." Since Diogenes Laertius does not mention a Caeneus as a source elsewhere, Jacoby (*FGrH* 338F18) suggested that the text be emended to Idomeneus, a source to whom Diogenes refers several times. There is absolutely no textual evidence for this change (Tarán 1981: 182 also points this out and discusses other conjectures), however, and nothing in the content of Diogenes' report would justify it. Idomeneus of Lampsacus did write a book on the Socratics, but the meager indications of its content suggests that it focused on Socrates' immediate pupils, Plato and Antisthenes, and surely it is a stretch to assume that Speusippus is a Socratic. All editors of Diogenes Laertius print Caeneus (see most recently Marcovich 1999). In fact this passage in Diogenes and Aristotle's reference to Caeneus in the *Posterior Analytics* support one another. They both make sense as a reference to a fourth-century author, who was the contemporary of Aristotle.

There is another feature of Diogenes' quotation from Caeneus, which is important to note. What are the forbidden things mentioned by Isocrates, which Speusippus is supposed to have revealed? Most scholars have assumed that these must be secrets of Isocrates' art, i.e. rhetoric (see Tarán 1981: 181–82 for references). This seems an odd thing of which to accuse Speusippus. There is, however, another more probable reference for "forbidden things." Speusippus was known for strong connections to the Pythagoreans and wrote a work entitled *On Pythagorean Numbers* (Fr. 28, Tarán). Moreover, there is a consistent theme in the Pythagorean tradition, which identified certain doctrines as "forbidden," i.e. as doctrines, which cannot be revealed to outsiders (Ar. Fr. 192 = Iam. *VP* 31; Aristox. Fr. 43 = D.L. VIII. 15). This would all make sense, if we supposed that Caeneus was accusing Speusippus of revealing certain forbidden Pythagorean doctrines. Can this scenario be made consistent with the reference to Isocrates? Yes. Isocrates discusses Pythagoras in a famous passage in his *Busiris* (28–29) and specifically refers to the silence of the Pythagoreans. In context, Isocrates might be referring to Pythagorean silence as an exercise in self-control rather than a reference to secret doctrines, but, at the least the passage shows Isocrates' interest in the Pythagoreans and it may be that in one of his lost works he specifically discussed the secret doctrines.

This brief passage in Diogenes Laertius thus suggests that Caeneus may be referring to Pythagorean doctrines, when he talks about forbidden things. This Pythagorean connection brings us full circle back to Aristotle's reference to Caeneus in *Posterior Analytics*. This Caeneus too is interested in a Pythagorean issue, the role of proportions in describing the natural world. It thus seems to be a reasonable conjecture that the Caeneus to whom Aristotle refers in the *Posterior Analytics* was a fourth-century writer with Pythagorean connections. Certainly there is much more evidence to support this conjecture than the proposal that he is the Lapith Caeneus improbably turned into a mathematician in Antiphanes' play. Whatever the case about the identity of Aristotle's Caeneus, the theory of proportion assigned to him certainly provides a parallel to Archytas' attempt to use the characteristics of proportions in order to explain natural phenomena. We have here either evidence for the influence of Archytas on Caeneus, or evidence for a broader tradition of which Archytas and Caeneus were parts.

Hett (1953: 361) suggests a different interpretation of the proportion of equality. Archytas is making the point that "if the cross section of a stalk were triangular and grew an equal amount in all directions, its shape would change." This is an interesting observation, but it is hard to connect directly to the text. The text does not seem, *prima facie*, to be making a point about preserving as opposed to changing shape in the process of growth. The reference to the proportion of equality would, on this reading, need to mean that in nature things grow equally in each direction, but this is, at the very least, an obscure way of expressing such an idea. If the same shape is to be preserved in this growth, so the reasoning goes, the initial shape must be circular. The only place that the conception of maintaining the same shape might be found in the text is in the verb ἀνακάμπτειν, but it is hard to see how "bending back on itself" is an appropriate way to describe a shape preserving itself through growth. We would expect to be told not that this proportion produces curves and circles but rather that it *maintains* its circular shape through growth (e.g. "this proportion alone bends back on itself so as to preserve its own circular shape through growth").

5–6 κινεῖσθαι γὰρ ἀνάλογον πάντα – Since this phrase continues the indirect statement dependent on "Archytas used to say," it is presented as an assertion of Archytas. It is thus a fundamental principle of his theory of motion that "all things are moved in proportion." Without any further context it is very difficult to know how Archytas would defend and further explain this assertion, but a few points can be made. First, Archytas is presumably not claiming that nothing is at rest but rather that "all things (that are in motion) are moved according to proportion." Second, since he believes that all motion is caused by some inequality (A23), it follows that there will be some sort of relationship of difference between the two things that are unequal. It would appear that Archytas thought that this relationship could always be expressed in an intelligible way, that it was *analogon*. Plato, on the other hand, seems to envisage the inequality that shakes the receptacle in the *Timaeus* (52e) as unintelligible and as having no order, until necessity submits to the demiurge, who establishes the proportions of the motions (56c). Archytas' position may be closer to that of Aristotle whose dynamics, if he can be said to have one (see Carteron 1975; Hankinson 1995; 144–48; Hussey 1983: 185–200), is based on principles of proportion. Thus, at *De Caelo* I. 6 (273b30–274a3), Aristotle says that velocity is proportional to the weight of the body in motion and, at *Physics* VII. 5 (249b27 ff.), he talks of the proportion between the forces of the movers and the distances through which and the times in which an object is moved. These passages are problematic and controversial in a number of ways, but they suggest that it may be the case that for Aristotle as well as Archytas "all things are moved according to proportion." Archytas' idea that all motion can be expressed in terms of proportion and that differences between types of motion are to be explained in terms of differences in types of proportion is appealing as an attempt to explain a complex body of phenomena (motions) by means of a relatively small number of mathematical rules.

6 ταύτην – Since both motion (κίνησις) and proportion (ἀναλογία) are feminine in Greek, "this" (ταύτην) could refer to either of them. Hett (1953) and Forster (1984) translate "this proportion" (see also Cambiano 1998: 322–23), while Flashar (1983) translates "this motion" (diese . . . Bewegung). At first sight, natural motion would seem to be the logical referent, since motion can be easily described as turning back on itself, whereas it is odd to talk of a proportion bending back on itself (but see on ἀνακάμπτειν below). There are, however, three reasons for supposing that proportion is the referent. First, ἀναλογίαν was mentioned last and is closest to ταύτην. Second, the immediately preceding clause has made the assertion that *all* things move in some sort of proportion, so that we now, in the clause introduced by ταύτην, need a statement which distinguishes the proportion of equality from other proportions (all things are moved in [some] proportion but this proportion alone . . .). Third, in line four, the proportion of equality is said to "be in" (ἐνεῖναι) natural motion, so that parallelism of structure would suggest that the subject of ἐγγένηται ("come to be in") is also the proportion of equality. Archytas is setting up a parallel between the proportion of equality and natural motion so that to some extent it does not matter which is indicated by the ταύτην. The structure of the passage, however, shows that Archytas is using the behavior of a certain type of proportion to explain a certain type of motion and thus that ταύτην refers back to ἀναλογίαν.

ἀνακάμπτειν – The basic meaning of this verb is "to bend back" or "to return." It does not appear in the Presocratics, occurs only once in Plato, but is used over thirty times in Aristotle. In some contexts ἀνακάμπτειν clearly refers to circular motion which bends back to its starting point (e.g. Arist. *De An.* 407a28 of Plato's view in the *Timaeus* that thinking involves circular motion). It does not always refer to circular motion, however. It can describe anything that reverses its direction in some sense (e.g. the wind at *Mete.* 364b12, cf. *EE* 1215b23 and *Ph.* 262b). In A23a Archytas appears to be appealing to this ambiguity in meaning. Since the motion produced has the form of circles and curves, we are clearly intended to think of the circular motion that bends back to its beginning, but the subject of the verb is the proportion of equality (see above), which does not literally move in a circle but bends back on itself in that it produces a smaller and smaller ratio, rather than increasing (see above).

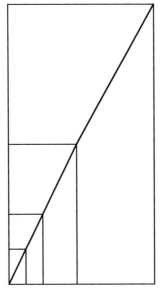

Figure A23a(1) Motion according to the geometric proportion (4:2 :: 8:4 :: 16:8 :: 32:16). A straight line with a constant slope of 2.

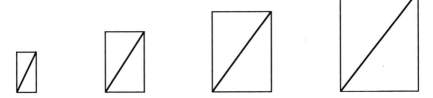

Figure A23a(2) Motion according to the arithmetic proportion (2:1 :: 3:2 :: 4:3 :: 5:4). Each segment will have a different slope and when combined they will produce a curve (see figure A23a(3)).

7 ἐγγένηται – The parallel with ἐνεῖναι in line five shows that this should be translated "whenever it comes to be in (something)" or "whenever it occurs" (see also Flashar 1983 and Forster 1984). Hett (1953) adopts the impersonal translation "whenever it is possible." This would give an odd twist to the meaning of the passage. Nature, through the use of the proportion of equality, tries to produce circles and curves but, in some circumstances (i.e under some sort of unnatural constraint), it is not possible for it to do so.

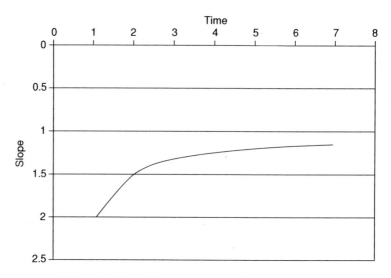

Figure A23a(3) Arithmetic proportion (2:1 :: 3:2 :: 4:3 . . .).

A24 Eudemus, *Physics* Fr. 65 Wehrli = Simplicius, *In Aristotelis Phys.* III. 4 (*CAG* IX. 467.26–468.3

"Ἀρχύτας δέ," ὥς φησιν Εὔδημος, "οὕτως ἠρώτα τὸν λόγον· 'ἐν τῷ   1
ἐσχάτῳ [οἷον τῷ ἀπλανεῖ] οὐρανῷ γενόμενος, πότερον ἐκτείναιμι ἂν   2
τὴν χεῖρα ἢ τὴν ῥάβδον εἰς τὸ ἔξω, ἢ οὔ;' καὶ τὸ μὲν οὖν μὴ ἐκτείνειν   3
ἄτοπον· εἰ δὲ ἐκτείνω, ἤτοι σῶμα ἢ τόπος τὸ ἐκτὸς ἔσται. διοίσει δὲ   4
οὐδέν, ὡς μαθησόμεθα. ἀεὶ οὖν βαδιεῖται τὸν αὐτὸν τρόπον ἐπὶ τὸ ἀεὶ   5
λαμβανόμενον πέρας, καὶ ταὐτὸν ἐρωτήσει, καὶ εἰ ἀεὶ ἕτερον ἔσται ἐφ' ὃ   6
ἡ ῥάβδος, δῆλον ὅτι καὶ ἄπειρον. καὶ εἰ μὲν σῶμα, δέδεικται τὸ προκεί-   7
μενον· εἰ δὲ τόπος, ἔστι δὲ τόπος τὸ ἐν ᾧ σῶμά ἐστιν ἢ δύναιτ' ἂν εἶναι,   8
τὸ δὲ δυνάμει ὡς ὂν χρὴ τιθέναι ἐπὶ τῶν ἀιδίων, καὶ οὕτως ἂν εἴη σῶμα   9
ἄπειρον καὶ τόπος." μήποτε δὲ οὗτος ὁ λόγος καὶ πρὸς ἡμᾶς ἀπορήσει   10
δριμέως τοὺς λέγοντας μηδὲν εἶναι ἔξω τοῦ οὐρανοῦ, ὡς τοῦ κοσμικοῦ   11
σώματος, οὗ πέρας ὁ οὐρανός, τὴν ὕλην χώραν κατειληφότος. εἰ οὖν ἐν   12
τῷ νώτῳ τοῦ οὐρανοῦ γενόμενος ἐκτείνοι τὴν χεῖρα, ποῦ ἂν ἐκταθείη;   13
οὐ γὰρ δὴ εἰς τὸ μηδέν· οὐδὲν γὰρ τῶν ὄντων ἐν τῷ μὴ ὄντι, ἀλλ' οὐδὲ   14
κωλυθήσεται ἐκτεῖναι· ὑπὸ γὰρ τοῦ μηδενὸς οὐ δυνατὸν κωλυθῆναι.   15

2 οἷον] ἤγουν a οὐρανοῦ a   3 ἢ οὔ. καὶ τὸ] Diels ἢ οὔ. καὐτὸ F ἢ οὐκ ἂν. τὸ aE
4 δὲ²] om. F   5 ὡς] aF   om. E ἀεὶ οὖν] aE εἰ οὖν F   6 ἐφ' ὃ E   13 ἐκτανθείη
aF   14 ἐν τῷ] εἰς τὸ F

"But Archytas," as Eudemus says, "used to propound the argument in this way: 'If I arrived at the outermost edge of the heaven [that is to say at the fixed heaven], could I extend my hand or staff into what is outside or not?' It would be paradoxical not to be able to extend it. But if I extend it, what is outside will be either body or place. It doesn't matter which, as we will learn. So then he will always go forward in the same fashion to the limit that is supposed in each case and will ask the same question, and if there will always be something else to which his staff [extends], it is clear that it is also unlimited. And if it is body, what was proposed has been demonstrated. If it is place, place is that in which body is or could be, but what is potential must be regarded as really existing in the case of eternal things, and thus there would be unlimited body and space." Perhaps this argument will keenly trouble us too who say that there is nothing outside the heaven, since the cosmic body, of which the limit is the heaven, has matter as its place. If then arriving at the back of the world he should stick out his hand, where would it be stuck? Not surely into nothing, for nothing of the things that are is in non-being. But neither will he be prevented from sticking it out. For it is not possible to be prevented by nothing. (See Heath 1949: 104, Barnes 1982: 204, and Urmson 2002: 87 for other translations.)

Authenticity
There is no reason to doubt the authenticity of this testimonium. Eudemus is an early and excellent source, who clearly had access to Archytas' work (see e.g. A14) and probably Aristotle's books on Archytas (see A13). The content of the testimonium, since it goes contrary to Platonic and Aristotelian views, is not in accord with the pseudo-Pythagorean literature that seeks to glorify Pythagoreans at the expense of Plato and Aristotle.

Context
This testimonium is drawn from Simplicius' (sixth century AD) commentary on Aristotle's *Physics* 203b15–203b29 (*CAG* IX. 465.23–468.18). In this passage of the *Physics*, Aristotle presents five arguments that have led people to believe in the existence of something unlimited. Simplicius discusses each of the five in turn. At the end of his discussion of the fifth argument, he adds this report about Archytas, the first nine lines of which, the actual report about Archytas, are identified as being from Eudemus, while Simplicius goes on for another six lines to give his own comments on Archytas' argument.

Eudemus of Rhodes, the ultimate source for the testimonium, was active in the second half of the fourth century and was the pupil of Aristotle. He wrote histories of arithmetic, astronomy, geometry and theology, but the majority of the fragments preserved come from his *Physics*. This work seems to have followed Aristotle very closely and to have taken the form of a paraphrase or commentary. It was used extensively by Simplicius (e.g. 466.8; 468.5). The testimony about Archytas is not explicitly said to be connected to Aristotle's fifth argument by either Eudemus or Simplicius and neither says that Aristotle had Archytas specifically in mind when writing the passage. However, since in Simplicius the reference to Archytas comes at the end of the sequential discussion of the five arguments and, since it is immediately followed by the transitional sentence, "thus Aristotle said that belief in something unlimited is based on five arguments, but Eudemus said there were six causes . . . ," it seems most likely that Simplicius saw it as relevant to Aristotle's fifth argument.

Nature and extent of the testimonium
Starting with μήποτε in line 10, the quotation from Eudemus ends and what follows is Simplicius' own comment (ἡμᾶς, line 10). Diels, in his edition of Simplicius, prints everything up to μήποτε as a quotation from Eudemus. The expression "fixed heaven" (τῷ ἀπλανεῖ, line 2), however, is not the idiom of the fourth century and almost surely does not belong to Archytas or Eudemus (see the detailed commentary). The use of οἷον ("that is to say") points to an explanatory gloss. The phrase "at the outermost edge of the heaven" (ἐν τῷ ἐσχάτῳ οὐρανῷ) probably belongs to Archytas, and Simplicius, or perhaps another late commentator, glossed this as "that is to say at the fixed heaven." Plato uses the expression "outermost edge of the heaven" (ἔσχατον οὐρανόν) in the *Timaeus* (36e), and Parmenides refers to "extreme olympus" (ὄλυμπος ἔσχατος), perhaps with a similar sense (Coxon 1986: 231–32), so that the expression ἐν τῷ ἐσχάτῳ οὐρανῷ would seem to be quite possible for Archytas, but οἷον τῷ ἀπλανεῖ must be a later addition.

What portion of the rest of lines 1–10 is due to Archytas and what to Eudemus? Ross assigned the whole argument to Archytas (1936: 547), but this is very unlikely. To begin with, it is unclear whether Eudemus was relying on any writing of Archytas for this report or whether his report is based ultimately on an oral source. The introductory words "Archytas used to propound the argument in this way" (οὕτως ἡρώτα τὸν λόγον – note the imperfect) support the latter alternative. Certainly there were a large number of anecdotes circulating about Archytas, many of which may go back to Aristoxenus' *Life of Archytas* (see A7 and A9). The first three lines up to ἢ οὔ, which contain the central insight of the argument, would seem to be the minimum that we can assign to Archytas himself (so DK, although they give οἷον τῷ ἀπλανεῖ οὐρανῷ to Archytas) and could well form part of an oral anecdote. We might perhaps extend this another half line to ἄτοπον. Beyond this point there are indications that Eudemus has intervened in the text to a considerable extent. Certainly the switch from first to third person in line five (βαδιεῖται) indicates that Eudemus is now paraphrasing, but there are strong reasons to believe that he has intervened in the text even earlier.

Furley regards everything after ἢ οὔ as Eudemus' own commentary on Archytas (1989: 113), and Cherniss long ago noted that Eudemus had recast Archytas' argument to correspond to Aristotle's account of the fifth reason for accepting the existence of something unlimited (1964: 20). Cherniss points to the "fully developed Aristotelian doctrine of space and pure actuality," but Furley shows that the argument which maintains that the potential is actual for eternal things may go back to Democritus. There is, however, another argument that does show conclusively that Eudemus has recast Archytas' argument from εἰ δὲ ἐκτείνω in line 4 onwards. In lines 7–8, Eudemus says that, if what is outside the cosmos is an unlimited body, then "what has been proposed has been demonstrated" (δέδεικται τὸ προκείμενον). This shows that, in Eudemus' mind, the problem under consideration is not whether space is unlimited or whether there is something outside the cosmos but rather whether an unlimited body exists or not. The emphasis on precisely this question betrays the Aristotelian provenance of the argument. At *Physics* 204b2 Aristotle explicitly says that "we are concerned with things cognizable by the senses and are inquiring whether there is or is not among them a body which is unlimited in augmentation." Furley has shown convincingly that it was Aristotle's rejection of the possibility of void that led him to consider the question of the unlimited solely in terms of an unlimited body (1989: 111). There is no reason to suppose that this was the central question for Archytas as well and some reason to think that it was not. Unlike Aristotle, Archytas is likely to have accepted the existence of void as did his predecessor Philolaus (Huffman 1993: 212 ff.). The thought experiment of extending the stick beyond the edge of the cosmos (i.e. the organized system bounded by the heavens) seems designed precisely to show that the universe (i.e. the sum total of everything) extends beyond the cosmos and in fact extends indefinitely (for the distinction between the cosmos and the universe, see Furley 1989: 2), but whether there is an infinitely large body is a different, peculiarly Aristotelian, question.

With this Aristotelian question in mind, it is possible to see more clearly how Eudemus has reworked the basic Archytan argument. Archytas' argument in something like his own words is contained in the thought experiment in lines 1–4, which shows that it is implausible to suppose that we could not stick our hand beyond the supposed limit of the universe. The experiment of Archytas is then continued in the generation of the infinite sequence in lines 5–7, although Eudemus is clearly paraphrasing: "He will always go forward in the same fashion to the limit that is supposed in each case and will ask the same question, and if there will always be something else to which his staff extends, it is clear that it is also unlimited." Eudemus introduces into this basic argument the further question of whether what is unlimited is body or space, for this question is used in lines 8–10, in order to show that in either case an unlimited body will result. Thus the words "if I extend it, what is outside will be either body or place" in line 4 are Eudemus' addition, as is the following comment that "It doesn't matter which, as we will learn," which looks forward to the conclusion of Eudemus' argument in lines 8–10, after he has finished summarizing Archytas. The only difficulty with this division of the argument between Archytas and Eudemus is the use of the first person in line 4 ("if I extend it"). Since the first person in line 2 clearly refers to Archytas ("could I extend"), we would have expected it to do so here in line 4 as well. It is clearly possible, however, for the first person in line 4 to refer to Eudemus. In line 5, he has switched to third-person narrative in describing Archytas' procedure, so that in line 4 he may well already have switched to presenting the argument from his own point of view.

Starting in line 10, the excerpt from Eudemus stops, and Simplicius continues with his own comment on the dilemma posed by Archytas' argument for those like himself, who say that there is nothing outside the cosmos. Simplicius' remarks in fact seem to be formulated in light of a response to Archytas' argument given by Alexander of Aphrodisias in the third century AD (*Quaestiones* III. 12, 106.35–107.4). Although he seems skeptical of Alexander's response here, Simplicius elsewhere endorses a slightly different interpretation of Alexander's point (*In Cael.* 285.21–7).

Archytas' argument

I will begin with a brief summary of Archytas' argument before turning to alternative interpretations and later developments of the argument, which will provide further clarification. Since Archytas' argument ends in line 7 with the assertion that "it [what is outside the cosmos] is unlimited," it seems reasonable to assume that Archytas was setting out to prove that there was something outside the cosmos and that it was unlimited, although Eudemus does not precisely identify Archytas' purpose at the beginning of the passage. The argument then appears to take the following form:

1. There is something outside the heaven and that something is unlimited.
2. For, suppose that there is not something outside the heaven (i.e. that the universe does not extend indefinitely), then there will be an outermost edge.
3. If I reached that edge, would I be able to extend my staff beyond the heaven or not?
4. It would be paradoxical, given our normal assumptions about the nature of space, if I could not extend it, so I can extend it.
5. The end of the staff, once extended, will mark a new limit.
6. I will advance to this new limit in each case and ask the same question (3 above).
7. There will always be something else to which the staff extends, since I will always answer the question as in 4 above.
8. That something is thus clearly unlimited.

Steps 1 and 2 above are not stated explicitly in Eudemus' report but are the necessary presuppositions for the argument he reports, which begins with step 3.

Simplicius lists Archytas' argument after his treatment of Aristotle's discussion of the fifth reason for which people have believed in the existence of the unlimited (i.e. that the imagination can always conceive a beyond). A number of scholars (Cherniss 1964: 20; Barnes 1982: 361–62; Solmsen 1960: 168 n. 32) have suggested, however, that Archytas' argument really fits Aristotle's "fourth reason" better (i.e. that whatever is limited reaches its limit by coming up against something else outside it). The "fourth reason" proceeds by conceptual analysis of what it means to be limited and concludes that there must always be something outside what is limited in order to limit it. Archytas' argument, however, does not proceed by conceptual analysis nor does it deal explicitly with the concept of the "limited" or what it means to limit something. Furley (1987: 137) has argued convincingly that the "fourth reason" goes back to Melissus.

Archytas' argument, in fact, fits Aristotle's description of the "fifth reason" so well that there can be little doubt that he was thinking of Archytas in formulating it. Aristotle's fifth reason (*Ph.* 203b22 ff.) is characterized by what takes place "in thought" or "in the imagination" (ἐν τῇ νοήσει) and this is a crucial characteristic of Archytas' argument. It asks us to imagine ourselves at the edge of the heavens. It is a thought experiment. Aristotle gives three examples of the fifth reason: numbers of which we can always imagine one more, mathematical magnitudes to which we can always add something in thought and finally "what is outside the heaven" (τὸ ἔξω τοῦ οὐρανοῦ). Again this third example fits Archytas exactly; he provides us with a thought experiment concerning what is outside the heaven. Aristotle in fact labels the fifth argument as the "most authoritative" or "most important" (κυριώτατον) and as that which causes a common difficulty for all thinkers. Cherniss argued (1964: 20) that the reference to "a common difficulty" showed that Aristotle was not thinking of a specific argument, but the fact that there were other versions of the argument or that its force was widely felt need not mean that Aristotle is not referring to its most influential formulation, i.e. Archytas' thought experiment. Eudemus' and Simplicius' quotation of Archytas' argument as their only example of the "fifth reason" suggests that it was the most famous version.

Archytas' argument had great influence and was taken up and adapted by the Stoics, Epicureans, Locke and Newton among others, while eliciting responses from Alexander and Simplicius (see Sorabji 1988: 125–41). It is instructive to compare Archytas' argument as we have reconstructed it with the Epicurean argument found in Lucretius' *De Rerum Natura* (1. 968–83). Lucretius' use of the argument is one of a number of connections between the Pythagoreans and the Atomists (see my discussion of Fr. 1). Furley even tries to claim the argument for Democritus rather than Archytas (1987: 137), but it then becomes inexplicable that our ancient sources assign it to Archytas. There are moreover some subtle differences between Archytas' version and that found in Lucretius. Lucretius' argument, like that of Archytas, starts from the assumption that the universe is limited and pictures someone at the furthest edge of the universe trying to hurl a javelin beyond the edge. Two possibilities are envisaged, either it will fly unhindered, in which case there is something beyond the edge into which it flies, or it will be stopped by some body, in which case there was something beyond the edge to stop it. In either case the person hurling the javelin was not at the edge to start with, which is contrary to the initial assumption. In order to avoid this paradox, we must assume that there is no edge and that the universe goes on without limit. Archytas' formulation is simpler. He seems to assume that, since his opponent treats the cosmos as limited, there can be no body outside the cosmos and accordingly does not consider the second possibility mentioned by Lucretius. Archytas just appeals to our normal assumptions about the nature of space and argues that it would be paradoxical if you could not stick out your hand or a stick, when you were at the supposed edge of the world.

The comparison with the Epicurean version of the argument raises a central puzzle about Archytas' argument: against whom was he arguing? It is possible, of course, that he is simply considering the logical possibilities about the nature of the cosmos and is not responding to any particular thinker. Still the *reductio ad absurdum* form of the argument suggests that he might have had a particular opponent in mind. The argument is likely to have been put forward between 400 and 350 BC, the years in which Archytas was active. Certainly in 400 the dominant view among Greek philosophers was that there was something outside our cosmos and that this something was unlimited in extent (see Huffman 1999b). Early Greek philosophers regarded the cosmos as arising from an unlimited which persisted outside, even after the cosmos arose. The clearest example is Anaximander, who posited the unlimited as the origin of the cosmos, but other thinkers, who adopted a single element from which the cosmos arose, regarded that element as unlimited and as persisting outside the cosmos (e.g. Anaximenes' air – A7). In the fifth century both Anaxagoras (B1) and Democritus (A1) embraced an unlimited outside our cosmos. Most importantly, Archytas' predecessor in the Pythagorean tradition, Philolaus, envisaged the spherical cosmos as surrounded by the unlimited, since he talks of the central fire breathing in air, void and time from the unlimited (Huffman 1993: 212–13).

The main exception to this vision of a cosmos surrounded by the unlimited was Parmenides. It is controversial as to whether we are to understand his comparison of what is to a "well-rounded sphere" which has a "final limit" (Fr. 8.42–49) as a statement about the cosmos or as a statement about possible objects of inquiry. Taken as a literal statement about the cosmos, Parmenides' comparison might invite Archytas' question (Barnes 1982: 204) as might the sphere into which Empedocles' four elements, each evidently finite in amount, combine as part of his cosmic cycle (see Furley 1987: 89 ff., however, for an argument that for Empedocles too the universe is unlimited). Sedley argues that Archytas' question is illegitimate as applied to Parmenides, since it assumes that space is infinite, whereas the Greeks were slow to develop the idea of space that exists independently of any occupying body (1999: 117; cf. also Sedley 1982). The fact that Archytas still has to put the question in the fourth century shows, so Sedley argues, just how slow to develop the idea of infinite space with no occupying body was. This is not totally convincing. Even if we grant that the early Greeks did not have a clear conception of infinite space, they clearly did have the conception of the universe extending indefinitely beyond the limits of our cosmos, and this was in fact the dominant picture of the cosmos (see the examples in the previous paragraph), to which Parmenides was the exception. In this environment, if Parmenides proposed that what is has a limit, it was inevitable that someone used to the conception of the universe as extending without limit would have asked what was outside that limit. No detailed conception of space need be assumed. Similarly, Archytas' question in the fourth century need not commit him to any particular theory of what might be outside the cosmos. Philolaus thought that the unlimiteds void, breath and time were outside the cosmos, so that Archytas too may have assumed that what is beyond the cosmos had a variety of natures. His question is simply, given the normal assumptions about space in our world, according to which we can extend our hand before us, if there is no body to prevent it, what would prevent us from extending our hand at the supposed edge of the cosmos?

Parmenides, however, wrote a hundred years before Archytas, and it would be more satisfying to find a more contemporary controversy to which Archytas is responding. The natural suggestion would be that Archytas is arguing with his contemporary, Plato, who paints a forceful picture of a cosmos outside of which there is nothing (*Ti.* 33c). As we have seen, Archytas does not consider the possibility that there might be a body outside the cosmos, which could stop us from extending the staff. This feature of his argument would make good sense, if Plato is the object, since Plato makes perfectly clear that all body has been used up in making the cosmos, so that no body can be left outside (*Ti.* 33c). Moreover, Plato uses the exact expression ("outermost limit of the heaven" *Ti.* 36e, τὸν ἔσχατον οὐρανόν) with which Archytas begins his argument. The *Timaeus* is generally regarded as one of Plato's latest dialogues, although there has been controversy. The current consensus is that it is likely to have been written in the period 365 to 347 (Kraut 1992: xii). This is also the period when Aristotle was active in the Academy so that, if Archytas developed his argument in this period, in response to Plato, this circumstance could explain Aristotle's emphatic statement that the "fifth reason" is "the most authoritative and provides a common problem for all" (*Ph.* 203b23).

This statement by Aristotle, Simplicius' clear respect for the argument and the later development of the argument by the Stoics and Epicureans all attest to how seriously the argument was taken in antiquity. Modern scholars are somewhat more divided about its value. Sorabji follows the ancient tradition and describes Archytas' argument as "the most compelling argument ever produced for the infinity of space" (1988: 125), whereas Barnes is more dismissive (1982: 362). Modern notions of space allow for it to be finite without having an edge, and without an edge, at which Archytas can stand, his argument will not work (Barnes 1982: 362 but see Sorabji's caveats 1988: 160–63). It is, however, perhaps unfair to judge Archytas' argument in terms of modern physics. Neither Aristotle nor Plato can give such a sophisticated response to Archytas. As Furley emphasizes, Aristotle's direct response to the "fifth reason" is disappointing (1987: 137).

Sorabji (1988: 126–28) argues that the most effective ancient response to Archytas is that of Alexander of Aphrodisias in the third century AD

(*Quaestiones* III. 12, 106, 35–107, 4). Alexander makes a distinction between empty space and nothing and argues that, if there is nothing beyond the edge of the universe, we cannot stretch our hand into nothing, for, as Sorabji puts it, "to stretch is by definition to stretch into something" (1988: 127). Moreover, Alexander argues, we would never have any desire to stretch our hand into nothing. Simplicius, immediately after mentioning Archytas' argument, refers to this response of Alexander, and points out that those (including himself) who take Alexander's line have to be careful to avoid saying that nothingness prevents someone from extending his hand, since "it is not possible to be prevented by nothing" (A24, 15). The point of Alexander's response is that Archytas is assuming in advance that there is empty space beyond the universe rather than nothing. As Sorabji points out, this response depends on the Aristotelian notion that there is no such thing as "three-dimensional extension which goes right through things" and that place is the two-dimensional inner surface of a thing's surroundings. Since the universe has no surrounding for Aristotle, there is no place into which to stretch the hand. The problem with all of this, as Sorabji points out, is that this will only be convincing if Archytas accepts Aristotle's denial of three-dimensional space (or, as I would prefer to put it, if he accepts Aristotle's view that our normal assumptions about space do not apply at the edge of the cosmos), and there is no obvious reason why Archytas is compelled to do so. Thus, it is far from clear that anyone in antiquity gave an effective response to Archytas' argument.

Barnes gives other reasons to suggest that Archytas' argument does not work, even if we ignore the position of modern science and grant that a finite extension must have edges. Barnes argues that something might prevent me from extending my staff. If we suppose that there is nothing outside the cosmos, then it could be gravity from inside the cosmos holding me back. This is not a very satisfying criticism. Gravity does not normally prevent us from extending our arm, why should it in this case? We might as well suppose that the dog Cerberus rises from Hades and eats us before we can extend our staff. Unless we can give a reason why we cannot extend our staff which is part of a coherent physical theory, it is illegitimate to respond to Archytas' argument with what amount to occult forces. Archytas' argument depends on our normal assumptions about how space works, and in order to counter his argument one has to present a coherent theory to replace it. Barnes says that, even if we ignore possible physical problems with extending our staff, nothing in Archytas' argument shows that there is a place in front of me in which to put my staff. Again the question is where the burden of proof lies. Experience tells us that Archytas is right: barring a physical obstacle there is a place in front of us in which to extend the staff. The burden of proof is on anyone who would argue that at the edge of the cosmos all of our previous experience and intuitions about space are invalid.

Detailed commentary

Line 2 οἶον – οἶον is used to mean "that is to say" already by Aristotle (LSJ v. 2d). ἤγουν, which appears in the Aldine edition, is used in glosses and has the same meaning.

[οἶον τῷ ἀπλανεῖ] οὐρανῷ – It is almost certain that this is not Archytas' own expression but rather an explanatory gloss introduced later in the tradition in order to explain more specifically what was meant by the phrase ἐν τῷ ἐσχάτῳ οὐρανῷ ("at the edge of the heaven"). It is doubtful that the words go back even to Eudemus, since the expression "fixed heaven" does not occur in Plato or Aristotle, although they talk of the "fixed stars" (e.g. *Ti.* 40b4; *Metaph.* 1073b19). On the other hand, the phrase "fixed heaven" occurs frequently in Simplicius (e.g. *CAG* VII. 58.36; 83.18; 408.3; 444.28), so that it seems most likely that it was introduced later in the tradition, perhaps by Simplicius himself.

A25 Apuleius, *Apology* 15–16 (see Butler and Owen 1914 and Helm 1912)

quid, quod nec ob haec debet tantummodo philosophus speculum invisere; 1
nam saepe oportet non modo similitudinem suam, verum etiam ipsius 2
similitudinis rationem considerare: num, ut ait Epicurus, profectae a nobis 3
imagines velut quaedam exuviae iugi fluore a corporibus manantes, cum 4
leve aliquid et solidum offenderunt, illisae reflectantur et retro expressae 5
contraversim respondeant an, ut alii philosophi disputant, radii nostri seu 6
mediis oculis proliquati et lumini extrario mixti atque ita uniti, ut Plato 7
arbitratur, seu tantum oculis profecti sine ullo foris amminiculo, ut Archytas 8
putat, seu intentu aëris facti, ut Stoici rentur, cum alicui corpori inciderunt 9
spisso et splendido et levi, paribus angulis quibus inciderant resultent ad 10
faciem suam reduces atque ita, quod extra tangant ac visant, id intra specu- 11
lum imaginentur. videnturne vobis debere philosophi haec omnia vestigare 12
et inquirere et cuncta specula, vel uda vel suda, soli <non> videre? 13

9 aëris] Pithoeus Colvius ueris F φ facti] F φ coacti Purser acti Helm **12–13** videnturne . . . philosophi . . . soli <non> videre] van der Vliet videturne . . . philosophia (videnturne . . . philosophi vulg.) . . . soli videre codd.

What about the further point that it is not just for these reasons that a philosopher ought to look in a mirror; for it is often required that he consider not only his own image but also the explanation of that very image. Is it the case that, as Epicurus says, images, as it were like sloughs, having originated from our bodies and streaming with a continual flow, when they strike something smooth and solid, are dashed against it and reversed, and giving back an image, correspond in reverse manner. Or, as other philosophers argue, do our rays, either filtered forth from the middle of our eyes, mixed with external light and thus made one, as Plato thinks, or derived from our eyes alone without any external support, as Archytas thinks, or made of the tensing of air, as the Stoics think, when they fall upon some body that is dense and shiny and smooth, rebound at angles equal to those at which they strike, returning to the face from which they started and thus form an image within the mirror of that which they touch and approach outside. Does it seem to you that philosophers ought to search out and investigate all these things and be the only ones not to look at all mirrors, whether solid or liquid?

Text A. Aëtius IV. 14.3 (Diels, *Dox.* 405. 15–22)

[Περὶ κατοπτρικῶν ἐμφάσεων]

οἱ ἀπὸ Πυθαγόρου καὶ τῶν μαθηματικῶν κατ᾽ ἀνάκλασιν τῆς ὄψεως. 1
φέρεσθαι μὲν γὰρ τὴν ὄψιν τεταμένην ὡς ἐπὶ τὸν χαλκόν, ἐντυ- 2
χοῦσαν δὲ πυκνῷ καὶ λείῳ πληχθεῖσαν ὑποστρέφειν αὐτὴν ἐφ᾽ ἑαυτὴν 3
ὅμοιόν τι πάσχουσαν τῇ ἐκτάσει τῆς χειρὸς καὶ τῇ ἐπὶ τὸν ὦμον 4
ἀντεπιστροφῇ. 5

---

1 οἵ] om. Stobaeus   καὶ τῶν μαθηματικῶν] om. [Plutarch]   ἀνάκλασιν] Stob.   ἀνακλάσεις
[Plut.]   2   τεταμένην] [Plut.]   τεταγμένην Stob. L   4–5   τῇ . . . ἀντεπιστροφῇ]
[Plut.] τῆς . . . ἀντεπιστροφῆς Stob. L

[On Images in Mirrors]

Those who follow Pythagoras and the mathematicians [say that images in mirrors come about] through reflection of the visual ray. For [they say] that the visual ray, directed, as it were, against the bronze, is struck when it encounters the dense and smooth bronze and turns back on itself. What happens is similar to someone extending their hand and then bending it back to their shoulder.

Text B. Aëtius IV. 13.9–10 (Diels, *Dox.* 404. 3–13)

[περὶ ὁράσεως]

Ἵππαρχος ἀκτῖνάς φησιν ἀφ᾽ ἑκατέρου τῶν ὀφθαλμῶν ἀποτεινομένας   1
τοῖς πέρασιν αὐτῶν οἷον χειρῶν ἐπαφαῖς περικαθαπτούσας τοῖς ἐκτὸς   2
σώμασι τὴν ἀντίληψιν αὐτῶν πρὸς τὸ ὁρατικὸν ἀποδιδόναι.   3
Ἔνιοι καὶ Πυθαγόραν τῇ δόξῃ ταύτῃ συνεπιγράφουσιν ἅτε δὴ   4
βεβαιωτὴν τῶν μαθημάτων καὶ πρὸς τούτῳ Παρμενίδην ἐμφαίνοντα   5
τοῦτο διὰ τῶν ποιημάτων.   6

1 ἀκτῖνάς] om. Stob.   φησιν ἀφ᾽ ἑκατέρου] Plut.   ἀφ᾽ ἑκατέρου φησί Stob.   2 αὐτῶν]
Meineke   αὐτῶν Plut., Stob.   οἷον] οἱονεί Stob.   περικαθαπτούσας] Stob.
περικαθαπτούσαις Plut.   4–6 Ἔνιοι . . . ποιημάτων.] om. Plut.   6 τοῦτο] ταὐτό
Meineke

[On Sight]

Hipparchus says that rays from each of the eyes reaching out with their
ends like the touch of hands, laying hold of the bodies outside return an
apprehension of them back to the sight.

Some also enroll Pythagoras as another advocate of this doctrine, since he
is the one who established the sciences, and in addition to him Parmenides,
since he displays this [theory] in his poems.

Text C. Iamblichus, *On General Mathematical Science* xxv (Festa 1891: 78.8–18)

οἱ δὲ Πυθαγόρειοι διατρίψαντες ἐν τοῖς μαθήμασι καὶ τό τε ἀκριβὲς   1
τῶν λόγων ἀγαπήσαντες, ὅτι μόνα εἶχεν ἀποδείξεις ὧν μετεχειρί-   2
ζοντο ἄνθρωποι, καὶ ὁμολογούμενα ὁρῶντες ἐξ ἴσου τὰ περὶ τὴν   3
ἁρμονίαν ὅτι δι᾽ ἀριθμῶν καὶ τὰ περὶ τὴν ὄψιν μαθήματα <ὅτι> διὰ   4
<δια>γραμμάτων, ὅλως αἴτια τῶν ὄντων ταῦτα ᾠήθησαν εἶναι καὶ   5
τὰς τούτων ἀρχάς· ὥστε τῷ βουλομένῳ θεωρεῖν τὰ ὄντα πῶς ἔχει, εἰς   6
ταῦτα βλεπτέον εἶναι, τοὺς ἀριθμοὺς καὶ τὰ γεωμετρούμενα εἴδη τῶν   7
ὄντων καὶ λόγους, διὰ τὸ δηλοῦσθαι πάντα διὰ τούτων.   8

3 ἐξ ἴσου] Burkert   ἐν ἴσῳ Burnyeat   ἐπ᾽ ἴσου Vitelli   ἔνισον codd.   4 <ὅτι>] add.
Burnyeat   4–5 διὰ <δια>γραμμάτων] Vitelli   διὰ γραμμάτων codd.   διὰ γραμμῶν
Thibodeau

The Pythagoreans devoted themselves to mathematics and both admired
the accuracy of its arguments, because it alone, of those things which
humans pursue, admitted of proofs, and also saw that the study of

harmonics was in a state of agreement, because it was based on numbers, no less than the study of optics, because it was based on diagrams. Therefore, they thought that these things and the principles of these things were the causes of the things that are, so that anyone who wishes to understand the true nature of the things that are must pay attention to these things: the numbers and the geometrical forms of the things that are and ratios, because it is by these that all things are made clear.

Authenticity

There is no reason to doubt the authenticity of this account of Archytas' views on optics. Apuleius' source may be Archimedes' *Catoptrics* (see below), which would be a relatively early and reliable source. Even if we suppose that Apuleius is relying on another source, the views on optics, which he assigns to Archytas, make good sense in terms of what we know of the development of optics in Archytas' time (see below). Both Texts A and C above also attest to early Pythagorean interest in optics. Finally, the optical theory assigned to Archytas by Apuleius is clearly distinguished from the theories of Plato and Aristotle, so that there is no trace of an attempt to assign later, more sophisticated views back to Archytas, as we would expect in the pseudo-Pythagorean tradition.

Context and source

Testimonium A25 is preserved in the *Apology* of Apuleius. Apuleius, who was born ca. AD 125, is most famous as the author of the *Metamorphoses* (*Golden Ass*) and as an orator. He also studied in Athens, however, and was called a *philosophus Platonicus*. His *De deo Socratis* was a declamation on Socrates' *daimonion* and he probably also wrote an exposition of Plato's philosophy in two books, a work on logic (*On Interpretation*), and a translation of the pseudo-Aristotelian *De Mundo*, but his authorship of each of the three has been contested (see Dillon 1977: 306–38 for an account of his philosophical works). He was brought to trial in 158/9 on the charge of having used magic to induce Pudentilla, the mother of a fellow pupil in Athens, to marry him. The *Apology* is his defense against the charge of using magic. He views this not just as an opportunity to defend himself but also as a chance to defend philosophy against the accusations brought against her by the uneducated (Chapters 1 and 3). In Chapter 13, he turns to the charge that he uses a mirror for magical purposes. He points out first that human beings naturally delight in seeing their own image and that, if we delight in statues, which preserve our image by art, we should all the more delight in the images of ourselves that nature provides in a mirror. In the middle of Chapter 15, he introduces a new defense, by pointing out that the philosopher has additional reasons for looking in a mirror. The philosopher looks in a mirror not just to see his own image but also to study the causes which produce that image. Apuleius then gives a brief overview of various theories of sight, which explain our ability to see images in a mirror. The theory of Archytas appears here, along with those of Epicurus, Plato and the Stoics. All the theories are presented very briefly and in broad strokes. Archytas' account of vision would appear to be cited primarily because it provides a clear contrast to the theories of Plato and the Stoics on a central point (see below).

What was Apuleius' source for his account of Archytas' theory of vision? In the next chapter, he raises a series of further questions about mirrors, which a philosopher should address (e.g. why do some mirrors kindle timber?). He says that these questions and very many others of the same type are treated by Archimedes, who was remarkable for his frequent and diligent inspection of mirrors, in a "huge volume" (*volumine ingenti*). This appears to be a reference to the lost *Catoptrics* of Archimedes, to which Theon of Alexandria and others also refer (cf. Heiberg 1910: II. 466; Heath 1953: XXXVII; Dijksterhuis 1987: 48). It is tempting to suppose that Apuleius derived his account of the theories of vision in the preceding chapter, including that of Archytas, from this work of Archimedes. Archimedes does not give such doxographies in his surviving works (I owe this observation to Phil Thibodeau), but those works deal largely with mathematics divorced from the physical world, and catoptrics as a subject matter more tied to physics might have led him to discuss theories of vision.

Knorr has recently argued that Archimedes wrote no such work and that his name had become falsely attached to the *Catoptrics* of Euclid by Apuleius' time (Knorr 1985). He points out the striking lack of reference to Archimedes' *Catoptrics*, either directly or indirectly, in all the major writers in the Greek tradition on optics (Diocles, Hero, Ptolemy). He also notes, however, that the ancient tradition is full of such surprising silences (1985: 32–33). The *Optics* and *Catoptrics* assigned to Euclid are not directly mentioned until the fourth and fifth centuries AD, respectively (Knorr 1985: 48), although Knorr shows that they were still likely to have been used by earlier writers on optics such as Ptolemy and Hero. Knorr's identification of the *Catoptrics* of "Archimedes" mentioned by Apuleius with the Euclidean *Catoptrics* relies most heavily on the similarity of the topics that Apuleius assigns to Archimedes in Chapter 16 of the *Apology* and the topics discussed in the *Catoptrics* handed down in Euclid's name (1985: 33 ff.). The weakness of the argument, however, is that the list of topics in Apuleius is what one would expect in any treatise on catoptrics and is not distinctive enough to show that Apuleius must be referring to Euclid's *Catoptrics* (Burnyeat 2004). Moreover, as Burnyeat (2004) has pointed out, Euclid's *Catoptrics* is exceedingly short (twenty-eight pages in the Teubner text) and, even if we suppose that part of it has been lost as argued by Knorr, it could hardly be described by Apuleius as a "huge volume." This huge volume that Apuleius consulted is thus likely to be a work by Archimedes after all, and it is quite possibly Apuleius' source for his account of Archytas' views on optics.

Archytas' theory of vision in Apuleius

Apuleius' admittedly exiguous testimony on Archytas' optics has been over-looked by most treatments of early Greek optics (e.g. Beare 1906, Lindberg 1976). Apuleius presents two basic ways of explaining the images of our-selves that we see in mirrors (*num . . . an*). These two sorts of explanation are in turn based on two fundamentally different theories of vision. Accord-ing to the first theory, vision is explained in terms of images coming to our eyes from outside. Earlier versions of such a theory can be found in Empedocles, Leucippus and Democritus, but Apuleius presents the theory in its Epicurean incarnation: the images that reach our eyes are films of atoms, which all bodies give off continuously and which have the form of the body from which they come, just like the skin sloughed by a snake. When we look into a mirror, the films of atoms that originate from our own face strike the mirror and are reflected back, albeit in reversed form, so as to hit our eyes, so that we see ourselves. According to the second theory, vision is explained in terms of visual rays, which extend from the eyes and which make contact with objects outside ourselves. When we look into a mirror, these visual rays are reflected back so as to come into contact with our own face. Since the rays are reflected back to us at the same angle with which they struck the mirror, they present the image as inside the mirror, although the rays are in fact touching our own face (or some other object) outside the mirror (line 11 – *quod extra tangant et visant*).

Archytas is presented as adopting the second sort of theory, along with Plato and the Stoics. It is assumed that all three of these theories explain our ability to see our own image in a mirror in the same way, i.e. by the reflection of the visual ray from the "dense, shiny and smooth" surface of the mirror. The theorem that the angle of incidence of the visual ray is equal to the angle of reflection is also assigned to all three. We might think that this was careless attribution of a later view back to Archytas, but this theorem is required in order for the explanation of the image in the mirror to work, i.e. for us to see the image at the appropriate place in the mirror.

Similarly at *Timaeus* 46a Plato does not refer to angles or equality, but the discussion clearly assumes some sort of rule of reflection. The three theories differ only in the way in which they explain the propagation of the visual ray itself. Plato is presented first. He argues that the visual ray is filtered by the middle of the eye and then mixed and made one with external light (cf. *Ti.* 45b ff.). Archytas is reported to have thought that the rays came from the eyes alone, without any external support. The Stoics argue that the rays are made by the tension of the air.

The description of Archytas' view is formulated in conscious contrast to the description of Plato's view. For Archytas the ray starts from the eye as it does for Plato (*oculis profecti* corresponds to *oculis proliquati*), but while for Plato the ray is then mixed with external light (*lumini extrario*), for Archytas the ray alone is sufficient without any external support (*foris* in the description of Archytas' view refers back to the *extrario* in the description of Plato's). In addition, Plato regards the visual ray as filtered (*proliquati*) by the eye (cf. *Ti.* 45c), while there is no reference to such a process in Archytas. The rays are simply said to "proceed" or "originate" (*profecti*) from the eye. That Plato did indeed think that the visual ray needs the support of the external light is shown by his claim in the *Timaeus* that the visual ray is extinguished when there is no external light (*Ti.* 45d). Thus, for Plato the visual ray falls apart without external support and ceases to exist. Archytas' position is that the ray continues to exist even without the support of external light. It is then unclear how Archytas would have explained our inability to see in the dark, but Apuleius' testimony indicates that he did not think that the visual ray ceased to exist, and we must suppose that he thought that it was hindered in some other way by the lack of light. Although Apuleius emphasizes this contrast between Plato and Archytas, they both share a belief in a visual ray that is emitted by the eye, in contrast to the Stoics. The Stoics regard the visual ray not as emitted from the eye but rather as acting on the air next to the eye, making it tense, so that the ray from our eye to the object is actually made by this tensing of the air (see the detailed commentary on *intentu aëris facti* in line 9).

The position of Archytas in the history of optics

A brief consideration of Archytas' connections both to his contemporary Plato and to his predecessors and successors in the tradition of Greek optics may help in understanding Archytas' contribution to optics. Two misconceptions about that tradition should be addressed at the beginning. First, attempts to assign a theory of vision to Pythagoras (e.g. Jablonski 1930: 309) should be rejected, since they are based on the *Pythagorean Memoirs*

excerpted by Alexander Polyhistor (D.L. VIII. 29), which have been shown
conclusively to be a product of the third century BC or later (Burkert 1972a:
53). There is no reliable evidence about any work by Pythagoras in optics.
Second, although it is certain that the notion of the visual ray predated both
Plato and Archytas, the ascription of the view to Alcmaeon and Empedocles
is mistaken. The case for Alcmaeon is based largely on an inference from his
supposed connection to the Pythagoreans (Beare 1906: 12), and there is, in
fact, no ancient source which assigns the visual ray to Alcmaeon (Stratton
1917: 161–62). With regard to Empedocles, Aristotle pointed out not only
that his use of the lantern as an image for the eye suggests that he accepts the
visual ray theory but also that, in other passages, he seems to explain vision
in terms of emanations coming from objects to the eye (*Sens.* 437b25 ff.).
The most recent consensus of scholars is that, while the fire in the eye had
a role to play for Empedocles, it was not a visual ray that went outside the
eye (Wright 1981: 242; Long 1966: 262–64). Empedocles like Democritus
seems to have explained vision primarily in terms of effluences from objects
striking our eyes.

   The visual ray theory does go back beyond Plato and Archytas into the
fifth century, however. Aristotle tells us that the mathematician Hippocrates
of Chios (fl. 450–430?) and his follower Aeschylus thought that the visual
ray was reflected (ἀνακλωμένης τῆς ἡμετέρας ὄψεως) from the moisture,
which a comet pulls after itself, to the sun, so that the visual ray reports light
as trailing the comet, when it is in fact "seeing" the light of the sun (*Mete.*
342b36 ff.). In his book on the Pythagoreans, Aristotle also reports that the
fifth-century Pythagoreans were impressed by the agreement produced in
the study of the visual ray (τὰ περὶ τὴν ὄψιν μαθήματα), because of the
use of geometrical diagrams (Text C above; see further below). These two
testimonia are a clear indication that explanations of visual phenomena in
terms of the geometry of the visual ray were already very successful in the
second half of the fifth century. It seems reasonable to believe that one of
the Pythagoreans who was impressed with Hippocrates' work in this area
was his contemporary Philolaus, since he explained the sun in terms of the
optics of a lens or a mirror (Huffman 1993: 266–70). The evidence for the
use of the visual ray by Hippocrates and fifth-century Pythagoreans is too
meager to indicate whether they relied solely on the visual ray or whether
they also took into account external light and the medium through which
the visual ray traveled.

   There is an important report in the doxography (Text A) stating that
"those from Pythagoras and the mathematicians" explain images in mirrors
as the result of the reflection of the visual ray (ἀνάκλασιν τῆς ὄψεως).

This is further explained by saying that the visual ray travels as if directed (τεταμένην, cf. e.g. Plato *R.* 581b) against the bronze (of the mirror), and encountering the density and smoothness of the bronze is struck and turns back on itself. This reflection of the visual ray is then compared to someone extending his hand and then bending it back to his shoulder. It seems to me quite plausible, in light of the evidence presented above, to regard "those from Pythagoras and the mathematicians" as the Pythagoreans of the fifth and fourth centuries such as Philolaus and Archytas and mathematicians such as Hippocrates. Burkert has suggested an alternative interpretation of the doxography on this point, however (1972a: 42 n. 76). He draws our attention to a nearby passage in Aëtius (Text B above), in which the second-century BC astronomer Hipparchus is said to have compared visual rays to hands, which reach out from the eyes to objects. The version of this report in Stobaeus goes on to say that some assign this same doctrine to Pythagoras, "since he is the one who established the sciences." This is a marvelous example of how the legend of Pythagoras grew. We see the tendency to assign later doctrines back to Pythagoras, simply because he was the supposed founder of the sciences. Text A can then be interpreted in light of Text B, since Text A also involves the comparison of the visual ray to a hand or an arm, which is found in Text B. "Those from Pythagoras" in Text A are not fifth-century Pythagoreans but rather the Pythagoreans of the legend that we have seen in the process of generation in Text B. "The mathematicians" are not fifth-century mathematicians such as Hippocrates but rather Hipparchus and other Hellenistic astronomer-mathematicians. In at least one other passage in the doxography (II. 31.2) "the mathematicians" does indeed seem to refer to the third-century astronomer Aristarchus (Burkert 1972a: 42 n. 76).

The evidence does not allow us to be certain which of the two explanations of Text A should be accepted. There are reasons to be skeptical of Burkert's explanation, however. First Text A, unlike Text B and other creations of the Pythagoras legend, does not refer to Pythagoras himself but rather to Pythagoreans. Second, while "the mathematicians" of the doxography clearly often refers to Hellenistic mathematicians, it is also plausible that it refers to the whole mathematical tradition going back to Euclid and before him to Hippocrates of Chios. Finally, Burkert seems unaware both of the evidence for Archytas' work in optics and of Hippocrates of Chios' use of the visual ray. Moreover, he tried to expunge all reference to optics from Aristotle's reports on the early Pythagoreans (see on Text C below). Without this evidence for work in optics by Pythagoreans and mathematicians of the fifth and early fourth centuries, Burkert's explanation of Text A would be compelling but, once that evidence is recognized, it is just as plausible that Text A is a reference to Hippocrates of Chios and the Pythagoreans of the fifth and early fourth centuries.

If we turn to the end of the fifth century and the first part of the fourth century, we see both Plato and Archytas adopting the visual ray theory. Archytas will have inherited an interest in optics from Philolaus. In addition he clearly knew of the work of Hippocrates of Chios in geometry (see A14), and he thus may have built on Hippocrates' work in optics as well. There is, however, a significant puzzle about both Archytas' and Plato's reception of earlier work in optics. Neither of them refers to optics as a science, although we might have expected them to do so. In Fragment 1, Archytas gives a hymn to the value of the sciences in general and specifically mentions the *quadrivium* of astronomy, logistic, geometry and harmonics. There is a resounding silence about optics. In *Republic* VII, Plato appears to quote from Fragment 1 of Archytas and to adopt Archytas' quadrivium, while also calling for a fifth science of stereometry. Again, there is not a trace of optics, yet, as we have seen, there is clear evidence for mathematical optics of some sort going back at least fifty years before the time of the writing of the *Republic*.

The most reasonable explanation of this silence about optics is that neither Archytas at the time of composition of the *Harmonics* (400–390?) nor Plato at the time of composition of the *Republic* in the 380s or 370s recognized optics as a distinct mathematical discipline. It may be that optics was regarded as an application of geometry to the physical world and there were as yet no treatises on optics such as Euclid was later to write. Instead there were geometrical explanations of optical phenomena, which were presented as parts of astronomy or cosmology. It is significant that the testimony for Hippocrates' use of the visual ray has to do with his explanation of comets. Plato is led to call for a new science of stereometry by mathematical considerations. He identifies a gap between geometry, which deals with two-dimensional figures, and astronomy, which deals with three-dimensional bodies in motion. Stereometry is needed to deal with three-dimensional bodies in themselves (*R.* 528a). There is no similarly compelling mathematical reason to propose a science of optics. Indeed, optics is the application of an already existing mathematical science, geometry, to one aspect of the physical world, visual phenomena. In *Republic* VII Plato is not doing physics but rather constructing a coherent set of mathematical sciences. Optics would have no role in this project, even if it did exist as a separate science at this time. Plato mentions empirical astronomy and harmonics but only to argue that we must go beyond them to purely mathematical sciences of harmony and figures in motion. There is no reason to mention empirical optics, because there is already a well-developed field of purely mathematical geometry.

In the *Timaeus*, Plato *is* doing physics and there he does refer to optical phenomena (45b ff.) and provides the explanation of vision which Apuleius summarizes in A25. He adopts the visual ray but clearly thinks that vision cannot be explained just in terms of the visual ray and gives an account in which the light outside the eye also plays an important role. At this point the question of the relation between Archytas' and Plato's work on optics appears once again. We might be inclined to suppose that Archytas' explanation in terms of the visual ray alone is earlier than Plato's more complicated theory. This is possible but not inevitable. The differences in the two theories may not tell a story of progress in the explanation of vision but rather reflect an ongoing controversy on the nature of optics. If we skip ahead to the end of the fourth century, we find that Euclid, in the earliest surviving treatise on optics, adopts the simple visual ray theory and makes no reference to the "more sophisticated" physical explanations of vision developed earlier not only in Plato's *Timaeus* but also in Aristotle, who apparently adopted the visual ray theory early in his career only to reject it and develop a more complicated theory later (Lindberg 1976: 217 n. 39).

Euclid's *Optics* is set out as a mathematical treatise, beginning with a set of seven postulates on the basis of which some fifty-eight propositions are proved. The postulates and the propositions make clear, however, that Euclid cannot be talking simply about mathematical lines. The visual ray is not a breadthless length, nor are there an unlimited number of such rays. There are spaces between rays and the rays are conceived of as making physical contact with visible bodies. Objects that fall in the spaces are not seen (see further Lindberg 1976: 13). At the same time, however, the physical properties of the visual ray and the process of vision are clearly kept to a minimum. The essence of the visual process is regarded as mathematical. Moreover, optics is now treated as a distinct branch of mathematics, which is of interest in its own right rather than as a part of cosmology or physics. Thus Archytas, like Euclid, may well have done his work in optics in full awareness of Plato's more complicated physical account of the visual ray and yet like Euclid have consciously chosen to adopt a visual ray with the bare minimum of physical characteristics. There are several pieces of evidence which suggest that this may have been the case.

First, Apuleius presents Archytas' theory as a response to Plato. This may, of course, be an ordering developed solely for rhetorical purposes by

Apuleius or his source. Nonetheless, there would be no reason for Archytas to have emphasized that the visual ray is derived from our eyes "without any external support" (*sine ullo foris amminiculo*), if someone else had not suggested that the visual ray did need support. The Latin word *amminiculum* ("support" or "prop"), which is used in describing Archytas' view, is rare enough to suggest that it represents a distinctive Platonic word, with which Archytas is taking issue. Indeed, in the passage on vision in the *Timaeus*, Plato uses the verb ἀντερείδω, which appears only here in Plato. This compound Greek verb is parallel to the Latin formation with the prefix ἀντί = "against" corresponding to the Latin *ad*, while the verb ἐρείδω has as a basic meaning "to prop" or "to support," which corresponds to the basic meaning of the Latin verb *munio*, "to build up." Archytas may therefore have repeated Plato's unusual word, perhaps in its noun form ἀντερείσμα, in order to ridicule the idea that the visual ray needed "propping up." The passage in which the verb occurs in Plato (*Ti.* 45c) is obscure enough, however, so that the correspondence between *amminiculum* and ἀντερείδω must remain a conjecture. Most translators of Plato take the verb to refer to the visual ray striking (Cornford) or "pressing against" (Zeyl) the object of vision. The visual ray is, however, already described as striking (προσπῖπτον) and meeting with (ξυνέπεσεν) the external object, so that I would suggest, in light of Archytas' criticism, that the subject of ἀντερείδει (A's reading for ἂν ἀντερείδῃ) is in fact the "one body" of the previous clause, which "props up" or "supports" the visual ray (". . . one kindred body is formed along the line of sight, in which way it supports that which flows from within to strike the external object which it meets"). Plato's use of ἀντερείδω to mean "support" is distinct from the later use of ἐπερείδω and ἐπερείσις by the Stoics to indicate the "pressure" of the tensed air on the object of sight (*SVF* ii. 868; cf. 863–64). In the Stoic term, ἐπι- indicates that the air presses "against" the object, whereas in Plato's term ἀντι- indicates not pressure "against" something static but the resistance that a support provides against or in response to pressure. At Xenophon *HG* v. 2.5, the verb is used of people leaning timbers against a tower to prop it up.

There is reason to at least conjecture, moreover, that the specifics of the formulation of the visual ray theory ascribed to the Pythagoreans and mathematicians by Aëtius (Text A) are based on a text of Archytas, which was also formulated in response to Plato. In Aëtius the reflection of the visual ray is compared to someone extending his hand and then bending it back to his shoulder. The comparison of the visual ray to the arm extending from the body would be a very apt response to Plato. Just as our arm can extend out into space beyond our body, without any need for support from outside the body, so the visual ray is an appendage of the eye needing no external support. Archytas' love of illustrations involving an extended hand or stick provides evidence that he might be behind this imagery. He is famous for his thought experiment to show that the universe is unlimited (A24), in which he asks whether, if we were at the supposed limit, we would be able to extend our hand or a stick into what is outside or not. Similarly, in Fragment 1, Archytas piles up illustrations for his theory of pitch and one of the most prominent is a waving stick. To be sure, other philosophers use such examples, but if we are looking for a Pythagorean who wrote on optics and might have originated the comparison of the visual ray to a hand, Archytas is a very plausible candidate, and such an illustration would make very good sense as a response to Plato.

Archytas' account of vision here in A25 is parallel to his account of sound in Fragment 1 in an even more important way than the use of striking examples. In both cases, Archytas presents a bare-bones physical theory, which seems designed largely as something upon which to hang a mathematical description of phenomena. The medium of sight (light) is ignored in his optics just as there is only an implicit reference to air as the medium of sound, in Archytas' account of acoustics in Fragment 1. Moreover, in neither case is the essential phenomenon, sound or the visual ray, analyzed. The basic conditions under which sound arises are defined and the existence of the visual ray is assumed, but there is no attempt to say what exactly a sound or a visual ray is. Archytas seems interested in formulating the basic laws governing the behavior of sound (e.g. his theory of pitch) and sight (e.g. that the angle of incidence is equal to the angle of reflection), and in particular in formulating those laws in a mathematical way (i.e. in terms of ratios of numbers or geometrical diagrams), but there are only limited traces of interest in the physics of sight or sound or in the physics of our perceptual processes. To this extent Archytas matches Aristotle's description of fifth-century Pythagoreans as focusing exclusively on the physical world but using principles which do not come from the physical world and in fact apply better to a higher class of realities (*Metaph.* 990b30). Archytas, as he did in the case of harmonics and perhaps in solid geometry, is looking for mathematics in things. As a result he tends to treat physical objects almost as mathematical objects and to reject Plato's excessively physical account of vision. Plato, in part because he has separated forms and mathematical entities from physical things in his metaphysics, is less willing to see the physical world, "the works of necessity," as simply mathematical in nature.

If we turn from Plato and Archytas to Aristotle, we encounter both a puzzling presence and a puzzling absence. The surprising presence is the appearance of a distinct discipline of optics, which Aristotle portrays as dependent on geometry, in the same way as harmonics is dependent on arithmetic (e.g. *APo.* 75b16). What has happened between the writing of the *Republic* and Aristotle's *Posterior Analytics* to lead Aristotle to recognize the discipline that is not mentioned by Plato or Archytas? The obvious answer is that someone has developed that discipline as a coherent whole for the first time. The natural suggestion is that this someone is Archytas (so Burnyeat 2004). We have seen that he may have developed a mathematical theory of optics later in his career in part as a response to the physics of the *Timaeus*. Archytas' use of the bare visual ray is parallel to Euclid's approach some fifty years later.

This suggestion leads to the puzzling absence, the lack of any reference to Archytas' work on optics by Aristotle. We know that Aristotle wrote three books on Archytas (A13) and that he also wrote an optics (D.L. v. 26). If Archytas had written on optics, surely Aristotle would be expected to refer to this work. The answer to this puzzle probably has most to do with the nature of the surviving treatises of Aristotle. His references to optics in the surviving works are relatively few in number and he mentions no names at all. Most of this treatment of optical phenomena is a treatment of the physical phenomenon of sight. Aristotle is thus consistent with his general views on explanation in science, in appealing only to physical explanations of optical phenomena. If Aristotle's work on optics had survived, we would expect a mathematical treatment of the phenomena, and it would indeed be a puzzle if Archytas were not mentioned there. Archytas' views on optics are not mentioned in Aristotle's surviving works, because Archytas in all probability dealt only with the mathematics of vision and had essentially nothing to say on the physics of sight. Aristotle's description of optics as dealing with mathematical lines but not *qua* mathematical but rather *qua* physical (*Ph.* 194a11) fits Euclid's *Optics* perfectly, but might also be a good description of the treatise on mathematical optics which we have hypothesized for Archytas. Indeed, Aristotle's description encapsulates Archytas' general approach to natural phenomena: he proceeds as if he is dealing with mathematical entities but treats all these entities *qua* physical rather than *qua* mathematical.

Aristotle's evidence for early Pythagorean work on optics
Text C provides important but neglected testimony for Pythagorean work in optics. Burkert argues convincingly that this passage in Iamblichus'

De Communi Mathematica Scientia (78. 8–18 Festa) is a fragment from Aristotle's books on the Pythagoreans (1972a: 50 n. 112). The passage in question comes between two passages derived from Aristotle and shows striking similarities both to Aristotle's presentation of the Pythagoreans elsewhere and to typical Aristotelian phraseology. Burkert, however, maintained that "the course of the argument is deranged" in two passages, which refer to optics and geometry, and bracketed these passages as additions of Iamblichus. He thus adopts a text that emphasizes the role of harmonics and number in Pythagoreanism and that corresponds closely to Aristotle's presentation of the Pythagoreans in the *Metaphysics* (985b31).

Even with Burkert's excisions, however, there is one important difference between Text C and Aristotle's presentation of the Pythagoreans elsewhere. Text C emphasizes not just that the Pythagoreans were impressed with mathematics because of the similarities which they saw between numbers and things, the theme stressed in the *Metaphysics*, but also that they admired the accuracy of the arguments of mathematics, because it alone, of the things which human beings pursue, admits of proof. This epistemological theme, which emphasizes the cognitive reliability of mathematical proof, is missing from Aristotle's account of Pythagoreanism outside of Text C. Burnyeat (2004) has argued that this discrepancy suggests that, in Text C, Aristotle is referring to a different brand of Pythagoreanism than in the *Metaphysics*, where he is referring primarily to the fifth-century Pythagoreanism associated with Philolaus. Burnyeat argues that Text C is describing Archytas, who is famous for his proof that there is no mean proportional between numbers in superparticular ratio (A19) and as the first person to solve the problem of the duplication of the cube (A14–A15; see also Fr. 4).

Since Archytas is the first Pythagorean whom we know to have carried out significant mathematical proofs Text C would certainly apply well to him, but the reference can apply to earlier Pythagoreans also. Hippocrates of Chios, as the first Greek to write on the elements of geometry, had already made advances in geometrical proof in the second half of the fifth century. Although he was not a Pythagorean, there is every reason to suppose that Pythagoreans such as Philolaus were familiar with his work and thus with rigorous mathematical proof. There is no direct reference to mathematical proof in Philolaus, but there is a strong emphasis on the epistemic role of number, a role that is also not reflected in Aristotle's reports of Pythagoreanism elsewhere than in Text C. Philolaus argues in Fragment 4 that "it is not possible that anything whatsoever be understood or known without [number]." We might conclude that Philolaus bases this assertion solely on the similarity between numbers and things, but why then should he suppose that numbers explain things rather than things numbers? Philolaus is clearly working on the assumption that numbers and mathematical relationships are more cognitively reliable than things. Where does this assumption come from? It seems quite plausible that it is because of the accuracy of the reasonings displayed in mathematical proof, which he had observed in the work on figures such as that of Hippocrates of Chios (Huffman 1993: 64 ff.; cf. 114–15). Thus, Text C with Burkert's excisions, while certainly a good description of Archytas' outlook, is also likely to reflect earlier Pythagoreanism as well.

What about Burkert's excisions? He suggests that Iamblichus added the references to geometry in order "to emphasize the many-sidedness of Pythagorean μαθήματα" (1972a: 448). Burkert's formulation slightly distorts what we find in Iamblichus, since, although there is a reference to geometry, it is geometry in the service of optics. The two subject matters that are put in parallel are "the facts about harmony" (τὰ περὶ τὴν ἁρμονίαν) and "the study of sight (the visual ray)" (τὰ περὶ τὴν ὄψιν μαθήματα). So, if Iamblichus is adding anything, it is a reference to optics and not to geometry. Burnyeat (2004) rightly objects, however, that, if Iamblichus' goal was to emphasize the breadth of the Pythagorean achievement, it is odd that he should seize upon such a minor science as optics rather than simply referring to geometry itself instead. Moreover, it is doubly strange that Iamblichus should introduce a reference to optics, since there is little evidence that Iamblichus himself was interested in mathematical optics. Although the word ὄψις appears a number of times elsewhere in *De Communi Mathematica Scientia*, it is always used in reference to vision in general and it is not connected to the visual ray or to the mathematical study of optics as it is here. Indeed there is only one reference to optics of any sort in any of Iamblichus' works (*VP* xxvi. 115.8; cf. Nicom. *Harm.* 6; Ptol. *Harm* I. 1–2). We can only conclude from this evidence that Iamblichus had little interest in mathematical optics, and it would be strange in the extreme if he had rewritten the passage from Aristotle to include references to optics in the way that Burkert suggests.

One might object that there is no evidence elsewhere that Aristotle connected the study of optics with the early Pythagoreans, so that it is just as problematic to suppose that the references to optics belong to him. The cases of Aristotle and Iamblichus are importantly different in two ways, however. First, as Burkert has shown, the language in the passage as a whole shows that it is from Aristotle. Thus, unless strong evidence can be given to show that individual phrases are not Aristotelian, we should accept the whole as coming from Aristotle. The onus of proof rests on anyone who argues that Iamblichus has intervened in the text, and it has been shown that there is no reason to believe that he would introduce a reference to optics. Second, although Aristotle does not connect the Pythagoreans to optics in other passages in his extant work, he does show a strong interest in optics. Even more importantly, in several passages he draws the same parallel between optics and harmonics, which we find in the passage from *De Communi Mathematica Scientia*. In the *Posterior Analytics*, Aristotle says that optics is subordinate to geometry in the same way that harmonics is subordinate to arithmetic (75b16 and 78b37) and related points are made in three passages in the *Metaphysics* (997b20, 1078a14, 1077a5). It is thus much more likely that the parallel between optics and harmonics which is drawn in Text C is due to Aristotle than to any intervention of Iamblichus.

Burkert also objects that the expression τὰ περὶ τὴν ὄψιν μαθήματα is both unclear and factually wrong (1972a: 448). His point is that the Pythagoreans were not impressed by mathematics being mathematical but rather that an everyday concern such as music should conform to mathematical rules; but this problem arises from two misreadings of the passage. First, Burkert translates τὰ περὶ τὴν ἁρμονίαν as "the facts about harmony," thus suggesting that we are dealing with everyday phenomena. Such an interpretation is not inevitable, however, and we may just as easily understand τὰ περὶ τὴν ἁρμονίαν as "the study of harmony" (i.e. with μαθήματα understood) in parallel with "the study of optics." Such study contains both an empirical and a mathematical component. This latter interpretation gains further support once we recognize a second way in which Burkert's reading of the passage is problematic As Burnyeat argues, the ὅτι in the preceding clause about harmony should be translated not "that" (Burkert) but rather "because." The point is that the Pythagoreans saw that the study of harmony was in a state of agreement, *because* it was based on numbers. In the next clause a similar point is made. They saw that the study of optics was in a state of agreement, *because* it was based on diagrams (i.e. proofs based on diagrams). (As Burnyeat notes, this requires us either to understand ὅτι before διὰ διαγραμμάτων or to suppose that ὅτι fell out of the text at that point. The manuscripts read the impossible διὰ γραμμάτων ["through letters"] and scholars have accepted Vitelli's emendation to διὰ διαγραμμάτων. In mathematical writing διάγραμμα regularly means "theorem" or "proof" rather than diagram [Netz 1999: 36], although in some philosophical contexts it clearly means diagram [e.g. Pl. *R.* 529e]. For the preposition διά followed by a word beginning with δια- see Hdt. III. 117.9 and Porph. *In Arist. Cat.*, *CAG* IV. 1.131.17. Asclepius, in his commentary on Nicomachus, uses the expression διὰ διαγράμματος [1. 125.12, p. 49 Tarán].)

Burkert also excised the phrase καὶ τὰ γεωμετρούμενα εἴδη τῶν ὄντων as an addition by Iamblichus. In this case his argument was that the phrase was a Platonism from late antiquity. However, Burnyeat argues convincingly that, although the passive γεωμετρούμενα is not paralleled elsewhere in Aristotle, the active form was in use in a transitive sense in the fifth century (Pl. *Tht.* 173e; Ar. *Av.* 995) and hence a use of the passive is perfectly plausible for Aristotle. Nor need we interpret the use of εἴδη as a suspicious reference to the Platonic theory of forms, since Aristotle elsewhere says that mathematics deals with εἴδη where he can hardly intend a reference to the Platonic forms (*APo.* 1. 13, 79a7–8). The Pythagoreans concluded from what they saw of harmonics and optics that, if we wish to understand the true nature of the things that are, we must look to "the numbers and the geometrical forms of the things that are." Harmonics discovers that sound behaves according to mathematical relations of numbers, and optics discovers that vision behaves according to the relations of geometrical shapes.

Two other minor difficulties raised by Burkert also need to be addressed briefly. First, he objects to the use of λόγους in the last sentence both because it lacks an article and because the introduction of "ratios" (Burkert translates "proportions") intrudes on the neat dichotomy that is set up between arithmetic and geometry; but the omission of the article is in fact the clue to the correct interpretation. The article is included with numbers and geometrical forms because each of these phrases goes with a dependent genitive (τῶν ὄντων, "the numbers and geometrical forms of the things that are"). Of course it makes little sense to talk of the ratios to one another of the things that are; ratios are relations between numbers or geometrical magnitudes. Hence there is no article with λόγους. Ratios are examples of mathematical first principles which the Pythagoreans came to see as first principles of the things that are as well. The mention of ratio does not interfere with the dichotomy, since it is a concept that applies to both arithmetic and geometry. Finally, the phrase ἔνισον which the manuscripts preserve in line 3 is indeed unparalleled, but it is likely to be a corruption of either the ἐν ἴσῳ proposed by Burnyeat (citing Th. IV. 65) or the ἐξ ἴσου suggested by Burkert himself (see S. *OC* 254–55).

Once the problems with the text have been solved, it becomes clear that Text C provides vital evidence for the history of early Pythagoreanism. What is strikingly new here is the emphasis on mathematical optics as a central concern of the early Pythagoreans. Testimonium A25 of Archytas, Text A above and the evidence for the optical questions raised by Philolaus' account of the sun all combine to support the plausibility of the role assigned to optics in Pythagoreanism by Aristotle in Text C. Whereas it has long been a commonplace to say that the Pythagoreans came to think that the world was governed by mathematical rules, because of the role numbers played in describing the sounds we hear, Text C tells us that this line of thought was paralleled by the discovery that our vision could be described in terms of geometrical relations. Who were these Pythagoreans who founded mathematical optics? Burnyeat argues that Archytas is the logical candidate. Borrowing the concept of the optical ray from Hippocrates of Chios and perhaps spurred by optical questions raised by Philolaus, he had both the necessary mathematical tools and the motivation to found optics and catoptrics (Burnyeat notes the plural in τὰ περὶ τὴν ὄψιν μαθήματα). Archytas is a plausible candidate to be the first person to write a treatise on mathematical optics, but I do not think that Aristotle is referring to Archytas in Text C. Text C is clearly from Aristotle's book on the Pythagoreans and his discussions of the Pythagoreans are always of fifth-century Pythagoreans, usually Philolaus (Huffman 1993: 28–31). Aristotle wrote separate books on Archytas (A13). Text C need not refer to a treatise in optics at all but, as I have suggested above, only to the geometrical explanation of optical phenomena in astronomy and cosmology, which preceded Archytas' work on optics proper.

Detailed commentary
(For the Apuleius passage as a whole see the commentary of Butler and Owen 1914.)

Line 8   amminiculo – *amminiculum*, "support," is derived from the root in the verb *munio* (to fortify, to support, to uphold). The preposition *ad* in the compound shows that the support is placed against something in order to prop it up. It is commonly used of the props on which vines grew (Cicero *N.D.* II. 120) but can be used of other objects used as supports or of support in a more metaphorical sense, such as the support given to beginning students (Quintilian *Inst.* II. 6.5). Cicero uses it of the "support" that our friends provide us, immediately after describing Archytas' emphasis on the value of friends (A7a), so that it is not impossible that Archytas used the equivalent Greek word in his discussion of friendship, as well as in his discussion of vision.

9   intentu aëris facti – This is the reading of all manuscripts, but scholars, unable to make sense of it, have proposed a number of emendations for *facti*.

Butler and Owen (1914) understand the Stoics to believe that the eye emits a visual ray, which is "held together" (Purser's emendation *coacti*) and kept from dissipating by the pressure of the external air (*intentu aëris*). There is nothing wrong with the manuscript reading, however, which indicates that the visual ray is literally "made" (*facti*) by the tensing of the air" (*intentu aëris*). The verb *intendo*, from which the rare noun *intentus* derives, has as a central meaning "to bring into a state of tension," and the suffix -*tus* is added to form a noun indicating the action of the verb (*OLD* -*tus*³), so that *intentu* means "tensing." On this account, the Stoics do not believe that a visual ray leaves the eye. Rather it acts on the air next to the eye in order to create a cone of tensed air stretching to the object of sight. The "ray" that extends from the eye to the object is thus literally made by the tensing of the air. This interpretation fits the evidence for Chrysippus. Some later testimonia, which suggest that the Stoics believed in a ray emitted by the eye, may be distortions of Chrysippus' view or later developments (Hahm 1978: 66 ff.).

CHAPTER VII

Miscellaneous testimonia

A10a Aulus Gellius, *Attic Nights* x. 12.8–10 (Marshall 1968)

Multa autem videntur ab hominibus istis male sollertibus huiuscemodi 1
commenta in Democriti nomen data, nobilitatis auctoritatisque eius 2
perfugio utentibus. Sed id, quod Archytam Pythagoricum commentum esse 3
atque fecisse traditur, neque minus admirabile neque tamen vanum aeque 4
videri debet. Nam et plerique nobilium Graecorum et Favorinus philoso- 5
phus, memoriarum veterum exsequentissimus, affirmatissime scripserunt 6
simulacrum columbae e ligno ab Archyta ratione quadam disciplinaque 7
mechanica factum volasse; ita erat scilicet libramentis suspensum et aura 8
spiritus inclusa atque occulta concitum. Libet hercle super re tam abhor- 9
renti a fide ipsius Favorini verba ponere: Ἀρχύτας Ταραντῖνος τὰ ἄλλα 10
καὶ μηχανικὸς ὢν ἐποίησεν περιστερὰν ξυλίνην πετομένην· ὁπότε καθί- 11
σειεν, οὐκέτι ἀνίστατο. μέχρι γὰρ τούτου *** (Fr. 66 Mensching; Fr. 62 12
Marres; Fr. 93 Barigazzi) 13

9 inclusa] F²O²X²N²Q inlusa rell. **10** τὰ] δ om. Fγ **11** ὁπότε] ΑΠΟΤΕ Fγ
om. δ ἦν ὁπότε Jacobi **11–12** καθίσειεν] ΚΑΘΗΣ (ΕΣ ΧΠ: ΝΣ F)ΕΙΕΝ Fγ (deficiunt δ)
12 μέχρι γὰρ τούτου] del. Hertz

Moreover, many fictions of this kind seem to have been ascribed to the name of Democritus by those men of misguided ingenuity, who availed themselves of the shelter of his renown and authority. But that which the Pythagorean Archytas is reported to have envisioned and made ought to seem neither less remarkable, nor equally groundless. For, many celebrated Greeks and in particular the philosopher Favorinus, a man very studious of ancient traditions, have written most positively that a model of a dove, which was made by Archytas out of wood with a special construction in accordance with the discipline of mechanics, flew. Evidently it was poised just so by counter weights and was set in motion by a puff of air concealed inside. In the case of a thing so hard to believe, I certainly want to quote the words of Favorinus himself: "Archytas of Tarentum, who was an expert in the field of mechanics, made a wooden dove which flew; whenever it alighted, it rose no more. For up to this point . . ."

Authenticity

Both Aulus Gellius and Favorinus are explicit in assigning the flying wooden dove to Archytas the Pythagorean from Tarentum. The only question is raised by Diogenes Laertius' report in A1 that there was a treatise in circulation entitled *On Mechanism*, which was by a different Archytas. Obviously the description of the wooden dove could have appeared in such a work and could have become mistakenly ascribed to Archytas of Tarentum (so Tannery 1887: 128). The dove is at about the same level of sophistication as and shows some similarities to the automata in the earliest surviving Greek treatises on the subject (see below), which date to the third century BC. Archytas' device would be a hundred years or more earlier, but there is evidence for the invention of isolated "marvelous devices" even before Archytas (see below). Thus, there is not sufficient reason for us to second-guess the testimony of Gellius and Favorinus, although there are grounds for doubts. If the dove is the invention of Archytas of Tarentum, this need not indicate that he wrote the treatise *On Mechanism*, which was in circulation, or any other treatise on the topic. The description of the wooden dove is so brief that it could have been derived even from a work like Aristoxenus' *Life of Archytas*.

Context

Testimonium A10a comes from Book Ten, Chapter 12 of the *Attic Nights* (ca. AD 180) of Aulus Gellius. Gellius was a Roman miscellanist, who was born in the 120s AD. The *Attic Nights* is a ". . . collection of mainly short chapters, based on notes or excerpts . . . made in reading, on a great variety of topics in philosophy, history, law, but above all in grammar in its ancient sense, including literary and textual criticism," which was intended for Gellius' children (L. S. Holford-Strevens in the *OCD*). Gellius was heavily influenced by the sophist and philosopher Favorinus, who wrote the earliest miscellany of the type, which also influenced Aelian and Athenaeus. As with all miscellanies there is a studied lack of order to the chapters in the *Attic Nights*, in order to produce a sense of variety. The chapters immediately preceding and succeeding it have no connection in subject to Chapter 12 and deal with points of Latin grammar.

Chapter Twelve itself is devoted to castigating Pliny the Elder for ascribing absurd views to the Greek philosopher Democritus. Gellius is so repulsed that he hesitates to report what Pliny says but goes on to give three examples, in order to illustrate the folly by which even keen minds are deceived. The last of these examples assigns to Democritus the view that some birds have a language and that, if we commingle the blood of these birds and eat the serpent, which arises when the blood is commingled, we will understand the language of birds (Plin. *Nat.* x. 137). Testimonium A10a is introduced at the end of the chapter, immediately after this last example. Gellius' mention of Archytas' dove in this context shows his hesitancy to believe the story. On the other hand he notes that, although as amazing as the other stories, it is not quite so incredible. He then admits that a number of Greeks including Favorinus (AD 85–155), who was an older friend of Gellius, have affirmed the truth of the story. After describing in a very cursory fashion how Archytas' wooden dove was supposed to have flown, he then feels compelled to end by quoting Favorinus as an authority for so incredible a story. It appears that the end of the quotation has been lost in the transmission of the text. It is uncertain whether the fragment of Favorinus came from his *Memoirs* (Ἀπομνημονεύματα — probably stories about philosophers) or from the *Miscellaneous History* (Παντοδαπὴ Ἱστορία).

The nature of Archytas' dove

Scholars have given surprisingly few reconstructions of the functioning of Archytas' flying wooden dove. By far the most convincing is that of Wilhelm Schmidt, although it is in need of some modifications. Schmidt gave two reconstructions, which agree concerning the basic mechanics of the dove but which differ in some details. The earliest is reported in DK (I. 425 note, from a letter of Jan. 23, 1903), while a somewhat later reconstruction is found in an article by Schmidt (1904). Schürmann (1991: 173–75) and Timpanaro Cardini (1958–64: II. 290–92) discuss the dove in some detail, but both basically favor Schmidt's reconstruction. Given the scanty evidence, any reconstruction must remain very conjectural. Here are the key points of Schmidt's reconstruction:

1. The wooden dove did not fly through the air independently but was part of a mechanism. In DK, Schmidt envisioned the mechanism in the form of a tree. The dove started from a perch on a lower branch and flew from branch to branch, until it alighted on an upper branch and stopped. In his later article, Schmidt pictured the dove as perched on the lip of a basin filled with water and positioned next to a wall. The dove flew up from the basin to a perch higher on the wall.

2. The dove was hollow and had a hidden tube leading into its center. Compressed air was introduced into the dove, and then the tube was sealed by turning a valve.

3. The dove was attached by a cord and a pulley to a counterweight, which was equal to the weight of the dove and which was hidden in or behind the tree (or the wall in the second version). The dove was then placed on a lower branch (or on the lip of the basin).

4. When the valve was opened, the air rushed out and by so doing caused the wings of the dove to flap (in the later reconstruction the dove was made with extended wings, and they did not flap) and lifted the dove off the branch. Once the compressed air had rushed out, the dove became lighter and was pulled upward by the counterweight, thus "flying" up to an upper branch (or a perch on the wall) and stopping, once the counterweight had reached the ground. In Schmidt's later version, the valve was opened by a lever extending through the wall, which was operated by someone hidden behind the wall.

5. Favorinus' comment that, once the dove alighted, it did not rise again presumably refers to the fact that the mechanism would have to be reset, with the dove returned to its lower perch and refilled with compressed air, before it could fly again. In his later article Schmidt uses Favorinus as a basis for his reconstruction of the dove as a trick used by a host to amaze his guests. The dove flies up from the basin causing other real doves drinking at the basin to scatter. The guests, realizing that the wooden dove was not real, then ask the host to have the dove fly again. The host replies that "the dove of Archytas flies only once," since he does not want to reveal the secret of the trick by resetting the mechanism in front of his guests.

Schmidt is clearly right to see the dove as part of a larger mechanism and not as flying independently. The sort of mechanism that he describes can be paralleled to some extent in the ancient evidence for mechanical devices both before and after Archytas. A free-flying wooden dove would be unparalleled (for interpretations along this line see Timpanaro Cardini 1958–64: II. 290–92). Gellius' incredulity concerning Archytas' dove might perhaps suggest that he thought it was free-flying, but the language that he uses to describe it, which is presumably a translation from a Greek original (most likely Favorinus), clearly suggests that the dove was not independent: *libramentis suspensum* is not easily understood as "equally balanced," as would be required if the dove flew independently, and is much more likely to refer to a dove which is put in a state of equipoise by the use of a counterweight (see the commentary below).

The area of Schmidt's reconstruction that seems most open to doubt is point 2 above. There is no mention of a valve or of compressed air in Gellius. It is, furthermore, far from clear how Archytas could have compressed the air inside the dove. Certainly there is no parallel for such a use of compressed air elsewhere in the ancient tradition on pneumatics (see below). Gellius' reference to a breath of air concealed within would not need to be a reference to air concealed in the dove. The breath of air could have been introduced through a tube concealed in the tree. The tube might have been in the branch of the tree which opened onto the perch where the dove was placed. If the dove was hollow, when someone behind the tree blew into the tube, the breath of air would cause the dove to jump up off the branch. Once the dove had jumped up off its perch, the counterweight attached to the dove would cause it to continue to fly up, until the counterweight reached the bottom, at which point the dove stopped flying.

Another problem with Schmidt's interpretation is that the difference in weight between the dove with compressed air and the dove without compressed air would not be significant enough to explain the ability of the counterweight to pull the dove up. The dove can only have held a very small amount of air. What gives the counterweight the impetus to lift the dove is simply the jump upward provided by the puff of air. If we ignored the friction of the cord on the pulley, the counterweight would pull the dove up, until the counterweight was stopped by some surface. In the actual functioning of the mechanism, there would be some friction so that the dove would only move up a limited distance before coming to a state of equipoise again. Nonetheless, it is plausible that the dove could have been pulled up enough by the counterweight so that it "flew" from a lower branch to an upper branch.

Archytas' dove in the context of the history of ancient automata

In order to fully understand the issues involved in the reconstruction of the workings of Archytas' dove, it is necessary to examine briefly the history of automata both before and after Archytas. Scholars typically assign the beginnings of sophisticated mechanical automata to Hellenistic Egypt and the figure of Ctesibius (fl. 270 BC), none of whose works have survived but whom we know through the reports of Vitruvius (see e.g. Hill 1984: 200; *OCD* under Ctesibius). Ctesibius, while designing a device to raise and lower a mirror in his father's barber shop, discovered that a counterweight falling in a narrow channel compressed the air, which made a sound as it came out of the mouth of the tube (Vitr. IX. 8.2–3). This interest in the force of air is characteristic of Greek treatises on automata, and the two most famous such treatises were in fact titled *Pneumatics* ("the study of air"). Philo of Byzantium's treatise (250–200 BC) survives only in an Arabic translation. Hero of Alexandria's (fl. ca. 50 BC) is preserved in Greek and is heavily dependent on Philo. Greek work on automata was in turn used and further developed in the Arabic tradition. Particularly important are the ninth-century AD *Book of Ingenious Devices* by three brothers known as the Banū Mūsā and the early thirteenth-century *Book of Knowledge of Ingenious Mechanical Devices* by al-Jazarī (Hill 1973 and 1978).

Examination of the automata described in these treatises reveals several points of connection with the dove of Archytas, but there are no precise parallels. First, birds are a particularly popular component of such automata. In several cases birds are made to sing by pouring liquid into a vessel and thus forcing air out through a narrow tube in the bird's mouth (Hero, *Pneumatics* 14 and 15). In other cases birds (or other animals) are made to drink (Hero, *Pneumatics* 28–30) or rotate back and forth (Hero, *Pneumatics* 15). There are, however, no instances of birds actually flying. The closest approximation to this is a bird that raises its wings in fright as a snake approaches its nest (Philo, *Pneumatics* 40 = Carra de Vaux 1902: 176–78; see also *Pneumatics* 42). This mechanism again works by pouring liquid into a vessel. In this case, the liquid causes a float to rise. The float is connected to the wings of the bird by a rod, and thus, as the float rises, the rod causes the wings to lift.

Second, there are many cases in which counterweights are used. In some instances doors are opened by counterweights (Hero, *Pneumatics* 37–38) or animals are made to rotate (Hero, *Pneumatics* 15). Although there are no examples of a bird or any other animal being lifted up by a counterweight, as is the case in Archytas, it certainly would appear to be within the capabilities of the ancient technology to use a counterweight to cause Archytas' dove to "fly" in the manner suggested in the reconstruction above.

Third, air pressure does play a role in a number of automata. For example, in one case heated air expands to drive out water from one vessel into another vessel, which serves as a counterweight to open a door (Hero, *Pneumatics* 37). Air pressure has a role to play in the very common concentric siphon (Hill 1984: 209), and Ctesibius' experiment with the mirror mentioned above involved the compression of air. In some devices air is compressed by blowing into a vessel partially filled with water, and, when a valve is turned, the compressed air causes the water to spurt out of the vessel (Hero, *Pneumatics* 42, 54 and cf. 9). It remains true, however, that there is no parallel among automata for the introduction of compressed air into an object without the use of a liquid as well. Nor is it clear how the air would have been compressed in the very small space afforded by a hollowed out model of a dove, which was presumably at most life size. Finally there is no parallel in the Hellenistic tradition for the use of compressed air to propel an object, which is surprising, if Archytas had already accomplished such a feat over a hundred years before the beginnings of that tradition (compressed air is used in a catapult invented by Ctesibius and described by Philo, but it is not clear whether the design is in fact practicable or how the technology would be relevant to Archytas' dove; see Drachmann 1963: 189 and Marsden 1971: 184).

How are we to understand Archytas' relation to this later Greek tradition of automata? He was active at least 100 years before Ctesibius, who is normally identified as the founder of the tradition. In part Ctesibius' primacy here is an accident of what has survived of the ancient tradition. Ctesibius' activities are described in some detail by Vitruvius, who evidently had access to Ctesibius' book. Ctesibius is in turn close in date to Philo whose *Pneumatics* we know and who influenced Hero. Thus it is possible to tell a coherent story about Greek automata and pneumatics starting with Ctesibius. As we have seen, however, Archytas' dove has many features in common with the later tradition. We are hampered in making any definitive claims for Archytas' contribution to this tradition by the lack of any other evidence for his work with automata besides the very skimpy description of his dove, nor is there any evidence for a treatise by Archytas on automata or pneumatics. It could be that Archytas' dove was an isolated invention rather than part of a larger body of work.

Supposing that we knew that Archytas had written a treatise on automata, it is not clear that even he can be identified as the originator of the tradition. A hundred years before Archytas, there are isolated examples of ingenious devices. Schmidt (1904: 346 ff.; cf. DK I. 425) cites as precursors of Archytas' work Cleotas' eagle used at Olympia in order to indicate the start of the horse race (Paus. VI. 20.12) and the stag which Canachus designed to rock in the hand of a statue of Apollo, without ever becoming detached (Plin. *Nat.* XXXIV. 75). The descriptions of these devices, which both belong to the early fifth century, are too brief to make clear even exactly what their purpose was let alone how they functioned, and reconstructions are highly conjectural. The stag appears to have no connection to Archytas' dove beyond the fact that it was a clever device, which depended on an initial state in which the object was poised just so (*suspendit*, cf. *suspensum* in Archytas A10a line 9). The Olympic eagle had wings permanently outstretched and employed a counterweight as did Archytas' dove. There is no mention of the use of air to initiate the movement of the eagle. It appears that it leaped up simply by the dropping of the counterweight in the form of a dolphin which was attached to the eagle through cords and a pulley (Schmidt 1904: 348 ff.).

It is unlikely that these creations of Canachus and Cleotas were the first or only such devices. It might be safe to say that Archytas and his predecessors differed from the later tradition precisely in that their efforts were isolated inventions rather than part of any sort of focused program of invention such as can be ascribed to Ctesibius, or coherent exposition of a series of related devices such as we find in Philo or Hero. These later three figures were in some sense professionals whereas Archytas remained an amateur. If Archytas wrote a treatise wholly or partially devoted to automata, it is clear that the Hellenistic tradition knew nothing of it, since neither Philo nor Hero mention Archytas.

Detailed commentary

Line 8 libramentis – *Libramentum* can be used to refer to an actual weight (e.g. of lead) used to operate a mechanism, i.e. a counterpoise (*OLD* 1) or to a more abstract notion of "equipoise," or "balance" (*OLD* 4). The best parallels for Gellius' usage appear to be Livy XXIV. 34.10 and Pliny, *Nat.* XXXVI. 117, where *suspensum* is used in the same context as it is in Gellius. In both cases the reference is to a weight used as a counterpoise. Livy is describing the mechanical device invented by Archimedes for the defense of Syracuse. From a crane located on the walls of the city, a grappling hook would be dropped onto the prow of enemy ships in the harbor. The hook would then be jerked back, catching hold of the prow of the ship, by a heavy lead counterweight (*gravique libramento*) on the walls, so that the ship was stood on its stern, with the prow suspended from the hook attached to the counterweight (*suspensa prora*). Lysippus (370–315 BC), some time after Archytas' death, constructed a sixty-foot tall statue of Zeus in Tarentum, which was so balanced (*ea ratio libramenti est*) that it could be moved by hand, while not being dislodged by storms (Pliny, *Nat.* XXXIV. 40).

Suspendo can mean "to hang" or "to suspend" an object from something. So Aeneas "hangs" a dove from a mast by a string in order to serve as a target in the archery contest (Vergil *Aen.* V. 489). *Suspendo* is also used of something "poised" like a bird above the waves (*Aen.* VII. 810). It can refer to something such as a millstone (Col. II. 10.35) or a dog's teeth (Lucr. V. 1069) which are "held poised" so as not to exert their full pressure. It is used by Pliny to describe Canachus' construction of a model of a stag: he so "poised" it in its tracks (*ita vestigiis suspendit*) as to allow a thread to pass under its feet (as it rocked back and forth). The common idea running through these usages is that of an object poised in a certain position by the action of a counter force. Gellius' words are thus most likely to mean that Archytas' wooden dove was part of a mechanism which used counterweights (*libramentis*) connected to the dove by a cord, in order to hold the dove unmoving but "poised" (*suspensum*) to be moved by the slightest change in the balance of the system. It is very hard to see how *libramentis suspensum* could refer to the wooden dove as simply well balanced in itself (i.e. equally balanced in weight, right to left and front to back) without any connection to a mechanism. Such a dove could be "well balanced" even when lying on a table and not "poised" at all, but *ita . . . suspensum* indicates that the dove was so poised as to be easily moved in the way that Gellius goes on to describe.

8–9   aura spiritus inclusa atque occulta concitum – *concitum* is set in contrast to *suspensum* and marks the next step in the process of making the dove fly. After being put into a state of equipoise by being connected to a mechanism of counterweights, it is set in motion (*concitum*) by a puff of air, which is "hidden within" (*inclusa atque occulta*). Hidden within what? The reference could be to air hidden within the dove itself. Thus, Schmidt suggested that there was compressed air in the dove, which was released with a valve. It is more likely, however, that the air was enclosed and hidden in the mechanism to which the dove was attached, perhaps a mechanism that looked like a tree. The use of *inclusa* does not indicate that the air was compressed, although Schmidt implies that it does (1904: 350). *Includo* regularly means "to enclose" without any further suggestion of compression. Thus at *N.D.* II . 24, when Cicero refers to the *calorem inclusum* in all living things, he is not saying that the heat is "compressed" but rather simply "contained" in each living thing.

11–12   ὁπότε καθίσειεν – The active of καθίζω is used intransitively elsewhere to describe birds alighting (Arist. *HA* 614a34–35 and 619b5), and καθίσειεν is thus best understood as intransitive here. The construction is a past general condition: "whenever it alighted, it rose no more." This interpretation works well with the interpretation of the functioning of Archytas' dove, which has been given above. The sentence describes the last phase. First, the dove is put into a state of equipoise by a mechanism, then that equipoise is disturbed and the dove is set in motion by a breath of air. The dove then flies up until the counterweight reaches the ground and, when the dove "alights," it will therefore rise no more until the mechanism is reset. DK adopt Jacobi's ἦν ὁπότε, which makes the verb transitive with Archytas as the subject: "Whenever, he set it down, it rose no more." It is odd that DK print this text, since it is hard to see how it would work with Schmidt's reconstruction of the dove which DK report. The only point at which Archytas would set the dove down would be at the beginning of the process, when he put the dove on the lower limb and attached it to the mechanism. It is precisely after Archytas does this that the dove does rise up, so that the assertion that "it rose no more" would make no sense.

12   μέχρι γὰρ τούτου *** – It is universally recognized that there is a lacuna here. There is not enough evidence to make a reliable guess as to how to complete the sense. Timpanaro Cardini (1958–64: II. 292–93) suggests that the import of the sentence was something like, "This was the extent of the mechanical art" (i.e. mechanics was able to design a dove that could fly so far but no further). It is also possible that the sense was "for the counterweight was able to lift it only to this point." Both of these suggestions suppose that only a few words have been lost. Another possibility is that Favorinus went on to describe the functioning of the dove in more detail and that several sentences rather than just a few words have fallen out. It is striking, however, that what is preserved from Favorinus exactly complements Gellius' report, not repeating the description of the counterweights and puff of air in Gellius but adding what happens at the end of the dove's flight, which is not in Gellius. This lack of repetition suggests that Gellius did not quote Favorinus' full description but just the salient fact that the wooden dove flew and the parts of Favorinus' description which Gellius had not already summarized in Latin. On this supposition, it appears likely that just a few words of Favorinus are missing.

A13 Text A. Diogenes Laertius, *Lives of the Philosophers* V. 25 (*Life of Aristotle*)

Περὶ φύσεως α΄ β΄ γ΄	1
Φυσικὸν α΄	2
Περὶ τῆς Ἀρχυτείου φιλοσοφίας α΄ β΄ γ΄	3
Περὶ τῆς Σπευσίππου καὶ Ξενοκράτους α΄	4
Τὰ ἐκ τοῦ Τιμαίου καὶ τῶν Ἀρχυτείων α΄	5
Πρὸς τὰ Μελίσσου α΄	6
Πρὸς τὰ Ἀλκμαίωνος α΄	7
Πρὸς τοὺς Πυθαγορείους α΄	8

3 ἀρχυτίου P   **5** τοῦ] om. F   ἀρχυτίων P   **7** Ἀλκμαίωνος] F   ἀκμαίωνος BP¹ (corr. P⁴)   **8** περὶ τῶν πυθαγορικῶν F²

Πρὸς τὰ Γοργίου ά 9
Πρὸς τὰ Ξενοφάνους ά 10
Πρὸς τὰ Ζήνωνος ά 11
Περὶ τῶν Πυθαγορείων ά 12

10 Ξενοφάνους] Menagius   Ξενοκράτους BPF   **12** πυθαγοριῶν B

On Nature – 3 books
Physics – 1 book
On the Archytan Philosophy – 3 books
On the Philosophy of Speusippus and Xenocrates – 1 book
A Summary of the Timaeus and the Works of Archytas – 1 book
A Response to the Writings of Melissus – 1 book
A Response to the Writings of Alcmaeon – 1 book
A Response to the Pythagoreans – 1 book
A Response to the Writings of Gorgias – 1 book
A Response to the Writings of Xenophanes – 1 book
A Response to the Writings of Zeno – 1 book
On the Pythagoreans – 1 book

Text B. Hesychius, *Life of Aristotle* (*Aristotelis . . . Fragmenta*, Rose 1886: 14)

Περὶ φύσεως ά 1
Περὶ φυσικῶν ά 2
Περὶ τῆς Ἀρχύτου φιλοσοφίας γ́ 3
Περὶ τῆς Σπευσίππου καὶ Ξενοκράτους ά 4
Ἐκ τῶν Τιμαίου καὶ Ἀρχύτου ά 5
Πρὸς τὰ Μελίσσου ά 6
Πρὸς τὰ Ἀλκμαίωνος ά 7
Περὶ τῶν Πυθαγορείων ά 8
Πρὸς τὰ Γοργίου <ά> 9

On Nature – 1 book
On Physics – 1 book
On the Philosophy of Archytas – 3 books
On the Philosophy of Speusippus and Xenocrates – 1 book
From the Writings of Timaeus and Archytas – 1 book
A Response to the Writings of Melissus – 1 book
A Response to the Writings of Alcmaeon – 1 book
On the Pythagoreans – 1 book
A Response to the Writings of Gorgias – <1 book>

Text C. Ptolemy, *Life of Aristotle* (*Aristotelis . . . Fragmenta*, Rose 1886: 20)

9　Ἀρχύτας γ′

. . .

19a　Περὶ τῶν Πυθαγορείων β′

9　*Archytas* – 3 books

. . .

19a　*On the Pythagoreans* – 2 books

Text D. Simplicius, *Commentary On Aristotle's De Caelo* II. 1 (*CAG* VII 379.14–17)

καὶ πάντων, οἶμαι, μᾶλλον ὁ Ἀριστοτέλης τὴν ἐν Τιμαίῳ περὶ τούτων τοῦ Πλάτωνος γνώμην ἠπίστατο, ὃς καὶ σύνοψιν ἢ ἐπιτομὴν τοῦ Τιμαίου γράφειν οὐκ ἀπηξίωσεν.

More than anyone, I suppose, Aristotle knew Plato's views on these matters in the *Timaeus*, since he did not think it beneath himself to write a synopsis or abridgement of the *Timaeus*.

Text E. Simplicius, *Commentary on Aristotle's De Caelo* I. 10 (*CAG* VII. 296.16–18)

. . . ταῦτα μὲν οὖν Ἀριστοτέλης οἶδε. τοιγαροῦν τὸν τοῦ Πλάτωνος Τίμαιον ἐπιτεμνόμενος γράφει, "φησὶ δὲ γενητὸν εἶναι· αἰσθητὸν γάρ, τὸ δὲ αἰσθητὸν γενητὸν ὑποτίθεται, τὸ δὲ νοητὸν ἀγένητον."

. . . Aristotle, then, knew these things. For certainly in abridging the *Timaeus* of Plato he writes, "He [Plato] says that it [the cosmos] is generated; for it is perceptible, and he assumes that what is perceptible is generated, but that what is intelligible is not generated."

Text F. Damascius, *Commentary on the Parmenides* (= *De Principiis* II. 172.16–22 Ruelle [Westerink and Combès 1986: LVI–LVII and CLI] = Rose 1886: 164–65)

βέλτιον ἄρα τῷ διορισμῷ αὐτοῦ ἐμμένειν, κατὰ τὴν Πυθαγορικὴν 1
συνήθειαν καὶ τὴν αὐτοῦ τοῦ Πλάτωνος, ἄλλα νοοῦντας τὰ ἔνυλα 2
πράγματα καὶ αὐτὴν τὴν ὕλην· ἔν τε γὰρ τῷ Φαίδωνι οὕτως ὀνομάζει 3
τὰ ἄλλα, τὰ εἴδη τὰ αἰσθητὰ λέγων ἄλλα, καὶ ἐν ἄλλοις. Ἀριστοτέλης 4

2 ἄλλα] Creuzer　ἀλλὰ codd.　　4 τὰ εἴδη] τὰ om. B

δὲ ἐν τοῖς Ἀρχυτείοις ἱστορεῖ καὶ Πυθαγόραν ἄλλο τὴν ὕλην καλεῖν 5
ὡς ῥευστὴν καὶ ἀεὶ ἄλλο καὶ ἄλλο γιγνόμενον. ὥστε δῆλός ἐστι καὶ ὁ 6
Πλάτων ταύτῃ τὰ ἄλλα ἀφοριζόμενος. 7

6 καὶ ἄλλο] om. BAP

It is better then to abide by his distinction [i.e. the distinction made by
Plato's Parmenides, cf.147b], in accordance with Pythagorean custom and
the custom of Plato himself, understanding embodied things and matter
itself as "others." For, in the *Phaedo*, he uses "the others" in this way, calling
the perceptible forms "others" and "in others" [83b]. Aristotle in the things
about Archytas reports that Pythagoras too called matter "other" as flowing
and always becoming other. So it is clear that Plato defined "the others" in
this way.

Text G. Porphyry, *Commentary on the Timaeus* Fr. 60 (Sodano) = Ioannes Philoponus, *De Aeternitate Mundi* (Rabe 1963: 522.16–23)

ὁ Πορφύριος . . . ἐπιφέρει ταῦτα "σαφῶς τὸν κόσμον ἐκ τῶν τεσσάρων
φησὶν [sc. Πλάτων] συνεστάναι στοιχείων· ὥστε τὸ πέμπτον σῶμα
δῆλός ἐστιν οὐχ ἡγούμενος τὸ ὑπὸ Ἀριστοτέλους καὶ Ἀρχύτου
εἰσαγόμενον· ἑξῆς δ᾽ ἀκριβέστερον ὀψόμεθα." ταῦτα μὲν οὖν καὶ ὁ
Πορφύριος.

Porphyry . . . adds this, "Clearly he [sc. Plato] says that the cosmos is
composed of the four elements, so that it is evident that he does not accept
the fifth body, which is introduced by Aristotle and Archytas. But in what
follows we will see this more accurately." This then is Porphyry.

Text H. Theophrastus, *Metaphysics* 6a15–27 (Ross-Fobes 1929: 12)

ἀπὸ δ᾽ οὖν ταύτης ἢ τούτων τῶν ἀρχῶν ἀξιώσειεν ἄν τις . . . τὰ 1
ἐφεξῆς εὐθὺς ἀποδιδόναι καὶ μὴ μέχρι του προελθόντα παύεσθαι· 2
τοῦτο γὰρ τελέου καὶ φρονοῦντος, ὅ περ Ἀρχύτας ποτ᾽ ἔφη ποιεῖν 3
Εὔρυτον διατιθέντα τινὰς ψήφους· λέγειν γὰρ ὡς ὅδε μὲν ἀνθρώπου ὁ 4
ἀριθμός, ὅδε δὲ ἵππου, ὅδε δ᾽ ἄλλου τινὸς τυγχάνει. νῦν δ᾽ οἵ γε πολλοὶ 5
μέχρι τινὸς ἐλθόντες καταπαύονται, καθάπερ καὶ οἱ τὸ ἓν καὶ τὴν ἀόρισ- 6
τον δυάδα ποιοῦντες· τοὺς γὰρ ἀριθμοὺς γεννήσαντες καὶ τὰ ἐπίπεδα 7
καὶ τὰ σώματα σχεδὸν τἆλλα παραλείπουσιν . . . 8

2 τοῦ προελθόντας L   τοῦ προελθόντος CΣ   παύσασθαι R   3 ὅπερ P   ὅπως Σ
4 λέγει LC   γάρ] om. J   5 δὲ ἵππου, ὅδε] om. Σ   ἀλλ᾽ οὔ τινος R   8 τἄλλα]
corr. Brandis   τὰ ἄλλα P   τ᾽ ἄλλα JCB   τἄλλα RHD

But one might expect that they would straightway give an account of the things which follow in succession from this principle or these principles and not advance to a certain point and stop. For this is the characteristic of an accomplished and sensible person, to do exactly what Archytas once said that Eurytus did by arranging certain pebbles. For he reports that Eurytus would say that this is the number of man, this of horse and this of something else. As it is, most people advance to a certain point and stop, just like those who make the one and the indefinite dyad principles. For, having generated numbers and surfaces and solids, they pretty nearly leave out the rest . . .

Text I. Aristotle, *Metaphysics* XV. 5 (1092b8–13)

οὐθὲν δὲ διώρισται οὐδὲ ὁποτέρως οἱ ἀριθμοὶ αἴτιοι τῶν οὐσιῶν καὶ 1
τοῦ εἶναι, πότερον ὡς ὅροι (οἷον αἱ στιγμαὶ τῶν μεγεθῶν, καὶ ὡς Εὔρυ- 2
τος ἔττατε τίς ἀριθμὸς τίνος, οἷον ὁδὶ μὲν ἀνθρώπου ὁδὶ δὲ ἵππου, 3
ὥσπερ οἱ τοὺς ἀριθμοὺς ἄγοντες εἰς τὰ σχήματα τρίγωνον καὶ τετράγ- 4
ωνον, οὕτως ἀφομοιῶν ταῖς ψήφοις τὰς μορφὰς τῶν φυτῶν), ἢ . . . 5

2 αἱ] E Al^p om. JA^b μεγεθῶν] codd. γραμμῶν Al^p Syr 5 τῶν φυτῶν] τῶν ζῴων καὶ
φυτῶν ex Al^p ci. Christ

Nor has it been defined how numbers are causes of substances and of being, whether as boundaries (as points are boundaries of magnitudes, and as Eurytus set out what was the number of what, e.g. that this is the number of man, this of horse, just as those who arrange numbers in the shapes triangle and rectangle, in this way portraying the shapes of creatures by means of pebbles) or . . .

Aristotle's treatises on Archytas and the Pythagoreans

All the texts in Testimonium 13 above (Texts A–I) are relevant to Aristotle's treatises on Archytas and the Pythagoreans. There are three primary ancient *Lives* of Aristotle, each of which includes a list of his works: the life by Diogenes Laertius, the life by Hesychius of Miletus (not the Hesychius who wrote the famous lexicon), and the life by Ptolemy (a Neoplatonist and not the famous astronomer), which only survives in the Syriac and Arabic tradition. The lists of Aristotle's works have been studied in detail by Moraux (1951) and Düring (1957). These lists provide a relatively coherent picture of Aristotle's writings on Archytas and the Pythagoreans (Texts A–C). All three lists agree that there was a work in three books on the philosophy of Archytas. There are slight differences in the description of this work (*The Archytan Philosophy*, D.L.; *The Philosophy of Archytas*, Hesychius; *Archytas*, Ptolemy), which are not significant (see Moraux 1951: 299–301 for decisive arguments against Baumstark's thesis that *Archytas* was a dialogue).

Diogenes Laertius and Hesychius both list a work that seems to have summarized points from Plato's *Timaeus* and the writings of Archytas. The title in Diogenes Laertius, *A Summary of the Timaeus and the Works of Archytas* (τὰ ἐκ τοῦ Τιμαίου καὶ τῶν Ἀρχυτείων α) looks like the original, because Hesychius' version can be explained as a development of Diogenes' title but not vice versa. Hesychius' title, *From the Writings of Timaeus and Archytas* (ἐκ τῶν Τιμαίου καὶ Ἀρχύτου α), makes sense as a simplification and regularization of Diogenes' title, in which both names are put in the genitive singular and only one article, in the genitive plural, is used. Hesychius' title, taken strictly, treats Timaeus as the name of an author rather than the title of a dialogue by Plato. This construal of Timaeus as an author once again suggests that Hesychius' title is a later inaccurate formulation, since the testimonia for the content of this treatise (Texts D–E above) show that it was, in fact, a précis of Plato's *Timaeus* (see below).

Finally the lists indicate that Aristotle wrote two books on the Pythagoreans. In the list of Diogenes Laertius, one work is *A Response to the Pythagoreans* while the other is simply *On the Pythagoreans*. In Ptolemy's list, it would appear that these two works have been combined under one title, since there is just one entry, *On the Pythagoreans*, but in two books. Hesychius' list has one work, *On the Pythagoreans*, in just one book. Hesychius' list, however, often lists only one work, where Diogenes gives two works with similar titles (Moraux 1951: 197–98). At any rate, later commentators quote from both the first (Aët. 1.18.6= Ar. Fr. 201) and second book (Alex. *In Metaph.* 75.16; Simpl. *In Cael.* 392.16 = Ar. Frs. 202 and 205) of Aristotle's work *On the Pythagoreans*, so that we can be sure that there were two books, at some point in the tradition.

Authenticity of Aristotle's works on Archytas and the Pythagoreans
The scholarly consensus is that all of these works on Archytas and the Pythagoreans by Aristotle are likely to be genuine (e.g. Burkert 1972a, Moraux 1951, Düring 1957), although there has been considerable controversy. It is, of course, impossible to be certain about the authenticity of works that have not survived and in particular about books such as Aristotle's three books on Archytas and *A Summary of the Timaeus and the Writings of Archytas*, of which we have virtually no fragments. Indeed, Rose, the editor of Aristotle's fragments, rejected the authenticity of all the lost works of Aristotle (1854: 81 ff.). On the other hand, Aristotle's standard

procedure of starting from his predecessors' views makes it very plausible that he should have devoted separate studies to important figures. Düring (1957: 47) draws attention to Aristotle's recommendation at *Topics* 105b12 that excerpts should be made from written texts and that the opinions of individual philosophers should be noted. Moraux (1951: 106–07) emphasizes that most of the authors to whom Aristotle is supposed to have devoted a special treatise are in fact frequently cited by Aristotle in the extant works, which makes it very plausible that he is drawing on his specialized treatises. This is certainly true of the Pythagoreans, to whom Aristotle refers frequently. In one case he explicitly refers to his more detailed treatment "in other writings" of an issue in the interpretation of Pythagoreanism (*Metaph.* 986a12). Moreover, such an extensive amount of material is quoted from Aristotle's two books on the Pythagoreans by later authors that we can form some idea of their contents, and there can be little doubt that they are genuine (see Burkert 1972a: 29 n. 5).

There is much less evidence for *A Summary of the Timaeus and the Writings of Archytas*. We have an explicit statement from Simplicius however, that Aristotle wrote a synopsis of the *Timaeus* as well as a quotation from that synopsis (Texts D–E above), so that there seems no good reason to deny its authenticity. The *prima facie* case for the authenticity of the three books on Archytas is weaker, in that we have only one clear reference to that book in the commentators (Text F), although a plausible case can be made for a second (Text G). The content of the secure reference has also raised some problems (see below). Moreover, Aristotle only refers to Archytas three times in the extant corpus (A10, A12, A22). This seems a surprisingly sparse yield, if Aristotle had devoted a detailed study in three books to him.

There are, however, more references to Archytas than first meet the eye, particularly if we take into account the evidence of Eudemus and the early Peripatos. Thanks to Theophrastus (A13H) we discover that Aristotle's report about Eurytus (A131 = *Metaph.* 1092b8) was derived from Archytas. Eudemus was known for following Aristotle's treatises very carefully in his own work, so that his accounts of Archytas' theory of motion (A23) and Archytas' argument that the universe is unlimited (A24) may ultimately rely on Aristotle. It is likewise Eudemus who preserves Archytas' solution to the duplication of the cube (A14). The further comments on Archytas' connection of proportion with motion (A23a) go back either to Aristotle himself or to the early Peripatos. We are thus approaching ten references to Archytas in Aristotle and early Peripatetics, who may be relying on Aristotle. The technical mathematical nature of much of Archytas' work may also contribute to the paucity of references to Archytas in Aristotle's extant works. Much of what Archytas had to say on music theory, including proofs such as that in A19, may have engaged Aristotle's attention in his special treatises, but Aristotle may not have found much occasion to mention this material in works such as the *Metaphysics* or *Physics*. Thus, since there is no positive reason to doubt their authenticity (see further on Texts F–G below) and since there is significant evidence of interest in Archytas by Aristotle and the early Peripatos, we should accept as genuine the three books on Archytas attributed to Aristotle.

The implications of Aristotle's writings on Archytas and the Pythagoreans for the study of Archytas

Several important conclusions can be drawn from the testimony about Aristotle's works on Archytas and the Pythagoreans. First, Aristotle must have thought Archytas' work to be of considerable importance, since he devoted three books to the study of it. There was in contrast only one book devoted to the study of Speusippus and Xenocrates together. Second, Aristotle clearly distinguished Archytas from the rest of the Pythagoreans, since he treated them in separate books and never calls Archytas a Pythagorean. This need not mean that Archytas was not a Pythagorean, but it surely suggests that for Aristotle he had an importance that was independent of his membership in the Pythagorean school. Third, the treatise on Archytas is grouped with other writings on physics in Diogenes Laertius' list of Aristotle's writings (Moraux 1951: 104 ff.). This classification does not go back to Aristotle, but it suggests that issues in physics bulked large in what Aristotle had to say about Archytas. Fourth, that there was an emphasis on physics is further supported by the conjunction of Archytas with Plato's *Timaeus* in Aristotle's *A Summary of the Timaeus and the Writings of Archytas*. We should be careful, however, not to rush to the conclusion that Archytas' account of the physical world was largely identical to what is found in the *Timaeus*. Where comparison between Archytas and the *Timaeus* is possible, it is more often the differences that are emphasized than the similarities (e.g. A23, A24). What seems to be implied is rather that Plato's *Timaeus* and the writings of Archytas are, in Aristotle's mind, two of the more important accounts of the physical world, irrespective of how similar they are to one another and irrespective of how much he disagrees with them (see the overview of Archytas' philosophy).

Aristotle's two treatises on Archytas

A Summary of the Timaeus and the Writings of Archytas. All of our knowledge of this book, beyond the title given in the lists of Diogenes

Laertius and Hesychius, is derived from two passages in Simplicius' commentary on Aristotle's *De Caelo* (Texts D–E). In the first passage Simplicius makes clear that he knows of a synopsis or epitome of the *Timaeus* made by Aristotle. So far he might be drawing on nothing more than the lists of Aristotle's works, but in the second passage he provides a quotation from Aristotle's epitome of the *Timaeus*. He thus may have had access to a copy of it, although the fact that he does not make further use of it suggests that he may only know of it at second hand through the references in other commentators. The passage from Aristotle's epitome is not a direct quotation from the *Timaeus* but rather summarizes in Aristotle's own words the argument of *Timaeus* 28c–d, which tries to demonstrate that the cosmos has come into existence. The quotation from Aristotle's book thus confirms what we might have deduced from Simplicius' description of the work as a synopsis or epitome, i.e. that the work was not a collection of excerpts from the *Timaeus* but rather a summary of its contents by Aristotle. At the same time the quotation suggests that Aristotle was trying to reproduce Plato's argument very accurately, and there is no suggestion that he attempted to provide any evaluation of it or commentary on it. Thus, it seems best not to translate the title, as is usually done, as *Excerpts from the Timaeus . . .*, which suggests literal quotation, but rather *A Summary of the Timaeus . . .*, which suggests that Aristotle was instead summarizing the main points made by Plato. Simplicius makes no mention of the part of the book that focused on the writings of Archytas. On analogy with what we have seen about the section on the *Timaeus*, we should suppose that it consisted of Aristotle's synopsis of some writings by Archytas, presumably writings that dealt with issues similar to those raised by Plato in the *Timaeus*.

Ryle (1965) ingeniously argued that Aristotle's work, *A Summary of the Timaeus and the Writings of Archytas*, was, in fact, the treatise which is known as the *Timaeus Locrus*, a précis of the *Timaeus* in Doric purporting to be the original document by Timaeus of Locri on which Plato drew (Marg 1972). Ryle demonstrates that this is more than just a précis of the *Timaeus*, since it "improves" on the *Timaeus* in a number of places. Ryle supposed that a youthful Aristotle had written it in Doric as a present for Dionysius II of Syracuse. As Ryle saw, Simplicius' quotation in Text E would refute this theory, if it really comes from *A Summary of the Timaeus and Writings of Archytas*, since the passage quoted is not to be found in the *Timaeus Locrus*. Ryle tries to deal with this problem by suggesting that Simplicius did not in fact know of any epitome of the *Timaeus* by Aristotle and that his introduction of the quotation (ἐπιτεμνόμενος) should not be taken to be a reference to an epitome of the *Timaeus* by Aristotle but only to indicate that Aristotle is summarizing the doctrine of the *Timaeus*, something that he might have done in a number of lost works, including *On Philosophy* (1965: 189–90). This is in itself a doubtful reading of ἐπιτεμνόμενος, but Ryle's argument is completely undercut by Text D, of which he seems to be unaware. Text D shows that Simplicius did know of an epitome of the *Timaeus* by Aristotle, and this must surely be the work that he quotes from in Text E. Since that quotation corresponds to nothing in the *Timaeus Locrus*, Ryle's thesis that *A Summary of the Timaeus and Writings of Archytas* is identical to the *Timaeus Locrus* is refuted.

On the Philosophy of Archytas. Three different sources give evidence about Aristotle's three-volume work on Archytas, and I will discuss each of these sources in turn.

Damascius (Text F): The only secure reference to Aristotle's three-volume work on Archytas is found in Damascius (Text F – properly from *In Parmenidem* rather than *De Principiis*; see Westerink 1976–77: II. 9–10), although I will argue that Text G and Text H might be based on it. Damascius refers to something that Aristotle reports ἐν τοῖς Ἀρχυτείοις (in the Archytan [books]). This phrasing could refer either to Aristotle's three books on the philosophy of Archytas or to *A Summary of the Timaeus and the Writings of Archytas*. The content of what Damascius reports, however, fits better with a critical discussion of Archytas' philosophy such as we might expect from Aristotle's three books on the philosophy of Archytas than with the bare summary of his doctrines in *A Summary . . .*

The content of what Damascius reports from Aristotle's books on Archytas ("Pythagoras too called matter 'other' as flowing and always becoming other") has caused considerable controversy and is contrary to what we would expect from Aristotle in three important ways. First, in the extant writings Aristotle does not refer to Pythagoras himself. His practice is to talk of the Pythagoreans (Burkert 1972a: 29 n. 6). Second, in his accounts of the Pythagoreans, Aristotle makes clear that, from his point of view, they have not adequately distinguished the material and formal cause. Yet, here in Text F, Pythagoras himself is presented as not only having distinguished matter from form but as having given a clear definition of it (Burkert 1972a: 45–46). Third, the view ascribed to Pythagoras here is ascribed to Platonists at *Metaphysics* 1087b26. Ross (1924: II. 471) follows pseudo-Alexander *In Metaph.* 798.23 in supposing that Aristotle is referring to Pythagoreans at 1087b26, but the "others" (οἱ δέ) to whom Aristotle refers must be Platonists. Throughout the preceding passage Aristotle has been referring to different Platonists with such expressions (οἱ δέ . . . οἱ μέν . . . οἱ δέ 1087b5–6; cf. 1087b14), and the view described in 1087b26 is at variance with Aristotle's presentation of Pythagoreans elsewhere (Burkert 1972a: 80 n. 164). Ross himself notes Alexander's mistaken identi-fication of the immediately following οἱ δέ (1087b27) with Pythagoreans or Pythagoras.

In the face of these significant divergences from Aristotle's usual practice in dealing with the Pythagoreans, some scholars have concluded that *On the Philosophy of Archytas* must be a spurious work, which was a product of the later pseudo-Pythagorean tradition (Zeller 1923: I. 470 n. 3; Cherniss 1964: 17 n. 68; De Vogel 1966: 215–16). Burkert has shown that the mention of Pythagoras himself in the doxography and, in particular, the conjunction of Pythagoras and Plato is usually an indication that we are dealing with the tradition about Pythagoreanism, which arose in the early Academy, which identified Plato's late metaphysics with Pythagoreanism, and which is the basis of much of the pseudo-Pythagorean tradition (1972a: 53–83, esp. 57, 79, 82–83). Burkert, however, rather than rejecting the authenticity of Aristotle's book on Archytas, suggests that Aristotle may have followed this Academic view of Pythagoras earlier in his career, before developing the view of the Pythagoreans found in the extant works (1972a: 80–81). There is a better explanation of the testimonium in Damascius, however, which suggests that *On the Philosophy of Archytas* was a genuine work of Aristotle.

Damascius is discussing Plato (*Parmenides* 147b and *Phaedo* 83b) and arguing that Plato is following Pythagorean custom in defining matter. In Damascius' reference to Aristotle's book on Archytas the καί before Pythagoras is particularly important. Aristotle reports that "Pythagoras *too* called matter other . . ." This "too" may be due to Damascius, but it is also possible that Aristotle joined Pythagoras (or rather Pythagoreans as I will argue) to Platonists in this passage from his book on Archytas. Damascius sees no need to include Aristotle's mention of Plato in this context and only sees fit to quote what he wants to emphasize, i.e. that Aristotle joined the Pythagoreans to Plato in saying that matter was other. Aristotle, like Damascius later, was connecting Pythagoreans with late Platonic doctrine, but there is a difference between Aristotle's approach and the approach of the early Academy, which assigned late Platonic metaphysics to Pythagoras himself.

Aristotle's distinct approach appears in his discussion of the definition of motion in the *Physics* (201b16–202a3). Aristotle wants to confirm his own definition by comparing it with definitions of his predecessors. He only considers one previous definition, which he ascribes to a vague "some" (ἔνιοι). The reference to the table of opposites (συστοιχίας 201b26) suggests that he might be thinking in part of the Pythagoreans (*Metaph.* 986a25), but other aspects of the report clearly allude to Plato. The ancient commentators conclude that Aristotle was referring both to Platonic passages in the *Sophist* and *Timaeus* and also to the Pythagoreans of the table of opposites (see further on A23). Aristotle may thus be connecting Plato and the Pythagoreans of the table of opposites as sharing a view that emphasized the indefinite nature of motion. Burkert collects other evidence which shows a consistent connection, at least in Aristotle's mind, between the "table of opposites" and Academic doctrines (1972a: 51–52). In explicating the passage from the *Physics*, Simplicius quotes Eudemus, who similarly joins Plato to the Pythagoreans of the table of opposites but also introduces Archytas into the discussion in contrast to the Platonic/Pythagorean view (see A23). Eudemus is known for following Aristotle very closely in his *Physics*. It is thus possible that Eudemus is reporting a discussion in Aristotle's book on Archytas, in which Aristotle contrasted Archytas' account of motion with the shared position of Plato and the Pythagoreans who adopted the table of opposites.

My suggestion regarding the text from Damascius (Text F) is then that it is based on something in Aristotle's book on Archytas, which is similar to the discussion of motion presented by Eudemus. Aristotle presented an account of matter which he ascribed to Plato (or Platonists cf. *Metaph.* 1087b26) and to the Pythagoreans of the table of opposites and which he compared to a conception of matter which he assigned to Archytas. According to this account, Plato regarded matter as "other," since it was flowing and always becoming other (in addition to *Metaph.* 1087b26 cf. the description of the receptacle at *Ti.* 49b ff., esp. 49d ἄλλοτε ἄλλη γιγνόμενον). Matter would thus have to fall in the indefinite column of the Pythagorean table of opposites, which includes what is changing (Arist., *Metaph.* 986a22). We simply have no way of knowing whether Aristotle presented Archytas' account of matter as similar to the account ascribed to Plato or whether there were significant differences, although Eudemus' account of Archytas' view on motion suggests that Aristotle was inclined to develop the differences between Archytas and Plato. For my suggestion to work we have to assume that Aristotle's original reference to Pythagoreans has been corrupted in the course of transmission, so that it has become Pythagoras in Damascius. This is exactly the sort of change that is to be expected in the later tradition where Pythagoras himself becomes all important. Something like this change may explain e.g. the reference to Pythagoras in the *Magna Moralia* (1182a11, cf. 1194a29). This interpretation of Damascius' testimonium saves us from having to suppose an otherwise unattested phase of Aristotle's development in which he ascribes to the Academic view in which mature Platonic metaphysics is to be assigned back to Pythagoras himself. Instead we have a relatively consistent Aristotle who does have a tendency to connect the Pythagoreans of the table of opposites with Plato and to contrast both of them with Archytas.

Frank (1923: 125, 179 n. 361) suggests that Aristotle's reference to Pythagoras here shows that Archytas was putting his own views in the mouth of Pythagoras. Text F thus becomes one of the cornerstones of Frank's reconstruction of Archytas' philosophy, in which matter is resolved into motion. This suggestion is purely arbitrary, however. There is not a trace of evidence elsewhere to suggest that Archytas adopted such a thesis and to assign it to him on the basis of what is ascribed to Pythagoras or the Pythagoreans in Text F is a leap in the dark.

Porphyry-Philoponus (Text G): This testimonium of Porphyry about Archytas is best understood as a garbled reference to Aristotle's book on Archytas (Frank 1923: 375 n. 335; Burkert 1972a: 237 n. 95; 331 n. 36). The reference to "the fifth body, which is introduced by Aristotle and Archytas" is probably a corruption of an original text that referred to "the fifth body, which is introduced by Aristotle in his book on Archytas." This need not mean that Aristotle introduced the fifth body for the first time in his book on Archytas. It only means that Aristotle introduced a discussion of the fifth body in that book.

The assertion about Aristotle, Archytas and the fifth body belongs to Porphyry and not to Philoponus, who is quoting Porphyry at this point. Philoponus, elsewhere in the *De Aeternitate Mundi*, makes it clear that he thinks Aristotle was the first to introduce the fifth element (e.g. 527.6), and he makes no allusion anywhere to any contribution of Archytas. There are no further references to the fifth body in the fragments that we have of Porphyry's commentary on the *Timaeus*, so we do not know how he presented it elsewhere. Modern scholarship in general assigns the conception of aether as a fifth element, which naturally moves in a circle and which is the material from which the heavenly bodies are made, to Aristotle. Some have wanted to see a similar conception of aether as implicit in Greek philosophy from the time of the Presocratics (Guthrie 1962: 270 ff.). Philolaus Fr. 12, however, which has sometimes been used as evidence that the Pythagoreans anticipated such doctrine of aether, is likely to be spurious (Huffman 1993: 392–95). References in the later tradition which assign the fifth body to Ocellus or Pythagoras are clear examples of the pseudo-Pythagorean tendency to assign mature Aristotelian and Platonic doctrine back to Pythagoras (Aët. II. 6.2; S.E. *M.* x. 316). The first clear attestation of aether as a fifth element is the *Epinomis* (984e). It is probable that Aristotle had already argued for his fifth element in his dialogue, *On Philosophy* (Jaeger 1948: 143 ff.). There is certainly evidence to suggest that members of the early Academy may have used Aristotle's new conception to interpret a problematic passage in the *Timaeus* in a way that assigns the theory to Plato (Sachs 1917: 64 ff.). Since a doctrine of aether can be seen developing in these texts from the early Academy, it is unlikely that any explicit doctrine of aether goes back to the fifth century. Even in the fourth century, it is probably not correct to talk as if there was a single theory of aether. As Solmsen rightly emphasizes, the concept of aether which appears in the *Epinomis* is totally different from Aristotle's, and there is no real evidence that Aristotle's conception was anticipated by earlier thinkers (1960: 287ff.).

Archytas is a different case from figures such as Pythagoras, Ocellus and Philolaus. As a contemporary of Plato it is not impossible that he played some role in the thinking of the Academy on the issue and, as Sachs comments (1917: 64 n. 1), certain theories can just be in the air at a given time, so that Archytas could have come up with a doctrine of a fifth element independently of Aristotle. There is no other evidence that assigns the fifth element or indeed any theory of elements to Archytas, but, given the sparsity of evidence for Archytas' views, this silence can hardly be conclusive. Two features of Archytas' account of motion in A23a, however, do not cohere very well with the idea that he argued for a fifth element, which had a circular motion. First, in A23a, Archytas explains circular motion not by appeal to the natural movement of a fifth element, as Aristotle did, but rather in terms of mathematical proportion. Second, in A23a, circular motion is used to explain the parts of animals and plants and not the motion of the heavens. Thus, if Archytas did introduce aether as a fifth element, he must have done so for somewhat different reasons from Aristotle, who uses it precisely to explain the circular motions of the heavens; yet surely the natural implication of Porphyry's conjunction of Aristotle and Archytas in Text G is that they meant the same thing by the fifth body.

Another possible explanation of the association of Archytas with Aristotle in Porphyry's assertion is that the original form of the testimonium read "the fifth element introduced by Aristotle in his book on Archytas," which became corrupted to "the fifth element introduced by Aristotle and Archytas." A very plausible case can be made that Aristotle would have discussed his new fifth element in his work on Archytas. As we have seen, this book included a discussion of "material principles" (Text F) and probably Archytas' account of motion (A23). It is very likely that Aristotle would have complained about Archytas' explanation of circular motion in terms of mathematical proportion (A23a) and argued instead that such motion, as a physical phenomenon, needs to be explained not in mathematical terms but rather in terms of physical elements, i.e. in terms of the introduction of a fifth element whose natural motion was circular (see the commentary on A23a). Thus, Text G may be better understood as a reflection of Aristotle's argument against Archytas' theory of motion in his *On the Philosophy of Archytas* than as testimony that Archytas himself adopted a fifth element.

Theophrastus–Aristotle (Texts H and I): The descriptions of Eurytus' procedure for identifying the number of individual things in the world, which are given by Theophrastus and Aristotle in these two texts, are essentially identical. Theophrastus, however, identifies Archytas as the source of the information, while Aristotle gives no source. Obviously Theophrastus did not get his information about the source from the passage in Aristotle's *Metaphysics*. It is tempting to suppose that he got it from Aristotle's book *On the Philosophy of Archytas*, which would also represent the original research on which Aristotle is drawing in his *Metaphysics*. Theophrastus' phrasing (note ποτ' = "once") suggests that the story was not found in Archytas' writings but was rather an oral anecdote. It is, of course, only a guess that Theophrastus was drawing on Aristotle's book. He could have derived the story from the oral tradition himself or he might have drawn on Aristoxenus' *Life of Archytas*.

Frank suggested that the view ascribed to Eurytus in these testimonia was in fact Archytas' own and that Archytas was simply following the practice of putting his own views in the mouth of earlier Pythagoreans (1923: 74 and n. 187). He then uses Texts H and I as central evidence in reconstructing the philosophy of Archytas (1923: 125). This is a purely arbitrary decision on Frank's part, however, and one that seriously undercuts the reliability of his picture of Archytas. There is no evidence that Archytas followed such a practice. Most importantly, Aristotle and Theophrastus both clearly take Archytas to be reporting the practice of Eurytus and not his own. Similarly the suggestion that Archytas invented the figure of Eurytus, whose name "well flowing" illustrates Archytas' supposed view of matter (Frank 1923: n. 187, n. 361; see on Text F above) founders on the evidence of Aristotle and Theophrastus, both of whom clearly regard Eurytus as an historical figure. The name Eurytus is found elsewhere in Greek literature and in inscriptions, particularly in the Doric speaking parts of Greece (Pape and Benseler 1959; Fraser and Matthews 1987–97: III).

What can we conclude about Archytas from his report about Eurytus? It illustrates Archytas' interest in his predecessors and perhaps his emphasis on the value of demonstrating in detail how a set of basic principles can be used to explain particular things in the world (see the overview of Archytas' philosophy). It is also interesting that Archytas here reports Eurytus' procedure in explaining animals and plants, since A23a suggests that Archytas himself may have had some interest in explaining the parts of animals and plants. Perhaps Archytas' report of Eurytus' procedure was a prelude to his own account of these matters.

Conclusion

Certainty about the contents of Aristotle's three books on Archytas is impossible, but we can make the following conjectures. They dealt prominently with issues in physics. Aristotle appears to have considered the extent to which Archytas achieved a conception of matter and to have compared Archytas' conception with that of Plato and the Pythagoreans who wrote the table of opposites. Aristotle may have considered Archytas' explanation of circular motion and, as part of that discussion, mentioned his own doctrine of aether. Finally, Aristotle may have discussed Archytas' conception of the relation between things and numbers. He perhaps included Archytas' report about Eurytus' attempt to demonstrate the number associated with individual things in the world by arranging pebbles in the shape of the particular thing.

Appendix 1
Spurious writings and testimonia

The standard collection of all the pseudo-Archytan writings is Thesleff (1965). New editions and commentaries on individual treatises have appeared since Thesleff and are cited below. In a few cases, where Thesleff has not provided the text, I provide enough of the text to reveal its nature. All of the following treatises are, in my judgment, surely spurious except *On Law and Justice*, where the evidence is more complicated. In the case of most treatises, I have given the main arguments for spuriousness. On the pseudo-Archytan treatises in general see Burkert 1972b, Centrone 1990 and 1994b, Moraux 1984: 605–83, and Thesleff 1972 and 1961.

I. TREATISES

A. Logic, epistemology and metaphysics

1. *Concerning the Whole System [sc. of Categories] or Concerning the Ten Categories* (Περὶ τοῦ καθόλου λόγου ἤτοι δέκα κατηγοριῶν), Thesleff 21.6–32.23. The best edition is Szlezak 1972. See also the comments of Gottschalk 1987: 1131–32. A complete manuscript of the treatise survives in a *koine* version, while a significant number of fragments of it are quoted by Simplicius and other commentators in a Doric version. This was the most commonly cited work of "Archytas" in antiquity, primarily because of the frequent citations of it by commentators on Aristotle's *Categories* (e.g. Simplicius, *CAG* VIII and IX; Syrianus, *In Hermogenem*; Olympiodorus, *CAG* XII. 1; Dexippus, *CAG* IV. 2; Elias, *CAG* XVIII. 1; Ammonios, *CAG* IV. 3; Anon. *In Cat.*, *CAG* XXIII. 2; Boethius, *In Cat.* 1; Boethius, *Arith.* II. 41). For the explanation of the meaning and various forms of the title of this work see Szlezak 1972: 94–95. This work, along with the pseudo-Archytan treatise *On Opposites* and the much later *Ten Universal Assertions*, represents the attempt to claim Aristotle's *Categories* for Pythagoreanism. *Concerning the Whole System* follows Aristotle very closely (e.g. at 22.14, it

identifies ten categories the names for which are essentially identical to the names Aristotle uses) but also takes into account divergences from Aristotle developed in the later tradition (e.g. it treats quality before quantity as did Eudorus [Simpl. *In Cat.* 206.8 ff.]). Since it is modeled on just the first nine chapters of Aristotle's *Categories*, while the separate pseudo-Archytan treatise *On Opposites* deals with the material in the later chapters, it can be dated after Andronicus of Rhodes (70–20 BC), who first separated the last six chapters (10–15), known as the *postpraedicamenta*, from the rest of Aristotle's *Categories*. It appears that Hippolytus (AD 170–236) refers to the work (*Refut.* VI. 24) and Iamblichus (AD 245–325) surely did (Simpl. *In Cat.* 2.9–25 (*CAG* VIII), so it was composed sometime between the second half of the first century BC and the third century AD. Szlezak shows that it has close ties to work on the categories in the first century BC and no references to later material and thus concludes that it is more likely to date to the first century BC than later (1972: 13–19). Although the work is an obvious forgery, both Iamblichus and Simplicius regarded it as a genuine work on which Aristotle relied (*CAG* VIII. 2. 9–25).

The treatise includes a discussion of time which is of some interest. See Sorabji 1983: 27, 38–43, 48 and Hoffmann 1980. In addition to Thesleff's voluminous list of citations of this work I have noticed the following: (1) Michael Psellus, *Opusc.* 7, line 130 (Duffy 1992: 26); (2) Arethas of Caesarea (AD 9–10), scholia on Porphyry's *Isagōgē* and Aristotle's *Categories*, scholion 214, line 28 and scholion 308, line 77 (Share 1994: 136.14 and 223.20).

2. *On Opposites* (Περὶ ἀντικειμένων), Thesleff 15.3–19.2. All six fragments come from Simplicius' commentary on Aristotle's *Categories*, *CAG* VIII. This treatise is based closely on Books 10–15 of Aristotle's *Categories*. For example, *On Opposites* (15.15–20) presents the same four-fold classification of opposition as Aristotle (*Cat.* 11b17–24), using the exact same names for each class and many of the same examples. It probably dates to the late first century BC (see *Concerning the Whole System* above). Simplicius thought that this was a genuine work from which Aristotle borrowed (*CAG* VIII. 382.7).

3. *The Ten Universal Assertions* (Καθολικοὶ λόγοι δέκα), Thesleff 3.9–8.19. Szlezak (1972) provides the best edition. He located one manuscript of the treatise and bases his text on that manuscript and the sixteenth-century edition by Pizimentius, which was based on a different, now lost, manuscript (pp. 11–13). Thesleff's account of this work, including his assertion that no manuscripts survive and that the dating is indeterminable (1961: 110–11, 114), should be rejected in light of Szlezak's further research. It has long been

clear that the work must have been composed after the third century AD, since it shows dependence on Porphyry's *Isagōgē* (3.17–18; Szlezak 1972: 162). In the afterword to his edition, Szlezak reports the stunning discovery that this supposed treatise of Archytas is essentially identical with the section devoted to categories in a Byzantine compendium of logic (1972: 184–88). The first edition of this compendium ascribed it to Gregorius Aneponymus, but the earliest manuscripts give no author and Heiberg treated it as an anonymous treatise. The subscription in the earliest manuscript dates to AD 1040 so that we know that the compendium, including the section on categories, was composed before that date. This text is not ascribed to Archytas and is not in Doric, so that it appears that the treatise was not originally written as a forgery in Archytas' name. At some point the section on categories was separated from the rest of the compendium, slightly edited (including the addition of the first sentence, which comes from a Christian treatise), given a superficial coloring of Doric dialect, assigned a new title and ascribed to Archytas. Szlezak dates this transformation of the text into a work by Archytas to the fifteenth century AD and the original Byzantine work to the sixth century AD (1972: 21, 25).

4. *On Principles* (Περὶ ἀρχῶν), Thesleff 19.3–20.17. One fragment preserved in Stobaeus (1. 41.2). It is likely that Syrianus, *CAG* VI. 1.166 (Thesleff 48. 3–6) refers to this text and Syrianus, *CAG* VI. 1.151 (Thesleff 47.27–48.2) may also come from it. This treatise sets out three basic principles: form, substance as what underlies, and a principle above the other two, god, who brings form and underlying substance together. The text betrays its post-Aristotelian date by its extensive use of the technical terminology of Aristotelian *Metaphysics* such as form, substance, what underlies (ὑποκείμενον), and τόδε τι εἶναι. See for example 19.19–20: ἁ μὲν μορφώ ἐστιν αἰτία τοῦ τόδε τι εἶμεν· ἁ δὲ ὡσία τὸ ὑποκείμενον, παραδεχόμενον τὰν μορφώ. On the connections between this treatise and Eudorus see Dillon 1977: 120–21.

5. *On Intelligence and Perception* (Περὶ νοῦ καὶ αἰσθάσιος), Thesleff 36.12–39.25. Two fragments preserved in Stobaeus. Part of the second fragment is also preserved in Iamblichus, along with additional material not in Stobaeus. Thesleff 38.24–39.25 (the section on the divided line) is paraphrased in the scholia to Plato's *Republic* 509d, with the heading "scholion taken from Archytas, Brontinus and Iamblichus" (Hermann, C. F. [1892] *Platonis Dialogi*, Vol. VI. 350). Since Iamblichus also quoted Brontinos immediately before quoting Archytas, the scholion appears to be simply drawing on Iamblichus as Thesleff suggests. Sophonias also paraphrases

Iamblichus. Burkert (1972b: 38–40) provides the best commentary on this text. As he points out, it ends with an almost word for word paraphrase of the divided line passage in the *Republic* (39.4–25 = R. 509d–511e). He concludes that the treatise belongs to the period of preparation for Neoplatonism (1st century BC–1st century AD).

6. *On Being* (Περὶ τοῦ ὄντος), Thesleff 40.1–16. One fragment from Stobaeus. Περὶ τοῦ ὄντος was the alternative title for Plato's *Sophist* in Thrasylus' classification (D.L. III. 58.7). The sole fragment from "Archytas'" work seems, like the *Sophist*, to be dealing with logic more than natural philosophy, so that *On Being* seems a better translation than *On Nature* (Thesleff). The treatise denies the assertion of those who claim that two opposing statements, which are both true, can be said about everything. This sounds like an attack on something like Protagoras' position that "there are two *logoi* about everything, opposite to one another" (D.L. IX. 51).

7. *On Wisdom* (Περὶ σοφίας), Thesleff 43.24–45.4. Five fragments preserved in Iamblichus' *Protrepticus*. The first fragment is also quoted in part by Porphyry in his commentary on Ptolemy. Two fragments of an *On Wisdom* by Periktione (Thesleff 146.1–22), in Doric, are preserved in Stobaeus and are very similar to Archytas' *On Wisdom*. Hense is right to suggest that the fragments are assigned to Periktione (whose other fragments are in Ionic) by mistake (Wachsmuth, Hense III: 85, note). Thesleff first rejected (1965: 146) and then later accepted (1972: 67) Hense's view. The treatment of wisdom and its relation to physics and mathematics in "Archytas'" *On Wisdom* is dependent on Aristotle's account of wisdom in the *Metaphysics*. "Archytas" emphasizes that wisdom deals with the principles of all things (τὰς τῶν ἐόντων ἀπάντων ἀρχάς 44.27–8, 146.15). In *Metaphysics* I Aristotle identifies wisdom with first philosophy or metaphysics and asserts that it deals with principles (ἀρχάς) and in particular with the first principles (τῶν πρώτων ἀρχῶν) of all things (982a2, 982b9). In *Metaphysics* IV Aristotle emphasizes that metaphysics studies being in general (καθόλου περὶ τοῦ ὄντος 1003a24), whereas the particular sciences divide off some portion of being (μέρος αὐτοῦ τι ἀποτεμνόμεναι) and study the characteristic of this portion (περὶ τούτου θεωροῦσι τὸ συμβεβηκός 1003a26). In *On Wisdom* it is said that wisdom studies the general characteristics of all things (τὰ ὦν καθόλω πᾶσι συμβεβηκότα . . . θεωρέν 44.26), and the mathematical sciences are described as the sciences concerned with something divided off (τι ἀφωρισμένον sc. from the rest of being) and as dealing with the particular characteristics of that division of being (τὰ δ' ἴδια καθ' ἕκαστον [συμβεβακότα] 146.14). The relation between wisdom, physics

and mathematics outlined in *On Wisdom* is recognizably the same as that proposed by Aristotle at *Metaphysics* 1061b18 ff. There are also some striking similarities in particular aspects of the treatment of wisdom. Thus *On Wisdom* says that wisdom is able to survey everything in the table of opposites (πάντα τὰ ἐν τᾷ συστοιχίᾳ, 44.35 and 146.21). It is true of course that the table of opposites is identified as Pythagorean by Aristotle (*Metaph.* 986a23 ff.), but Aristotle himself uses the table in places, and he particularly refers to it in his discussion of wisdom/first philosophy in *Metaphysics* IV. He says that it will belong to first philosophy to study both unity and its opposite plurality (1004a10) as well as the other basic oppositions, and he refers explicitly to the table of opposites at 1004b28 (συστοιχία).

B. Ethics and politics

1. *On the Good and Happy Man* (Περὶ ἀνδρὸς ἀγαθοῦ καὶ εὐδαίμονος), Thesleff 8.26–15.2. Twelve fragments preserved in Stobaeus. The best edition is now Centrone 1990. Burkert (1972b: 35–38) shows the general connections of this treatise to Antiochus and Arius Didymus as well as illustrating its Peripatetic and Stoic terminology. He would date it to the first century BC, which Centrone also accepts as the most probable date (1990: 42). There are numerous examples that show the treatise's dependence on Aristotle and later philosophy. *On the Good and Happy Man* makes a distinction between what is praised and what is blessed (8.32–33) which clearly draws on the *Nicomachean Ethics* (1101b10 ff.), and some of the language is very similar (1101b32 ὁ μὲν γὰρ ἔπαινος τῆς ἀρετῆς; 8.32 ὁ μὲν ἔπαινος ἐπ' ἀρετᾷ). The treatise moves from the good of man to the goods of the parts of man, i.e. body and soul (11. 8–9). The exact same move is found in Arius Didymus (Stobaeus 11. 122.11 Wachsmuth). Arius Didymus goes on to distinguish four goods of the soul and four goods of the body (11. 125.2). *On the Good and Happy Man* (11.9–10) has an identical list except that the later text has the rare word εὐεκτία for "strength" instead of ἰσχύς. See Centrone's commentary for further examples.

2. *On Law and Justice* (Περὶ νόμου καὶ δικαιοσύνης), Thesleff 33.1–36.11. Five fragments are preserved in Stobaeus, to which should probably be added the passage attributed to Archytas, without identifying the text from which it comes, at Stobaeus IV. 1.132 = Thesleff 47. 23–26. See also Boethius, *Inst. Arithm.* 11. 45, which does not mention Archytas but gives the same content as 34. 3–10. Of all the works whose fragments are collected by Thesleff, *On Law and Justice* is the treatise whose spuriousness is most

difficult to assert with confidence. Delatte, who has carried out the only detailed study of the fragments, shows convincingly that the treatise uses the political conceptions of the fourth-century *polis* and focuses on problems which are easy to parallel in fourth-century authors, although it shows some originality and independence in the solutions which it proposes for those problems. While recognizing that it is impossible to prove a work authentic, Delatte comes to the modest conclusion that it is not impossible that the work is by Archytas, since there are no indications of apocryphal or late composition (1922: 71–24, esp. 121–24). Minar, on the basis of Delatte's arguments asserted that it "has an excellent claim to authenticity" (1942: 111). Morrison sees no reason to reject the fragments and regards them as illustrating the principle of calculation (*logismos*) introduced in Fragment 3 of Archytas (1956: 155). Thesleff seems influenced by Delatte in dating *On Law* to the middle or late fourth century and says that it "may be authentic or at least comparatively old" (1961: 112, 114).

DK, on the other hand, did not include the fragments of *On Law and Justice*, in accordance with the principle of only accepting fragments from mathematical works as genuine, since they were less likely to be forged. Zeller rejected its authenticity on the grounds of similarity to Platonic and Aristotelian conceptions (1923: 111. 2.114 ff., esp. 158–59; cf. von Fritz (1954: 83). Gruppe (1840: 11) was troubled by an apparent reference to Plato's theory of forms (see below) but also rejected the treatise for poor reasons, including the claim that the image of the leader as shepherd was of eastern, Hebraic, origin (91–92; see Delatte 1922: 121). Theiler (1926), in his review of Delatte, showed that there were significant ties between *On Law and Justice* and surely pseudo-Pythagorean writings. Among more recent scholars, Sinclair rejected *On Law*, on the grounds that it was full of echoes of Plato, Aristotle and Hellenistic philosophy (1951: 293–95). Aalders has provided the most detailed case against authenticity. He does not, however, carry out a complete study of the fragments but provides eight reasons why the treatise cannot go back to the fourth century and suggests that, because of its agreement with Polybius in proposing a mixed constitution, it may date to the third or second century BC (1968: 13–20; see also 1975: 27–39). Burkert says that the spuriousness is shown by the use "of such a word as ἀπάθεια" but gives no further discussion of the treatise (1972a: 78 n. 156).

Moraux (1984: 670–77) documents certain shared questions and themes between *On Law* and Aristotle's *Politics*, such as the necessity of not looking just for the best constitution but also the constitution that best fits an individual people. What he does not show, however, is that the presentation in *On Law* need be derived from Aristotle rather than being Archytas' response to common issues in the political philosophy of the fourth century. Archytas' presentation differs in significant ways from Aristotle and his simpler presentation of the issues could represent an earlier stage in the development of these ideas rather than being a simplification carried out by a later inferior author. The supposed similarities in language that he presents are not convincing (673, n. 317). Finally, Centrone (2000) assumes the spuriousness of *On Law* (Centrone 1994b seems to leave the issue open) but also implicitly argues for its spuriousness by showing its similarity to the spurious treatises on kingship by Diotogenes, Sthenidas and Ecphantus.

My analysis of the arguments for and against authenticity suggests that at present the treatise should be regarded as spurious, although the evidence is almost equally divided. The surely spurious treatises such as the *Timaeus Locrus* or Archytas' writings on categories are characterized by straightforward borrowing of distinctively Platonic and Aristotelian distinctions such as the tripartite soul or Aristotle's system of categories. There is nothing this clear cut in *On Law and Justice*. The claim, raised initially by Hartenstein (1833: 64) and Gruppe (1840: 11), that *On Law* embraces the theory of forms is inconclusive. It is true that, at 34. 10–11, a contrast is set up between ἰδέαι and εἰκόνες, which, taken out of context, could be understood as a reference to forms and their images. Examination of the context shows, however, that ἰδέαι cannot be a reference to forms in the Platonic sense of metaphysical entities, which have independent existence, but instead has its common meaning of "kinds." The text is asserting that there are three kinds of distribution (διανομᾶς), those governed by the arithmetic, harmonic and geometric proportions respectively, not that there are three distinct metaphysical entities. Representations or examples (εἰκόνες) of these three kinds of distribution are then said to be observed both in constitutions and in households. The term εἰκόνες does not suggest the form–image relationship as in Plato, because there is none of the language of participation such as we find in spurious treatises like *On Intelligence* (Thesleff 38.14–15).

Three of Aalders' arguments for spuriousness (numbers 2–4) have to do with the use of Sparta as a model government in *On Law* and all are weak. The argument that Archytas, as a moderate democrat, could not have appealed to Sparta as a model has little force. Tarentum was after all a Spartan colony and had maintained good relations with Sparta during the Peloponnesian war. Aalder's suggestion that Tarentum was at odds with Syracuse and hence with Sparta is not supported by the evidence (see the section on Archytas' life). The Spartan constitution was open to a wide variety of interpretations, and a moderate democrat could see what he wanted in it. In Plato's *Laws*, the Spartan Megillus, says that sometimes it seems to him that the Spartan state is closest of all states to democracy (712d). Some indeed have argued that the use of Sparta as a model suggests authenticity, since a eulogy of Sparta makes most sense in the first part of the fourth century when Sparta's fortunes were higher than later, but it was possible to idealize Sparta even later (Delatte 1922: 72).

Aalders objects that *On Law*, treats the *koroi* and *hippargetai* in a contradictory fashion both as democratic elements in the state and also as what holds other elements together (including the ephors as the democratic element). Moreover, in treating *koroi* and *hippargetai* as democratic elements, the author regards them as political organs, which they were not. Aristotle, however, reports that other interpreters regarded the educational system and common messes as democratic elements (*Pol.* 1266a1). Such interpreters are doing something similar to what we find in *On Law*, since they find democratic features in aspects of Spartan society which are not literally political organs. Aristotle also makes clear that the various elements in the Spartan state were open to widely different interpretations. Thus the ephors are viewed in one sense as an oligarchic element and in another as a democratic element (*Pol.* 1265b35 ff.). It seems not at all implausible for the author of *On Law* to view the *koroi* as in one sense a democratic element and in another sense as providing a moderating role between elements. At any rate, our ignorance of exactly how bodies such as the *koroi* did work and the wide range of evaluations of different aspects of the Spartan constitution by fourth-century authors, take away all the force from Aalders' objections to *On Law* on the basis of its treatment of Sparta. In its prominent use of the Spartan constitution *On Law* fits very well into fourth-century political discourse.

On Law's suggestion that the parts of the Spartan constitution balance each other has often been seen as parallel to Polybius' treatment of Roman government, and hence as evidence of a Hellenistic date of composition (Aalders 1968: 19). As Aalders himself points out, however, the notion that the *koroi* at Sparta take up a middle position (34.25) to ensure this equilibrium has its closest parallels with Aristotle (*Pol.* 1295b2 ff.; Aalders 1975: 30–31; Delatte 1922: 113). One must remember that Aristotle studied Archytas' work carefully and wrote three books on Archytas so that Archytan influence on Aristotle is always a possibility.

Turning to Aalders' remaining objections, as well as objections raised by other scholars, there seem to me to be two primary considerations which speak in favor of the authenticity of *On Law and Justice* and two against. I will begin with the arguments in favor. First, the use of the term *apatheia* in the fragments (33.18), which Burkert and Aalders treat as a sign of spuriousness, is in fact the strongest argument for authenticity. Presumably Burkert sees *apatheia* ("impassivity') as an indication of the influence of Hellenistic philosophy on the author of *On Law*, since it was a prominent concept especially in Scepticism and Stoicism (Long and Sedley 1987: 1. 21–22). Aalders, however, correctly notes that what we find in *On Law* has very close connections to the earliest use of *apatheia*, a passage in Aristotle (*EN* 1104b24). In *On Law*, virtue is said to lead the soul into impassivity and tranquility (*apatheia* and *aremia*), whereas Aristotle reports that some people define virtues as certain states of impassivity and tranquility, using just the same pair of terms as in *On Law* (ἀρεμίαν, ἀπάθειαν). Aalders' suggestion that the author of *On Law* is drawing on Aristotle (see also Theiler 1926: 152), however, is not very plausible. Aristotle is not stating his own view here but reporting that some (i.e. of his contemporaries or predecessors) define virtues in this way. Later forgers usually seize on prominent Aristotelian or Platonic distinctions and claim them for the Pythagoreans. It is not typical for them to seize on passing remarks in Plato and Aristotle, which report the views of others. It is more plausible to suppose that in this passage Aristotle is referring precisely to the views of Archytas stated in *On Law*. Aristotle is clearly assigning the use of the terms *apatheia* and *aremia* to a contemporary or predecessor. He also specifically talks of people who *define* virtue in this way, and we know that Aristotle was interested in Archytas' definitions (see A22). It may be more than coincidence that another of those definitions involves precisely the concept of tranquility ("windlessness" is defined as *aremia* in a quantity of air). Commentators have typically said that Aristotle was referring to Speusippus in this passage of the *Nicomachean Ethics* (e.g. Irwin 1985: 312), but the terms *apatheia* and *aremia* are not associated with Speusippus elsewhere, and it is much more plausible that Aristotle is referring to Archytas.

Second, as all commentators notice, the application of the mathematical means used in music theory to types of political constitutions by the author of *On Law* is paralleled by a number of texts in the fourth century (Plato, Aristotle, Isocrates). In these other texts, however, geometric equality is associated with aristocracy and arithmetic equality with democracy (see the commentary on Fragment 3), while in *On Law and Justice* we find a unique system in which the geometric mean is associated with democracy, the harmonic mean with aristocracy and the arithmetic mean with oligarchy. Aalders argues that this peculiar system is an indication of a clumsy attempt by a forger to transfer the proportions of music theory to political theory. Such originality is not typical of the Pythagorean forgeries, however, since they are trying to claim that Platonic and Aristotelian distinctions are really

Pythagorean. Innovation of this sort is more plausibly regarded as Archytas's own contribution to a fourth-century debate.

Another reason for regarding the system of connections between means and constitutions in *On Law* as that of Archytas is its close connection to Archytas Fragment 2. It is not simply that Fragment 2 defines the same three means. What is odd about Fragment 2, at first sight, is not its definitions of the means but its evaluation of each of the means in terms of whether the ratios of the larger terms in each of the means are greater than, or smaller than, or equal to the ratios of the smaller terms. There is no obvious reason for making this comparison in the context of Fragment 2. *On Law and Justice*, however, picks up on precisely this point in connecting constitutions with means, so that e.g. the harmonic mean (12:8 :: 8:6) is associated with aristocracy, because the larger terms (12:8 = the better members of society) have a greater ratio (more privileges) than the smaller terms (8:6 = the lesser members of society). It is possible that the similarity between Fragment 2 and *On Law* is to be explained by supposing that *On Law* was forged partially on the basis of Fragment 2 (Theiler 1926: 152), but it is then hard to explain why Fragment 2 chose to compare the means in the way it does, independently of the application to politics in *On Law*. On these grounds it is more plausible that both texts are genuine works of Archytas.

One argument that weighs against *On Law* is the connections which it shows with surely spurious Pythagorean treatises. Two passages in Diotogenes are almost identical to passages in *On Law*. Thus in Diotogenes' treatise *On Piety* it is asserted that the laws should not be [written] on houses and doors but in the character of the citizens (76.2–3), and we find the same statement word for word in *On Law* (34.30–31). There is also a similarity between the assertion in Diotogenes' *On Kingship* that the king is either animate law (νόμος ἔμψυχος) or lawful rule (71.21–22) and the assertion in *On Law* that there are two kinds of law, the animate (ἔμψυχος) and inanimate, one being represented by the king and the other by the written letter (33.8–9). It is possible to explain these similarities on the assumption that the pseudepigrapha under Diotogenes' name are quoting the genuine treatise by Archytas, in an attempt to appear more authentic. There are fourth-century parallels for both the personification of law (Arist. *EN* 1132a22; Xen. *Cyr.* VII. 1.22) and also the idea that the law should be written in the character of the citizens (Isoc. VII. 39 ff.), so there would be nothing surprising in Archytas having made similar assertions. Centrone on the other hand sees the similarity as part of the basic homogeneity of the Pythagorean treatises on politics, which suggests that they had a common origin (2000: 574–75). A number of scholars have argued that the description of the ruler as *philanthrōpon* in *On Law* (36.4) betrays Hellenistic influence (Sinclair 1951: 289–94, who compares the *Letter of Aristeas*, and Aalders 1968: 19–20) but Aalders himself admits that there are fourth-century parallels for the application of the term to a king. The usage may be more common in the Hellenistic context, but it is not impossible for Archytas.

Theiler (1926: 152) has pointed out some strong parallels between the definition of virtue in *On Law* (the harmony of the rational and irrational part of the soul 33.15–17) and the definition given in the surely spurious treatises of Damippos (Thesleff 68.26 – ἁ συναρμογὰ τῶ ἀλόγω μέρεος τᾶς ψυχᾶς ποτὶ τὸ λόγον ἔχον, ἀρετά) and Metopos (Thesleff 119.28–120.2; see also Theages 190.1 ff.). Again *On Law* says that it is characteristic of the better to rule and of the worse to be ruled but of both to have power (33.14–15), and the same thing is said in pretty much the same words in the pseudo-Pythagorean treatise by Kriton/Damippos (Thesleff 68.29–69.1). Even more significantly, the definition of virtue as harmony which is common to *On Law*, Damippos and Metopos plays a prominent role in the later Peripatetic tradition, especially in Arius Didymus (Stobaeus II. 128.23 τὴν δ᾽ ἀμφοῖν [sc. τοῦ λόγου καὶ τοῦ ἀλόγου] ἁρμονίαν καὶ συμφωνίαν ἀρετήν), with whom other pseudo-Pythagorean writings show strong connections. It is always possible to claim again that both the later Peripatetic tradition and the pseudo-Pythagorean writings are drawing on the genuine *On Law* of Archytas, but the evidence can also be well explained by supposing that *On Law* was a forgery composed in the same milieu as Damippos and Metopos.

The second reason for doubting the authenticity of *On Law* is its failure to connect with the genuine fragments and testimonia of Archytas which deal with ethical and political issues. There is nothing flatly inconsistent, and, at the general level, there is a great deal of agreement between *On Law* and what is said in Fragment 3 about justice and the state and what is said in A9 and A9a about pleasure. The difficulty is that there is almost no overlap in terminology and distinctions. Thus, calculation, concord, greed, equality, and the split between the rich and the poor, which are prominent in Fragment 3 either do not appear or are marginal in *On Law*. Nor do the ideas of impassivity and tranquility appear directly in Archytas' speech against pleasure in A9a. This can of course be explained by arguing that *On Law* is a much more detailed treatment of issues presented more generally in Fr. 3 and A9–A9a or by arguing that Fr. 3 focuses more on justice, while the fragments we have from *On Law and Justice* focus most on law. The fact remains that *On Law* shows surprisingly little agreement on specifics with Archytas' genuine fragments and testimonia.

There are also a few minor reasons for doubting the authenticity of *On Law*. For example, *On Law* uses the word ζῳοφόρος to refer to the zodiac (35.24–25), whereas the earliest usage elsewhere is in the pseudo-Aristotelian *De Mundo* (392a11), which is usually dated somewhere between the first century BC and the first century AD. There is evidence that Archytas' pupil Eudoxus was the first to make use of the concept of the zodiac, which was borrowed from Babylonia (Barton 1994: 22), and some would date its use in the Greek world even earlier, so the reference to the zodiac may not be impossible for Archytas, but it is used in *On Law* as if it were not a novelty but a common conception.

In the case of most Greek authors (e.g. Plato or Aristotle) the assumption is that a work handed down in the manuscript tradition is a genuine work, unless a significant preponderance of evidence indicates that it is spurious. Thus, in the case of most authors, if the evidence for authenticity and spuriousness were equally balanced, we would accept the ancient tradition and regard the work as genuine. In the Pythagorean tradition, however, spurious works far outnumber genuine treatises in general and this is certainly true in the case of Archytas in particular. In such a situation, in order for a work to be regarded as genuine, there must either be no significant grounds for suspicion of the authenticity of a fragment or there must be a clear preponderance of evidence in favor of authenticity. My conclusion is that, given our present understanding of the evidence, the arguments for the authenticity or spuriousness of *On Law and Justice* are about equally balanced. Accordingly it cannot be treated as a genuine treatise of Archytas.

3. *On Moral Education* (Περὶ παιδεύσεως ἠθικῆς), Thesleff 40.17–43.23. Three fragments preserved in Stobaeus. A short fragment cited in Philostratus (*V. Apoll.* VI. 31 = Thesleff 47.18–22) as from a writing of Archytas on the training of children (ὑπὲρ παίδων ἀγωγῆς) may also be from this treatise (Zeller 1923: III. 2.120). There are two recent editions of this work with commentary: Giani 1993 and Centrone 1990. Burkert (1972b: 30–35) shows that this treatise (43.8–18) has marked similarities to Carneades' discussion of final ends (Cic. *Fin.* v. 16–23). *On Moral Education* presents two of Carneades' three ends, pleasure and lack of pain and also considers each in connection with moral good as does Carneades. See also Annas 1999: 52–53, nn. 3 and 5. Annas also notes that at 40.22 *On Moral Education* treats the indifferents as the material (*hulē*) of which someone can make good or bad use. This conception is paralleled in Plutarch (*On Common Conceptions* 1069e, 1070f–1071e) and Cicero (*Fin.* III. 60–61). On this treatise see also Praechter 1897. For further parallels between this treatise and later Greek

philosophy see Burkert 1972b, Centrone 1990 and Giani 1993. The treatise should be dated to the late first century BC or the first century AD.

II. MISCELLANEOUS REFERENCES TO SPURIOUS WORKS OF ARCHYTAS

1. Stobaeus I. 369.9–11 (quoting from Iamblichus, *On the Soul*), reports that Plato and his followers, Archytas, and the rest of the Pythagoreans, regarded the soul as tripartite and divided it into the rational, spirited and appetitive parts.

2. Censorinus (4.3) reports that Pythagoras, Ocellus, Archytas, and pretty nearly all the Pythagoreans thought that the human race had always existed.

3. Claudianus Mamertus, *De statu animae* 2.7 (Thesleff 47.8–13) reports that Archytas, "in that magnificent work which he published on nature" (*de rerum natura*), said that the soul is composed according to the model of the unit and rules the body as the one rules numbers. Thesleff suggests that this work may have been entitled *On Nature* (Περὶ φύσεως).

4. John the Lydian, *De mensibus* 2.9 (Thesleff 47. 14–17), reports that, whereas Pythagoras said that the soul was a square, Archytas defined it in terms of the circle. The soul is that which moves itself and must be the first mover, but this is the circle or sphere.

5. Thesleff 77.1–9, which is assigned to the *On Piety* of Diotogenes in two different passages of Stobaeus (IV. 1.133 and I. 7.10), is attributed to Archytas by Arsenius, *Apophthegmata* 34a (*Corpus Paroemiographorum Graecorum* II. 667). There is some similarity to *The Ten Universal Assertions* (Thesleff 7.10).

For the treatises *On Flutes*, *On Farming*, *On the Decad*, *On Machines* and *On Cooking* see the chapter on Archytas' life and writings.

III. LETTERS

1. D.L. VIII. 79–80 (Thesleff 46.1–7) contains a letter of Archytas to Plato, which Diogenes presents as the letter to which Plato is responding in *Letter XII*. This and the following letter refer to certain notes or treatises (ὑπομνήματα) of the Lucanian Ocellus. Ocellus might be an historical person, who lived ca. 400 BC and was a non-Greek Pythagorean, but all we

know about him is that he is listed under Lucania in Iamblichus' catalogue of Pythagoreans (*VP* 267). A certainly spurious treatise (it borrows from Aristotle's *On Generation and Corruption*) under his name has survived along with a fragment from another spurious work (Harder 1966, Thesleff 1965: 124.11–138.22). This and the following letter look suspiciously like an attempt to authenticate the spurious treatise (Harder 1966: 39–43 supports this view which goes back to Zeller and Diels). Thesleff (1962) regards the letters as spurious but gives a different explanation of their origin. For commentary see also Brisson 1987.

2. Plato, *Letter XII*, also preserved at D.L. VIII. 80–81 (Thesleff 46.8–15), is the response to the above letter of Archytas. This is the only letter of Plato about which doubts are expressed in the manuscript tradition. The manuscripts add the remark, which may go back to Thrasyllus, that this letter "is rejected as not Plato's" (ἀντιλέγεται ὡς οὐ Πλάτωνος). Accordingly few scholars have regarded it as authentic (only six of thirty-two on Brisson's list [1987: 72]). The reasons for regarding it as spurious are given in the note on Archytas' letter above. For commentary see Thesleff 1962 and Brisson 1987.

3. D.L. III. 21–22 (Thesleff 45.20–30) is Archytas' letter to Dionysius II asking for Plato's release, which is preserved in Diogenes' life of Plato. This purports to be a letter sent with Lamiscus, in which Archytas identifies himself as one of "the friends of Plato" who have sent Lamiscus to take Plato away in accordance with the agreement made with Dionysius. It asks that Plato be returned unhurt and reminds Dionysius of how eagerly he had wanted Plato to come and that he had undertaken to insure Plato's safety. The letter is in Doric. Nothing in it is anachronistic or *per se* suspicious. The grounds for doubting it are simply that it looks very much like a later elaboration on the story told in the *Seventh Letter*, in which Lamiscus' mission is described. In the *Seventh Letter*, there is no mention of a letter from Archytas accompanying Lamiscus. It would be easy for a forger to compose this short letter and present it as a copy of a genuine document which Lamiscus brought, or it may be that the letter is a rhetorical exercise, the exercise being to compose an appropriate letter for Archytas to have written to Dionysius. The contents of the letter are very general in nature and could easily be derived directly or by implication from the *Seventh Letter*. The only surprise is that a certain Photidas, who is not mentioned in the *Seventh Letter* and is otherwise unknown, is identified as the compatriot of Lamiscus.

4. Plato, *Letter IX*. There is nothing about the contents of the letter that make it impossible to suppose that Plato wrote it. The Echecrates referred to at the end need not be the Echecrates of Phlius mentioned in the *Phaedo*, who could not be described as young at the putative time of composition of the letter (after 387). Another Echecrates of Tarentum is mentioned at Iamblichus *VP* 267. The letter is open to suspicion, however, on the general grounds upon which all short letters are suspect, i.e. they are easy to forge for profit and were used as exercises in rhetorical schools. The advice that Plato gives Archytas, who is weary of his public duties, i.e. that we live not just for ourselves but also our country, is very banal and just the sort of thing we would expect from a rhetorical exercise. The advice can also be easily derived from statements of Plato in the *Republic*, and, while some of it might be appropriate to a general audience, one would not think that Plato would feel it necessary to preach it to a figure of Archytas' prominence. Ten of the thirty-two authors in Brisson's table have regarded it as authentic (1987: 72). Cicero clearly accepted the letter as authentic (*Fin.* II. 14; *Off.* I. 7). For commentary on the letter see Brisson 1987.

5. Plato, *Letter XIII*. In this letter, addressed to Dionysius II, Plato says that he is sending a certain Helicon, a pupil of Eudoxus, "of whom you [sc. Dionysius] and Archytas, if Archytas has come to you, may be able to make use." The authenticity of this letter is contested (eleven of thirty-two scholars on Brisson's list accept it [1987: 72]). Even if it is authentic, it tells us little about Archytas. See Morrow 1962 and Brisson 1987.

6. *Letters of Socrates and the Socratics*, 24 (Hercher 1873: 626). Archytas is mentioned in the first line of this short letter, purporting to be by Plato. Plato says that he is unable to send to Syracuse the things which Archytas needed.

7. *Letters of Socrates and the Socratics*, 37 (Hercher 1873: 635 = Thesleff 1965: 46.20–47.6). This is an anonymous letter appended to the collection of Socratic letters. Since it is in Doric and mentions a Cleinias, who is plausibly identified with the Pythagorean Cleinias (Iamb., *VP* 127, 198, 239), it is likely that the supposed author had Pythagorean connections. Thesleff argues that this author was Archytas, because of similarities which he sees to Archytas' letter to Plato, which is discussed above. I see no significant similarity between the letters of which Archytas is the supposed author and this letter and therefore would not assign it to him. See Sykutris (1933: 104) for other suggestions about the author.

IV. MEDIEVAL WRITINGS

1. Pseudo-Boethius, *Ars geometriae* line 379 Folkerts (393.7 Friedlein); 645 (408.14); 723 (412.20); 741 (413.22); 926 (425.23). This work has been shown to be a mathematical compendium, which was compiled in the eleventh century AD and then ascribed to Boethius by the compiler (Folkerts 1970: 105). These testimonia were rejected by DK (so also Tannery 1887: 128–29) but accepted by Timpanaro Cardini (1958–64: II. 354 ff.). The compiler ascribes a version of an abacus table to the Pythagoreans and Archytas, but no source independent of ps.-Boethius supports this attribution. Folkerts points out that the abacus described by the compiler shows strong similarities to that of Gerbert in the ninth century and argues that the compiler introduced Architas' name in connection with the abacus (line 379), because it was obviously impossible for Gerbert's name to appear in a work by "Boethius" who lived over 400 years earlier (1970: 89). Archytas was mentioned as a prominent mathematician in the authentic works by Boethius and the compiler probably drew the name from these works. The compiler is very confused about Architas, dating him after Euclid (723 ff.) and asserting that Architas made the Pythagorean discovery of the abacus available to the Roman world (translated it into Latin? *ab Archita* depends on *Latio accommodatam* not on *traditionem* as Timpanaro Cardini's translation suggests). The compiler's description of Architas in line 380 has been influenced by Horace I. 28. See also Burkert 1972a: 406 and n. 31: "The *Ars geometriae* bearing the name of Boethius, though obviously not composed before the High Middle Ages, even presents an early version of the Arabic numerals as an invention of the 'Pythagorici', and describes the method of calculating with these *apices* on an abacus, called *mensa Pythagorea* – perhaps the most striking of the anachronisms in which the Pythagorean tradition is so rich." When pseudo-Boethius assigns to Architas what Proclus (*In Eucl.* 428.10) and Hero (*Geom.* 8, p. 218 Heiberg) call the method of Plato for determining the sides of scalene right triangles, we would have to be very credulous indeed, given what we have seen of pseudo-Boethius, to think that this is based on an accurate ancient tradition, attested nowhere else.

2. ps.-Albertus Magnus, *The Marvels of the World* (*De mirabilibus mundi* – thirteenth century AD). There is no modern edition of the Latin text. I have taken the text from Wellmann 1921: 2, n. 7, who cites it from "Ausgabe vom Jahre 1492, Argent.", and I have also consulted a microfilm of an anonymous edition of 1514. For an English translation see Best and Brightman 1973.

et dixit Architas, si accipiatur cor lupi dum vivit et suspendatur super patientem quartanam, eradicat eam. Fol. 20v (para. 39, Best and Brightman 1973: 91)

And Architas said, if the heart be taken from a wolf ["snake" – Best and Brightman; no animal is specified in the edition of 1514], while it is alive, and hung on a person suffering a quartan fever, it utterly removes the fever.

et dixit Architas, quod si accipiatur cerumen sinistrae auris canis et suspendatur febricitantibus periodice, confert, maxime quartanae. Fol. 21r (para. 45, Best and Brightman 1973: 94)

And Architas said that if the wax of the left ear of a dog be taken and hung on people with a periodic fever, it is beneficial, especially for a quartan fever.

Wellmann (1921: 4) thought that these magical recipes were similar to those of Bolus of Mendes and suggested that they came from a treatise on agriculture forged in Archytas' name (D.L. VIII. 82), which Wellmann would assign to the second century BC at the latest. The material in ps.-Albertus is very similar to what we find ascribed to Architas a little later in *Lumen Animae* (see below), and it seems more likely that these texts represent medieval magical/medical texts, which are here ascribed to the great name of Architas in order to give them authority, than that they belong to an otherwise unattested ancient tradition concerning Archytas.

3. *On Events in Nature* (*De eventibus in natura*, also cited as *De effectibus in natura* and as *De eventibus futurorm*) by Archita Tharentinus (or Tharentinus, or just Tharen). There are numerous selections from this supposed book by Archita in the medieval texts known as *The Light of the Soul* (*Lumen Animae*). Rouse and Rouse 1971 (to whom this account is heavily indebted) have identified three main versions of *The Light of the Soul* (A, B, C), which are related but far from identical. All were composed in the fourteenth century and were very popular in a circumscribed region of central Europe during the fifteenth century. Some 195 manuscripts of various versions of it survive. *The Light of the Soul* was a manual for preachers that contained bits of lore/science about the natural world, which were then given an explanation in terms of Christian moral doctrine. This explanation was in turn supported by reference to ecclesiastical authorities (see the example below). Neither version A nor C has been published. An edition of version B was edited and published by Matthias Farinator in 1477, and three more incunabula editions of B followed in 1477, 1479 and 1482. Rouse and Rouse 1971 have examined manuscripts of all versions, but most scholars know the work only through the incunabula editions of version B

(e.g. Thorndike 1934: III. 546–560). I have consulted a microfilm of this but have not studied it in detail.

The idea that a treatise by Archytas entitled *On Events in Nature* had survived to the medieval period is problematic, since we have no indication of it in the earlier tradition. We might imagine it to be similar to the Aristotelian *Problems* and to reflect the wide range of interest in natural science suggested by the testimonia for Archytas. A number of the excerpts cited in the *Light of the Soul* deal with topics on which we know Archytas worked. Thus one excerpt says that a dying man emits fiery rays from his eyes (*Lumen* B, Farinator xlix. Cg), which reminds us of Archytas' explanation of sight in terms of the visual ray (A25). Another excerpt asserts that voices carry further in groves, at night, in times of grief and under water (*Lumen* B, Farinator iii. V). This might be connected to Archytas' prominent work in acoustics attested in Fragment 1. On the other hand, none of the excerpts refers to doctrines that are peculiarly Archytan, and some excerpts do not connect to anything else we know of Archytas and are somewhat bizarre, such as the assertion that "a feather placed on hot gold is soon transformed and resolved into water" (*Lumen* B, Farinator ii. Aa) or that "if someone looks into a mirror, before which a white flower has been placed, he cries" (*Lumen* B, Farinator ii. Da). Other selections deal with the effect of the stars or sun on the earth (*Lumen* B, Farinator vii. R; xxi. G). The following are further examples but not a complete list: strong passion makes the body white but the eyes red (xxxi. Aa); when lead vases sweat, rain follows soon (xxxxix. B); someone at the bottom of a well sees the stars in the middle of the day (xxxxix. O); a sweet liquid becomes sweeter, if put in a gold or silver vase, but more bitter if put in any other sort of vase (xlix. Ec). See also Thorndike 1934: III. 552–53.

The difficulty with accepting *On Events in Nature* as a genuine treatise of Archytas is not just the content of these excerpts but even more the nature of *The Light of the Soul* itself and the way it treats sources. The prologue to the work refers to important sources used by the author. The earliest version (A) includes selections from Architas in the text but does not mention him as a source in the prologue. Version B clearly bases its prologue on A but expands on it in a largely fictitious way. In particular the author of this version out-does "his predecessor in describing the ways in which he acquired his sources. His description amounts to a fictitious voyage littéraire . . ." (Rouse and Rouse 1971: 28). As part of this expansion of the prologue in B, the author reports that "certain books were brought to me from a monastery in Germany, including Architas Tharentinus, *On Events in Nature*." Given the nature of the expansion of the prologue in B, the story of obtaining the Architas manuscript looks like an invention for dramatic effect.

There are, however, much more serious problems with the use of sources in the *Lumen Animae*. In a number of cases the selections are drawn from sources which do survive, yet nothing corresponding to the selections quoted in *The Light of the Soul* can be found in the original text from which they supposedly come (e.g. Seneca, *Hercules Furens* and Sallust, *Bellum Jugurthinum* – Rouse and Rouse 1971: 20). Plato is cited from Books 5 and 10 of the *Phedrone*, although the selections do not correspond to anything in the *Phaedo* or *Phaedrus* or any other Platonic dialogue (Thorndike 1934: 552 suggests that they are perversions of material in the *Timaeus*, but they correspond to nothing in the *Timaeus*). Some of the most interesting cases are the selections supposed to come from the medieval author Theophilus, who wrote a work *De Diversis Artibus*, sometime in the first half of the twelfth century. *The Light of the Soul* A cites some forty-two passages from a work *On Various Arts* by Theophilus, but none of them can be found in the extant text of Theophilus nor is their content at all similar to the extant work. What is even more striking is that *The Light of the Soul* B also quotes forty-two extracts from Theophilus, but only one of these overlaps with what is found in A, and again none correspond to what is found in the extant text of Theophilus. Dodwell charitably supposed that the author of *Light* B had a manuscript in front of him which included Theophilus' work but also other completely different works on alchemical themes, which were not identified as separate works, so that the author thought he was excerpting from Theophilus, when he was not (1961: l–lii). Rouse and Rouse argue that there is too little uniformity in the selections supposedly drawn from Theophilus to suppose that they came from one source and suggest that the author of *Light* B simply "attributed extracts to Theophilus at random, regardless of their actual sources" (1971: 34 n. 55). A third version of *The Light of the Soul* (C) drew heavily on *Light* A, but the cavalier attitude towards the selections is shown by the fact that *Light* C changes the name of the author for 40 percent of the selections which it draws from *Light* A (Rouse and Rouse 1971: 44).

The *Light of the Soul* still needs further study; the Rouses' evaluation depends on a survey of only parts of the text. Nonetheless, it appears that in the *Light of the Soul* what was important was the truth contained in the natural lore cited and especially the moral truth derived therefrom. There was little concern for accurate citation of sources. Certain authors and texts were selected as authorities, some of these being actual texts and some invented. Then various bits of natural lore were assigned to these authorities in order to bolster the truth of the natural lore, whether or not the lore actually came from that author or not. The references to Archita in *The Light of the Soul* tell us then that Archytas' name had survived into the Middle Ages as that of an important authority on topics in natural science. It is quite possible that the treatise *On Events in Nature* was a total invention and never existed in any form. If a treatise with that name ascribed to Archytas did exist, it is still doubtful whether the selections quoted in *The Light of the Soul* came from it, as the case of Theophilus' *On Various Arts* shows. What *The Light of the Soul* presents are, in all probability, bits of natural lore which were in circulation and which are assigned to Archytas in order to gain the authority of a great figure from antiquity.

Rouse mentions two further works ascribed to Archita in *The Light of the Soul*, which I have not been able to confirm: (1) de machina mundiali (Rouse and Rouse 1971: 93); (2) veritatis et fidelitatis (Rouse and Rouse 1971: 93). The following is an example of the selections from Archita Tharentinus, *De eventibus in natura* found in *The Light of the World*. The first chapter of *Light of the World* A begins with an excerpt from Architas (quoted from Rouse and Rouse 1971: 17, compare with *Lumen* B, Farinator xlix. Ga):

Archita Tharentinus in libro de eventibus in natura. Incendio grandi facto rubescit super zenith nostrum perpendiculariter totum caelum. Sic, intra nos facto incendio dei amantissime caritatis fulgebit in nos mox caelum beatissime trinitatis. Unde Damascenus in libro contra errores graecorum: Cumque divina accendimur caritate mox toti intus perfundimur felicissima caritate.

As Archita the Tarentine says in his book *On Events in Nature*, when a great fire is lit, the entire heaven grows red perpendicularly above our heads. In the same way, when the fire of the most loving charity of god is lit within us, the heaven of the most blessed trinity will soon shine upon us. As Damascenus says on the same topic, in his book against the errors of the Greeks, whenever we are kindled by divine charity, we are soon thereafter filled with most felicitous charity. (tr. Rouse, slightly modified)

4. An apocryphal work of Archytas, which has never been published in full, is preserved in Codex Ambrosianus D 27 sup. (See *Catalogus Codicum Astrologorum Graecorum*, ed. F. Cumont et al., Vol. iii, p. 11). The treatise begins on folio 81 with the heading: The first of four books of *The Circular Theory of the Things in the Heaven* by Archytas Maximus [!] (Ἀρχύτου τοῦ Μαξίμου κυκλικῆς θεωρίας μετεώρων τῶν εἰς τέσσαρα τὸ πρῶτον). The second book begins on folio 88, the third on folio 97 and the fourth book covers f. 109v–115r. The treatise is in Attic rather than Doric Greek.

Antonius Elter discussed this work and published the first few pages of it (1899: 39–48). In line 60 of Elter's edition, the author refers to Aristotle and his *Meteorologica* by name, so that the work cannot be by Archytas. The treatise starts out with a definition of the sphere as a solid body contained by one surface and goes on to talk about the sphere of the cosmos, dividing it into two regions, that of aither and that of the elements.

V. TESTIMONIA FROM THE ARABIC TRADITION

1. Ḥunayn ibn Isḥāq, *Maxims of the Philosophers*, 20 (Loewenthal [1896] 83). Ḥunayn, "the most important mediator of ancient Greek science to the Arabs" (Lewis et al. 1971: III. 578–81), gives the following report concerning a certain Qiṭos or Qiros (Loewenthal [1896: 17] reports both variants). Qiṭos, as Loewenthal suggested, could be a reference to Archytas, if we supposed that the name corresponds to -chytas in Ar-chytas, but certainty is not possible (Qiṭos is mentioned as a cognomen of a certain Husayn b. Hillel in Gil 1992: 214). Because of this uncertainty, the report cannot be treated as reliable evidence for Archytas. There is no edition of the Arabic text, but Loewenthal published an edition of a medieval Hebrew translation of the Arabic along with a German translation of the Hebrew. The English translation of the Hebrew given below was kindly carried out for me by Dr. Friedrich Niessen, to whom I am also indebted for the expert commentary and the reference to Gil above.

Qiṭos [Archytas?] said, "However, we have mentioned four strings (only), corresponding to the natures which are combined in a human being, since they are four. Their names (are as follows): (1) the whistling string, which is called "zir" (note one), corresponding to strength and strength corresponding to the yellow bile, (2) the second string, which is called "mathna" (note two), corresponding to justice and justice corresponding to the blood, (3) the third string, which is called "mathlath" (note three), corresponding to righteousness and righteousness corresponding to the phlegm, (4) the silent string, which is called "bamm" (note four), corresponding to forgiveness and magnanimity and forgiveness and magnanimity corresponding to the black bile. [A reference to the first string has evidently fallen out of the text at this point.] Joy and rejoicing depend on the second string; fear and timidity depend on the third string; sorrow and joy [sic] depend on the silent string, corresponding to the black bile.

Note one: "zir," meaning "below, high pitched" (Persian), is the technical term for the highest pitched string of a stringed instrument.
Note two: "mathna," means "second place" (from the Arabic root "ṭanā" meaning "to double").

Note three: "mathlath" or "mithlath" meaning "third place" (from the Arabic root "t̲alāt̲" meaning "three").

Note four: The consonants "b'm" appear to be a wrong transcription of the Persian "bamm," meaning "thick, low sound," the term for the lowest pitched string.

2. Ibn Abī Uṣaybiʿa, *Sources of Information on the Classes of Physicians* ('Uyūn al-anbāʾ fī ṭabaḳāt al-aṭibbāʾ). This thirteenth-century work contained the biographies of over 380 physicians (Arabic, Greco-Roman, and Near Eastern). At the end of the biography of Pythagoras, the author gives the following quotation from Porphyry, which evidently comes from his *History of Philosophy* (see Smith 1993: 220–47, although he does not include this fragment). The translation below is based on a French translation kindly and expertly carried out for me by Marwan Rashed and based on the 1884 edition of the Arabic text by August Müller.

And I have handed down from Porphyry's book, *On the History of the Philosophers*, their accounts and their opinions. He said, "As regards the books of Pythagoras the sage, in the collection of which Archytas the philosopher from Tarentum distinguished himself, there are eighty books. As regards those (books), which, at the price of all his efforts, he collected, compiled and gathered, man by man, from all the men of mature age, who were of the kindred of Pythagoras the philosopher, of his sect and who inherited his knowledge, their number is two hundred. And he who distinguished himself by the clear-sightedness of his understanding and by the putting aside of the false books, which were put in the mouth of Pythagoras and circulated under his name and which were invented by unscrupulous individuals (among those books which they used to fabricate a tradition are: The Book of Solitary Prayers, The Book of the Characterization of Detestable Professions, The Science of Prodigies, The Book of Rules for the Composition of Symposia, The Book of the Construction of Drums, Cymbals and Magadeis [? ma ʿāzif in Arabic], The Book of Priestly Orders, The Book of the Sowing of Plants, The Book of Instruments, The Book of Poems, The Book on the Generation of the Universe, The Book of Hands, The Book of Virility, as well as a number of other books resembling these books), may he enjoy eternal happiness." And he [i.e. Porphyry] said, "Regarding those wicked men who invented those false books which we have mentioned, they are, according to the accounts which have reached us, Aristippus the Young, Nikos, who was nick-named 'one eye,' as well as a man of the Cretan people, who is called Konios, and Magillos and FWKHJWAQA [the Arabic is not clear] and others still more impudent. And that which incited them to the invention of these false books, put in the mouth of Pythagoras the philosopher and under his name, was in order to be well received among the moderns and because of that to be honored, to influence them and to establish personal connections with them. Regarding the books of the sage which are beyond suspicion, there are two hundred and eighty of them, which were forgotten until the world saw the birth of wise men possessing determination and fervor, who acquired, gathered and compiled them. They were not known previously in the land of Hellas (? Adha), but were preserved in Italy."

This report is not clear in all aspects, but the following seem to be the main points: (1) Archytas played an important role in collecting the books of Pythagoras. (2) Initially it appears that he collected eighty books of Pythagoras and two hundred books from followers of Pythagoras. (3) The exact nature of the two hundred books is unclear. Are they original works by these followers of Pythagoras or are they collections of the master's writings and reports of his sayings? Later all two-hundred and eighty books are ascribed to Pythagoras. (4) Archytas is praised for distinguishing these genuine works from other works which were forgeries and wrongly attributed to Pythagoras. (5) Pythagoras' two-hundred and eighty books were forgotten, after the time of Archytas, until some determined men collected and compiled them. Before that time they were not known in Greece but only preserved in Italy.

This account would make excellent sense as someone's attempt to explain a corpus of pseudo-Pythagorean writings similar to that reflected in Thesleff's collection. The eighty books by Pythagoras himself would explain the works forged in Pythagoras' name; the 200 books would explain the books forged in the names of other Pythagoreans. Archytas would be singled out as the one who collected them, both because a large number of works ascribed to him figured in the collection and because he was the last prominent early Pythagorean. These books are then said to have been forgotten everywhere except southern Italy, which explains the failure of fourth-century and later Greek philosophical authors to mention them. They were then rediscovered by some wise men, who could plausibly be dated to the first centuries BC and AD, when the pseudo-Pythagorean texts start to appear. If this report is an accurate account of Porphyry, it would appear that he accepted essentially all of what we regard as the pseudo-Pythagorean treatises, including many by Archytas, as genuine. He did recognize that there were some forgeries, but the names of the treatises and the names of forgers which he lists, with a few exceptions (e.g. Magilos = Megillos, Thesleff 1965: 115), do not correspond to the pseudo-Pythagorean writings that have survived. This suggests that the pseudo-Pythagorean treatises excerpted by Stobaeus (ca. AD 400) are the treatises accepted by Porphyry and that the treatises regarded as spurious by Porphyry had already disappeared.

The conclusion that Porphyry accepted as authentic a great number of treatises that modern scholarship regards as spurious is supported by his description of Archytas, in his commentary on Ptolemy's *Harmonics*, as the Pythagorean "whose works are most of all said to be indeed genuine" (*In Ptol.* Düring 1932: 56) and his quotation, in the same work, of what is undoubtedly a spurious treatise of Archytas (*In Ptol.* Düring 1932: 31–32). On the other hand, for the most part he both quotes from and refers to Archytas' genuine work on harmonics (e.g. Fr. 1), and there is evidence that he did not think that all treatises assigned to Archytas were likely to be genuine. It is striking, for instance, that, in his commentary on Aristotle's *Categories*, he never refers to the pseudo-Archytan treatise, which deals with categories. It might be that Porphyry does not know of the treatise, but the other possibility is that he does not refer to it because he does not regard it as authentic. For other discussions of this testimonium see van der Waerden, *RE* Suppl. x (1965) 862–64 and Thesleff 1972: 78–79.

Appendix 2
Archytas' name

The ancient evidence unambiguously shows that the upsilon in Archytas' name is long. Herodian, the great Greek grammarian of the second century AD, explicitly says in two places that the upsilon in Ἀρχύτας is long (*Hdn. Gr.* III. 1, p. 77.12 Lentz; III. 2, p. 851.33; see also III. 1, p. 57.9–10; 3.2, p. 654.27–28; 3.2, p. 656.15. See also [ps- ?] Arcadius, *De Accentibus* 28.17 and Theognostus, *Canones sive De Orthographia* 244.2 and 249.5). Moreover, the name Archytas appears in poems by Bion of Borysthenes (335–245 BC) and Eratosthenes of Cyrene (285–194 BC) and in each case the upsilon is shown to be long by the meter. The first line of Bion's poem (A3d) is a parody of Homer and is thus in dactylic hexameter: ὦ πέπον Ἀρχύτα, ψαλληγενές, ὀλβιότυφε. The phrase ὦ πέπον Ἀρχύτα has replaced the Homeric ὦ μάκαρ Ἀτρείδη and both Ἀτρείδη and Ἀρχύτα are scanned as three long syllables (Kindstrand 1976: 194–95). Similarly in Eratosthenes' epigram on the duplication of the cube (see Archytas A15, line 50: μηδὲ σύ γ' Ἀρχύτεω δυσμήχανα ἔργα κυλίνδρων) the upsilon is treated as long in the hexameter. Note that the ending -εω of Ἀρχύτεω is a single syllable by synizesis (Smyth 1956: 214D5). Wilamowitz (1962: 67) comments on the intentional use of consecutive spondees in the second and third foot of this line, in order to give it a certain weight, which underlines the difficulty of Archytas' solution to the duplication of the cube.

There has been some confusion in modern scholarship on the length of the upsilon. Marcovich (1999), Long (1964), and Hicks (1959) all treat it as short when they print the form Ἀρχύται at D.L. VIII. 82 rather than Ἀρχῦται, which is correct (so DK). Pape and Benseler (1959) and LSJ (s.v. Ἀρχύτειος) correctly recognize that the upsilon is long. According to the standard rules for pronouncing Greek names in English, after the form is Latinized, the accent should be on the second syllable from the end of the word, the y, since it is long.

The Doric forms of Archytas' name are much more common than the Attic in the nominative, dative and accusative. With one exception

(A8 = Athenaeus XII. 519b), the Attic forms are found only in the seventh and thirteenth Platonic letters (n.b. that they are not used in the ninth and twelfth letter) and the late grammarians (e.g. Herodian). Some have suggested that the use of the Attic form in the *Seventh Letter* is a small point in favor of its authenticity (Brisson 1987: 224 n. 107; Harward 1932: 209), but the same argument would also suggest that the thirteenth letter is authentic. The Attic forms may be due to the manuscript transmission with the Doric forms being replaced by the more familiar Attic endings. If the Attic form does go back to the original author, there is no reason to suspect that Plato would use the Attic spelling of Archytas' name more than a forger writing in Attic. In fact, since Plato had met and spent time with Archytas, one would rather suspect that he would use the Doric form. Aristotle uses the Doric forms.

In the genitive case, on the other hand, the Attic Ἀρχύτου is much more common than the Doric Ἀρχύτα. The Doric form is most common in the pseudo-Archytan tradition, although it is used in giving the title of Aristoxenus' life of Archytas in Athenaeus (A9). In Porphyry's commentary on Ptolemy's *Harmonics* the Attic form is generally used but the Doric appears once (56.2). It seems likely that the Doric form was preserved in the cases other than the genitive, because the Doric differed from the Attic only in having a alpha rather than an eta. In the genitive, the Doric alpha was radically different than the Attic ου, and accordingly individual authors and copyists in the manuscript tradition may have fallen back to using the more familiar Attic form. In the pseudo-Pythagorean tradition both authors and copyists were very aware that the text was supposed to be in Doric, and accordingly the Doric genitive was more carefully preserved.

Bibliography

Aalders, G. J. D. (1968) *Die Theorie der Gemischten Verfassung im Altertum* (Amsterdam)

(1975) *Political Thought in Hellenistic Times* (Amsterdam)

Ackrill, J. L. (1970) "A Defence of Platonic Division," in Wood, Oscar P. and Pitcher, George eds., *Ryle: A Collection of Critical Essays* (New York) 373–92

(1973) *Aristotle's Ethics* (London)

Adam, J. (1929) *The Republic of Plato* (Cambridge)

Aerts, W. J. (1990) *Michaelis Pselli Historia Syntomos* (Berlin)

Annas, Julia (1976) *Aristotle's Metaphysics: Books M and N* (Oxford)

(1999) *Platonic Ethics, Old and New* (Ithaca and London)

Anton, J. ed. (1980) *Science and the Sciences in Plato* (New York)

Anton, J. P. and Kustas, G. L., eds. (1971) *Essays on Ancient Greek Philosophy* (Albany)

Atti 10 Convegno, 1970: Taranto nella Civiltà della Magna Grecia (Naples)

Bailey, C. (1947) *Titi Lucreti Cari De Rerum Natura Libri Sex*, 3 vols. (Oxford)

Barbera, A. (1984) "Placing *Sectio Canonis* in Historical and Philosophical Contexts," *Journal of Hellenic Studies* 104: 157–61

(1991) *The Euclidean Division of the Canon* (Lincoln)

Barker, A. D. (1979) "ΣΥΜΦΩΝΟΙ ΆΡΙΘΜΟΙ: A Note on *Republic* 531c1–4," *Classical Philology* 73: 337–42

(1981) "Methods and Aims in the Euclidean *Sectio Canonis*," *Journal of Hellenic Studies* 101: 1–16

(1984) *Greek Musical Writings*, Vol. I: *The Musician and His Art* (Cambridge)

(1987) "Archita di Taranto e l' armonica pitagorica," in Cassio, A. C. and Musti, D. eds., *Tra Sicilia e Magna Grecia* (Pisa) 159–78

(1989) *Greek Musical Writings*, Vol. II: *Harmonic and Acoustic Theory* (Cambridge)

(1992) "Three Approaches to Canonic Division," in Mueller (1992a) 49–83

(1994) "Ptolemy's Pythagoreans, Archytas, and Plato's Conception of Mathematics," *Phronesis* 39.2: 113–35

(2001) *Scientific Method in Ptolemy's Harmonics* (Cambridge)

Barnes, J. (1982) *The Presocratic Philosophers* (London)

(1984) ed., *The Complete Works of Aristotle: The Revised Oxford Translation*, 2 vols. (Princeton)

(1994) *Aristotle: Posterior Analytics*, 2nd edn. (Oxford)

(1995) *The Cambridge Companion to Aristotle* (Cambridge)

Barnes, J., Schofield, M., and Sorabji, R., eds. (1975) *Articles on Aristotle*, Vol. I (London)

(1979) eds., *Articles on Aristotle*, Vol. III (London)

Baron, W., ed. (1967) *Beiträge zur Methodik der Wissenschaftsgeschichte* (Wiesbaden)

Barton, Tamsyn (1994) *Ancient Astrology* (London)

Beare, J. I. (1906) *Greek Theories of Elementary Cognition* (Oxford)

Bélis, A. (1986) *Aristoxène de Tarente et Aristote: le Traité d' Harmonique* (Paris)

Best, Michael R. and Brightman, Frank H. (1973) *The Book of Secrets of Albertus Magnus* (Oxford)

Blass, F. (1884) "De Archytae Tarentini fragmentis mathematicis," in *Mélanges Graux* (Paris) 573–84

Bluck, R. S. (1947) *Plato's Seventh and Eighth Letters* (Cambridge)

(1964) *Plato's Meno* (Cambridge)

Bodnár, István (2004) "The Mechanical Principles of Animal Motion," in Laks and Rashed (2004) 137–147

Bonitz, H. (1955) *Index Aristotelicus* (Graz), repr. of first edition of 1870 (Berlin)

Bostock, David (1994) *Aristotle: Metaphysics, Books Z and H* (Oxford)

Bowen, A. C. (1982) "The Foundations of Early Pythagorean Harmonic Science: Archytas, Fragment 1," *Ancient Philosophy* 2: 79–104

(1991a) *Science and Philosophy in Classical Greece* (New York)

(1991b) "Euclid's *Sectio canonis* and the History of Pythagoreanism," in Bowen (1991a) 164–87

Bower, C. M. (1978) "Boethius and Nicomachus: An Essay Concerning the Sources of *De institutione musica*," *Vivarium* 16.1: 1–45

(1989) tr. *Anicius Manlius Severinus Boethius, Fundamentals of Music* (New Haven)

Brandwood, L. (1969) "Plato's Seventh Letter," *Revue de l'Organisation Internationale pour l'Étude des Langues anciennes par Ordinateur* 4: 1–25

Brauer, George C. Jr. (1986) *Taras: Its History and Coinage* (New Rochelle)

Briggs, W. W. (1983) "Housman and Polar Errors," *American Journal of Philology* 104: 268–77

Brisson, Luc (1987) *Platon: Lettres* (Paris)

Brown, M. S. (1967) "Plato Disapproves of the Slave-boy's Answer," *Review of Metaphysics* 21: 57–93

Brumbaugh, Robert S. (1966) *Ancient Greek Gadgets and Machines* (New York)

Brunt, P. A. (1993) *Studies in Greek History and Thought* (Oxford)

Buck, C. D. (1955) *The Greek Dialects* (Chicago)

Bulmer-Thomas, I. (1971a) "Eutocius of Ascalon," in Gillispie (1971) IV. 488–91

(1971b) "Hippocrates of Chios," in Gillispie (1971) VI. 410–18

Burkert, W. (1960) "Platon oder Pythagoras? Zum Ursprung des Wortes 'Philosophie'," *Hermes* 88: 159–77

(1961) "Hellenistische Pseudopythagorica," *Philologus* 105: 16–43, 226–46

(1972a) *Lore and Science in Ancient Pythagoreanism*, tr. E. Minar (Cambridge, Mass.), 1st German edn., 1962

(1972b) "Zur geistesgeschichtlichen Einordnung einiger Pseudopythagorica," *Pseudepigrapha I*, Fondation Hardt Entretiens XVIII (Vandoeuvres–Genève) 25–55, discussion 88–102

(1985) *Greek Religion* (Cambridge, Mass.)

(1992) *The Orientalizing Revolution: Near Eastern Influence on Greek Culture in the Early Archaic Age* (Cambridge, Mass.)

Burnet, J. (1900) *The Ethics of Aristotle* (London)

Burnyeat, M. F. (2000) "Plato on Why Mathematics is Good for the Soul," in Smiley (2000) 1–81

(2001) *A Map of Metaphysics Zeta* (Pittsburgh)

(2004) "Archytas and Optics," forthcoming in *Science in Context*

Butler, H. E., tr. (1920) *Quintilian: Insitutio Oratoria* (Cambridge, Mass.)

Butler, H. E. and Owen, A. S. (1914) *Apulei Apologia sive Pro Se de Magia Liber, With Introduction and Commentary* (Oxford)

Cambiano, Giuseppe (1996) "Alle origini della meccanica: Archimede e Archita," *Eredità della Magna Grecia, Atti del Trentacinquesimo Convegno di Studi sulla Magna Grecia* (Taranto) 459–95

(1998) "Archimede Meccanico et La Meccanica di Archita," *Elenchos* 19.2: 291–324

Cancik, H. and Schneider, H., eds. (1996) *Der Neue Pauly: Enzyklopädie der Antike*, Vol. 1 (Stuttgart)

Carra de Vaux, B. (1902) *Le Livre des Appareils Pneumatiques et des Machines Hydrauliques par Philon de Byzance* (Paris)

Carteron, H. (1975) "Does Aristotle have a Mechanics?," in Barnes et al. (1975) 161–74

Caskey, Elizabeth Gwyn (1974) "Again – Plato's Seventh Letter," *Classical Philology* 69.3: 220–27

Cassio, Albio Cesare (1988) "Nicomachus of Gerasa and the Dialect of Archytas, Fr. 1," *Classical Quarterly* n.s. 38: 135–39

Caston, Victor and Graham, Daniel W., eds. (2002) *Presocratic Philosophy: Essays in Honour of Alexander Mourelatos* (Aldershot)

Caven, Brian (1990) *Dionysius I: War-Lord of Sicily* (New Haven and London)

Centrone, Bruno (1990) *Pseudopythagorica Ethica* (Naples)

(1994a) "Archytas De Tarente," in Goulet (1994) 339–42

(1994b) "Pseudo-Archytas," in Goulet (1994) 342–45

(2000) "Platonism and Pythagoreanism in the Early Empire," in Rowe and Schofield (2000) 559–84

Chadwick, H. (1981) *Boethius* (Oxford)

Cherniss, H. (1944) *Aristotle's Criticism of Plato and the Academy* (Baltimore)

(1945) *The Riddle of the Early Academy* (Berkeley)

(1951) "Plato as Mathematician," *Review of Metaphysics* 4: 395–425

(1964) *Aristotle's Criticism of Presocratic Philosophy* (New York)

Ciaceri, E. (1927–32) *Storia della Magna Grecia*, I–III (Milan–Rome)

Clagett, M. (1964) *Archimedes in the Middle Ages*, Vol. 1 (Madison)

Clark, G., tr. (1989) *Iamblichus: On the Pythagorean Life* (Liverpool)

Clavaud, Robert (1974) *Démosthène: Discours d'apparat (Épitaphios, Éroticos)* (Paris)

Cohen, M. R. and Drabkin, I. E., eds. (1948) *A Source Book in Greek Science* (New York)

Colson, F. H. (1924) *M. Fabii Quintiliani Institutionis Oratoriae Liber I* (Cambridge)

Cooper, Guy L. (1998) *Attic Prose Syntax* (Ann Arbor)

Cornford, F. M. (1937) *Plato's Cosmology* (London)

Cougny, E. (1890) *Epigrammatum anthologia Palatina cum Planudeis et appendice nova*, Vol. III (Paris)

Coxon, A. H. (1986) *The Fragments of Parmenides* (Assen)

Cuomo, S. (2000) *Pappus of Alexandria and the Mathematics of Late Antiquity* (Cambridge)

Davies, M. (1990) *Sophocles: Trachiniae* (Oxford)

Deane, Philip (1973) "Stylometrics do not Exclude the Seventh Letter," *Mind*, n.s. 82: 113–17

Delatte, A. (1922) *Essai sur la politique pythagoricienne* (Liège and Paris)

Denniston, J. D. (1959) *The Greek Particles*, 2nd edn. (Oxford)

Despotopoulos, Constantin (1987) "La signification des mots λογισμός et λογιστικά chez Archytas," Πρακτικὰ τῆς Ἀκαδημίας Ἀθηνῶν 62.1: 291–303

Deubner, L., ed. (1937) *Iamblichi De Vita Pythagorica Liber*, 2nd edn. 1975, ed. U. Klein (Stuttgart)

Dicks, D. R. (1970) *Early Greek Astronomy to Aristotle* (Ithaca)

Diehl, E., ed. (1904) *Proclus Diadochus in Platonis Timaeum Commentaria* (Leipzig)

Diels, H. (1879) *Doxographi Graeci* (Berlin)

(1952) *Die Fragmente der Vorsokratiker*, 6th edn., rev. W. Kranz, 3 vols. (Berlin), first edn. 1903

(1965) *Antike Technik*, 3rd edn. (Osnabrück)

Diès, Auguste (1959) *Platon: Philèbe* (Paris)

Dihle, Albrecht (1970) *Studien zur Griechischen Biographie* (Göttingen)

Dijksterhuis, E. J. (1987) *Archimedes* (Princeton)

Dillon, J. (1977) *The Middle Platonists* (London)

Dillon, J. and Hershbell, J., trs. (1991) *Iamblichus: On The Pythagorean Way of Life* (Atlanta)

Dilts, M. R., ed. (1974) *Claudii Aeliani Varia Historia* (Leipzig)

Dirlmeier, Franz (1967) *Aristoteles: Nikomachische Ethik* (Berlin)

Dixsaut, M., ed. (1999) *La Fêlure du Plaisir: Études sur le Philèbe de Platon*, Vol. II: *Contextes* (Paris)

Dodds, E. R. (1959) *Plato: Gorgias* (Oxford)

Dodwell, C. R. (1961) *Theophilus: The Various Arts* (London)

D'Ooge, M. L., Robbins, F. E., and Karpinski, L. C. (1926) *Nicomachus of Gerasa: Introduction to Arithmetic* (New York)

Dorandi, Tiziano (1991) *Filodemo: Storia dei Filosofi, Platone e l'Academia* (Naples)

Drachmann, A. G. (1963) *The Mechanical Technology of Greek and Roman Antiquity* (Copenhagen)

Duffy, J. M., ed. (1992) *Michaelis Pselli Philosophica Minora*, Vol. 1: *Opuscula Logica, Physica, Allegorica, Alia* (Leipzig)

Dunbabin, T. J. (1948) *The Greeks in the West* (Oxford)

Düring, I. (1930) *Die Harmonielehre des Klaudios Ptolemaios* (Göteborg)
(1932) *Porphyrios Kommentar zur Harmonielehre des Ptolemaios* (Göteborg)
(1934) *Ptolemaios und Porphyrios über die Musik* (Göteborg)
(1957) *Aristotle in the Ancient Biographical Tradition* (Göteborg)

Edelstein, Ludwig (1966) *Plato's Seventh Letter* (Leiden)

Einarson, Benedict and De Lacy, Phillip, trs. (1967) *Plutarch: Moralia*, Vol. XIV (Cambridge, Mass.)

Elter, A. (1899) *Analecta Graeca*, Natalicia regis Guilelmi II concelebranda (Bonn)

Fantham, E. (1981) "The Synchronistic Chapter of Gellius (*NA* 17.21) and Some Aspects of Roman Chronology and Cultural history Between 60 and 50 BC," *Liverpool Classical Monthly* 6.1: 7–17

Festa, N., ed. (1891) *Iamblichus: De communi mathematica scientia*, 2nd edn. 1975, ed. U. Klein (Stuttgart)

Finley, M. I. (1977) *Aspects of Antiquity*, 2nd edn. (New York)

Flashar, H., ed., (1983) *Aristoteles: Problemata Physica* (Berlin)

Folkerts, M. (1970) *"Boethius" Geometrie II: Ein Mathematisches Lehrbuch des Mittelalters* (Wiesbaden)

Fornara, Charles W. (1971) *The Athenian Board of Generals from 501 to 404* (Wiesbaden)

Forster, E. S., tr. (1927) *The Works of Aristotle*, ed. W. D. Ross: Volume VII, *Problemata* (Oxford)
(1928) "The Pseudo-Aristotelian *Problems*: Their Nature and Composition," *Classical Quarterly* 22: 163–65
(1984) tr., *[Aristotle] Problems* in Barnes (1984) II. 1319–1527

Fowler, D. H. (1987) *The Mathematics of Plato's Academy* (Oxford)

Frank, E. (1923) *Plato und die sogenannten Pythagoreer: Ein Kapitel aus der Geschichte des griechischen Geistes* (Halle)

Fraser, P. M. (1972) *Ptolemaic Alexandria*, 3 vols. (Oxford)

Fraser, P. M. and Matthews, E. (1987–97) *A Lexicon of Greek Personal Names* (Oxford)

Frede, M. (1996) "Ps.-Archytas," in Cancik and Schneider (1996) 1031

Freeman, K. (1946) *The Pre-Socratic Philosophers: A Companion to Diels, Fragmente der Vorsokratiker* (Cambridge, Mass.)
(1948) *Ancilla to the Pre-Socratic Philosophers* (Cambridge, Mass.)

Friedlein, G., ed. (1867) *Anicii Manilii Torquati Severini Boetii De institutione arithmetica libri duo, De institutione musica libri quinque, accedit Geometria quae fertur Boetii* (Leipzig)
(1873) ed., *Procli Diadochi in primum Euclidis Elementorum librum commentarii* (Leipzig)

Frischer, Bernard (1984) "Horace and the Monuments: A New Interpretation of the Archytas Ode (C.1.28)," *Harvard Studies in Classical Philology* 88: 71–102

von Fritz, K. (1940) *Pythagorean Politics in Southern Italy* (New York)

(1945a) "The Discovery of Incommensurability by Hippasos of Metapontum," *Annals of Mathematics* 46: 242–64. Reprinted in Furley and Allen (1970) 382–412

(1945b) "*Nous, Noein,* and their Derivatives in Pre-Socratic Philosophy," *Classical Philology* 40: 223–42; 41: 12–34. Reprinted in Mourelatos (1993) 23–85

(1954) *The Theory of the Mixed Constitution in Antiquity* (New York)

(1971) "The Philosophical Passage in the Seventh Platonic Letter," in Anton and Kustas (1971) 408–47

Furley, D. J. (1987) *The Greek Cosmologists,* Vol. 1 (Cambridge)

(1989) *Cosmic Problems* (Cambridge)

Furley, D. J. and Allen, R. E., eds. (1970) *Studies in Presocratic Philosophy* (New York)

Gaiser, Konrad (1988) *Philodems Academica* (Stuttgart)

Gallop, David (1975) *Plato: Phaedo* (Oxford)

Gauthier, R. A. and Jolif, J. Y. (1970) *Aristote: L' Éthique à Nicomaque,* 2nd edn., 4 vols. (Paris)

Gautier, Paul, ed. (1986) *Théophylacte D' Achrida: Lettres* (Thessalonica)

Giangrande, G., ed. (1956) *Eunapii Vitae Sophistarum* (Rome)

Giani, Simona (1993) *Pseudo Archita: L' Educazione Morale* (Rome)

Gigante, M. (1971) "La cultura a Taranto," in *Atti 10 Convegno, 1970: Taranto nella Civiltà della Magna Grecia* (Naples) 67–131

Gil, Moshe (1992) *A History of Palestine, 634–1099,* tr. Ethel Broido (Cambridge)

Gillispie, C. C., ed. (1970–80) *Dictionary of Scientific Biography,* 16 vols. (New York)

Goldstein, B. R. and Bowen A. C. (1983) "A New View of Early Greek Astronomy," *Isis* 74: 330–40

Gomme, A. W. (1956) *A Historical Commentary on Thucydides,* Vol. II (Oxford)

Gomme, A. W., Andrewes, A., and Dover, K. J. (1970) *A Historical Commentary on Thucydides,* Vol. IV (Oxford)

Gomperz, T. (1905) *Greek Thinkers,* 4 vols., tr. G. G. Berry (London)

Gosling, J. C. B. and Taylor, C. C. W. (1982) *The Greeks on Pleasure* (Oxford)

Gottschalk, H. B. (1982) "Diatribe Again," *Liverpool Classical Monthly* 7.6: 91–92

(1983) "More on DIATRIBAI," *Liverpool Classical Monthly* 8.6: 91–92

(1987) "Aristotelian Philosophy in the Roman World from the Time of Cicero to the End of the Second Century AD," *Aufstieg und Niedergang der römischen Welt* II. 36. 2: 1079–1174

Goulet, Richard, ed. (1994) *Dictionnaire des Philosophes Antiques,* Vol. 1 (Paris)

Gow, A. S. F. (1952) *Theocritus: Edited With a Translation and Commentary,* 2 vols. (Cambridge)

Griffith, G. T. (1935) *The Mercenaries of the Hellenistic World* (Cambridge)

Gruppe, O. F. (1840) *Über die Fragmente des Archytas und der ältern Pythagoreer* (Berlin)

Gudeman, A. (1913) "Ein chronologischer Irrtum bei Cicero," *Berliner Philologische Wochenschrift* 33: 1343–44

Gulick, Charles Burton, tr. (1933) *Athenaeus: The Deipnosophists* (London)
Gulley, Norman (1972) "The Authenticity of the Platonic Epistles," in *Pseude-pigrapha I*, Fondation Hardt, Entretiens xviii (Vandoeuvres–Genève) 105–30
Guthrie, W. K. C. (1962) *A History of Greek Philosophy*, Vol. i (Cambridge)
  (1965) *A History of Greek Philosophy*, Vol. ii (Cambridge)
  (1969) *A History of Greek Philosophy*, Vol. iii (Cambridge)
  (1975) *A History of Greek Philosophy*, Vol. iv (Cambridge)
  (1978) *A History of Greek Philosophy*, Vol. v (Cambridge)
Haas, Arthur Erich (1907) "Antike Lichttheorien,"*Archiv für Geschichte der Philoso-phie* 20: 345–86
Hahm, David F. (1978) "Early Hellenistic Theories of Vision and the Perception of Color," in Machamer and Turnbull (1978) 60–95
Hankinson, R. J. (1995) "Philosophy of Science" and "Science" in Barnes (1995) 107–67
Harder, Richard (1966) *Ocellus Lucanus* (Zürich)
Hartenstein, G. (1833) *De Archytae Tarentini fragmentis philosophicis* (Leipzig)
Harvey, F. D. (1965–66) "Two Kinds of Equality," *Classica et Mediaevalia* 26: 101–46; corrigenda, ibid. 27: 99–100
Harward, J. (1932) *The Platonic Epistles* (Cambridge)
Heath, T. L. (1913) *Aristarchus of Samos* (Oxford)
  (1921) *A History of Greek Mathematics*, 2 vols. (Oxford)
  (1925) *The Thirteen Books of Euclid's Elements*, 3 vols. (Cambridge)
  (1949) *Mathematics in Aristotle* (Oxford)
  (1953) *The Works of Archimedes with the Method of Archimedes*, repr. of the Cambridge University Press editions of 1897 and 1912 (New York)
Heiberg, J. L., ed. (1910–15) *Archimedis Opera Omnia*, 3 vols. (rev. 1972 E. S. Stammatis) (Leipzig)
  (1925) *Geschichte der Mathematik und Naturwissenschaften im Altertum* (Munich)
  (1976) ed., *Heronis Alexandri opera quae supersunt omnia*, Vol. iv: *Definitiones . . . Geometrica* (Stuttgart)
Heiberg, J. L. and Menge, H., eds. (1883–1916) *Euclidis Opera Omnia*, 8 vols. (1–5 rev. E. S. Stammatis 1969–77) (Leipzig)
Heinimann, Felix (1945) *Nomos und Physis* (Basel)
Helm, Rudolf, ed. (1912) *Apulei Platonici Madaurensis Opera quae Supersunt:* Vol. ii, Fasc. i: *Pro Se de Magia Liber (Apologia)* (Leipzig)
Hense, C. (1907) "Ein Fragment des Athenodorus von Tarsus," *Rheinisches Museum* 62: 313–15
Hercher, R. (1873) *Epistolographi Graeci* (Paris)
Herman, Gabriel (1987) *Ritualized Friendship and the Greek City* (Cambridge)
Hermann, C. F., ed. (1892) *Platonis Dialogi*, 6 vols. (Leipzig)
Hett, W. S., tr. (1953) *Aristotle: Problems, Books I–XXI*, rev. edn. (Cambridge, Mass.)
Hicks, R. D., tr. (1959) *Diogenes Laertius: Lives of Eminent Philosophers* (Cambridge, Mass.)
Hignett, C. (1952) *A History of the Athenian Constitution* (Oxford)
Hilberg, I., ed. (1910) *Sancti Eusebii Hieronymi Epistulae* (Leipzig)

Hill, Donald, ed. (1973) *The Book of Knowledge of Ingenious Mechanical Devices by Ibn al-Razzāz al-Jazari* (Dordrecht–Boston)

(1978) ed., *The Book of Ingenious Devices by the Banu Musa bin Shakir* (Dordrecht–Boston)

(1984) *A History of Engineering in Classical and Medieval Times* (London)

Hiller, E. (1870) "Der Πλατωνικός des Eratosthenes," *Philologus* 30: 60–72

(1878) ed., *Theonis Smyrnaei Expositio rerum Mathematicarum ad Legendum Platonem Utilium* (Leipzig)

Hoche, R., ed. (1864) *Joannes Philoponus: In Nicomachi Arithmeticam Introductionem*, lib. 1 (Leipzig)

(1866) ed., *Nicomachi Geraseni Pythagorei Introductionis Arithmeticae Libri II* (Leipzig)

Hoffmann, Philippe (1980) "Jamblique Exégète du Pythagoricien Archytas: trois originalitiés d' une doctrine du temps," *Les Études Philosophiques* 307–23

Holder, Alfred, ed. (1894) *Scholia Antiqua in Q. Horatium Flaccum:* Volumen I: *Porfyrionis Commentum* (Leipzig)

Hornblower, Simon (1991) *A Commentary on Thucydides*, Vol. 1 (Oxford)

Hornblower, Simon and Spawforth, Antony, eds. (1996) *The Oxford Classical Dictionary*, 3rd edn. (Oxford)

Hort, Arthur, tr. (1916) *Theophrastus: Enquiry into Plants* (Cambridge, Mass.)

Hubert, C., ed. (1971) *Plutarchi Moralia* IV (Leipzig)

Huby, Pamela (1999) *Theophrastus of Eresus, Sources for His Life, Writings, Thought and Influence. Commentary*, Vol. IV: *Psychology* (Leiden)

Huffman, C. A. (1985) "The Authenticity of Archytas Fr. 1," *Classical Quarterly* 35.2: 344–48

(1993) *Philolaus of Croton: Pythagorean and Presocratic* (Cambridge)

(1999a) "The Pythagorean Tradition," in Long (1999) 66–87

(1999b) "Limite et illimité chez les premiers philosophes grecs," in Dixsaut (1999) 11–31

(2001) "The Philolaic Method: The Pythagoreanism behind the *Philebus*," in Preus (2001) 67–85

(2002a) "Polyclète et les Présocratiques," in Laks and Louguet (2002) 303–27

(2002b) "Archytas and the Sophists," in Caston and Graham (2002) 251–70

Hussey, Edward (1983) *Aristotle's Physics: Books III and IV* (Oxford)

Irwin, T. (1977) *Plato's Moral Theory* (Oxford)

(1979) *Plato: Gorgias* (Oxford)

(1985) tr., *Aristotle: Nicomachean Ethics* (Indianapolis)

Isnardi Parente, Margherita (1979) *Città e regimi politici nel pensiero greco* (Torino)

Jablonski, W. (1930) "Die Theorien des Sehens im griechischen altertum bis auf Aristoteles," *Sudhoffs Archiv für Geschichte der Medizin* 23: 306–61

Jaeger, W. (1948) *Aristotle*, 2nd edn. (Oxford)

Jan, K., ed. (1962) *Musici Scriptores Graeci* (Leipzig)

Joachim, H. H. (1955) *Aristotle: The Nicomachean Ethics* (Oxford)

Jocelyn, H. D. (1982) "Diatribes and Sermons," *Liverpool Classical Monthly* 7.1: 3–7

(1983) "'Diatribes' and the Greek Book-title Διατριβαί," *Liverpool Classical Monthly* 8.6: 89–91

Joly, R. (1961) "La Question hippocratique et le témoinage du Phèdre," *Revue des Études Grecques* 74: 69–92

Jones, W. H. S., tr. (1918) *Pausanias: Description of Greece*, 6 vols. (London)

Junge, G. and Thomson, W., eds. (1930) *The Commentary of Pappus on Book X of Euclid's Elements* (Cambridge, Mass.)

Kahn, C. (1985) *Anaximander and the Origins of Greek Cosmology* (Philadelphia). First printed in 1960

(1996) *Plato and the Socratic Dialogue* (Cambridge)

(2001) *Pythagoras and the Pythagoreans* (Indianapolis)

Kaibel, G., ed. (1887) *Athenaei Naucratitae Dipnosophistarum libri XV* (Leipzig)

Kayser, C. L., ed. (1870) *Flavii Philostrati Opera . . . Eusebius, Adversus Hieroclem* (Leipzig)

Keller, Otto, ed. (1902) *Pseudacronis Scholia in Horatium Vetustiora* (Leipzig)

Keuls, Eva (1976) "Aspetti religiosi della Magna Grecia nell'età romana," *La Magna Grecia nell'età romana, Atti del Quindicesimo Convegno di Studi sulla Magna Grecia* (Naples) 439–58

(1979) "The Apulian 'Xylophone': A Mysterious Musical Instrument Identified," *American Journal of Archaeology* 83: 476–77

Keyser, Paul T. (1998) "Orreries, the Date of [Plato] Letter ii, and Eudorus of Alexandria," *Archiv für Geschichte der Philosophie* 80.3: 241–67

Kilpatrick, Ross S. (1968) "Archytas at the Styx (Horace *Carm.* 1.28)," *Classical Philology* 63.3: 201–26

Kindstrand, Jan Fredrik (1976) *Bion of Borysthenes* (Uppsala)

Kingsley, P. (1990) "The Greek Origin of the Sixth-Century Dating of Zoroaster," *Bulletin of the School of Oriental and African Studies* 53.2: 245–65

(1995a) *Ancient Philosophy, Mystery, and Magic: Empedocles and Pythagorean Tradition* (Oxford)

(1995b) "Artillery and Prophecy: Sicily in the Reign of Dionysius I," *Prometheus* 21: 15–23

Kirk, G. S., Raven, J. E., and Schofield, M. (1983) *The Presocratic Philosophers*, 2nd edn. (Cambridge)

Klein, J. (1968) *Greek Mathematical Thought and the Origin of Algebra*, tr. E. Braun (Cambridge, Mass.)

Knorr, W. R. (1975) *The Evolution of the Euclidean Elements* (Dordrecht)

(1985) "Archimedes and the pseudo-Euclidean *Catoptrics*," *Archives Internationales d'Histoire des Sciences* 35: 28–105

(1986) *The Ancient Tradition of Geometric Problems* (Boston)

(1989) *Textual Studies in Ancient and Medieval Geometry* (Boston)

Kopff, E. C. (1975) "An Emendation in Herodotus 7.9.β.2," *American Journal of Philology* 96: 117–20

Krafft, Fritz (1967) "Die Anfänge einer theoretischen Mechanik und die Wandlung ihrer Stellung zur Wissenschaft von der Natur," in Baron (1967) 12–33

(1970) *Dynamische und Statische Betrachtungsweise in der Antiken Mechanik* (Wiesbaden)

Kraut, R., ed. (1992) *The Cambridge Companion to Plato* (Cambridge)

(1997) *Aristotle: Politics, Books VII and VIII* (Oxford)

Krischer, Tilman (1995) "Die Rolle der Magna Graecia in der Geschichte der Mechanik," *Antike und Abendland* 41: 60–71

Krohn, F., ed. (1912) *Vitruvii De Architectura Libri Decem* (Leipzig)

Kucharski, P. (1939) "La 'méthode d'Hippocrate' dans le Phèdre," *Revue des Études Grecques* 52: 301–57

Kühner, R. and Gerth, G. (1887) *Ausführliche Grammatik der griechischen Sprache II, Satzlehre* (Hanover), repr. 1966 (Darmstadt)

Kurtz, Eduard, ed. (1903) *Die Gedichte des Christophoros Mitylenaios* (Leipzig)

Laks, André and Louguet, Claire, eds. (2002) *Qu' est-ce que La Philosophie Présocratique?* (Lille)

Laks, André and Rashed, Marwan, eds. (2004) *Aristote et le mouvement des animaux: Dix études sur le De motu animalium* (Lille)

Lamb, W. R. M., tr. (1925) *Plato: Lysis, Symposium, Gorgias* (Cambridge, Mass.)

Lasserre, François (1954) *Plutarque de la Musique* (Olten)

(1966a) *The Birth of Mathematics in the Age of Plato* (Cleveland)

(1966b) *Die Fragmente des Eudoxus von Knidos* (Berlin)

Le Blond, J. M. (1979) "Aristotle on Definition," in Barnes, Schofield, and Sorabji (1979) 63–79

Ledger, Gerard R. (1989) *Re-counting Plato: A Computer Analysis of Plato's Style* (Cambridge)

Lentz, A., ed. (1867) *Grammatici Graeci*, Vol. III. 1, *Herodiani Technici Reliquae . . . De Prosodia Catholica* (Leipzig)

Lenz, F. W. and Behr, C. A., eds. (1978) *P. Aelii Aristidis Opera Quae Exstant Omnia:* Vol. 1 (Leiden)

Leone, P. A. M., ed. (1968) *Ioannis Tzetzae Historiae* (Naples)

(1972) ed., *Ioannis Tzetzae Epistulae* (Leipzig)

Lesher, J. H. (1992) *Xenophanes of Colophon* (Toronto)

Levin, F. (1990) "Unity in Euclid's *Sectio Canonis*," *Hermes* 118: 430–43

Levison, M., Morton, A. Q., and Winspear, A. D. (1968) "The Seventh Letter of Plato," *Mind*, n.s. 77: 309–25

Lewis, B., Ménage, V. L., Pellat, Ch., and Schacht, J., eds. (1971) *The Encyclopedia of Islam* (Leiden)

Lewis, D. M., Boardman, John, Hornblower, Simon, and Ostwald, M., eds. (1994) *The Cambridge Ancient History:* Volume VI: *The Fourth Century* BC (Cambridge)

Lewis, V. Bradley (2000) "The Seventh Letter and the Unity of Plato's Political Philosophy," *The Southern Journal of Philosophy* XXXVIII: 231–51

Lieberg, Godo (1958) *Die Lehre von der Lust in den Ethiken des Aristoteles* (Munich)

Lindberg, David C. (1976) *Theories of Vision from Al-Kindi to Kepler* (Chicago)

Lintott, A. W. (1982) *Violence, Civil Strife and Revolution in the Classical City* (Baltimore)

Lippman, E. A. (1964) *Musical Thought in Ancient Greece* (New York)
Lloyd, G. E. R. (1975) "The Hippocratic Question," *Classical Quarterly* 25: 171–92
  (1979) *Magic, Reason, and Experience* (Cambridge)
  (1987a) *The Revolutions of Wisdom* (Cambridge)
  (1987b) "The Alleged Fallacy of Hippocrates of Chios," *Apeiron* 20: 103–28
  (1990) "Plato and Archytas in the Seventh Letter," *Phronesis* 35.2: 159–74
  (1991) *Methods and Problems in Greek Science* (Cambridge)
  (1996) *Aristotelian Explorations* (Cambridge)
Lloyd-Jones, H. and Parsons, P. (1983) *Supplementum Hellenisticum* (Berlin)
Loewenthal, A. (1896) *Honein Ibn Ishâk: Sinnsprüche der Philosophen* (Berlin)
Lombardo, M. (1987) "La Magna Grecia dalla fine del v secolo a. C. alla conquista romana," in Pugliese Carratelli (1987) 55–88
Long, A. A. (1966) "Thinking and Sense-Perception in Empedocles: Mysticism or Materialism?," *Classical Quarterly* 16: 256–76
  (1999) ed., *The Cambridge Companion to Early Greek Philosophy* (Cambridge)
Long, A. A. and Sedley, D. N. (1987) *The Hellenistic Philosophers*, 2 vols. (Cambridge)
Long, H. S., ed. (1964) *Diogenis Laertii Vitae Philosophorum*, 2 vols. (Oxford)
Lynch, John Patrick (1972) *Aristotle's School* (Berkeley)
MacDowell, Douglas M. (1978) *The Law in Classical Athens* (London)
Machamer, Peter K. and Turnbull, Robert G., eds. (1978) *Studies in Perception* (Columbus)
MacKay, L. A. (1977) "Horatiana: *Odes* 1.9 and 1.28," *Classical Philology* 72.4: 316–18
McKirahan, Richard D. (1978) "Aristotle's Subordinate Sciences," *British Journal for the History of Science* 11.39: 197–220
Maddalena, Antonio (1954) *I Pitagorici* (Bari)
Mansfeld, J. (1980) "Plato and the Method of Hippocrates," *Greek, Roman and Byzantine Studies* 2: 341–62
  (1998) *Prolegomena Mathematica: From Apollonius of Perga to Late Neoplatonism* (Leiden)
Marcovich, M., ed. (1999) *Diogenes Laertius: Vitae Philosophorum* (Stuttgart)
Marg, Walter, ed. (1972) *Timaeus Locrus: De Natura Mundi et Animae* (Leiden)
Marrou, H. I. (1956) *A History of Education in Antiquity* (New York)
Marsden, E. W. (1969) *Greek and Roman Artillery: Historical Development* (Oxford)
  (1971) *Greek and Roman Artillery: Technical Treatises* (Oxford)
Marshall, P. K., ed. (1968) *A. Gellii Noctes Atticae* (Oxford)
Martin, A. and Primavesi, O. (1999) *L' Empédocle de Strasbourg* (Berlin)
Mastronarde, Donald J. (1994) *Euripides' Phoenissae* (Cambridge)
Mathiesen, T. J. (1975) "An Annotated Translation of Euclid's Division of a Monochord," *Journal of Music Theory* 19: 236–58
  (1999) *Apollo's Lyre* (Lincoln)
Mathieu, Bernard (1987) "Archytas de Tarente pythagoricien et ami de Platon," *Bulletin de l' Association G. Budé* 239–55

Mejer, Jørgen (1978) *Diogenes Laertius and His Hellenistic Background* (Wiesbaden)

Mele, A. (1981) "I pitagorici e Archita," *Storia della società italiana* 1: 272–84

Mercken, H. P. F. (1990) "The Greek Commentators on Aristotle's *Ethics*," in Sorabji (1990a) 407–44

Merlan, Philip (1953) *From Platonism to Neoplatonism* (The Hague)

Minar, Edwin L. (1942) *Early Pythagorean Politics in Practice and Theory* (Baltimore)

Moles, J. L. (1996) "Diatribe," in Hornblower and Spawforth (1996) 463–64

Momigliano, Arnaldo (1993) *The Development of Greek Biography*, 2nd edn. (Cambridge, Mass.)

Moraux, P. (1951) *Les Listes anciennes des ouvrages d'Aristote* (Louvain)

    (1973) *Der Aristotelismus bei den Griechen von Andronikos bis Alexander von Aphrodisias*, Erster Band: *Die Renaissance des Aristotelismus im I. Jh. v. Chr.* (Berlin)

    (1984) *Der Aristotelismus bei den Griechen von Andronikos bis Alexander von Aphrodisias*, Zweiter Band: *Der Aristotelismus im I. und II. Jh. n. Chr.* (Berlin)

Morrison, J. S. (1956) "Pythagoras of Samos," *Classical Quarterly* 50: 135–56

    (1958) "The Origins of Plato's Philosopher Statesman," *Classical Quarterly* 52: 198–218

Morrow, Glenn R., tr. (1962) *Plato's Epistles* (Indianapolis and New York)

Mourelatos, A. P. D. (1980) "Plato's 'Real Astronomy': *Republic* vii 527d–531d," in Anton (1980) 33–73

    (1993) ed., *The Pre-Socratics* (Princeton), a revised version of the 1974 edition

Moutsopoulos, E. (1959) *La Musique dans l'oeuvre de Platon* (Paris)

Mueller, I. (1980) "Ascending to Problems: Astronomy and Harmonics in *Republic* vii," in Anton (1980) 103–22

    (1992a) ed., Περὶ τῶν μαθημάτων (Edmonton) = *Apeiron* 24.4 (1991)

    (1992b) "Mathematics and Education: Some Notes on the Platonic Program," in Mueller (1992a) 85–104

    (1992c) "Mathematical Method and Philosophical Truth," in Kraut (1992) 170–99

    (1997) "Greek Arithmetic, Geometry and Harmonics: Thales to Plato," in Taylor (1997) 271–322

Mueller-Goldingen, C. (1985) *Untersuchungen zu den Phonissen des Euripides* (Stuttgart)

Mullach, F. A., ed. (1860–81) *Fragmenta philosophorum graecorum*, 3 vols. (Paris)

Müller, A. (1884) *Ibn Abi Useibia* (Königsberg)

Münzer, F. (1905) "Atticus als Geschichtschreiber," *Hermes* 40: 50–100

Mustilli, D. (1964) "Civiltà della Magna Grecia," in *Atti del terzo Convegno di studi sulla Magna Grecia* (Naples) 5–47

Netz, R. (1999) *The Shaping of Deduction in Greek Mathematics* (Cambridge)

    (2003) "Plato's Mathematical Construction," *Classical Quarterly* 53.2: 500–09

Neuenschwander, E. (1974) "Zur Ueberlieferung der Archytas-Lösung des delischen Problems," *Centaurus* 18: 1–5

Neugebauer, O. (1975) *A History of Ancient Mathematical Astronomy*, 3 vols. (Berlin)

Nisbet, R. G. M. and Hubbard, M. A. (1970) *A Commentary on Horace: Odes, Book 1* (Oxford)

Nolle, J. (1914) *Ps.-Archytae Fragmenta* (Tubingen)

O'Brien, D. (1981) *Theories of Weight in the Ancient World*, Vol. 1: *Democritus: Weight and Size* (Paris)

O'Meara, D. J. (1989) *Pythagoras Revived. Mathematics and Philosophy in Late Antiquity* (Oxford)

Ostwald, M., tr. (1962) *Aristotle: Nicomachean Ethics* (Indianapolis)

(1969) *Nomos and the Beginnings of the Athenian Democracy* (Oxford)

Pais, E. (1932) "Questioni Catoniane, il Filosofo Pitagorico Nearco," in *Mélanges Glotz*, II (Paris) 681–98

Pape, W. and Benseler, G. E. (1959) *Wörterbuch der Griechischen Eigennamen* (Graz)

Parker, Robert (1996) *Athenian Religion: A History* (Oxford)

Patton, W. R., Pohlenz, M., and Sieveking, W., eds. (1929) *Plutarchi Moralia* III (Leipzig)

Peck, A. L., tr. (1942) *Aristotle: Generation of Animals* (Cambridge, Mass.)

Philip, J. A. (1966) *Pythagoras and Early Pythagoreanism* (Toronto)

Pistelli, H., ed. (1894) *Iamblichus: In Nicomachi arithmeticam introductionem*, 2nd edn. 1975, ed. U. Klein (Stuttgart)

Powell, J. G. F. (1988) *Cicero: Cato Maior De Senectute* (Cambridge)

(1990) *Cicero: Laelius, On Friendship and The Dream of Scipio* (Warminster)

(1995) ed., *Cicero the Philosopher* (Oxford)

Praechter, K. (1897) "Krantor und Ps. Archytas," *Archiv für Geschichte der Philosophie* 10: 186–90

Preus, A., ed. (2001) *Essays in Ancient Greek Philosophy VI: Before Plato* (Albany)

Pritchett, W. Kendrick (1974) *The Greek State at War*, Part II (Berkeley)

Pugliese Carratelli, G., ed. (1987) *Magna Grecia, lo sviluppo politico, sociale ed economico* (Milan)

Purcell, Nicholas (1994) "South Italy in the Fourth Century BC," in Lewis, D. M. et al. (1994) 381–403

Rabe, H., ed. (1963) *Ioannes Philoponus De Aeternitate Mundi* (Hildesheim)

Raeder, Hans (1906) "Über die Echtheit der Platonischen Briefe," *Rheinisches Museum*, n.f. LXI: 427–71, 511–42

Reid, James S. (1897) *M. Tulli Ciceronis: Laelius, De Amicitia* (Cambridge)

Reifferscheid, A., ed. (1875) *Arnobii Adversus Nationes Libri VII* (Vienna)

Rhodes, P. J. (1972) *The Athenian Boule* (Oxford)

Ribezzo, Francesco (1951) "La Spedizione di Archita di Taranto contro Mesania (Mesagne)," *Arch. Stor. Pugl.* 4: 7–21

Riedweg, C. (1996) "Archytas," in Cancik and Schneider (1996) 1029–31

Riginos, A. S. (1976) *Platonica* (Leiden)

Ritter, Constantin (1888) *Untersuchungen über Platon: Die Echtheit und Chronologie der Platonischer Schriften* (Stuttgart) de Romilly, J. (1972) "Vocabulaire et Propagande ou les premiers emplois du mot 'ὁμόνοια'," in *Mélanges de Linguistique et de Philologie Grecques Offerts à Pierre Chantraine* (Paris) 199–209

(1992) *The Great Sophists in Periclean Athens* (Oxford)

Rose, V. (1854) *De Aristotelis Librorum Ordine et Auctoritate Commentatio* (Berlin) (1886) ed., *Aristotelis . . . Fragmenta* (Leipzig)

Ross, W. D. (1924) *Aristotle's Metaphysics* (Oxford)

(1936) *Aristotle's Physics* (Oxford)

(1949) *Aristotle: Prior and Posterior Analytics* (Oxford)

Ross, W. D. and Fobes, F. H., eds. (1929) *Theophrastus: Metaphysics* (Oxford)

Rouse, M. A. and R. H. (1971) 'The Texts called *"Lumen Animae,"'* *Archivum Fratrum Praedicatorum* 41: 5–113

Rowe, Christopher and Schofield, Malcolm, eds. (2000) *The Cambridge History of Greek and Roman Political Thought* (Cambridge)

Ruelle, C. A., Knoellinger, H., and Klek, J., eds. (1922) *Aristotelis quae feruntur Problemata Physica* (Leipzig)

Ryle, G. (1965) "The *Timaeus Locrus*," *Phronesis* 10: 174–90

Sachs, E. (1917) *Die fünf Platonischen Körper* (Berlin)

Salanitro, G., ed. (1987) *Theodorus Gaza: M. Tulli Ciceronis Liber De Senectute in Graecum Translatus* (Leipzig)

Salmon, E. T. (1967) *Samnium and the Samnites* (Cambridge)

Santirocco, Matthew S. (1986) *Unity and Design in Horace's Odes* (Chapel Hill)

Sayre, Kenneth M. (1995) *Plato's Literary Garden* (Notre Dame and London)

Schaefer, G. H. (1811) *Gregorii Corinthii et aliorum Grammaticorum libri De Dialectis Linguae Graecae* (Leipzig)

Schenkel, H. and Downey, G., eds. (1965) *Themistii Orationes Quae Supersunt* (Leipzig)

Schmidt, W. (1904) "Aus der antiken Mechanik," *Neue Jahrbücher für das Klassische Altertum* 13: 329–51

Schneider, R., ed. (1912) *Griechische Poliorketiker*, Vol. 1., *Abhandlungen der Königlichen Gesellschaft der Wissenschaften zu Göttingen, Philol.-hist. Kl.*, n.f. 12, no. 5 (Berlin)

Schofield, M. (1991) *The Stoic Idea of the City* (Cambridge)

(2000) "Plato and Practical Politics," in Rowe and Schofield (2000) 293–302

Schulte, F. (1906) *Archytae qui ferebantur de notionibus universalibus et de oppositis libellorum reliquiae* (Marburg)

Schürmann, Astrid (1991) *Griechische Mechanik und Antike Gesellschaft* (Stuttgart)

Sedley, D. (1973) "Epicurus, *On Nature book XXXVIII*," *Cronache Ercolanesi* 3: 5–83

(1982) "Two Conceptions of Vacuum," *Phronesis* 27: 175–93

(1999) "Parmenides and Melissus" in Long (1999) 113–33

Senn, G. (1929) "Über Herkunft und Stil der Beschreibungen von Experimenten im Corpus Hippocraticum," *Sudhoffs Archiv für Geschichte der Medizin* 22: 217–89

Seyffert, M. and Müller, C. F. W. (1965) *M. Tullii Ciceronis Laelius de Amicitia Dialogus* (Hildesheim)

Share, Michael, ed. (1994) *Arethas of Caesarea's Scholia on Porphyry's Isagoge and Aristotle's Categories* (Athens)

Shorey, P. (1933) *What Plato Said* (Chicago)

(1935) tr., *Plato: The Republic*, 2 vols. (Cambridge, Mass.)

Sinclair, R. K. (1988) *Democracy and Participation in Athens* (Cambridge)

Sinclair, T. A. (1951) *A History of Greek Political Thought* (London)

Singer, Charles et al. (1956) *A History of Technology* (Oxford)

Smiley, Timothy, ed. (2000) *Mathematics and Necessity: Essays in the History of Philosophy* (Oxford)

Smith, A., ed. (1993) *Porphyrii Philosophi Fragmenta* (Leipzig)

Smith, H. W. R. (1976) *Funerary Symbolism in Apulian Vase Painting* (Berkeley)

Smith, R. (1995) "Logic," in Barnes (1995) 27–65

Smyth, H. W. (1956) *Greek Grammar* (Cambridge)

Sodano, A. R., ed. (1964) *Porphyrii in Platonis Timaeum Commentariorum Fragmenta* (Naples)

Solmsen, F. (1942) "Eratosthenes as Platonist and Poet," *Transactions and Proceedings of the American Philological Association* 73: 192–213

(1960) *Aristotle's System of the Physical World* (Ithaca)

(1969) Review of Edelstein 1966, *Gnomon* 41: 29–34

Sorabji, Richard (1983) *Time, Creation and the Continuum* (Ithaca)

(1988) *Matter, Space and Motion* (Ithaca)

(1990a) *Aristotle Transformed: The Ancient Commentators and Their Influence* (Ithaca)

(1990b) "The Ancient Commentators on Aristotle," in Sorabji (1990a) 1–30

Spence, I. G. (1994) *The Cavalry of Ancient Greece: A Social and Military History With Particular Reference to Athens* (Oxford)

Stewart, J. A. (1892) *Notes on the Nicomachean Ethics of Aristotle* (Oxford)

Stillwell, Richard, ed. (1976) *The Princeton Encyclopedia of Classical Sites* (Princeton)

Strange, Steven (1985) "The Double Explanation in the *Timaeus*," *Ancient Philosophy* 5: 25–39

(1992) tr., *Porphyry: On Aristotle's Categories* (Ithaca)

Stratton, G. M. (1917) *Theophrastus: De Sensibus* (London)

Sturm, A. (1895–97) *Das Delische Problem* (Linz)

Sykutris, J., ed. (1933) *Die Briefe des Sokrates und der Sokratiker* (Paderborn)

Szlezak, T. A. (1972) *Pseudo-Archytas über Die Kategorien* (Berlin)

Tannery, P. (1887) *La Géométrie Grecque* (Paris)

(1905) "Un traité Grec d' arithmétique antérieur à Euclide," *Bibliotheca Mathematica* 3.6: 225–29, reprinted in *Mémoires scientifiques* III: 244–50 (Paris)

(1912–43) *Mémoires scientifiques*, 16 vols. (Paris)

Tarán, L. (1981) *Speusippus of Athens* (Leiden)

(1969) ed., *Asclepius of Tralles: Commentary to Nicomachus' Introduction to Arithmetic* (Philadelphia)

Taylor, A. E. (1928) *A Commentary on Plato's Timaeus* (Oxford)

Taylor, C. C. W., ed. (1997) *Routledge History of Philosophy*, Vol. 1: *From the Beginning to Plato* (London)

Terzaghi, N., ed. (1944) *Synesii Cyrenensis opuscula* (Rome)

Theiler, W. (1926) Review of Delatte 1922, *Gnomon* 2: 147–56

Thesleff, H. (1961) *An Introduction to the Pythagorean Writings of the Hellenistic Period* (Åbo)

    (1962) "Okkelos, Archytas and Plato," *Eranos* 60: 8–36

    (1965) ed., *The Pythagorean Texts of the Hellenistic Period* (Åbo)

    (1972) "On the Problem of the Doric Pseudo-Pythagorica. An Alternative Theory of Date and Purpose," *Pseudepigrapha I*, Fondation Hardt Entretiens XVIII (Vandoeuvres–Genève) 59–87

Thomas, I., tr. (1939) *Selections Illustrating the History of Greek Mathematics*, 2 vols. (Cambridge, Mass.)

Thorndike, Lynn (1934) *A History of Magic and Experimental Science* (New York)

Timpanaro Cardini, Maria (1958–64) *Pitagorici: Testimonianze e Frammenti*, 3 fascs. (Florence)

Tredennick, H., tr. (1960) *Aristotle: Posterior Analytics* (Cambridge, Mass.)

Trendall, A. D. and Cambitoglou, Alexander (1978) *The Red-Figured Vases of Apulia*, Vol. 1 (Oxford)

Urmson, J. O., tr. (2002) *Simplicius: On Aristotle's "Physics 3"* (Ithaca)

Usener, H. (1887) *Epicurea* (Leipzig)

Vlastos, G. (1970) "Equality and Justice in Early Greek Cosmologies," in Furley and Allen (1970) 56–91

    (1981) *Platonic Studies* (Princeton)

    (1991) *Socrates: Ironist and Moral Philosopher* (Ithaca)

De Vogel, C. J. (1966) *Pythagoras and Early Pythagoreanism* (Assen)

Vogel, M. (1963) *Die Enharmonik der Griechen* (Düsseldorf)

Wachsmuth, C. and Hense, O., eds. (1884–1912) *Stobaeus: Anthologium*, 5 vols. (Berlin)

Wackernagel, J. (1914) "Akzentstudien III," *Nachr. Kön. Ges. Wiss. Gött.*, Philol.-hist. Klasse: 97–130 = *Kleine Schriften* 2 (Göttingen, no date) 1154–87

van der Waerden, B. L. (1943) "Die Harmonielehre der Pythagoreer," *Hermes* 78: 163–99

    (1947–49) "Die Arithmetik der Pythagoreer," *Mathematische Annalen* 120: 127–53, 676–700

    (1963) *Science Awakening*, tr. A. Dresden (New York)

Wallach, Barbara Price (1997) "Diatribe," in Zeyl (1997) 181–83

Watson, John Selby, tr. (1887) *Quintilian's Institutes of Oratory* (London)

Wehrli, F. (1945) *Die Schule des Aristoteles*, Vol. II: *Aristoxenos* (Basle)

    (1955) *Die Schule des Aristoteles*, Vol. VIII: *Eudemos* (Basle)

Wellmann, M. (1921) "Die Georgika des Demokritos," *Abhandlungen der Preussischen Akademie der Wissenschaften* IV: 1–58

West, David (1995) *Horace: Odes 1* (Oxford)

West, M. L. (1983) *The Orphic Poems* (Oxford)

    (1992) *Ancient Greek Music* (Oxford)

Westerink, L. G. (1961) "Elias on the Prior Analytics," *Mnemosyne* S. IV, 14: 126–39
(1962) ed., *Anonymous Prolegomena to Platonic Philosophy* (Amsterdam)
(1976–77) ed., *The Greek Commentaries on Plato's Phaedo*, 2 vols. (Amsterdam)
Westerink, L. G., ed. and Combès, J., tr. (1986) *Damascius: Traité des Premiers Principes*: Vol. 1 (Paris)
Westlake, H. D. (1994) "Dion and Timoleon," in Lewis, D. M. et al. (1994) 693–706
White, Nicholas P. (1976) *Plato on Knowledge and Reality* (Indianapolis)
von Wilamowitz-Moellendorff, U. (1894) "Ein Weihgeschenk des Eratosthenes," *Nachrichten der K. Gesellschaft der Wissenschaften zu Göttingen, Phil.-hist. Klasse*, 15–35; repr. in *Kleine Schriften* Vol. II (Berlin) 1962: 48–70
(1919–20) *Platon* (Berlin)
Wilkinson, L. P. (1945) *Horace and His Lyric Poetry* (Cambridge)
Williams, Gordon (1980) *Figures of Thought in Roman Poetry* (New Haven)
Wilpert, Paul (1949) *Zwei aristotelische Frühschriften über die Ideenlehre* (Regensburg)
Wilson, N. G., tr. (1997) *Aelian: Historical Miscellany* (Cambridge, Mass.)
Winnington-Ingram, R. P. (1932) "Aristoxenus and the Intervals of Greek Music," *Classical Quarterly* 26: 195–208
Wolfer, E. P. (1954) *Eratosthenes von Kyrene als Mathematiker und Philosoph* (Groningen)
Wright, M. R. (1981) *Empedocles: The Extant Fragments* (New Haven)
Wuilleumier, Pierre (1939) *Tarente des origines à la conquète Romaine* (Paris)
Zeller, E. (1923) *Die Philosophie der Griechen in ihrer geschichtlichen Entwicklung* (Leipzig) I⁷, ed. Wilhelm Nestle, repr. Darmstadt 1963
Zeyl, Donald J., tr. (1987) *Plato: Gorgias* (Indianapolis)
(1997) ed., *Encyclopedia of Classical Philosophy* (Westport)
Zhmud, L. (1997) *Wissenschaft, Philosophie und Religion im frühen Pythagoreismus* (Berlin)
(1998) "Plato as Architect of Science," *Phronesis* 43.3: 210–44
(2002) "Eudemus' History of Mathematics," in Fortenbaugh, W. W. and Bodnar, I., eds. *Eudemus of Rhodes* (New Brunswick) 263–306
Ziegler, K., ed. (1994) *Plutarchi Vitae Parallelae*, Vol. II, Fasc. 2 (Stuttgart)

Select index of Greek words and phrases discussed in the text

Index locorum

(Entries in bold refer to the page on which the Greek or Latin text is provided).

General index

Reference should also be made to the Index Locorum for the names of ancient authors. General references to an author's works are given at the end of the listing for each author. Specific references are found in the Index Locorum.

Aalders, G. J. D., 600, 601–05
abacus table, 610
Academy, xi, 42, 95, 319–20, 377, 501, 589–90, 592; on the one, 484
Ackrill, J. L., 61, 335
acoustics, 30, 99, 113–14, **129–48**; Archytas' theory in A19a, **473–75**
Adam, J., 210, 385, 386, 390, 439, 442
adminiculum, 297, 561, 568
Adrastus, commentator on the *Timaeus*, 180, 472
Aelian, as source for A8, 298–99
aether, 526, 591, 594
Agesilaus, 34
agriculture, 27–28, 31
air, compressed, 573–79; as the medium of sound, 131, 133–34, 140–41, 562; and the visual ray, 569
pseudo-Albertus Magnus, *The Marvels of the World*, 25, 610–11
Alcibiades, 34
Alcmaeon, 527, 557
Alcman, 27
Alexander of Aphrodisias, Archytas' argument for an unlimited universe, response to, 544, 548–49; Plato's theory of motion, criticism of, 510–11
Alexander the Molossian, 10
Alexander Polyhistor, 94; *Pythagorean Memoirs*, 556
altar, Archytas' definition of, 497–99, 500, 507
amminiculum, see *adminiculum*
Ammonius son of Hermeias, 125
analogy, 341
Anaxagoras, 34, 134, 547
Anaximander, 547
Andronicus of Rhodes, 93, 596

anecdotes, 18–19, 100, 287, 338–41, 542, 593; and Archytas' theory of definition, 504
anger, 19, 73, **288–90**, 339–40
angle of incidence, 555
animals, 594; parts of, 517–20, 525–28
Annas, J., 487, 606
Anonymus Iamblichi, 208
Antiochus of Ascalon, 93, 599
Antiphanes, 535, 536
antiphonoi, 445
Antisthenes, 230
apatheia, 602–03, 605
Aphrodite, 160
apotomē, 455
appearance vs. reality, 152
Apuleius, 25, 86, 99; Archimedes as a source for Archytas' optics, use of, 554–55; as a source for A25, 553–54, 560; *Apology*, 553
arbitrator, Archytas' definition of, 497–99, 500, 507
Archedemus, 8, 37–38
Archelaus, 54; on sound, 134
Archestratus of Gela, 318
Archimedes, 14, 23, 78, 384, 577; *Catoptrics*, 553, 554–55; *On the Sphere and Cylinder*, 345; *Sand Reckoner*, 22, 374
Archippus, 6
Archita Tharentinus, *On Events in Nature*, 611–14
Architas (later spelling of Archytas), 25, 610–14
Archytas (*This is a selective listing. Please also consult the table of contents and other subject headings*), acoustic theory, **129–48**, **473–75**, 562; and aether, 591–93; on agriculture, 27–28, 31; anger of, **288–90**; on arithmetic, 31, 32, 48; and artillery, 14, 17, 82;

651